Organico's
Income Statement
For Month Ended March 31, 2017

Revenues:		
Food services revenue	$ 3,800	
Teaching revenue...	300	
Total revenues		$ 4,100
Operating expenses:		
Rent expense	$ 1,000	
Salaries expense	700	
Total operating expenses		1,700
Profit		$ 2,400

Organico
Statement of Changes in Equity
For Month Ended March 31, 2017

Hailey Walker, capital, March 1		$ -0-
Add: Investments by owner...	$ 10,000	
Profit	2,400	12,400
Total		$ 12,400
Less: Withdrawals by owner...		600
Hailey Walker, capital, March 31		$ 11,800

Organico
Balance Sheet
March 31, 2017

Assets		Liabilities	
Cash	$ 8,400	Accounts payable..............	$ 200
Supplies....................	3,600	Notes payable	6,000
Equipment	6,000	Total liabilities	$ 6,200
		Equity	
		Hailey Walker, capital	11,800
Total assets...............	$18,000	Total liabilities and equity ..	$ 18,000

Organico
Statement of Cash Flows
For Month Ended March 31, 2017

Cash flows from operating activities		
Cash received from clients	$ 4,100	
Cash paid for supplies	(3,400)	
Cash paid for rent...	(1,000)	
Cash paid to employee	(700)	
Net cash used by operating activities		$ (1,000)
Cash flows from investing activities...		-0-
Cash flows from financing activities		
Investment by owner...	$10,000	
Withdrawal by owner	(600)	
Net cash provided by financing activities.............................		9,400
Net increase in cash...		$ 8,400
Cash balance, March 1...		-0-
Cash balance, March 31..		$ 8,400

The arrows are provided for education purposes only to emphasize the link between statements.

DIFFERENTIATING THE FINANCIAL STATEMENTS

Fundamental Accounting Principles uses a colour scheme to help students differentiate among the four key financial statements.

Fundamental
ACCOUNTING PRINCIPLES

Volume 2

Fifteenth Canadian Edition

Kermit D. Larson
University of Texas—Austin

Tilly Jensen
Athabasca University—Alberta

Heidi Dieckmann
Kwantlen Polytechnic University—British Columbia

Fundamental Accounting Principles
Volume 2
Fifteenth Canadian Edition

The Internet addresses listed in the text were accurate at the time of publication. The inclusion of a Web site does not indicate an endorsement by the authors or McGraw-Hill Ryerson, and McGraw-Hill Ryerson does not guarantee the accuracy of the information presented at these sites.

ISBN-13: 978-1-25-908736-3
ISBN-10: 1-25-908736-0

3 4 5 6 7 8 9 10 WC 1 9 8 7

Printed and bound in Canada.

Care has been taken to trace ownership of copyright material contained in this text; however, the publisher will welcome any information that enables them to rectify any reference or credit for subsequent editions.

Director of Product Management: Rhondda McNabb
Product Manager: Keara Emmett
Executive Marketing Manager: Joy Armitage Taylor
Product Developer: Sarah Fulton
Senior Product Team Associate: Stephanie Giles
Supervising Editor: Jessica Barnoski
Photo/Permissions Editor: Tracy Leonard
Copy Editor: Karen Rolfe
Plant Production Coordinator: Scott Morrison
Manufacturing Production Coordinator: Emily Hickey
Cover Design: Michelle Losier
Cover Image: Rachel Idzerda
Interior Design: Michelle Losier
Page Layout: Aptara®, Inc.
Printer: Webcom

About the Authors

Kermit D. Larson, University of Texas—Austin

Kermit D. Larson is the Arthur Andersen & Co. Alumni Professor of Accounting Emeritus at the University of Texas at Austin. He served as chair of the University of Texas, Department of Accounting, and was visiting associate professor at Tulane University. His scholarly articles have been published in a variety of journals, including *The Accounting Review, Journal of Accountancy,* and *Abacus.* He is the author of several books, including *Financial Accounting* and *Fundamentals of Financial* and *Managerial Accounting,* both published by Irwin/McGraw-Hill.

Professor Larson is a member of the American Accounting Association, the Texas Society of CPAs, and the American Institute of CPAs. His positions with the AAA have included vice president, southwest regional service president, and chair of several committees, including the Committee of Concepts and Standards. He was a member of the committee that planned the first AAA doctoral consortium and served as its director.

Tilly Jensen, Athabasca University—Alberta

Tilly Jensen graduated from the University of Alberta with a Bachelor of Commerce and later attained the designation of Certified Management Accountant. She worked in private industry for a number of years before making teaching her full-time career. Tilly was an accounting instructor at the Northern Alberta Institute of Technology (NAIT) in Edmonton, Alberta, for a number of years and is now an Assistant Professor of Accounting at Athabasca University, Canada's open, online university. She obtained her M.Ed. at the University of Sheffield in Britain while travelling abroad and completed her doctoral studies at the University of Calgary focusing on how educational technologies might be used to enhance critical thinking. Tilly spent four years in the Middle East teaching at Dubai Men's College of the Higher Colleges of Technology in the United Arab Emirates. While overseas, she also taught financial accounting to students enrolled in the Chartered Institute of Management Accountants (CIMA) program, a British professional accounting designation. During a sabbatical, Tilly also taught accounting in China to ESL students at Shenyang Ligong University. She authored LIFA—Lyryx Interactive Financial Accounting—a dynamic, leading-edge, Web-based teaching and learning tool produced by Lyryx. Tilly has also authored material for CGA-Canada. In addition to her professional interests, Tilly places a priority on time spent with her family and friends.

Heidi Dieckmann, Kwantlen Polytechnic University—British Columbia

Heidi Dieckmann graduated from Simon Fraser University in Burnaby, BC with a BBA in Accounting and carried on her studies in the Masters of Professional Accountancy Program at the University of Saskatchewan. Heidi attained her CA designation while working in public practice at KPMG in Burnaby before beginning her career in education as an Accounting instructor at Kwantlen Polytechnic University. While at KPU, Heidi has served as Department Chair and has sat on several committees. Her major initiatives at KPU included spearheading the Accounting Society of Kwantlen, an impressive accounting student club that has created opportunities for students to network with professional accountants in industry and public practice. She was also actively involved in the redesign of KPU's new BBA program and managed the detailed competency mapping for the new CPA designation. She is currently involved as a CPA Mentor, coaching upcoming CPAs through the new CPA education and experience requirements.

Heidi has a passion for student engagement and learning outcomes and is inspired by Eric Mazur's research on the Flipped Classroom and Peer Instruction, and Dee Fink's research in Creating Significant Learning Experiences. Heidi is a member of the Canadian Accountants Academics Association and has presented at the Learning Strategies Exchange for her work in student engagement through online education. She has been inspired to embrace international education through participating in the award-winning Canadian Academics Studying Europe conference led by Catherine Vertesi and Robert Buttery; visiting the European Union and the Council of Europe; and studying Swiss Banking at the University of Zurich, and political and education systems at the University of Applied Sciences and Arts Northwestern Switzerland. In her spare time Heidi enjoys volunteering through teaching art classes at her children's school. She loves to create new dishes; travel; and, most of all, spending time with her husband Andrew, her two children, and her close family and friends.

Brief Contents

Contents

CHAPTER 17
Analyzing Financial Statements 1054

APPENDIX I
Payroll Liabilities A-1

APPENDIX II
Financial Statement Information A-2

APPENDIX III
Chart of Accounts A-24

Preface

A Note About Our Cover

The cover of the Fifteenth Canadian Edition is the work of Rachel Idzerda. Rachel's playful illustration spotlights many of the companies, entrepreneurs, and organizations featured in *Fundamental Accounting Principles'* 17 chapter opening vignettes. See if you can spot the images representing Zane Caplansky's food truck (Chapter 1), Frogbox's green moving supplies (Chapter 3), Kicking Horse Coffee (Chapter 11), or ZooShare (Chapter 14). Rachel is a freelance illustrator specializing in editorial illustration and portraiture. She combines clean, delicate linework with bold colours and graphic elements to create a sense of energy and mood in her work. Rachel received her BAA in Illustration from Sheridan College in 2012, and currently lives and works in Montreal, QC with her partner and their two pampered dogs.

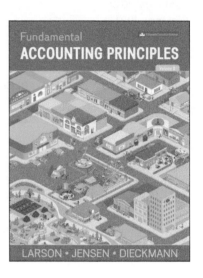

Inside the Chapters

As educators, instructors strive to create an environment that fosters learning and provides students with the tools they need to succeed. The Fifteenth Canadian Edition continues to meet and surpass the high standards the market expects from *Fundamental Accounting Principles*. We continue to put learning first, with student-centred pedagogy and critical thinking lessons throughout the text.

All the pedagogical tools are carefully designed for ease of use and understanding, helping the instructor teach and giving the students what they need to succeed.

Pedagogy

STUDENT SUCCESS CYCLE

Student success at the post-secondary level is not measured by how much knowledge a student has acquired, but rather by how well a student can *use* knowledge. The Student Success Cycle, illustrated by a circular icon, reinforces decision-making skills by highlighting key steps toward understanding and critically evaluating the information the student has just read. **Read–Do–Check–Apply** reinforces active learning rather than passive learning. This tool is integrated throughout the text, including the chapter opening page, Checkpoint questions, Demonstration Problems, and end-of-chapter material.

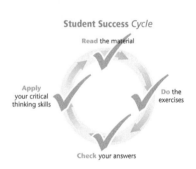

CRITICAL THINKING CHALLENGE

An essential element of critical thinking is the ability to ask questions while reading (or listening or speaking). These exercises are designed to help students develop the skills related to questioning. Suggested answers are posted on **Connect**.

> CRITICAL THINKING CHALLENGE
> Would Amazon have a merchandise turnover similar to Lululemon Athletica's? Explain why or why not. What does "inventory demand planning" refer to? What would the effect be of cost-saving strategies on the weighted average cost of inventory?

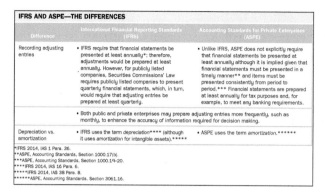

IFRS AND ASPE—THE DIFFERENCES

IFRS AND ASPE—THE DIFFERENCES

This box appears at the end of every chapter to highlight any differences or important points about reporting and terminology as they relate to the financial accounting course. The chapter content is IFRS 2014 compliant for Volume I and IFRS 2015 compliant throughout Volume 2; references are provided where appropriate.

REAL-WORLD FOCUS

The Fifteenth Canadian Edition has increased the use of real business examples to reflect the most current information available. This contin-

> A **business** is an entity represented by one or more individuals selling products or services for profit. Products sold include anything from athletic apparel (CCM, Bauer, Lululemon, NIKE, Reebok), to electronic devices (Apple, Dell, Hewlett-Packard, Samsung), and clothing (Abercrombie and Fitch, GAP, Zara). Service providers such as data communication providers (Bell, Rogers, and Telus), food services (McDonald's, The Keg, Starbucks, Tim Hortons), and internet services (Google, Twitter, Skype, Facebook, Instagram) make our lives more connected. A business can be as small as an in-home

ues the text's strong ties to the real world of accounting, be it through detailed interviews with businesspeople for the chapter opening vignettes, examples of ethical standards and treatments, or annual reports for both in-chapter example disclosures and end-of-chapter material. When an actual business is used, its name is highlighted in **bold magenta** for emphasis. This integration with real-world companies helps engage students while they read.

Food Truck Frenzy

Across the country, major urban centres are experiencing an industry trend to go to the street to entice customers with a wide range of made-to-order food options. In Canada, the street vendor industry is in the growth phase of its industry life cycle, according to IBISWorld, a global market research firm. IBISWorld estimates the market for street vendors in Canada to be strong over the next five years with revenues expected to reach $281 million in 2018 and expected annual growth to cap out at 4.2% in 2015. The market is dominated by new market entrants—in most cases individual owners operating as sole proprietors. The most successful street vendors will take advantage of effective marketing and branding toward health-conscious consumers looking for unique dining options.

Thundering Thelma received her initial debut on CBC's *Dragons' Den* when owner Zane Caplansky decided to expand his famous brick-and-mortar deli in downtown Toronto and enter the trendy urban food truck business. After being labelled "insane Zane" by Kevin O'Leary, and the other Dragons balking at the 15% ownership interest at a proposed cost of $350,000, Zane decided to continue his new business venture on his own. A year later, Caplansky returned to *Dragons' Den* and boasted achieving profit margins between 30 and 40% and achieving $110,000 in sales in his first six months of operation. Caplansky's business continues to thrive with two new locations opening at the Toronto Pearson Airport, one modelled after his brick-and-mortar restaurant and the other modelled after his food truck.

Sources: http://clients1.ibisworld.ca/reports/ca/industry/industryoutlook.aspx?entid=1683, accessed April 15, 2014; http://www.torontolife.com/daily-dish/people-dish/2011/11/03/zane-caplansky-on-dragons-den, accessed April 15, 2014; http://www.postcity.com/Eat-Shop-Do/Eat/November-2013/Weekly-Restaurant-Recap-Harvest-Kitchen/CBC Dragon's Den, Season 7, Episode 11, aired January 7, 2013.

Video Link: http://www.cbc.ca/dragonsden/episodes/season-7/episode-11-season-7

NEW VIDEO LINKS

This text features interactive digital links directing students and instructors to helpful videos to provide students with real world application of the chapter content and enhance student exposure to valuable online resources.

NEW: A LOOK BACK, A LOOK AT THIS CHAPTER, A LOOK AHEAD

In these brief paragraphs, students are directed to reflect on their learning from previous chapters; provided with a high-level summary of the current chapter; and introduced to the concepts covered in the following chapter. These helpful learning summaries help students focus on how their learning ties into big-picture objectives.

Receivables

A Look Back

Chapter 7 provides an introduction to Internal Control and Cash with a detailed analysis of internal control guidelines, banking activities, accounting for petty cash funds, and reconciling the differences between cash reported in the bank account and cash in the company's accounting records.

A Look at This Chapter

Chapter 8 takes a look at accounting for customer accounts receivable and short-term notes receivable, specifically investigating tools such as initial recognition of the receivables and subsequent measurement at the end of the accounting period. Valuation is assessed through methods to estimate bad debts, including the benefits of an A/R aging report, and using the accounts receivable turnover ratio and days' sales uncollected ratios to evaluate financial statements.

A Look Ahead

Chapter 9, the first chapter of Volume 2, investigates accounting issues for fixed assets under the following major categories: property, plant and equipment, and intangible assets. The chapter focuses on identifying all items that are included in their asset cost and analyzes options for matching their usage costs over their useful lives. Other considerations such as how to handle asset disposals, exchanges, and sales are analyzed.

LEARNING OBJECTIVES

Learning Objectives have long been a standard in this textbook. By giving students a head start on what the following material encompasses, the text readies them for the work ahead.

CHECKPOINT

This series of questions within the chapter reinforces the material presented immediately before it. These questions allow students to "Do" problem material by referencing what they

CHECKPOINT

5. What is the difference between private and public accountants?
6. What are the four broad fields of accounting?
7. What is the purpose of an audit?
8. Distinguish between managerial and financial accounting.
9. What is the difference between external and internal users of accounting information?
10. Why are internal controls important?

Do Quick Study question: QS 1-5

have just learned. Answers at the end of each chapter will then allow them to "Check" their work, further supporting the Student Success Cycle. Under each set of Checkpoints is a reference to the Quick Study questions (single-topic exercises) available at the end of each chapter. Students can go ahead and try them at this point. Checkpoint solutions are at the end of the chapter. Quick Study solutions are available on **Connect**.

NEW: IMPORTANT TIPS

Important tip boxes have been incorporated throughout the text to direct students' attention to critical concepts that students often miss in their initial reading of the text.

Important Tip: Ensure you know the following rules as illustrated in Exhibit 2.7 before reading Chapter 3. For a helpful learning tool, review the following video by Colin Dodds, an educational music video enthusiast.
Video Link: https://youtu.be/7EuxfW76BWU

DECISION INSIGHT

Social responsibility continues to be important for students to learn early in their accounting courses. Through the Decision Insight feature, accounting's role in ethics and social responsibility is described by both reporting and assessing its impact. Relating theory to a real-life situation piques interest and reinforces active learning.

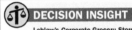

DECISION INSIGHT

Loblaw's Corporate Grocery Stores Go Perpetual

Loblaw Companies Limited, identifies its upgrade of its IT infrastructure as a positive move to enable the company to develop a more precise estimate through a "system-generated average cost." The company estimates "the impact of this inventory measurement and other conversion differences associated with implementation of a perpetual inventory system to be a $190 million decrease to the value of the inventory."

DECISION MAKER   Answer—End of chapter

Inventory Manager—Ethical Dilemma

You are the inventory manager for a trendy urban retail inventory merchandiser. Your compensation includes a bonus plan based on the amount of gross profit reported in the financial statements. Your supervisor comes to you and asks your opinion about changing the inventory costing method from moving weighted average to FIFO. Since costs have been rising and are expected to continue to rise, your superior predicts the company will be more attractive to investors because of the reported higher profit using FIFO. You realize this proposed change will likely increase your bonus as well. What do you recommend?

DECISION MAKER

This feature requires students to make accounting and business decisions by using role-playing to show the interaction of judgment and awareness, as well as the impact of decisions made. Guidance answers are available at the end of each chapter.

EXTEND YOUR KNOWLEDGE (EYK)

Supplementary material has been developed to explore some topics in more detail than the textbook can allow. A list of EYKs relevant to each chapter is presented at the end of the chapter, alerting students to visit **Connect** if they choose to delve deeper into the material.

For further study on some topics of relevance to this chapter, please see the following Extend Your Knowledge supplements:

EYK 4-1 Work Sheet Demonstration
EYK 4-2 Corporate Supplement
EYK 4-3 Summary of Business Activities
EYK 4-4 Examples of Classified Balance Sheets

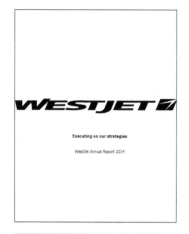

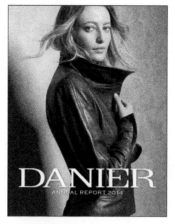

FINANCIAL STATEMENTS

Features and assignments that highlight companies such as **WestJet** (a company that provides services) and **Danier** (a merchandiser) show accounting in a modern and global context. Because students go directly to the financial statements of real companies, they remain engaged in the active learning process. The audited annual financial statement section of these annual reports (with notes to the financial statements), as well as those of **Indigo Books & Music**, and **Telus** (without the notes), are reproduced at the end of Volume 1. In Volume 2, the annual audited financial statements, **excluding** notes to the financial statements, for WestJet, Danier, Indigo, and Telus are included.

End-of-Chapter Material

Fundamental Accounting Principles sets the standard for quantity and quality of end-of-chapter material.

SUMMARY

Each chapter includes a Summary of the chapter by Learning Objective, to reinforce what students have just learned.

Summary

LO1 Explain the accounting cycle. The accounting cycle includes the steps in preparing financial statements for users that are repeated each reporting period.

LO2 Describe an account, its use, and its relationship to the ledger. An account is a detailed record of increases and decreases in a specific asset, liability, or equity item. Information is taken from accounts, analyzed, summarized, and presented in useful reports and financial statements for users.

LO3 Define debits and credits and explain their role in double-entry accounting. Debit refers to left, and credit refers to right. The following table summarizes debit and credit effects by account type:

Double-entry accounting means that every transaction affects at least two accounts. The total amount debited must equal the total amount credited for each transaction. The system for recording debits and credits follows from the accounting equation. The debit side is the normal balance for assets, owner's withdrawals, and expenses, and the credit side is the normal balance for liabilities, owner's capital, and revenues.

LO4 Describe a chart of accounts and its relationship to the ledger. A ledger is a record that contains all accounts used by a company. This is what is referred to as *the books*. The chart of accounts is a listing of all accounts and usually includes an identification number that is assigned to each account.

LO5 Analyze the impact of transactions on accounts, record entries in a journal, and post

Guidance Answer to DECISION MAKER

Accounting Clerk

The business entity principle is being violated because it requires that the owner's personal expenses be recorded separately from those of his business. By debiting the entire amount to Office Supplies, assets will be overstated on the balance sheet. By crediting Accounts Payable for the whole amount, liabilities will also be overstated. At the end of the accounting period when the amount of supplies used is recorded, Office Supplies Expense will be overstated on the income statement, causing profit to be understated. When profit is too low, equity is also understated.

GUIDANCE ANSWERS TO DECISION MAKER

These discuss the Decision Maker boxes presented earlier in the chapter, and reinforce the need for decision making and critical thinking skills. This feature fits into the Student Success Cycle by reinforcing the "Apply" step.

Guidance Answers to CHECKPOINT

1. Best Buy.
2. Total cost is $12,180, calculated as:
   $11,400 + $130 + $150 + $100 + $400.
3. The matching principle.
4. Businesses that sell unique, high dollar–value merchandise in relatively low volume levels might choose specific identification. Car dealerships are a good example because each car received as merchandise inventory is unique in terms of both features and identification number. Using specific identification allows the business to accurately tag each item coming in and going out.
5. Moving weighted average gives a lower inventory figure on the balance sheet as compared to FIFO. FIFO's inventory amount will approximate current replacement costs. Moving weighted average costs increase but more slowly because of the effect of averaging.
6. Because these units are the same ones that were originally written down, a reversal is appropriate and would be recorded as:

Merchandise Inventory 2,000
    Cost of Goods Sold............ 2,000
$1,800 − $1,300 = $500/unit
original write-down; $500 × 4 =
$2,000 maximum reversal

7. The reported inventory amount is $540, calculated as (20 × $5) + (40 × $8) + (10 × $12).
8. Cost of goods sold is understated by $10,000 in 2017 and overstated by $10,000 in 2018.
9. The estimated ending inventory (at cost) is $327,000 and is calculated as:
   Step 1: ($530,000 + $335,000) − $320,000 = $545,000
   Step 2: $\frac{$324,000 + $195,000}{$530,000 + $335,000} = 60\%$
   Step 3: $545,000 × 60% = $327,000
10. Company B is more efficient at selling its inventory because it has higher merchandise turnover.

GUIDANCE ANSWERS TO CHECKPOINT
The Checkpoint material throughout the chapter allows students to pause and check their progress. This feature reinforces the "Do," "Check," and "Apply" steps of the Student Success Cycle.

Glossary

Consignee One who receives and holds goods owned by another party for the purpose of acting as an agent and selling the goods for the owner. The consignee gets paid a fee from the consignor for finding a buyer.
Consignor An owner of inventory goods who ships them to another party who will then find a buyer and sell the goods for the owner. The consignor retains title to the goods while they are held offsite by the consignee.
Consistency principle The accounting requirement that a company use the same accounting policies period after period so that the financial statements of succeeding periods will be comparable.

Days' sales in inventory A financial analysis tool used to estimate how many days it will take to convert the inventory on hand into accounts receivable or cash; calculated by dividing the ending inventory by cost of goods sold and multiplying the result by 365.
Faithful representation The accounting principle that requires information to be complete, neutral, unbiased, and free from error.
First-in, first-out (FIFO) The pricing of an inventory under the assumption that inventory items are sold in the order acquired; the first items received are the first items sold.

GLOSSARY
All terms highlighted in the chapter are included.

Problem Material

DEMONSTRATION PROBLEM

This Demonstration Problem is based on the same facts as the Demonstration Problem at the end of Chapter 1 except for two additional items: (b) August 1 and (k) August 18. The following activities occurred during the first month of Joanne Cardinal's new haircutting business called The Cutlery:

a. On August 1, Cardinal put $16,000 cash into a chequing account in the name of The Cutlery. She also invested $10,000 of equipment that she already owned.
b. On August 1, Cardinal paid $2,400 for six months of insurance effective immediately.
c. On August 2, she paid $2,000 cash for furniture for the shop.
d. On August 3, she paid $3,200 cash to rent space in a strip mall for August.
e. On August 4, she furnished the shop by installing the old equipment and some new equipment that she bought on credit for $21,000. This amount is to be repaid in three equal payments at the end of August, September, and October.

DEMONSTRATION PROBLEMS
These problems reinforce the chapter material and further bolster the Student Success Cycle.

ANALYSIS COMPONENT
An analysis component is included in each Mid- and End-of-Chapter Demonstration Problem, as well as several Exercises, Problems, and Focus on Financial Statements questions. These promote critical thinking and give students opportunities to practise their analytical skills.

Analysis Component:
Refer to The Cutlery's August 31, 2017, financial statements. What do each of *equity* and *liabilities* represent?

Concept Review Questions

1. What tasks are performed with the work sheet?
2. What two purposes are accomplished by recording closing entries?
3. What are the four closing entries?
4. Daniel is having trouble determining whether withdrawals, the owner's capital, interest income and prepaid insurance are temporary or permanent accounts. Explain to him the difference between a temporary and a permanent account in accounting and classify the accounts into each category.
9. Refer to Danier's income statement in Appendix III at the end of the book. What journal entry was recorded as of June 28, 2014, to close the revenue account?
10. What is a company's operating cycle?
11. Why is a classified balance sheet more useful to financial statement users than a non-classified balance sheet?
12. What classes of assets and liabilities are shown on a typical classified balance sheet?

CONCEPT REVIEW QUESTIONS
These short-answer questions reinforce the chapter content by Learning Objective.

QUICK STUDY
These single-topic exercises give students a quick test of each key element in the chapter and are referenced to Learning Objectives. Answers to these items are available on **Connect**.

Quick Study

QS 6-1 Inventory ownership LO1
1. At year-end Carefree Company has shipped, FOB destination, $500 of merchandise that is still in transit to Stark Company. Which company should include the $500 as part of inventory at year-end?
2. Carefree Company has shipped goods to Stark and has an arrangement that Stark will sell the goods for Carefree. Identify the consignor and the consignee. Which company should include any unsold goods as part of inventory?

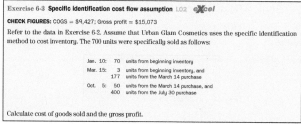

Exercise 6-3 **Specific identification cost flow assumption** LO2 *eXcel*

CHECK FIGURES: COGS = $9,427; Gross profit = $15,073

Refer to the data in Exercise 6-2. Assume that Urban Glam Cosmetics uses the specific identification method to cost inventory. The 700 units were specifically sold as follows:

Jan. 10:	70	units from beginning inventory
Mar. 15:	3	units from beginning inventory, and
	177	units from the March 14 purchase
Oct. 5:	50	units from the March 14 purchase, and
	400	units from the July 30 purchase

Calculate cost of goods sold and the gross profit.

EXERCISES

Exercises provide students with an additional opportunity to reinforce basic chapter concepts by Learning Objective. Note: Selected end-of-chapter exercises and problems are marked with this icon: *eXcel*. These have Excel templates located on **Connect**.

PROBLEMS

Problems typically incorporate two or more concepts. As well, there are two groups of Problems: A Problems and Alternate or B Problems. B Problems mirror the A Problems to help improve understanding through repetition.

Problems

Problem 1-1A **Identifying type of business organization** LO2

Complete the chart below by placing a checkmark in the appropriate column.

	Type of Business Organization		
Characteristic	Sole Proprietorship	Partnership	Corporation
Limited liability			
Unlimited liability			
Owners are shareholders			
Owners are partners			
Taxed as a separate legal entity			

Ethics Challenge

EC 5-1

Claire Phelps is a popular high school student who attends approximately four dances a year at her high school. Each dance requires a new dress and accessories that necessitate a financial outlay of $100 to $200 per event. Claire's parents inform her that she is on her own with respect to financing the dresses. After incurring a major hit to her savings for the first dance in her second year, Claire developed a different approach. She buys the dress on credit the week before the dance, wears it to the dance, and returns the dress the next week to the store for a full refund on her charge card.

Required

1. Comment on the ethics exhibited by Claire and possible consequences of her actions.
2. How does the store account for the dresses that Claire returns?

ETHICS CHALLENGE

Each chapter includes at least one Ethics Challenge to reinforce critical thinking skills for students and open up discussion about various ethical topics.

FOCUS ON FINANCIAL STATEMENTS

Each chapter includes two technical and analytical questions that incorporate into the financial statements all major topics covered up to that point. Additional questions are available online on **Connect**.

Focus on Financial Statements

FFS 2-1

Travis McAllister operates a surveying company. For the first few months of the company's life (through April), the accounting records were maintained by an outside bookkeeping service. According to those records, McAllister's equity balance was $75,000 as of April 30. To save on expenses, McAllister decided to keep the records himself. He managed to record May's transactions properly, but was a bit rusty when the time came to prepare the financial statements. His first versions of the balance sheet and income statement follow. McAllister is bothered that the company apparently operated at a loss during the month, even though he was very busy.

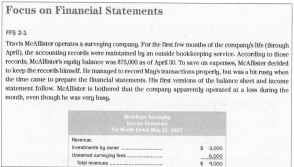

McAllister Surveying
Income Statement
For Month Ended May 31, 2017

Revenue:		
Investments by owner	$	3,000
Unearned surveying fees		6,000
Total revenues	$	9,000

Critical Thinking Mini Case

Prairie Insurance sells life insurance, disability insurance, vehicle insurance, crop insurance, and homeowners' insurance. You are employed by Prairie Insurance and have been promoted to sales division manager for the Western Canadian division. You will be supervising approximately 25 salespeople, along with five administrative assistants at various locations. The salespeople travel extensively and submit expense reports along with sales information monthly. A sample expense report for September shows:

Prairie Insurance—Western Canadian Division
Sales Report: John Bishop
Month Ended September 30, 2017

Sales revenue*	$56,000
Expenses**	34,000

*Sales invoices attached
**Receipts attached

CRITICAL THINKING MINI CASES

These cases give students the opportunity to apply critical thinking skills to concepts learned in the chapter, thus further reinforcing the "Apply" step of the Student Success Cycle.

HELP ME SOLVE IT

New *Help Me Solve It* tutorials are available on **Connect** for Larson's *Fundamental Accounting Principles*. The tutorials guide students through one or two of the more challenging end-of-chapter problems per chapter, providing them with an engaging visual and audio walkthrough of the problem.

What's New

The Accounting Standard

We listened! Through extensive reviewing and consultations with the market, we have heard the issues and concerns instructors like you have about the materials you use to teach introductory financial accounting. Here you will find a list of new changes to specific chapters that our author has made to ensure the content of *Fundamental Accounting Principles* remains current and fresh. Whether you are new to using *Fundamental Accounting Principles* or new to this edition, you can see that McGraw-Hill Education and Larson/Jensen/Dieckmann are setting the accounting standard in *Fundamental Accounting Principles*. We know you'll like what you see.

General Updates

- Appendix III for Volume 1 includes the complete annual audited financial statements, including notes to the financial statements, for WestJet and Danier Leather, as well as the audited financial statements *without* the notes for Indigo Books & Music and Telus. Appendix II for Volume 2 includes the annual audited financial statements, *excluding* notes to the financial statements, for WestJet, Danier Leather, Indigo, and Telus.

- Throughout Volumes 1 and 2, the exercises and problems have been refreshed in terms of numbers and/or business name/owner with a focus on providing relevant company examples to connect with today's students. Company scenarios have been expanded and updated to provide students with more information and updated examples to enhance student engagement. Volume 1 end-of-chapter content was revised by Praise Ma of Kwantlen Polytechnic University, and Volume 2 by Laura Dallas, also of Kwantlen Polytechnic University.

- Various end-of-chapter exercises/problems have been adjusted to incorporate instructor and reviewer suggestions.

- The chapter content is IFRS 2014 compliant throughout Volume I and IFRS 2015 compliant throughout Volume 2; IFRS 2014/2015 references are included where appropriate.

- The 15th edition includes 14 exciting *new* chapter opening vignettes, featuring a range of engaging topics, and including inspiring stories from company startups to success stories of well-known businesses and not-for-profit organizations. Additionally, Chapter 7's vignette features an analysis titled "What Is Cash?" outlining the vast array of Canadian payment options available today. Nearly all of the vignettes now include relevant video links for students to broaden their real-world exposure to critical business decisions.

- Actual businesses used as examples throughout Volumes 1 and 2 are bolded and highlighted in magenta at first mention to emphasize integration of accounting concepts with actual business practice.

- IFRS and ASPE differences are identified at the end of each chapter.

- Important tip boxes have been incorporated throughout the text to direct students' attention to critical concepts that students often miss in their initial reading of the text.

- Many new exhibits have been added, including several new learning summaries to assist students in tying together chapter concepts. Many existing exhibits have been refreshed as appropriate with updated information.

- Several new excerpts have been added to direct students' attention to real-company example disclosures in their most recent published annual financial statement reports.

- The number of actual business examples has increased based on review requests; these have been bolded and highlighted in magenta at first mention for emphasis.
- *New* presentation displays all formulas students need to pay attention to in purple boxes.

Chapter-by-Chapter Updates

CHAPTER 9 (FORMER CHAPTER 10)

- New chapter opening vignette featuring Vancouver International Airport, includes a Video Link spotlighting YVR's state-of-the-art Airside Operations Building.
- Updated critical thinking challenge on the Airside Operations Building at YVR.
- New engaging chapter preview to help students understand capital investments in PPE.
- Updated Decision Maker to enhance student engagement.
- New example of obsolescence, to aid in student understanding.
- Updated presentation of accounting for acquired buildings versus constructed buildings to enhance student comprehension.
- Updated mid-chapter and end-of-chapter Demonstration Problems.
- Updated financial statement excerpts, featuring presentation of Indigo Books & Music Inc.'s accounting policy and depreciation schedule for property, plant, and equipment and Microsoft's presentation and disclosure over intangible assets.
- Updated coverage of Patents and Copyrights to reflect current Canadian laws over intellectual property rights.
- New example of acquisition: Shoppers Drug Mart by Loblaw Companies, Ltd. is provided with example note disclosure to help students understand accounting for goodwill.
- New Exhibit 9.23: World's Most Valuable brands.

CHAPTER 10 (FORMER CHAPTER 11)

- New chapter opening vignette spotlighting Pebble Technology Corp. and its efforts to raise capital through Kickstarter fundraising campaigns. Vignette includes video links to further student engagement.
- Updated excerpt of Second Cup Ltd.'s balance sheet, featuring presentation of current liabilities.
- New presentation of Exhibit 10.6 featuring Sales Tax Rates, effective January 1, 2016.
- New Exhibit 10.8: GST-Exempt and Zero-Rated Products, including an explanation of zero-rated goods and GST-exempt products.
- New section illustrating collection, payment, and final remittance of HST.
- New section outlining accounting for customer awards/loyalty programs and gift cards.
- Terminology updated from *long-term* liabilities to *non-current*.
- Updated chapter Demonstration Problem, enhancing student engagement.

CHAPTER 11 (FORMER CHAPTER 12)

- New chapter opening vignette featuring Canadian-born start-up Kicking Horse Coffee includes video links featuring an interview on entrepreneurship and expansion into the United States and an inside look at Kicking Horse Coffee.
- New Critical Thinking challenge.
- Updated terminology from partnership *income*/loss to partnership *profit*/loss.
- Updated Exhibit 11.10.

CHAPTER 12 (FORMER CHAPTER 13)

- Updated chapter opening vignette features new video link to Dragon's Den episode and CBC interview.
- New Decision Insight features Cara Operations and its decision to go public.
- New excerpt from Telus Corporation's financial statements illustrates disclosure of declared dividends.

- New Financial Statement Analysis section for ROE and book value per share to provide more real world application context for the chapter content.

CHAPTER 13 (FORMER CHAPTER 14)

- New chapter opening vignette highlights the history of Apple Inc. from its origins as a tech start-up to the recent 7:1 stock split, including a Video Link highlighting what investors should know about the impact of the Apple Inc. stock split.

- Expanded discussion of stock splits incorporates an analysis of the impact of the Apple Inc. stock split to shareholders, enhancing student engagement by demonstrating the impact through investigating the event.

- New Financial Statement Analysis section includes the dividend payout ratio, featuring the dividend payout ratio for Telus Corporation and providing more real-world context for chapter content.

- Removed appendix covering treasury shares

- New table featuring several examples of classifying changes to accounting estimates and accounting policy changes.

CHAPTER 14 (FORMER CHAPTER 15)

- New chapter opening vignette features two examples of real bond issuance by ZooShare with different risk profiles; it includes video link helping students to understand the business model of ZooShare's renewable energy cooperative.

- New example bond issuance for Telus Corporation to enhance real-world application of the bond issuance procedures.

- New Decision Insight covering the over-the-counter trading options for the sale of or determination of market pricing for corporate bonds in Canada.

- New example of a bond issuance by Telus Corp., with the current trading information.

- Updated chapter demonstration example to illustrate the present value of a premium bond to enhance student engagement.

- New Important Tip box on calculating bond interest expense.

- New financial statement note excerpt from WestJet.

- Content covering leases, previously in the appendix, has been moved into the main chapter with expanded examples to help students understand the accounting differences for the lessee and lessor based on the terms of the lease agreement.

- Added Financial Statement Analysis section for debt to equity Ratio, to provide more real-world application context for the chapter content.

CHAPTER 15 (FORMER CHAPTER 16)

- New chapter opening vignette features Saskatchewan craft brewery start-up Farmery; it includes video links to CBC Dragon's Den episode and a CBC interview.

- New Exhibits 15.1 and 15.2, financial statement disclosure excerpts for PMC-Sierra and Indigo, providing context to students and aiding comprehension of chapter topics.

- New Exhibit 15.3 highlights an example stock quote for Spin Master Corp.

- Updated Accounting for Investments section based on IFRS 9.

- New Decision Insight box spotlights Bernie Madoff and Ponzi Schemes (repurposed from chapter opening vignette in 14th edition).

- Updated Investments section based on new IFRS 9, effective January 1, 2018. Terminology is updated to reflect new standards.

- New Exhibit 15.7, Accounting for Investments Summary Chart, outlines the key issues of accounting for strategic and non-strategic investments and corresponding journal entries and financial statement presentation.

CHAPTER 16 (FORMER CHAPTER 17)

- New chapter opening vignette features Butter Avenue patisserie and includes Video Link for students to learn more about the company.

- New Decision Insight on top 10 cash flow management tips for small businesses.

- Coverage of direct method of cash flow statements moved from appendix into main chapter with an emphasis on the key differences and similarities between the direct and indirect methods highlighted through Important Tip boxes to aid student comprehension.

- New financial statement excerpt provides an example cash flow statement for Brick Brewing Company Ltd. to help students understand the real-world application of the material.

- New summary chart (Exhibit 16.14) provides key information to students on preparing a cash flow statement and highlighting key differences between direct and indirect methods of statement of cash flow.

- Mid-Chapter Demonstration Problem and Demonstration Problem now feature both direct and indirect methods.

CHAPTER 17 (FORMER CHAPTER 18)

- New chapter opening vignette features Lululemon Athletica Inc. and analyzes its growth from inception to a $1.8 billion company, providing analysis of its profit and gross margins and analyzing its key success factors.

- Financial statement analysis is illustrated with a more detailed and engaging example, including heightened company detail to capture student interest and demonstrate real world applicability.

- New introductory section focussing on the basics of analysis encourages students to perform a more holistic approach to their analysis and provides a brief overview of tools such as PESTLE, SWOT, and Porter's Five Forces.

- New terminology: *acid-test ratio* is referred to as the *quick ratio*.

- Formulas requiring memorization are highlighted in purple boxes and key rules of thumb and commentary on favourable versus unfavourable results have been added to help students in interpreting their results.

APPENDIX I

- All rates (i.e., EI, CPP, Provincial Tax, Federal Tax) are updated to 2015.

APPENDIX II

- Includes annual audited financial statements (*excluding* notes to the financial statements) for WestJet, Danier Leather, Telus Corporation, and Indigo Books & Music. (See Volume 1 for WestJet and Danier audited financial statements with notes.)

APPENDIX III

- Sample chart of accounts updated to reflect textbook content.

Market Leading Technology

connect

Learn without Limits

McGraw-Hill Connect® is an award-winning digital teaching and learning platform that gives students the means to better connect with their coursework, with their instructors, and with the important concepts that they will need to know for success now and in the future. With Connect, instructors can take advantage of McGraw-Hill's trusted content to seamlessly deliver assignments, quizzes, and tests online. McGraw-Hill Connect is the only learning platform that continually adapts to each student, delivering precisely what they need, when they need it, so class time is more engaging and effective. Connect makes teaching and learning personal, easy, and proven.

Connect Key Features:

SMARTBOOK®

As the first and only adaptive reading experience, SmartBook is changing the way students read and learn. SmartBook creates a personalized reading experience by highlighting the most important concepts a student needs to learn at that moment in time. As a student engages with SmartBook, the reading experience continuously adapts by highlighting content based on what each student knows and doesn't know. This ensures that he or she is focused on the content needed to close specific knowledge gaps, while it simultaneously promotes long-term learning.

CONNECT INSIGHT®

Connect Insight is Connect's new one-of-a-kind visual analytics dashboard—now available for both instructors and students—that provides at-a-glance information regarding student performance, which is immediately actionable. By presenting assignment, assessment, and topical performance results together with a time metric that is easily visible for aggregate or individual results, Connect Insight gives the user the ability to take a just-in-time approach to teaching and learning, which was never before available. Connect Insight presents data that empowers students and helps instructors improve class performance in a way that is efficient and effective.

SIMPLE ASSIGNMENT MANAGEMENT

With Connect, creating assignments is easier than ever, so instructors can spend more time teaching and less time managing.

- Assign SmartBook learning modules
- Instructors can edit existing questions and create their own questions
- Draw from a variety of text-specific questions, resources, and test bank material to assign online
- Streamline lesson planning, student progress reporting, and assignment grading to make classroom management more efficient than ever

SMART GRADING

When it comes to studying, time is precious. Connect helps students learn more efficiently by providing feedback and practice material when they need it, where they need it.

- Automatically score assignments, providing students immediate feedback on their work and comparisons with correct answers
- Access and review each response, manually change grades, or leave comments for students to review

- Track individual student performance—by question or assignment, or in relation to the class overall—with detailed grade reports.

- Reinforce classroom concepts with practice tests and instant quizzes.

- Integrate grade reports easily with Learning Management Systems including Blackboard, D2L, and Moodle.

INSTRUCTOR LIBRARY

The Connect Instructor Library is a repository for additional resources to improve student engagement in and out of the class. It provides all the critical resources instructors need to build their course. Instructors can

- Access Instructor resources

- View assignments and resources created for past sections

- Post their own resources for students to use

Instructor Resources

Instructor supplements are available within **Connect**.

SOLUTIONS MANUAL

Fundamental Accounting Principles continues to set the standard for accuracy of its problem material. The Solutions Manual has been revised by Praise Ma, Kwantlen Polytechnic University (Volume 1) and Laura Dallas, Kwantlen Polytechnic University (Volume 2). Additional accuracy checking was provided by Rhonda Heninger, SAIT Polytechnic, Elizabeth Hicks, Douglas College, and Michelle Young, CPA. Available in both Microsoft Word and PDF format, solutions for all problem material are included.

COMPUTERIZED TEST BANK

The test bank has been revised and technically checked for accuracy to reflect the changes in the Fifteenth Canadian Edition. Carol Tristani, Mohawk College, revised the test bank for this edition. Grouped according to Learning Objective, difficulty level, and by level of Bloom's Taxonomy, the questions in the computerized test bank include true/false, multiple choice, matching, short essay, and problem material.

POWERPOINT® PRESENTATIONS

These presentation slides, revised by Betty Young, Red River College, are fully integrated with the text to visually present chapter concepts.

INSTRUCTOR'S MANUAL

The Instructor's Manual, revised by Denise Cook, Durham College (Volume 1) and Joe Pidutti, Durham College (Volume 2), cross-references assignment materials by Learning Objective and also provides a convenient chapter outline.

FOCUS ON FINANCIAL STATEMENTS

These include technical and analytical questions that incorporate major topics covered. These, and accompanying solutions in the Solutions Manual, have been revised by Stephanie Ibach, MacEwan University. Two additional Focus on Financial Statement exercises for each chapter are included on Connect.

EXTEND YOUR KNOWLEDGE

This supplemental material has been developed to delve into more detail for specific topics. These have been revised by Stephanie Ibach, MacEwan University.

EXCEL TEMPLATE SOLUTIONS
Solutions to the problems using Excel templates are available for instructors. These have been revised by Ian Feltmate, Acadia University.

IMAGE BANK
All exhibits and tables displayed in the text are available for your use, whether for creating transparencies or handouts, or customizing your own PowerPoint presentations.

Other Supplements for Students

WORKING PAPERS
Available for purchase by students, printed Working Papers for Volumes 1 and 2 match the end-of-chapter material. They include papers that can be used to solve all of the Quick Study questions, Exercises, and A and B Problem sets. The Working Papers for the Fifteenth Canadian Edition have been revised by Praise Ma, Kwantlen Polytechnic University (Volume 1) and Laura Dallas, Kwantlen Polytechnic University (Volume 2). Additional technical checking was completed by Michelle Young.

Superior Learning Solutions and Support

The McGraw-Hill Education team is ready to help instructors assess and integrate any of our products, technology, and services into your course for optimal teaching and learning performance. Whether it's helping your students improve their grades, or putting your entire course online, the McGraw-Hill Education team is here to help you do it. Contact your Learning Solutions Consultant today to learn how to maximize all of McGraw-Hill Education's resources.

For more information, please visit us online: http://www.mheducation.ca/highereducation/educators/digital-solutions

Developing a Market-Driven Text

The success of this text is the result of an exhaustive process, which has gone beyond the scope of a single edition. Hundreds of instructors and educators across the country have been involved in giving their feedback to help develop the most successful accounting fundamentals text in the country. We owe thanks to all of those who took the time to evaluate this textbook and its supplemental products.

Fifteenth Canadian Edition Reviewers

Joan Baines	Red River College	Rod Delcourt	Algonquin College
Les Barnhouse	Grant MacEwan University	Kevin deWolde	University of the Fraser Valley
Maria Belanger	Algonquin College	Han Donker	University of Northern British Columbia
Robert Briggs	New Brunswick Community College	David Fleming	George Brown College
Lewis Callahan	Lethbridge College	Brent Groen	University of Fraser Valley
Barb Chapple	St. Clair College	Kerry Hendricks	Fanshawe College
Shiraz Charania	Langara College	Rhonda Heninger	Southern Alberta Institute of Technology
Denise Cook	Durham College		
Derek Cook	Okanagan College	Elizabeth Hicks	Douglas College
Heather Cornish	Northern Alberta Institute of Technology	Darcie Hillebrand	Capilano University
		Gwen Hoyseth	Grande Prairie Regional College

Yvonne Jacobs	*College of the North Atlantic*	Doug Ringrose	*Grant MacEwan University*
Lauren Kirychuk	*Bow Valley College*	Pina Salvaggio	*Dawson College*
Laurette Korman	*Kwantlen Polytechnic University*	David Scott	*Niagara College*
Michelle Nicholson	*Okanagan College*	Glen Stanger	*Douglas College*
Tariq Nizami	*Champlain Regional College*	Doug Thibodeau	*Nova Scotia Community College*
Joe Pidutti	*Durham College*	Peggy Wallace	*Trent University*
Traven Reed	*Canadore College*	Patricia Zima	*Mohawk College*
James Reimer	*Lethbridge College*		

Fundamental Accounting Principles continues to set the bar in terms of its leading-edge approach to educating today's students through outstanding quality, dependable accuracy, and state-of-the-art supplemental resources.

This has been possible only because of the outstanding efforts and contributions of a dedicated team of exceptional individuals. I owe many thanks to their expertise and commitment as it was extensively drawn upon during the process of writing this textbook. Particular thanks go out to Maria Belanger, Shannon Butler, Denise Cook, Ian Feltmate, Rhonda Heninger, Elizabeth Hicks, Stephanie Ibach, Joe Pidutti, Don Smith, Carol Tristani, Betty Young, and Michelle Young. A big thanks to the many entrepreneurs, financial experts, and business owners who devoted their precious time to making our chapter opening vignettes compelling and captivating. Thanks also to our brilliant illustrator, Rachel Idzerda (www.rachelidzerda.com), for sharing our vision and for her tireless efforts in crafting our cover illustration with creativity and vibrant energy. A special thanks to my close friends and colleagues Praise Ma and Laura Dallas for approaching the project with a fresh perspective. Their innovative spirits and their outstanding dedication ensure the end-of-chapter questions are accurate, relevant, and engaging for today's students. I am thankful to McGraw-Hill Ryerson's exceptional team, including Rhondda McNabb, Joy Armitage Taylor, Keara Emmett, Sarah Fulton May, Jessica Barnoski, and freelance copyeditor Karen Rolfe, who have been exceptionally responsive, supportive, and dedicated to producing a phenomenal product.

I am incredibly appreciative to my colleagues across Canada and current and past students who have inspired enhancements for this edition. Their knowledge and expertise in identifying student learning hurdles in the classroom and suggestions for enhancing student comprehension are invaluable in our continuous improvement initiative to maintain this textbook as the industry standard.

With heartfelt appreciation,
Heidi Dieckmann

CHAPTER 9

Property, Plant, and Equipment and Intangibles

A Look Back

Chapters 7 and 8 focused on current assets: cash, cash equivalents, and receivables. We explained why they are known as liquid assets and described how companies account and report for them.

A Look at This Chapter

This chapter introduces us to non-current assets. We explain how to account for a non-current asset's initial cost, the allocation of an asset's cost to periods benefiting from it, the recording of additional costs after an asset is purchased, and the disposal of an asset.

Photo Courtesy of Vancouver International Airport and Larry Goldstein.

LEARNING OBJECTIVES

LO1 Describe property, plant, and equipment (PPE) and calculate their cost.

LO2 Explain, record, and calculate depreciation using the methods of straight-line, units-of-production, and double-declining-balance.

LO3 Explain and calculate depreciation for partial years.

LO4 Explain and calculate revised depreciation.

LO5 Explain and record impairment losses.

LO6 Account for asset disposal through discarding, selling, or exchanging an asset.

LO7 Account for intangible assets and their amortization.

*Appendix 9A

LO8 Explain and calculate revised depreciation when there is a subsequent capital expenditure that creates partial-period depreciation.

Vancouver International Airport—Canadian Leaders in Customer Experience and Innovation

Vancouver Airport Authority is a community-based, not-for-profit organization that manages Vancouver International Airport (YVR). Since its inception in 1992, the Airport Authority has experienced an incredible history of growth, innovation, and leadership along with industry excellence.

Canada's second-busiest airport, YVR served more than 19 million passengers in 2014, with 53 airlines connecting people and businesses to more than 110 non-stop destinations worldwide. The Airport Authority continues to build a world-class, sustainable airport to fulfill its mission to connect British Columbia to the world.

YVR was voted Best Airport in North America for the sixth consecutive year, and Best Airport in the World for its size category of 10 to 20 million passengers, in the 2015 Skytrax World Airport Awards, the global benchmark of airport excellence. YVR is the only airport to have ever received this honour for six consecutive years. "This award is a powerful testament to the commitment of the YVR community—24,000 strong—to go beyond, every day," said Craig Richmond, president & CEO, Vancouver Airport Authority.

The Airport Authority reinvests all earnings into airport operations and development. The Airport Authority continues to ensure airport operations are optimized through its 10-year, $1.8 billion capital plan to upgrade terminal facilities and infrastructure, including hundreds of metres of moving walkways and high-speed baggage systems, with a focus on decreasing connection times between international and domestic flights.

YVR's new, state-of-the-art Airside Operations Building (AOB) opened in winter 2014. The AOB replaced the existing 50-year-old fire hall and consolidated all airside operations, from emergency response to snow removal, into one, central airside location. The AOB is 117,101 square feet, slightly smaller than seven hockey rinks.

In addition to terminal and airside improvements, the Airport Authority formed a joint venture with McArthurGlen Group to develop Greater Vancouver's first luxury designer outlet, which opened in summer 2015.

YVR also recently launched an innovative solution to passenger flow issues—BorderXpress Automated Passport Control (APC) kiosks. These kiosks are able to efficiently process passengers through customs based on self-serve, touchscreen prompts, significantly reducing passenger wait times. Since its product launch in September 2013, YVR has successfully deployed more than 600 BorderXpress kiosks in over 23 international airports across Canada, the United States, and the Caribbean, serving over 20 million travellers.

With continued investment in capital assets, the Airport Authority has developed policies and procedures to ensure they are captured effectively in its accounting records. In its 2014 audited consolidated financial statements, the Airport Authority reported net capital assets of $1.83 billion, representing 86.6% of total assets. Major categories include buildings and structures, runways, rapid transit infrastructure, machinery and equipment, furniture and fixtures, computer equipment and systems, construction in progress, and the Airport Authority's impressive art collection. Based on the significant accounting policies, capital assets are amortized on a straight-line basis, at cost less estimated salvage value, over a period not exceeding the estimated useful lives. Capitalized costs include the purchase price and acquisition and construction costs such as "installation costs, design and engineering fees, legal fees, survey costs, site preparation, transportation charges, labour, insurance and duties."

From new buildings to improved infrastructure and innovative services, the Airport Authority is committed to creating an airport that British Columbia can be proud of—a premier global gateway.

Source: www.yvr.ca

Video Link: https://www.youtube.com/watch?v=xS60bqgB8VM

CRITICAL THINKING CHALLENGE	You are asked by the CFO of YVR to evaluate the newest capital asset, the Airside Operations Building at YVR, and to break it into major components for depreciation purposes. Identify at least five major components and determine an expected life for each of those components.

CHAPTER PREVIEW

Why do companies like Facebook Inc. and Google Inc. have less than 20% of total assets in PPE while other companies like WestJet and Air Canada have over 50% of total assets invested in PPE? The difference is that airlines are capital intensive and technology companies require a greater investment in research and development. *Property, plant, and equipment* and *intangible assets* are often the key areas requiring investment of capital resources for newly established businesses. Over time, the major assets held in this category require repairs, improvements, and replacements with newer, more efficient assets or more physical capacity due to expansion. As the items held in this category are material in relation to their total assets, it is essential that we are cautious to effectively capture the initial costs on the balance sheet and subsequently record the usage of these assets on the income statement as an expense, referred to as *depreciation expense,* in the period the asset is utilized.

This chapter focuses on non-current assets used in the operation of a business: *property, plant, and equipment* and *intangible assets.* Property, plant, and equipment represent a major investment for most companies and make up a large portion of assets on the balance sheet. They also affect the income statement because their costs are charged to depreciation expense, often one of the largest expenses on the income statement. This chapter will describe the purchase and use of these assets. We also explain what distinguishes property, plant, and equipment assets from other types of assets, how to determine their cost, how to allocate their costs to periods benefiting from their use, and how to record their disposal.

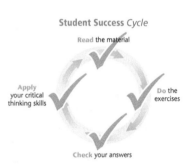

Student Success *Cycle*

Read the material

Do the exercises

Check your answers

Apply your critical thinking skills

Property, Plant, and Equipment (PPE)

LO1   Describe property, plant, and equipment (PPE) and calculate their cost.

Non-current assets that are used in the operations of a business and have a useful life of more than one accounting period are divided into three groups:

1. Tangible assets known as property, plant, and equipment[1]

2. Intangible assets[2]

3. Goodwill[3]

Property, plant, and equipment (PPE), sometimes referred to as **capital assets** or **fixed assets**, includes land, buildings, equipment, machinery, and leasehold improvements. For instance, WestJet's $2,793,194 of net PPE as at December 31, 2014, includes aircraft, ground property and equipment, spare engines and parts, buildings, and leasehold improvements as shown in the financial statements located in

---

[1]   IFRS 2015, IAS 16.

[2]   IFRS 2015 IAS 38.

[3]   **Goodwill** is an asset representing the future economic benefits arising from other assets acquired in a business combination that are not individually identified and separately recognized.

Appendix II. **Intangible assets** lack physical substance and include patents, copyrights, leaseholds, drilling rights, and trademarks and are discussed in a later section of this chapter.

For many businesses, PPE make up the single largest asset category on the balance sheet. For example, on its September 28, 2014, balance sheet, Starbucks Ltd. shows total assets of $10.75 billion with net PPE comprising $3.52 billion of this amount. Telus Corporation reported $8.4 billion of net property, plant, and equipment at December 31, 2013, representing 39% of total assets.

PPE are set apart from other assets by two important features:

1. *These assets are used in business operations to help generate revenue.* This makes them different from *inventory*, for instance, which is an asset that is *not used* in operations but rather held for the purpose of resale. A company that purchases a computer for the purpose of selling it reports the computer on the balance sheet as inventory. But if the same company purchases this computer for use in operations, it is classified as PPE.

2. *PPE are in use and provide benefits for more than one accounting period.* This makes PPE different from *current assets* such as *supplies* that are usually consumed soon after they are placed in use. The cost of current assets is assigned to a single period as they are used.

Accounting for PPE reflects these two important features. We must initially record the cost of each PPE item (balance sheet focus) and allocate its estimated period cost to each appropriate period benefiting from its use (income statement focus) in the manner in which the asset is consumed/used.

Exhibit 9.1 shows the *three main accounting issues with PPE*. They are:

1. Calculating and accounting for the initial and subsequent costs of PPE

2. Allocating the costs of PPE against revenues for the periods they benefit in the manner in which the asset is consumed/used

3. Recording the disposal of PPE

This chapter focuses on the decisions and factors surrounding these three important issues.

EXHIBIT 9.1

Issues in Accounting for PPE

© Paha_l/Dreamstime.com/GetStock.com

© 6thgearadvertising/Dreamstime.com/
GetStock.com

© Hartphotography/Dreamstime.com/
GetStock.com

Decline in book value over service life

Acquisition	Use	Disposal
• Calculate initial cost	• Account for subsequent costs • Allocate cost to periods benefited	• Record disposal

Cost of PPE

Consistent with the *cost principle*, PPE are recorded at **cost**, which includes all normal and reasonable expenditures necessary to get the asset in place and ready for its intended use.[4] The cost of a piece of manufacturing equipment, for instance, includes the following:

1. Its invoice price, less any cash discount for early payment

2. Freight, unpacking, and assembling costs

3. Non-refundable sales taxes (PST, HST)

4. All necessary costs of installing and testing the equipment before placing it in use. Examples are the costs of building a base or foundation for the equipment, of providing electrical hook-ups, and of adjusting the equipment before using it in operations.

The above example highlights serveral types of *capital expenditures*. **Capital expenditures** are costs of PPE that provide material benefits extending beyond the current period.[5] They are debited to PPE accounts and reported on the balance sheet.

When expenditures regarding PPE are *not* considered a normal part of getting the asset ready for its intended use, they are expensed as a current-period cost. For example, if a machine is damaged during unpacking, the **repairs** are recorded as an expense. Also, a traffic fine paid for moving heavy machinery on city streets without a proper permit is an expense and *not* part of the machinery's cost. These are **revenue expenditures**: costs that maintain an asset but do not materially increase the asset's life or productive capabilities. They are recorded as expenses and deducted from revenues in the current period's income statement. Consistent with this rule, **WestJet** reports:

> Major overhaul expenditures are capitalized and depreciated over the expected life between overhauls. All other costs relating to the maintenance of fleet assets are charged to the consolidated statement of earnings on consumption or as incurred.
>
> Source: WestJet Airlines, 2013 Annual Report

Subsequent Expenditures

When PPE is acquired and put into service, additional or *subsequent* expenditures often are incurred after the acquisition to operate, maintain, repair, and improve it. In recording these subsequent expenditures, we must decide whether they are to be accounted for as capital or *revenue* expenditure. Exhibit 9.2 can be used to determine if a subsequent expenditure is capital or revenue in nature. Examples of subsequent capital expenditures include roofing replacement, plant expansion, and major overhauls of machinery and equipment. These expenditures either extend the life of the asset or improve efficiency; therefore, they are capitalized and depreciated. Examples of subsequent revenue expenditures that would be recorded as an expense on the income statement are supplies, fuel, minor repairs, and costs relating to routine testing.

For example, consider the following expenses Dealz Wheelz, an Ontario rental car rental agency, incurs in its normal course of business.

1. Its 2015 Toyota Yaris experiences a battery failure and the mechanic installs a new battery to fix the problem. This would be classified as a current-period revenue expenditure and is recorded as a

---

4 IFRS 2015 IAS 16, para. 16.

5 IFRS 2015, IAS 16, para. 29–42, discusses the use of the cost and revaluation models of measurement after recognition of PPE. The cost model has been adopted in this chapter. The revaluation model is beyond the scope of this text and is left for discussion in a more advanced course.

EXHIBIT 9.2

Is It a Capital or Revenue Expenditure?

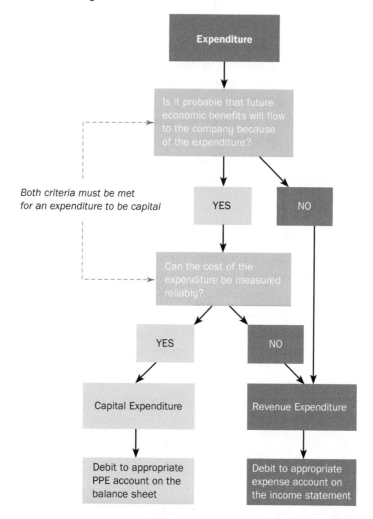

current-period expense. Revenue expenditures like the purchase of the battery do not materially improve the future value of the economic benefits obtained from the car but help to *maintain the asset*, keeping it in good working order over its estimated useful life.

2. Dealz Wheelz had a customer drive the 2011 Ford Fusion from Toronto to Halifax in humid August weather, without getting an oil change, requiring the mechanic to do a complete engine replacement upon its return to the rental depot. Replacing the engine in this situation *does* improve the future economic benefits of the car because its useful life is extended. Therefore, the new engine is recorded as a capital expenditure.[6]

A subsequent capital expenditure does not always increase an asset's useful life. An example is replacing manual controls on a machine with automatic controls to reduce labour costs. This machine will still wear out just as fast as it would with manual controls, but because the automatic controls improve the machine's efficiency in terms of labour cost savings, it is a capital expenditure.

---

6 IFRS 2015, IAS 16, para. 13, requires the carrying amount of those parts that are replaced to be removed from the accounting records. The removal of PPE from the accounting records, also known as the disposal of PPE, is discussed in a later section of this chapter.

Financial statements are affected for several years as a result of the choice to record costs as revenue expenditures or as capital expenditures. Therefore, managers must be careful when classifying costs.

PPE Subledger

For accounts payable, accounts receivable, and merchandise inventory, we discussed and illustrated the benefits in maintaining both a control account in the general ledger and a corresponding subledger. In the case of accounts receivable, the subledger recorded the detailed transactions by customer. Many companies also keep a subledger for PPE. The PPE subledger details information such as cost, residual value, estimated useful life, date of purchase, depreciation, serial number, and other relevant data for each item of PPE or group of PPE. This information is useful in recording depreciation and preparing related notes to the financial statements, but is also a valuable form of internal control over PPE. The subledger can be used to verify recorded PPE against a physical count.

Low-Cost Asset Purchases

Maintaining individual PPE records can be expensive, even in the most advanced system. For that reason, many companies do not keep detailed records for assets costing less than some minimum amount such as $100. Instead, these low-cost PPE items are treated as revenue expenditures. This means their costs are directly charged to an expense account at the time of purchase. This practice is acceptable under the *materiality principle*. Treating immaterial capital expenditures as revenue expenditures is unlikely to mislead users of financial statements. As an example, in a recent annual report **Coca-Cola** disclosed that it capitalizes only *major* or material betterments:

> Additions and major replacements or betterments are added to the assets at cost. Maintenance and repair costs and minor replacements are charged to expense when incurred.
>
> Source: Coca-Cola

DECISION MAKER
Answer—End of chapter

Restaurant Results

You are a new grad who recently opened your own restaurant. Because of a cash shortage, you are preparing financial statements in the hope of getting a short-term loan from the bank. A friend of yours suggests that you treat as many expenses as possible as capital expenditures. What are the effects on financial statements of treating expenses as capital expenditures? What do you think of your friend's proposal?

CHECKPOINT

1. What is included in the cost of a PPE asset?
2. Explain the difference between revenue expenditures and capital expenditures and how they are recorded.
3. What is a subsequent capital expenditure and how is it recorded?

Do Quick Study questions: QS 9-1, QS 9-2

In the remainder of this section we explain how to determine the capital costs for each of five types of PPE: land (property), land improvements, buildings (plant), leasehold improvements, and machinery and equipment.

Land

When land is purchased for a building site, its cost includes the total amount paid for the land, including any real estate commissions, fees for insuring the title, legal fees, and any accrued property taxes paid by the purchaser. Payments for surveying, clearing, grading, draining, and landscaping[7] are also included in the cost of land. Other costs of land include assessments by the local government, whether incurred at the time of purchase or later, for items such as roadways, sewers, and sidewalks. These assessments are included because they permanently add to the land's value.

Land purchased as a building site sometimes includes a building or other obstructions that must be removed. In such cases, the total purchase price is capitalized under the Land account along with the cost of removing the building, less any amounts recovered through sale of salvaged materials. To illustrate, assume a company bought land for a retail store for $170,000. This land contains an old service garage that is removed at a net cost of $15,000 ($20,000 in costs less $5,000 proceeds from salvaged materials). Additional closing costs totalled $10,000, and consisted of brokerage fees ($8,000), legal fees ($1,500), and title costs ($500). The cost of this land is $195,000, calculated as:

Net cash price of land	$170,000
Net cost of service garage removal	15,000
Closing costs	10,000
Cost of land	**$195,000**

Land Improvements

Because land has an unlimited life and is not consumed when used, it is not subject to depreciation. But **land improvements** such as parking lot surfaces, driveways, fences, and lighting systems have limited useful lives. While these costs increase the usefulness of the land, they are charged to a separate PPE account called Land Improvements so their costs can be allocated to the periods they benefit.

Buildings

ACQUIRED BUILDINGS

A Building account is charged for the costs of purchasing or constructing a building when it is used in operations. When purchased, the costs of a building usually include its *purchase price, brokerage fees, taxes, title fees, and legal costs.* Its costs also include all expenditures to make it ready for its intended use, such as repairs or renovations that include wiring, lighting, flooring, and wall coverings.

CONSTRUCTED BUILDINGS

When a building, or any PPE item, is constructed by a company for the company's own use, its cost includes construction-related materials and labour costs; heat, electricity and other utilities consumed during construction; plus a reasonable amount of depreciation expense on machinery used to construct the

---

[7] Landscaping is included in the cost of land if it is considered permanent in nature. Landscaping costs with a finite life of greater than one accounting period are charged to the Land Improvements account.

asset. Cost of construction also includes design fees, building permits, and interest and insurance costs applicable to the period of construction. All interest and insurance costs incurred *after* the asset is placed in use are expensed as operating expenses.

Leasehold Improvements

Many businesses rent their facilities under a contract called a **lease**. The property's owner grants the lease and is called the **lessor**. The one who secures the right to possess and use the property is called the **lessee**. Non-current leases sometimes require the lessee to pay for alterations or improvements to the leased property—such as interior modifications, enhancements, painting, and storefronts—these costs are referred to as **leasehold improvements**. Leasehold improvements become part of the property and revert to the lessor at the end of the lease. These costs are debited to a *Leasehold Improvements* account and are depreciated over either the life of the lease or the life of the improvements, whichever is shorter. In its notes to the financial statements, **Lululemon Athletica Inc.** reports net leasehold improvements at February 2, 2014, of $140,748,000 at cost, depreciated using the straight-line method over the lesser of the length of the lease to a maximum of five years.

Machinery and Equipment

The cost of machinery and equipment consists of all costs normal and necessary to purchase it and prepare it for its intended use. It includes the purchase price, less discounts, plus non-refundable sales taxes, transportation charges, insurance while in transit, and the costs of installing, assembling, and testing of machinery and equipment.

Lump-Sum Asset Purchase

A **lump-sum purchase**, also called a **basket purchase**, is the purchase of PPE in a group with a single transaction for a lump-sum price. When this occurs, we allocate the cost of the purchase among the different types of assets acquired based on their *relative values*. Their values can be estimated by appraisal or by using the tax-assessed valuations of the assets. To illustrate, assume **David's Tea** paid $630,000 cash to acquire land appraised at $210,000, land improvements appraised at $70,000, and a building appraised at $420,000. The $630,000 cost was allocated on the basis of appraised values as shown in Exhibit 9.3:

EXHIBIT 9.3

Calculating Costs in a Lump-Sum Purchase

	Appraised Value	Percent of Total		Apportioned Cost	
Land...	$210,000	30	($210,000/$700,000)	$189,000	($630,000 × 30%)
Land improvements	70,000	10	($ 70,000/$700,000)	63,000	($630,000 × 10%)
Building	420,000	60	($420,000/$700,000)	378,000	($630,000 × 60%)
Totals	$700,000	100		$630,000	

Alternatively, the calculation can be done by dividing the total cost by the total appraised value ($630,000/$700,000 = 0.90 or 90%) and applying the 90% to the individual appraised values as follows:

Land...	$210,000	×	90% =	$189,000
Land improvements	70,000	×	90% =	63,000
Building	420,000	×	90% =	378,000

CHECKPOINT

4. Identify the account charged for each of the following expenditures: (a) purchase price of a vacant lot, and (b) cost of paving that vacant lot.

5. What amount is recorded as the cost of a new machine given the following items related to its purchase: gross purchase price, $700,000; sales tax, $49,000; purchase discount taken, $21,000; freight to move machine to plant, $3,500; assembly costs, $3,000; cost of foundation for machine, $2,500; cost of spare parts used in maintaining machine, $4,200?

Do Quick Study question: QS 9-3

Depreciation

LO2 Explain, record, and calculate depreciation using the methods of straight-line, units-of-production, and double-declining-balance.

Because PPE (except for land) wear out or decline in usefulness as they are used, an expense must be recorded. **Depreciation**[8] is the process of matching (or allocating) the depreciable cost of an asset in a rational and systematic manner over the asset's estimated useful life.[9]

To illustrate why the allocation of an asset's cost is required, assume that a delivery van is purchased for $40,000 on January 1, 2017. It is estimated that the van will help generate $30,000 in revenues each year for four years. At the end of the four-year period, it is estimated that the van will be worthless. We could record the $40,000 as an expense in the year it was purchased as illustrated in Exhibit 9.4. However, profit is distorted because we have not matched the expense of the delivery van over the four years that it is creating revenue. The treatment in Exhibit 9.4 is therefore *not in conformance with GAAP.*

EXHIBIT 9.4

Cost of the Delivery Van Recorded as an Expense in Year of Purchase

	2017	2018	2019	2020
Revenues	$30,000	$30,000	$30,000	$30,000
Expense	40,000	-0-	-0-	-0-
Profit (Loss)	($10,000)	$30,000	$30,000	$30,000

Estimated four-year life of the delivery van.

If instead we apply the matching principle and allocate the cost of the delivery van against the periods it generates revenue, we achieve a more accurate reflection of performance across time, as Exhibit 9.5 illustrates.

---

8 The term *depreciation* is used to describe the allocation of the cost of a tangible asset over its useful life, and *amortization* is used to describe the allocation of the cost of an intangible asset. The amortization of intangible assets is discussed in more detail in a later section.

9 IFRS 2015, IAS 16, para. 50.

EXHIBIT 9.5

Cost of the Delivery Van Matched Against Revenues Generated Over Its Four-Year Useful Life

	2017	2018	2019	2020
Revenues	$30,000	$30,000	$30,000	$30,000
Expense	10,000*	10,000*	10,000*	10,000*
Profit (Loss).....................	$20,000	$20,000	$20,000	$20,000

Estimated four-year life of the delivery van.

*$40,000 ÷ 4 years = $10,000 per year.

This allocation of the delivery van's cost is *depreciation.*

Note that depreciation is a process of cost allocation, not asset valuation. *Depreciation does not measure the decline in the van's value each period.* Nor does it measure the physical deterioration of the van. Depreciation is a process of allocating an asset's cost to expense over its useful life, nothing more. Because depreciation reflects the cost of using a plant and equipment asset, we do not begin recording depreciation charges until the asset is available for use within the company.

Reporting Depreciation on Assets

Both the cost and accumulated depreciation of PPE must be reported. Many companies show PPE on one line at the net amount of cost less accumulated depreciation. When this is done, the amount of accumulated depreciation is disclosed in a footnote. **Indigo Books & Music Inc.** reports $3,507,000 as the net amount of its property, plant, and equipment on its March 29, 2014, balance sheet. To satisfy the full disclosure principle,[10] it also describes its depreciation methods in Note 3 as follows:

Property, plant and equipment

All items of property, plant and equipment are initially recognized at cost, which includes any costs directly attributable to bringing the asset to the location and condition necessary for it to be capable of operating in the manner intended by the Company. Subsequent to initial recognition, property, plant and equipment assets are shown at cost less accumulated depreciation and any accumulated impairment losses.

Depreciation of an asset begins once it becomes available for use. The depreciable amount of an asset, being the cost of an asset less the residual value, is allocated on a straight-line basis over the estimated useful life of the asset. Residual value is estimated to be zero unless the Company expects to dispose of the asset at a value that exceeds the estimated disposal costs. The residual values, useful lives, and depreciation methods applied to assets are reviewed annually based on relevant market information and management considerations.

The following useful lives are applied:

Furniture, fixtures and equipment	5–10 years
Computer equipment	3–5 years
Equipment under finance leases	3–5 years
Leasehold improvements	over the lease term and probable renewal periods to a maximum of 10 years

Items of property, plant and equipment are assessed for impairment as detailed in the accounting policy note on impairment and are **derecognized** (removed from the accounting records) either upon disposal or when no future economic benefits are expected from their use. Any gain or loss arising on derecognition is included in profit in the period the asset is disposed of.

---

10   IFRS 2015, IAS 16, para. 73.

A detailed schedule outlining the breakdown of the net book values for each category of PPE is found in Note 8 of Indigo's 2014 Annual Report, an excerpt of which is shown below.

8. Property, Plant and Equipment

(thousands of Canadian dollars)	Furniture fixtures and equipment	Computer equipment	Leasehold improvements	Equipment under finance leases	Total
Gross carrying amount					
Balance, March 31, 2012	56,273	15,756	58,773	6,146	136,948
Additions	4,296	2,439	2,706	465	9,906
Transfers/reclassifications	(4)	(411)	415	—	—
Disposals	(161)	(20)	(110)	(2,976)	(3,267)
Assets with zero net book value	(5,113)	(3,279)	(5,015)	—	(13,407)
Balance, March 30, 2013	55,291	14,485	56,769	3,635	130,180
Additions	10,008	3,451	5,241	137	18,837
Transfers/reclassifications	16	(465)	449	—	—
Disposals	(478)	(217)	(208)	(948)	(1,851)
Assets with zero net book value	(2,719)	(6,174)	(7,922)	—	(16,815)
Balance, March 29, 2014	62,118	11,080	54,329	2,824	130,351
Accumulated depreciation and impairment					
Balance, March 31, 2012	25,953	8,895	31,240	3,932	70,020
Depreciation	5,208	3,092	8,129	1,209	17,638
Transfers/reclassifications	—	5	(5)	—	—
Disposals	(130)	(9)	(109)	(2,976)	(3,224)
Net impairment losses and reversals	—	—	250	—	250
Assets with zero net book value	(5,113)	(3,279)	(5,015)	—	(13,0407)
Balance, March 30, 2013	25,918	8,704	34,490	2,165	71,277
Depreciation	5,422	2,631	7,495	810	16,358
Transfers/reclassifications	—	5	(5)	—	—
Disposals	(216)	(197)	(188)	(948)	(1,549)
Net impairment losses and reversals	1,007	60	1,537	—	2,604
Assets with zero net book value	(2,719)	(6,174)	(7,922)	—	(16,815)
Balance, March 29, 2014	29,412	5,029	35,407	2,027	71,875
Net carrying amount					
April 1, 2012	30,320	6,861	27,533	2,214	66,928
March 30, 2013	29,373	5,781	22,279	1,470	58,903
March 29, 2014	32,706	6,051	18,922	797	58,476

Reporting both the cost and accumulated depreciation of PPE helps balance sheet readers compare the assets of different companies. For example, a company holding assets costing $50,000 and accumulated depreciation of $40,000 is likely in a different situation than a company with new assets costing $10,000. The **book value** (original cost of the asset less its accumulated depreciation) is the same in both cases, but the first company may have more productive capacity available but is likely is facing the need to incur costs to replace older assets.

Factors in Calculating Depreciation

Three factors are relevant in determining depreciation. They are (1) cost, (2) estimated residual value, and (3) estimated useful (service) life.

COST

The *cost* of PPE, as described earlier in this chapter, consists of all necessary and reasonable expenditures to acquire it and to prepare the asset for its intended use. Where an asset consists of parts (or components) with costs that are significant in relation to the total cost of the asset, each part or common group of parts are required to be depreciated separately under the IFRS standards.[11] To illustrate, assume an apartment building and land are purchased for a total cost of $1,650,000; $1,000,000 of the total $1,650,000 represented the cost of the land, which is not depreciated. It was determined that the remaining $650,000 could be broken down into the following significant parts and related costs: carpets, $25,000; appliances, $50,000; windows and doors, $100,000; cabinets, $75,000; roof $40,000; and the building structure, $360,000. Each of these significant parts must be depreciated separately. As discussed previously, it would be helpful to use a PPE subledger to record information related to assets and parts of assets.

RESIDUAL VALUE

Residual value is an estimate of the amount we expect to receive from selling the asset or trading it in at the end of its useful life or benefit period.[12] The total amount of depreciation to be expensed over an asset's benefit period equals the asset's cost minus its estimated residual value. For example, if the cost and estimated residual value of a forklift is $20,000 and $4,000 respectively, the total amount of depreciation to be expensed over the van's useful life is $16,000 (= $20,000 − $4,000). If we expect an asset to be traded in on a new asset, its residual value is the expected trade-in value.

USEFUL (SERVICE) LIFE

The **useful life** of an asset is the length of time it is productively used in a company's operations. Useful life, also called **service life**, is not necessarily as long as the asset's total productive life. As an example, the productive life of a computer may be four years. Yet some companies trade in old computers for new ones every two years. In this case, these computers have a two-year useful life. This means the cost of these computers (less their expected trade-in value) is charged to depreciation expense over a two-year period.

Several variables often make the useful life of an asset hard to predict, such as wear and tear from use in operations, *inadequacy*, and *obsolescence*. **Inadequacy** refers to the condition where the capacity of a company's PPE is too small to meet the company's productive needs. **Obsolescence** refers to a condition where, because of new inventions and improvements, an asset is no longer useful in producing goods or services with a competitive advantage. A company usually disposes of an obsolete asset before it wears out. For example Silver Town, a Canadian movie theatre chain, purchases new projection equipment and expects its useful life to be 10 years. After using the projection equipment for two years, the technology changes from film-based projection to digital projection. The major production companies stop issuing the old film format and go entirely digital. The film-based equipment becomes obsolete and Silver Town needs to upgrade to digital projection to continue its operations. Obsolescence, like inadequacy, is hard to predict.

To predict the useful life of a new asset, a company uses its past experience or, when it has no experience with a type of asset, it relies on the experience of others or on engineering studies and judgment.

DECISION INSIGHT

The life expectancy of PPE is often in the eye of the beholder. Take **Imperial Oil** and **Suncor Energy**, for instance. Both compete in the oil industry, yet their refineries' life expectancies are quite different. Imperial depreciates its refineries over 25 years, but Suncor depreciates its refineries over an average of 32 years. Such differences can dramatically impact their financial statement numbers.

---

11   IFRS 2015, IAS 16, para. 43–47.
12   IFRS 2015 IAS 16, para. 6.

Depreciation Methods

There are many *depreciation methods* for allocating an asset's cost over the accounting periods in its useful life. Companies are required to select a method that most closely reflects the expected pattern of consumption of the benefits of the underlying asset.[13] The depreciation method chosen is applied consistently from period to period unless there is a change in use or a change in expected future benefits. Depreciation methods based on revenue produced from operations where the asset is being used are not permitted.[14]

We explain three methods in this section:

1. Straight-line, the most frequently used method of depreciation
2. Units-of-production
3. Double-declining-balance,[15] an accelerated method

 **DECISION INSIGHT**

On Trend

About 87% of companies use straight-line depreciation for plant assets, 4% use units-of-production, and 4% use declining-balance. Another 5% use an unspecified method.

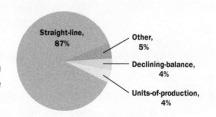

SOURCE: John Wile, Ken Shaw, and Barbara Chiapetta, "Decision Insight—In Vogue," *Fundamental Accounting Principles* 20e, 2011, The McGraw-Hill Companies, Inc.

The calculations in this section use information from an athletic shoe manufacturer whose year-end is December 31. The term **depreciable cost** refers to the cost to be depreciated, which equals the total asset cost minus the estimated residual value. In particular, we look at equipment used for producing shoes. This equipment is used by manufacturers such as Asics, Adidas, Nike, New Balance and Saucony, and its data for depreciation are shown in Exhibit 9.6.

EXHIBIT 9.6

Data for Shoe-Production Equipment

Cost	$10,000
Estimated residual value	1,000
Depreciable cost	$ 9,000
Estimated useful life:	
Accounting periods	5 years
Units produced	36,000 shoes

STRAIGHT-LINE METHOD

Straight-line depreciation charges the same amount to expense for each period of the asset's useful life.

The formula and calculation for straight-line depreciation of the production equipment just described is shown in Exhibit 9.7.

---

13 IFRS 2015 IAS 16, para. 62
14 IFRS 2015 IAS 16, para. 62A.
15 IFRS 2015, IAS 16, para. 62 uses the term *diminishing balance* instead of *declining balance*.

EXHIBIT 9.7

Straight-Line Depreciation Formula

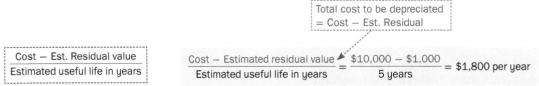

Total cost to be depreciated
= Cost − Est. Residual

$$\frac{\text{Cost} - \text{Est. Residual value}}{\text{Estimated useful life in years}}$$

$$\frac{\text{Cost} - \text{Estimated residual value}}{\text{Estimated useful life in years}} = \frac{\$10,000 - \$1,000}{5 \text{ years}} = \$1,800 \text{ per year}$$

If this equipment is purchased on January 1, 2017, and used throughout its predicted useful life of five years, the straight-line method allocates an equal amount of depreciation to each of the years 2017 through 2021. We make the following adjusting entry at the end of each of these five years to record straight-line depreciation of this equipment:

Dec.	31	Depreciation Expense	1,800	
		Accumulated Depreciation, Equipment		1,800
		To record annual depreciation over its		
		five-year useful life.		

The $1,800 Depreciation Expense appears on the income statement among operating expenses. This entry credits Accumulated Depreciation, Equipment, a contra account to the Equipment account under the property, plant and equipment asset line item on the balance sheet.

The net balance sheet amounts are the asset's book values for each of those years and are calculated as the asset's original cost less its accumulated depreciation. At the end of year two, its book value is $6,400 and is reported in the PPE section of the balance sheet as shown in Exhibit 9.8:

EXHIBIT 9.8

Balance Sheet Presentation After Two Years of Depreciation

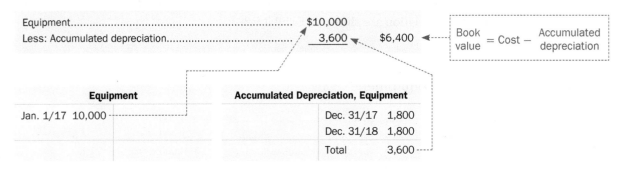

Equipment..	$10,000	
Less: Accumulated depreciation..	3,600	$6,400

Book value = Cost − Accumulated depreciation

Equipment		
Jan. 1/17 10,000		

Accumulated Depreciation, Equipment		
	Dec. 31/17	1,800
	Dec. 31/18	1,800
	Total	3,600

Instead of listing the cost less accumulated depreciation, many balance sheets show PPE *net* of accumulated depreciation. The *net* means *after* accumulated depreciation has been subtracted from the cost of the asset. Recall that cost less accumulated depreciation is *book value*. Exhibit 9.9 shows this alternative form of presentation for the equipment of Exhibit 9.8 (cost of $10,000 less accumulated depreciation of $3,600).

EXHIBIT 9.9

Alternative Balance Sheet Presentation

Equipment (net)..	$6,400

The graphs in Exhibit 9.10 show (1) why this method is called straight-line depreciation, and (2) the decline in book value by $1,800 depreciation each year.

EXHIBIT 9.10

Financial Statement Effects of Straight-Line Depreciation

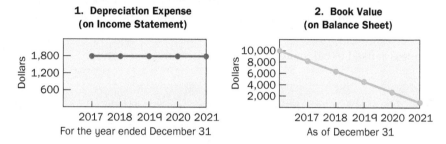

The straight-line depreciation *rate* is calculated as 100% divided by the number of periods in the asset's useful life. In the case of our shoe production equipment, this rate is 20% (100% ÷ 5 years). We use this rate and other information on the equipment to calculate the machine's *straight-line depreciation schedule* shown in Exhibit 9.11.

EXHIBIT 9.11

Straight-Line Depreciation Schedule

	Depreciation for the Period			End of Period	
Period	Cost to be Depreciated	Depreciation Rate	Depreciation Expense	Accumulated Depreciation	Book Value
	—	—	—	—	10,000*
2017	$9,000**	20%	$1,800	$1,800	8,200
2018	9,000	20	1,800	3,600	6,400
2019	9,000	20	1,800	5,400	4,600
2020	9,000	20	1,800	7,200	2,800
2021	9,000	20	1,800	9,000	1,000

*Cost on January 1, 2017
**$10,000 − $1,000

Note three items in this schedule that are distinguishing features of the straight line method:

1. Depreciation expense is the same each period.
2. Accumulated depreciation is the sum of current and prior periods' depreciation expense.
3. Book value declines each period until it equals the residual value at the end of its useful life.

Straight-line is by far the most frequently applied depreciation method in financial reporting.

UNITS-OF-PRODUCTION METHOD

If PPE are used about the same amount in each accounting period, the straight-line method produces a systematic allocation of the asset's cost over its useful life. Yet the use of some assets varies greatly from one accounting period to the next. A builder, for instance, may use a piece of construction equipment for a month and then not use it again for several months.

When use of equipment varies from period to period, the units-of-production depreciation method can provide a better allocation of the asset's cost than straight-line depreciation. **Units-of-production depreciation** charges a varying amount to expense for each period of an asset's useful life depending on its usage.

A two-step process is used to calculate units-of-production depreciation:

1. Calculate the depreciation per unit by subtracting the asset's residual value from its total cost, and then dividing by the total number of units expected to be produced during its useful life. Units of production can be expressed in units of product or in any other unit of measure such as hours used or kilometres driven. This gives us the amount of depreciation per unit of service provided by the asset.

2. Calculate depreciation expense for the period by multiplying the units used in the period by the depreciation per unit.

Exhibit 9.12 shows the formula and calculation for units-of-production depreciation for the production equipment described in Exhibit 9.6 as having an estimated production capacity of 36,000 units (assume 7,000 shoes produced in 2017).

EXHIBIT 9.12

Units-of-Production Depreciation Formula

Step 1:

$$\text{Depreciation per unit} = \frac{\text{Cost} - \text{Est. residual value}}{\text{Total est. units}} = \text{Deprec. per unit}$$

$$\text{Depreciation per unit} = \frac{\text{Cost} - \text{Estimated residual value}}{\text{Total estimated units of production}} = \frac{\$10,000 - \$1,000}{36,000 \text{ units}}$$

$$= \$0.25 \text{ per shoe}$$

Step 2:

$$\text{Depreciation expense} = \text{Depreciation per unit} \times \text{Units produced in period}$$
$$\$0.25 \text{ per shoe} \times 7,000 \text{ shoes} = \mathbf{\$1,750}$$

Using the production estimates for the equipment, we calculate the *units-of-production depreciation schedule* shown in Exhibit 9.13. If the equipment produces 7,000 shoes in 2017, its first year, depreciation for 2017 is $1,750. If the equipment produces 8,000 shoes in 2018, depreciation for 2018 is $2,000, calculated as 8,000 shoes times $0.25 per shoe.

Note that depreciation expense depends on unit output, that accumulated depreciation is the sum of current and prior-periods' depreciation expense, and that book value declines each period until it equals residual value at the end of the asset's useful life.

The units-of-production depreciation method is not as frequently applied as straight-line. **Suncor Energy Inc.** uses units-of-production in addition to straight-line as reported in its December 31, 2013, annual report:

Capital expenditures are not depleted until assets are substantially complete and ready for their intended use.

Costs to develop oil and gas properties other than oil sands properties, including costs of dedicated infrastructure, such as well pads and wellhead equipment, are depleted on a unit-of-production basis over proved developed reserves. A portion of these costs may not be depleted if they relate to undeveloped reserves. Costs to develop and construct oil sands mines are depreciated on a straight-line basis over the life of the mine.

Major components of property, plant, and equipment are depreciated on a straight-line basis over their expected useful lives.

Natural gas processing plants	15 years
Oil sands upgraders, extraction plants and mine facilities	20 to 40 years
Oil sands mine equipment	5 to 15 years
Oil sands in situ processing facilities	30 years
Power generation and utility plants	30 to 40 years
Refineries, ethanol, and lubricants plants	20 to 40 years
Marketing and other distribution assets	20 to 40 years

The costs of major inspection, overhaul, and turnaround activities that are capitalized are depreciated on a straight-line basis over the period next to the scheduled activity, which varies from two to five years.

Depreciation, depletion, and amortization rates are reviewed annually, or when events or conditions occur that impact capitalized costs, reserves, or estimated service lives.

Source: Suncor Energy Inc., http://www.suncor.com/pdf/Suncor_financial_statements_2013_en.pdf

EXHIBIT 9.13

Units-of-Production Depreciation Schedule

	Depreciation for the Period			End of Period	
Period	Number of Units	Depreciation Per Unit	Depreciation Expense	Accumulated Depreciation	Book Value
	—	—	—	—	$10,000*
2017	7,000	$0.25	$1,750	$1,750	8,250
2018	8,000	0.25	2,000	3,750	6,250
2019	9,000	0.25	2,250	6,000	4,000
2020	7,000	0.25	1,750	7,750	2,250
2021	6,000**	0.25	1,250***	9,000	1,000

*Cost on January 1, 2017
**6,000 units were actually produced, but the maximum number of units on which depreciation can be calculated in 2021 is 5,000 [36,000 total estimated units less 31,000 units depreciated to date (7,000 + 8,000 + 9,000 + 7,000)]. Recall that an asset must not be depreciated below its residual value.
***5,000 × $0.25 = $1,250

DECLINING-BALANCE METHOD

An **accelerated depreciation method** provides higher depreciation expenses in the early years of an asset's life and lower charges in later years. While several accelerated methods are used in financial reporting, the most common is the **declining-balance depreciation**, which uses depreciation rates of up to twice the straight-line rate and applies it to the asset's beginning-of-period book value. Because book value *declines* each period, the amount of depreciation also declines each period.

Double-declining-balance depreciation (DDB) or **diminishing-balance depreciation** is applied in two steps:[16]

> 1. Calculate the double-declining-balance rate (= 2 ÷ Estimated years of useful life), and
> 2. Calculate depreciation expense by multiplying the rate by the asset's beginning-of-period book value.

It is important to note that residual value is not used in these calculations. We adjust depreciation expense in the final year to depreciate the asset down to the residual value, as illustrated in Exhibit 9.15.

Returning to the shoe production equipment, we can apply the double-declining-balance method to calculate its depreciation expense. Exhibit 9.14 shows this formula and its first-year calculation for the production equipment. The abbreviated two-step process is:

> 1. 2 divided by the estimated useful life, and
> 2. Calculate annual depreciation expense as the declining-balance rate multiplied by the book value at the beginning of each period (see Exhibit 9.15).

EXHIBIT 9.14

Double-Declining-Balance Depreciation Formula

Double-declining-balance depreciation = Book value × $\dfrac{2}{n}$,

where n = estimated useful life

Step 1:

Double-declining-balance rate = 2 ÷ Estimated useful life = 2 ÷ 5 years = 0.40 or 40%

Step 2:

Depreciation expense $\quad$ = Double-declining-balance rate × Beginning period book value
$\qquad\qquad\qquad\qquad$ = 40% × \$10,000 = **\$4,000**

The *double-declining-balance depreciation schedule* is shown in Exhibit 9.15. The schedule follows the formula except in the year 2021, when depreciation expense is \$296. The \$296 is calculated by subtracting the \$1,000 residual value from the \$1,296 book value at the beginning of the fifth year. This is done because an asset is *never* depreciated *below* its residual value. If we had used the \$518.40 (40% × \$1,296) for depreciation expense in 2021, then ending book value would equal \$777.60, which is less than the \$1,000 residual value.

Maximum accumulated depreciation*
= Cost − Residual
ALTERNATIVELY
Minimum book value*
= Residual value
regardless of method

COMPARING DEPRECIATION METHODS

Exhibit 9.16 shows depreciation expense for the shoe-production equipment under each of the three depreciation methods.

---

16 The double-declining-balance method is also described as being *twice the straight-line rate* because it can be alternatively applied as follows to get the same results:
    1. Calculate the asset's straight-line depreciation rate (100% ÷ Estimated useful life in years),
    2. Double it, and
    3. Calculate depreciation expense by multiplying this doubled rate by the asset's beginning-of-period book value.

EXHIBIT 9.15

Double-Declining-Balance Depreciation Schedule

Period	Depreciation for the Period			End of Period		
	Beginning-of-Period Book Value	Depreciation Rate	Depreciation Expense	Accumulated Depreciation	Book Value	
	—	—	—	—	$10,000*	
2017	$10,000	40%	$4,000	$4,000	6,000	
2018	6,000	40	2,400	6,400	3,600	
2019	3,600	40	1,440	7,840	2,160	
2020	2,160	40	864	8,704	1,296	
2021	1,296	40	296**	9,000**	1,000	

*Cost on January 1, 2017
**Year 2021 depreciation is $1,296 − $1,000 = $296. This is because maximum accumulated depreciation equals cost minus residual as we depreciate the asset only up to the residual value.

EXHIBIT 9.16

Depreciation Methods Compared: Annual Depreciation Expense

Period	Straight-Line	Units-of-Production		Double-Declining-Balance
	$\dfrac{\text{Cost} - \text{Est. residual}}{\text{Est. useful life}}$	$\dfrac{\text{Cost} - \text{Est. residual}}{\text{Total est. units of production}}$	$\times$ Actual units produced in period	Book value $\times\ 2/n$, where n = Est. useful life
2017	$ 1,800	$ 1,750		$ 4,000
2018	1,800	2,000		2,400
2019	1,800	2,250		1,440
2020	1,800	1,750		864
2021	1,800	1,250		296
	$ 9,000	$ 9,000		$ 9,000

While the amount of depreciation expense per period is different for different methods, *total* depreciation expense is the same ($9,000) for the machine's useful life. Each method starts with a total cost of $10,000 and ends with a residual value of $1,000. The difference is the *pattern* in depreciation expense over the useful life. This pattern is graphically represented in Exhibit 9.17. The book value of the asset when using straight-line is always greater than book value from using double-declining-balance, except

EXHIBIT 9.17

Graphic Comparison of Depreciation Methods

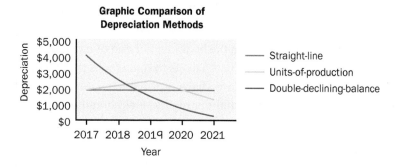

at the beginning and end of an asset's useful life. Also, the straight-line method yields a steady pattern of depreciation expense, while units-of-production does not because it depends on the number of units produced. All of these methods are acceptable as they allocate cost in a rational and systematic manner.

CHECKPOINT

6. On January 1, 2017, Laser Renew Inc. pays $77,000 to purchase office furniture with a residual value of zero. The furniture's useful life is somewhere between 7 and 10 years. What is the 2017 straight-line depreciation on the furniture using (a) a 7-year useful life, and (b) a 10-year useful life?

7. What is the meaning of the accounting term *depreciation*?

8. Laser Renew Inc. purchases a new machine for $96,000 on January 1, 2017. Its predicted useful life is 5 years or 100,000 units of product, and its residual value is $8,000. During 2017, 10,000 units of product are produced. Calculate the book value of this machine on December 31, 2017, assuming (1) straight-line depreciation, and (2) units-of-production depreciation.

9. A specialized piece of laser therapy equipment was purchased for $340,000. Its components A, B, and C had respective costs estimated to be 20%, 50%, and 30% of the total cost. The estimated useful lives of the components were determined to be 4 years, 8 years, and 15 years, respectively. The residual value for each component was $0. Calculate the annual depreciation for each component assuming straight-line.

Do Quick Study questions: QS 9-4, QS 9-5, QS 9-6, QS 9-7, QS 9-8

DEPRECIATION FOR INCOME TAX REPORTING

The rules a company follows for financial reporting purposes are usually different from the rules it follows for income tax reporting purposes. Financial accounting aims to report useful information on financial performance and position, whereas income tax accounting reflects government-established requirements developed to raise public revenues and encourage public interests. Differences between these two bases are normal and expected. Depreciation is an example of one of these common differences between financial statement profit and taxable income.

The *Income Tax Act* requires that companies use a declining-balance method for calculating the maximum *capital cost allowance* that may be claimed in any period. **Capital cost allowance (CCA)** is the term used to describe depreciation for tax purposes. CCA reduces taxable income in the early years of an asset's life because depreciation is greatest in the early years. The money a company saves in taxes in the early years means a company has the resources to earn additional profit. The *Income Tax Act* specifies the rates for various groups of assets. For example, a rate of 20% would be used for general machinery and equipment, and a rate of 4% for most buildings.

Partial-Year Depreciation

LO3 Explain and calculate depreciation for partial years.

Assets are purchased and disposed of at various times during an accounting period. When an asset is purchased (or disposed of) at a time other than the beginning or end of a period, depreciation is recorded only for the part of the year the asset was in use. This is to make sure that the year of purchase or the year of disposal is charged with its appropriate share of the asset's depreciation. There are different ways to account for the depreciation for partial years. The most common method used is the nearest whole month. We are going to look at two methods:

1. Nearest whole month, and   2. Half-year convention.

NEAREST WHOLE MONTH

When calculating depreciation for partial years to the nearest whole month, depreciation for a month is calculated if the asset was in use for more than half of that month. To illustrate, let's return to the athletic shoe–production equipment. Assume this equipment is purchased and placed in service on April 8, 2017, and the annual accounting period ends on December 31. This equipment costs $10,000, has a useful life of five years, and has a residual value of $1,000. Because this equipment is purchased and used for more than half of April plus all of May through December, in 2017 the amount of depreciation reported is based on nine months (if the purchase date had been April 28, the depreciation would have been calculated for eight months since the asset was not in use for more than half of April). Depreciation is not calculated by taking into account specific days of use because this would imply that depreciation is precise, when in fact it is based on estimates of the useful life and residual values. Using straight-line depreciation, we calculate nine months' depreciation of $1,350 as follows:

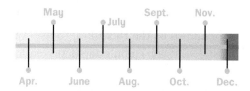

$$\frac{\text{Cost} - \text{Estimated residual value}}{\text{Estimated useful life in years}} = \frac{\text{Depreciation}}{\text{per year}} \times \frac{\text{Fraction}}{\text{of year}} \quad \frac{\$10,000 - \$1,000}{5 \text{ years}} = \$1,800/\text{year} \times \frac{9}{12}$$
$$= \$1,350$$

A similar calculation is necessary when disposal of an asset occurs during a year. As an example, let's suppose the equipment described above is sold on June 4, 2021. Depreciation for 2021 is recorded for the period January 1 through June 4, or five months. Because the asset was held for less than half of June, depreciation is not calculated for June. This partial year's depreciation, calculated to the nearest whole month, is:

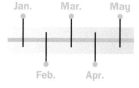

$$\frac{\$10,000 - \$1,000}{5 \text{ years}} = \$1,800/\text{year} \times \frac{5}{12} = \$750$$

Exhibit 9.18 demonstrates the calculations for a partial year's depreciation to the nearest month for the units-of-production and double-declining-balance methods. *Notice that the depreciation expense calculation for units-of-production is not affected by the partial year.* This is because the units-of-production method is a function of use, not of time.

Partial Year's Depreciation Calculated to Nearest Month Under the Units-of-Production and Double-Declining-Balance Methods

Date of Purchase	Units-of-Production	Double-Declining-Balance
April 8, 2017	$\dfrac{\$10,000 - \$1,000}{36,000 \text{ units}}$	Rate $= \dfrac{2}{5} = 0.40$ or 40%
		$40\% \times \$10,000$
	$= \$0.25/\text{unit} \times 7,000 \text{ units} = \textbf{\$1,750}$	$= \$4,000/\text{year } \dfrac{9}{12} = \textbf{\$3,000}$

HALF-YEAR CONVENTION

For companies that have a large number of PPE expenditures year after year, tracking when individual assets were put into use and then calculating depreciation to the nearest month can be a costly process. Because this kind of accuracy would not necessarily increase the usefulness of information related to depreciation, the *materiality principle* allows us the flexibility to use a method more appropriate for the situation, such as the *half-year convention*. When calculating depreciation for partial years using the **half-year convention**, six months' depreciation is recorded for the partial period regardless of when during the period the asset was acquired or disposed of. Exhibit 9.19 illustrates the application of the half-year convention assuming the shoe-production equipment was purchased and put into use on April 8, 2017.

Partial Year's Depreciation Calculated Using the Half-Year Convention Under the Straight-Line, Units-of-Production, and Double-Declining-Balance Methods

Date of Purchase	Straight-Line	Units-of-Production	Double-Declining-Balance
April 8, 2017	$\dfrac{\$10,000 - \$1,000}{5 \text{ years}}$	$\dfrac{\$10,000 - \$1,000}{36,000 \text{ units}}$	Rate $= \dfrac{2}{5} = 0.40$ or 40%
			$40\% \times \$10,000$
	$= \$1,800/\text{year} \times \dfrac{6}{12} = \textbf{\$900}$	$= \$0.25/\text{unit} \times 7,000 \text{ units} = \textbf{\$1,750}$	$= \$4,000/\text{year} \times \dfrac{6}{12} = \textbf{\$2,000}$

Notice again that the calculation of units-of-production is not affected by partial years.

CHECKPOINT

10. Why is depreciation for a partial year not calculated to the nearest day?

Do Quick Study questions: QS 9-9, QS 9-10, QS 9-11

Revising Depreciation Rates

LO4   Explain and calculate revised depreciation.

Depreciation is based on the original cost of an asset, estimated residual value, and estimated useful life. If the cost of the asset changes because the estimates for residual value and/or useful life are adjusted or because of a subsequent capital expenditure, *revised depreciation* for current and future periods must be calculated.

REVISING DEPRECIATION RATES WHEN THERE IS A CHANGE IN THE ESTIMATED RESIDUAL VALUE AND/OR ESTIMATED USEFUL LIFE

Because depreciation is based on predictions of residual value and useful life, depreciation expense is an estimate. If our estimate of an asset's useful life and/or residual value changes, we use the new estimate(s) to calculate **revised depreciation** for the current and future periods. This means we calculate a new depreciation expense calculation by spreading the cost that has not yet been depreciated over the remaining useful life. This approach is used for all depreciation methods.

Let's return to our athletic shoe–production equipment using straight-line depreciation. At the beginning of this asset's third year, its book value is $6,400, calculated as:

Cost	$10,000
Less: Prior two years' accumulated depreciation (2017, 2018)...	3,600*
Book value	$ 6,400

*Calculated as $1,800 per year as determined above using the straight-line approach for two years.

At the beginning of its third year, in 2019, the predicted number of years remaining in its useful life changes from three to four years and its estimate of residual value changes from $1,000 to $400. Depreciation for each of the equipment's four remaining years is now recalculated as shown in Exhibit 9.20.

EXHIBIT 9.20

Calculating Revised Depreciation Rates When There Is a Change in Estimated Residual Value and/or Estimated Useful Life

$$\frac{\text{Remaining book value} - \text{Revised residual value}}{\text{Revised remaining useful life}} = \frac{6,400 - 400}{4 \text{ years}} = \textbf{1,500 per year}$$

This means $1,500 of depreciation expense is recorded for the equipment at the end of 2019 through 2022, the remaining six years of its useful life.

We do not revise the previous years depreciation expense, as these expenses reflected the best information available at the time they were recorded, based on management's estimate.

Revising estimates of the useful life or residual value of an asset is referred to as a **change in an accounting estimate**. A change in an accounting estimate results when a review of the asset shows that "expectations differ from previous estimates."[17] Accountants refer to change in an accounting estimate as being applied *prospectively*. This means that it is reflected in current and future financial statements only; no adjustments are made to prior year financial statements.[18]

REVISING DEPRECIATION RATES WHEN THERE IS A SUBSEQUENT CAPITAL EXPENDITURE

We also calculate revised depreciation if the cost of the asset changes because of a subsequent capital expenditure, such as the installation of a new engine. Depreciation is the allocation of an asset's cost. Subsequent capital expenditures cause the cost of an asset to change. Revised depreciation must therefore be calculated when there is a subsequent capital expenditure.

A subsequent capital expenditure can be the *addition* of a component to an existing asset or the *replacement* or *overhaul* of a component. In the case where there is an addition, such as adding a

---

17 IFRS 2015, IAS 16, para. 51.
18 IFRS 2015, IAS 8, para. 36.

computer panel to a machine to improve its efficiency, the cost of the addition is debited to the appropriate PPE account and depreciation for the asset is revised to incorporate the additional cost and any change in the estimated useful life and/or residual value.[19]

For example, on January 3, 2017, Natural Foods paid $15,000 cash for a refrigeration unit installed on its delivery van to improve the shelf life of its products upon reaching the customer. The delivery van had a book value of $32,000 at December 31, 2016, and an estimated remaining useful life of 10 years and no residual value. Assume the refrigeration unit had an estimated life of five years and no residual value and that its addition to the delivery van did not change the van's useful life or residual value. The entries to record the addition of the refrigeration unit on January 3 and revised depreciation at December 31, Natural Food's year-end, are:

2017					
Jan.	3	Delivery Van—Refrigeration Unit....................	15,000	
		Cash...		15,000
		To record addition of refrigeration unit to the van.		
Dec.	31	Depreciation Expense, Van	6,200	
		Accumulated Depreciation, Van...............		6,200
		To record revised depreciation on the van; Van: $32,000 ÷ 10 yrs = $3,200; Refrigeration unit: $15,000 ÷ 5 yrs = $3,000; $3,200 + $3,000 = $6,200 total depreciation.		

When a subsequent capital expenditure results in the replacement of a component of PPE, the cost and accumulated depreciation of the replaced component must be removed from the accounting records and any resulting loss or gain must be recorded. To demonstrate the accounting entries, assume that on January 2, 2017, Natural Foods purchased equipment with several components including an engine. The engine had a cost of $50,000, an estimated useful life of five years, and a residual value of $8,000. On January 5, 2019, the engine suffered major damage and was replaced with a new one for $55,000 on account with an estimated useful life of six years and residual value of $7,000. If the old engine was scrapped (no cash was received), two entries are required on January 5, 2019. First, the old engine must be removed from the accounting records, which is recorded as:

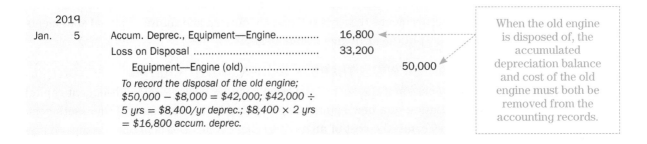

2019					
Jan.	5	Accum. Deprec., Equipment—Engine..............	16,800	
		Loss on Disposal	33,200	
		Equipment—Engine (old)		50,000
		To record the disposal of the old engine; $50,000 − $8,000 = $42,000; $42,000 ÷ 5 yrs = $8,400/yr deprec.; $8,400 × 2 yrs = $16,800 accum. deprec.		

When the old engine is disposed of, the accumulated depreciation balance and cost of the old engine must both be removed from the accounting records.

Because the asset was not fully depreciated at the time of the replacement and it was scrapped, the $33,200 book value (calculated as the $50,000 cost less the $16,800 accumulated depreciation) represents

19 IFRS 2015, IAS 16, para. 37

a loss. Losses are reported separately from Revenue in the *Other Revenues and Expenses* section of the income statement.[20]

The purchase of the new engine on the same date must also be recorded as shown below:

	2019			
Jan.	5	Equipment—Engine (new)................................	55,000	
		Accounts Payable		55,000
		To record the new engine on the equipment.		

These two entries could be combined as:

	2019			
Jan.	5	Accum. Deprec., Equipment—Engine..............	16,800	
		Equipment—Engine (new)	55,000	
		Loss on Disposal	33,200	
		Accounts Payable		55,000
		Equipment—Engine (old)		50,000
		To record the disposal of the old engine *and the acquisition of the new engine.*		

If we assume the old engine was sold for $5,000 cash instead of being scrapped at the time of replacement, the combined entry would be:

	2019			
Jan.	5	Cash	5,000	
		Accum. Deprec., Equipment—Engine..............	16,800	
		Equipment—Engine (new)............................	55,000	
		Loss on Disposal.....................................	28,200	
		Accounts Payable		55,000
		Equipment—Engine (old)		50,000
		To record the disposal of the old engine for *$5,000 cash and the acquisition of the* *new engine.*		

> Again, notice that the accumulated depreciation and cost of the old engine are removed from the accounting records because the old engine has been disposed of.

Notice that the $28,200 *Loss on Disposal* represents the difference between the $33,200 book value of the component being replaced and the $5,000 cash proceeds.

Depreciation on the equipment at year-end would be revised to incorporate depreciation on the replacement component. For example, depreciation on the new engine at December 31, 2019, would be:

$$\frac{\$55,000 - \$7,000}{6 \text{ years}} = \$8,000$$

When a subsequent capital expenditure occurs partway through the accounting period, partial-period depreciation must be calculated on the component being replaced up to the time of the replacement to update the accumulated depreciation account. Revised depreciation for the year would be based on the new component for the part of the year it was in use. These calculations are illustrated in Appendix 9A.

---

[20] IFRS 2015, IAS 16, para. 68.

CHECKPOINT

11. In early January 2017, a cell phone repair shop acquires equipment at a cost of $3,800. The company estimates this equipment to have a useful life of three years and a residual value of $200. Early in 2019, the controller at the shop changes its estimate to a total four-year useful life and zero residual value. Using straight-line depreciation, what is depreciation expense on this equipment for the year ended December 31, 2019?

12. Assume the Fairmont Hotel had a desktop computer with a book value at its December 31, 2016, year-end of $5,000. The computer had an estimated remaining useful life of two years and a $500 residual value. On January 12, 2017, a second monitor costing $800 was added to the computer to enhance the booking agent's productivity. The second monitor had an estimated life of two years and no residual value. Record the addition on January 12 and the revised depreciation on the computer at December 31. Assume the second monitor was purchased on account.

Do Quick Study questions: QS 9-12, QS 9-13

DECISION MAKER   Answer—End of chapter

Controller Constraints

Assume you are the controller for Cabinet World in the year 2017. Cabinet World has struggled financially for more than two years, losing market share to three key players in its market (Ikea, Home Depot, and Lowes) and there are no signs of improvement. The company's operations require major investments in equipment, and depreciation is a large item in calculating profit. Cabinet World normally requires frequent replacements of equipment, and equipment is typically depreciated over three years. Cabinet World's President Belinda Hayer recently instructed you to revise estimated useful lives of equipment from three to six years and to use a six-year life on all new equipment. You suspect this instruction is motivated by a desire to improve reported profit. What actions do you take?

Impairment of PPE Assets

LO5 Explain and record impairment losses.

If the book value (or carrying amount) of a PPE item is *greater* than the amount to be recovered through the asset's use or sale, the difference is recognized as an **impairment loss**, as the asset's value is impaired.[21] Impairment can result from a variety of situations that include a significant decline in an asset's market value or a major adverse effect caused by technological, economic, or legal factors. PPE must be assessed for impairment annually to ensure that assets and profit are not overstated. When an impairment loss is recorded, revised depreciation must be calculated and recorded in future periods because of the decrease in the carrying amount of the asset caused by the impairment loss.[22]

To demonstrate, assume that on its December 31, 2017, adjusted trial balance, Fitbit Inc. has specialized manufacturing equipment with a cost of $50,000 and accumulated depreciation of $27,000. As part of its December 31, 2017, year-end procedures, Fitbit Inc. performed an annual asset impairment assessment and found that the equipment had a recoverable value of $15,000. Because the $23,000 book value

---

21 IFRS 2015, IAS 36, para. 8.

22 IFRS 2015, IAS 36, para. 63.

of the equipment ($50,000 cost less $27,000 accumulated depreciation) is greater than the $15,000 recoverable value, the $8,000 difference is recorded as an impairment loss on December 31, 2017, as follows:

2017			
Dec. 31	Impairment Loss..	8,000	
	Equipment..		8,000
	To record impairment loss on equipment.		

At December 31, 2018, revised depreciation must be calculated and recorded on the equipment because of the impairment loss recorded in 2017. Assuming Fitbit Inc. applies straight-line depreciation and that the remaining useful life was four years and the residual value of the equipment was zero, revised depreciation is:

2018			
Dec. 31	Depreciation Expense, Equipment..................	3,750	
	Accum. Deprec., Equipment..................		3,750
	To record revised depreciation caused by impairment loss; $50,000 − $8,000 = $42,000 revised cost of equipment; $42,000 − $27,000 = $15,000 remaining book value; $15,000 ÷ 4 years = $3,750 revised depreciation.		

Impairment losses may be reversed in subsequent periods if the recoverable amount of the asset exceeds the book value (or carrying amount). Reversal of impairment losses is beyond the scope of this course and is covered in more advanced courses.

CHECKPOINT

13. At its December 31, 2017, year-end, Solartech Ltd. assessed its assets for impairment and found that two machines had recoverable amounts that differed from book value: Machine A and Machine B had respective book values of $107,000 and $238,000, and recoverable values of $136,000 and $92,000, respectively. Assuming the business had recorded no impairment losses in previous years, what accounting treatment is required for the impairment loss?

Do Quick Study question: QS 9-14

MID-CHAPTER DEMONSTRATION PROBLEM

Part 1

Chaps Bikes purchased manufacturing equipment for $160,000 on September 3, 2017. The estimated life of the equipment is 10 years but due to technological advances, Chaps expects to replace the equipment in five years when the residual value is estimated to be $40,000. Chaps' year-end is December 31.

Required

Complete a schedule similar to the following for each year of the asset's estimated useful life using the (a) straight-line, and (b) double-declining-balance methods (round calculations to the nearest whole dollar).

	2017	2018	2019	2020	2021	2022
Cost						
Less: Accumulated depreciation.....................						
Book value						
Depreciation expense.................................						

Analysis Component:

Which depreciation method, straight-line or double-declining-balance, will give the highest total profit over the asset's useful life? Explain your answer.

Part 2

Chaps Bikes purchased a sales vehicle for $30,000 on August 21, 2017. The company planned to use it for 100,000 kilometres or about three years and then trade it in for $10,000. The actual kilometres driven were:

2017	10,250
2018	33,700
2019	37,980
2020	19,710

Required

Complete a schedule similar to that required in Part 1 using the units-of-production method.

Part 3

On March 21, 2015, Chaps purchased a customized paint machine for $60,000 and it was estimated to have a useful life of six years and a residual value of $15,000. During 2017, it was determined that the total useful life of the machine should be revised to eight years and the residual value decreased to $5,000.

Required

Record depreciation expense on the machine for the year ended December 31, 2017.

Part 4

As part of its December 31, 2017, year-end procedures, Chaps assessed its assets for impairment and found that a piece of its gear manufacturing equipment had a recoverable value of $14,000 and a remaining useful life of two years and residual value of zero. The December 31, 2017, adjusted trial balance showed that the equipment had a cost of $114,000 and accumulated depreciation of $62,000. Chaps recorded no impairment losses in previous years.

Required

Record the impairment loss at December 31, 2017, and the revised depreciation at December 31, 2018.

Solution

Part 1

a. Straight-line

	2017	2018	2019	2020	2021	2022
Cost	160,000	160,000	160,000	160,000	160,000	160,000
Less: Accum. deprec............	8,000[1]	32,000[2]	56,000	80,000	104,000	120,000
Book value	152,000	128,000	104,000	80,000	56,000	40,000
Depreciation expense..........	8,000[1]	24,000[3]	24,000	24,000	24,000	16,000[4]

[1] $(\$160,000 - \$40,000)/5$ years $= \$24,000$/year $\times \dfrac{4}{12} = \$8,000$

[2] $\$8,000 + \$24,000 = \$32,000$

[3] $(\$160,000 - \$40,000)/5$ years $= \$24,000$/year

[4] $(\$160,000 - \$40,000)/5$ years $= \$24,000$/year $\times \dfrac{8}{12} = \$16,000$

b. Double-declining-balance

	2017	2018	2019	2020	2021	2022
Cost	160,000	160,000	160,000	160,000	160,000	160,000
Less: Accum. deprec............	21,333	76,800[2]	110,080	120,000	120,000	120,000
Book value	138,667	83,200	49,920	40,000	40,000	40,000
Depreciation expense..........	21,333[3]	55,467[4]	33,280[5]	9,920[6]	-0-	-0-

[1] Double declining rate $= 2/5 = 40\%$

[2] $40\% \times \$160,000 = \$64,000 \times \dfrac{4}{12} = \$21,333$

[3] $\$21,333 + \$55,467 = \$76,800$

[4] $40\% \times \$138,667 = \$55,467$

[5] $40\% \times \$83,200 = \$33,280$

[6] $40\% \times \$49,920 = \$19,968$. However, this exceeds the maximum accumulated depreciation allowed of $120,000 (cost less residual of $160,000 − $40,000). Therefore, depreciation expense in 2020 is $9,920 (= $120,000 maximum allowable accumulated depreciation less $110,080 accumulated depreciation to date).

Analysis Component:

Because both methods will have a total depreciation expense of $120,000 over the life of the asset, total profit over the asset's useful life will be identical regardless of depreciation method used. Over the life of the asset, the straight-line approach provides a consistent expense, whereas the double declining balance method charges more depreciation in the early years of the manufacturing equipment's life.

Part 2

	2017	2018	2019	2020
Cost	30,000	30,000	30,000	30,000
Less: Accumulated depreciation...................	2,050	8,790[2]	16,386	20,000
Book value	27,950	21,210	13,614	10,000
Depreciation expense...................	2,050[1]	6,740[3]	7,596[4]	3,614[5]

[1] $(\$30,000 - \$10,000)/100,000$ km $= \$0.20$/km; 10,250 km $\times \$0.20$/km $= \$2,050$

[2] $\$2,050 + \$6,740 = \$8,790$

[3] 33,700 km $\times \$0.20$/km $= \$6,740$

[4] 37,980 km $\times \$0.20$/km $= \$7,596$

[5] 19,710 km $\times \$0.20$/km $= \$3,942$. However, this would exceed the maximum allowed accumulated depreciation of $20,000 (= $30,000 − $10,000). Therefore, depreciation expense is limited to $3,614 (= $20,000 − $16,386).

Part 3

	2017			
	Dec. 31	Depreciation Expense, Equipment.................	6,700	
		Accumulated Depreciation, Equipment....		6,700
		To record revised depreciation.		

Calculations:

1. Depreciation expense for 2015:

$$\frac{\$60,000 - \$15,000}{6 \text{ years}} = \$7,500/\text{year} \times \frac{9}{12} = \$5,625$$

2. Accumulated depreciation at December 31, 2016:
   $$\$5,625 + \$7,500 = \$13,125$$

3. Revised depreciation for 2017:

$$\frac{(\$60,000 - \$13,125) - \$5,000}{8 \text{ years} - 1\frac{9}{12}\text{years} = 6.25 \text{ years}} = \$6,700$$

Part 4

	2017			
	Dec. 31	Impairment Loss...	38,000	
		Equipment...		38,000
		To record impairment loss on equipment; $\$114,000 - \$62,000 = \$52,000$ *book value;* $\$52,000 - \$14,000 = \$38,000.$		
	2018			
	Dec. 31	Depreciation Expense, Equipment.................	7,000	
		Accumulated Depreciation, Equipment....		7,000
		To record revised depreciation caused by impairment loss; $\$114,000 - \$38,000 = \$76,000$ *revised cost of equipment;* $\$76,000 - \$62,000 = \$14,000$ *remaining book value;* $\$14,000 \div 2$ *years* $= \$7,000$ *revised depreciation.*		

Disposals of PPE

LO6 Account for asset disposal through discarding, selling, or exchanging an asset.

Assets are disposed of for several reasons. Many assets eventually wear out or become obsolete. Other assets are sold because of changing business plans. Sometimes an asset is discarded or sold because it is damaged by fire or accident. Regardless of the cause, disposals of PPE occur in one of three ways: discarding, sale, or exchange. The accounting for disposals of PPE is described in Exhibit 9.21.

Discarding PPE

A PPE asset is *discarded* when it is no longer useful to the company and it has no market value. To illustrate, assume a machine costing $9,000 with accumulated depreciation of $9,000 is discarded on June 5.

EXHIBIT 9.21

Accounting for Disposals of PPE

1. Record depreciation expense up to the date of disposal. This updates the accumulated depreciation account.
2.* Compare the asset's book value with the net amount received or paid at disposal and record any resulting gain or loss.
3.* Remove the balances of the disposed asset and related accumulated depreciation accounts. *Why? If the asset is gone, all accounts related to the asset (the asset account and its related accumulated depreciation) must be taken off the books as well.*
4.* Record any cash (and other assets) received or paid in the disposal.

*Steps 2, 3, and 4 are recorded in one journal entry.

When accumulated depreciation equals the asset's cost, the asset is fully depreciated and the entry to record the discarding of this asset is:

June	5	Accumulated Depreciation, Machinery............	9,000
		Machinery		9,000
		To record the discarding of fully depreciated machinery.		

This entry reflects all four steps of Exhibit 9.21. Step 1 is not needed since the machine is fully depreciated. Since book value is zero and no cash is involved, no gain or loss is recorded in Step 2. Step 3 is shown in the debit to *Accumulated Depreciation* and credit to *Machinery.* Since no cash is involved, Step 4 is irrelevant.

How do we account for discarding an asset that is not fully depreciated or whose depreciation is not up to date? Consider equipment costing $8,000 with accumulated depreciation of $6,000 on December 31, 2017. This equipment is being depreciated using the straight-line method over eight years with zero residual value. On July 1, 2018, it is discarded. Step 1 is to bring depreciation expense up to date:

July	1	Depreciation Expense, Equipment..................	500
		Accumulated Depreciation, Equipment.....		500
		To record six months' depreciation;		
		Jan. 1/18 to July 1/18; $1,000 \times \frac{6}{12}$.		

The July 1 balance in the Accumulated Depreciation, Equipment account after posting this entry is:

Accumulated Depreciation, Equipment					Acct. No. 168
Date	Explanation	PR	Debit	Credit	Balance
2017 Dec. 31	Balance	✓			6,000
2018 July 1		G8		500	6,500

The second and final entry reflects Steps 2 to 4 of Exhibit 9.21.

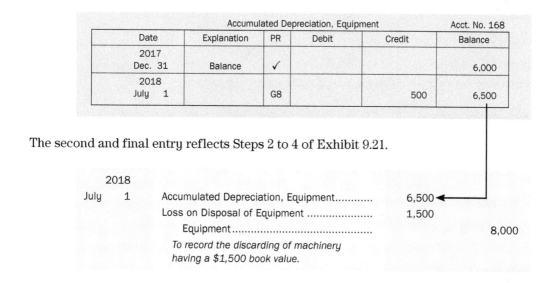

2018 July	1	Accumulated Depreciation, Equipment............	6,500
		Loss on Disposal of Equipment	1,500
		Equipment...		8,000
		To record the discarding of machinery having a $1,500 book value.		

The loss is calculated by comparing the equipment's book value of $1,500 (= $8,000 − $6,500) with the zero net cash proceeds. The loss on disposal is reported in the *Other Revenues and Expenses* section of the income statement.[23]

Gain (loss)			
on disposal*	=	Cash proceeds	− Book value

* A gain occurs when proceeds are greater than book value; a loss occurs when proceeds are less than book value.

Selling PPE

To illustrate the accounting for selling assets, we consider SportsWorld's April 1, 2018, sale of its delivery equipment costing $16,000 with accumulated depreciation of $12,000 on December 31, 2017. Annual depreciation on this equipment is $4,000 calculated using straight-line depreciation. The entry (Step 1) to record depreciation expense and update accumulated depreciation to April 1 is:

2018			
April 1	Depreciation Expense, Equipment..................	1,000	
	Accumulated Depreciation, Equipment.....		1,000

To record three months' depreciation;
Jan. 1/18 to April 1/18; $4,000 \times \dfrac{3}{12}$.

The April 1 balance in the Accumulated Depreciation, Equipment account after posting this entry is:

	Accumulated Depreciation, Equipment				Acct. No. 168
Date	Explanation	PR	Debit	Credit	Balance
2017 Dec. 31	Balance	✓			12,000
2018 Apr. 1		G11		1,000	13,000

The second entry to reflect Steps 2 to 4 of Exhibit 9.21 depends on the amount received in the sale. We consider three different possibilities:

		Book Value = $16,000 − $13,000 = $3,000			
	Sale at Book Value (Cash Proceeds = $3,000)		Sale Above Book Value (Cash Proceeds = $7,000)		Sale Below Book Value (Cash Proceeds = $2,500)

2018						
Apr. 1	Cash	3,000	Cash......................................	7,000	Cash	2,500
	Accum. Deprec., Equip.	13,000	Accum. Deprec., Equip.	13,000	Accum. Deprec., Equip.	13,000
	Equipment......................	16,000	Gain on Disposal of Equip.*	4,000	Loss on Disposal of Equip. ...	500
	To record the sale of .... equipment for $3,000.		Equipment........................	16,000	Equipment	16,000
			To record the sale of .... equipment for $7,000...............		*To record the sale of equipment for $2,500.*	

*The gain on disposal is reported in the *Other Revenues and Expenses* section of the income statement.[24]

 **CHECKPOINT**

14. A company acquires equipment on January 10, 2017, at a cost of $42,000. The CFO selected the straight-line depreciation method and assumed a five-year life and $7,000 residual value for the equipment. On June 27, 2018, the company sold this equipment for $32,000. Prepare the entry or entries for June 27, 2018.

Do Quick Study question: QS 9-15

---

23   IFRS 2015, IAS 16, para. 68.

24   IFRS 2015, IAS 16, para. 68.

Exchanging PPE

Many assets such as machinery, automobiles, and office equipment are disposed of by exchanging them (also referred to as a trade-in) for new assets. The exchange of assets is treated as both a sale of the old asset and a purchase of a new asset. Both the cost and related accumulated depreciation of the old asset must be removed from the books. The cost of the new asset will be recorded at the fair value of the asset(s) received. If the fair value cannot be reliably determined, then the new asset will be recorded at the carrying value of the asset(s) given up.[25] Any gains or losses realized on the exchange are also recorded at the time of disposal.

In a typical exchange of PPE, a trade-in allowance is received on the old asset and the balance is paid in cash. Often, the trade-in allowance offered *does not* reflect the fair value of the asset being traded in. For example, when buying a new car and trading in your old vehicle, the sales department at the dealership may decide to set the trade-in value of your car at a price higher than its fair value to make you feel they are giving you extra value in an attempt to win your business.

To illustrate, on January 2, 2017, Pizza Express trades in a 2015 Honda Accord for a 2017 Honda Pilot that has a list price of $41,000, which has been determined to be a reliable fair value. The original cost of the 2015 Accord was $30,000 and accumulated depreciation is $12,000 up to the date of the trade-in, resulting in a book (or carrying) value of $18,000 (= $30,000 − $12,000). The dealership provides Pizza Express with a trade-in allowance of $20,000 on the Honda Accord and the $21,000 balance is to be in cash. The entry to record this transaction is as follows:

2017			
Jan. 2	Equipment: Honda Pilot..................................	41,000	
	Accumulated Depreciation, Equipment:		
	Honda Accord...	12,000	
	Equipment: Honda Accord.......................		30,000
	Cash..		21,000
	Gain on Asset Exchange		2,000
	To record exchange of 2015 Honda Accord		
	and cash for 2017 Honda Pilot.		

Notice that the 2017 Honda Pilot received by Pizza Express was recorded at $41,000, the fair value of the asset received. The difference between the assets received by Pizza Express ($41,000) and the book (or carrying) value of the total assets exchanged by Pizza Express ($18,000 2015 Honda Accord + $21,000 cash) represents the gain on the exchange ($2,000).

If instead the $41,000 list price of the Honda Pilot is determined to be unreliable, as most dealers negotiate on price, the entry would be:

2017			
Jan. 2	Equipment: Honda Pilot..................................	39,000	
	Accumulated Depreciation, Equipment:		
	Honda Accord...	12,000	
	Equipment: Honda Accord.......................		30,000
	Cash..		21,000
	To record exchange of 2015 Honda Accord		
	and cash for 2017 Honda Pilot.		

---

[25]   IFRS 2015, IAS 16, para. 24.

In this situation, the Honda Pilot received by Pizza Express was recorded at $39,000, the fair value of the assets given up ($18,000 + $21,000); no gain or loss is recorded.

CHECKPOINT

15. On March 3, a local organic apple orchard trades an old truck for a new tractor. The original cost of the old truck is $30,000, and its accumulated depreciation at the time of the trade is $23,400. The new tractor has a list price of $45,000 and the trade-in allowance being offered is $5,000. Prepare entries to record the trade under two different assumptions where the list price of the new tractor is (1) representative of its fair value, or (2) not representative of its fair value.

Do Quick Study questions: QS 9-16, QS 9-17

Intangible Assets

LO7   Account for intangible assets and their amortization.

Intangible assets are rights, privileges, and competitive advantages held by a company that are separately identifiable, have no physical substance, are non-monetary (meaning they have no fixed cash flows attached) and provide future economic benefits as a result of their use in operations. Examples are patents, copyrights, leaseholds, drilling rights, and trademarks. Lack of physical substance is not sufficient grounds for an asset to be an intangible. Note: Goodwill is excluded from the intangible asset category as it represents the future economic benefits that may result from the extra benefits achieved through the identifiable assets when operating together.[26] Exhibit 9.22 outlines the note disclosure for **Microsoft** from its 2014 annual report. Numbers presented are stated in millions of US dollars.

Depreciation is the systematic allocation of the cost of *plant and equipment* over its useful life.

Amortization is the systematic allocation of the cost of an *intangible asset* over its useful life.

EXHIBIT 9.22

Note 11–Intangible Assets
The components of intangible assets, all of which are finite-lived, as follows:

(in millions)	Gross Carrying Amount	Accumulated Amortization	Net Carrying Amount	Gross Carrying Amount	Accumulated Amortization	Net Carrying Amount
Year Ended June 30,			**2014**			**2013**
Technology-based (a)	$ 6,440	$ (2,615)	$ 3,825	$ 3,760	$ (2,110)	$ 1,650
Marketing-related	1,518	(324)	1,194	1,340	(211)	1,137
Contract-based	2,266	(716)	1,550	823	(688)	135
Customer-related	732	(320)	412	380	(219)	161
Total	$10,956	$ (3,975)	$ 6,981	$ 6,311	$ (3,226)	$ 3,083

(a) Technology-based intangible assets included $98 million as of June 30, 2014 and 2013, respectively, of net carrying amount of software to be sold, leased, or otherwise marketed.

We estimated that we have no significant residual value related to our intangible assets. No material impairments of intangible assets were identified during any of the periods presented.

Source: Microsoft 2014 Annual Report: http://www.microsoft.com/investor/reports/ar14/index.html#notes-intangible-assets

---

26   IFRS 2015, IAS 38, para. 11, indicates that goodwill "may result from the synergy between the identifiable assets acquired or from assets that, individually, do not qualify for recognition in the financial statements."

Accounting for Intangible Assets

An intangible asset is recorded at cost when the asset is acquired.[27] Its cost must be systematically allocated to expense over its estimated useful life through the process of **amortization**.[28] The amortization period for intangible assets is estimated based on legal, regulatory, contractual, competitive, economic, or other factors that might limit its useful life. Disposal of an intangible asset is accounted for using the approach previously introduced for disposal of fixed assets. It involves removing its cost and accumulated amortization, recording any asset received, and recognizing any gain or loss for the difference.

Intangible assets are amortized in a similar manner to fixed assets. The straight-line method is generally used *unless* another method better reflects the use of the intangible asset.[29] Intangible assets are assumed to have a residual value of zero.[30]

Intangible assets are shown on the balance sheet separately from goodwill and property, plant, and equipment. The long-term asset section of the 2014 balance sheet for Microsoft Inc. shows the following in millions of US dollars:

Property and equipment, net of accumulated depreciation of $14,793 and $12,513	13,011	9,991
Equity and other investments	14,597	10,844
Goodwill	20,127	14,655
Intangible assets, net	6,981	3,083
Other long-term assets	3,422	2,392

Intangible assets, as is the case for PPE, must be assessed annually for impairment.

Patents

The federal government grants patents under the federal *Patent Act* to encourage the invention of new products or processes. According to the Canadian Intellectual Property Office, to be granted a patent the intellectual property rights must relate to something that is new, inventive (non-obvious to a person of average skill in the related field) and useful. A **patent** is a legally protected exclusive right to an invention[31] that prevents others from manufacturing, selling, or unauthorized use of the invention for 20 years. When patent rights are purchased, the cost of acquiring the rights is debited to an account called *Patents*. If the owner successfully engages in lawsuits to defend a patent, the cost of lawsuits is debited to the Patents account. The costs of exploratory research and development leading to a new patent are expensed when incurred.[32]

While a patent gives its owner exclusive rights to it for 20 years, its cost is amortized over the shorter of its legal life of 20 years or estimated useful life. If we purchase a patent from an inventory for $25,000

---

27 IFRS 2015, IAS 38, para. 72, permits the use of either the cost model or revaluation model after recognition. The cost model is used in this text and the revaluation model is left for discussion in more advanced courses.

28 IFRS 2015, IAS 38, para. 107–109, indicates that for intangible assets with indefinite useful lives, no amortization is recorded. Intangible assets with indefinite useful lives are assessed for impairment annually. Intangible assets with indefinite useful lives are beyond the basics of financial accounting and are left for discussion in more advanced courses.

29 IFRS 2015, IAS 38, para. 97.

30 IFRS 2015, IAS 38, para. 100.

31 http://www.ic.gc.ca/eic/site/cipointernet-internetopic.nsf/eng/wr03716.html?Open&wt_src=cipo-home, accessed February 2015.

32 IFRS 2015, IAS 38, para. 56, 57; 126–127.

with an expected useful life of 10 years, the following entries are made to record the acquisition of the patent and the annual adjusting entry over the 10-year period to amortize one-tenth of its cost:

Jan.	2	Patents..	25,000	
		Cash		25,000
		To record purchase of patents.		
Dec.	31	Amortization Expense, Patents	2,500	
		Accumulated Amortization, Patents		2,500
		To write off patent cost over its 10-year useful life.		

The debit of $2,500 to Amortization Expense, Patents appears on the income statement as a cost of the product or service provided under the protection of the patent. This entry credits the Accumulated Amortization, Patents account.

Copyrights

A copyright is granted by the Canadian Intellectual Property Office of the federal government or by international agreement. A **copyright** gives its owner the exclusive right to publish and sell musical, dramatic, literary, or artistic work during the life of the creator plus 50 years.[33] Yet the useful life of most copyrights is much shorter. The costs of a copyright are amortized over its useful life. The only identifiable cost of many copyrights is the fee paid to the Copyright Office and, if immaterial, the cost is charged directly to an expense account; if material, such as the cost of purchasing the copyrights to songs by the Beatles, costs are capitalized and periodically amortized by debiting an account called *Amortization Expense, Copyrights.*

Mineral Resources

Companies like **Spry Energy Ltd.** and **Yoho Resources Inc.**, both with their head offices in Calgary, Alberta, are involved in the extraction of oil and gas from the earth. In order to engage in this activity, a company must obtain legal permissions known as **drilling rights**. Other names related to drilling rights are mineral rights, mining rights, or oil rights. The owner of land has legal rights to the surface and perhaps to the subsurface. Often, a government body has the legal rights to the subsurface even when someone else might have legal rights to the surface. Companies wanting to drill for oil or other minerals must pay for the legal right to do so. These rights provide the company with a future economic benefit that is necessary for operating activities and, given that the rights are intangible in nature, they are accounted for as intangible assets.[34]

Oil and gas are *natural resources*. **Natural resources** include trees, mineral deposits, and water and are consumed when used. Trees are used to produce pulp and paper and lumber. **Alberta-Pacific Forest Industries Inc.**, more commonly known as **Alpac**, is one of the largest pulp and paper mills in the world and is owned by **Mitsubishi and Oji Paper Group**. Alpac purchases *timber rights*, an intangible asset, to cut trees for its operations. **Barrick Gold Corporation**, with its head office in Toronto, is the gold industry leader and reported more than $37.4 billion of total assets on its December 31, 2013, balance sheet. Of that amount, $116 million represented the book value of an intangible asset Barrick calls *Water Rights in South America.* Large volumes of water are needed in the extraction of gold.

---

33 http://www.ic.gc.ca/eic/site/cipointernet-internetopic.nsf/eng/wr03719.html?Open&wt_src=cipo-cpyrght-main
34 IFRS 2015, IFRS 6, para. 15.

Property, plant, and equipment used by companies in their consumption of natural resources are depreciated.[35]

Trademarks and Trade Names

Companies often adopt unique symbols or select unique names and brands in marketing their products. A **trademark** or *trade name* is a symbol, name, phrase, or jingle identified with a company, product, or service. According to Forbes, "Trademarks serve as an information shortcut for consumers" and "in many cases the trademark theoretically accounts for a significant chunk of its owner's overall worth."[36] Exhibit 9.23 outlines The World's Most Valuable Brands as assessed by Forbes. Ownership and exclusive rights to use a trademark or trade name are often established by showing that one company used it before another. But ownership is best established by registering a trademark or trade name with the Canadian Intellectual Property Office. The cost of developing, maintaining, or enhancing the value of a trademark or trade name by means such as advertising is expensed at the time the costs are incurred. If a trademark or trade name is purchased outright or as part of a business acquisition, its cost is debited to an asset account and amortized.

EXHIBIT 9.23

Rank	Brand	Brand Value ($ bil)	1-Yr Value Change (%)	Brand Revenue ($ bil)	Company Advertising ($ mil)	Industry
1	Apple	124.2	19	170.9	1,100	Technology
2	Microsoft	63.0	11	86.7	2,300	Technology
3	Google	56.6	19	51.4	2,848	Technology
4	Coca-Cola	56.1	2	23.8	3,266	Beverages
5	IBM	47.9	−5	99.8	1,294	Technology
6	McDonald's	39.9	1	89.1	808	Restaurants
7	General Electric	37.1	9	126.0	—	Diversified
8	Samsung	35.0	19	209.6	3,818	Technology
9	Toyota	31.3	22	182.2	4,200	Automotive
10	Louis Vuitton	29.9	5	9.7	4,707	Luxury

Source: http://www.forbes.com/powerful-brands/. Top brands determined based on companies with a brand presence in the United States.

Leaseholds

A **leasehold** refers to the rights granted to the lessee to use a specific asset by the lessor in the lease. A leasehold is an intangible asset for the lessee if a non-current lease requires the lessee to pay a bonus in advance. The resulting debit to a Leasehold account is amortized over the term of the lease by debiting Rent Expense and crediting Leaseholds.

---

35 IFRS 2015, IFRS 6, para. 16.

36 http://www.forbes.com/sites/seanstonefield/2011/06/15/the-10-most-valuable-trademarks/

Goodwill

Goodwill arises as a result of a business acquisition and reflects the amount paid for a business that exceeds the fair market value of the company's net assets (assets minus liabilities) if purchased separately. It is accounted for separately from other identifiable intangible assets on the financial statements. This usually implies that the company has certain valuable attributes not measured among its net assets. These can include superior management, skilled workforce, superior suppliers and customer loyalty, quality products or services, excellent location, or other competitive advantages. Goodwill is subject to a high degree of scrutiny by the acquirer, which wants to pay a reasonable amount for its acquisition. For instance, **Google** shows goodwill on its December 31, 2014, balance sheet of $15.6 billion.

Goodwill is recognized only when a company acquires another business.[37] Internally created goodwill is not recorded in the financial statements, due to the high level of difficulty in determining true value. Permission to do so could lead to abuse and values arrived at would lack objectivity. The amount paid by the acquirer on the acquisition date provides objective evidence that goodwill exists and sets a value to be recognized.

In 2014 **Loblaw Companies Ltd.** acquired the shares of **Shoppers Drug Mart Ltd.** Note 17 of Loblaws 2014 annual report reveals the following breakdown of the group's carrying value of goodwill, with a $2,294 million addition of goodwill attributable to the newly acquired Shoppers Drug Mart.

Goodwill is attributable to synergies expected following the integration of Shoppers Drug Mart, improved competitive positioning in the retail market, and future growth of the company's customer base as a result of the acquisition. The goodwill arising from this acquisition is not deductible for tax purposes.

The carrying amount of goodwill attributed to each CGU grouping was as follows:

(millions of Canadian dollars)	As at January 3, 2015	As at December 28, 2013
Shoppers Drugs Mart	$2,294	$ —
Market	337	—
Discount	459	—
Quebec region	—	700
T&T Supermarket Inc.	129	129
All other	24	114
Carrying amount of goodwill	$3,243	$ 943

Goodwill is not depreciated or amortized. Instead, goodwill is decreased only if its value has been determined by management to be impaired. Impairment of goodwill results when the current value of goodwill (fair value of the organization less the fair value of its net assets) is less than the carrying value of goodwill.

Causes of impairment might include ongoing past or potential cash flow losses, product obsolescence or negative changes in variables supporting original calculations of goodwill. Testing for impairment should be done at least annually.

---

37 IFRS 2015, IFRS 3, para. 3, 32.

CHECKPOINT

16. On January 6, 2017, assume Lego pays $120,000 for a patent with a 20-year legal life to produce a new electronic Lego product that is expected to be marketable for about three years. Prepare entries to record its acquisition and the December 31, 2017, adjustment.

Do Quick Study questions: QS 9-18, QS 9-19

CRITICAL THINKING CHALLENGE

Refer to the Critical Thinking Challenge questions at the beginning of the chapter. Compare your answers to those suggested on Connect.

IFRS AND ASPE—THE DIFFERENCES

Difference	International Financial Reporting Standards (IFRS)	Accounting Standards for Private Enterprises (ASPE)
Depreciation	• *Depreciation* is the term used to describe how costs are allocated for plant and equipment.	• The term *depreciation* or *amortization* may be used to describe how costs are allocated for plant and equipment.
Impairment of PPE and intangible assets	• Impairment must be reviewed annually. • The reversal of an impairment loss is permitted.	• Impairment is reviewed when apparent. • The reversal of an impairment loss is not permitted.
Goodwill	• Impairment must be reviewed annually. • The reversal of an impairment loss is not permitted.	• Same as for PPE.

A Look Ahead

Chapter 10 focuses on current liabilities. We explain how they are computed, recorded, and reported in financial statements. We also explain the accounting for company payroll and contingencies.

For further study on some topics of relevance to this chapter, please see the following Extend Your Knowledge supplement:

EYK 9-1   Presentation of Property, Plant, and Equipment and Intangibles on the Balance Sheet

Summary

LO1 Describe property, plant, and equipment (PPE) and calculate their cost. PPE (1) are used in the operations of a company, and (2) have a useful life of more than one accounting period. There are three main accounting issues with PPE: (1) calculating and accounting for their initial and subsequent costs, (2) allocating their costs to the periods they benefit, and (3) recording their disposal. PPE are recorded at cost when purchased. Cost includes all normal and reasonable expenditures necessary to get the asset in place and ready

for its intended use. Revenue expenditures expire in the current period and are debited to expense accounts. Capital expenditures benefit future periods and are debited to asset accounts. The cost of a lump-sum purchase is allocated among its individual assets based on their relative values.

LO2 Explain, record, and calculate depreciation using the methods of straight-line, units-of-production, and double-declining-balance. Depreciation is the process of allocating to expense the cost of plant and equipment over the accounting periods benefiting from use of the asset. Depreciation does not measure the asset's decline in market value, nor does it measure its physical deterioration. Three factors determine depreciation: cost, residual value, and useful life. Residual value is an estimate of the asset's value at the end of its benefit period. Useful (service) life is the length of time an asset is productively used in operations.

Straight-line: $\dfrac{\text{Cost} - \text{Est. Residual value}}{\text{Estimated useful life in years}}$

Units-of-production: $\dfrac{\text{Cost} - \text{Estimated residual value}}{\substack{\text{Total estimated units} \\ \text{of production}}} \times \substack{\text{Units used} \\ \text{in period}}$

Double-declining-balance: Book value $\times\ 2/n$, where n = Estimated useful life

The amount of depreciation expense per period is usually different for different methods but total depreciation expense is the same. The difference is in the pattern in depreciation expense over the asset's useful life. The straight-line method yields a steady pattern of depreciation expense, while units-of-production does not because it depends on the number of units produced. DDB is an accelerated depreciation method.

LO3 Explain and calculate depreciation for partial years. When PPE are bought and sold throughout the year, depreciation can be calculated either to the nearest whole month *or* by applying the half-year convention.

LO4 Explain and calculate revised depreciation. Depreciation is revised when material changes occur in the estimated residual value and/or useful life and/or there is a subsequent capital expenditure. Revised depreciation is calculated by spreading the *remaining* cost to be depreciated over the remaining useful life of the asset.

LO5 Explain and record impairment losses. If the book value of an asset is greater than its recoverable amount, an impairment loss is recorded. When an impairment loss is recorded, revised depreciation is calculated and recorded in the subsequent period because of the change in the asset's book value. Assets must be assessed annually for impairment.

LO6 Account for asset disposal through discarding, selling, or exchanging an asset. When PPE is discarded, sold, or exchanged, its cost and accumulated depreciation are removed from the accounts. Any cash proceeds from discarding or selling an asset are recorded and compared to the asset's book value to determine a gain or loss. When assets are exchanged, the new asset is recorded at its fair value, and any gain or loss on disposal is recognized.

LO7 Account for intangible assets and their amortization. An intangible asset is recorded at the cost incurred to purchase the asset. Amortization is normally recorded using the straight-line method. Intangible assets include patents, copyrights, drilling rights, leaseholds, franchises, and trademarks. Goodwill is not an intangible asset and is presented separately on the financial statements.

Guidance Answers to DECISION MAKER

Restaurant Results

Treating an expense as a capital expenditure results in lower reported expenses and higher profit. This is because, unlike an expense, a capital expenditure is not expensed immediately. Instead, the cost of a capital expenditure is spread out over the asset's life. Treating an expense as a capital expenditure also means asset and equity totals are reported at a larger amount. This continues until the asset is fully depreciated. Your friend is probably trying to help, but the suggestion hints at unethical behaviour. You must remember that only an expenditure benefiting future periods is a capital expenditure. If an item is truly an "expense" not benefiting future periods, then it must not be treated as a capital expenditure.

Controller Constraints

Before you conclude that this instruction is unethical, you might tell the president of your concern that the longer estimate doesn't seem realistic in light of past experience with three-year replacements. You might ask if the change implies a new replacement plan. Depending on the president's response, such a conversation might eliminate your concern. It is possible the president's decision to change estimated useful life reflects an honest and reasonable prediction of the future. Since the company is struggling financially, the president may have concluded that the normal pattern of replacing assets every three years can't continue. Perhaps the strategy is to avoid costs of frequent replacements and stretch use of the equipment a few years longer until financial conditions improve. Even if you doubt the company will be able to use the equipment for six years, you should consider the possibility that the president has a more complete understanding of the situation and honestly believes a six-year life is a good estimate.

On the downside, you may be correct in suspecting that the president is acting unethically. If you conclude the president's decision is unethical, you might confront the president with your

opinion that it is unethical to change the prediction just to increase profit. This is a personally risky course of action and you may want to remind the president of her own ethical responsibility. Another possibility is to wait and see if the auditor will insist on not changing the estimate. You should always insist the statements be based on reasonable estimates.

Guidance Answers to CHECKPOINT

1. Consistent with the cost principle, PPE assets are recorded at cost, which includes all normal and reasonable expenditures needed to get the asset ready for use.

2. A revenue expenditure benefits only the current period and should be charged to expense of the current period. A capital expenditure has a benefit that extends beyond the end of the current period and should be charged to an asset.

3. A subsequent capital expenditure involves enhancing the economic benefits of an existing PPE asset, usually by replacing part of the asset with an improved or superior part. A subsequent capital expenditure should be debited to the improved asset's account.

4. **a.** Land

   b. Land Improvements

5. $700,000 + $49,000 − $21,000 + $3,500 + $3,000 + $2,500 = $737,000

6. **a.** Straight-line with 7-year life: ($77,000/7) = $11,000

   b. Straight-line with 10-year life: ($77,000/10) = $7,700

7. Depreciation is a process of allocating and charging the cost of assets to the accounting periods that benefit from the assets' use.

8. **a.** Book value using straight-line depreciation: $96,000 − [($96,000 − $8,000)/5] = $78,400

   b. Book value using units-of-production: $96,000 − [($96,000 − $8,000) × (10,000/100,000)] = $87,200

9. Component A: $340,000 × 20% = $68,000 ÷ 4 years = $17,000/year; Component B: $340,000 × 50% = $170,000 ÷ 8 years = $21,250/year; Component C: $340,000 × 30% = $102,000 ÷ 15 years = $6,800/year.

10. Depreciation is based on an estimated useful life, so to calculate it to the nearest day would imply a degree of accuracy that is neither possible nor required.

11. ($3,800 − $200)/3 = $1,200
    $1,200 × 2 = $2,400
    ($3,800 − $2,400)/2 = $700

12.

2017			
Jan. 12	Computer – Monitor	800	
	Accounts Payable		800
	To record the addition of a second monitor to the computer.		
Dec. 31	Depreciation Expense, Computer.............................	2,650	
	Accum. Deprec., Computer..		2,650
	*To record revised depreciation on the computer caused by the addition of a second monitor; $5,000 − $500 = $4,500 ÷ 2 years = $2,250 **PLUS** $800 ÷ 2 years = $400; Total depreciation = $2,250 + $400 = $2,650.*		

13. Machine A's book value is less than its recoverable amount so there is no impairment. There is an impairment loss of $146,000 ($238,000 book value less $92,000 recoverable amount) that must be recorded for Machine B. Additionally, revised depreciation will have to be calculated and recorded for Machine B.

14.

Jan. 27	Depreciation Expense	3,500	
	Accum. Depreciation		3,500
27	Cash.....................................	32,000	
	Accum. Depreciation	10,500	
	Gain on Sale of Equip.		500
	Equipment.........................		42,000

15. a.

Mar. 3	Tractor (new)	45,000	
	Loss on Trade-In	1,600	
	Accum. Depreciation (old)	23,400	
	Truck (old)		30,000
	Cash		40,000

b.

Mar. 3	Tractor (new)	46,600	
	Accum. Depreciation (old)	23,400	
	Truck (old)		30,000
	Cash		40,000

16.

Jan. 6	Patents	120,000	
	Cash		120,000
Dec. 31	Amortization Expense	40,000	
	Accum. Amort., Patents		40,000
	[Amortization calculation:		
	$120,000/3 = $40,000]		

DEMONSTRATION PROBLEM

Health Smart Limited (HSL) purchased a manufacturing assembly machine for its new product launch: The Total Health Watch on March 2, 2017 for $62,000 cash. It had an estimated useful life of five years and a residual value of $14,000. On February 25, 2020, the machine was disposed of. HSL's year-end is December 31, and it calculates depreciation to the nearest whole month using straight-line depreciation.

Required

1. Prepare the entry to record the disposal under each of the following independent assumptions:

   a. The machine was sold for $26,000 cash.

   b. The machine was sold for $33,200 cash.

   c. The machine was sold for $34,180 cash.

   d. The old machine was exchanged for tools with a market value of $88,000. A trade-in allowance of $25,000 was offered on the old machine and the balance was paid in cash. Assume the $88,000 market value of the tools represents their fair value.

   Additional company transaction:

2. On January 4, 2020, the company purchases with cash a patent from a biomedical engineering firm in Winnipeg for $100,000 to enable the launch of a new Total Health Watch for individuals with diabetes that incorporates glucose/insulin monitoring into the equipment. The company estimates the useful life of the patent to be 10 years. Journalize the patent acquisition and amortization for the year.

Analysis Component:

Regarding the purchase of the patent in Part 2, explain what potential adjustment might be necessary at the end of 2020 other than amortization.

Planning the Solution

- Remember that all depreciation must be recorded before removing a disposed asset from the books. Calculate and record the depreciation expense for 2017 through to 2020 using the straight-line method calculated to the nearest whole month. Record the gain/loss on the disposal as well as the removal of the asset and its related accumulated depreciation from the books.

- Record the patent as an intangible asset for its purchase price. Use straight-line amortization over the years of useful life to calculate amortization expense.

Solution

1a.

2020			
Feb. 25	Depreciation Expense, Machine	1,600	
	Accumulated Depreciation, Machine		1,600
	To update depreciation to date of sale.		
25	Accumulated Depreciation, Machine[1]	28,800	
	Cash...	26,000	
	Loss on Disposal[2].......................................	7,200	
	Machine		62,000
	To record sale of machine.		

1b.

Feb. 25	Depreciation Expense, Machine	1,600	
	Accumulated Depreciation, Machine		1,600
	To update depreciation to date of sale.		
25	Accumulated Depreciation, Machine..............	28,800	
	Cash...	33,200	
	Machine		62,000
	To record sale of machine.		

1c.

Feb. 25	Depreciation Expense, Machine	1,600	
	Accumulated Depreciation, Machine		1,600
	To update depreciation to date of sale.		
25	Accumulated Depreciation, Machine..............	28,800	
	Cash...	34,180	
	Machine		62,000
	Gain on Disposal[3]		980
	To record sale of machine.		

[1] 2017: $(\$62,000 - \$14,000)/5 \times \dfrac{10}{12} = \$\ 8,000$

2018: $(\$62,000 - \$14,000)/5 \qquad = \quad 9,600$

2019: $\qquad\qquad\qquad\qquad\qquad = \quad 9,600$

2020: $(\$62,000 - \$14,000)/5 \times \dfrac{2}{12} = \quad 1,600$

Accumulated Depreciation $\qquad\qquad \underline{\$28,800}$

[2] Gain (loss) = Proceeds − Book value
= $\$26,000 - (\$62,000 - \$28,800) = (\underline{\$7,200})$

[3] Gain (loss) = $\$34,180 - (\$62,000 - \$28,800) = \underline{\underline{\$\ \ 980}}$

1d.

Feb.	25	Depreciation Expense, Machine	1,600	
		Accumulated Depreciation, Machine		1,600
		To update depreciation to date of exchange.		
	25	Accumulated Depreciation, Machine..............	28,800	
		Tools	88,000	
		Loss on Disposal[4]......................................	8,200	
		Machine		62,000
		Cash..		63,000
		To record exchange of machine.		

[4] Gain (loss) = $88,000 - [$63,000 + ($62,000 - $28,800)] = ($8,200)

2.

	2020			
Jan.	4	Patent..	100,000	
		Cash		100,000
		To record patent acquisition.		
Dec.	31	Amortization Expense, Patent	10,000	
		Accumulated Amortization, Patent		10,000
		To record amortization expense		
		($100,000/10 years = $10,000).		

Analysis Component:

The adjustment that might be necessary at the end of 2020 other than amortization relates to impairment. Both PPE and intangible assets must be assessed annually for impairment. If the book value (or carrying value) of the asset is greater than the recoverable amount, an impairment loss will need to be recorded. Additionally, if an impairment loss is recorded, revised amortization will need to be calculated and recorded.

APPENDIX 9A

Revised Depreciation When There Is a Subsequent Capital Expenditure That Creates Partial-Period Depreciation

LO8 Explain and calculate revised depreciation when there is a subsequent capital expenditure that creates partial-period depreciation.

Learning Objective 4 in the chapter discussed calculating revised depreciation when there is a change in the estimated useful life and/or estimated residual value *or* when there is a subsequent capital expenditure. What it did not consider is the calculation of revised depreciation when a subsequent capital expenditure occurs during the accounting period such that depreciation is for a partial period.

Calculating and recording revised depreciation involves a multi-step process when there has been a subsequent capital expenditure partway through the accounting period. First, depreciation on the asset must be updated to the date of the subsequent capital expenditure. Then, the subsequent capital expenditure is recorded and, if the subsequent capital expenditure is a replacement, the component being replaced must be removed from the books with any resulting gain or loss also recorded.[38] Finally, revised depreciation is calculated. To demonstrate, assume the following information is available regarding a piece of equipment:

Equipment:						
Component	**Date of Purchase**	**Depreciation Method**[39]	**Cost**	**Estimated Residual Value**	**Estimated Life**	**Accum. Dep. At Dec. 31, 2016, Year-End**
Computer panel	Jan. 2/16	Straight-line	$ 16,000	-0-	8 years	$2,000
Engine	Jan. 2/16	Units-of-prod.	140,000	10,000	50,000 hrs	3,900
			$156,000			$5,900

On September 1, 2017, the computer panel was replaced with a new one costing $20,000 purchased on account. The new computer panel had an estimated residual value of $2,000 and an estimated useful life of six years. During 2017, the equipment had been used 1,200 hours from January 1 to August 31 and 650

---

38 IFRS 2015, IAS 16, para. 13, 67–72.

39 IFRS 2015, IAS 16, para. 45, indicates that the components of a given asset may have different depreciation methods.

hours from September 1 to December 31. To record the replacement of the computer panel and record depreciation on the equipment for 2017, these steps are followed:

1. Update depreciation on the equipment to September 1, the date of the subsequent capital expenditure.

Sept.	1	Depreciation Expense, Equipment	4,453	
		Accumulated Depreciation, Equipment		4,453
		To update depreciation on the equipment.		

Calculations:

Computer panel $16,000 cost − $0 residual = $16,000;

$16,000 ÷ 8 years = $2,000/year $\times \dfrac{8}{12} =$ $1,333[40]

Engine $140,000 cost − $10,000 residual = $130,000 ÷ 50,000 hrs
= $2.60/hr; $2.60/hr × 1,200 hrs =   3,120
          $4,453

Notice that when depreciation is updated to September 1, *it is based on the original rates of depreciation.*

2. Record the subsequent capital expenditure and remove the component being replaced.

Sept.	1	Equipment (new computer panel)	20,000	
		Accumulated Depreciation, Equipment............	3,333	
		Loss on Disposal of Equipment	12,667	
		Equipment (old computer panel)..............		16,000
		Accounts Payable		20,000
		To record the replacement of the computer panel; $2,000 + $1,333 = $3,333.		

3. Calculate and record revised depreciation on the equipment from September 1 to December 31.

Dec.	31	Depreciation Expense, Equipment	2,690	
		Accum. Deprec., Equipment..................		2,690
		To record depreciation from Sept. 1 to Dec. 31.		

Calculations:

Computer panel: $20,000 cost − $2,000 residual = $18,000;

$18,000 ÷ 6 years = $3,000/year $\times \dfrac{4}{12} =$ $1,000

Engine: $140,000 cost − $10,000 residual = $130,000;
$130,000 ÷ 50,000 hrs = $2.60/hr; $2.60/hr × 650 hrs =   1,690
          $2,690

 **CHECKPOINT**

17. Explain the accounting treatment when a significant component of a machine is replaced by a new one.

Do Quick Study question: *QS 9-20

---

40   Depreciation is rounded to the nearest whole dollar because it is based on estimates.

Summary of Appendix 9A

*LO8 Explain and calculate revised depreciation when there is a subsequent capital expenditure that creates partial-period depreciation. Depreciation is revised when there is a subsequent capital expenditure since the book value of the asset has changed. Depreciation must be updated/recorded to the time the capital expenditure was made. Then, if the capital expenditure resulted in the replacement of a component, the cost and accumulated depreciation related to the replaced component must be removed from the books. Revised depreciation is then calculated based on the revised values.

Guidance Answer to CHECKPOINT

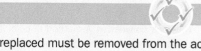

17. When a significant component of a machine is replaced by a new one, the cost of the replacement is considered to be a capital expenditure and debited to the machine account. Additionally, the accumulated depreciation of the component being replaced must be updated to the point in time when the replacement occurred. Then, the component being replaced must be removed from the accounting records by debiting accumulated depreciation for the updated amount and crediting the machine account for the cost of the component being replaced; any resulting gain or loss is also recorded. Finally, revised depreciation is calculated for the machine that incorporates the new component.

Glossary

Accelerated depreciation method A depreciation method that produces larger depreciation charges during the early years of an asset's life and smaller charges in the later years.

Amortization A process of systematically allocating the cost of an intangible asset to expense over its estimated useful life.

Basket purchase See *lump-sum purchase*.

Book value The original cost of plant and equipment (or intangible asset) less its accumulated depreciation (or amortization).

Capital assets See *property, plant, and equipment*.

Capital cost allowance (CCA) The system of depreciation required by federal income tax law for federal income tax purposes.

Capital expenditures Costs of PPE that provide material benefits extending beyond the current period. They are debited to PPE asset accounts and reported on the balance sheet.

Change in an accounting estimate A change in a calculated amount used in the financial statements that results from new information or subsequent developments and from better insight or improved judgment.

Copyright A right granted by the federal government or by international agreement giving the owner the exclusive privilege to publish and sell musical, literary, dramatic, or artistic work during the life of the creator plus 50 years.

Cost Includes all normal and reasonable expenditures necessary to get a PPE asset or intangible asset in place and ready for its intended use.

Declining-balance depreciation A depreciation method in which an asset's depreciation charge for the period is determined by applying a constant depreciation rate (up to twice the straight-line rate) each year to the asset's book value at the beginning of the year. Also known as *diminishing-balance depreciation*.

Depreciable cost The total asset cost less the residual value of the asset. Reflects the amount to be depreciated over the assets useful life.

Depreciation The process of matching (or allocating) the depreciable cost of a tangible asset in a rational and systematic manner over the asset's estimated useful life.

Derecognize Assets are removed from accounting records either upon disposal or when no future economic benefits are expected from their use. Any gain or loss arising on derecognition is included in earnings in the period the asset is disposed or void of future economic benefits.

Diminishing-balance depreciation See *double-declining-balance depreciation*.

Double-declining-balance depreciation A depreciation method in which depreciation is determined at twice the straight-line rate. It is calculated as:

Book value $\times$ 2/n, where n = Estimated useful life.

Drilling rights An intangible asset that gives the holder legal permission to extract oil and gas and/or other minerals from the subsurface. Other forms of legal permission similar to drilling rights include mineral rights, mining rights, timber rights, and water rights.

Fixed assets See *property, plant, and equipment*.

Goodwill The amount by which the value of a company exceeds the fair market value of the company's net assets if purchased separately; goodwill is not an intangible asset; goodwill is *not* amortized or depreciated but is instead subject to an annual impairment test.

Half-year convention A method of calculating depreciation for partial periods. Six months' depreciation is taken for the partial period regardless of when the asset was acquired or disposed of. Also known as the *half-year rule*.

Impairment loss Results when the book value (or carrying value) of PPE or an intangible asset is greater than its recoverable amount because of the annual impairment test.

Inadequacy A condition in which the capacity of the company's PPE is too small to meet the company's productive demands.

Intangible assets Rights, privileges, and competitive advantages to the owner of identifiable assets used in operations that have a useful life of more than one accounting period but have no physical substance; examples include patents, copyrights, drilling rights, leaseholds, franchises, and trademarks. Goodwill is not an intangible asset.

Land improvements Assets that increase the usefulness of land but that have a limited useful life and are subject to depreciation.

Lease A contract allowing property rental.

Leasehold A name for the rights granted to the lessee by the lessor in a lease.

Leasehold improvement An asset resulting from a lessee paying for alterations or improvements to the leased property.

Lessee The party to a lease that secures the right to possess and use the property.

Lessor The party to a lease that grants to another the right to possess and use property.

Lump-sum purchase Purchase of PPE in a group with a single transaction for a lump-sum price. The cost of the purchase must be allocated to individual asset accounts; also called a *basket purchase*.

Natural resources Assets that are physically consumed when used; examples include timber, mineral deposits, and oil and gas fields; also called *wasting assets*.

Obsolescence A condition in which, because of new inventions and improvements, a PPE item can no longer be used to produce goods or services with a competitive advantage.

Patent An exclusive right granted to its owner by the federal government to manufacture and sell a machine or device, or to use a process, for 20 years.

PPE A common abbreviation for *property, plant, and equipment*.

Property, plant, and equipment (PPE) Tangible assets used in the operations of a company that have a useful life of more than one accounting period; often abbreviated as *PPE*; sometimes referred to as *fixed assets*.

Repairs Expenditures made to keep a PPE asset in normal, good operating condition; treated as a revenue expenditure.

Residual value Management's estimate of the amount that will be recovered at the end of a PPE item's useful life through a sale or as a trade-in allowance on the purchase of a new asset.

Revenue expenditures Expenditures that should appear on the current income statement as expenses and be deducted from the period's revenues because they do not provide a material benefit in future periods.

Revised depreciation Recalculated depreciation because of a change in cost, residual value, and/or useful life.

Service life See *useful life*.

Straight-line depreciation A method that allocates an equal portion of the total depreciation for an asset; calculated as:

$$\frac{\text{Cost} - \text{Residual value}}{\text{Estimated useful life in years}}$$

Trademark A symbol, name, phrase, or jingle identified with a company, product, or service. Also referred to as a trade name.

Units-of-production depreciation A method that charges a varying amount to expense for each period of an asset's useful life depending on its usage; expense for the period is calculated as:

$$\frac{\text{Cost} - \text{Estimated residual value}}{\text{Total estimated units of production}} \times \text{Units used in period}$$

Useful life The estimated length of time in which a PPE item or intangible asset will be productively used in the operations of the business; also called *service life*.

Concept Review Questions

1. What characteristics of a property, plant, and equipment item make it different from other assets, such as accounts receivable or inventory?

2. What is the balance sheet classification of land held for future expansion? Why is the land not classified as property, plant, and equipment?

3. What are some examples of items to include in the cost of a property, plant, and equipment purchase?

4. What is the difference in how to account for land and land improvements?

5. Does the balance of the Accumulated Depreciation, Machinery account represent funds accumulated to replace the machinery when it wears out?

6. What is the difference in profit between a subsequent revenue expenditure and a subsequent capital expenditure, and how are each recorded?

7. What accounting principle justifies charging the $75 cost of PPE immediately to an expense account?

8. Refer to the statements of cash flows for Danier Leather in Appendix II. What was the gain or loss

on disposal of assets reported for the 2014 year-end?

9. What are some of the events that might lead to the disposal of PPE?

10. What are the characteristics of an intangible asset?

11. What are two types of intangible assets?

12. Refer to the balance sheet for WestJet in Appendix II. What amount did it report as intangible assets at December 31, 2014?

13. When is the only time a business can record goodwill?

14. Refer to the balance sheet for WestJet in Appendix II. What amount did it report as goodwill at December 31, 2014?

15. In the chapter opening vignette, YVR refers to several capital initiatives that are underway. What types of construction costs can YVR capitalize for self-constructed assets such as the development of a new runway for the international terminal?

Quick Study

QS 9-1 **Cost of PPE** LO1

Sydney Lanes, a local bowling alley, installed automatic scorekeeping equipment. The electrical work required to prepare for the installation was $18,000. The invoice price of the equipment was $180,000. Additional costs were $3,000 for delivery and $600 for insurance during transportation. During the installation, a component of the equipment was damaged because it was carelessly left on a lane and hit by the automatic lane cleaning machine. The cost of repairing the component was $2,250. What is the cost that should be capitalized of the automatic scorekeeping equipment?

QS 9-2 **Revenue and capital expenditures** LO1

1. Classify the following expenditures as revenue (R) or capital expenditures (C):

   a. The monthly replacement cost of filters on an air conditioning system, $120.

   b. The cost of replacing a compressor for an ice cream firm's refrigeration system that extends the estimated life of the system by four years, $40,000.

   c. The cost of annual tune-ups for delivery trucks, $200.

   d. The cost of $175,000 for an addition of a new wing on an office building.

2. Prepare the journal entry to record each of the above (assume all transactions occurred on March 15, 2017, and were on account).

QS 9-3 Lump-sum purchase L01   eXcel

On April 14, 2017, Orchid Company, a new Thai Restaurant, purchased land and a building for a total price of $540,000, paying cash of $85,000 and borrowing the balance from the bank. The bank appraised the land at $320,000 and the building at $180,000. Complete the following table and prepare the entry to record the purchase.

PPE Item	(a) Appraised Values	(b) Ratio of Individual Appraised Value to Total Appraised Value (a) ÷ Total Appraised Value	(c) Cost Allocation (b) × Total Actual Cost
Land			
Building			
Totals			

QS 9-4 Balance sheet presentation L02

TechCom has provided the following selected account information, in alphabetical order, from its adjusted trial balance at October 31, 2017 (assume normal balances):

Accounts receivable	$16,400
Accumulated depreciation, equipment	3,800
Accumulated amortization, patent	3,100
Accumulated depreciation, vehicles	13,800
Allowance for doubtful accounts	800
Cash	9,000
Equipment	25,000
Land	48,000
Patent	20,100
Vehicles	62,000

Prepare the asset section of the classified balance sheet at October 31, 2017.

QS 9-5 Calculating depreciation—straight-line L02

On January 2, 2017, Crossfire acquired sound equipment for concert performances at a cost of $55,900. The rock band estimated that it would use this equipment for four years, and then sell the equipment for $1,900. Calculate depreciation for each year of the sound equipment's estimated life using the straight-line method. Crossfire's year-end is December 31.

QS 9-6 Calculating depreciation—units-of-production L02   eXcel

Papaya, a specialty greeting card company, purchased a photocopier costing $45,000 on January 1, 2017. The equipment is expected to produce a total of 4,000,000 copies over its productive life. Its residual value at the end of its useful life is estimated to be $5,000. The equipment actually produced:

Fiscal Year	Copies Produced
2017	650,000
2018	798,000
2019	424,000
2020	935,000
2021	1,193,000

Calculate depreciation for 2017 through to 2021 using the units-of-production method. Papaya's year-end is December 31.

QS 9-7 Calculating depreciation—double-declining-balance LO2 e**X**cel

Patty's Pies acquired a delivery truck on January 1, 2017, for $86,000. It is expected to last five years and then sell for about $16,000. Calculate depreciation for each year of the truck's life using the double-declining-balance method. Patty's Pies year-end is December 31.

QS 9-8 Calculating depreciation on components LO2

Crystal Cleaners is an eco-friendly dry cleaner. The following excerpt from its PPE subledger shows the component details regarding the dry cleaning equipment:

Dry Cleaning Equipment:

Component	Depreciation Method[1]	Cost	Estimated Residual	Estimated Life
Computer panel	SL	$ 4,000	$ -0-	8 years
Dry cleaning drum	Units	70,000	5,000	400,000 garments
Stainless steel housing	SL	85,000	10,000	20 years
Miscellaneous parts	SL	26,000	-0-	2 years
		$185,000		

[1] SL = Straight-line; Units = Units-of-production.

Calculate depreciation on the dry cleaning equipment for the year ended December 31, 2017. Assume the equipment was purchased on January 2, 2017, and that 62,000 garments were dry cleaned during 2017.

QS 9-9 Calculating depreciation—partial periods LO2,3

Equipment with an estimated life of 10 years and no expected residual value was purchased on account for $60,000 on March 6, 2017. Assuming a year-end of December 31, calculate depreciation for 2017 and 2018 using the straight-line method:

    a. To the nearest whole month   **b.** Using the half-year convention

QS 9-10 Double-declining-balance—partial periods LO2,3

Refer to the information in QS 9-9. Assume the equipment is depreciated using the double-declining-balance method. Calculate depreciation for 2017 and 2018:

    a. To the nearest whole month   **b.** Using the half-year convention

QS 9-11 Units-of-production—partial periods LO2,3

AbeCo, a luggage manufacturing company, borrowed $75,000 from the bank to purchase a machine that was estimated to produce 120,000 suitcases; its expected residual value is $15,000. During 2017 and 2018, the machine produced 20,000 and 28,000 units, respectively. Calculate depreciation for 2017 and 2018 assuming the units-of-production method is used:

    a. To the nearest whole month   **b.** Using the half-year convention

QS 9-12 Revised depreciation—change in useful life and residual value LO4

On January 1, 2017, Kaldex Company purchased for $35,720 equipment with an estimated useful life of eight years and an estimated residual value at the end of its life of $4,200. Early in January 2020, it was determined that the total estimated useful life on the equipment should be 10 years with a revised estimated residual value of $1,570. Kaldex uses the straight-line method to calculate depreciation and its year-end is December 31. Calculate revised depreciation for 2020.

QS 9-13 Revised depreciation—subsequent capital expenditure LO4

A Catering Company had a deluxe, portable barbecue with a book value of $7,000 at its December 31, 2016, year-end. The barbecue had an estimated remaining useful life of five years and a $200 residual value. On January 3, 2017, a customized electronic rotisserie unit costing $1,000 was added to the barbecue to improve the quality of the barbecuing process. The rotisserie had an estimated life of five years and no residual value. Record the addition on January 3 and the revised depreciation on the barbecue at December 31. Assume cash was paid for the rotisserie and that it represents a significant expenditure.

QS 9-14 Impairment losses LO5

Phantom Company was preparing the annual financial statements and, as part of its year-end procedures, prepared the following alphabetized schedule based on adjusted values at March 31, 2017:

Asset	Cost	Accumulated Depreciation	Recoverable Amount
Building	$1,200,000	$465,000	$735,000
Computer.............................	3,500	1,800	200
Furniture	79,000	53,000	5,000
Land.......................................	630,000	-0-	790,000
Machine.................................	284,000	117,000	172,000

What, if any, impairment losses need to be accounted for? Assume Phantom Company recorded no impairment losses in previous years.

QS 9-15 Disposal of PPE LO6

Huang Furniture Company showed the following adjusted account balances on September 30, 2017:

Equipment	$ 56,000
Accumulated depreciation, equipment...	39,000
Machinery	109,000
Accumulated depreciation, machinery	96,000
Delivery truck	48,000
Accumulated depreciation, delivery truck..	33,000
Furniture	26,000
Accumulated depreciation, furniture	21,000

Prepare the entries to record the following on October 1, 2017:

   a. Equipment was sold for cash of $17,000.

   b. Machinery was sold for cash of $27,000.

   c. Delivery truck was sold for cash of $11,000.

   d. Furniture was given to a charity.

QS 9-16 Exchanging PPE LO6

Dean Carpet Stores owned an automobile with a $15,000 cost that had $13,500 accumulated depreciation as of December 31, 2017. Its fair value on this date was $3,000. On the same day, Dean exchanged this auto for a computer with a fair value of $5,800. Dean was required to pay an additional $2,750 cash. Prepare the entry to record this transaction for Dean.

QS 9-17 Exchanging PPE LO6

On March 1, 2017, Wallace Company purchased a new machine with a suggested retail price of $123,000. The new machine was to replace an old machine that originally cost $90,000 and had $36,000 of accumulated depreciation at the time of the exchange. The retailer was offering Wallace a trade-in allowance of $60,000. Record the exchange assuming the fair values are not known.

QS 9-18 Intangible assets and amortization LO7

On January 4, 2017, Amber's Boutique paid cash of $95,000 for a 10-year franchise. Prepare the entry to record the purchase of the franchise and the adjusting entry at December 31, 2017.

QS 9-19 Intangible assets and amortization LO7

Assume Barrick Gold Corporation purchased mineral rights for a gold mine in Peru on October 1, 2017, by paying cash of $5,000,000 and incurring a non-current note payable for the $30,000,000 balance. Barrick also paid $4,000,000 cash for water rights needed to mine the gold. Barrick is planning to mine this area for 10 years. Record the purchase of the mineral rights and water rights on October 1, 2017, and the amortization on December 31, 2017, Barrick's year-end. Assume Barrick uses the straight-line method to amortize intangibles.

*QS 9-20 Revised depreciation—subsequent capital expenditure creating partial-period depreciation *LO8

Flint Solar Energy showed the following information in its Property, Plant, and Equipment subledger regarding a machine.

Machine:						
Component	Date of Purchase	Depreciation Method	Cost	Est. Residual	Est. Life	Accum. Dep. at Dec. 31, 2016, Year-End
Motor	Jan. 1/13	Straight-line	$ 45,000	$ 5,000	10 years	$16,000
Metal housing	Jan. 1/13	Straight-line	68,000	15,000	25 years	8,480
Misc. parts	Jan. 1/13	Straight-line	15,000	-0-	5 years	12,000
			$128,000			$36,480

On September 1, 2017, the motor was replaced with a new one costing $60,000; it was purchased on account. The new motor had an estimated residual value of $10,000 and an estimated life of eight years. Calculate the *total* depreciation expense to be recorded on the machine for 2017.

Exercises

Exercise 9-1 Cost included in PPE LO1

CHECK FIGURE: Total acquisition costs = $16,250

Dalton Company purchased a machine for $15,000, terms 2/10, n/60, FOB shipping point. The seller prepaid the freight charges, $260, and sent a second invoice for the freight. Dalton took advantage of the discount on the first invoice, but the discount was not available on the freight invoice. The machine required a special steel mounting and power connections costing $795, and another $375 was paid to assemble the machine and get it into operation. In moving the machine onto its steel mounting, it was

An asterisk (*) identifies assignment material based on Appendix 9A.

dropped and damaged. The repairs cost $190. Also, $120 of raw materials were used in calibrating (adjusting) the machine so that it would produce the correct quality product. The adjustments were normal for this type of machine and were not the result of the damage. However, the items produced while the adjustments were being made were not saleable. Prepare a calculation to show the cost of this machine for accounting purposes.

Exercise 9-2 **Recording costs of real estate—land versus building costs** LO1

CHECK FIGURE: Dr Land $1,860,000

After planning to build a new plant, Kallisto Backpack Manufacturing purchased a large lot on which a small building was located. The negotiated purchase price for this real estate was $1,200,000 for the lot plus $480,000 for the building. The company paid $75,000 to have the old building torn down and $105,000 for levelling the lot. Finally, it paid $2,880,000 in construction costs, which included the cost of a new building plus $215,000 for lighting and paving a parking lot next to the building. Present a single journal entry to record the costs incurred by Kallisto, all of which were paid in cash (assume a date of March 10, 2017, for your entry).

Exercise 9-3 **Lump-sum purchase** LO1 eXcel

CHECK FIGURE: Dr Land $244,346

On April 12, 2017, Prism Ltd., a camera lens manufacturer, paid cash of $552,375 for real estate plus $29,400 cash in closing costs. The real estate included land appraised at $249,480; land improvements appraised at $83,160; and a building appraised at $261,360. Prepare a calculation similar to QS 9-3 showing the allocation of the total cost among the three purchased assets and present the journal entry to record the purchase.

Exercise 9-4 **Lump-sum purchase** LO1

CHECK FIGURE: Dr Tools $388,800

On January 1, 2017, Bona Vista Co. purchased land, a building, equipment, and tools for a total price of $4,320,000, paying cash of $1,104,000 and borrowing the balance from the bank. The bank appraiser valued the assets as follows: $1,152,000 for the land; $1,344,000 for the building; $998,400 for the equipment; and $345,600 for the tools. Prepare the entry to record the purchase.

Exercise 9-5 **Cost of PPE, straight-line depreciation** LO1,2

CHECK FIGURE: Dr Truck $63,000

On January 1, 2017, Land's End Construction purchased a used truck for $37,500. A new motor had to be installed to get the truck in good working order; the costs were $13,500 for the motor and $6,750 for the labour. The truck was also painted for $5,250. It was ready for use by January 4. A 12-month insurance policy costing $3,600 was purchased to cover the vehicle. The driver filled it with $180 of gas before taking it on its first trip. It is estimated that the truck has a five-year useful life and a residual value of $7,500. Land's End uses the straight-line method to depreciate all of its vehicles. Prepare the entry to record the purchase of truck, insurance, and gas, and record the depreciation at year-end, December 31, 2017.

Exercise 9-6 **Alternative depreciation methods—straight-line, double-declining-balance, and units-of-production** LO2 eXcel

CHECK FIGURES: b. 2019 = $18,300; c. 2020 = $39,560

On January 2, 2017, Wavepoint Systems, a cell phone manufacturer, installed a computerized machine in its factory at a cost of $169,200. The machine's useful life was estimated at four years or a total of 181,500 units with a $24,000 trade-in value. Wavepoint's year-end is December 31. Calculate depreciation for each year of the machine's estimated useful life under each of the following methods:

a. Straight-line

b. Double-declining-balance

c. Units-of-production, assuming actual units produced were:

2017	38,300	2019	52,600
2018	41,150	2020	56,000

Exercise 9-7 **Calculating depreciation** LO2 **eXcel**

CHECK FIGURE: b. $95,360

Jackal Energy purchased a transport truck on January 1, 2017, for $238,400 cash. Its estimated useful life is five years or 240,000 kilometres with an estimated residual value of $46,400.

Required Calculate depreciation expense for the year ended December 31, 2017, using each of the following methods:

a. Straight-line

b. Double-declining-balance

c. Units-of-production (assume 38,000 kilometres were actually driven in 2017)

Analysis Component: Which depreciation method will produce the highest profit for Jackal in 2017?

Exercise 9-8 **Alternative depreciation methods** LO2 **eXcel**

CHECK FIGURES: Deprec. exp. 2019: Straight-line = $21,250; DDB = $18,036; Units = $30,000

On January 3, 2017, Xenex Innovations purchased computer equipment for $125,250. The equipment will be used in research and development activities for five years or a total of 8,500 hours and then sold for about $19,000. Prepare a schedule with headings as shown below. Calculate depreciation and book values for each year of the equipment's life for each method of depreciation. Xenex's year-end is December 31.

	Straight-Line		Double-Declining-Balance		Units-of-Production*	
Year	Depreciation Expense	Book Value at December 31	Depreciation Expense	Book Value at December 31	Depreciation Expense	Book Value at December 31

*Assume actual usage in hours of:

2017	1,350	2020	2,980
2018	1,780	2021	2,700
2019	2,400		

Analysis Component: Which method will result in the greatest:

a. Total assets being reported on the balance sheet in 2017? in 2020?

b. Operating expenses being reported on the income statement in 2017? in 2020?

Exercise 9-9 **Lump-sum purchase, double-declining-balance** LO1,2

CHECK FIGURES: 2018 depreciation: Land = $0; Building = $215,040; Equipment = $60,480; Tools = $18,667

On January 1, 2017, Creative Calligraphy Inc. purchased land, building, equipment, and tools for a total of $2,520,000. An appraisal identified the fair values to be $700,000 (land), $1,120,000 (building), $210,000 (equipment), and $70,000 (tools). The estimated useful life and residual value of the building was 10 years and $700,000; for the equipment, five years and $42,000; and for the tools, three years and $7,000. Calculate depreciation for 2017 and 2018 using the double-declining-balance method. Creative Calligraphy's year-end is December 31.

Analysis Component: Explain depreciation as it applies to land.

Exercise 9-10 **Calculating depreciation** LO2 e**X**cel

CHECK FIGURE: Depreciation expense, truck = $8,672

At December 31, 2016, Dynamic Exploration's balance sheet showed total PPE assets of $802,000 and total accumulated depreciation of $339,980 as detailed in the PPE subledger below. Dynamic calculates depreciation to the nearest whole month.

	Cost Information					Depreciation		
Description	Date of Purchase	Depreciation¹ Method	Cost²	Residual	Life	Balance of Accum. Deprec. Dec. 31, 2016	Depreciation Expense for 2017	Balance of Accum. Deprec. Dec. 31, 2017
Building	May 2, 2011	S/L	$650,000	$250,000	10 yr.	$226,667		
Modular furniture	May 2, 2011	S/L	72,000	-0-	6 yr.	68,000		
Truck	Jan. 25, 2014	DDB	80,000	10,000	8 yr.	45,313		

¹ S/L—Straight-line; DDB—double-declining-balance
² There have been no disposals or subsequent capital expenditures since the date of purchase.

Required Complete the schedule by calculating depreciation expense for 2017 for each asset and then determining the balance of accumulated depreciation at December 31, 2017 (round to the nearest whole dollar).

Analysis Component: The depreciation methods used by Dynamic are not consistent between the building, modular furniture, and truck. Is this in accordance with GAAP? Explain why or why not.

Exercise 9-11 **Balance sheet presentation** LO2

CHECK FIGURE: Total assets = $800,020

Refer to Exercise 9-10. Assume that the only other assets at December 31, 2016, were total current assets of $338,000. Prepare the asset section of Dynamic Exploration's classified balance sheet at December 31, 2016.

Exercise 9-12 **Income statement effects of alternative depreciation methods** LO2 e**X**cel

CHECK FIGURE: b. Depreciation expense, Year 3 = $64,344

Kenartha Oil recently paid $470,400 for equipment that will last five years and have a residual value of $105,000. By using the machine in its operations for five years, the company expects to earn $171,000 annually, after deducting all expenses except depreciation. Complete the schedule below assuming each of (a) straight-line depreciation and (b) double-declining-balance depreciation.

	Year 1	Year 2	Year 3	Year 4	Year 5	5-Year Totals
Profit before depreciation						
Depreciation expense						
Profit						

Analysis Component: If Kenartha Oil wants the Year 1 balance sheet to show the highest value possible for the equipment, which depreciation method will it choose? Explain.

Exercise 9-13 Partial-period depreciation—nearest month L03 eXcel

CHECK FIGURES: Straight-line, 2018 = $21,600; Units, 2018 = $43,416

VanHoutte Foods bought machinery on September 10, 2017, for $156,000. It was determined that the machinery would be used for six years or until it produced 200,000 units and then would be sold for about $26,400. Complete the schedule below by calculating annual depreciation to the nearest whole month for 2017, 2018, and 2019. VanHoutte's year-end is December 31.

| | Depreciation | |
Year	Straight-Line	Double-Declining-Balance

*Round the per unit depreciation expense to three decimal places.

Assume actual units produced of:

2017	31,000	2019	52,000
2018	67,000		

Analysis Component: If depreciation is not recorded, what is the effect on the income statement and balance sheet?

Exercise 9-14 Partial-period depreciation—half-year convention L03 eXcel

CHECK FIGURES: Straight-line, 2019 = $22,000; DDB, 2019 = $21,120

Design Pro purchased on October 1, 2017, $110,000 of furniture that was put into service on November 10, 2017. The furniture will be used for five years and then donated to a charity. Complete the schedule below by calculating annual depreciation for 2017, 2018, and 2019, applying the half-year convention for partial periods. The year-end is December 31.

| | Depreciation | |
Year	Straight-Line	Units-of-Production*

Analysis Component: What effect would it have on the 2017 financial statements if the furniture had been debited to an expense account when purchased instead of being recorded as PPE?

Exercise 9-15 Alternative depreciation methods—partial year's depreciation L03 eXcel

CHECK FIGURES: a. 2018 = $22,500; b. 2018 = $35,000

On April 1, 2017, Ice Drilling Co. purchased a trencher for $125,000. The machine was expected to last five years and have a residual value of $12,500.

Required Calculate depreciation expense for 2017 and 2018 to the nearest month, using (a) the straight-line method, and (b) the double-declining-balance method. The company has a December 31 year-end.

Exercise 9-16 Revising depreciation rates—change in useful life and residual value L04 eXcel

CHECK FIGURE: 2. $6,800

The Hilton Skating Club used straight-line depreciation for a used Zamboni* that cost $43,500, under the assumption it would have a four-year life and a $5,000 trade-in value. After two years, the club

*"Zamboni" is a trademark name for an ice resurfacing machine.

determined that the Zamboni still had three more years of remaining useful life, after which it would have an estimated $3,850 trade-in value.

Required

1. Calculate the Zamboni's book value at the end of its second year.

2. Calculate the amount of depreciation to be charged during each of the remaining years in the Zamboni's revised useful life.

Exercise 9-17 **Revising depreciation rates—change in useful life and residual value** LO4

CHECK FIGURE: Revised depreciation = $7,624

On April 3, 2017, David's Chocolates purchased a machine for $71,200. It was assumed that the machine would have a five-year life and a $15,200 trade-in value. Early in January 2020, it was determined that the machine would have a seven-year useful life and the trade-in value would be $8,000. David's Chocolates uses the straight-line method to the nearest month for calculating depreciation.

Required Record depreciation at December 31, 2020, David's Chocolate's year-end. Round to the nearest whole dollar.

Exercise 9-18 **Revised depreciation—subsequent capital expenditure** LO2,4

CHECK FIGURE: 2. $14,700

At its December 31, 2016, year-end, Athletic Apparel had a warehouse with an adjusted book value of $292,500 and an estimated remaining useful life of 15 years and residual value of $90,000. Because of pick-up and delivery issues at the warehouse, a contractor was hired to construct a new door into the east wall during the week of January 5, 2017, for $25,500 on account. The estimated useful life of the door is 15 years with an estimated residual value of $7,500. Athletic uses the straight-line method to depreciate assets.

Required

1. Record the installation of the new door.

2. Record total depreciation on the warehouse at December 31, 2017.

Exercise 9-19 **Impairment losses** LO2,5

Kane Biotech was preparing the annual financial statements and, as part of the year-end procedures, assessed the assets and prepared the following alphabetized schedule based on adjusted values at December 31, 2017:

Asset	Date of Purchase	Deprec. Method*	Cost	Residual Value	Useful Life	Accum. Deprec.	Recoverable Amount
Equipment	May 1/12	Units	$40,000	$ 5,000	7,000 units	$20,000	$ 8,000
Furniture	Jun. 28/12	DDB	12,000	2,000	8 yrs	9,509	2,950
Land	Apr. 5/12	N/A	85,000	N/A	N/A	N/A	101,800
Office building	Apr. 5/12	SL	77,000	17,000	15 yrs	23,000	52,500
Warehouse	Apr. 5/12	SL	55,000	10,000	20 yrs	12,938	45,100

*DDB = Double-declining-balance; SL = Straight-line; Units = Units-of-production; N/A = Not applicable

Required

1. Record any impairment losses at December 31, 2017. Assume Kane Biotech has recorded no impairment losses in previous years.

2. Record depreciation for each asset at December 31, 2018. Assume that there was no change in the residual values or useful lives regardless of any impairment losses that might have occurred. The equipment produced 1,800 units during 2018.

Exercise 9-20 **Disposal of PPE** LO6

CHECK FIGURES: b. Gain = $1,450; c. Loss = $950

Macho Taco sold a food truck on March 1, 2017. The accounts showed adjusted balances on February 28, 2017, as follows:

Food Truck	$42,000
Accumulated Depreciation, Food Truck	21,850

Required Record the sale of the food truck assuming the cash proceeds were:

    a. $20,150   **b.** $21,600   **c.** $19,200   **d.** $0 (the food truck was scrapped).

Exercise 9-21 **Partial year's depreciation; disposal of PPE** LO2,3,6

CHECK FIGURES: a. Gain = $6,000; b. Loss = $10,000

Candy Craze purchased and installed a machine on January 1, 2017, at a total cost of $296,800. Straight-line depreciation was taken each year for four years, based on the assumption of a seven-year life and no residual value. The machine was disposed of on July 1, 2021, during its fifth year of service. Candy Craze's year-end is December 31.

Required Present the entries to record the partial year's depreciation on July 1, 2021, and to record the disposal under each of the following unrelated assumptions:

    a. The machine was sold for $112,000 cash.

    b. Candy Craze received an insurance settlement of $96,000 resulting from the total destruction of the machine in a fire.

Exercise 9-22 **Exchanging PPE** LO6

CHECK FIGURE: b. Loss = $29,000

On October 6, 2017, Western Farms Co. traded in an old tractor for a new one, receiving a $56,000 trade-in allowance and paying the remaining $164,000 in cash. The old tractor cost $190,000, and straight-line depreciation of $105,000 had been recorded as of October 6, 2017. Assume the fair value of the new tractor was equal to the trade-in allowance of the old tractor plus the cash paid.

Required

    a. What was the book value of the old tractor?

    b. What is the gain or loss on the exchange?

    c. What amount should be debited to the new Tractor account?

    d. Record the exchange.

Exercise 9-23 **Exchanging PPE** LO6

CHECK FIGURE: b. Loss = $1,000

On November 3, 2017, Gamez 2 Go Media exchanged an old computer for a new computer that had a list price of $190,000. The original cost of the old computer was $150,000 and related accumulated depreciation was $65,000 up to the date of the exchange. Gamez 2 Go Media received a trade-in allowance of $100,000 and paid the balance in cash.

Required

    a. Record the exchange assuming the fair values are unknown.

    b. Assume that the fair value of the new asset was $174,000. Record the exchange.

Analysis Component: What is the dollar value that will be used to depreciate the new computer in part (b)? Explain which GAAP helped you answer the question correctly.

Exercise 9-24 **Recording PPE disposal or exchange** L06

CHECK FIGURES: a. Loss = $6,250; c. Loss = $2,750; d. Gain = $11,250

On January 2, 2017, Direct Shoes Inc. disposed of a machine that cost $84,000 and had been depreciated $45,250. Present the journal entries to record the disposal under each of the following unrelated assumptions:

    a. The machine was sold for $32,500 cash.

    b. The machine was traded in on new tools having a $117,000 cash price. A $40,000 trade-in allowance was received, and the balance was paid in cash. Since the tools have been customized, the fair values are not known.

    c. The machine plus $68,000 was exchanged for a delivery van having a fair value of $104,000.

    d. The machine was traded for vacant land adjacent to the shop to be used as a parking lot. The land had a fair value of $75,000, and Direct Shoes Inc paid $25,000 cash in addition to giving the seller the machine.

Exercise 9-25 **Amortization of intangible assets** L07

CHECK FIGURE: Amortization Expense, Copyright = $14,790

The Jazzy Antiques purchased the copyright on a watercolour painting for $177,480 on January 1, 2017. The copyright legally protects its owner for 19 more years. However, Jazzy plans to market and sell prints of the original for the next 12 years only. Prepare journal entries to record the purchase of the copyright and the annual amortization of the copyright on December 31, 2017. The company uses the straight-line method to amortize intangibles.

Exercise 9-26 **Amortization of intangible assets** L02,3,7

CHECK FIGURES: 2. Timber rights, Dec. 31, 2017 = $48,000; Dec. 31, 2018 = $144,000

On September 5, 2017, Nelson Lumber purchased timber rights in Northern Quebec for $432,000, paying $96,000 cash and the balance by issuing a non-current note. Logging the area is expected to take three years, and the timber rights will have no value after that time. On September 27, 2017, Nelson Lumber, purchased a patent for new logging equipment on account. It is expected that the patent will be technologically obsolete in 10 years. Nelson's year-end is December 31 and it uses the straight-line method to amortize intangibles.

Required

  1. Record the acquisition of the timber rights and the patent.

  2. Record amortization on the timber rights and the patent at December 31, 2017, and December 31, 2018.

Exercise 9-27 Balance sheet LO2,7

CHECK FIGURE: Total assets = $302,080

Huang Resources showed the following alphabetized adjusted trial balance at October 31, 2017:

Account	Balance
Accounts payable	$ 18,400
Accounts receivable	27,200
Accumulated amortization, mineral rights	30,400
Accumulated amortization, trademark	22,400
Accumulated depreciation, building	81,600
Accumulated depreciation, equipment	110,400
Allowance for doubtful accounts	1,920
Sally Huang, capital	221,280
Building	147,200
Cash	9,600
Equipment	184,000
Expenses	1,443,200
Land	89,600
Mineral rights	57,600
Note payable	72,000
Revenues	1,433,600
Trademark	33,600

Other information:

a. All accounts have normal balances.

b. $38,000 of the note payable is due after October 31, 2018.

Required Prepare a classified balance sheet at October 31, 2017.

Exercise 9-28 Balance sheet LO2,3,7

CHECK FIGURE: Total assets = $80,460

Montalvo Bionics showed the following alphabetized unadjusted trial balance at April 30, 2017:

Account	Balance
Accounts payable	$ 4,860
Accounts receivable	16,200
Accumulated depreciation, furniture	10,080
Accumulated depreciation, machinery	20,088
Allowance for doubtful accounts	900
Cash	9,000
Expenses	88,200
Furniture	21,600
Josh Montalvo, capital	22,572
Josh Montalvo, withdrawals	82,800
Machinery	48,600
Note payable	13,500
Patent	21,600
Prepaid rent	12,960
Revenues	223,200
Unearned revenue	5,760

Other information:

    a. All accounts have normal balances.

    b. The furniture was depreciated using the straight-line method and had a useful life of five years and residual value of zero.

    c. The machinery was depreciated using the double-declining-balance method and had a useful life of 10 years and residual value of $27,000.

    d. The patent was purchased on November 2, 2016, and is expected to be used for 15 years, after which it will have no value.

    e. The balance in Prepaid Rent represents rent from June 1, 2016, to May 31, 2017.

    f. $5,400 of the note payable will be paid by April 30, 2018.

Required Prepare a classified balance sheet at April 30, 2017.

Exercise 9-29 Purchase Equipment, Depreciation, Disposal of Equipment LO2,3,6

CHECK FIGURES: 2015 deprec oven $750; 2016 deprec truck $8,400

Jessica Grewal decided to open a food truck business, the Samosa Shack. She encountered the following transactions in managing her equipment over the first 2 years of her business.

April 1,	2015	Purchased food truck for $48,000 and paid $6,000 to have a commercial oven installed. Other costs that she incurred are $3,600 for insurance on the truck for the first year, and $4,000 to have the truck painted with her Samosa Shack logo. Jessica estimates that the truck would last 5 years and have a $10,000 residual value. The oven is also expected to last 5 years and have a $1,000 residual value.
October 1,	2015	The oven broke down and cost $1,800 to repair.
December 31, 2015		Recorded the adjusting entry for depreciation and insurance.
April 1,	2016	Replaced all of the tires with all-season tires for $2,100 and paid another year of insurance for $3,600.
December 31, 2016		Recorded the adjusting entry for depreciation, and insurance.
March 31,	2017	Jessica was exhausted from the food truck business, and decided to go back to school and sell the food truck to her friend Mark. He paid her $21,000 for the truck and oven, which included $1,000 for the oven component.

Record all the entries for the 2 years that Jessica owned the truck, including the disposal of the truck and oven. The company calculates depreciation using the straight-line method to the nearest month.

*Exercise 9-30 Revised depreciation—subsequent capital expenditure LO2,3,*8

CHECK FIGURES: 2. Tool carrier, Dec. 31, 2017 = $600; Dec. 31, 2018 = $1,200

Nova Scotia Telecom Company had a truck that was purchased on July 7, 2015, for $36,000. The PPE subledger shows the following information regarding the truck:

An asterisk (*) identifies assignment material based on Appendix 9A.

Truck:						
Component	**Date of Purchase**	**Deprec. Method**	**Cost**	**Est. Residual**	**Est. Life**	**Accum. Dep. at Dec. 31/17**
Truck body	Jul. 7/15	SL	$28,000	-0-	10 yr	$4,200
Motor	Jul. 7/15	SL	8,000	-0-	10 yr	1,200
			$36,000			$5,400

A customized tool carrier was constructed and permanently fitted to the truck on July 3, 2017, at a cost of $9,600 cash. The tool carrier adds to the economic value of the truck. It will be used for the truck's remaining life and have a zero residual value. The useful life and residual value of the truck did not change as a result of the addition of the tool carrier.

Required

1. Record the installation of the tool carrier assuming it is a component of the truck.

2. Calculate depreciation on the truck and its new component, the tool carrier, for the company's December 31, 2017, and December 31, 2018, year-ends.

3. Calculate the book value of the truck at December 31, 2017 and 2018.

Problems

Problem 9-1A **Real estate costs** L01

CHECK FIGURE: 2. Land = $3,810,880

On March 31, 2017, Kornet Investment Advisors paid $4,480,000 for land with two buildings on it. The plan was to demolish Building 1 and build a new store (Building 3) in its place. Building 2 was to be used as a company office and was appraised at a value of $1,026,080. A lighted parking lot near Building 2 had improvements (Land Improvements 1) valued at $652,960. Without considering the buildings or improvements, the tract of land was estimated to have a value of $2,984,960. Kornet incurred the following additional costs:

Cost to demolish Building 1	$ 676,160
Cost of additional landscaping	267,520
Cost to construct new building (Building 3)	3,230,400
Cost of new land improvements near Building 2 (Land Improvements 2)	252,800

Required

1. Prepare a schedule having the following column headings: Land, Building 2, Building 3, Land Improvements 1, and Land Improvements 2. Allocate the costs incurred by Kornet to the appropriate columns and total each column.

2. Prepare a single journal entry dated March 31, 2017, to record all the incurred costs, assuming they were paid in cash on that date.

Problem 9-2A Balance sheet presentation LO2

CHECK FIGURES: 2016 Total assets = $371,920; 2017 Total assets = $443,120

The adjusted balances at December 31, 2017, for Derlak Enterprises are shown in alphabetical order below:

	2017	2016		2017	2016
Accounts payable	$ 56,800	$ 9,600	Lee Derlak, withdrawals	$ 32,000	$ 38,400
Accumulated amortization, franchise	19,200	11,200	Notes payable, due in 2023	240,000	129,600
Accumulated amortization, patent	4,000	2,400	Office supplies	2,400	2,320
Accumulated depreciation, equipment	72,800	64,800	Operating expenses	780,800	571,200
Accumulated depreciation, tools	44,800	42,400	Patent	16,000	16,000
Accumulated depreciation, vehicles	108,800	97,600	Prepaid rent	40,000	48,000
Cash	12,000	28,800	Salaries payable	32,800	26,400
Equipment	184,000	100,000	Service revenue	720,000	753,600
Franchise	41,600	41,600	Tools	143,920	100,800
Lee Derlak, capital*	206,320	62,320	Vehicles	252,800	252,800

*The owner, Lee Derlak, made no additional investments during the year.

Required Prepare a comparative classified balance sheet at December 31, 2017.

Analysis Component: Are Derlak's assets financed mainly by debt or equity in 2016? in 2017? Is the change in how assets were financed from 2016 to 2017 favourable or unfavourable? Explain.

Problem 9-3A Calculating depreciation—partial periods LO2,3 eXcel

CHECK FIGURES: 1B. 2019 Depreciation expense = $39,063 2A. 2019 Depreciation expense = $61,524

Yorkton Company purchased for $375,000 equipment having an estimated useful life of eight years with an estimated residual value of $62,500. Depreciation is calculated to the nearest month. The company has a December 31 year-end.

Required Complete the following schedules (round calculations to the nearest whole dollar):

1. Assuming the purchase was made on January 1, 2017.

2. Assuming the purchase was made on July 1, 2017.

	2017	2018	2019
A. Double-declining-balance method			
Equipment	_____	_____	_____
Less: Accumulated depreciation	_____	_____	_____
Year-end book value	_____	_____	_____
Depreciation expense for the year	_____	_____	_____
B. Straight-line method	_____	_____	_____
Equipment	_____	_____	_____
Less: Accumulated depreciation	_____	_____	_____
Year-end book value	_____	_____	_____
Depreciation expense for the year	_____	_____	_____

Problem 9-4A Calculating depreciation—partial periods LO2,3 eXcel

CHECK FIGURES: DDB 2019 = $110,400

West Coast Tours runs boat tours along the West Coast of British Columbia. On March 5, 2017, it purchased, with cash, a cruising boat for $828,000, having a useful life of 10 years or 13,250 hours, with a residual value of $192,000. The company's year-end is December 31.

Required Calculate depreciation expense for the fiscal years 2017, 2018, and 2019 by completing a schedule with the following headings (round to the nearest whole dollar):

	Depreciation Method[1]		
Year	Straight-Line	Double-Declining-Balance	Units-of-Production[2]

[1] Depreciation is calculated to the nearest month.
[2] Assume actual hours of service were 2017, 720; 2018, 1,780; 2019, 1,535.

Analysis Component: If you could ignore the matching principle, how could you record the purchase of the boat? What impact would this have on the financial statements in the short and long term?

Problem 9-5A Calculating depreciation—partial periods LO2,3 e**X**cel

CHECK FIGURE: DDB 2019 = $119,232

Refer to the information in Problem 9-4A. Redo the question assuming that depreciation for partial periods is calculated using the half-year convention.

Problem 9-6A Calculating depreciation LO2

CHECK FIGURES: 1. Dr. Depreciation Expense, Building $65,000. 1. Dr. Depreciation Expense, Equipment $86,400. 2. Total PPE = $1,190,600.

BigSky Farms Partial Balance Sheet April 30, 2017		
Property, plant and equipment:		
Land		$650,000
Building[1]	$975,000	
Less: Accumulated depreciation	715,000	260,000
Equipment[2]	750,000	
Less: Accumulated depreciation	318,000	432,000
Total property, plant and equipment		$1,342,000

[1] The building was purchased on May 3, 2006, and is depreciated to the nearest whole month using the straight-line method. Depreciation is based on a 15-year life, after which it will be demolished and replaced with a new one.

[2] The equipment was purchased on November 3, 2014, and is depreciated to the nearest whole month using the double-declining-balance method. The total estimated useful life is 10 years with a residual value of $250,000.

Required

1. Calculate *and* record depreciation for the year just ended April 30, 2018, for both the building and equipment.

2. Prepare the property, plant, and equipment section of the balance sheet at April 30, 2018.

Problem 9-7A PPE costs; partial year's depreciation; alternative methods LO1,2,3 e**X**cel

CHECK FIGURES: 2. $31,320; 3. $21,000

Logic Co. recently negotiated a lump-sum purchase of several assets from a company that was going out of business. The purchase was completed on March 1, 2017, at a total cash price of $1,260,000 and included a building, land, certain land improvements, and 12 vehicles. The estimated market values of the assets were building, $652,800; land, $462,400; land improvements, $68,000; and vehicles, $176,800. The company's fiscal year ends on December 31.

Required

1. Prepare a schedule to allocate the lump-sum purchase price to the separate assets that were purchased. Also present the journal entry to record the purchase.

2. Calculate the 2017 depreciation expense on the building using the straight-line method to the nearest whole month, assuming a 15-year life and a $41,040 residual value.

3. Calculate the 2017 depreciation expense on the land improvements assuming a five-year life, $12,000 residual, and double-declining-balance depreciation calculated to the nearest whole month.

Analysis Component: Assume the assets purchased on March 1, 2017, were not put into service until May 23, 2017. Would this affect your answers in parts 2 and 3 above? Explain.

Problem 9-8A Alternative depreciation methods; partial year's depreciation LO2,3 e**X**cel

CHECK FIGURES: 2017 SL = $38,000; 2021 Units = $89,664; 2021 DDB = $4,500

A machine that cost $504,000, with a four-year life and an estimated $48,000 residual value, was installed in Haley Company's factory on September 1, 2017. The factory manager estimated that the machine would produce 475,000 units of product during its life. It actually produced the following units: 2017, 21,400; 2018, 122,400; 2019, 119,600; 2020, 118,200; and 2021, 102,000. The company's year-end is December 31.

Required Prepare a form with the following column headings:

Year	Straight-Line	Units-of-Production	Double-Declining-Balance

Show the depreciation for each year and the total depreciation for the machine under each depreciation method calculated to the nearest whole month. Round to the nearest whole dollar.

Problem 9-9A Calculating depreciation; partial year's depreciation LO2,3 e**X**cel

CHECK FIGURES: Deprec. Expense 2018: Office equip. = $3,800; Machinery = $19,638; Truck = $23,664

At December 31, 2017, Halifax Servicing's balance sheet showed capital asset information as detailed in the schedule below. Halifax calculates depreciation to the nearest whole month.

Cost Information						Depreciation		
Description	Date of Purchase	Depreciation Method	Cost[1]	Residual	Life	Balance of Accum. Deprec. Dec. 31, 2017	Depreciation Expense for 2018	Balance of Accum. Deprec. Dec. 31, 2018
Office Equip.	March 27/14	Straight-line	$ 52,000	$14,000	10 yr.			
Machinery	June 4/14	Double-declining-balance	275,000	46,000	6 yr.			
Truck	Nov. 13/17	Units-of-production	113,000	26,000	250,000 km[2]			

[1] There have been no disposals or subsequent capital expenditures since the date of purchase.
[2] Actual kilometres driven were 2017, 14,000; 2018, 68,000.

Required Complete the schedule (round only your final answers).

Problem 9-10A **Partial year's depreciation; revising depreciation rates** LO1,2,4

CHECK FIGURE: Dec. 31, 2018 Deprec. Exp. = $22,220

Never Late Ltd completed the following transactions involving delivery trucks:

2017

Mar. 26 Paid cash for a new delivery truck, $97,075 plus $5,825 of freight costs. The truck was estimated to have a five-year life and a $15,000 trade-in value.

Dec. 31 Recorded straight-line depreciation on the truck to the nearest whole month.

2018

Dec. 31 Recorded straight-line depreciation on the truck to the nearest whole month. However, due to new information obtained early in January, the original estimated useful life of the truck was changed from five years to four years, and the original estimated trade-in value was increased to $17,500.

Required Prepare journal entries to record the transactions.

Problem 9-11A **Revising depreciation rates** LO4

CHECK FIGURES: Deprec. Exp., Machinery = $95,200; Deprec. Exp., Office Furn. = $11,733

The December 31, 2017, adjusted trial balance of Maritime Manufacturing showed the following information:

Machinery...	$556,800
Accumulated depreciation, machinery[1]...	246,400
Office furniture..	89,600
Accumulated depreciation, office furniture[2]...	49,600

[1] Remaining useful life four years; estimated residual $64,000
[2] Remaining useful life five years; estimated residual $11,200.

Early in 2018, the company made a decision to stop making the items produced by the machinery and buy the items instead. As a result, the remaining useful life was decreased to two years and the residual value was increased to a total of $120,000. At the beginning of 2018, it was determined that the estimated life of the office furniture should be reduced by two years and the residual value decreased by $6,400. The company calculates depreciation using the straight-line method to the nearest month.

Required Prepare the entries to record depreciation on the machinery and office furniture for the year ended December 31, 2018 (round calculations to the nearest whole dollar).

Problem 9-12A **Revised depreciation—change in life/residual and subsequent capital expenditure** LO2,3,4

CHECK FIGURES: 1. Loss = $5,032; 2. 2017 Deprec. on Machine #5027 = $6,908

Pete's Propellers Company showed the following information in its Property, Plant, and Equipment sub-ledger regarding Machine #5027.

Machine #5027					
Component	**Date of Purchase**	**Depreciation Method***	**Cost**	**Est. Residual**	**Est. Life**
Metal housing	Jan. 12/15	SL	$44,000	$8,000	15 yrs
Motor	Jan. 12/15	DDB	26,000	2,000	10 yrs
Blade	Jan. 12/15	SL	7,720	1,000	5 yrs
			$77,720		

*SL = Straight-line; DDB = Double-declining-balance

On January 7, 2017, the machine blade cracked and it was replaced with a new one costing $10,400 purchased for cash (the old blade was scrapped). The new blade had an estimated residual value of $1,000 and an estimated life of five years and would continue to be depreciated using the straight-line method. During 2017, it was determined that the useful life on the metal housing should be increased to a total of 20 years instead of 15 years and that the residual value should be increased to $8,600.

Required

1. Prepare the entry to record the purchase of the replacement blade.

2. Calculate the *total* depreciation expense to be recorded on Machine #5027 for 2017.

Problem 9-13A Depreciation and impairment losses LO1,2,3,5

CHECK FIGURE: 2. Total assets = $271,920

Safety-First Company completed all of its October 31, 2017, adjustments in preparation for preparing its financial statements, which resulted in the following trial balance.

Account	Balance
Accounts payable	$ 11,220
Accounts receivable	19,800
Accumulated depreciation, building	79,200
Accumulated depreciation, equipment	37,400
Accumulated depreciation, furniture	20,900
Allowance for doubtful accounts	880
Building	136,400
Cash	11,000
Equipment	90,200
Expenses, including cost of goods sold	761,200
Furniture	50,600
Land	105,600
Merchandise inventory	35,200
Note payable	85,800
Sales	904,200
Tarifa Sharma, capital	62,480
Unearned revenues	7,920

Other information:

1. All accounts have normal balances.

2. $26,400 of the note payable balance is due by October 31, 2018.

The final task in the year-end process was to assess the assets for impairment, which resulted in the following schedule.

Asset	Recoverable Value
Land	$136,400
Building	105,600
Equipment	28,600
Furniture	15,400

Required

1. Prepare the entry (entries) to record any impairment losses at October 31, 2017. Assume the company recorded no impairment losses in previous years.

2. Prepare a classified balance sheet at October 31, 2017.

Analysis Component What is the impact on the financial statements of an impairment loss?

Problem 9-14A **Partial-period depreciation; disposal of PPE** LO2,3,6

CHECK FIGURES: 1. GAIN = $67,350; 2. LOSS = $23,867

Endblast Productions showed the following selected asset balances on December 31, 2017:

Land	$396,800
Building	526,400
Accumulated depreciation, building[1]	393,600
Equipment	171,200
Accumulated depreciation, equipment[2]	74,400

[1] Remaining estimated useful life is eight years with a residual value of $80,000; depreciated using the straight-line method to the nearest whole month.

[2] Total estimated useful life is 10 years with a residual value of $16,000; depreciated using the double-declining-balance method to the nearest whole month.

Required Prepare the entries for each of the following (round final calculations to the nearest whole dollar).

1. The land and building were sold on September 27, 2018, for $592,000 cash.

2. The equipment was sold on November 2, 2018, for $56,800 cash.

Problem 9-15A **Disposal of PPE** LO1,2,3,6

CHECK FIGURES: 2. Dec. 31, 2017 = $17,080; 3a. Loss = $3,990; 3b. Gain = $2,310; 3c. Gain = $770

Vita Water purchased a used machine for $116,900 on January 2, 2017. It was repaired the next day at a cost of $4,788 and installed on a new platform that cost $1,512. The company predicted that the machine would be used for six years and would then have a $20,720 residual value. Depreciation was to be charged on a straight-line basis to the nearest whole month. A full year's depreciation was recorded on December 31, 2017. On September 30, 2022, it was retired.

Required

1. Prepare journal entries to record the purchase of the machine, the cost of repairing it, and the installation. Assume that cash was paid.

2. Prepare entries to record depreciation on the machine on December 31 of its first year and on September 30 in the year of its disposal (round calculations to the nearest whole dollar).

3. Prepare entries to record the retirement of the machine under each of the following unrelated assumptions:

   a. It was sold for $21,000.

   b. It was sold for $27,300.

   c. It was destroyed in a fire and the insurance company paid $25,760 in full settlement of the loss claim.

Problem 9-16A **Partial year's depreciation; exchanging PPE** LO2,3,6

CHECK FIGURE: Dec. 31, 2017: Deprec. Exp. = $3,236

In 2017, Staged Home Ltd. completed the following transactions involving delivery trucks:

July 5 Traded-in an old truck and paid $25,600 in cash for furniture. The accounting records on July = showed the cost of the old truck at $36,000 and related accumulated depreciation of $6,000. The furniture was estimated to have a six-year life and a $6,268 trade-in value. The invoice for the exchange showed these items:

Price of the furniture (equal to its fair value)	$45,100
Trade-in allowance	(19,500)
Total paid in cash	$25,600

Dec. 31 Recorded straight-line depreciation on the furniture (to nearest whole month).

Required Prepare journal entries to record the transactions.

Problem 9-17A **Partial year's depreciation; alternative methods; exchange/disposal of PPE** LO2,3,6

CHECK FIGURES: a. Machine 1550 = $6,075; Machine 1795 = $22,646; Machine BT-311 = $77,810

Zephyr Minerals completed the following transactions involving machinery.

Machine No. 1550 was purchased for cash on April 1, 2017, at an installed cost of $52,900. Its useful life was estimated to be six years with a $4,300 trade-in value. Straight-line depreciation was recorded for the machine at the ends of 2017, 2018, and 2019. On March 29, 2020, it was traded for Machine No. 1795, with an installed cash price of $62,000. A trade-in allowance of $30,210 was received for Machine No. 1550, and the balance was paid in cash. The fair values of Machine No. 1550 and Machine No. 1795 could not be determined.

Machine No. 1795's life was predicted to be four years with a trade-in value of $8,200. Double-declining-balance depreciation on this machine was recorded each December 31. On October 2, 2021, it was traded for Machine No. BT-311, which had an installed cash price of $537,000, the machine's fair value. A trade-in allowance of $20,000 was received for Machine No. 1795, and the balance was paid in cash.

It was estimated that Machine No. BT-311 would produce 200,000 units of product during its five-year useful life, after which it would have a $35,000 trade-in value. Units-of-production depreciation was recorded for the machine for 2021, a period in which it produced 31,000 units of product. Between January 1, 2022, and August 21, 2024, the machine produced 108,000 more units. On August 21, 2024, it was sold for $81,200.

Required Round calculations to the nearest dollar and prepare journal entries to record:

    a. The depreciation expense recorded to the nearest whole month on the first December 31 of each machine's life.

    b. The purchase/exchange/disposal of each machine.

Problem 9-18A **Intangible assets** LO7

CHECK FIGURE: b. $24,000

On October 1, 2017, Kingsway Broadcasting purchased for $288,000 the copyright to publish the music composed by a local Celtic group. Kingsway expects the music to be sold over the next three years. The company uses the straight-line method to amortize intangibles.

Required Prepare entries to record:

    a. The purchase of the copyright

    b. The amortization for the year ended December 31, 2017, calculated to the nearest whole month

Problem 9-19A **Intangible assets** LO2,3,6,7

CHECK FIGURES: 2. Accum. Amort., Mineral Rights = $57,200; Accum. Deprec., Equip. = $224,400; Accum. Deprec., Truck = $87,450

Copper Explorations recently acquired the rights to mine a new site. Equipment and a truck were purchased to begin mining operations at the site. Details of the mining assets follow:

Asset	Date of Purchase	Cost	Est. Residual	Est. Life
Mineral rights	Mar. 1/17	$ 62,400	$ -0-	4 yrs
Equipment	Mar. 1/17	244,800	-0-	4 yrs
Truck	Mar. 1/17	95,400	-0-	4 yrs

Copper's year-end is December 31 and it uses the straight-line method for all mining assets including intangibles.

Required

1. Record amortization and depreciation at December 31, 2017, on the mining assets, including the mineral rights.

2. Assume the mine was closed on October 31, 2020, and the assets were scrapped. Record the disposal of the assets.

*Problem 9-20A **Revised depreciation—change in useful life/residual and subsequent capital expenditure** LO2,3,4,*8

CHECK FIGURES: 1. Loss = $9,310; 2. Total 2017 deprec. = $5,773

Ocean Fishers Ltd had a 22-foot fishing boat with an inboard motor that was purchased on April 9, 2009, for $77,000. The PPE subledger shows the following information regarding the boat:

Fishing Boat – 22 Foot With Inboard Motor:					
Component	Date of Purchase	Deprec. Method	Cost	Est. Residual	Est. Life
Fibreglass body	Apr. 9/09	SL	$23,800	$7,000	15 yr
Motor	Apr. 9/09	SL	53,200	-0-	10 yr
			$77,000		

On June 27, 2017, $63,000 cash was paid for a new motor to replace the old one, which was scrapped. The new motor had an estimated useful life of 12 years and a residual value of $4,200. Early in 2017, it was determined that the useful life of the boat's fibreglass body should be adjusted to a total of 20 years with no change in the residual value.

Required

1. Record the appropriate entries regarding the

    a. Purchase of the replacement motor on June 27, 2017, and

    b. Depreciation taken on the fishing boat (body plus motor) on December 31, 2017, the company's year-end.

2. Calculate *total* depreciation taken on the fishing boat (body plus motor) for the company's year ended December 31, 2017.

Alternate Problems

Problem 9-1B **Real estate costs** L01 e**X**cel

CHECK FIGURE: 2. Dr. Land $423,600

In 2017, DelCano Properties paid $540,000 for a tract of land on which two buildings were located. The plan was to demolish Building A and build a new factory (Building C) in its place. Building B was to be used as a company office and was appraised at a value of $189,108. A lighted parking lot near Building B had improvements valued at $50,058. Without considering the buildings or improvements, the tract of land was estimated to have a value of $317,034.

The company incurred the following additional costs:

Cost to demolish Building A	$ 46,800
Cost to landscape new building site	69,000
Cost to construct new building (Building C)	542,400
Cost of new land improvements (Land Improvements C)	40,500

Required

1. Prepare a schedule having the following column headings: Land, Building B, Building C, Land Improvements B, and Land Improvements C. Allocate the costs incurred by the company to the appropriate columns and total each column.

2. Prepare a single journal entry dated June 1 to record all the incurred costs, assuming they were paid in cash on that date.

Problem 9-2B **Balance sheet presentation** L02

CHECK FIGURES: 2016 Total assets = $290,610; 2017 Total assets = $453,420

The adjusted balances at September 30, 2017, for Xentel Interactive are shown in alphabetical order below:

	2017	2016		2017	2016
Accounts payable	$ 4,320	$ 3,150	Land	$ 68,400	$ 68,400
Accounts receivable	1,800	4,320	Machinery	295,200	115,200
Accumulated amortization, copyright	1,080	540	Mason Xentel, capital*	226,080	270,252
Accumulated depreciation, building	54,000	50,400	Mason Xentel, withdrawals	72,000	41,400
Accumulated depreciation, machinery	90,000	82,800	Notes payable, due October 2022	230,220	55,800
Building	225,000	225,000	Operating expenses	558,000	625,572
Cash	900	2,700	Prepaid insurance	-0-	1,530
Consulting revenue earned	540,000	622,800	Unearned fees	82,800	5,580
Copyright	7,200	7,200			

*The owner, Mason Xentel, made no additional investments during the year ended September 30, 2017.

Required Prepare a comparative classified balance sheet at September 30, 2017.

Analysis Component: How were Xentel's assets mainly financed in 2016? in 2017? Has the change in how assets were financed from 2016 to 2017 *strengthened* the balance sheet? (To strengthen the balance sheet is to decrease the percentage of assets that are financed by debt as opposed to equity.)

Problem 9-3B **Calculating depreciation; partial periods** L02,3 e**X**cel

CHECK FIGURES: 1B. 2019 Depreciation Expense = $53,200; 2A. 2019 Depreciation Expense = $84,672

LiveReel Media purchased for $588,000 machinery having an estimated useful life of 10 years with an estimated residual value of $56,000. The company's year-end is December 31. Depreciation is calculated using the half-year rule.

Required Complete the following schedules:

1. Assuming the purchase was made on January 1, 2017

2. Assuming the purchase was made on April 1, 2017

	2017	2018	2019
A. Double-declining-balance method			
Machinery...	____	____	____
Less: Accumulated depreciation	____	____	____
Year-end book value...	____	____	____
Depreciation expense for the year	____	____	____
B. Straight-line method...			
Machinery...	____	____	____
Less: Accumulated depreciation	____	____	____
Year-end book value...	____	____	____
Depreciation expense for the year	____	____	____

Problem 9-4B Calculating depreciation; partial periods LO2,3

CHECK FIGURE: DDB 2019 = $32,480

Tundra Tours runs tundra buggy expeditions in northern Manitoba for tourists to catch a glimpse of the abundant caribou, polar bears, and other wildlife. Tundra purchased a tundra buggy on October 19, 2017, for cash of $145,000. Its estimated useful life is five years or 100,000 kilometres with a residual value estimated at $25,000. Tundra Tours' year-end is December 31.

Required Calculate depreciation expense for each fiscal year of the asset's useful life by completing a schedule with the following headings *(round calculations to the nearest whole dollar)*:

		Depreciation Method[1]	
Year	Straight-Line	Double-Declining-Balance	Units-of-Production[2]

[1] Deprecation is calculated to the nearest month
[2] ssumes actual kilometres of use were 2017, 5,800; 2018, 19,400; 2019, 22,850; 2020, 25,700; 2021, 19,980; 2022, 14,600.

Problem 9-5B Calculating depreciation; partial periods LO2,3

CHECK FIGURE: DDB 2019 = $27,840

Refer to the information in Problem 9-4B. Redo the question assuming that depreciation for partial periods is calculated using the half-year convention.

Problem 9-6B Calculating depreciation LO2

CHECK FIGURES: 1. Dr. Depreciation Expense, Machinery $55,000; 1. Dr. Depreciation Expense, Equipment $126,667; 2. Total PPE = $241,666

Westfair Foods Partial Balance Sheet December 31, 2017		
Property, plant, and equipment:		
Machinery[1]	$ 500,000	
Less: Accumulated depreciation	330,000	$ 170,000
Equipment[2]	1,280,000	
Less: Accumulated depreciation	1,026,667	253,333
Total property, plant, and equipment		$423,333

[1] The machinery was purchased on January 1, 2012, and is depreciated to the nearest whole month using the straight-line method. Its total estimated useful life is eight years with a $60,000 residual value.

[2] The equipment was purchased on August 1, 2015, and is depreciated to the nearest whole month using the double-declining-balance method. The useful life is estimated to be four years with a residual value of $36,000.

Required

1. Calculate and record depreciation for the year ended December 31, 2018, for both the machinery and equipment (round calculations to the nearest whole dollar).

2. Prepare the property, plant, and equipment section of the balance sheet at December 31, 2018.

Problem 9-7B PPE costs; partial year's depreciation; alternative methods LO1,2,3

CHECK FIGURES: 2. $8,820; 3. $6,525

ID Watchdog Inc. recently negotiated a lump-sum purchase of several assets from a contractor who was planning to change locations. The purchase was completed on September 30, 2017, at a total cash price of $1,044,000, and included a building, land, certain land improvements, and a heavy general-purpose truck. The estimated market values of the assets were building, $663,300; land, $397,980; land improvements, $120,600; and truck, $24,120. The company's fiscal year ends on December 31.

Required

1. Prepare a schedule to allocate the lump-sum purchase price to the separate assets that were purchased. Also present the journal entry to record the purchase.

2. Calculate the 2017 depreciation expense on the building using the straight-line method to the nearest whole month, assuming a 15-year life and a $45,000 residual value.

3. Calculate the 2017 depreciation expense on the land improvements assuming an eight-year life, $36,000 residual, and double-declining-balance depreciation to the nearest whole month (round calculations to the nearest whole dollar).

Problem 9-8B Alternative depreciation methods; partial year's depreciation LO2,3 eXcel

CHECK FIGURES: 2017 SL = $31,304; 2022 Units = $21,140; 2019 DDB = $48,048

On May 2, 2017, Uniglobe Satellite Company purchased and installed a new machine that cost $273,000, with a five-year life and an estimated $38,220 residual value. Management estimated that the machine would produce 168,000 units of product during its life. Actual production of units was as follows:

2017	23,520
2018	36,960
2019	33,600
2020	31,920
2021	26,600
2022	30,940

Required Prepare a schedule with the following column headings.

Year	Straight-Line	Units-of-Production	Double-Declining-Balance

Show the depreciation for each year (calculated to the nearest whole month) and the total depreciation for the machine under each depreciation method. For units-of-production, round the depreciation charge per unit to two decimal places. The company's year-end is December 31.

Problem 9-9B **Calculating depreciation; partial year's depreciation** LO2,3 *eXcel*

CHECK FIGURES: Deprec. Expense: Equipment = $2,280; Machinery = $38,124; Tools = $3,432

At April 30, 2017, Hackney Building Products' year-end, the balance sheet showed PPE information as detailed in the schedule below. The company calculates depreciation for partial periods using the half-year convention.

	Cost Information					Depreciation		
Description	Date of Purchase	Depreciation Method	Cost[1]	Residual	Life	Balance of Accum. Deprec. Dec. 31, 2017	Depreciation Expense for 2018	Balance of Accum. Deprec. Dec. 31, 2018
Equipment	Oct. 3/14	Straight-line	$ 62,400	$ 16,800	20 yr.			
Machinery	Oct. 28/14	Units-of-production	540,000	180,000	100,000 units			
Tools	Nov. 3/14	Double-declining-balance	64,000	15,000	5 yr.			

[1] There have been no disposals or subsequent capital expenditures since the date of purchase.
[2] Actual units produced were (for years ended April 30): 2015, 940; 2016, 10,150; 2017, 9,280; 2018, 10,590.

Required Complete the schedule.

Problem 9-10B **Partial year's depreciation; revising depreciation rates** LO1,2,4

CHECK FIGURE: Dec. 31, 2018 Deprec. Exp. = $10,600

Fab-Form Industries completed the following transactions involving the purchase of delivery equipment.

2017

June 26 Paid cash for a new truck, $68,400 plus $3,420 in freight costs. The truck was estimated to have a four-year life and an $18,000 residual value.

27 Paid $3,780 for special racks installed on the truck.* The racks will enhance the economic benefits flowing from the truck.

Dec. 31 Recorded straight-line depreciation on the truck to the nearest whole month.

2018

Jan. 5 It was determined that the estimated useful life of the truck should be revised to a total of six years and the residual value changed to $10,100.

Mar. 15 Paid $660 for repairs to the truck's fender damaged when the driver backed into a loading dock.

Dec. 31 Recorded straight-line depreciation on the truck to the nearest whole month.

*Assume the special racks depreciate in an identical manner as the truck.

Required Prepare journal entries to record the transactions.

Problem 9-11B Revising depreciation rates LO4

CHECK FIGURES: Deprec. Exp., Building = $1,620; Deprec. Exp., Equip. = $7,320

The December 31, 2017, adjusted trial balance of Biomedics Inc showed the following information:

Building	$274,800
Accumulated depreciation, building[1]...	134,400
Equipment...	117,600
Accumulated depreciation, equipment[2]	38,400

[1] Remaining useful life 15 years; estimated residual value $60,000.
[2] Remaining useful life 6 years; estimated residual value $18,000.

During 2018, a major increase in market demand for building space caused the company to assess the useful life and residual value of the building. It was decided that the useful life would be increased by five years and the residual value increased by $48,000. At the beginning of 2018, it was determined that the remaining estimated life of the equipment should be 10 years and the residual value $6,000. Biomedics calculates depreciation using the straight-line method to the nearest month (round calculations to the nearest whole dollar).

Required Prepare the entries to record depreciation on the building and equipment for the year ended December 31, 2018.

Problem 9-12B Revised depreciation—change in life/residual and subsequent capital expenditure LO2,3,4

CHECK FIGURES: 1. Loss = $8,847; 2. 2017 Deprec. on doors = $7,950; Total 2017 deprec. = $28,185

Brainium Technologies showed the following information in its Property, Plant, and Equipment subledger regarding a warehouse.

Warehouse:					
Component	Date of Purchase	Depreciation Method*	Cost	Est. Residual	Est. Life
Windows	Jan. 8/12	SL	$ 51,750	-0-	15 yrs
Doors	Jan. 8/12	SL	105,000	-0-	20 yrs
Roofing	Jan. 8/12	SL	43,500	-0-	10 yrs
Siding	Jan. 8/12	SL	54,000	-0-	25 yrs
Framing/walls	Jan. 8/12	SL	222,000	60,000	30 yrs
Furnace	Jan. 8/12	DDB	27,000	-0-	10 yrs
Misc.	Jan. 8/12	DDB	61,500	7,500	5 yrs
			$564,750		

*SL = Straight-line; DDB = Double-declining-balance

During 2017, it was determined that the original useful life on the warehouse doors should be reduced to a total of 12 years and that the residual value should be $23,100. On January 3, 2017, the furnace broke down unexpectedly. It was replaced the next day with a new one costing $39,000, purchased on account (the old furnace was scrapped). The new furnace had an estimated residual value of $7,500 and an estimated life of 16 years and would continue to be depreciated using the double-declining-balance method.

Required

1. Prepare the entry to record the purchase of the new furnace.

2. Calculate the *total* depreciation expense to be recorded on the warehouse for 2017.

Problem 9-13B Depreciation and impairment losses LO1,2,3,5

CHECK FIGURE: 2. Total assets = $481,125

La Mancha Enterprises completed all of its March 31, 2017, adjustments in preparation for compiling its financial statements, which resulted in the following trial balance.

Account	Balance
Accounts payable	$ 14,750
Accounts receivable	57,500
Accumulated depreciation, computer equipment	40,250
Accumulated depreciation, machinery	152,500
Accumulated depreciation, warehouse	286,500
Allowance for doubtful accounts	6,000
Cash	35,000
Computer equipment	72,500
Expenses, including cost of goods sold	1,246,750
Joy La Mancha, capital	407,875
Land	145,000
Machinery	241,250
Mortgage payable	93,750
Office supplies	4,875
Revenues	1,227,500
Salaries payable	33,750
Warehouse	460,000

Other information:

1. All accounts have normal balances.

2. $34,200 of the mortgage balance is due beyond March 31, 2018.

The final task in the year-end process was to assess the assets for impairment, which resulted in the following schedule.

Asset	Recoverable Value
Computer equipment	$ 6,250
Land	172,500
Machinery	65,000
Warehouse	243,750

Required

1. Prepare the entry (entries) to record any impairment losses at March 31, 2017. Assume the company recorded no impairment losses in previous years.

2. Prepare a classified balance sheet at March 31, 2017.

Analysis Component: How does the recording of an impairment loss affect equity, if at all?

Problem 9-14B Partial-period depreciation; disposal of PPE LO2,3,6

CHECK FIGURES: 1. Accum. Deprec. = $42,175; 2. Accum. Deprec. = $33,082; 3. Accum. Deprec. = $48,300

EveryWhere Development Co. showed the following selected PPE balances on January 31, 2017:

Van	$64,400
Accumulated depreciation, van[1]	40,600
Machinery	128,800
Accumulated depreciation, machinery[2]	20,440
Equipment	75,600
Accumulated depreciation, equipment[3]	44,800

[1] Remaining estimated useful life is 40,000 kilometres with a residual value of $9,800; depreciated using the units-of-production method.
[2] Total estimated useful life is 10 years with a residual value of $16,800; depreciated using the double-declining-balance method to the nearest whole month.
[3] Remaining estimated useful life is three years with a residual value of $5,600; depreciated using the straight-line method to the nearest whole month.

Required Prepare the entries to record the following disposals:

1. The van was sold on March 2, 2017, for cash of $17,920. It had been driven 4,500 kilometres from January 31, 2017, to the date of sale.

2. The machinery was sold on August 27, 2017, for cash of $95,718.

3. The equipment was sold on June 29, 2017, for cash of $27,720.

Problem 9-15B Disposal of PPE LO1,2,3,5

CHECK FIGURES: 2. Dec. 31, 2017 = $20,604; Apr. 1, 2022 =$5,151; 3A. Loss = $21,657; 3B. Gain = $2,343; 3C. Loss = $33,657

On January 1, 2017, Ultra Green Packaging purchased a used machine for $156,000. The next day, it was repaired at a cost of $4,068 and mounted on a new platform that cost $5,760. Management estimated that the machine would be used for seven years and would then have a $21,600 residual value. Depreciation was to be charged on a straight-line basis to the nearest whole month. A full year's depreciation was charged on December 31, 2017, through to December 31, 2021, and on April 1, 2022, the machine was retired from service.

Required

1. Prepare journal entries to record the purchase of the machine, the cost of repairing it, and the installation. Assume that cash was paid.

2. Prepare entries to record depreciation on the machine on December 31, 2017, and on April 1, 2022 (round calculations to the nearest whole dollar).

3. Prepare entries to record the retirement of the machine under each of the following unrelated assumptions:

   a. It was sold for $36,000.

   b. It was sold for $60,000.

   c. It was destroyed in a fire and the insurance company paid $24,000 in full settlement of the loss claim.

Problem 9-16B **Partial year's depreciation; revising depreciation; exchanging PPE** LO2,3,4,6

CHECK FIGURES: Aug. 31, 2017, Computer equip. = $72,600; Dec. 31, 2017, Deprec. Exp. = $7,240

During 2017, Global Designs Inc. had the following transactions.

2017

Aug. 31 Global traded-in furniture with a cost of $42,000 and accumulated depreciation of $25,800 recorded in the accounting records on this date. Global paid $56,400 in cash for a computer system that was estimated to have a three-year life and a $19,200 residual value. The invoice for the exchange showed these items:

Price of the computer equipment	$ 74,400
Trade-in allowance granted on the furniture..	(18,000)
Total paid in cash	$ 56,400

Sept. 4 Paid $11,760 for upgrades to the computer equipment, which increased the economic benefits flowing from the equipment.

Dec. 31 Recorded straight-line depreciation on the computer equipment to the nearest whole month. Round calculations to the nearest whole dollar.

Required Prepare journal entries to record the transactions. Assume that the fair values were *not* known at the time of the exchange.

Problem 9-17B **Partial year's depreciation; alternative methods; exchange/disposal of PPE** LO2,3,6

CHECK FIGURES: 1. Machine 6690 = $10,800; Machine 6691 = $8,325; Machine 6711 = $7,155

Vidéotron Ltée completed the following transactions involving printing equipment.

Machine 6690 was purchased for cash on May 1, 2017, at an installed cost of $72,900. Its useful life was estimated to be four years with an $8,100 trade-in value. Straight-line depreciation was recorded for the machine at the end of 2017 and 2018.

On August 5, 2019, it was traded for Machine 6691, which had an installed cash price of $54,000. A trade-in allowance of $40,500 was received and the balance was paid in cash. The new machine's life was estimated at five years with a $9,450 trade-in value. The fair values of Machines 6690 and 6691 were not reliably determined at the time of the exchange. Double-declining-balance depreciation was recorded on each December 31 of Machine 6691's life. On February 1, 2022, it was sold for $13,500.

Machine 6711 was purchased on February 1, 2022, at an installed cash price of $79,650. It was estimated that the new machine would produce 75,000 units during its useful life, after which it would have an $8,100 trade-in value. Units-of-production depreciation was recorded on the machine for 2022, a period in which it produced 7,500 units of product. Between January 1 and October 3, 2023, the machine produced 11,250 more units. On October 3, 2023, it was sold for $54,000.

Required Prepare journal entries to record:

1. The depreciation expense recorded to the nearest whole month on the first December 31 of each machine's life (for units-of-production, round the rate per unit to three decimal places).

2. The purchase/exchange/disposal of each machine.

Problem 9-18B **Intangible assets** LO7

CHECK FIGURE: 2. Total PPE = $735,000

On February 3, 2017, Secure Software Group purchased the patent for a new software for cash of $220,800. The company expects the software to be sold over the next five years and uses the straight-line method to amortize intangibles.

Required

1. Prepare entries to record the:

   a. Purchase of the software patent.

   b. Straight-line amortization for the year ended December 31, 2017, calculated to the nearest whole month. Round to the nearest dollar.

2. On December 31, 2017, the company's adjusted trial balance showed the additional asset accounts shown below. Prepare the asset section of the balance sheet at December 31, 2017, including the patent purchased on February 3, 2017.

Accounts receivable	$285,600
Accumulated depreciation, equipment	259,200
Accumulated depreciation, building	189,000
Allowance for doubtful accounts	8,400
Cash	103,200
Equipment	477,600
Building	595,200
Land	110,400
Merchandise inventory	135,600

Problem 9-19B Intangible assets LO2,3,6,7

CHECK FIGURES: 2. Accum. Amort., Patent = $42,000; Accum. Deprec., Equipment = $70,560; Accum. Deprec., Computer = $63,840

RangeStar Telecommunications recently acquired a patent regarding a new telecommunications application. Additional equipment and a computer were purchased to begin making the application available to consumers. Details of the assets follow:

Asset	Date of Purchase	Cost	Est. Residual	Est. Life
Patent	Feb. 12/17	$210,000	$ -0-	20 yrs
Equipment	Feb. 12/17	320,600	56,000	15 yrs
Computer	Feb. 12/17	79,800	-0-	5 yrs

The company's year-end is December 31 and it uses the straight-line method for all production assets including intangibles, calculated to the nearest whole month.

Required

1. Record amortization and depreciation at December 31, 2017, on the production assets, including the patent.

2. Assume that because a highly superior alternative telecommunications application became available from a competitor, RangeStar's application no longer had value and was officially discontinued on January 27, 2021. The equipment was sold for $252,000 cash and the patent and computer were scrapped. Record the disposal of the assets.

*Problem 9-20B Revised depreciation—change in useful life/residual and subsequent capital expenditure LO2,3,4,*8

CHECK FIGURES: 1. Gain = $4,800; 2. Total 2017 deprec. = $26,210

On August 26, 2012, Race World International purchased a piece of equipment for a total of $426,000. The PPE subledger shows the following information regarding the equipment:

Equipment					
Component	Date of Purchase	Deprec. Method	Cost	Est. Residual	Est. Life
Metal frame	Aug. 26/12	SL	$144,000	$36,000	20 yrs
Engine	Aug. 26/12	DDB	96,000	6,000	10 yrs
Fan	Aug. 26/12	SL	32,400	3,600	5 yrs
Conveyor system	Aug. 26/12	SL	126,000	39,600	10 yrs
Misc. parts	Aug. 26/12	DDB	27,600	4,800	5 yrs
			$426,000		

Early in 2017, it was determined that the useful life of the metal frame should be adjusted to a remaining life of 20 years with a reduction of $12,000 in the residual value. On October 3, 2017, the company paid $36,000 cash for a new fan to replace the old one, which was sold on the same day to a competitor for $8,400 cash. The new fan had an estimated useful life of five years and a residual value of $4,800.

Required

1. Record the appropriate entries regarding the:

    a. Purchase of the replacement fan on October 3, 2017, and sale of the old fan

    b. Depreciation taken on the fan component on December 31, 2017, the company's year-end

2. Calculate *total* depreciation taken on the equipment for Race World's year ended December 31, 2017.

Analytical and Review Problem

A & R Problem 9-1

At the last meeting of the executive committee of Kearins, Ltd., the controller was severely criticized by both the president and vice-president of production about the recognition of periodic depreciation. The president was unhappy with the fact that what he referred to as "a fictitious item" was deducted, resulting in depressed profit. In his words, "Depreciation is a fiction when the assets being depreciated are worth far more than we paid for them. What the controller is doing is unduly understating our profit. This in turn is detrimental to our shareholders because it results in the undervaluation of our shares on the market."

The vice-president was equally adamant about the periodic depreciation charges; however, she presented a different argument. She said, "Our maintenance people tell me that the level of maintenance is such that our plant and equipment will last virtually forever." She further stated that charging depreciation on top of maintenance expenses is double-counting—it seems reasonable to charge either maintenance or depreciation but not both.

The time taken by other pressing matters did not permit the controller to answer; instead, you were asked to prepare a report to the executive committee to deal with the issues raised by the president and vice-president.

Required As the controller's assistant, prepare the required report.

Ethics Challenge

Marcia Diamond is a small business owner who handles all the books for her business. Her company just finished a year in which a large amount of borrowed funds were invested into a new building addition as well as numerous equipment and fixture additions. Marcia's banker requires that she submit semiannual financial statements for his file so he can monitor the financial health of her business. He has warned her that if profit margins erode, making the loan riskier from the bank's point of view, he might raise the interest rate on the borrowed funds. Marcia knows that her profit margin is likely to decline in this current year. As she posts year-end adjusting entries, she decides to apply the following depreciation rule: All property, plant, and equipment would be depreciated using the straight-line method over 50 years with 50% of each asset's cost representing the residual value. Marcia knows that most of the assets have a useful life of less than 20 years and little or no residual value but says to herself, "I plan on being in business for the next 50 years so that's my justification."

Required

1. Identify the decisions managers like Ms. Diamond must make in applying depreciation methods.

2. Is Marcia's decision an ethical violation, or is it a legitimate decision that managers make in calculating depreciation?

3. How will Marcia's depreciation rule affect the profit margin of her business?

Focus on Financial Statements

FFS 9-1

CHECK FIGURES: Deprec. Exp.—Bldg. = $46,000; Deprec. Exp.—Mach. = $31,200; Deprec. Exp.—Truck = $38,400; Deprec. Exp.—Furn. (old) = $576; Amort. Exp.—Patent = $20,760; Deprec. Exp.—Equip. = $24,429; Deprec. Exp.—Furn. (new) = $14,657; Post-closing capital balance = $661,974

Times TeleCom's PPE subledger at January 1, 2017, appeared as follows:

Description	Date of Purchase[1]	Deprec./ Amort. Method[2]	Original Cost[3]	Residual	Life	Accum. Balance Dec. 31, 2016	Expense for 2017
Land[4]	July 3/14		$280,000				
Building[4]	July 3/14	S/L	454,000	40,000	15 yr.		
Machinery[5]	Mar 20/14	Units	150,000	30,000	250,000 units		
Truck	Mar 01/14	S/L	298,800	30,000	7 yr.		
Furniture[6,7]	Feb 18/14	DDB	24,000	3,000	5 yr.		
Patent	Nov 7/15	S/L	103,800	-0-	5 yr.		

Table header spanning: **Cost Information** (Description through Life), **Depreciation/Amortization** (Accum. Balance Dec. 31, 2016 and Expense for 2017).

Additional information:

[1] The company calculates depreciation and amortization to the nearest whole month.

[2] S/L = Straight-line; DDB = Double-declining-balance; Units = Units-of-production

[3] There were no disposals, revisions, or impairments prior to January 1, 2017.

[4] At the beginning of 2017, it was determined that the land and building would be used for five years less than originally estimated due to the need to expand.

[5] Actual units produced: 2014, 45,000; 2015, 55,000; 2016, 52,000; 2017, 65,000.

[6] Used office equipment and furniture were purchased on April 10, 2017, for a total of $114,000 at a bankruptcy sale. The appraised value of the office equipment was $96,000 and of the furniture $72,000. The old furniture was given to a charitable organization on April 12, 2017.

[7] The estimated useful lives and residual values of the April 10 purchases were four years and $10,000 for the office equipment, and five years and $4,000 for the furniture. These assets will be depreciated using the DDB method.

Required

a. Complete the PPE subledger; round calculations to the nearest dollar.

b. Using the information from the PPE subledger completed in part (a) and the following December 31, 2017, adjusted account balances, prepare a single-step income statement and statement of changes in equity for the year ended December 31, 2017, along with the December 31, 2017, classified balance sheet: Cash, $30,000; Accounts Receivable, $72,000; Prepaid Insurance, $15,600; Accounts Payable, $68,000; Unearned Revenue, $53,800; Notes Payable due in 2020, $284,000; Susan Times, Capital, $421,180; Susan Times, Withdrawals, $204,000; Revenue Earned, $950,000; Salaries Expense, $294,000; Insurance Expense, $30,000; Loss on disposal of furniture, $5,184. Susan Times, the owner, made no investments during 2017.

FFS 9-2

Refer to the financial statements for each of **Danier Leather**, **Indigo**, and **WestJet** in Appendix II.

Required Answer the following questions.

Part 1

The June 28, 2014, balance sheet for Danier Leather reports $16,826 (thousand) of PPE.

    a. What does the $16,826 (thousand) represent (i.e., is it the cost of the PPE)?

    b. Which generally accepted accounting principle (GAAP) requires that information in addition to the $16,826 (thousand) must be reported and where must it be reported?

    c. What amount did Danier report as depreciation expense for the year ended June 28, 2014? (*Hint: Refer to the statements of cash flow in Appendix II. Alternatively, go to www.sedar.com, retrieve the complete set of audited annual financial statements, and refer to the appropriate note to the statements.*)

Part 2

    a. WestJet's balance sheet reports $2,793,194 (thousand) of property and equipment on the same date. What percentage is this of its total assets?

    b. Indigo's balance sheet reports $58,476 (thousand) of property and equipment at March 29, 2014. What percentage is this of its total assets?

    c. Compare Westjet and Indigo's inventory, and property and equipment each as a percentage of total assets. Why do these percentages differ between firms? (*Hint: Review the asset section of each company's balance sheet.*)

Critical Thinking Mini Case

Two years ago, on March 1, 2015, General Recycling Management Systems purchased five used trucks and debited the Trucks account for the total cost of $180,000. The estimated useful life and residual value per truck were determined to be five years and $5,000, respectively. $36,000 was paid for a two-year insurance policy covering the trucks effective March 1, 2015; this amount was also debited to the Trucks account since it related to the trucks. On February 1, 2016, new motors were installed in the trucks; parts cost $33,000, and labour was $7,000. New tires were also installed on this date at a total cost of $32,000, and each truck was given an oil change in addition to some minor brake work; the total cost was $2,500. All of these costs were debited to the Trucks account. Profit for the years ended December 31, 2016, and 2017 were $78,000 and $85,000. The manager of the business was paid a bonus equal to 15% of profit; the 2016 bonus was paid on February 1, 2017, and recorded on that date as a debit to Bonus Expense and credit to Cash; the 2017 amount was paid on February 1, 2018, and recorded on that date as a debit to Bonus Expense and credit to Cash.

Required Using the elements of critical thinking, comment on whether all of these items should have been recorded to the truck account. What would the impact be to profit if some of the items were recorded as expense? And, what would the difference be to the manager's bonus paid? What are your thoughts on the Ethics involved in this situation?

Current Liabilities

A Look Back

Chapter 9 focused on non-current assets including plant assets, intangibles, and goodwill. We showed how to account for and analyze those assets.

A Look at This Chapter

This chapter explains how to identify, compute, record, and report current liabilities in financial statements. We also analyze and interpret these liabilities, including those related to employee costs.

Source: © Copyright 2015 Pebble.

LEARNING OBJECTIVES

LO1 Describe the characteristics of liabilities and explain the difference between current and non-current liabilities.

LO2 Identify and describe known current liabilities.

LO3 Prepare entries to account for current notes payable.

LO4 Account for estimated liabilities, including customer awards/loyalty programs, warranties, and corporate income taxes.

Canadian-Born Tech Start-up Breaks Funding Records on Kickstarter

One of the biggest challenges entrepreneurs and inventors face is managing their cash flow, especially funding the current liabilities incurred in manufacturing of the initial acquisition of sufficient inventory to enter the market. This is because the high costs of manufacturing inventory precedes the collection of cash flow from sales of goods. Companies need the inventory before they can sell their product to the consumer. Venture capitalists specialize in providing funds to start-ups, but generally capture a significant percentage of equity or impose high royalty costs.

The crowdfunding platform Kickstarter has revolutionized the ability for start-ups to raise funds, while maximizing the owner's control over the business. Filmmakers, artists, musicians, and inventors have both access to funding opportunities and the benefit of completely controlling their projects. The entrepreneur establishes a funding goal and a deadline, and individual people can choose to pledge money to help the project. If entrepreneurs are able to reach their funding goal they receive the money raised net of a 5% fee collected by Kickstarter, and Amazon.com takes between 3% and 5% to process payments. To entice people to contribute to the project, the inventor/creator offers rewards such as a sample of the product or a copy of the book or film to be produced. People rally around projects as supporters to help others' dreams come true, to be inspired, and to gain access to leading-edge technology. According to Kickstarter.com, the company's belief is that "creative projects make for a better world and [we're] thrilled to help support new ones."

Canadian entrepreneur and founder/CEO of Pebble Technology Corp. Eric Migicovsky has successfully launched two smartphone products through Kickstarter funding. His incredible story comes from humble beginnings and signifies an important lesson in managing working capital (current assets − current liabilities).

As a student in the Systems Design Engineering Program at the University of Waterloo, he developed a prototype of his first smartwatch while on a co-op term at the Netherlands' Delft Industrial School. When he returned to Waterloo, local high school students helped him fabricate the smartwatch branded the InPulse, designed to sync text notifications from BlackBerry devices. Its product launch in 2011 proved unsuccessful as it was linked to the BlackBerry platform, which at that time was beginning to lose significant market share to Android and iPhone devices. Migicovsky expended nearly all the company resources, raised through angel investor seed money (approximately $350,000) to respond to enthusiastic customer pre-orders. "Disastrously, only 50 percent of the pre orders came through, leaving him choking on inventory he couldn't sell."

Migicovsky's next product launch was under the company Pebble Technology Corp. When the company was unable to raise funds through venture capitalists, it decided to try Kickstarter to fund the Android- and iPhone-compatible new and improved smartwatch. Pebble broke funding records at Kickstarter, raising more than $10 million in 2012, drastically overachieving its funding goal of $100,000 for its smartwatch called the Pebble. In the first two years, the Pebble shipped over 1 million devices, dominating the smartwatch market.

In 2015 Pebble used Kickstarter a second time to market its latest smartwatch, the Pebble Time. The company set a funding goal of $500,000 and reached its goal within the first 33 minutes on Kickstarter, raising more than $2 million in an hour, and setting a new record for Kickstarter with the final total funds raised reaching $20,338,986. The company offered the Pebble Time to all funding backers who contributed $159 in funding. The product launched in 2015 with a retail price of $199. A huge benefit of the Kickstarter program is to enable Pebble to raise cash flow to meet the high current liabilities incurred in the initial manufacturing phase of the product without sacrificing ownership equity.

Sources: www.kickstarter.com; http://www.theglobeandmail.com/report-on-business/careers/careers-leadership/high-tech-tailor-measures-up-in-the-silicon-valley/article20378020/?page=all; www. mashable.com/2015/02/24/pebble-time-smartwatch/; www.getpebble.com; http://www.theglobeandmail.com/technology/tech-news/back-on-kickstarter-pebble-raises-2-million-in-an-hour-for-new-smartwatch/article23179085/; http://www.huffingtonpost.com/michaelprice/heres-how-the-pebble-smar_b_5798406.html

Video Link: http://www.theglobeandmail.com/technology/technology-video/video/article23040405/

Video Link Bloomberg Interview: https://www.youtube.com/watch?v=PrOXw-O_E3g

Why is management of working capital especially critical for new businesses launching consumer products? Explain and provide examples.

CHAPTER PREVIEW

Accrual accounting was introduced in Chapter 3 and emphasized the accounting entries required to present current liabilities for accounts payable, notes payable, wages, and unearned revenues effectively at period-end. In this chapter we define, classify, and measure these liabilities that are expected to be settled in the next year for the purpose of reporting useful information about them to decision makers. We outline proper accounting treatment for warranties, taxes, payroll liabilities, and contingent liabilities. Capturing and recording current liabilities is critical, as it significantly impacts a company's financial liquidity. Banks, investors, and other users of financial statements rely on accurately reported current liabilities to analyze the risk position of the client.

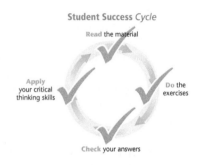

Student Success *Cycle*

Characteristics of Liabilities

LO1 Describe the characteristics of liabilities and explain the difference between current and non-current liabilities.

This section discusses important characteristics of liabilities, how they are classified, and how they are reported.

Defining Liabilities

A **liability** is a future payment of assets or services that a company is currently obligated to make as a result of past transactions or events.[1] This definition includes three crucial elements as portrayed in Exhibit 10.1.

EXHIBIT 10.1

Characteristics of a Liability

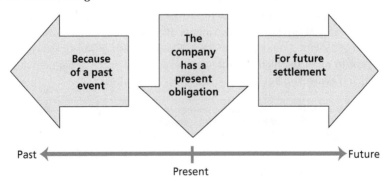

---

1 IFRS 2015, IAS 37, para. 10.

Liabilities do not include *all* expected future settlements, as all three criteria must be met for the obligation to be recognized. The liability is recorded at the point in time when it is probable or likely that a future outflow of resources is required to settle a past transaction. For example, most companies expect to pay wages to their employees in upcoming months and years. But these future amounts are not liabilities because the obligation is triggered at the time the employee performs the work. At this time it will be matched to the period in which the corresponding revenue will be recognized, following the matching principle.

Classifying Liabilities as Current or Non-Current

Information about liabilities is more useful when the balance sheet identifies them as either current or non-current. Decision makers need to know when obligations are due so they can plan for them and take appropriate action. Improper classification of liabilities can affect key ratios, such as the working capital ratio, which is used extensively in financial statement analysis and decision making.

Current Liabilities

Current liabilities are obligations expected to be settled:

1. Within one year of the balance sheet date, or within the company's next operating cycle, whichever is longer,
2. Using current assets or by creating other current liabilities (e.g., replacing an account payable with a note payable).[2]

Examples of current liabilities are accounts payable, current notes payable, wages payable, warranty liabilities, lease liabilities, payroll and other taxes payable, unearned revenues, and the portion of long-term debt that is due within the next period.

Current liabilities and their classification on financial statements vary depending on the types of operations performed by the company and the financial statement presentation. For instance, Empire Company Limited, the parent company of the grocery chain Sobeys and, as of 2014, Safeway grocery stores in Canada, reported current liabilities on its May 3, 2014, balance sheet as shown in Exhibit 10.2. This means that Empire Companies expected to pay $2,567 million of current liabilities during the year after the balance sheet date of May 3, 2014.

Non-Current Liabilities

A company's obligations *not* expected to be settled within the longer of one year of the balance sheet date or the next operating cycle are reported as **non-current liabilities**, also referred to as *long-term liabilities*. Non-current liabilities include obligations such as long-term debt, notes payable, lease commitments, and provisions, all due more than one year in the future. Empire Company Limited's long-term debt obligations, as reported on its May 3, 2014, balance sheet, illustrated in Exhibit 10.2, indicate the company has outstanding obligations of $3,929 million ($6496.5 − $2,567.4) that are due after May 3, 2015.

---

2 IFRS 2015, IAS 1, para. 69.

EXHIBIT 10.2

Liabilities of Empire Company Limited at May 3, 2014, in millions of CDN dollars:

Liabilities		
Current		
Bank indebtedness (*Note 14*)	$ —	$ 6.0
Accounts payable and accrued liabilities	2,246.0	1,765.8
Income taxes payable	21.0	75.2
Provisions (*Note 15*)	82.4	30.6
Long-term debt due within one year (*Note 16*)	218.0	47.6
	2,567.4	1,925.2
Provisions (*Note 15*)	140.7	52.9
Long-term debt (*Note 16*)	3,279.9	915.9
Other long-term liabilities (*Note 17*)	389.2	309.7
Deferred tax liabilities (*Note 13*)	119.3	180.6
	6,496.5	3,384.3

Source: http://www.empireco.ca/site/media/Empireco/EmpireAR14_SEDAR%20secured(1).pdf

Non-current liabilities are discussed in greater detail in Chapter 14 but are introduced here because of their relationship to current liabilities.

Current Portion of Long-Term Debt

The **current portion of long-term debt** is the part of long-term debt that is due within the longer of one year of the balance sheet date or the next operating cycle and is reported under current liabilities. Exhibit 10.2 shows Empire Company Limited's "*long term debt due within one year*" as part of current liabilities as $218 million. This represents the principal amount of debt that will be paid by Empire Company Limited by May 3, 2014, which is *within one year from the balance sheet date*. The portion due after *May 3, 2015*, $3,279.9 million is reported on the non-current liabilities section of the balance sheet and is classified as long-term debt due within one year. Exhibit 10.3 illustrates the timing of current vs. non-current debt in comparison to the balance sheet date for Empire Company.

To illustrate further, Exhibit 10.4 illustrates a scenario where a long-term debt agreement for $7,500 is incurred on January 1, 2017. Based on the debt agreement, it is to be repaid in installments

EXHIBIT 10.3

Timing Analysis of Current vs. Non-Current Liabilities on Empire Company Limited's May 3, 2014, Balance Sheet

The May 3, 2014, balance sheet reports that $2,567.4 million of current liabilities are due during the year after the balance sheet date.

The May 3, 2014, balance sheet reports that non-current liabilities of $3,929 million are due beyond one year of the balance sheet date.

May 3, 2014
Balance Sheet Date   May 3, 2015   May 3, 2016

EXHIBIT 10.4

Determining Current vs. Non-current Portions of Liabilities

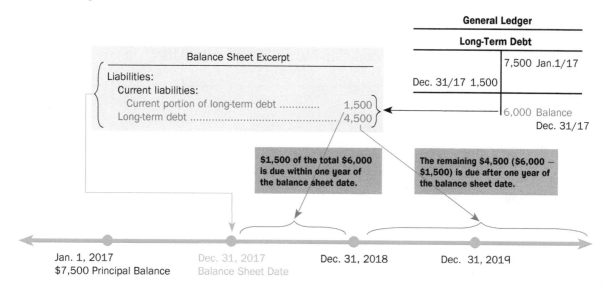

of $1,500 per year for the next five years each December 31. On December 31, 2017, the first principal payment of $1,500 was made (ignore interest), leaving a principal balance owing on December 31, 2017, of $6,000 (= $7,500 − $1,500). The December 31, 2017, balance sheet reports the $1,500 principal payment due in 2018 as the current portion of long-term debt under current liabilities, as shown in Exhibit 10.4. The *remaining* $4,500 long-term portion of the principal (= $6,000 total liability − $1,500 current portion) will be reported under long-term liabilities on the December 31, 2017, balance sheet. The sum of the current and long-term portions equals the $6,000 total principal of the liability outstanding on December 31, 2017.

No journal entry is necessary to split the current portion from the non-current portion. It is a presentation issue considered when the financial statements are compiled. At the time of financial statement preparation, we ensure proper classification of the amounts for long-term debt as either current or noncurrent when the balance sheet is prepared.

Dividing a liability between its current and non-current portions involves only the principal amount of the debt and not the anticipated future interest payments. Any interest that has accrued up to the date of the balance sheet is reported as *interest payable* under current liabilities. Interest relating to future periods is expensed in the period incurred.

Liabilities not having a fixed due date that are payable on the creditor's demand are known as **demand loans**. They are reported as current liabilities because the creditor may *demand* or require payment within a year from the balance sheet date or the company's next operating cycle; whichever is longer.

Balance Sheet Presentation of Current Liabilities

Exhibit 10.5 is based on the December 31, 2013, balance sheet of **The Second Cup Ltd.** The actual balance sheet provides more extensive detail regarding the assets and equity items and contains notes corresponding to items on the balance sheet. Our focus is on the liability section of the balance sheet. Note that current liabilities are listed according to their maturity or due dates similar to the current liabilities listed in Exhibit 10.2.[3]

EXHIBIT 10.5

Partial Balance Sheet of The Second Cup Ltd. in Thousands $CDN

Total assets	$77,340
Liabilities	
Current Liabilities	
Accounts payable and accrued liabilities (note 12)	$ 4,586
Provisions (note 13)	847
Other liabilities (note 14)	717
Income tax payable	138
Gift card liability	3,895
Deposits from franchise partners	878
	11,061
Non-current liabilities	
Provisions (note 13)	1,380
Other liabilities (note 14)	428
Long-term debt (note 15)	11,089
Deferred income taxes	7,418
Total liabilities	31,376
Shareholders' equity	45,964
Total liabilities and shareholders' equity	$77,340

 **CHECKPOINT**

1. What is a liability?
2. Is every expected future payment a liability?
3. If a liability is payable in 15 months, is it classified as current or non-current?

Do Quick Study questions: QS 10-1, QS 10-2

Known (Determinable) Liabilities

LO2   Identify and describe known current liabilities.

Accounting for liabilities involves addressing three important questions: Who to pay? When to pay? How much to pay? Answers to these questions often are decided when a liability is incurred. For example, suppose a company has an account payable to a specific individual for $5,000, due on August 15, 2017. This liability is definite with respect to all three questions. The company *knows* whom to pay, when to pay, and how much to pay; these liabilities are called **known liabilities**. They are set by agreements, contracts, or laws, and are measurable and include accounts payable, payroll, sales taxes, unearned revenues, and notes payable. For other types of liabilities there may be *uncertainty* with respect to one or

---

3   Listing current liabilities according to their maturity dates is not an IFRS requirement; there are alternatives for how current liabilities can be listed.

more of these three questions. This section discusses how we account for *known* liabilities. The next section will look at *uncertain* liabilities.

Trade Accounts Payable

Trade accounts payable, frequently shortened to *accounts payable*, are amounts owed to suppliers with whom we engage in *trade* regarding products or services purchased on credit. Much of our discussion of merchandising activities in earlier chapters dealt with accounts payable. To review, assume **Danier Leather** purchases $12,000 of office supplies from **Staples** on November 14, 2017, on credit, terms n/30. Danier would record the transaction as follows:

2017				
Nov. 14	Office Supplies..	12,000		
	Accounts Payable—Staples....................		12,000	
	To record the purchase of office supplies			
	on credit: terms n/30.			

Because this account payable is due within 30 days (which is within the current period), it is reported as a current liability on the balance sheet.

Payroll Liabilities

A more detailed discussion of payroll liabilities than what follows is included in EYK 10-1 which, for your convenience, is available in PDF format on Connect, including reinforcement materials.

Payroll represents employee compensation for work performed. **Payroll liabilities** are employee compensation amounts owed to employees for work performed. Employers are required by law to deduct (withhold) amounts regarding the employee's income taxes payable and Canada Pension Plan (CPP) (or Quebec Pension Plan in Quebec) and Employment Insurance (EI) contributions. Employers may withhold other amounts such as union dues and hospital insurance as authorized by the employee. All amounts withheld are remitted by the employer to the appropriate authorities. The difference between an employee's gross earnings and deductions taken equals an employee's net pay (or take-home pay).

To illustrate the journal entry to record payroll liabilities, assume that on January 5, the end of its first weekly pay period in the year, Chandler Company's payroll records showed that its one office employee and two sales employees had earned gross pay of $688, $880, and $648, respectively. The payroll records showed the following details:

	Deductions						Payment	Distribution	
Gross Pay	EI Premium[4]	Income Taxes[4]	Hosp. Ins.	CPP[4]	Union Dues	Total Deductions	Net Pay	Office Salaries	Sales Salaries
688.00	14.45	137.50	40.00	30.72	15.00	237.67	450.33	688.00	
880.00	18.48	203.35	40.00	40.23	15.00	317.06	562.94		880.00
648.00	13.61	124.80	40.00	28.74	15.00	222.15	425.85		648.00
2,216.00	46.54	465.65	120.00	99.69	45.00	776.88	1,439.12	688.00	1,528.00

---

4 These values are based on assumed payroll deductions.

The journal entries to record the January 5 payroll liabilities are:

Jan.	5	Office Salaries Expense	688.00	
		Sales Salaries Expense.................................	1,528.00	
		EI Payable...		46.54
		Employees' Income Tax Payable		465.65
		Employees' Hospital Insurance		
		Payable...		120.00
		CPP Payable..		99.69
		Employees' Union Dues Payable...........		45.00
		Salaries Payable....................................		1,439.12
		To record January 5 payroll.		
	5	EI Expense	65.16	
		CPP Expense..	99.69	
		EI Payable...		65.16
		CPP Payable..		99.69

To record the employer's payroll taxes;
$46.54 × 1.4* = $65.16 EI;
$99.69 × 1* = $99.69 CPP.

*The employer's portions of EI and CPP are,
respectively, 1.4 times and 1 times the
employee's portion.

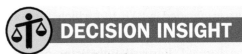

DECISION INSIGHT

Don't Delay!

A company's delay or failure to pay withholding taxes to the government has severe consequences. For example, a financial penalty can be levied, with interest, on the unpaid balance. The government can even close a company, take its assets, and pursue legal actions against those involved. The guilty party may even go to jail.

Provincial Sales Tax (PST), Federal Goods and Services Tax (GST) Payable, and Harmonized Sales Tax (HST)

Canada has two levels of government—provincial and federal—that impose sales taxes on the same transactions. We will introduce and demonstrate *each independently*.

PROVINCIAL SALES TAX (PST)

Provincial Sales Tax (PST) is a tax applied on sales to the *final* consumers of products. This means that a business does not incur PST on its purchases. PST is calculated as a percentage of the sale price of the item being sold. PST percentages vary across the country, as detailed in Exhibit 10.6. British Columbia, Manitoba, Quebec, and Saskatchewan require retailers to collect PST from their customers and to forward this tax periodically to the appropriate provincial authority.

To demonstrate, assume that Z Galleria Furniture, located in Kelowna, British Columbia, is a retailer of household furnishings. Z Galleria purchases merchandise inventory from several manufacturers including Holt Industries. Because Z Galleria is not the final consumer, it does not pay PST on purchases made from Holt Industries and its other suppliers. Customers purchasing from Z Galleria Furniture are the final consumer and will therefore pay the applicable PST. Idea Furniture is required to collect and remit PST charged

EXHIBIT 10.6

Sales Tax Rates, Effective January 1, 2016

	PST Rate	GST Rate	HST Rate*
Regions with GST Only			
Alberta	-0-	5%	—
Northwest Territories	-0-	5%	—
Nunavut	-0-	5%	—
Yukon	-0-	5%	—
Regions with GST and PST			
British Columbia	7%	5%	—
Manitoba	8%	5%	—
Quebec	9.975%	5%	—
Saskatchewan	5%	5%	—
Regions with HST			
New Brunswick	—	—	13%
Newfoundland and Labrador**	—	—	15%
Nova Scotia	—	—	15%
Ontario	—	—	13%
Prince Edward Island	—	—	14%

*A Harmonized Sales Tax (HST) is applied in place of PST and GST. HST is the combination of the PST with the GST for a total sales tax. For example, for both New Brunswick and Ontario the PST rate of 8% is combined with the GST of 5%, resulting in an overall HST of 13%.
**The Newfoundland 2015 budget announced that the rate increases from 13% to 15%, effective January 1, 2016.

on sales to its customers. If Z Galleria Furniture's total cash sales on July 14, 2017, were $16,000 (cost of sales $12,000), the company would record the following entry (assuming a perpetual inventory system):

2017				
July	14	Cash	17,120	
		Furniture Sales		16,000
		PST Payable		1,120
		To record cash sales plus applicable PST;		
		$16,000 × 7% = $1,120.		
	14	Cost of Goods Sold	12,000	
		Merchandise Inventory		12,000
		To record cost of sales.		

When Z Galleria Furniture *remits* or forwards this tax to the British Columbia Ministry of Finance, the entry is (assume for simplicity that it is remitted on the same day):

2017				
July	14	PST Payable	1,120	
		Cash		1,120
		To record remittance of sales tax payable to		
		provincial authority—BC Ministry of Finance.		

Any balance in PST Payable at the end of the period is reported as a current liability on the balance sheet.

FEDERAL GOODS AND SERVICES TAX (GST)

The federal government levies a **Goods and Services Tax (GST)**, which is a tax on nearly all goods and services sold in Canada and is charged to the end consumer. GST applies to most property and services in Alberta, British Columbia, Manitoba, Northwest Territories, Nunavut, Quebec, Saskatchewan, and Yukon. The GST rate in these provinces is 5%. To discuss GST, the related terminology must be understood and is summarized in Exhibit 10.7.

EXHIBIT 10.7

Terminology Related to GST

Exempt Supplies	GST-exempt services are educational, health care, and financial services.
Harmonized Sales Tax (HST)	A combined GST and PST rate is applied to taxable supplies. In most cases HST applies to the same property and services as GST.
Input Tax Credit (ITC)	GST paid by the *registrant* on purchases of *taxable supplies*. Input tax credits are applied against (reduce) GST Payable. Input tax credits are also known as and recorded by the *registrant* as GST Receivable.
Receiver General for Canada	Federal government authority to which GST Payable is remitted.
Registrant	Registered[5] individual or entity selling *taxable supplies* that is responsible for collecting the GST on behalf of the government.
Taxable Supplies	Taxable goods or services on which GST is calculated and includes everything except *zero-rated* and *exempt* supplies.
Zero-Rated Supplies	Goods including groceries, prescription drugs, and medical devices, which have zero GST.

GST is calculated as 5% of taxable supplies. A registrant collects GST on sales of taxable supplies. The same registrant also *pays* GST on purchases of taxable supplies but records an input tax credit (or GST Receivable) for the amount of GST paid. GST collected less input tax credits (GST paid) equals the balance to be remitted to (or refunded from) the Receiver General for Canada.[6]

Consumers are not charged any GST on zero-rated goods and services and GST-exempt products (refer to Exhibit 10.8 for an example of GST-exempt and zero-rated products). Zero-rated goods sold to customers enable the supplier to claim the input tax credits to recover the GST/HST paid on products purchased and used within the business, even though they did not charge customers GST. Exempt products sold to customers do not provide the company with input tax credits on goods or services acquired to supply the exempt product.

EXHIBIT 10.8

GST-Exempt and Zero-Rated Products

GST/HST Zero-Rated Goods and Services	GST/HST Exempt Products
Basic groceries (milk, bread, vegetables)	Music lessons
Prescription drugs and dispensing fees	Educational Services that lead to certificate or diploma
Fishery products	Childcare services
Agricultural products (grain, wool)	Most services provided by financial institutions
Exports to foreign countries	Medical devices
Issuing insurance policies	
For a full list of zero-rated goods and services refer to: www.cra-arc.gc.ca/E/pub/gm/4-3/4-3-e.html	
For a full list of GST-exempt products refer to www.cra-arc.gc.ca/tx/bsnss/tpcs/gst-tps/gnrl/txbl/xmptgds-eng.html	

5   A business with sales of less than $30,000 per year does not have to register for GST purposes.

6   Businesses are required to remit quarterly, or for larger businesses, monthly. Certain businesses may elect to pay annually.

We will now demonstrate the collection, payment, and final remittance of GST (*for simplicity, PST will be ignored for the moment*). On August 3, 2017, Z Galleria Furniture purchased $20,000 of merchandise inventory on credit from Holt Industries; terms n/30. Z Galleria Furniture records this transaction as:

2017				
Aug.	3	Merchandise Inventory...............................	20,000	
		GST Receivable	1,000	
		Accounts Payable—Holt Industries........		21,000
		To record purchase on credit plus applicable ITC; $20,000 × 5% = $1,000.		

The balance in GST Receivable after posting the August 3 transaction is (assuming a zero beginning balance):

GST Receivable (or ITC)

Aug. 3	1,000

On August 6, Z Galleria Furniture recorded total sales (all cash) of $45,000 (cost of sales $33,750) as:

2017				
Aug.	6	Cash	47,250	
		Sales...		45,000
		GST Payable......................................		2,250
		To record cash sales plus applicable GST; $45,000 × 5% = $2,250.		
	6	Cost of Goods Sold.......................................	33,750	
		Merchandise Inventory		33,750
		To record cost of sales.		

The balance in GST Payable after posting the August 6 transaction is (assuming a zero beginning balance):

GST Payable

	2,250 Aug. 6

After posting the August 6 transaction, the GST accounts show a net balance *owing* to the Receiver General for Canada of $1,250 (GST Payable of $2,250 less GST Receivable or ITC of $1,000).[7]

---

7 Some businesses combine GST Receivable and GST Payable to achieve the same net result. For example, if Z Galleria Furniture had combined the GST accounts, as shown below, the same $1,250 net balance results.

GST Receivable/Payable

Aug. 3	1,000	2,250	Aug. 6
		1,250	Balance

Assume Z Galleria Furniture remitted the balance to the Receiver General for Canada on August 7. The entry to record this transaction is:

Aug.	7	GST Payable	2,250	
		Cash...		1,250
		GST Receivable....................................		1,000
		To record remittance of GST to Receiver General for Canada.		

The balances in GST Receivable and GST Payable would be zero after posting the August 7 entry.

If the balance in GST Receivable (ITC) exceeds the balance in GST Payable, Z Galleria Furniture would be entitled to receive a refund.

A net credit balance in the GST Payable account at the end of the period would be shown on the balance sheet as a current liability; a net debit balance would appear under current assets as GST Receivable.

Additional examples demonstrating PST/GST, by region in Canada, can be found online in Extend Your Knowledge 10-2 along with reinforcement exercises.

HARMONIZED SALES TAX (HST)

The **Harmonized Sales Tax (HST)** is a combined GST and PST rate applied to taxable supplies. Ontario, New Brunswick, Nova Scotia, Newfoundland and Labrador, and Prince Edward Island apply HST in lieu of PST and GST. In most cases HST applies to the same property and services as GST and, similar to GST remittances, HST is remitted directly to CRA.

We will now demonstrate the collection, payment, and final remittance of HST. On August 3, 2017, Z Galleria Furniture purchased $20,000 of merchandise inventory on credit from Holt Industries located in Ontario; terms n/30. Z Galleria Furniture records this transaction as:

2017				
Aug.	3	Merchandise Inventory..................................	20,000	
		HST Receivable	2,600	
		Accounts Payable—Holt Industries........		22,600
		To record purchase on credit plus applicable ITC; $20,000 \times 13\% = \$2,600.		

The balance in HST Receivable after posting the August 3 transaction is (assuming a zero beginning balance):

HST Receivable (or ITC)	
Aug. 3 2,600	

On August 6, Z Galleria Furniture recorded total sales (all cash) of $45,000 (cost of sales $33,750) as:

2017				
Aug.	6	Cash..	50,850	
		Sales		45,000
		HST Payable.......................................		5,850
		To record cash sales plus applicable HST; $45,000 \times 13\% = \$5,850.		
	6	Cost of Goods Sold.......................................	33,750	
		Merchandise Inventory		33,750
		To record cost of sales.		

The balance in HST Payable after posting the August 6 transaction is (assuming a zero beginning balance):

HST Payable	
	5,850 Aug. 6

After posting the August 6 transaction, the HST accounts show a net balance *owing* to the Receiver General for Canada of $3,250 (HST Payable of $5,850 less HST Receivable or ITC of $2,600).[8]

Assume Z Galleria Furniture remitted the balance to the Receiver General for Canada on August 7. The entry to record this transaction is:

2017				
Aug.	7	HST Payable	5,850	
		Cash...		3,250
		HST Receivable.....................................		2,600
		To record remittance of HST to Receiver General for Canada.		

The balances in HST Receivable and HST Payable would be zero after posting the August 7 entry.

If the balance in HST Receivable (ITC) exceeds the balance in HST Payable, Z Galleria Furniture would be entitled to receive a refund.

Unearned Revenues

Unearned revenues[9] are amounts received in advance from customers for future products or services and are reported as current liabilities. Unearned revenues include advance ticket sales for sporting events, music concerts, or airline flights. For example WestJet, in Appendix II, reported "Advance ticket sales" of $551,022,000 in its December 31, 2013, annual report. For example, on March 5, 2017 WestJet sold $100,000 of advance tickets; its entry is:

2017				
Mar.	5	Cash	100,000	
		Advance ticket sales		100,000
		To record airline tickets sold in advance.		

If $40,000 in airline tickets purchased in advance are redeemed in April, the entry is:

2017				
April		Advance ticket sales	40,000	
		Passenger revenues.............................		40,000
		To record redemption of airline tickets sold in advance.		

---

8 Some businesses combine GST Receivable and GST Payable to achieve the same net result. For example, if Z Galleria Furniture had combined the GST accounts, as shown below, the same $1,250 net balance results.

GST Receivable/Payable			
Aug. 3	1,000	2,250	Aug. 6
		1,250	Balance

9 Unearned revenues are also called **deferred revenues, collections in advance,** or **customer deposits**.

Unearned revenues also arise with magazine publishers, construction projects, hotel reservations, and custom orders. Unearned revenue accounts are reported as current liabilities.

CHECKPOINT

4. Eldorado Co. collected $1,130 including taxes from a customer. Assuming that Eldorado Co. pays a combined PST/GST rate of 13%, calculate (a) sales, and (b) harmonized sales taxes payable.

Do Quick Study questions: QS 10-3, QS 10-4, QS 10-5, QS 10-6, QS 10-7

MID-CHAPTER DEMONSTRATION PROBLEM

Centrum Advertising Services, a Montreal advertising firm, has a December 31 year-end and prepares financial statements annually. Centrum gathered the following information to prepare the current liability section of its December 31, 2017, balance sheet.

a. Centrum borrowed $48,000 on January 2, 2017. Payments are made annually for five years each January 2.

Year	Annual Payment	Principal Portion of Payment	Interest Portion of Payment	Principal Balance at Year-End
2018	11,395	8,515	2,880	39,485
2019	11,395	9,026	2,369	30,459
2020	11,395	9,567	1,828	20,892
2021	11,395	10,142	1,253	10,750
2022	11,395	10,750	645	-0-

b. Property taxes of $8,650 were unpaid and unrecorded at December 31, 2017.

c. The payroll register showed the following total unpaid amounts as at December 31, 2017.

	Deductions					Pay	Distribution	
Gross Pay	EI Premiums*	Income Taxes*	United Way	CPP*	Total Deductions	Net Pay	Office Salaries	Sales Salaries
7,840.00	164.64**	3,196.25	320.00	384.75**	4,065.64	3,774.36	1,900.00	5,940.00

*These values are based on assumed payroll deductions.
**The employer's portions of EI and CPP are 1.4 times and 1 times the employee's portion respectively.

d. Centrum Advertising Services operates out of a small building in downtown Montreal. Total services provided to clients during the month of December were $186,000 excluding sales taxes. Assume GST and PST are paid on the fifteenth day of the month following sales.

e. The unadjusted trial balance showed Unearned Service Revenue of $7,800. $5,200 of this amount had been earned by December 31.

Required

For each of the above, determine what will be included in the current liabilities section of Centrum's December 31, 2017, balance sheet. (*Hint: For (d), refer to Exhibit 10.6 to determine the appropriate PST rate.*)

Analysis Component:

If the current portion of the non-current debt described in (a) above is not reported under current liabilities but reported as part of non-current liabilities, total liabilities would be correct. Therefore, is it acceptable to report the current portion of non-current liabilities as part of long-term debt? Why or why not?

Solution

a. Two amounts will appear in the current liabilities section as a result of this information:

Interest payable of $2,880; and
Current portion of long-term note payable $8,515.

b. Property taxes payable of $8,650

c. Five amounts will be included in the "Payroll liabilities" amount appearing in the current liabilities section as a result of this information:

EI payable	$ 395.14*
Employees' income taxes payable	3,196.25
United Way payable	320.00
CPP payable	769.50**
Salaries payable	3,774.36
Total payroll liabilities	$8,455.25

*$164.64 × 1.4 = $230.50 Employer's portion plus $164.64 Employees' portion.
**$384.75 Employer's portion plus $384.75 Employees' portion.

d. GST = $186,000 × 5% = $ 9,300.00
PST = ($186,000) × 9.975% = 18,553.50

Total sales taxes payable = $27,853.50

e. Unearned revenue = $7,800 − $5,200 = $2,600

Analysis Component:

It is not acceptable to report the current portion of non-current liabilities as part of long-term debt even though total liabilities would be unaffected. Why? Because if current liabilities are understated then the liquidity position is overstated, which has the potential to create the impression that the business has the ability to cover its current obligations when it may not.

Current Notes Payable

LO3 Prepare entries to account for current notes payable.

A **current note payable** is a written promise to pay a specified amount on a specified future date within one year or the company's operating cycle, whichever is longer, and is reported as a current liability on the balance sheet. Notes payable are typically interest-bearing to compensate the supplier/issuer of the note for the time until payment is made.

A common use of notes payable is in the purchase merchandise inventory and other assets or to replace an account payable. Current notes payable also arise when money is borrowed from a bank.

NOTE GIVEN TO GRANT EXTENDED CREDIT

A company can substitute an interest-bearing note payable to replace an overdue account payable that does not bear interest.

To illustrate, assume that on November 23, 2017, West Holdings Inc. asks to extend its past-due $6,000 account payable to TechNology Inc. After some negotiation, TechNology Inc. agrees to accept $1,000 cash and a 60-day, 12%, $5,000 note payable to replace the account payable. West Holdings Inc. records this transaction as:

2017			
Nov. 23	Accounts Payable—TechNology Inc...............	6,000.00	
	Cash..		1,000.00
	Notes Payable		5,000.00
	Gave $1,000 cash and a 60-day note to extend due date on account.		

Signing the note changes the form of the debt from an account payable to a note payable.

On December 31, 2017, West Holding Inc.'s year-end, accrued interest on the note (38 days from November 23 to December 31) is recorded as follows:

Dec. 31	Interest Expense...	62.47	
	Interest Payable		62.47
	Accrued interest expense on note; $5,000 × 12% × 38/365.		

To calculate interest, we used the formula in Exhibit 10.9.

EXHIBIT 10.9

Formula to Calculate Interest $(I = Prt)$

Interest	=	Principal of the Note	×	Annual Interest Rate	×	Time[10]
$62.47	=	$5,000	×	12%	×	38/365

The balance sheet presentation on December 31, 2017, of the liabilities regarding the note payable is shown under current liabilities as in Exhibit 10.10. Interest is rounded to the nearest whole dollar for financial statement presentation purposes.

EXHIBIT 10.10

Balance Sheet Presentation of Current Notes Payable and Interest Payable

Current liabilities:	
Notes payable, current	$5,000
Interest payable	62

---

10 Time = number of days since last payment to period-end divided by 365.

On the due date[11] of January 22, 2018, Weston pays the note and interest by giving TechNology a cheque for $5,098.63; $5,000 represents payment for the note payable and $98.63 is payment of the total interest for the 60-day note calculated at the rate of 12%.

The payment is recorded as:

Jan. 22	Notes Payable	5,000.00	
	Interest Payable	62.47	
	Interest Expense	36.16	
	Cash		5,098.63

Paid note with interest;
$5,000 × 12% × 22/365 = $36.16.

Notice that $62.47 of the total interest being paid is for the interest liability that appeared on the December 31 balance sheet in Exhibit 10.10. $36.16 of the total interest is the interest expense for the accounting period beginning January 1, 2018. The matching principle requires that the total interest expense be allocated over the term of the note as illustrated in Exhibit 10.11.

EXHIBIT 10.11

Matching of Interest Expense to the Proper Accounting Periods

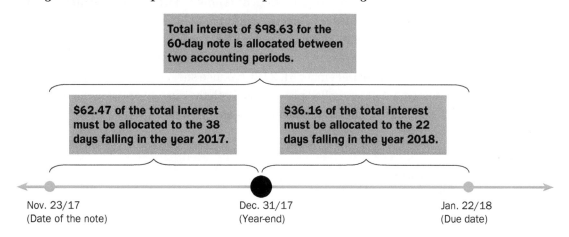

Total interest of $98.63 for the 60-day note is allocated between two accounting periods.

$62.47 of the total interest must be allocated to the 38 days falling in the year 2017.

$36.16 of the total interest must be allocated to the 22 days falling in the year 2018.

Nov. 23/17
(Date of the note)

Dec. 31/17
(Year-end)

Jan. 22/18
(Due date)

NOTE PAYABLE—BORROWING FUNDS FROM A BANK

A bank requires a borrower to sign a promissory note when making a loan. The borrowing company records its receipt of cash and the new liability with this entry:

| Sept. 30 | Cash | 2,000.00 | |
| | Notes Payable | | 2,000.00 |

Borrowed $2,000 cash with a 60-day,
12%, $2,000 note.

---

11 The due date or *maturity date* of a note was discussed in Chapter 8. To review the calculation of the due date, assume the 60-day note above that is dated November 23. The due date or maturity date is January 22, calculated as:

Days in November	30
Minus date of note	23
Days remaining in November	7
Add days in December	31
	38
Days to equal 60 days or	
Maturity date, January 22	22
Period of the note in days	60

When the note matures (or becomes due), the borrower repays the note plus interest. Journal entries regarding the accrual of interest expense at the end of the accounting period and repayment of the note on the due date are the same as described in the previous section for a note given to extend a credit period.

CHECKPOINT

5. Why would a creditor want a past-due account replaced by a note?

6. A company borrows $10,000 by signing a note payable promising to repay the principal plus interest calculated at the rate of 5% in 180 days. What is the total interest expense?

Do Quick Study questions: QS 10-8, QS 10-9

Estimated Liabilities (or Provisions)

LO4 Account for estimated liabilities, including customer awards/loyalty programs, warranties, and corporate income taxes.

An **estimated liability** is a known obligation of an uncertain amount, but one that can be reasonably estimated. Estimated liabilities are also referred to as **provisions**.[12] Two common examples of provisions are manufacturer product warranties and income taxes payable. We discuss each of these in this section. Other examples of estimated liabilities include property taxes and certain contracts to provide future services. **Canadian National Railway Company**, more commonly referred to as **CN**, reported total *Accounts payable and other* on its December 31, 2013, balance sheet of $1.48 billion. Included in this amount were several estimated liabilities, called provisions. Both the current and non-current portion of CN's provisions are disclosed in its financial statement notes as follows:

In millions December 31,	2013	2012
Personal injury and other claims provision, current................................	$ 45	$ 82
Personal injury and other claims provision, net of current portion...........	271	232
Environmental provisions, current	41	31
Environmental provisions, net of current portion..................................	78	92

DECISION INSIGHT

Reward Programs

Reward programs, also known as loyalty programs, are incentives offered by credit card companies and retailers to entice consumers to make purchases. There are numerous reward programs in Canada. Many, such as **Air Miles** and **Aeroplan**, offer travel rewards such as flights, cruises, and holiday packages. **Shoppers Drug Mart** offers Optimum Points on purchases made at its stores that can be redeemed for a cash discount once set point levels have been met. Some reward programs, such as **President's Choice MasterCard**, offer merchandise through a points-based system. Reward programs offer in the range of 1 to 3% points or rewards per dollar spent. Reward programs create a liability for the credit card company or retailer. Because consumers don't always take advantage of redeeming rewards/points earned, the liability associated with rewards is typically estimated as an amount less than 100% of the actual eligible reward value.

---

12   IFRS 2015, IAS 37, para. 13.

Customer Awards/Loyalty Programs

CUSTOMER LOYALTY PROGRAMS

Under customer loyalty programs businesses offer customers points and other awards to encourage long-term customer relationships and encourage customer loyalty. Shoppers Optimum points enable customers to save up points earned on purchases made and redeem the points at specific rewards levels for a cash value on purchases made. Starbucks' rewards program enables coffee drinkers the benefit of a free drink for every 12th purchase made. Canadian Tire also provides Canadian Tire Money, rewarding customers who pay for purchases with cash.

As these programs provide a direct benefit to consumers, the company must record a current liability to account for the value of customer redemptions. Since there is uncertainty with respect to when customers will redeem their awards and the potential exists that some customers may opt to never redeem their rewards, companies need to make an estimate of this liability.

For example, assume based on past experience that All Sports expects of its customers 400,000 points outstanding, 50% will choose to redeem their points for cash reductions on future purchases. Each point is worth 20 cents off their purchase, therefore the following redemption liability will be established for its December 31, 2017, year-end:

2017			
Dec. 31	Sales Discount for Redemption of		
	Rewards Points	40,000	
	(400,000 × 50% × $0.20)		
	Redemption Rewards Points Liability		40,000

When the customers later redeem their points, an entry will be recorded to reduce the rewards point liability and record the sales transaction. For example, assume January 20, 2018 All Sports customers redeem a total of 1,000 points on sales of $2,000 worth of sporting goods. The following entry will be recorded:

2018			
Jan. 20	Redemption Rewards Points Liability..............	200	
	Cash	1,800	
	Sporting Goods Sales Revenue		2,000

GIFT CARDS

Gift cards are becoming an increasingly popular gift item, enabling the individual receiving the card flexibility to purchase items that meet his or her needs. According to Executiveboard.com, "In 2014 $124 billion will be loaded onto gift cards in the U.S." Executiveboard.com anticipates the future of gift cards to be linked to e-gifting where mobile transaction volumes are expected to increase significantly over the next five years, reducing the need for a plastic gift card. Lost value from unclaimed, unused, or expired cards accounts for less than 1% of total gift card values.[13] Gift card sales that are unredeemed by the customer are referred to as **breakage**. Retailers recognize the revenue for unredeemed gift cards based on their experience with customer redemption patterns or when the likelihood of the customer redeeming the gift card becomes remote.[14] The accounting entries to record the redemption will be covered in a future course in intermediate accounting.

---

13 http://www.executiveboard.com/exbd/financial-services/tower-group/gift-cards/index.page
14 IFRS 2015, IFRS 15 Revenue from Contracts with Customers para. B46

Indigo Books & Music Inc. discloses the following policy with respect to gift cards in its 2014 annual report:

Gift cards

The Company sells gift cards to its customers and recognizes the revenue as gift cards are redeemed. The Company also recognizes gift card breakage if the likelihood of gift card redemption by the customer is considered to be remote. The Company determines its average gift card breakage rate based on historical redemption rates. Once the breakage rate is determined, the resulting revenue is recognized over the estimated period of redemption based on the company's experience, commencing when the gift cards are sold. Gift card breakage is included in revenues in the Company's consolidated statements of earnings (loss) and comprehensive earnings (loss).

All Sports decided to begin offering store gift cards. On January 25, 2018, the company sold $100 worth of gift cards. The amount collected when the gift cards are sold is recorded as follows:

	2018			
Jan.	25	Cash	100	
		Unearned Revenue – Gift Card Liability		100

When the gift cards are subsequently redeemed they are recorded in the same manner as traditional unearned revenue (unearned revenue is debited and revenue is credited for the sale of goods).

Warranty Liabilities

A **warranty** obligates a seller to pay for replacing or repairing the product (or service) when it fails to perform as expected within a specified period. Most cars, for instance, are sold with a warranty covering service and parts for a specified period of time. This arrangement results in an obligation for the seller to service the product resulting in a probable outflow of goods/services on the part of the seller, meeting the definition of a *provision*.[15] As a provision, a warranty needs to be estimated and recorded in the financial statements as a liability.

To comply with the *matching principle*, the seller reports the estimated expense of providing the warranty in the period when revenue from the sale of the product (or service) is reported. The seller reports this warranty obligation, even though there is uncertainty about existence, amount, payee, and date the obligation will be satisfied. The seller's warranty obligation does not require payments unless products fail and are returned for repairs. But future payments are probable and the amount of this liability can be estimated using, for instance, past experience with warranties. **Apple Inc.**, the popular company that manufactures the iPhone, iPad, and other products, showed a warranty liability of $US4.16 billion for its year ended September 27, 2014.

ILLUSTRATION OF WARRANTY LIABILITIES

To illustrate, let's consider the dealership Car and Truck World, which sells a used car for $16,000 on December 1, 2017, with a one-year or 15,000-kilometre warranty covering parts and labour. Car and

---

15   IFRS 2015, IAS 37, para. 13.

Truck World's experience shows warranty expense averages 4% of a car's selling price or $640 (= $16,000 × 4%). The dealer records this estimated expense and liability with this entry:

2017				
Dec.	1	Warranty Expense..	640	
		Estimated Warranty Liability		640
		To record warranty expense and liability		
		at 4% of selling price.		

This entry alternatively could have been made as part of end-of-period adjustments. Either way, it causes the estimated warranty expense to be reported on the 2017 income statement. Also, it results in a warranty liability on the balance sheet for December 31, 2017.

Suppose the customer returns the car for warranty repairs on January 9, 2018. The dealership's service department performs the work by replacing parts costing $200 and using $180 for labour regarding installation of the parts. The entry to record partial settlement of the estimated warranty liability is:

2018				
Jan.	9	Estimated Warranty Liability	380	
		Auto Parts Inventory.............................		200
		Wages Payable....................................		180
		To record costs of warranty repairs.		

This entry does not record any additional expense in the year 2018 but instead reduces the balance of the estimated warranty liability. Warranty expense was already recorded in 2017, the year the car was sold. The balance in the Estimated Warranty Liability account on January 9, 2018, after posting this entry is:

Estimated Warranty Liability

Jan. 9/18	380	640	Dec. 1/17
		260	Balance

What happens if total warranty costs turn out to be more or less than the estimated 4% or $640? The answer is that management should monitor actual warranty costs to see whether the 4% rate is accurate. If experience reveals a large difference from estimates, the rate should be changed for future sales. This means that while differences are expected, they should be small.

The preceding example illustrated estimating warranty expense based on a percentage of sales dollars. Warranty expense can also be based on a percentage of *units* sold. For example, assume that Buxton Snowboards sold 7,600 snowboards during November 2015 for an average of $185 (cost: $120). Buxton provides a warranty that replaces any defective board with a new one. This company's experience shows that warranty expense averages 0.5% of the snowboards sold. The entry on November 30 to record the estimated warranty would be:

2017				
Nov.	30	Warranty Expense..	4,560	
		Estimated Warranty Liability		4,560
		To record warranty expense and liability		
		at 0.5% of units sold; 0.005 × 7,600		
		= 38 snowboards; 38 snowboards		
		× $120 cost/board = $4,560.		

Notice that the journal entries are the same for recording warranty expense based on a percentage of sales dollars or on a percentage of units sold. Which method is used depends on whether warranty expense is to be matched to sales dollars or units sold.

7. Estimated liabilities (or provisions) include an obligation to pay:
  a. An uncertain but reasonably estimated amount to a specific entity on a specific date.
  b. A known amount to a specific entity on an uncertain due date.
  c. A known amount to an uncertain entity on a known due date.
  d. All of the above.

8. A car is sold for $15,000 on June 1, 2016, with a one-year warranty covering parts and labour. Warranty expense is estimated at 1.5% of selling price. On March 1, 2017, the car is returned for warranty repairs for parts costing $75 and labour costing $60. The amount recorded as warranty expense at the time of the March 1 repairs is:
  a. $0   **d.** $135
  b. $60   **e.** $225
  c. $75

Do Quick Study questions: QS 10-10, QS 10-11

Income Tax Liabilities for Corporations

Financial statements of both single proprietorships and partnerships do not include income taxes because these organizations do not directly pay income taxes. Instead, taxable profit for these organizations is carried to the owners' personal tax returns and taxed at that level. But corporations are subject to income taxes and must estimate their income tax liability when preparing financial statements. We explain this process in this section.

Income tax expense for a corporation creates a liability until payment is made to the government. Because this tax is created through earning taxable profit, a liability is incurred as taxable profit is earned. This tax must usually be paid monthly under federal regulations. The monthly installment is equal to one-twelfth of the corporation's estimated income tax liability for the year. The *actual* total income tax for the period is not known until immediately after the accounting period when information is finalized.

ILLUSTRATION OF INCOME TAX LIABILITIES

To illustrate, let's consider a corporation that prepares monthly financial statements. Based on its taxable profit for 2016, this corporation estimates it will owe income taxes of $144,000 in 2017. In January 2017, the following adjusting entry records the estimated income tax:

2017			
Jan. 31	Income Tax Expense	12,000	
	Income Tax Payable		12,000
	Accrued income tax based on 1/12 of		
	total estimated; $144,000 × 1/12.		

Assume that the tax installment is paid the next day and the entry to record its payment is:

Feb. 1	Income Tax Payable	12,000	
	Cash		12,000
	Paid income tax installment for January 2017.		

This process of accruing and then paying tax installments continues through the year. By the time annual financial statements are prepared at year-end, the corporation knows its total taxable profit and the actual amount of income taxes it must pay. This information allows it to update the expense and liability accounts.

Suppose this corporation determines that its income tax liability for 2017 is a total of $156,700. The Income Tax Expense account reflects estimated taxes of $132,000 based on installments recorded at the rate of $12,000 per month for each of January to November. The entry to record the additional income tax for 2017 is as follows:

Dec. 31	Income Tax Expense	24,700	
	Income Tax Payable		24,700
	To record additional tax expense and		
	liability; $156,700 − $132,000 = $24,700		
	balance owing.		

This liability of $24,700 is settled when the corporation makes its final payment, assumed to be on January 1, 2018.

CHECKPOINT

9. Why does a corporation accrue an income tax liability for quarterly reports?

Do Quick Study questions: QS 10-12, QS 10-13

Contingent Liabilities

As discussed in the previous sections, an estimated liability, also known as a provision, is recorded when the liability is probable *and* it can be reliably estimated. A **contingent liability** exists when the liability is not probable *or* it cannot be estimated.[16] Contingent liabilities are *not* recorded as a liability on the balance sheet because they do not meet the recognition criteria. For a liability to be recognized and recorded, there must be a present obligation with a probability of a determinable outflow of resources. Estimated liabilities such as warranties are not contingencies since they satisfy the recognition criteria: they are probable *and* they can be reliably estimated.[17] Contingent liabilities are disclosed to the users of the financial statements in the notes *unless* the possibility is remote that there will be an outflow of resources. Exhibit 10.12 shows how to differentiate a provision from a contingency along with the accounting treatment for each.

In practice, the accounting treatment for contingencies requires the application of judgment, as illustrated in Exhibit 10.12. Management recognizes that disclosing a contingent liability could affect decisions made by users of financial statements. For example, note disclosure regarding a pending lawsuit may cause share prices to decline. In applying judgment, the unethical manager may withhold information regarding uncertain future events.

A **contingent asset** should never be recorded until it is actually realized.[18] Contingent assets that are probable are disclosed in the notes to the financial statements but we should avoid any misleading implications about their realization. For example, a plaintiff in a lawsuit should not disclose any expected inflow until the courts settle the matter. Disclosure of contingent assets that are not probable is prohibited.

---

16 IFRS 2015, IAS 37, para. 27–30.
17 IFRS 2015, IAS 37, para. 11–14.
18 IFRS 2015, IAS 37, para. 31–35.

EXHIBIT 10.12

Estimated Liabilities—Differentiating Provisions from Contingencies

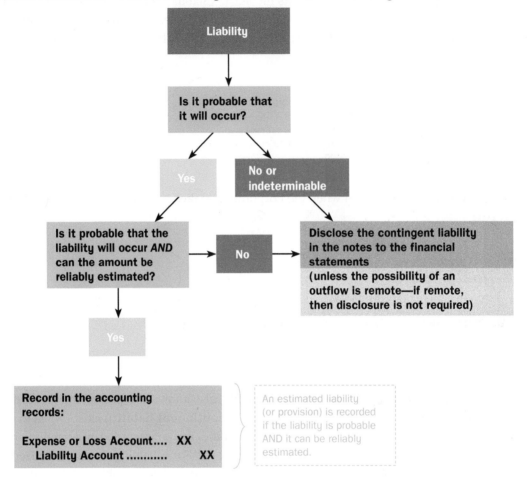

**CHECKPOINT**

10. Under what circumstances is a future payment reported in the notes to the financial statements as a contingent liability?

Do Quick Study question: QS 10-14

DECISION INSIGHT

Eco Cops

What is it worth to be able to ski at Lake Louise? What is the cost when beaches are closed due to pollution? What is the life of a seal worth? These questions are part of measuring environmental liabilities of polluters. One method of measuring these liabilities is called contingent valuation, in which people are surveyed and asked to answer questions like these. Their answers are used by regulators to levy hefty fines, assess punitive damages, measure costs of cleanup, and assign penalties for damage to "environmental intangibles."

Refer to the Critical Thinking Challenge questions at the beginning of the chapter. Compare your answers to those suggested on Connect.

IFRS AND ASPE—THE DIFFERENCES

Difference	International Financial Reporting Standards (IFRS)	Accounting Standards for Private Enterprises (ASPE)
Contingent liabilities	• The term *probable* is used as one of the characteristics of a contingent liability.	• The term *likely* is used as one of the characteristics of a contingent liability; *likely* is more certain than *probable*.

A Look Ahead

Chapter 11 explains the partnership form of organization. It also describes the accounting concepts and procedures for partnership transactions.

For further study on some topics of relevance to this chapter, please see the following Extend Your Knowledge supplements:

EYK 10-1 Payroll Liabilities
EYK 10-2 PST/GST Comprehensive Exercises

Summary

LO1 Describe the characteristics of liabilities and explain the difference between current and non-current liabilities. Liabilities are highly probable future settlements of assets or services an entity is currently obligated to make as a result of past transactions or events. Current liabilities are due within one year of the balance sheet date or the next operating cycle, whichever is longer, and are settled using current assets. All other liabilities are non-current liabilities.

LO2 Identify and describe known current liabilities. Known current liabilities are set by agreements or laws and are measurable with little uncertainty. They include accounts payable, sales taxes payable, unearned revenues, notes payable, payroll liabilities, and the current portion of long-term debt.

LO3 Prepare entries to account for current notes payable. Current notes payable are current liabilities and most bear interest. When a current note is interest-bearing, its face value equals the amount borrowed. This type of note also identifies a rate of interest to be paid at maturity.

LO4 Account for estimated liabilities, including customer awards/loyalty programs, warranties and corporate income taxes. Liabilities for warranties, and corporate income taxes are recorded with estimated amounts and are recognized as expenses when incurred; they are also known as provisions. Contingent liabilities are not recorded but disclosed in the notes to the financial statements.

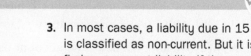

Guidance Answers to CHECKPOINT

1. Liabilities are probable future settlements of assets or services that an entity is currently obligated to make as a result of past transactions or events.

2. No, an expected future payment is not a liability unless an existing obligation was created by a past event or transaction.

3. In most cases, a liability due in 15 months is classified as non-current. But it is classified as a current liability if the company's operating cycle is 15 months or longer.

4. **a.** Sales = $1,130 ÷ 1.13 = $1,000
   b. HST = $1,130 − $1,000 = $130

5. A creditor might want to have a note payable instead of an account payable in order to (a) start charging interest and/or (b) have positive evidence of the debt and its terms.

6. The interest expense was $10,000 × 5% × 180/365 = $246.58.

7. *a*

8. *a*

9. A corporation accrues an income tax liability for its interim financial statements because income tax expense is incurred when profit is earned, not just at the end of the year.

10. A liability that is determined to be contingent is disclosed in the notes to the financial statements unless payment is remote.

DEMONSTRATION PROBLEM

The following series of transactions and other events took place at the Vitablend, located in Prince George, British Columbia, during its calendar reporting year. Describe their effects on the financial statements by presenting the journal entries described in each situation, if any.

a. In September 2017, Vitablend sold $140,000 of merchandise that was covered by a 180-day warranty. Prior experience shows that the costs of fulfilling the warranty will equal 5% of the sales revenue. Calculate September's warranty expense and the increase in the warranty liability and show how it would be recorded with a September 30 adjusting entry. Also show the journal entry that would be made on October 8 to record an expenditure of $300 cash to provide warranty service on an item sold in September.

b. On October 12, 2017, Vitablend arranged with a supplier to replace an overdue $10,000 account payable by paying $2,500 cash and signing a note for the remainder. The note matured in 90 days and had a 12% interest rate. Show the entries that would be recorded on October 12, December 31, and the date the note matures.

c. In late December, the company learns that it is facing a product liability suit filed by an unhappy customer. The company's lawyer is of the opinion that although the company will probably suffer a loss from the lawsuit, it is not possible to estimate the amount of the damages at the present time.

d. Vitablend Company recorded estimated income taxes at the end of each month, January through December inclusive, at the rate of 28% of income before tax. Total profit before taxes for the year was estimated to be $896,000. At year-end, the actual income tax expense was determined to be $273,880. Record the year-end income tax expense adjustment entry for the company.

e. On November 1, Vitablend borrows $5,000 from the bank on a 90-day, 14% note. Record the issuance of the note on November 1, interest accrual on December 31, and repayment of the note with interest on the maturity date.

f. As of November 30, 2017, the account balances for GST Receivable, GST Payable, and PST Payable were $16,800, $9,660, and $8,280 respectively. During December, Vitablend Company purchased $196,000 of merchandise on credit and recorded credit sales of $295,000 (cost of sales $177,000). Vitablend Company remits GST and PST on the last day of each month regarding the previous month's transactions. Record the remittance or refund of sales taxes on December 31 as well as summary entries for the purchase and sale of merchandise during December. (Date the summary entries Dec. 31 for simplicity.)

Analysis Component:

Part (a) requires that a warranty liability be recorded for September yet no warranty work regarding September sales has yet been performed and may not even result in the future. Would it be acceptable to defer recording warranty liabilities and related expenses until the warranty work actually results? Why or why not?

Planning the Solution

- For part (a), calculate the warranty expense for September and record it with an estimated liability. Record the October expenditure as a decrease in the liability.

- For part (b), eliminate the liability for the account payable and create the liability for the note payable. Calculate the interest expense for the 80 days that the note is outstanding in 2017 and record it as an additional liability. Determine the maturity date of the note. Record the payment of the note, being sure to include the interest for the 10 days in 2018.

- For part (c), decide if a contingent liability exists for the company and needs to be disclosed; if it is remote, disclosure of a contingent liability is not required.

- For part (d), determine how much of the income tax expense is payable for the current year.

- For part (e), record the note. Make the year-end adjustment for 60 days' accrued interest. Record the repayment of the note, being sure to include the interest for the 30 days in 2018.

- For part (f), four entries are required. First, prepare separate entries to record the remittance or refund of GST and PST on December 31 based on the November 30, 2017, account balances. Next, prepare the entry to record the purchase of merchandise during December, including GST. Finally, prepare the entry to record the sale of merchandise during December, including GST and appropriate PST for Manitoba.

- Prepare an answer for the analysis component.

Solution

a. Warranty expense = 5% × $140,000 = $7,000

Sept.	30	Warranty Expense...	7,000.00	
		Estimated Warranty Liability		7,000.00
		To record warranty expense and liability at 5% of sales for the month.		
Oct.	8	Estimated Warranty Liability	300.00	
		Cash...		300.00
		To record the cost of the warranty service.		

b. Interest expense for 2017 = 12% × \$7,500 × 80/365 = \$197.26

Interest expense for 2018 = 12% × \$7,500 × 10/365 = \$24.66

Oct.	12	Accounts Payable	10,000.00	
		Notes Payable		7,500.00
		Cash...		2,500.00
		Paid \$2,500 cash and gave a 90-day, 12% note to extend the due date on the account.		
Dec.	31	Interest Expense...	197.26	
		Interest Payable		197.26
		To accrue interest on note payable; \$7,500 × 0.12 × 80/365 = \$197.26.		
Jan.	10	Notes Payable..	7,500.00	
		Interest Payable	197.26	
		Interest Expense...	24.66	
		Cash...		7,721.92
		Paid note with interest, including accrued interest payable; \$7,500 × 0.12 × 10/365 = \$24.66.		

c. The pending lawsuit is a contingent liability and should be disclosed in the notes to the financial statements. Although the loss cannot be reasonably estimated, it is probable according to the lawyer so it is a contingent liability.

d.

Dec.	31	Income Tax Expense	23,000.00	
		Income Taxes Payable.........................		23,000.00
		To record income tax expense; \$273,880 − (\$896,000 × 28% = \$250,880) = \$23,000.		

e.

Nov.	1	Cash	5,000.00	
		Notes Payable		5,000.00
		Borrowed cash with a 90-day 14% note.		
Dec.	31	Interest Expense...	115.07	
		Interest Payable		115.07
		To record accrued interest; \$5,000 × 14% × 60/365 = \$115.07.		
Jan.	30	Notes Payable..	5,000.00	
		Interest Expense...	57.53	
		Interest Payable	115.07	
		Cash...		5,172.60
		To record payment of note and accrued interest; \$5,000 × 14% × 30/365 = \$57.53.		

f.

Dec.	31	GST Payable	9,660	
		Cash	7,140	
		GST Receivable		16,800
		To record refund of GST from Receiver General for Canada; $16,800 − $9,660 = $7,140.		
	31	PST Payable	8,280	
		Cash		8,280
		To record remittance of sales tax payable to provincial authority.		
	31	Merchandise Inventory	196,000	
		GST Receivable	9,800	
		Accounts Payable		205,800
		To record the purchase of merchandise on credit; $196,000 × 5% = $9,800 GST.		
	31	Accounts Receivable	330,400	
		Sales		295,000
		PST Payable		20,650
		GST Payable		14,750
		To record the sale of merchandise on credit; $295,000 × 5% GST = $14,750 GST; $295,000 × 7% PST = $20,650 PST.		
	31	Cost of Goods Sold	177,000	
		Merchandise Inventory		177,000
		To record the cost of sales.		

Analysis Component:

Although warranty costs regarding September sales will not occur until a future date, the matching principle requires that expenses (and the related liability) be recorded in the period in which the corresponding sales were realized. Warranty work done in the future regarding September sales must be matched against September sales, otherwise profit for September will be overstated.

Glossary

Breakage The dollar value of unredeemed gift cards or customer loyalty program points. These amounts are recognized into revenue based on expected customer redemption patterns or after the probability of customer redemption is remote.

Collections in advance See *unearned revenues*.

Contingent asset A potential asset that depends on a future event arising out of a past transaction. Contingent assets are never recorded until actually realized but, if probable, can be disclosed in the notes to the financial statements.

Contingent liability A potential liability that depends on a future event arising out of a past transaction.

Current liabilities Obligations due within a year of the balance sheet date or the company's next operating cycle, whichever is longer; paid using current assets or by creating other current liabilities.

Current note payable A current obligation in the form of a written promissory note.

Current portion of non-current debt The portion of non-current debt that is due within one year of the balance sheet date; reported under current liabilities on the balance sheet.

Customer deposits See *unearned revenues*.

Deferred revenues See *unearned revenues*.

Demand loans Liabilities not having a fixed due date that are payable on the creditor's demand.

Estimated liability An obligation of an uncertain amount that can be reasonably estimated; also known as a *provision*.

Exempt supplies GST-exempt services are educational, health care, and financial services.

Goods and Services Tax (GST) A value-added tax on nearly all goods and services sold in Canada. The tax is levied by the federal government.

Harmonized Sales Tax (HST) A combined GST and PST rate applied to taxable supplies. Currently, New Brunswick, Newfoundland and Labrador, and Ontario apply HST of 13%. Nova Scotia applies HST of 15%.

Input Tax Credit (ITC) GST paid by the registrant on purchases of taxable supplies. Input tax credits are applied against (reduce) GST Payable. Also known as *GST Receivable*.

Known liabilities A company's obligations that have little uncertainty and are set by agreements, contracts, or laws; also called *definitely determinable liabilities*.

Liability A future payment of assets or services that a company is currently obligated to make as a result of past transactions or events.

Non-current liabilities Obligations of a company that do not require payment within the longer of one year or an operating cycle. Also known as long-term liabilities.

Payroll Employee compensation for work performed.

Payroll liabilities Employee compensation amounts owing to employees and government and other agencies.

Provincial Sales Tax (PST) A consumption tax levied by provincial governments on sales to the final consumers of products; calculated as a percentage of the sale price of the item being sold.

Provisions See *estimated liability*.

Receiver General for Canada The federal government authority to which GST Payable is remitted.

Registrant Registered individual or entity selling taxable supplies that is responsible for collecting the GST on behalf of the government. A business with sales of less than $30,000 per year does not have to register for GST purposes.

Taxable supplies Taxable goods or services on which GST is calculated and includes everything except zero-rated and exempt supplies.

Trade accounts payable Amounts owed to suppliers regarding products or services purchased on credit. Commonly referred to as *accounts payable*.

Unearned revenues Amounts received in advance from customers for future products or services. Also called collections in advance, deferred revenues, or customer deposits.

Warranty An agreement that obligates the seller or manufacturer to repair or replace a product when it breaks or otherwise fails to perform properly within a specified period.

Zero-rated supplies Goods including groceries, prescription drugs, and medical devices that have zero GST.

Concept Review Questions

1. What is the difference between a current and a non-current liability?

2. What are the three important questions concerning the certainty of liabilities?

3. What amount does WestJet, in Appendix II, report as the current portion of long-term debt as at December 31, 2014? In what accounting period will this amount be paid?

4. Refer to the Indigo Books balance sheet in Appendix II. Does Indigo Books show any unredeemed gift card liability tax? If so, what is the balance in the account and what does the liability represent?

5. Refer to the balance sheet for Telus in Appendix II. What percentage is accounts payable and accrued liabilities at December 31, 2014, of the total current liabilities? of total liabilities?

6. Suppose that a company has a facility located in an area where disastrous weather conditions often occur. Should it report a probable loss from a future disaster as a liability on its balance sheet? Explain.

7. Why are warranty liabilities usually recognized on the balance sheet as liabilities even when they are uncertain?

8. What is the benefit of a company like Pebble Technology Corp., featured in the vignette, raising funds through Kickstarter, as opposed to through finding equity investors or obtaining a loan from the bank?

Quick Study

QS 10-1 Distinguishing between current and non-current liabilities LO1

Which of the following items should normally be classified as a current liability for Prairie Brewing Company? Prairie has a 15-month operating cycle.

    a. A note payable due in 18 months.

    b. Salaries payable.

    c. A payable that matures in two years.

    d. A note payable due in 10 months.

    e. The portion of a long-term note that is due to be paid in 12 months.

QS 10-2 Current portion of long-term debt LO1

On January 1, 2017, La Petite Macaron, a local French bakery, borrowed $84,000 from the bank. Interest is calculated at the rate of 4% and the term of the note is four years. Four equal annual payments will be made in the amount of $23,141 each December 31. The payment schedule is shown below:

Year	Annual Payment	Principal Portion of Payment	Interest Portion of Payment	Principal Balance at Year-End
2017	$23,141	$19,781	$3,360	$64,219
2018	23,141	20,572	2,569	43,647
2019	23,141	21,395	1,746	22,252
2020	23,141	22,252	889	-0-

Show how La Petite Macaron will show the note on its year-end balance sheet:

  1. December 31, 2017

  2. December 31, 2018

QS 10-3 Unearned revenue LO2

MetroConcerts receives $2,000,000 in advance cash ticket sales for a four-date tour for Diana Krall. Record the advance ticket sales as a lump sum as of October 31, 2017. The concerts sold out and no additional ticket sales have been recorded. Record the revenue earned for the first concert date, November 16, 2017, assuming each concert date brings in the same amount of revenue.

QS 10-4 Accounting for sales tax payable LO2

Suppose Mink Make-up sells $5,600 of make up (merchandise with a cost of $4,800) for cash on September 30. The sales tax law requires Mink to collect 13% harmonized sales tax on every dollar of merchandise sold. Record Mink's entries for the $5,600 sale and applicable sales tax (assume a perpetual inventory system).

QS 10-5 Sales tax payable LO2

Hinton Designers, located in Quebec, provided $7,300 of services on credit to a client on May 7, 2017. Record Hinton's entry, including the appropriate GST and PST. (*Hint: Refer to Exhibit 10.6 for PST rates.*)

QS 10-6 Sales tax payable LO2

On September 3, 2017, Reynolds Retailers, operating out of Nunavut, sold $14,700 of goods for cash with a cost of $12,380. Record Reynolds's entries, including all appropriate sales taxes.

QS 10-7 Payroll liabilities LO2

Laser Tag Palace has two employees and the payroll register showed the following information for the biweekly pay period ended March 23, 2017:

Employee	Gross Pay	EI* Premium	Income Taxes*	CPP*	Total Deductions	Net Pay	Salaries Expense
Bently, A.	$2,010.00	$34.77	$416.45	$ 92.83	$ 544.05	$1,465.95	$2,010.00
Craig, T.	2,115.00	36.59	456.85	98.03	591.47	1,523.53	2,115.00
Totals	$4,125.00	$71.36	$873.30	$190.86	$1,135.52	$2,989.48	$4,125.00

*These values are based on assumed payroll deductions.

Prepare the entry to record the payroll liability on March 23, 2017. Ignore employer's contributions payable on CPP and EI.

QS 10-8 Notes payable LO3

Jackson Textiles had an outstanding account in the amount of $14,800 owing to Huang Manufacturing. On October 1, 2017, Huang agreed to convert Jackson's account to an 8%, 45-day note having a face value of $14,800. Record Jackson's entries on October 1, 2017, and on the due date.

QS 10-9 Current note transactions LO3

On December 11, 2017, the Sydney Company borrowed $42,000 and signed a 60-day, 5.5% note payable. Calculate the accrued interest payable on December 31, 2017.

QS 10-10 Warranty liabilities LO4

Vision Wear's product warranties state that defective glasses will be replaced free of charge for the life of the product. Vision Wear estimates that 2% of the pairs of glasses sold will require replacement. Each pair of glasses costs Vision Wear on average $40. During October 2017, Vision Wear sold 1,300 pairs of glasses at an average price of $120 per pair. Record the estimated warranty liability for October.

QS 10-11 Warranty liabilities LO4

On December 20, 2017, The Net Department Store sold a computer for $3,500 with a one-year warranty that covers parts and labour. Warranty expense was estimated at 2% of sales dollars. On March 2, 2018, the computer was taken in for repairs covered under the warranty that required $30 in parts and $10 of labour. Prepare the March 2 journal entry to record the warranty repairs.

QS 10-12 Recording an income tax liability LO4

Wang Corp. estimates income tax expense to be $285,600 for the year 2017. Record estimated income tax for January on January 31, 2017, and the payment on February 1, 2017.

QS 10-13 Recording an income tax liability LO4

During 2017, Victory Bubble Tea House recorded $36,000 in estimated income taxes on the last day of each month and made the payment on the 15th of the following month. On December 31, 2017, Victory's year-end, it was determined that total income tax expense for the year was $402,000. Record the income tax expense on December 31 (assuming no entry has yet been made in December to record tax) and the payment on January 15, 2018.

QS 10-14 **Reporting contingent liabilities** LO4

The following legal claims exist for the Doucet Advertising Agency. Classify the required accounting treatment for each legal situation as (a) a liability should be recorded, or (b) the legal claim need only be described in the notes to the financial statements.

a. Doucet faces a probable loss on a pending lawsuit; however, the amount of the judgment cannot be reasonably estimated.

b. A plaintiff is suing Doucet Company for a damage award of $1,200,000; it is not probable that the plaintiff will win the case.

c. Doucet Company estimates damages of another case at $3,000,000 and it is probable that Doucet will lose the case.

Exercises

Exercise 10-1 **Classifying liabilities** LO1

The following list of items appear on the balance sheet of Crunched Auto Body Repair Shop, which has a 12-month operating cycle. Identify the proper classification of each item. In the space beside each item write a *C* if it is a current liability, an *L* if it is a non-current liability, or an *N* if it is not a liability.

_____ **a.** Wages payable.

_____ **b.** Notes payable in 60 days.

_____ **c.** Mortgage payable (payments due in the next 12 months).

_____ **d.** Notes receivable in 90 days.

_____ **e.** Note payable (matures in 5 years).

_____ **f.** Mortgage payable (payments due after the next 12 months).

_____ **g.** Notes payable due in 18 months.

_____ **h.** Income taxes payable.

_____ **i.** Estimated warranty liability.

_____ **j.** Allowance for doubtful accounts.

Exercise 10-2 **Financial statement presentation—current liabilities** LO1

CHECK FIGURE: Total current liabilities = $305,000

The Creative Electronics Company shows the following selected adjusted account balances as at December 31, 2017:

Accounts Payable	$ 95,000
Salaries Payable...	136,000
Accumulated Depreciation, Equipment.............	23,000
Estimated Warranty Liability	18,000
Mortgage Payable	275,000
Notes Payable, 6 months..............................	21,000

Required Prepare the current liability section of Creative's balance sheet. $35,000 in principal is due during 2018 regarding the mortgage payable. For simplicity, order the liabilities from largest to smallest.

Exercise 10-3 Current versus non-current portions of debt LO1

On January 2, 2017, the Casual Elite Co. acquired land, to build a distribution centre, by issuing a 6%, three-year note for $200,000. The note will be paid in three annual payments of $74,822 each December 31. The payment schedule follows:

Year	Annual Payment	Principal Portion of Payment	Interest Portion of Payment	Principal Balance at Year-End
2017	$74,822	$62,822	$12,000	$137,178
2018	74,822	66,591	8,231	70,587
2019	74,822	70,587	4,235	-0-

Required

1. Prepare the entry to:

   a. Issue the note on January 2, 2017.

   b. Record the annual payment on December 31, 2017.

2. Show how the note will appear on the December 31, 2017, balance sheet.

Exercise 10-4 Financial statement presentation—current liabilities LO1

CHECK FIGURE: Total current liabilities = $155,700

The following alphabetized list of selected adjusted account balances is from the records of Jasper Company on December 31, 2017:

Accounts Payable	$ 71,000
Accumulated Depreciation—Equipment	46,000
Estimated Warranty Liability	16,500
GST Payable	9,800
Mortgage Payable, $35,000 due Dec. 31, 2018	370,000
Notes Payable, due April 1, 2018	15,800
Notes Payable, due April 1, 2021	114,000
PST Payable	7,600
Warranty Expense	11,200

Required Prepare the current liability section of Jasper Company's 2017 balance sheet (for simplicity, list the accounts from largest to smallest).

Analysis Component: Why is it important to classify assets and liabilities in current and non-current categories?

Exercise 10-5 Unearned revenues LO2

CHECK FIGURE: 2. $71,333

Stone Works is a paving stone installation business that operates from about April to October each year. The company has an outstanding reputation for the quality of its work and as a result pre-books customers a full year in advance. Customers must pay 40% at the time of booking and the balance on the completion date of the job. Stone Works records the 40% cash advance received from customers in the Unearned Revenues account. The December 31, 2017, balance sheet shows Unearned Revenues totalling $129,000.

During 2018, $284,000 of cash was collected in total from customers: $205,000 regarding work completed during the year for customers who paid 40% down in 2017, and the balance representing the 40% prepayments for work to be done in 2019.

Required

1. Prepare the entry to record the collection of cash in 2018.

2. Determine the balance in Unearned Revenue at December 31, 2018.

Exercise 10-6 **Various liabilities** LO2

Designer Architects had the following additional information at its November 30, 2017, year-end:

    a. The Unearned Revenue account showed a balance of $62,000, which represented four months of services paid in advance by a client for services beginning on October 15, 2017.

    b. The payroll register showed the following unpaid amounts as at November 30:

EI* Premium	Income Taxes*	CPP*	Total Deductions	Net Payable	Office Salaries	Sales Salaries
80.41**	1,290.00	183.98**	1,554.39	2,745.61	2,500.00	1,800.00

*These values are based on assumed payroll deductions.
**The employer's portions of EI and CPP are 1.4 times and 1 times the employees' portion respectively.

    c. The November utility bill in the amount of $2,160 was unpaid and unrecorded at November 30.

Required Prepare the appropriate entries at year-end based on the above information.

Analysis Component: If the above entries are not recorded on November 30, 2017, what is the effect on the income statement and the balance sheet? Identify which GAAP would be violated.

Exercise 10-7 **Gift card journal entries** LO2

Sarah's Pottery and Gift store had the following transactions:

    a. On November 15 2015, Katie, from a small office business, Custom Graphics, contacted Sarah to purchase gift cards for the holiday season. Katie's boss gave her $2,000 to purchase 40 gift cards with a value of $50 each from Sarah.

    b. During the month of December, 15 of the $50 gift cards were used in full by staff members of Custom Graphics.

Prepare the journal entries for each of the transactions. Calculate the liability that will remain on the December 31, 2015 balance sheet for Sarah's Pottery and Gift Store.

Exercise 10-8 **Loyalty program journal entries, balance sheet impact** LO2

Real People Sporting (RPS) Co-op introduced a loyalty program in 2015. Every customer who signed up would receive 1% of their total purchases as a cheque, each February for the previous year, that could be used in-store store on any merchandise, within the next 9 months. The customers could look online during the year and check their balance at any time. Laura signed up for the program in 2015, when she purchased a kayak in July for $1,000. Later, in September, she purchased a mountain bike for $2,300. In March 2016, she purchased a paddle board for $2,200 and used her cheque towards the purchase.

> **a.** Prepare the journal entries for RPS Co-op for each of the transactions on July 2015, September 2015, and March 2016.

> **b.** In 2015 RPS Co-op had a total of $482,000 in sales to customers who had signed up with the loyalty program. What is the amount of liability that would be created by these sales?

Exercise 10-9 **Sales taxes payable** LO2

CHECK FIGURES: a. HST Payable = $27,000; b. PST Payable = $12,600; c. PST Payable = $18,900

Sunnyside Solar Consultants provided $180,000 of consulting services to Delton Developments on April 14, 2017, on account.

Required Journalize Sunnyside's April 14 transaction including applicable PST and GST or HST assuming it is located in:

> **a.** Nova Scotia   **c.** Prince Edward Island
> **b.** British Columbia   **d.** Alberta

Use the PST rates in Exhibit 10.6.

Exercise 10-10 **Sales tax payable** LO2

Assume Pebble Inc. on October 15 purchased $2,500 of merchandise on credit. The next day, it recorded sales of $1,700; cost of sales was $1,200. Record the October 15 and October 16 entries assuming each of the geographical areas noted in Exhibit 10.6. A chart similar to the following might be useful in organizing your answer, where those regions with the same sales taxes are combined in one column.

Date	Description	Alberta/NWT/ Nunavut/Yukon	Saskatchewan	Etc.

Exercise 10-11 **Asset purchased with a note** LO2,3

Snowbot Snow Removal Company of Halifax purchased some snow-plow equipment on March 10, 2017, that had a cost of $100,000 (ignore GST/PST). Show the journal entries that would record this purchase and payment under these three separate situations:

> **a.** The company paid cash for the full purchase price.

> **b.** The company purchased the equipment on credit with terms 1/30, n/60. Payment was made on April 9, 2017.

> **c.** The company signed a 10%, one-year note for the full purchase price. The note was paid on March 10, 2018, the maturity date. Ignore year-end accruals.

Exercise 10-12 **Notes payable** LO3

CHECK FIGURE: 1. October 30

Mercedes Boats borrowed $100,000 on September 15, 2017, for 45 days at 8% interest by signing a note.

> **1.** On what date will this note mature?

> **2.** How much interest expense is created by this note?

> **3.** Prepare the journal entries for September 15, 2017, and the maturity date.

Exercise 10-13 **Notes payable with year-end adjustments** LO3

CHECK FIGURE: 1. March 1

Trista and Co. borrowed $180,000 on December 1, 2017, for 90 days at 5% interest by signing a note to buy jewelry inventory.

1. On what date will this note mature?

2. How much interest expense is created by this note in 2017?

3. How much interest expense is created by this note in 2018?

4. Prepare the journal entries on December 1, December 31 (Trista and Co.'s year-end), and the maturity date.

Exercise 10-14 **Estimated warranties** LO4

CHECK FIGURES: c. $15,470; d. $9,750

Shefford Cutlery extends a lifetime replacement warranty on all units sold. Using past experience, the company estimates that 0.5% of units sold will be returned and require replacement at an average cost of $130 per unit. On January 1, 2017, the balance in Shefford's Estimated Warranty Liability account was $15,600. During 2017, sales totalled $3,600,000 or 15,000 units. The actual number of units returned and replaced was 76.

Required

   a. Prepare the entry to estimate warranty liabilities based on the units sold for 2017. Assume the adjustment is made on December 31.

   b. Record the replacement of the units returned in 2017 (use a date of December 31).

   c. Calculate the balance in the Estimated Warranty Liability account at December 31, 2017.

   d. What is the warranty expense that will appear on the income statement for the year ended December 31, 2017?

Exercise 10-15 **Warranty expense and liability** LO4

CHECK FIGURE: 4. Ending 2018 balance = $42

On December 6, 2017, Norwood Co., an office equipment supplier, sold a copier for cash of $12,000 (cost $9,400) with a two-year parts and labour warranty. Based on prior experience, Norwood expects eventually to incur warranty costs equal to 5% of the selling price. The fiscal year coincides with the calendar year. On January 20, 2018, the customer returned the copier for repairs that were completed the same day. The cost of the repairs consisted of $198 for the materials taken from the parts inventory and $360 of labour that was fully paid with cash. These were the only repairs required in 2018 for this copier.

Required

1. How much warranty expense should the company report in 2017 for this copier?

2. How much is the warranty liability for this copier as of December 31, 2017?

3. How much warranty expense should the company report in 2018 for this copier?

4. How much is the warranty liability for this copier as of December 31, 2018?

5. Show the journal entries that would be made to record (a) the sale (assume a perpetual inventory system); (b) the adjustment on December 31, 2017, to record the warranty expense; and (c) the repairs that occurred in January 2018. Ignore sales taxes.

Exercise 10-16 Income taxes payable LO4

CHECK FIGURE: 5. $978,000

Music Media Ltd. prepares statements quarterly.

Part A:

Required

1. Based on 2016 results, Music's estimated tax liability for 2017 is $285,960. Music will accrue 1/12 of this amount at the end of each month (assume the installments are paid the next day). Prepare the entry on January 31, 2017, to accrue the tax liability and on February 1 to record the payment.

2. At year-end, December 31, the actual income tax for 2017 was determined to be $291,420. Prepare the adjusting entry on December 31 to record the accrual (assume 11 months have been accrued to date in 2017). Record the payment on January 1, 2018.

Part B:

Required

3. Complete the following table assuming Music estimates its tax liability for the year 2017 to be $640,000.

	Jan.–Mar.	Apr.–June	July–Sept.	Oct.–Dec.
Actual profit before tax..................................	$280,000	$410,000	$430,000	$510,000
Estimated income tax expense				
Profit				

4. Assuming that actual tax for the year 2017 was determined to be $652,000, prepare the appropriate adjusting entry at year-end to bring the balance in the Income Tax Expense account to the correct balance, assuming no accrual has yet been recorded for the fourth quarter.

5. Calculate Music's actual profit for the year 2017.

Exercise 10-17 Various liabilities LO2,4

CHECK FIGURE: c. HST Payable = $273,000

Superior Skateboard Company, located in Ontario, is preparing adjusting entries at December 31, 2017. An analysis reveals the following:

a. During December, Superior sold 6,500 skateboards that carry a 60-day warranty. The skateboard sales totalled $390,000. The company expects 8% of the skateboards will need repair under warranty and it estimates that the average repair cost per unit will be $38.

b. A disgruntled employee is suing the company. Legal advisors believe that it is probable that Superior will have to pay damages, the amount of which cannot be reasonably estimated.

c. Superior needs to record previously unrecorded cash sales of $2,100,000 (cost of sales 65%) plus applicable HST.

d. Superior recognizes that $95,000 of $160,000 received in advance for skateboards has now been earned.

Required Prepare any required adjusting entries at December 31, 2017, for each of the above.

Exercise 10-18 **Various liabilities** LO2,4

Mackenzie Corp. is preparing the December 31, 2017, year-end financial statements. Following are selected unadjusted account balances:

Estimated warranty liability	$ 6,460	120-day note payable, 4%	$ 80,000
Income tax expense	118,800	Unearned revenues	296,000
Mortgage payable, 5%	440,000	Warranty expense	6,400

Additional information:

a. $10,800 of income tax was accrued monthly from January through to November inclusive and paid on the 15th day of the following month. The actual amount of tax expense for the year is determined to be $126,040.

b. A customer is suing the company. Legal advisors believe it is probable that the company will have to pay damages, the amount of which will approximate $140,000 given similar cases in the industry.

c. During December, Mackenzie had sales of $710,000. 5% of sales typically require warranty work equal to 20% of the sales amount.

d. Mortgage payments are made on the first day of each month.

e. $111,500 of the Unearned Revenues remain unearned at December 31, 2017.

f. The 120-day note payable was dated November 15, 2017.

Required

1. Prepare any required adjusting entries at December 31, 2017, for each of the above.

2. Determine the adjusted amounts for total liabilities and profit assuming these were $940,000 and $620,000, respectively, prior to preparing the adjustments in (a) to (f) above.

Analysis Component: What is the effect on the income statement and balance sheet if the above entries are not recorded? Identify which GAAP, if any, would be violated if these entries are not recorded.

Exercise 10-19 **Comprehensive balance sheet** LO1,2,3,4

CHECK FIGURES: Total current assets = $230,255; Total current liabilities = $127,030

Domino Company showed the following adjusted trial balance information for its December 31, 2017, year-end.

Account	Balance[1]	Account	Balance[1]
Accounts payable	$ 41,700	Interest receivable	$ 55
Accounts receivable	36,000	Jake Bedoe, capital	257,125
Accum. deprec., building	346,000	Land	81,400
Accum. deprec., machinery	119,000	Machinery	289,000
Allowance for doubtful accounts	1,100	Merchandise inventory	119,000
Building	520,000	Notes payable[2]	184,000
Cash	18,300	Notes receivable, due 2018	22,000
Estimated warranty liabilities	10,300	Operating expenses	895,900
Income taxes payable	7,100	Prepaid rent	36,000
Income tax expense	118,600	Revenue	1,140,000
Interest payable	530	Unearned revenue	29,400

[1]Assume all accounts have a normal balance.

[2]$146,000 of the note payable is due beyond December 31, 2018.

Required Prepare a classified balance sheet for Domino Company at December 31, 2017.

Problems

Problem 10-1A Current versus non-current portions of debt LO1

On January 2, 2017, Brook Company acquired machinery by issuing a 3%, $360,000 note due in five years on December 31, 2020. Annual payments are $78,608 each December 31. The payment schedule is:

Year	Annual Payment	Principal Portion of Payment	Interest Portion of Payment	Principal Balance at Year-End
2017	$78,608	$67,808	$10,800	$292,192
2018	78,608	69,842	8,766	222,350
2019	78,608	71,937	6,671	150,413
2020	78,608	74,096	4,512	76,317
2021	78,608	76,317	2,291	-0-

Required Using the information provided, complete the following liabilities section of Brook Company's balance sheet at December 31:

	December 31			
	2017	2018	2019	2020
Current liabilities:				
Current portion of non-current debt...				
Interest payable............................				
Non-current liabilities				
Long-term debt...............................				

Problem 10-2A Transactions with current notes payable LO3 eXcel

Zing Cell Phone Company entered into the following transactions involving current liabilities during 2017 and 2018:

2017

Mar. 14 Purchased merchandise on credit from Ferris Inc. for $130,000. The terms were 1/10, n/30 (assume a perpetual inventory system).

Apr. 14 Zing paid $20,000 cash and replaced the $110,000 remaining balance of the account payable to Ferris Inc. with a 4%, 60-day note payable.

May 21 Borrowed $120,000 from Scotia Bank by signing a 3.5%, 90-day note.

? Paid the note to Ferris Inc. at maturity.

? Paid the note to Scotia Bank at maturity.

Dec. 15 Borrowed $95,000 and signed a 4.25%, 120-day note with National Bank.

Dec. 31 Recorded an adjusting entry for the accrual of interest on the note to National Bank.

2018

? Paid the note to National Bank at maturity.

Required

1. Determine the maturity dates of the three notes just described.

2. Present journal entries for each of the preceding dates.

Problem 10-3A Estimated product warranty liabilities LO4

CHECK FIGURES: 2. $1,750; 3. $40,600; 4. $40,145

On November 10, 2017, Singh Electronics began to buy and resell scanners for $55 each. Singh uses the perpetual system to account for inventories. The scanners are covered under a warranty that requires the company to replace any non-working scanner within 90 days. When a scanner is returned, the company simply throws it away and mails a new one from inventory to the customer. The company's cost for a new scanner is only $35. Singh estimates warranty costs based on 18% of the number of units sold. The following transactions occurred in 2017 and 2018 (ignore GST and PST):

2017		
Nov.	15	Sold 2,000 scanners for $110,000 cash.
	30	Recognized warranty expense for November with an adjusting entry.
Dec.	8	Replaced 150 scanners that were returned under the warranty.
	15	Sold 5,500 scanners.
	29	Replaced 40 scanners that were returned under the warranty.
	31	Recognized warranty expense for December with an adjusting entry.
2018		
Jan.	14	Sold 275 scanners.
	20	Replaced 63 scanners that were returned under the warranty.
	31	Recognized warranty expense for January with an adjusting entry.

Required

1. How much warranty expense should be reported for November and December 2017?

2. How much warranty expense should be reported for January 2018?

3. What is the balance of the estimated warranty liability as of December 31, 2017?

4. What is the balance of the estimated warranty liability as of January 31, 2018?

5. Prepare journal entries to record the transactions and adjustments (ignore sales taxes).

Problem 10-4A Determining the effects of various liabilities on financial statements LO1,4

Part 1:

Okanagan Refrigeration manufactures and markets commercial refrigeration systems for food trucks and specialized transport trucks. It was disclosed in notes to the company's financial statements that estimated warranty costs are accrued at the time products are sold. Assume that in 2017 warranty costs are estimated at $315,000 and that the related warranty work was actually paid for during 2018.

Required Explain how financial statements are affected due to warranties in 2017 and 2018.

Part 2:

Assume that Fabfit Enterprises collected $1,950,000 during 2017 for fitness magazines that will be delivered in future years. During 2018, Fabfit delivered magazines based on these subscriptions amounting to $1,835,000.

Required Explain how financial statements are affected in 2017 and 2018 by these subscriptions.

Problem 10-5A Sales taxes payable LO2

CHECK FIGURES: a. HST Receivable = $6,500; b. PST Payable = $2,800

Modern Electronics Company purchases merchandise inventory from several suppliers. On April 1, 2017, Modern Electronics purchased from Speedy Supplies $50,000 of inventory on account. On May 15, 2017,

Modern Electronics sold inventory to a Jones Apartment Complex for $40,000 cash, which included $25,000 COGS for the inventory. On June 15, 2017 Modern Electronics remitted the applicable PST and GST or HST.

Required Journalize Modern Electronics Company transactions on April 1, 2017, May 15, 2017 and June 15, 2017, including applicable PST and GST or HST assuming it is located in:

   a. Ontario

   b. British Columbia

   c. Alberta

Use the PST, GST and HST rates in Exhibit 10.6.

Problem 10-6A Comprehensive LO1,2,3,4   Help Me SOLVE IT

CHECK FIGURE: Total liabilities = $769,033

Eyelash Extension Co.'s liabilities as reported on the June 30, 2017, balance sheet are shown below, along with its statement of changes in equity.

Accounts payable	$179,400
Notes payable, due 2019	480,000
Total liabilities	$659,400

Eyelash Extension Co. Statement of Changes in Equity For Year Ended June 30, 2017	
Jan Suzette, capital, June 30, 2016	$481,000
Add: Profit	196,400
Total	$677,400
Less: Withdrawals	285,000
Jan Suzette, capital, June 30, 2017	$392,400

Jan is selling the business. A potential buyer has hired an accountant to review the accounting records and the following was discovered:

   a. Eyelash Extension Co. began selling a new product line this past year that offered a warranty to customers. It is expected that $48,000 of warranty work will result next year based on first-year sales. No entry was prepared on June 30 to show this.

   b. Annual property taxes of $20,690 are due July 31, 2017; the income statement shows only one month of property expense resulting from an entry correctly recorded on July 31, 2016.

   c. Interest on the notes payable is paid quarterly. No entry has been recorded since the last quarterly payment of $8,200 on May 1, 2017.

   d. $16,200 of new office furniture was purchased on account and received on June 28. This transaction has not been recorded.

   e. Unearned revenue of $21,000 has been included on the income statement.

Required Using the information provided, prepare a corrected statement of changes in equity and liabilities section of the balance sheet (ignore PST/GST and round all calculations to the nearest whole dollar).

Analysis Component: Which GAAP is violated when accrued liabilities are not recorded? Explain your answer.

Problem 10-7A Comprehensive—balance sheet LO1,2,3,4

CHECK FIGURES: 2. Total current assets = $219,386; Total assets = $926,386;
Total current liabilities = $235,451

Golden Wedding Dress Company designs custom wedding dresses for brides to be. The person preparing the adjusting entries at year-end was unable to complete the adjustments due to illness. You have been given the following unadjusted trial balance along with some additional information for the December 31, 2017, year-end.

Account	Unadjusted Balance	Account	Unadjusted Balance
Accounts receivable	$ 71,400	Income tax expense	$ 33,660
Accum. deprec., building	116,000	Land	121,000
Accum. deprec., equipment	332,000	Merchandise inventory	69,800
Advance sales	216,000	Mortgage payable	217,997
Allowance for doubtful accounts	500	Sarah Golden, capital	204,863
Building	415,000	Note payable	150,000
Cash..	87,100	Other operating expenses	1,161,000
Equipment..	619,000	Sales	1,345,000
Estimated warranty liability	3,200	Sales returns and allowances	7,600

Other information:

1. Assume all accounts have a normal balance.

2. 75% of the balance in the Advance Sales account is for wedding dresses to be made and delivered by Golden during 2018; the remaining 25% is from sales earned during 2017.

3. Golden warranties its wedding dresses against defects and estimates its warranty liability to be 2.5% of adjusted net sales.

4. The 3.5%, 5-year note payable was issued on October 1, 2017; interest is payable annually each September 30.

5. A partial amortization schedule for the mortgage follows:

Year	Interest Expense	Principal Portion	Annual Payment*	Principal Balance at Dec. 31
2015	$11,346	$21,033	$32,379	$262,620
2016	10,505	21,874	32,379	240,746
2017	9,630	22,749	32,379	217,997
2018	8,720	23,659	32,379	194,338
2019	7,774	24,605	32,379	169,733

*Payments are made annually each January 2.

6. Uncollectible accounts are estimated to be 1% of outstanding receivables.

7. A physical count of the inventory showed a balance actually on hand of $61,600.

8. The balance in Income Tax Expense represents taxes accrued and paid for the 2017 year at the rate of $3,060 per month. Assume the income tax rate is 20%.

Required

1. Based on the information provided, journalize the adjusting entries at December 31, 2017.

2. Prepare a classified balance sheet (round all values on the balance sheet to whole numbers).

Alternate Problems

Problem 10-1B **Current versus non-current portions of debt** LO1

On January 2, 2017, Redbook Manufacturing acquired machinery by issuing a 5%, $350,000 note due in six years on January 2, 2023. Annual payments are $68,956 each January 2. The payment schedule is:

Year	Annual Payment	Principal Portion of Payment	Interest Portion of Payment	Principal Balance at Year-End
2018	$68,956	$51,456	$17,500	$298,544
2019	68,956	54,029	14,927	244,515
2020	68,956	56,730	12,226	187,785
2021	68,956	59,567	9,389	128,218
2022	68,956	62,545	6,411	65,673
2023	68,956	65,673	3,283	-0-

Required Using the information provided, complete the following liabilities section of Redbook Manufacturing's balance sheet:

	December 31			
	2017	2018	2019	2020
Current liabilities:				
Current portion of non-current debt				
Interest payable.............................				
Non-current liabilities				
Long-term debt................................				

Problem 10-2B **Transactions with current notes payable** LO3   e**X**cel

Brad's Building Supplies entered into the following transactions involving current liabilities during 2017 and 2018.

2017

Feb.	4	Purchased merchandise on credit from Shape Products for $68,600. The terms were 2/10, n/60. Assume Brad uses a perpetual inventory system; ignore sales taxes.
Mar.	2	Borrowed $215,000 from the First Provincial Bank by signing a note payable for 30 days at 3.5%.
Apr.	1	Paid the First Provincial Bank note.
	5	Gave Shape Products $18,600 cash and a $50,000, 30-day, 5% note to secure an extension on Brad's past-due account.
May	5	Paid the note given to Shape on April 5.
Nov.	16	Borrowed $216,000 at First Provincial Bank by signing a note payable for 60 days at 4%.
Dec.	1	Borrowed money at the Bank of Montreal by giving a $300,000, 90-day, 5% note payable.
	31	Recorded an adjusting entry for the accrual of interest on the note to the First Provincial Bank.
	31	Recorded an adjusting entry for the accrual of interest on the note to the Bank of Montreal.

2018

Jan.	15	Paid the November 16 note to First Provincial Bank.
Mar.	1	Paid the principal and interest on the December 1 note given to the Bank of Montreal.

Required Prepare journal entries to record these transactions for Brad's Building Supplies.

Problem 10-3B **Estimated product warranty liabilities** LO4

CHECK FIGURES: 2. $5,400; 3. $11,340; 4. $2,700

On November 9, 2017, Snowbot Snow Removal began to buy and resell snow blowers for $700 each. Snowbot uses the perpetual system to account for inventories. The snow blowers are covered under a warranty that requires the company to replace any non-working snow blower within 60 days. When a snow blower is returned, the company simply discards it and sends a new one from inventory to the customer. The company's cost for a new snow blower is $540. The manufacturer has advised the company to expect warranty costs to equal 20% of the total units sold. These transactions occurred in 2017 and 2018.

2017		
Nov.	16	Sold 60 snowblowers each for $700.
	30	Recognized warranty expense for November with an adjusting entry.
Dec.	10	Replaced two snowblowers that were returned under the warranty.
	20	Sold 140 snowblowers.
	30	Replaced 17 snowblowers that were returned under the warranty.
	31	Recognized warranty expense for December with an adjusting entry.
2018		
Jan.	6	Sold 50 snowblowers for $35,000 cash.
	20	Replaced 26 snowblowers that were returned under the warranty.
	31	Recognized warranty expense for January with an adjusting entry.

Required

1. How much warranty expense should be reported for November and December 2017?

2. How much warranty expense should be reported for January 2018?

3. What is the balance of the estimated warranty liability as of December 31, 2017?

4. What is the balance of the estimated warranty liability as of January 31, 2018?

5. Prepare journal entries to record the transactions and adjustments (ignore sales taxes).

Problem 10-4B Contingencies and warranties LO4

Tara Kim is the new manager of accounting and finance for a medium-sized manufacturing company. Now that the end of the year is approaching, her problem is determining whether and how to describe some of the company's liabilities in the financial statements. The general manager, Serge Warack, raised objections to the treatment of one warranty estimate and a contingency in the preliminary proposal.

First, Warack objected to the proposal to report nothing about a patent infringement suit that the company has filed against a competitor. Warack's written comment on Tara's proposal was, "We KNOW that we have them cold on this one! We're almost guaranteed to win a very large settlement!"

Second, he objected to Tara's proposal to recognize an expense and a liability for warranty service on units of a new product that was just introduced in the company's fourth quarter. His scribbled comment on this point was, "There is no way that we can estimate this warranty cost. Besides, we don't owe anybody anything until the products break down and are returned for service. Let's just report an expense if and when we do the repairs."

Required Develop a written response from Tara Kim regarding the two objections raised by Serge Warack.

Problem 10-5B Sales taxes payable LO2

CHECK FIGURES: a. HST Receivable = $6,000; b. PST Payable = $800

Appleton Electronics Company purchases merchandise inventory from several suppliers. On October 1, 2017, Appleton Electronics purchased from Digital Wiring $40,000 of inventory on account. On November 10, 2017, Appleton Electronics sold inventory to Disco Sound Company for $16,000 cash, which included $10,000 COGS for the inventory. On December 15, 2017 Appleton Electronics remitted the applicable PST and GST or HST.

Required Journalize Appleton Electronics Company transactions on October 1, 2017, November 10, 2017 and December 15, 2017, including applicable PST and GST or HST assuming it is located in:

    a. Nova Scotia

    b. Saskatchewan

    c. Yukon

Use the PST, GST, and HST rates in Exhibit 10.6.

Problem 10-6B Comprehensive LO1,2,3,4

CHECK FIGURE: Total liabilities = $492,363

Zest Company is a Montreal HR firm. Its condensed income statement for the year ended November 30, 2017, is shown below.

Zest Company Income Statement For Year Ended November 30, 2017	
Consulting revenue	$863,500
Operating expenses	512,800
Profit	$350,700

The liabilities reported on the November 30, 2017, balance sheet were:

Accounts payable	$ 26,230
Mortgage payable	328,698
Total liabilities	$354,928

Marie Martin, the owner, is looking for additional financing. A potential lender has reviewed Zest's accounting records and discovered the following:

    a. Mortgage payments are made annually each December 1. The December 1, 2017, payment has not yet been made or recorded. A partial amortization schedule for the mortgage follows:

Year	Payment	Interest	Principal	Principal Balance, December 1
2016	$46,244	$17,854	$28,390	$328,698
2017	46,244	16,435	29,809	298,889
2018	46,244	14,944	31,300	267,589
2019	46,244	13,379	32,865	234,724

    b. Consulting revenue included $85,000 received for work to be done in January and February 2018.

    c. Accrued salaries at November 30, 2017, totalling $11,500 have not been recorded.

    d. $7,000 of office supplies purchased on account were received November 28; this transaction was not recorded.

    e. Annual property taxes of $17,500 are due each December 1; no property taxes have been included on the income statement.

Required Using the information provided, prepare a corrected income statement and liabilities section of the balance sheet.

Analysis Component: If you were paid an annual bonus based on profit, what ethical dilemma would you face regarding the above items?

Problem 10-7B **Comprehensive—balance sheet** LO1,2,3,4

CHECK FIGURES: 2. Total current assets = $400,138; Total assets = $757,738; Total current liabilities = $164,547

Merano Wool Company manufactures clothing from merino wool. The person preparing the adjusting entries at year-end left for a vacation prior to completing the adjustments. You have been given the following unadjusted trial balance along with some additional information for the December 31, 2017, year-end.

Account	Unadjusted Balance	Account	Unadjusted Balance
Accounts payable	$ 26,300	Gina Lejeune, capital...................	$ 136,175
Accounts receivable	65,100	Income tax expense	176,000
Accum. deprec., equipment..................	110,000	Merchandise inventory	157,800
Accum. deprec., furniture	71,400	Note payable.............................	109,325
Allowance for doubtful accounts	900	Office supplies..........................	1,200
Cash...	119,000	Other operating expenses............	1,439,000
Equipment...	416,000	Prepaid rent..............................	17,600
Estimated warranty liabilities................	9,100	Sales	2,015,000
Furniture	123,000	Unearned sales..........................	36,500

Other information:

1. Assume all accounts have a normal balance.

2. 30% of the balance in Unearned Sales is from sales earned during 2017; the remaining balance is for 2018 sales.

3. Merano warranties its clothing against manufacturer defects and estimates that 4.5% of the 18,800 garments sold during 2017 will be returned for replacement. The average cost of the garments is $75.

4. A partial amortization schedule for the note payable follows:

Year	Interest Expense	Principal Portion	Annual Payment*	Principal Balance at Dec. 31
2015	$10,188	$29,959	$40,147	$173,810
2016	8,691	31,456	40,147	142,354
2017	7,118	33,029	40,147	109,325
2018	5,466	34,681	40,147	74,644
2019	3,732	36,415	40,147	38,229

*Payments are made annually each January 2.

5. 3% of outstanding receivables are estimated to be uncollectible.

6. A physical count of the inventory showed a balance actually on hand of $143,940.

7. The balance in Income Tax Expense represents taxes accrued and paid for the 2017 period at the rate of $16,000 per month. Assume the income tax rate is 24%.

Required

1. Based on the information provided, journalize the adjusting entries at December 31, 2017.

2. Prepare a classified balance sheet (round all values on the balance sheet to whole numbers).

Ethics Challenge

EC 10-1

Mike Li is a sales manager for an electric car dealership in Alberta. Mike earns a bonus each year based on revenue generated by the number of vehicles sold in the year less related warranty expenses. The quality of electric cars sold each year seems to vary since the warranty experience related to cars sold is highly variable. The actual warranty expenses have varied over the past 10 years from a low of 3% of an electric car's selling price to a high of 10%. In the past, Mike has tended toward estimating warranty expenses on the high end just to be prudent. It is the end of the year and once again he must work with the dealership's accountant in arriving at the warranty expense accrual for the electric cars sold this year.

Required

1. Does the warranty accrual decision present any kind of ethical dilemma for Mike Li?

2. Since the warranty experience is not constant, what percentage do you think Mike should choose for this year? Justify your response.

Focus on Financial Statements

FFS 10-1

CHECK FIGURES: Part 1. Total liabilities = $167,260; Part 2. Total current assets = $48,640; Total assets = $452,640

On August 31, 2017, World Travel Consulting showed the following adjusted account balances in alphabetical order:

Accounts payable	$ 2,800
Accounts receivable	22,500
Accumulated depreciation, building	37,000
Accumulated depreciation, equipment	13,000
Building	271,000
Cash	15,000
Charles World, capital	?
Equipment	38,000
GST receivable	840
Interest payable	1,400
Land	145,000
Long-term mortgage payable	111,860
Notes payable, due December 1, 2018	26,000
Notes payable, due March 1, 2018	17,000
Office supplies	1,800
Office supplies expense	14,000
Other operating expenses (including depreciation)	101,000
Prepaid expenses	8,500
Salaries expense	126,000
Salaries payable	8,200
Sales	631,500

Required

1. Prepare the liability section of the balance sheet at August 31, 2017 based on the above trial balance.

2. Prepare a corrected balance sheet at August 31, 2017. Charles World, the owner, is planning on expanding the business and has applied for a $2,000,000 bank loan. John Tanner, a CPA and Certified Fraud Examiner, was contracted by the bank to review the financial statements of World Travel Consulting. John discovered that included in sales were the following:

Advance air ticket sales	$106,000
Accommodation prepayments...	49,000
Unearned bus tour revenue	41,800

He also noted the following excerpt from the amortization schedule of the long-term mortgage payable:

Year	Principal Balance at August 31
2016	$146,320
2017	111,860
2018	70,040
2019	41,820

Analysis Component: Using your answers from Parts 1 and 2, discuss the implications of John's findings on the financial statements.

FFS 10-2

Part I:

Required Answer the following questions by referring to the December 31, 2014, and June 28, 2014, respective balance sheets for each of **WestJet** and **Danier Leather** in Appendix II.

    a. WestJet shows *Advance ticket sales* of $575,781 (thousand) under current liabilities. Explain what this is.

    b. WestJet shows *Current portion of long-term debt* of $159,843 (thousand) under current liabilities. Explain what this is and why it is classified as a current liability. Why is some of the debt listed as a current liability and the balance as non-current debt?

    c. Danier's Payables and accruals at June 28, 2014, is $9,185,000. What percentage is this of total liabilities on the same date?

Part 2:

Required Answer the following questions by referring to the December 31, 2014, balance sheet for **Telus** and the March 29, 2014 balance sheet for **Indigo** in Appendix II.

    a. Telus shows a December 31, 2014, balance of $255,000,000 of current maturities of long-term. Calculate the total long-term debt.

    b. Calculate what percentage of Indigo's assets at March 29, 2014, was financed by current liabilities.

Critical Thinking Mini Case

Selected information taken from the December 31, 2017, financial statements for Mesa Company is shown below for the year just ended:

Current assets	$120,000	Non-current liabilities..............................	$660,000
Property, plant, and equipment	840,000	Equity...	278,000
Intangibles..	50,000	Revenues	960,000
Current liabilities	72,000	Expenses...	890,000

The accountant was not sure about how to handle a few transactions and has listed the details here.

Inventory

Purchased $34,000 of merchandise inventory on December 28, 2017, shipped FOB destination on December 28, and received on January 5, 2018. (Recorded as a debit to Merchandise Inventory and a credit to Accounts Payable).

Because this liability was not due until 2018, it was listed as a non-current liability on the December 31, 2017, balance sheet.

Revenue

On December 15, 2017 $80,000 was collected for services to be provided in February and March 2018 and was recorded as a debit to Cash and a credit to Revenue.

On December 31, 2017, $50,000 of revenue earned but not collected or recorded was recorded as a debit to Accounts Receivable and a credit to Revenue.

Liabilities

On January 5, 2018, $5,000 of interest accrued on a note payable during December and was recorded when it was paid as a debit to Interest Expense and a credit to Interest Payable.

Payroll liabilities of $40,000 had accrued as of December 31, 2017, but had not been recorded.

Liabilities of $430,000 were due after December 31, 2018 and the balance was included in current liabilities.

Required Using the elements of critical thinking described on the inside front cover, discuss the impact on the current ratio, and specifically calculate the ratio before and after the changes you determine are needed. For each item, determine what the correct balance should be. What should the profit really be? Comment on the reliability of the financial statements. Who are the financial statement users that might be significantly impacted by these errors?

Comprehensive Problem

CHECK FIGURES: 4. Profit = $28,690; Total assets = $218,200

Interior Design Company **(Review of chapters 1–10)**

Interior Design Company specializes in home staging consulting services and sells furniture built by European craftsmen. The following six-column table contains the company's unadjusted trial balance as of December 31, 2017.

| Interior Design Company Six-Column Table December 31, 2017 | | | | | |
	Unadjusted Trial Balance		Adjustments		Adjusted Trial Balance
Cash..	$ 32,000				
Accounts receivable	47,000				
Allowance for doubtful accounts		$ 6,128			
Merchandise inventory................................	35,000				
Trucks..	40,000				
Accum. depreciation, trucks...........................		-0-			
Equipment..	150,000				
Accum. deprec., equipment		43,000			
Accounts payable		12,000			
Interest payable		-0-			
Estimated warranty liability		2,400			
Unearned extermination services revenue.......		-0-			
Long-term notes payable.............................		120,000			
Ken Jones, capital		85,804			
Ken Jones, withdrawals...............................	42,000				
Extermination services revenue		140,000			
Interest revenue		872			
Sales...		270,000			
Cost of goods sold	162,000				
Deprec. expense, trucks..............................	-0-				
Deprec. expense, equipment	-0-				
Wages expense	89,000				
Interest expense...	-0-				
Rent expense	33,000				
Bad debts expense	-0-				
Miscellaneous expenses	12,404				
Repairs expense...	26,000				
Utilities expense...	11,800				
Warranty expense.......................................	-0-				
Totals	$680,204	$680,204			

The following information applies to the company and its situation at the end of the year:

  a. The bank reconciliation as of December 31, 2017, includes these facts:

Balance per bank..	$28,400
Balance per books...	32,000
Outstanding cheques	5,200
Deposit in transit...	7,000
Interest revenue	88
Service charges (miscellaneous expense)	34

Included with the bank statement was a cancelled cheque that the company had failed to record. (This information allows you to determine the amount of the cheque, which was a payment of an account payable.)

  b. An examination of customers' accounts shows that accounts totalling $5,000 should be written off as uncollectible. In addition, it has been determined that the ending balance of the Allowance for Doubtful Accounts account should be $8,600.

c. A delivery truck was purchased and placed in service on July 1, 2017. Its cost is being depreciated with the straight-line method using these facts and predictions:

Original cost..	$40,000
Expected residual value...	12,000
Useful life (years)	4

d. A special computer for floor layout design was purchased and put into service early in January 2015 and is being depreciated with the straight-line method using these facts and predictions:

	Sprayer	Injector
Original cost..	$90,000	$60,000
Expected residual value...................................	6,000	5,000
Useful life (years)	8	5

e. On October 1, 2017, the company was paid $5,280 in advance to provide monthly staging service on an apartment complex for one year. The company began providing the services in October. When the cash was received, the full amount was credited to the Home Staging Consulting Revenue account.

f. The company offers a warranty for all of the products it sells. The expected cost of providing warranty service is 2% of sales. No warranty expense has been recorded for 2017. All costs of servicing products under the warranties in 2017 were properly debited to the liability account.

g. The $120,000 long-term note is a five-year, 4% note that was given to National Bank on December 31, 2015.

h. The ending inventory of merchandise was counted and determined to have a cost of $33,600. The difference is due to shrinkage; assume a perpetual inventory system.

Required

1. Use the preceding information to determine the amounts of the following items:

   a. The correct ending balance of Cash and the amount of the omitted cheque.

   b. The adjustment needed to obtain the correct ending balance of the Allowance for Doubtful Accounts.

   c. The annual depreciation expense for the delivery truck that was acquired during the year (calculated to the nearest month).

   d. The annual depreciation expense for the equipment that was in use during the year.

   e. The correct ending balances of the Home Staging Consulting Revenue and Unearned Home Staging Consulting Revenue accounts.

   f. The correct ending balances of the accounts for Warranty Expense and Estimated Warranty Liability.

   g. The correct ending balance of the Interest Expense account. (Round amounts to the nearest whole dollar.)

   h. The cost of goods sold for the year.

2. Use the results of requirement 1 to complete the six-column table by first entering the appropriate adjustments for items (a) through (h) and then completing the adjusted trial balance columns. (*Hint: Item (b) requires two entries.*)

3. Present general journal entries to record the adjustments entered on the six-column table.

4. Present a single-step income statement, a statement of changes in equity, and a classified balance sheet.

Partnerships

Chapter 10 focused on how current liabilities are identified, computed, recorded, and reported. Attention was directed at notes, payroll, sales taxes, warranties, employee benefits, and contingencies.

© Stephanie Van de Kemp, stephanievandekemp.com

A Look at This Chapter

This chapter explains the partnership form of organization. Important partnership characteristics are described along with the accounting concepts and procedures for its most fundamental transactions.

LEARNING OBJECTIVES

LO1 Identify characteristics of partnerships.

LO2 Prepare entries when forming a partnership.

LO3 Allocate and record profit and loss among partners.

LO4 Account for the admission and withdrawal of a partner.

LO5 Prepare entries for partnership liquidation.

Kicking Horse Coffee—An Incredible Canadian Success Story

Like many entrepreneurs, Elana Rosenfeld and Leo Johnson's focus was on doing what they love and they were determined to find a way to make a living doing it. Elana and Leo graduated from university in Montreal and headed off on a cross-country adventure. When they reached Invermere, BC, they fell in love with the organic beauty of the little mountain town and bought a small acreage where they built a little cabin in the woods. Shortly after, the couple decided to buy a local café, getting a mortgage from the local banker and a loan from the café owner's accountant. A year later they sold the café at a small profit and travelled for a year, which gave them "the space to think, to be creative and to plan."

Elana and Leo returned from their travels with a new vision. The adventurous partners saw a market opportunity for premium, organic, fair-trade coffee beans, as they realized this market was not being satisfied by the grocery stores at that time. They returned to the same local banker and negotiated a loan for $75,000 to start a coffee company, literally out of their garage. The grocery chain Thrifty Foods agreed to stock their coffee within the company's first year and the business quickly grew in popularity with a quality product and trendy names like Kick Ass, Hoodoo Joe, Kootenay Crossing, 454 Horse Power, and Grizzly Claw. The partners divided their responsibilities, maximizing each other's strengths. Leo focused on roasting, design, and operations, and Elana managed sales, marketing and finance. Early on, Elana determined how much profit they needed to make on each bag of coffee sold and they stuck to it.

In 2010, the original partners decided to part ways and Elana engaged a Deloitte partner in mid-market corporate finance to identify a financial partner that would enable the business to grow and expand into the U.S. market. In 2012, the company's strong brand recognition, and history of impressive growth and profitability, led it to attract a number of offers. In selecting a partner, Elana indicates that she relied on gut instinct and focused on an equity partner that shared her vision and values. Under the agreement, Elana maintains her leadership as the chief executive officer and participates in the company's continued success, maintaining a significant ownership of the shares in Kicking Horse Coffee.

In her role as company founder and CEO, Elana continues to focus on ensuring Kicking Horse keeps its corporate vision alive and she represents the company as the external voice of Kicking Horse. Elana also works with the CFO in the establishment and oversight of the budget. Elana oversees strategic planning and ensures Kicking Horse Coffee embodies the following Core Values in every aspect of its operations: genuine/authentic, sense of belonging, world friendly, life-long learning, and drive for perfection. She ensures the management team is strong and is effectively executing its corporate strategy and values.

After 18 years of growth and four garage expansions, the once little cabin in the woods is now the biggest employer in Invermere with a 60,000 square foot facility, and expects to roast an impressive 3.4 million pounds of coffee in 2014. You can find the company's full-bodied beans in all major grocery chains across Canada and it is successfully expanding strategically through paced, organic growth into the U.S. market.

Elana advises future business owners considering a partnership to avoid a 50/50 split, as it can lead to issues when conflicting views surface. She also suggests obtaining good legal counsel to develop a partnership agreement. Elana found a legal firm that specializes in entrepreneurship and that shares her approach to business, which has proven to be a valuable resource for the company. As for her advice to future accountants, she encourages "people first and the numbers will follow." To be successful, Elana recommends that corporate values are "fully integrated into the way the company operates financially" and strongly suggests everyone should take an ethics-oriented course to ensure effective decision making.

Sources: http://www.theglobeandmail.com/report-on-business/small-business/sb-growth/small-town-success-kicking-horse-coffee-brews-bold-move-to-the-us/article20707819/; http://www.vancouversun.com/business/smallbusiness/Vancouver+entrepreneur+celebrates+sweet+smell/7617938/story.html; www.kickinghorsecoffee.com; interview with Elana Rosenfeld, November 29, 2014.

Video Links: BDC Interview with Elana on Entrepreneurship and Expansion into the US: https://www.youtube.com/watch?v=56FiZHU_AaQ&feature=youtu.be

An inside look at Kicking Horse Coffee: https://www.youtube.com/watch?v=mnG7-5RUexg

CRITICAL THINKING CHALLENGE What were the advantages of Elana and Leo choosing the partnership form of business organization?

CHAPTER PREVIEW

There are three common types of business organizations: corporations, partnerships, and proprietorships. In Chapter 1, we briefly discussed the following characteristics of these organizations:

	Sole Proprietorship	Partnership	Corporation
Business entity	Yes	Yes	Yes
Legal entity	No	No	Yes
Limited liability	No	No	Yes
Unlimited life	No	No	Yes
Business taxed	No	No	Yes
One owner allowed	Yes	No	Yes

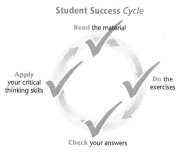

Student Success *Cycle*

Read the material

Apply your critical thinking skills

Do the exercises

Check your answers

The opening article revealed Elana and Leo's decision to open up Kicking Horse Coffee as a partnership, but there are disadvantages as well as advantages to this form of business organization. This chapter focuses on the partnership form of organization.

Partnership Form of Organization

A **partnership** is an unincorporated association of two or more persons to pursue a business for profit as co-owners. General partnerships are governed by provincial law and registration requirements. Partnerships are especially common in Canada for small retail and service-based businesses. Many professional practitioners such as physicians, lawyers, and accountants also organize their practices as partnerships.

Two forms of partnerships are recognized by Canadian law: *general partnerships* and *limited partnerships*.

Characteristics of General Partnerships

LO1 Identify characteristics of partnerships.

General partnerships offer certain advantages and disadvantages with their unique characteristics, as described in this section.

PARTNERSHIP AGREEMENT

Forming a partnership requires that two or more legally competent persons agree to be partners. Their agreement becomes a **partnership contract**. While it should be in writing to protect partners in the event of disagreement or dissolution of the business, the contract is binding even if it is only expressed orally.[1] Partnership agreements normally include the partners':

- Names and contributions
- Rights and duties
- Sharing of profit and losses
- Withdrawal provisions

---

1 Some courts have ruled that partnerships are created by the actions of partners even when there is no expressed agreement to form one.

- Dispute procedures
- Procedures for admission and withdrawal of new partners
- Rights and duties of surviving partners in the event of a partner's death

Lawyers prepare partnership contracts but it is common for public accountants to review these contracts and advise partners on tax matters relating to their share of partnership profit.

LIMITED LIFE

The life of a partnership is limited. Death,[2] bankruptcy, or any event taking away the ability of a partner to enter into or fulfill a contract ends a partnership. A partnership can also be terminated at will by any one of the partners. Conditions of termination may be specified in the partnership contract.

TAXATION

A partnership is not subject to taxes on its profit. It has the same tax status as a proprietorship. The profit or loss of a partnership is allocated to the partners according to the partnership agreement, and is included for determining the taxable profit of each partner's tax return.[3] Allocation of partnership profit or loss is done each year whether or not cash is distributed to partners.

CO-OWNERSHIP OF PROPERTY

Partnership assets are owned jointly by all partners. Any investment by a partner becomes the joint property of all partners. Partners have a claim on partnership assets based on the balances in their capital accounts.

MUTUAL AGENCY

The relationship between partners in a general partnership involves **mutual agency**. This means each partner is a fully authorized agent of the partnership. As its agent, a partner can commit or bind the partnership to any contract within the scope of the partnership's business. For instance, a partner in a merchandising business can sign contracts binding the partnership to buy merchandise, lease a store building, borrow money, or hire employees. These activities are all within the scope of business of a merchandising firm. However, a partner in a law firm, acting alone, cannot bind the other partners to a contract to buy snowboards for resale or rent an apartment for parties. These actions are outside the normal scope of a law firm's business.

Partners can agree to limit the power of any one or more of the partners to negotiate contracts for the partnership. This agreement is binding on the partners and on outsiders who know it exists, but it is not binding on outsiders who do not know it exists. Outsiders unaware of the agreement have the right to assume each partner has normal agency powers for the partnership. Because mutual agency exposes all partners to the risk of unwise actions by any one partner, people should evaluate each potential partner before agreeing to join a partnership.

UNLIMITED LIABILITY

When a general partnership cannot pay its debts, the creditors can apply their claims to all *personal* assets of partners, such as their homes. If a partner does not have enough assets to meet his or her share of the partnership debt, the creditors can apply their claims to the assets of the *other* partners. Because

---

2 Partnership agreements may include special provisions regarding the death of a partner so that the partnership can continue after that event.

3 The *Canada Income Tax Act* requires that proper records be maintained by partnerships and all other forms of business ownership that fall under its provisions.

partners can be called on to pay the debts of a partnership, each partner is said to have **unlimited liability** for the partnership's debts. This represents a major risk of the partnership form of business. Mutual agency and unlimited liability are two main reasons that most partnerships have only a few members. Unlimited liability is considered a major disadvantage of the partnership form of organization. For a summary of advantages and disadvantages of partnerships see Exhibit 11.1.

EXHIBIT 11.1

Advantages and Disadvantages of Partnerships

Partnerships	
Advantages	**Potential Disadvantages**
• Ease of formation	• Unlimited liability for general partnerships creating personal obligations
• Low start-up costs	• Hard to find suitable partners
• Access to more capital sources	• Possible development of conflict among partners
• Broader base of management talent	• Divided authority, resulting in potential problems if disagreements arise in management decisions
• Increased effectiveness from pooling talent	
• Shared business risk	• Partners can legally bind each other without prior approval
• Less bureaucracy than corporations	• Lack of continuity (or limited life)

Limited Partnerships

Some individuals who want to invest in a partnership are unwilling to accept the risk of unlimited liability. Their needs may be met with a **limited partnership**. Limited partnerships are established under provincial statutes that require registration. A limited partnership has two classes of partners: general and limited. At least one partner must be a **general partner** who assumes management duties and unlimited liability for the debts of the partnership. The **limited partners** have no personal liability beyond the amounts they invest in the partnership. A limited partnership is managed by the general partner(s). Limited partners have no active role except as specified in the partnership agreement. A limited partnership agreement often specifies unique procedures for allocating profits and losses between general and limited partners. The same basic accounting procedures are used for both limited and general partnerships.

Limited Liability Partnerships

Some provinces such as Ontario allow professionals such as lawyers and accountants to form a **limited liability partnership**. This is identified with the words "Limited Liability Partnership" or by "L.L.P." This type of partnership is designed to protect innocent partners from malpractice or negligence claims resulting from the acts of another partner. When a partner provides service resulting in a malpractice claim, that partner has personal liability for the claim. The remaining partners who are not responsible for the actions resulting from the claim are not personally liable. However, all partners are personally liable for other partnership debts. Accounting for a limited liability partnership is the same as for a general partnership.

1. Prepare a summary of the characteristics of a general partnership.
2. What is the difference between a *limited partnership* and a *limited liability partnership*?

Do Quick Study questions: QS 11-1, QS 11-2

Basic Partnership Accounting

Accounting for a partnership is the same as accounting for a proprietorship except for transactions directly affecting equity. Because ownership rights in a partnership are divided among partners, partnership accounting:

- Uses a capital account for each partner
- Uses a withdrawals account for each partner
- Allocates profit or loss to partners according to the partnership agreement

This section describes partnership accounting for organizing a partnership, distributing profit and losses, and preparing financial statements.

Organizing a Partnership

LO2 Prepare entries when forming a partnership.

When partners invest in a partnership, their capital accounts are credited for the invested amounts. Partners can invest both assets and liabilities. Each partner's investment is recorded at an agreed upon value, normally the fair market value of the assets and liabilities at their date of transfer to the partnership.

To illustrate, on January 11, 2017, Olivia Tsang and David Breck organize as a partnership called the Landing Zone. Their business offers year-round facilities for skateboarding and snowboarding. Tsang's initial net investment in the Landing Zone is $30,000, made up of $7,000 in cash, equipment with a fair value of $33,000, and a $10,000 note payable reflecting a bank loan for the business due in six months. Breck's initial investment is cash of $10,000. These amounts are the values agreed upon by both partners. The entries to record these investments are:

2017				
Jan.	11	Cash	7,000	
		Equipment...	33,000	
		Notes Payable		10,000
		Olivia Tsang, Capital...............................		30,000
		To record investment of Tsang.		
	11	Cash	10,000	
		David Breck, Capital...............................		10,000
		To record investment of Breck.		

The balance sheet for the partnership would appear as follows immediately after the initial investment on January 11, 2017:

The Landing Zone			
Balance Sheet			
January 11, 2017			

Assets		Liabilities		
Current assets:		Notes payable...............................		$10,000
Cash..	$17,000	**Equity[4]**		
Property, plant, and equipment:		Olivia Tsang, capital........................	$30,000	
Equipment..................................	33,000	David Breck, capital	10,000	
Total assets	$50,000	Total equity................................		40,000
		Total liabilities and equity		$50,000

 **CHECKPOINT**

3. Original Works Partnership was formed by three friends with the vision of selling cell phone cases to artists embellished with original artwork. Partner A invested $50,000 cash, Partner B contributed equipment worth $75,000, and Partner C transferred land worth $180,000 along with the related $100,000 note payable to the partnership. Calculate the total equity for Partners A, B, and C.

Do Quick Study question: QS 11-3

After a partnership is formed, accounting for its transactions is similar to that for a proprietorship. The differences include:

1. Partners' withdrawals of assets are debited to their *individual* withdrawals accounts (as opposed to *one* withdrawals account for a sole proprietorship).

2. In closing the accounts at the end of a period, *each* partner's capital account is credited or debited for his or her share of profit or loss (as opposed to *one* capital account for a sole proprietorship).

3. The withdrawals account of *each* partner is closed to that partner's capital account (as opposed to *one* withdrawals account and *one* capital account for a sole proprietorship).

In the following sections, we will demonstrate that the basic accounting procedures related to the recording of withdrawals and closing of the accounts at the end of a period are similar for a partnership as for a proprietorship.

Dividing Profit or Loss

LO3 Allocate and record profit and loss among partners.

Partners are not employees of the partnership. They are its owners. Partnership agreements generally include a provision for rewarding partners for their service and capital contributions to the partnership.

---

4 To clarify who holds the equity of the organization, the equity section of a partnership's balance sheet can be called *Partners' Equity* just as the equity section of a sole proprietorship's balance sheet can be called *Owner's Equity*. In this textbook, the equity section for all types of business organizations (sole proprietorships, partnerships, and, in Chapter 12) is called Equity.

If partners devote their time and services to their partnership, they are understood to do so for profit, not for salary. This means that when partners calculate the profit of a partnership, the amounts that they withdraw from the partnership assets are *not* expenses on the income statement.[5] They are recorded by debiting the partner's withdrawals account. Assume, for example, that on December 15, 2017, Olivia Tsang withdrew $20,000 and David Breck withdrew $18,000. The journal entry to record the withdrawals is:

2017				
Dec. 15	Olivia Tsang, Withdrawals	20,000	
	David Breck, Withdrawals	18,000	
	Cash		38,000
	To record the withdrawal of cash		
	by each partner.		

When profit or loss of a partnership is allocated among partners, the partners can agree to be assigned *salary allowances* as part of their allocation. *These salary allowances simply represent allocations of profit; they are not actual distributions of cash.* Partners also can agree that division of partnership earnings includes a return based on the amount invested. These are called *interest allowances.* Their partnership agreement can provide for interest allowances based on their capital balances. For instance, since Tsang contributes three times the investment of Breck, it is only fair that this fact be considered when earnings are allocated between them. Like salary allowances, these interest allowances are *not* expenses on the income statement and they are *not* actual distributions of cash.

Partners can agree to any method of dividing profit or loss. In the absence of an agreement, the law says that profit or loss of a partnership is shared equally by the partners. If partners agree on how they share profit but say nothing about losses, then losses are shared in the same way as profit. Several methods of sharing partnership profit or loss are used. Three frequently used methods divide profit or loss using (1) a stated fractional basis, (2) the ratio of capital investments, or (3) salary and interest allowances and any remainder in a fixed ratio.

EXHIBIT 11.2

Illustration of 3:2 Ratio

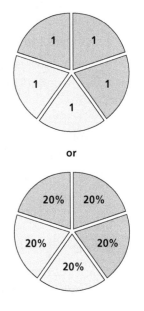

or

1. ALLOCATED ON A STATED FRACTIONAL BASIS

One way to divide partnership profit or loss is to give each partner a fraction of the total. Partners must agree on the fractional share each receives. A fractional basis can be expressed as a ratio, a fraction, or a percentage. As an example, assume a 3:2 ratio as illustrated in Exhibit 11.2. This means that 3/5 or 60% (3 ÷ 5 = 0.60 × 100% = 60%) is allocated to one partner and 2/5 or 40% (2 ÷ 5 = 0.40 × 100% = 40%) is allocated to the other partner.

Assume the partnership agreement of Olivia Tsang and David Breck is based on a ratio of 3:2. This means Tsang receives three-fifths or 60%, and Breck two-fifths or 40%, of partnership profit and loss. If their partnership's profit for the year ended December 31, 2017, is $70,000, it is allocated to the partners and the Income Summary account is closed with the following entry:

---

[5] Withdrawals are frequently called *salary allowances* but they should not be confused with salary expense. Salaries taken out of the partnership are simply withdrawals.

2017				
Dec. 31	Income Summary	70,000		
	Olivia Tsang, Capital..............................		42,000	
	David Breck, Capital		28,000	
	To allocate profit and close the Income Summary account.			

2. ALLOCATED ON THE RATIO OF CAPITAL INVESTMENTS

Partners can also allocate profit or loss on the ratio of the relative capital investments of each partner. Assume Tsang and Breck agreed to share earnings on the ratio of their beginning capital investments. Since Tsang invested $30,000 and Breck invested $10,000, this means Tsang receives three-fourths [$30,000/($30,000 + $10,000)] or 75% of any profit or loss and Breck receives one-fourth [$10,000/($30,000 + $10,000)] or 25%.

3. ALLOCATED USING SALARIES, INTEREST ALLOWANCE, AND A FIXED RATIO

Service contributions (the amount of work each partner does) and capital contributions of partners often are not equal. Salary allowances can make up for differences in service contributions, evening out the imbalance created when one partner contributes more time, energy, expertise, or leadership to the business. Interest allowances can make up for unequal capital contributions, providing a higher return to partners who invest more of their resources in the business. When both service and capital contributions are unequal, the allocation of profit and loss can include *both* salary and interest allowances.

In the new partnership formed by Olivia Tsang and David Breck, assume both partners agree that Tsang's services are worth an annual salary of $40,000. Since Breck is less experienced in the business, his services are valued at $25,000 annually. To compensate Tsang and Breck fairly given these differences in service and capital contributions, they agree to share profit or loss as per Exhibit 11.3.

EXHIBIT 11.3

Example Partnership Agreement Between Tsang and Breck

1. Annual salary allowances of $40,000 to Tsang and $25,000 to Breck.
2. Interest allowances equal to 10% of each partner's beginning-of-year capital balance.
3. Any remaining balance of profit or loss to be shared 3:1.

The provisions for salaries and interest in this partnership agreement are called *allowances*. Allowances are *not* reported as salaries and interest expense on the profit statement. They are a means of dividing the profit or loss of a partnership so each partner's capital account can be allocated its share.

ILLUSTRATION WHEN PROFIT EXCEEDS ALLOWANCE

Recall that Tsang's original investment was $30,000 and Breck's $10,000. If the Landing Zone has first-year profit of $70,000 and Tsang and Breck apply the partnership agreement as per Exhibit 11.3, they would allocate profit or loss as shown in Exhibit 11.4 with the accompanying entry following.

Tsang is *allocated* $43,750 and Breck $26,250 of the $70,000 total; they do not *receive* these amounts. Remember that the purpose of the calculation in Exhibit 11.4 is to determine the amount of profit or loss to be allocated to each partner's capital account at the end of the accounting period. Therefore, the entry to allocate the $70,000 profit between the partners and to close the Income Summary account on December 31, 2017, is as shown in Exhibit 11.4.

The balance in each of Tsang's and Breck's capital accounts at December 31, 2017, after posting all closing entries, is reflected in Exhibit 11.5.

EXHIBIT 11.4

Allocating Profit When Profit Exceeds Allowances

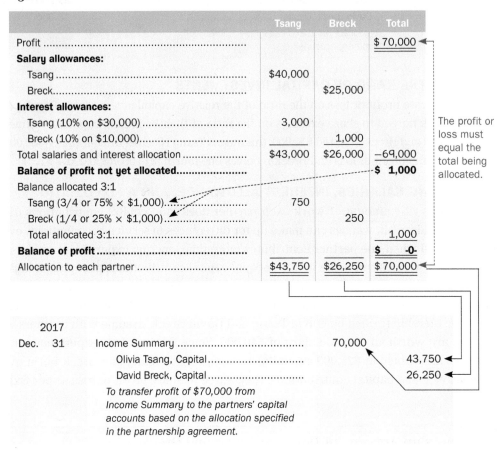

	Tsang	Breck	Total
Profit			$ 70,000
Salary allowances:			
Tsang	$40,000		
Breck		$25,000	
Interest allowances:			
Tsang (10% on $30,000)	3,000		
Breck (10% on $10,000)		1,000	
Total salaries and interest allocation	$43,000	$26,000	−69,000
Balance of profit not yet allocated			$ 1,000
Balance allocated 3:1			
Tsang (3/4 or 75% × $1,000)	750		
Breck (1/4 or 25% × $1,000)		250	
Total allocated 3:1			1,000
Balance of profit			$ -0-
Allocation to each partner	$43,750	$26,250	$ 70,000

The profit or loss must equal the total being allocated.

	2017				
Dec.	31	Income Summary		70,000	
		Olivia Tsang, Capital			43,750
		David Breck, Capital			26,250

To transfer profit of $70,000 from Income Summary to the partners' capital accounts based on the allocation specified in the partnership agreement.

EXHIBIT 11.5

Partners' Post-Closing Capital Balances at December 31, 2017

Olivia Tsang, Capital

		30,000	Jan. 11/17 Partner investment
Dec. 31/17 Withdrawal[6]	20,000		
		43,750	Dec. 31/17 Allocation of income
		53,750	Post-Closing Balance Dec. 31/14

David Breck, Capital

		10,000	Jan. 11/17 Partner investment
Dec. 31/17 Withdrawal[6]	18,000		
		26,250	Dec. 31/17 Allocation of income
		18,250	Post-Closing Balance Dec. 31/17

---

6 The closing entry for withdrawals is as follows:

	2017				
Dec.	31	Olivia Tsang, Capital	20,000		
		David Breck, Capital	18,000		
		Olivia Tsang, Withdrawals		20,000	
		David Breck, Withdrawals		18,000	

To record withdrawals to each partner's capital account.

ILLUSTRATION WHEN ALLOWANCES EXCEED PROFIT

The method of sharing agreed to by Tsang and Breck must be followed even if profit is less than the total of the allowances. If the Landing Zone's first-year profit is $50,000 instead of $70,000, it is allocated to the partners as shown in Exhibit 11.6. The profit or loss must equal the total being allocated.

EXHIBIT 11.6

Allocating Profit When Allowances Exceed Profit

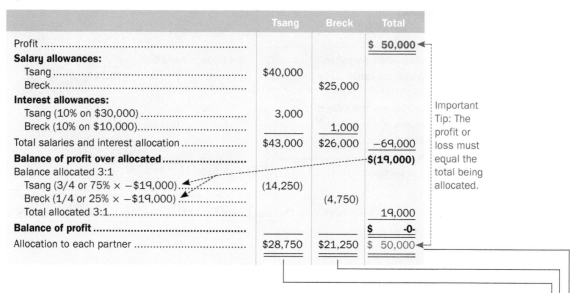

	Tsang	Breck	Total	
Profit			$ 50,000	
Salary allowances:				
Tsang	$40,000			
Breck...		$25,000		
Interest allowances:				
Tsang (10% on $30,000)	3,000			Important Tip: The profit or loss must equal the total being allocated.
Breck (10% on $10,000)..................................		1,000		
Total salaries and interest allocation	$43,000	$26,000	−69,000	
Balance of profit over allocated			$(19,000)	
Balance allocated 3:1				
Tsang (3/4 or 75% × −$19,000).......................	(14,250)			
Breck (1/4 or 25% × −$19,000)		(4,750)		
Total allocated 3:1...			19,000	
Balance of profit			$ -0-	
Allocation to each partner	$28,750	$21,250	$ 50,000	

Calculations for salaries and interest are identical to those in Exhibit 11.4. When we apply the total allowances against profit, the balance of profit is negative. This negative $19,000 balance is allocated in the same manner as a positive balance. The 3:1 sharing agreement means negative $14,250 and negative $4,750 are allocated to the partners to determine the final allocation. In this case, Tsang's capital account is credited with $28,750 and Breck's capital account with $21,250 as reflected in the following closing entry:

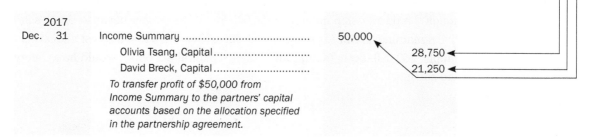

2017			
Dec. 31	Income Summary	50,000	
	Olivia Tsang, Capital...............................		28,750
	David Breck, Capital...............................		21,250

To transfer profit of $50,000 from Income Summary to the partners' capital accounts based on the allocation specified in the partnership agreement.

ILLUSTRATION WHEN THERE IS A LOSS

If the Landing Zone had experienced a loss, then it would be shared by Tsang and Breck in the same manner as the $50,000 profit. The only difference is that they would have begun with a negative amount because of the loss. Specifically, the partners would still have been allocated their salary and interest allowances, further adding to the negative balance of the loss. This *total* negative balance *after* salary and interest allowances would have been allocated 3:1 (75% and 25%) between the partners. These allocations would have been applied against the positive numbers from any allowances to determine each partner's share of the loss. Exhibit 11.7 illustrates how a $6,000 loss would be divided between Tsang and Breck.

EXHIBIT 11.7

Allocating a Loss

	Tsang	Breck	Total
Loss			$ (6,000)
Salary allowances:			
Tsang	$ 40,000		
Breck..		$25,000	
Interest allowances:			
Tsang (10% on $30,000)	3,000		
Breck (10% on $10,000)................................		1,000	
Total salaries and interest allocation	$ 43,000	$26,000	−69,000
**Balance of loss over allocated..........................			$(75,000)
Balance allocated 3:1			
Tsang (3/4 or 75% × −$75,000)......................	(56,250)		
Breck (1/4 or 25% × −$75,000)		(18,750)	
Total allocated 3:1..			75,000
**Balance of loss			$ -0-
Allocation to each partner	$(13,250)	$ 7,250	$ (6,000)

The net profit or loss must equal the total being allocated.

The entry to allocate the loss between the partners and to close the Income Summary account is as follows:

2017			
Dec. 31	Olivia Tsang, Capital	13,250	
	David Breck, Capital		7,250
	Income Summary..................................		6,000
	To allocate loss and close the Income Summary account.		

When a loss is allocated to the partners' capital accounts, you would expect each partner's capital account to decrease (a debit). However, notice that this entry causes Breck's capital account to increase (a credit) even though the partnership incurred a $6,000 loss. This occurs because Breck's 25% share of the $75,000 negative remaining balance is less than his $26,000 salaries and interest allocation. If the loss had been, for example, $60,000, both Tsang's and Breck's capital accounts would have decreased as a result of the closing entry.

CHECKPOINT

4. Ben and Jerry form a partnership by contributing $70,000 and $35,000, respectively. They agree to an interest allowance equal to 10% of each partner's capital balance at the beginning of the year with the remaining profit shared equally. Allocate first-year profit of $40,000 to each partner.
5. What fraction does each partner receive if three partners share on a 1:2:2 basis?
6. What percentage does each partner receive if three partners share on a 1:2:2 basis?

Do Quick Study questions: QS 11-4, QS 11-5, QS 11-6

Partnership Financial Statements

Partnership financial statements are very similar to those of a proprietorship. The statement of changes in equity for a partnership is one exception. It shows each partner's capital balance at the beginning of the period, any additional investments made by each partner, each partner's allocation of the profit or loss, withdrawals made by each partner, and the ending capital balance for each partner. To illustrate, Exhibit 11.8 shows the statement of changes in equity for the Landing Zone prepared according to the sharing agreement of Exhibit 11.3. Recall that the Landing Zone's first-year profit was $70,000. Also, Tsang withdrew $20,000 and Breck $18,000 at the end of the first year as reflected in the T-accounts of Exhibit 11.5.

EXHIBIT 11.8

Statement of Partners' Equity

The Landing Zone
Statement of Changes in Equity
For Year Ended December 31, 2017

	Tsang	Breck	Total
Capital, January 1	$ -0-	$ -0-	$ -0-
Add: Investments by partners	30,000	10,000	40,000
Profit	43,750	26,250	70,000
Total	$ 73,750	$ 36,250	$110,000
Less: Partners' withdrawals	(20,000)	(18,000)	(38,000)
Capital, December 31	$ 53,750	$ 18,250	$ 72,000

The equity section of the balance sheet of a partnership usually shows the separate capital account balance of each partner. In the case of the Landing Zone, both Olivia Tsang, Capital and David Breck, Capital are listed in the equity section along with their balances of $53,750 and $18,250, respectively. This information appears on the December 31, 2017, balance sheet as shown in Exhibit 11.9.

EXHIBIT 11.9

The ending capital balances on the statement of changes in equity are listed on the balance sheet.

Balance Sheet for the Landing Zone at December 31, 2017

The Landing Zone
Balance Sheet
December 31, 2017

Assets			Liabilities		
Current assets:			Long-term notes payable		$ 8,000
Cash		$50,000	**Equity**		
Property, plant, and equipment:			Olivia Tsang, capital	$53,750	
Equipment	$33,000		David Breck, capital	18,250	
Less: Accumulated depreciation	3,000	30,000	Total equity		72,000
Total assets		$80,000	Total liabilities and equity		$80,000

MID-CHAPTER DEMONSTRATION PROBLEM

Claudia Parker and Alex Craig began a partnership several years ago called the Gift Consultants. Adjusted trial balance information for the year ended September 30, 2017, appears below.

Account	Balance*
Accounts payable	$ 18,000
Accounts receivable	47,000
Accumulated depreciation, office furniture	6,000
Accumulated depreciation, vehicles	21,000
Allowance for doubtful accounts	3,000
Cash	34,000
Claudia Parker, capital	47,000
Claudia Parker, withdrawals	50,000
Consulting revenue	214,000
Expenses	$ 94,000
Notes payable, due March 2020	25,000
Office furniture	33,000
Prepaid rent	12,000
Alex Craig, capital	72,000**
Alex Craig, withdrawals	75,000
Unearned revenue	7,000
Vehicles	68,000

*Assume all account balances are normal.
**Alex Craig invested $10,000 during the year.

1. Prepare calculations that show how the profit should be allocated to the partners assuming the partnership agreement states that profits/losses are to be shared by allowing an $85,000 per year salary allowance to Parker, a $15,000 per year salary allowance to Craig, 10% interest on beginning of the year capital balances, and the remainder equally.
2. Prepare the journal entry to close the Income Summary account to the partners' capital accounts.
3. Prepare a statement of changes in equity and a classified balance sheet.

Analysis Component:

Why are each of the partners' withdrawals different from the salary allowance identified in the partnership agreement?

Planning the Solution

- Set up a column for each partner as well as a column to keep track of allocated profit.
- Allocate profit to each partner according to the terms of the partnership agreement.
- Prepare the entry to close the Income Summary to the partners' capital accounts.
- Prepare the statement of changes in equity for the year ended September 30, 2017, and a classified balance sheet for September 30, 2017.
- Answer the analysis question.

Solution

1.

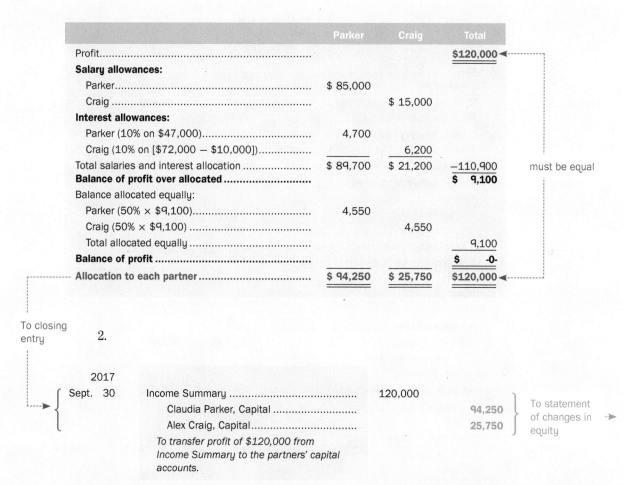

	Parker	Craig	Total	
Profit..			$120,000	
Salary allowances:				
Parker..	$ 85,000			
Craig		$ 15,000		
Interest allowances:				
Parker (10% on $47,000).................................	4,700			
Craig (10% on [$72,000 − $10,000])................		6,200		
Total salaries and interest allocation	$ 89,700	$ 21,200	−110,900	must be equal
Balance of profit over allocated			$ 9,100	
Balance allocated equally:				
Parker (50% × $9,100)....................................	4,550			
Craig (50% × $9,100)		4,550		
Total allocated equally			9,100	
Balance of profit			$ -0-	
Allocation to each partner	$ 94,250	$ 25,750	$120,000	

To closing entry

2.

2017				
Sept. 30	Income Summary	120,000		
	Claudia Parker, Capital		94,250	To statement of changes in equity
	Alex Craig, Capital...................................		25,750	
	To transfer profit of $120,000 from Income Summary to the partners' capital accounts.			

3.

From profit
allocation in
Part 1 and
resulting
closing entry
in Part 2

The Gift Consultants Statement of Changes in Equity For Year Ended September 30, 2017			
	Parker	**Craig**	**Total**
Capital, October 1, 2016...	$ 47,000	$ 62,000	$109,000
Plus:			
Investments by owners...................................	-0-	10,000	10,000
Profit	94,250	25,750	120,000
Total...	$ 141,250	$ 97,750	$239,000
Less: Partners' withdrawals.................................	50,000	75,000	125,000
Capital, September 30, 2017	$ 91,250	$ 22,750	$114,000

The Gift Consultants Balance Sheet September 30, 2017			
Assets			
Current assets:			
Cash		$34,000	
Accounts receivable..	$47,000		
Less: Allowance for doubtful accounts...........	3,000	44,000	
Prepaid rent..		12,000	
Total current assets			$ 90,000
Property, plant, and equipment:			
Vehicles	$68,000		
Less: Accumulated depreciation...................	21,000	$47,000	
Office furniture..	$33,000		
Less: Accumulated depreciation...................	6,000	27,000	
Total property, plant, and equipment			74,000
Total assets			$164,000
Liabilities			
Current liabilities:			
Accounts payable...	$18,000		
Unearned revenue	7,000	$25,000	
Total current liabilities			
Long-term liabilities:			
Notes payable, due March 2020......................		25,000	
Total liabilities..			$ 50,000
Equity			
Claudia Parker, capital...................................		$91,250	
Alex Craig, capital...		22,750	
Total equity			114,000
Total liabilities and equity.....................................			$164,000

Analysis Component:

The withdrawals represent the assets actually withdrawn by the partners from the partnership. The salary allowance in the partnership agreement is *assumed* and used only as one of the variables for calculating how much of the profit is to be allocated to each partner's capital account.

Admission and Withdrawal of a Partner

LO4 Account for the admission and withdrawal of a partner.

A partnership is based on a contract between individuals. When a partner is added or a partner withdraws, the old partnership ends. Still, the business can continue to operate as a new partnership among the remaining partners. This section looks at how we account for the addition and withdrawal of a partner.

Admission of a Partner

There are two ways in which a new partner is admitted to a partnership. First, a new partner can purchase an interest from one or more current partners. Second, a new partner can invest cash or other assets in the partnership.

PURCHASE OF A PARTNERSHIP INTEREST

The purchase of a partnership interest is a *personal transaction between one or more current partners and the new partner* that involves a reallocation of the capital of the current partners who sold their portion of the partnership. The partnership allocation results in the new partner accessing his or her purchased portion of the profit and interest allocations. To become an official partner in the business with a voice in decision making, the purchaser must be accepted by the current partners. If the existing partners agree to the new partner joining, a new partnership is formed and a new partnership agreement is created, outlining profit and loss allocations for the newly formed partnership.

To illustrate, assume that at the end of the Landing Zone's third year David Breck has a capital balance of $20,000 and he sells *one-half* of his partnership interest to Cris Davis for $18,000 on January 4, 2020. Breck is selling a $10,000 recorded interest (= $20,000 × 1/2) in the partnership. The partnership records this as:

2020				
Jan.	4	David Breck, Capital......................................	10,000	
		Cris Davis, Capital..................................		10,000
		To record admission of Davis by purchase.		

The effect of this transaction on equity is as follows:

	Olivia Tsang, Capital	David Breck, Capital	Cris Davis, Capital	Total Equity
Balance *before* January 4 transaction......................	$52,000	$20,000	$ -0-	$72,000
January 4 transaction	-0-	(10,000)	+10,000	-0-
Balance *after* January 4 transaction........................	$52,000	$10,000	$10,000	$72,000

Two aspects of this transaction are important. First, the $18,000 Davis paid to Breck is *not* recorded by the partnership. The partnership's assets, liabilities, and total equity are not affected by this transaction. Second, Tsang and Breck must agree if Davis is to become a partner. If they agree to accept Davis into the partnership, a new partnership is formed and a new contract with a new profit-and-loss-sharing agreement is prepared. If either Tsang or Breck refuse to accept Davis as a partner, then Davis still is able to keep Breck's sold share of partnership profit and loss. If the partnership is liquidated, Davis gets her share of partnership assets. However, Davis gets no voice in managing the company until she is admitted as a partner.

INVESTING ASSETS IN A PARTNERSHIP

Admitting a partner by an investment of assets is a *transaction between the new partner and the partnership*. The invested assets become partnership property. To illustrate, if Tsang (with a $52,000 interest) and Breck (with a $20,000 interest) agree to accept Davis as a partner in the Landing Zone with her investment of $28,000, the entry to record Davis's investment is:

2020				
Jan.	4	Cash	28,000	
		Cris Davis, Capital.................................		28,000
		To record admission of Davis by investment.		

After this entry is posted, both assets (cash) and equity (Cris Davis, Capital) increase by $28,000 as shown in the following schedule:

	Net Assets	Olivia Tsang, Capital	David Breck, Capital	Cris Davis, Capital	Total Equity
Balance *before* January 4 transaction...	$ 72,000	$52,000	$20,000	$ -0-	$ 72,000
January 4 transaction	+28,000	-0-	-0-	+28,000	+28,000
Balance *after* January 4 transaction	$100,000	$52,000	$20,000	$28,000	$100,000

Davis now has 28% equity in the net assets of the business, calculated as $28,000 divided by the total equity of $100,000 (= $52,000 + $20,000 + $28,000). However, she does not necessarily have a right to 28% of profit. Dividing profit and loss is a separate matter on which partners must agree and document formally in their partnership agreement.

BONUS TO OLD PARTNERS

When the current market value of a partnership is greater than the recorded amounts of equity, the partners usually require a new partner to pay a bonus (premium) for the privilege of joining. This situation exists when the market value of net assets exceeds their book value., which is often the case once a partnership has established customers and has a proven track record of profitable growth. To illustrate, let's say Tsang and Breck agree to accept Davis as a partner with a 25% interest in the Landing Zone, but they require Davis to invest $48,000. Recall that the partnership's accounting records show Tsang's equity in the business to be $52,000 and Breck's equity to be $20,000. Davis's equity is determined as follows:

Equities of existing partners ($52,000 + $20,000)	$ 72,000
Investment of new partner...	48,000
Total equity	$120,000
Equity of Davis (25% × $120,000)	$ 30,000

Although Davis invests $48,000, her equity in the recorded net assets of the partnership is only $30,000. The difference of $18,000 is called a bonus (or premium) and is allocated to the existing partners according to their profit/loss share ratio. Assume this to be 50:50. The entry to record this is:

2020				
Jan.	4	Cash	48,000	
		Cris Davis, Capital.................................		30,000
		Olivia Tsang, Capital.............................		9,000
		David Breck, Capital		9,000
		To record admission of Davis and bonus to old partners; $18,000 × 1/2 = $9,000.		

The effects of this transaction on the accounts are summarized as follows:

	Net Assets	Olivia Tsang, Capital	David Breck, Capital	Cris Davis, Capital	Total Equity
Balance *before* January 4 transaction...	$ 72,000	$52,000	$20,000	$ -0-	$ 72,000
January 4 transaction	+48,000	+9,000	+9,000	+30,000	+48,000
Balance *after* January 4 transaction.....	$120,000	$61,000	$29,000	$30,000	$120,000

BONUS TO NEW PARTNER

Existing partners can give a bonus (premium) to a new partner so that the new partner gets a larger equity than the amount invested. This usually occurs when additional cash is needed or the new partner has exceptional talents or business connections. To illustrate, let's say Tsang and Breck agree to accept Davis as a partner with a 25% interest in total equity, but they require Davis to invest only $18,000. Davis's equity is determined as:

Equities of existing partners ($52,000 + $20,000)	$72,000
Investment of new partner..	18,000
Total equity	$90,000
Equity of Davis (25% × $90,000)	$22,500

Davis receives a bonus of $4,500 (= $22,500 − $18,000). The entry to record Davis's investment is:

2020				
Jan.	4	Cash	18,000	
		Olivia Tsang, Capital	2,250	
		David Breck, Capital......................................	2,250	
		Cris Davis, Capital.................................		22,500
		To record Davis's admission and bonus; *$4,500 × 1/2 = $2,250.*		

The effect of this transaction on the accounts follows:

	Net Assets	Olivia Tsang, Capital	David Breck, Capital	Cris Davis, Capital	Total Equity
Balance *before* January 4 transaction...	$72,000	$52,000	$20,000	$ -0-	$72,000
January 4 transaction	+18,000	−2,250	−2,250	+22,500	+18,000
Balance *after* January 4 transaction.....	$90,000	$49,750	$17,750	$22,500	$90,000

Davis's bonus of $4,500 is contributed by the old partners in their profit-and-loss-sharing ratio. Davis's 25% equity doesn't necessarily entitle her to 25% of any profit or loss. This is a separate matter for agreement by the partners.

 **CHECKPOINT**

7. When a "bonus"' is given to a new partner being admitted, what is the effect on the existing partners' capital accounts?

Do Quick Study questions: QS 11-7, QS 11-8, QS 11-9, QS 11-10

Withdrawal of a Partner

There are generally two ways in which a partner withdraws from a partnership. First, the withdrawing partner can sell his or her interest to another person who pays for it in cash or other assets. For this, we debit the withdrawing partner's capital account and credit the new partner's capital account (as already described in our discussion on the purchase of partnership interests). The second case is when cash or other assets of the partnership are given to the withdrawing partner in settlement of his or her equity interest. This section explains the accounting for the second case.

To illustrate, let's assume that on October 31, 2020, Breck withdraws from the partnership of the Landing Zone. The three partners share profit and loss equally. The accounts show the following capital balances immediately prior to Breck's withdrawal:

	Olivia Tsang, Capital	David Breck, Capital	Cris Davis, Capital	Total Equity
Capital balances immediately *prior* to Breck's withdrawal	$84,000	$38,000	$38,000	$160,000

Accounting for the withdrawal depends on whether a bonus is paid or not. We describe three possibilities, summarized as follows:

1. NO BONUS

If Breck withdraws and receives cash of $38,000

Oct.	31	David Breck, Capital......................................	38,000	
		Cash		38,000

2. BONUS TO REMAINING PARTNERS

If Breck withdraws and receives cash of $34,000

Oct.	31	David Breck, Capital......................................	38,000	
		Cash		34,000
		Olivia Tsang, Capital...............................		2,000
		Cris Davis, Capital.................................		2,000

3. BONUS TO WITHDRAWING PARTNER

If Breck withdraws and receives cash of $40,000

Oct.	31	David Breck, Capital......................................	38,000	
		Olivia Tsang, Capital	1,000	
		Cris Davis, Capital	1,000	
		Cash		40,000

A withdrawing partner is sometimes willing to take less than the recorded value of his or her equity just to get out of the partnership or because the recorded values of some assets are overstated. When this occurs, the withdrawing partner in effect gives a bonus to remaining partners equal to the equity left behind as shown in the second situation above.

The third case shows a bonus to the withdrawing partner. This bonus might arise for two reasons:

- If the recorded book value of the equity of the partnership is understated, or

- If the remaining partners want to remove a partner, which may require giving assets of greater value than the withdrawing partner's recorded equity.

Death of a Partner

A partner's death dissolves a partnership if the partnership agreement does not provide otherwise. A deceased partner's estate is entitled to receive his or her equity based on provisions that are stated in the partnership contract. These provisions include methods for (1) closing of the books to determine profit or loss since the end of the previous period up to the date of death, and (2) determining current values for assets and liabilities. The remaining partners and the deceased partner's estate then must agree to a settlement of the deceased partner's equity. This can involve selling the equity to remaining partners or to an outsider, or it can involve withdrawing assets. The journal entries regarding the death of a partner are the same as those for the withdrawal of a partner.

DECISION MAKER

Answer—End of chapter

Lawyer

You are a lawyer hired by the two remaining partners of a three-member partnership. The third partner recently died. The three partners shared profit and loss in the ratio of their capital balances, which were equal. The partnership agreement says a deceased partner's estate is entitled to the "partner's percentage share of partnership assets." The estate argues it is entitled to one-third of the current value of the partnership's total assets. The remaining partners say the distribution should use the assets' book values, which are only 75% of current value. They also point to partnership liabilities, which equal 40% of the assets' book value, and 30% of current value. How would you resolve this situation?

CHECKPOINT

8. Partners Taylor and Swift have respective capital balances of $40,000 and $20,000. If Partner Taylor withdraws and receives cash from the partnership of $30,000, what is the journal entry?

Do Quick Study questions: QS 11-11, QS 11-12, QS 11-13

Liquidation of a Partnership

 Prepare entries for partnership liquidation.

Partnership liquidation is the process of closing down a business; it involves selling partnership assets, paying business debts, and distributing any remaining cash to owners. When a partnership is liquidated, its business is ended. Four steps are involved:

1. Non-cash assets are sold for cash and a gain or loss on liquidation is recorded.
2. Gain or loss on liquidation is allocated to partners using their profit-and-loss ratio.
3. Liabilities are paid.
4. Remaining cash is distributed to partners based on their capital balances.

Partnership liquidation often follows one of two different cases described next.

No Capital Deficiency

No capital deficiency means that all partners have credit balances in their capital accounts before final distribution of cash. To illustrate, let's assume Tsang, Breck, and Davis operate their partnership in the Landing Zone for several years, sharing profit and losses equally. The partners decide to liquidate on January 15, 2022. On that date, the books are closed, and profit is transferred to the partners' capital accounts. A summary of account balances immediately *prior* to liquidation is:

	Assets				= Liabilities +	Equity		
	Cash	Sporting Facilities	Accum. Deprec. Sporting Facilities	Land	Accounts Payable	Olivia Tsang, Capital	David Breck, Capital	Cris Davis, Capital
Account balances immediately *prior* to liquidation..................	$168,000	$33,000	$18,000	$25,000	$20,000	$70,000	$66,000	$52,000

Following the four-step liquidation process, we first record the sale of the non-cash assets that occurred on January 15 for cash of $46,000. The entry is:

2022				
Jan.	15	Cash	46,000	
		Accumulated Depreciation,		
		Sporting Facilities..	18,000	
		Sporting Facilities		33,000
		Land		25,000
		Gain From Liquidation.............................		6,000
		Sold non-cash assets at a gain.		

Second, we record the allocation of the resulting gain from liquidation against the partners' capital accounts:

Jan.	15	Gain From Liquidation	6,000	
		Olivia Tsang, Capital..............................		2,000
		David Breck, Capital...............................		2,000
		Cris Davis, Capital.................................		2,000
		To allocate liquidation gain to partners.		

The balances in the accounts after Steps 1 and 2 are recorded and summarized in Exhibit 11.10.

Step 3 in the liquidation process requires that liabilities be paid. Because creditors have claim to partnership assets before the partners do, they are paid first. The entry to record payment to the creditors is:

Jan.	15	Accounts Payable	20,000	
		Cash..		20,000
		To pay claims of creditors.		

Exhibit 11.10 shows the account balances after Step 3, payment of creditors.

EXHIBIT 11.10

Liquidation of a Partnership—No Capital Deficiency

	Assets				= Liabilities +	Equity		
	Cash	Sporting Facilities	Accum. Deprec., Sporting Facilities	Land	Accounts Payable	Olivia Tsang, Capital	David Breck, Capital	Cris Davis, Capital
Account balances immediately *prior* to liquidation	$168,000	$33,000	$18,000	$25,000	$20,000	$70,000	$66,000	$52,000
1. & 2. Sale of non-cash assets for a gain of $6,000	+46,000	−33,000	−18,000	−25,000		+2,000	+2,000	+2,000
Balance	$214,000	$ -0-	$ -0-	$ -0-	$20,000	$72,000	$68,000	$54,000
3. Payment of Accounts Payable	−20,000				−20,000			
Balance	$194,000	$ -0-	$ -0-	$ -0-	$ -0-	$72,000	$68,000	$54,000
4. Distribution of cash to partners	−194,000					−72,000	−68,000	−54,000
Final balance	$ -0-	$ -0-	$ -0-	$ -0-	$ -0-	$ -0-	$ -0-	$ -0-

Step 4 in the liquidation process is to *divide the remaining cash of $194,000 among the partners according to their capital account balances* as follows:

Jan.	15	Olivia Tsang, Capital	72,000	
		David Breck, Capital	68,000	
		Cris Davis, Capital	54,000	
		Cash		194,000
		To distribute remaining cash to partners.		

The account balances after distribution of cash to the partners are summarized in Exhibit 11.10.

Capital Deficiency

Capital deficiency means that at least one partner has a debit balance in his or her capital account before the final distribution of cash. This can arise from liquidation losses, excessive withdrawals before liquidation, or recurring losses in prior periods.

Assume that the partners of the Landing Zone decide to liquidate. Davis's capital account shows a deficiency of $3,000 immediately prior to the final distribution of cash. Davis's capital deficiency means that she owes the partnership $3,000. The final distribution of cash depends on whether the deficient partner can pay the deficiency or not.

PARTNER PAYS DEFICIENCY

Davis should pay $3,000 into the partnership to cover the deficiency. If Davis is willing and able to pay, the partners' capital balances after the payment are:

	Cash	Olivia Tsang, Capital	David Breck, Capital	Cris Davis, Capital
Account balances immediately *prior* to distribution of cash to partners	$24,000	$19,000	$8,000	$ (3,000)
Davis pays deficiency	+3,000			+3,000
Balance	$27,000	$19,000	$8,000	$ -0-

The entry to record the final cash distributions to partners is:

Jan.	15	Olivia Tsang, Capital	19,000	
		David Breck, Capital.....................................	8,000	
		Cash...		27,000
		To distribute remaining cash to partners.		

PARTNER CANNOT PAY DEFICIENCY

Because of unlimited liability in a partnership, a partner's unpaid deficiency is absorbed by the remaining partners who have credit balances in their partnership capital. If Davis is unable to pay the $3,000 deficiency, it is shared by Tsang and Breck based on their profit-and-loss-sharing ratio. Since they share equally, this is recorded as:

Jan.	15	Olivia Tsang, Capital	1,500	
		David Breck, Capital.....................................	1,500	
		Cris Davis, Capital.................................		3,000
		To transfer Davis's deficiency to Tsang and Breck.		

After Davis's deficiency is absorbed by Tsang and Breck, the capital account balances of the partners are:

	Cash	Olivia Tsang, Capital	David Breck, Capital	Cris Davis, Capital
Account balances immediately *prior* to distribution of cash to partners............................	$24,000	$19,000	$8,000	$(3,000)
Transfer Davis's deficiency to Tsang and Breck		−1,500	−1,500	+3,000
Balance	$24,000	$17,500	$6,500	$ -0-

The entry to record the final cash distributions to the partners is:

Jan.	15	Olivia Tsang, Capital	17,500	
		David Breck, Capital.....................................	6,500	
		Cash...		24,000
		To distribute remaining cash to partners.		

The inability of Davis to cover her deficiency does not relieve her of the liability. If she becomes able to pay at some future date, Tsang and Breck can each collect $1,500 from her. If Davis does not comply, then Tsang and Breck may have to resort to legal action.

The sharing of an insolvent partner's deficit by the remaining partners in their original profit-and-loss-sharing ratio is generally regarded as equitable.

 **CHECKPOINT**

9. Assume that assets, liabilities, and equity prior to liquidation were $50,000, $10,000, and $40,000. Calculate total assets, liabilities, and equity after the payment of the liabilities.

Do Quick Study questions: QS 11-14, QS 11-15

Refer to the Critical Thinking Challenge question at the beginning of the chapter. Compare your answer to that suggested on Connect.

IFRS AND ASPE—THE DIFFERENCES

Difference	International Financial Reporting Standards (IFRS)	Accounting Standards for Private Enterprises (ASPE)
None to note within the scope of this course.		

A Look Ahead

Chapter 12 extends our discussion to the corporate form of organization. We describe the accounting and reporting for stock issuances, dividends, and other equity transactions.

Summary

LO1 Identify characteristics of partnerships. A partnership is a voluntary association between the partners that is based on a contract. The life of a partnership is limited by agreement or by the death or incapacity of a partner. Normally, each partner can act as an agent of the other partners and commit the partnership to any contract within the apparent scope of its business. All partners in a general partnership are personally liable for all the debts of the partnership. Limited partnerships include one or more general partners plus one or more (limited) partners whose liabilities are limited to the amounts of their investments in the partnership. The risk of becoming a partner results in part from the fact that partnership characteristics include mutual agency and unlimited liability.

LO2 Prepare entries when forming a partnership. The initial investment of partnership assets is recorded by debiting the assets contributed at the fair market value and crediting the partners' capital accounts.

LO3 Allocate and record profit and loss among partners. A partnership's profits or losses are allocated to the partners according to the terms of the partnership agreement. The agreement may specify that each partner will receive a given fraction, or that the allocation of profits and losses will reflect salary allowances and/or interest allowances. When salary and/or interest allowances are granted, the residual profit or loss usually is allocated equally or on a stated fractional basis.

LO4 Account for the admission and withdrawal of a partner. When a new partner buys a partnership interest directly from one or more of the existing partners, the amount of cash paid from one partner to another does not affect the total recorded equity of the partnership. The recorded equity of the selling partner(s) is simply transferred to the capital account of the new partner. Alternatively, a new partner may purchase an equity interest in the partnership by investing additional assets in the partnership. When this occurs, part of the new partner's investment may be credited as a bonus to the capital accounts of the existing partners. Also, to gain the participation of the new partner, the existing partners may give the new partner a bonus whereby portions of the existing partners' capital balances are transferred to the new partner's capital account.

LO5 Prepare entries for partnership liquidation. When a partnership is liquidated, losses and gains from selling the partnership assets are allocated to the partners according to the partnership profit-and-loss-sharing ratio. If a partner's capital account has a deficit balance that the partner cannot pay, the other partners must share the deficit in their relative profit-and-loss-sharing ratio.

Guidance Answer to DECISION MAKER

Lawyer

The partnership agreement apparently fails to mention liabilities or use the term *net assets*. Still, to give the estate one-third of total assets is not fair to the remaining partners. This is because if the partner had lived and the partners had decided to liquidate, the liabilities would have had to be paid first. Also, a settlement based on the re-

corded equity of the deceased partner would fail to recognize excess of current value over book value. These value increases would be realized if the partnership were liquidated. A fair settlement would be a payment to the estate for the balance of the deceased partner's equity based on the *current value of net assets*.

Guidance Answers to CHECKPOINT

1. A summary of the characteristics of a general partnership is as follows:

Partnership	A contract exists between the partners according to the partnership agreement and, in its absence, profits and losses are shared equally.
Limited life	The life of a partnership is limited subject to terms in the partnership contract.
Taxation	A partnership is not subject to tax. Taxation occurs upon distribution of profit to its owners.
Co-ownership of property	Partnership assets are owned jointly by the partners.
Mutual agency	Each partner is an authorized agent of the partnership.
Unlimited liability	Partners can be called on to pay the debts of the partnership.

2. A limited partnership has at least one general partner who assumes management duties and unlimited liability for the debts of the partnership; the limited partners have no personal liability beyond the amounts they invest in the partnership. In a limited liability partnership, liability is limited to the partner(s) responsible for any malpractice or negligence claims; innocent partners are not liable. However, all partners in a limited liability partnership are personally liable for other partnership debts.

3. $50,000 + $75,000 + ($180,000 − $100,000) = $205,000

4.

	Ben	Jerry	Total	
Profit			$40,000	
Interest allowance	$ 7,000	$ 3,500	−10,500	must be equal
Remaining balance...			**$29,500**	
Balance allocated equally	14,750	14,750	29,500	
Remaining balance ...			$ -0-	
Shares of partners....	**$21,750**	**$18,250**	**$40,000**	

5. 1/5, 2/5, 2/5

6. 20%, 40%, 40%

7. A bonus to a new partner being admitted causes the existing partners' capital accounts to decrease.

8.

Partner Taylor	40,000	
Partner Swift		10,000
Cash		30,000

9. Assets = $50,000 − $10,000 = $40,000; Liabilities = $10,000 − $10,000 = $0; Equity = $40,000.

DEMONSTRATION PROBLEM

Part 1

On a work sheet similar to that shown below, include eight columns to show the effects of the following on the partners' capital accounts over a four-year period.

Date	Transaction	Ries, Capital	Bax, Capital	Royce, Capital	Murdock, Capital	Elway, Capital	Total Equity

Apr. 13/17	Ries, Bax, and Royce create RB&R Co., an architect design firm focusing on high-end commercial real estate projects. Ries and Bax each invest $10,000 while Royce invests $24,000. They agree that each will get a 10% interest allowance on each partner's beginning-of-year capital balance. In addition, Ries and Bax are to receive $5,000 salary allowances. The remainder of the profit is to be divided evenly.
Dec. 31/17	The partnership's profit for the year is $39,900, and withdrawals at year-end are Ries, $5,000; Bax, $12,500; and Royce, $11,000.
Jan. 1/18	Ries sells her interest to Murdock for $20,000, who is accepted by Bax and Royce as a partner in the new BR&M Co. The profits are to be shared equally after Bax and Royce each receive $25,000 salaries.
Dec. 31/18	The partnership's profit for the year is $35,000, and their withdrawals are Bax, $2,500; and Royce, $2,000.
Jan. 1/19	Elway is admitted as a partner after investing $60,000 cash in the new Elway & Associates partnership. Elway is given a 60% interest in capital after the other partners transfer $9,180 to his account from each of theirs. A 20% interest allowance (on the beginning-of-year capital balances) will be used in sharing profits, but there will be no salaries. Elway will get 40% of the remainder, and the other three partners will each get 20%. (**Note:** The interest allowance is to be calculated on each partner's capital balance immediately after the admission of Elway.)
Dec. 31/19	Elway & Associates earns $127,600 for the year, and year-end withdrawals are Bax, $25,000; Royce, $27,000; Murdock, $15,000; and Elway, $40,000.
Jan. 1/20	Elway buys out Bax and Royce for the balances of their capital accounts, paying them $92,000 cash from personal funds. Murdock and Elway will share future profits on a 1:9 ratio.
Feb. 29/20	The partnership has earned $10,000 of profit since the beginning of the year. Murdock retires and receives partnership cash equal to her capital balance. Elway takes possession of the partnership assets in his own name, and the business is dissolved.

Part 2

Journalize the transactions affecting the partnership for the year ended December 31, 2018.

Analysis Component:

Why would the partnership agreement allocate different salary allowances to each of Bax, Royce, and Murdock ($25,000, $25,000, and $0, respectively)?

Planning the Solution

- Evaluate each transaction's effects on the capital accounts of the partners.
- Each time a new partner is admitted or a partner withdraws, allocate any bonus based on the profit-or-loss-sharing agreement.
- Each time a new partner is admitted or a partner withdraws, allocate subsequent profits or losses in accordance with the new partnership agreement.
- Prepare the journal entries to record the transactions for the year 2018.
- Answer the analysis question.

Solution

Part 1

Date	Event	Ries, Capital	Bax, Capital	Royce, Capital	Murdock, Capital	Elway, Capital	Total Equity
Apr. 13/17	Investment	$ 10,000	$10,000	$24,000			$ 44,000
Dec. 31/17	$39,900 profit allocation:						39,900
	– 10% interest	1,000	1,000	2,400			
	– Salary allowance	5,000	5,000	-0-			
	– $25,500 remainder equally	8,500	8,500	8,500			
	Withdrawals:	(5,000)	(12,500)	(11,000)			(28,500)
	Balance:	$ 19,500	$12,000	$23,900			$ 55,400
Jan. 1/17	Ries sells to Murdock	(19,500)			$19,500		-0-
Dec. 31/17	$35,000 profit allocation:						35,000
	– Salary allowance		25,000	25,000	-0-		
	– ($15,000) remainder equally		(5,000)	(5,000)	(5,000)		
	Withdrawals:		(2,500)	(2,000)	-0-		(4,500)
	Balance:		$29,500	$41,900	$14,500		$ 85,900
Jan. 1/19	Elway admitted as partner		(9,180)	(9,180)	(9,180)	$ 87,540	60,000
Dec. 31/19	$127,600 profit allocation:						127,600
	– 20% interest allowance		4,064	6,544	1,064	17,508	
	– Remainder 40% Elway; 20% others		19,684	19,684	19,684	39,368	
	Withdrawals:		(25,000)	(27,000)	(15,000)	(40,000)	(107,000)
	Balance:		$19,068	$31,948	$11,068	$104,416	$166,500
Jan. 1/20	Elway buys out Bax and Royce		(19,068)	(31,948)		51,016	-0-
	Balance:		$ -0-	$ -0-	$11,068	$155,432	$166,500
Feb. 29/20	$10,000 profit allocation:				1,000	9,000	10,000
	Adjusted balance:				$12,068	$164,432	$176,500
	Murdock retires:				(12,068)	-0-	(12,068)
	Adjusted balance:				$ -0-	$164,432	$164,432
	Partnership dissolved					(164,432)	(164,432)
	Final balance					$ -0-	$ -0-

Part 2

Analysis Component:

The partnership agreement allocates different salary allowances to each of the partners likely because each partner's direct involvement in the operation of the partnership varies.

	2018			
Jan.	1	Ries, Capital...	19,500	
		Murdock, Capital....................................		19,500
		To record entrance of Murdock in place of Ries.		
Dec.	31	Bax, Withdrawals	2,500	
		Royce, Withdrawals	2,000	
		Cash		4,500
		To record the withdrawal of cash by each partner.		
Dec.	31	Bax, Capital...	2,500	
		Royce, Capital..	2,000	
		Bax, Withdrawals		2,500
		Royce, Withdrawals...............................		2,000
		To close partners' withdrawal accounts to their capital.		
Dec.	31	Income Summary	35,000	
		Murdock, Capital	5,000	
		Bax, Capital...		20,000
		Royce, Capital		20,000
		To close Income Summary to partners' capital.		

Glossary

General partner A partner who assumes unlimited liability for the debts of the partnership; also, the general partner in a limited partnership is responsible for its management.

General partnership A partnership in which all partners have mutual agency and unlimited liability for partnership debts.

Interest allowances Provide a specified return based on each partner's level of invested capital. The allowance represents a distribution of capital and does not involve actual distribution of cash.

Limited liability partnership A partnership in which each partner is not personally liable for malpractice or negligence claims unless the partner was responsible for providing the service that resulted in the claim.

Limited partners Partners who have no personal liability for debts of the partnership beyond the amounts they have invested in the partnership.

Limited partnership A partnership that has two classes of partners: limited partners and general partners.

Mutual agency The legal relationship among the partners whereby each partner is an agent of the partnership and

is able to bind the partnership to contracts within the apparent scope of the partnership's business.

Partnership An unincorporated association of two or more persons to pursue a business for profit as co-owners.

Partnership contract The agreement between partners that sets forth the terms under which the affairs of the partnership will be conducted.

Partnership liquidation The dissolution of a business partnership by (1) selling non-cash assets for cash, (2) allocating the gain or loss according to partners' profit-and-loss ratio, (3) paying liabilities, and (4) distributing remaining cash to partners based on capital balances.

Salary allowances Partnership allocation of profit that is based on a specified dollar value, compensating partners for service contributions via allocation of profit to the partners' capital accounts.

Unlimited liability The legal relationship among general partners that makes each of them responsible for paying all the debts of the partnership if the other partners are unable to pay their shares.

Concept Review Questions

1. Amie and Lacey are partners. Lacey dies, and her son claims the right to take his mother's place in the partnership. Does he have this right? Why?

2. If a partnership contract does not state the period of time over which the partnership is to exist, when does the partnership end?

3. As applied to a partnership, what does the term *mutual agency* mean?

4. Can partners limit the right of a partner to commit their partnership to contracts? Would the agreement be binding (a) on the partners, and (b) on outsiders?

5. What does the term *unlimited liability* mean when it is applied to members of a partnership?

6. How does a general partnership differ from a limited partnership?

7. Leung, Lidder, and Lang have shared an equal stake as partners in a sports bar for the past three years. The partnership is being dissolved, as Leung is moving to England and leaving the firm. Lidder and Lang plan to carry on the business. In the final settlement, Leung places a $75,000 salary claim against the partnership. He contends that he has a claim for a salary of $25,000 for each year because he devoted all of his time for three years to the affairs of the partnership. Is his claim valid? Why?

8. The partnership agreement of lawyers Jenny Nelmida and Fei Abella provides for a two-thirds/one-third sharing of profit but says nothing about losses. The first year of partnership operations resulted in a loss and Nelmida argues that the loss should be shared equally because the partnership agreement said nothing about sharing losses. What do you think?

9. If the partners in Bloom Partnership, a floral design shop, want the financial statements to show the procedures used to allocate the partnership profit among the partners, on what financial statement should the allocation appear?

10. After all partnership assets are converted to cash and all liabilities have been paid, the remaining cash should equal the sum of the balances of the partners' capital accounts. Why?

11. Kay, Kat, and Kim are triplets who own a dance studio. In a liquidation, Kay's share of partnership losses exceeds her capital account balance. She is unable to meet the deficit from her personal assets, and the excess losses are shared by her partners. Does this relieve Kay of liability?

12. A partner withdraws from a partnership and receives assets of greater value than the book value of his equity. Should the remaining partners share the resulting reduction in their equities in the ratio of their relative capital balances or in their profit-and-loss-sharing ratio?

13. In the chapter opening vignette featuring Kicking Horse Coffee, Elana advises that partners avoid a 50/50 partnership split and she strongly suggests obtaining legal counsel in drafting partnership agreements. What are the advantages and disadvantages of a 50/50 split and what benefits can partnerships gain from obtaining legal counsel prior to forming the business?

Quick Study

QS 11-1 Partnership liability LO1

Bowen and Campbell are partners in operating a store. Without consulting Bowen, Campbell enters into a contract for the purchase of merchandise for the store. Bowen contends that he did not authorize the order and refuses to take delivery. The vendor sues the partners for the contract price of the merchandise. Will the partnership have to pay? Why? Does your answer differ if Bowen and Campbell are partners in a public accounting firm?

QS 11-2 Liability in limited partnerships LO1

Stanley organized a limited partnership and is the only general partner. Hillier invested $20,000 in the partnership and was admitted as a limited partner with the understanding that he would receive 10% of the profits. After two unprofitable years, the partnership ceased doing business. At that point, partnership liabilities were $85,000 larger than partnership assets. How much money can the creditors of the partnership obtain from the personal assets of Hillier in satisfaction of the unpaid partnership debts?

QS 11-3 Journal entry when forming a partnership LO2

Len Peters and Beau Silver form a partnership to operate a catering business, called A Catered Affair. Peters invests $20,000 cash and Silver invests $30,000 cash on March 1, 2017. Prepare the journal entry to record the establishment of the partnership.

QS 11-4 Partnership profit allocation LO3

Bill Ace and Dennis Bud are partners in an urban restaurant called Salt. Profit for the year ended March 31, 2017, is $120,000.

    a. How much profit should be allocated to each partner assuming there is no partnership agreement?

    b. Prepare the entry to allocate the profit.

    c. Prepare the entry to allocate the $120,000 assuming it is a loss.

QS 11-5 Allocation of profit LO3

Lisa Montgomery and Joel Chalmers established a coffee bean distribution business. Their partnership shared profits and losses based on an agreement that gave Lisa a salary allowance of $45,000 and Joel $10,000 with any unallocated profit (loss) shared equally. Prepare the entry to close the Income Summary account at December 31, 2017, assuming a credit balance of $48,000.

QS 11-6 Allocation of loss LO3

Jenn Smith and Mike Yang have a small business consulting partnership. They share profits and losses as detailed in their partnership agreement that gave Jenn a salary allowance of $115,000 and Mike $90,000 with any unallocated profit (loss) shared 3:2. Prepare the entry to close the Income Summary account at December 31, 2017, assuming a debit balance of $80,000.

QS 11-7 Admission of a partner LO4

Ramos and Bailey have a frozen yogurt shop in Victoria, BC. They are equal partners, with $30,000 in each of their partnership capital accounts. Bailey's sister Kate is admitted to the partnership on October 1, 2017, after paying $30,000 to the partnership for a one-third interest. Prepare the entry to show Kate's admission to the partnership.

QS 11-8 Admission of a partner LO4

Suppose on March 12, 2017, Kate agrees to pay Ramos and Bailey $12,000 each for a one-third interest in the existing Ramos–Bailey partnership. At the time Kate is admitted, each partner has a $30,000 capital balance. Prepare the journal entry to record Kate's purchase of the partners' interest. *Note: Kate is paying Ramos and Bailey; she is not paying the partnership.*

QS 11-9 Admission of a partner—bonus to new partner LO4

On June 17, 2017, Bishop agrees to invest $30,000 into an online custom T-shirt print shop business for a 40% interest in total partnership equity. At the time Bishop is admitted, the existing partners, Pollard and Mission, each have a $30,000 capital balance. Prepare the entry on June 17 to record admission to the partnership. Any bonus is to be shared equally by Pollard and Mission.

QS 11-10 Admission of a partner—bonus to old partners LO4

On April 21, 2017, Wilson agrees to invest $30,000 into Quest, a land development partnership in Niagara-on-the-Lake for a 20% interest in total partnership equity. At the time Wilson is admitted, the existing partners, Beacon and Metcalf, each have a $30,000 capital balance. Prepare the entry on April 21 to record Wilson's admission to the partnership. Any bonus is to be shared equally by Beacon and Metcalf.

QS 11-11 Partner withdrawal LO4

Hector, Wilson, and Stuart are partners in What's Your Beef?, a local vegan burger chain, with capital balances of $25,000, $40,000, and $35,000, respectively. Based on their partnership agreement, they share profit and losses equally. Stuart is retiring and has agreed to accept $35,000 cash for his share of the partnership. Record Stuart's withdrawal on November 23, 2017.

QS 11-12 Partner withdrawal—bonus to remaining partners LO4

Oliver, Peter, and Wendell are partners in NewTech Company an R&D firm specializing in cloud storage. Their capital balances are $30,000, $22,000, and $15,000, respectively, on November 23, 2017. They share profit and losses in the ratio of 3:2:1. Peter retires on November 23, 2017, and has agreed to accept $15,000 for his share of the partnership. Record Peter's retirement and calculate the resulting balances in the capital accounts.

QS 11-13 Partner withdrawal—bonus to leaving partner LO4

Linda, Sue, and Darlene are partners in Designs Unlimited. Their capital balances are $150,000, $140,000, and $250,000 respectively on March 15, 2017. They share profit and losses in the ratio of 2:2:2. Darlene retires on March 15, 2017, and has agreed to accept $300,000 for her share of the partnership. Record Darlene's retirement and calculate the resulting balances in the capital accounts.

QS 11-14 Partnership liquidation—gain on sale of equipment LO5 eXcel

Sam, Andrew, and Mary were partners in Gem Skateboard Company. The partners shared profits and losses 3:2:3, respectively. On April 1, 2017, the partnership showed the following account balances just prior to liquidation:

	Cash	Equipment	Accum. Deprec. Equipment	Sam, Capital	Andrew, Capital	Mary, Capital
Account balances immediately *prior* to liquidation...	$32,000	$151,000	$36,000	$65,000	$48,000	$34,000

Equipment was sold for $175,000. Prepare the journal entry to record the final distribution of cash.

QS 11-15 Partnership liquidation—loss on sale of equipment LO5 eXcel

Assume the same information as in QS 11-14 except that the Equipment was sold for $85,000 on April 1, 2017. Prepare the journal entry to record the final distribution of cash.

Exercises

Exercise 11-1 Forms of organization LO1

For each scenario below, recommend a form of business organization: sole proprietorship, partnership, or corporation. Along with each recommendation, explain how business profits would be taxed if the form of organization recommended were adopted by the owners. Also list several advantages that the owners would enjoy from the form of business organization that you recommend.

1. Keith, Scott, and Brian are new university graduates in computer science. They are thinking of starting an app design firm. They all have university debt and currently do not own any of the computer equipment that they will need to get the company started.

2. Dr. Marble and Dr. Sampson are new graduates from medical residency programs. They are both family practice physicians and would like to open a clinic in an underserved rural area. Although neither has any funds to bring to the new venture, a banker has expressed interest in making a loan to provide start-up funds for the practice.

3. Matthew has been out of school for about five years and has become quite knowledgeable about commercial real estate development. Matthew would like to organize a company that buys and sells commercial properties in Calgary. Matthew feels that he has the expertise to manage the company but needs funds to invest in the commercial property.

Exercise 11-2 Journalizing partnership entries LO2,3

CHECK FIGURES: 1. Share of profit: Williams: $116,000; Xie: $44,000

On February 1, 2017, Tessa Williams and Audrey Xie formed a partnership in Ontario. Williams contributed $80,000 cash and Xie econtributed land valued at $120,000 and a small building valued at $180,000. Also, the partnership assumed responsibility for Xie's $130,000 long-term note payable associated with the land and building. The partners agreed to share profit or loss as follows: Williams is to receive an annual salary allowance of $90,000, both are to receive an annual interest allowance of 20% of their original capital investments, and any remaining profit or loss is to be shared equally. On November 20, 2017, Williams withdrew cash of $60,000 and Xie withdrew $45,000. After the adjusting entries and the closing entries to the revenue and expense accounts, the Income Summary account had a credit balance of $160,000.

Required
1. Present general journal entries to record the initial capital investments of the partners, their cash withdrawals, and the December 31 closing of the Income Summary and withdrawals accounts.

2. Determine the balances of the partners' capital accounts as of the end of 2017.

Exercise 11-3 Profit allocation in a partnership LO3 eXcel

CHECK FIGURES: c. Dallas: $229,500; Weiss: $164,500

Dallas and Weiss formed a partnership to manage rental properties, by investing $115,000 and $135,000, respectively. During its first year, the partnership recorded profit of $394,000.

Required Prepare calculations showing how the profit should be allocated to the partners under each of the following plans for sharing profit and losses:

a. The partners failed to agree on a method of sharing profit.

b. The partners agreed to share profits and losses in proportion to their initial investments.

c. The partners agreed to share profit by allowing a $140,000 per year salary allowance to Dallas, a $70,000 per year salary allowance to Weiss, 25% interest on their initial investments, and sharing the balance equally.

Exercise 11-4 Profit allocation in a partnership LO3

CHECK FIGURES: 1. Jensen: $255,800; Stafford: $164,200; 2. Jensen: $(53,200); Stafford: $(41,800)

Jensen and Stafford began a partnership to start a hardwood flooring installation business, by investing $160,000 and $200,000, respectively. They agreed to share profits/(losses) by providing yearly salary allowances of $150,000 to Jensen and $75,000 to Stafford, 20% interest allowances on their investments, and sharing the balance 3:2.

Required

1. Determine each partner's share if the first-year profit was $420,000.

2. Independent of (1), determine each partner's share if the first-year loss was $95,000.

Exercise 11-5 **Profit allocation** LO3 eXcel

CHECK FIGURES: 1. Share of profit: Liam: $126,750; Katano: $(96,750)

Liam and Katano formed a partnership to open a sushi restaurant by investing $95,000 and $105,000 respectively. They agreed to share profit based on an allocation to Liam of an annual salary allowance of $150,000, interest allowance to both Liam and Katano equal to 15% of their beginning-of-year capital balance, and any balance based on a 1:3 ratio respectively. At the end of their first year, December 31, 2017, the Income Summary had a credit balance of $30,000. Liam withdrew $7,000 during the year and Katano $24,000.

Required

1. Prepare the entry to close the Income Summary on December 31, 2017.

2. Calculate the balance in each partner's capital account at the end of their first year.

Exercise 11-6 **Profit allocation** LO3

Debra and Glen are partners who agree that Debra will receive a $100,000 salary allowance after which remaining profit or losses will be shared equally in their flower shop. If Glen's capital account is credited $8,000 as his share of the profit (loss) in a given period, how much profit (loss) did the partnership earn?

Exercise 11-7 **Profit allocation, statement of changes in equity, balance sheet** LO3

CHECK FIGURES: 1. Share of profit: To Williams: $172,800; To Adams: $205,200; 3. Total assets = $449,000

Keith Williams and Brian Adams were students when they formed a partnership several years ago for a part-time business called Music Works. Adjusted trial balance information for the year ended December 31, 2017, appears below.

Account	Balance*	Account	Balance*
Accounts payable	$ 9,500	Keith Williams, capital**	$ 28,300
Accumulated depreciation	75,000	Keith Williams, withdrawals	50,000
Brian Adams, capital**	22,000	Note payable, due May 2019***	120,000
Brian Adams, withdrawals	60,000	Office supplies	16,000
Cash	208,000	Revenues	480,000
Equipment	300,000	Utilities payable	1,200
Expenses	102,000		

  *Assume all account balances are normal.
 **The partners made no investments during the year.
***$40,000 of the note payable is due in May 2018.

Required

1. Prepare calculations that show how the profit should be allocated to the partners assuming the partnership agreement states that profit/(losses) are to be shared by allowing a $90,000 per year salary allowance to Williams, a $150,000 per year salary allowance to Adams, and the remainder on a 3:2 ratio.

2. Prepare the journal entry to close the Income Summary account to the partners' capital accounts.

3. Prepare a statement of changes in equity and a classified balance sheet.

Analysis Component: Why might the partners' capital accounts be so small relative to the amount of the withdrawals made?

Exercise 11-8 **Admission of a new partner** LO4

CHECK FIGURES: b. Cr Reynolds, Capital: $8,000; c. Dr Reynolds, Capital: $16,000

Talent, a local HR consulting firm, has total partners' equity of $760,000, which is made up of Hall, Capital, $600,000, and Reynolds, Capital, $160,000. The partners share profit/(losses) in a ratio of 75% to Hall and 25% to Reynolds. On July 1, Morris is admitted to the partnership and given a 20% interest in equity.

Required Prepare the journal entry to record the admission of Morris under each of the following unrelated assumptions, in which Morris invests cash of:

    a. $190,000

    b. $230,000

    c. $110,000

Exercise 11-9 **Admission of a new partner** LO4

Keri & Nick Consulting's partners' equity accounts reflected the following balances on August 31, 2017:

Keri Lee, Capital..	$ 50,000
Nick Kalpakian, Capital	195,000

Lee and Kalpakian share profit/losses in a 2:3 ratio respectively. On September 1, 2017, Liam Court is admitted to the partnership with a cash investment of $105,000.

Required Prepare the journal entry to record the admission of Liam under each of the following unrelated assumptions, where he is given:

    a. A 30% interest in equity

    b. A 20% interest in equity

    c. A 50% interest in equity

Exercise 11-10 **Sale of a partnership interest** LO4

The partners in the Majesty partnership have agreed that partner Prince may sell his $140,000 equity in the partnership to Queen, for which Queen will pay Prince $110,000. Present the partnership's journal entry to record the sale on April 30.

Exercise 11-11 **Retirement of a partner** LO4

CHECK FIGURES: b. Dr Holt, Capital: $3,750; c. Cr Holt, Capital: $1,875

Barth, Holt, and Tran have been partners of a ski, snowboard, and mountain bike shop in Whistler, BC, called Storm. Based on the partnership agreement, they share profit and losses in a 6:2:2 ratio. On November 30, the date Tran retires from the partnership, the equities of the partners are Barth, $300,000; Holt, $195,000; and Tran, $75,000. Present general journal entries to record Tran's retirement under each of the following unrelated assumptions:

    a. Tran is paid $75,000 in partnership cash for his equity.

    b. Tran is paid $90,000 in partnership cash for his equity.

    c. Tran is paid $67,500 in partnership cash for his equity.

Exercise 11-12 **Retirement of a partner** LO4

Brenda Roberts, Lacy Peters, and Aarin MacDonald are partners in RPM Dance Studios. They share profit and losses in a 40:40:20 ratio. Aarin retires from the partnership on October 14, 2017, and receives $80,000 cash plus a car with a book value of $40,000 (original cost was $84,000).

Required For each of the following unrelated situations, present the journal entry to record Aarin's retirement assuming the equities of the partnership on October 14 are:

a. Roberts, $300,000; Peters, $400,000; MacDonald, $120,000

b. Roberts, $100,000; Peters, $120,000; MacDonald; $160,000

c. Roberts, $130,000; Peters, $160,000; MacDonald; $60,000

Exercise 11-13 **Liquidation of a partnership** LO5 e**X**cel

David Wallace, Olena Dunn, and Danny Lin were partners in a commercial architect firm and showed the following account balances as of December 31, 2017:

	Cash	Equipment	Accum. Deprec. Equipment	Accounts Payable	Notes Payable	David Wallace, Capital	Olena Dunn, Capital	Danny Lin, Capital
Account balances December 31, 2017.............	$13,000	$152,000	$89,000	$7,000	$12,000	$31,000	$14,000	$12,000

Due to several unprofitable periods, the partners decided to liquidate the partnership. The equipment was sold for $56,000 on January 1, 2018. The partners share any profit (loss) in the ratio of 2:1:1 for Wallace, Dunn, and Lin respectively.

Required Prepare the liquidation entries (sale of equipment, allocation of gain/loss, payment of creditors, final distribution of cash).

Exercise 11-14 **Liquidation of a partnership** LO5 e**X**cel

CHECK FIGURE: Dr. Martha Wheaton, Capital: $380,000

Martha Wheaton, Bess Chen, and Sam Smith were partners in an urban Calgary tea shop called Wake and showed the following account balances as of December 31, 2017:

	Cash	Building	Accum. Deprec. Building	Land	Accounts Payable	Martha Wheaton, Capital	Bess Chen, Capital	Sam Smith, Capital
Account balances December 31, 2017.........	$184,000	$824,000	$480,000	$208,000	$128,000	$316,000	$(52,000)	$344,000

Due to difficulties, the partners decided to liquidate the partnership. The land and building were sold for $680,000 on January 1, 2018. The partners share any profit (loss) in the ratio of 2:1:1 for Wheaton, Chen, and Smtih respectively.

Required Prepare the entry to distribute the remaining cash to the partners assuming any deficiencies are paid by the partners.

Exercise 11-15 **Liquidation of a partnership** L05 e**X**cel

CHECK FIGURE: Dr. Martha Wheaton, Capital: $366,667

Assume the same information as in Exercise 11-14 except that capital deficiencies at liquidation are absorbed by the remaining partners in Wake according to their profit (loss) ratio.

Required Prepare the entry to distribute the remaining cash to the partners. Round calculations to the nearest whole dollar.

Exercise 11-16 **Liquidation of a partnership** L05

CHECK FIGURE: 3b. Dr Sophia, Capital: $10,200

Toast, a Belleville Ontario, restaurant, began with investments by the partners as follows: Lea, $231,200; Eva, $177,200; and Sophia, $191,600. The first year of operations did not go well, and the partners finally decided to liquidate the partnership, sharing all losses equally. On December 31, after all assets were converted to cash and all creditors were paid, only $60,000 in partnership cash remained.

Required

1. Calculate the capital account balances of the partners after the liquidation of assets and payment of creditors.

2. Assume that any partner with a deficit pays cash to the partnership to cover the deficit. Present the general journal entries on December 31 to record the cash receipt from the deficient partner(s) and the final disbursement of cash to the partners.

3. Assume that any partner with a deficit is not able to reimburse the partnership. Present journal entries: (a) to transfer the deficit of any deficient partners to the other partners, and (b) to record the final disbursement of cash to the partners.

Problems

Problem 11-1A **Methods of allocating partnership profit** L03 e**X**cel

CHECK FIGURE: c. Cr Jenkins, Capital: $195,000

Jenkins, Willis, and Trent invested $200,000, $350,000, and $450,000, respectively, in a partnership. During its first year, the firm recorded profit of $600,000.

Required Prepare entries to close the firm's Income Summary account as of December 31 and to allocate the profit to the partners under each of the following assumptions:

    a. The partners did not produce any special agreement on the method of distributing profits.

    b. The partners agreed to share profit and losses in the ratio of their beginning investments.

    c. The partners agreed to share profit by providing annual salary allowances of $110,000 to Jenkins, $120,000 to Willis, and $55,000 to Trent; allowing 15% interest on the partners' beginning investments; and sharing the remainder equally.

Problem 11-2A **Allocating partnership profits and losses; sequential years** L03

CHECK FIGURES: d. Year 1: Phillip: $(86,000); Case: $(14,000); d. Year 2: Phillip: $39,000; Case: $111,000; d. Year 3: Phillip: $89,000; Case: $161,000

Phillip and Case are in the process of forming a partnership to import Belgian chocolates, to which Phillip will contribute one-third time and Case full time. They have discussed the following alternative plans for sharing profit and losses.

a. In the ratio of their initial investments, which they have agreed will be $160,000 for Phillis and $240,000 for Case.

b. In proportion to the time devoted to the business.

c. A salary allowance of $5,000 per month to Case and the balance in accordance with their initial investment ratio.

d. A $5,000 per month salary allowance to Case, 15% interest on their initial investments, and the balance equally.

The partners expect the business to generate profit as follows: Year 1, $100,000 loss; Year 2, $150,000 profit; and Year 3, $250,000 profit.

Required Prepare four schedules with the following column headings:

Year	Calculations	Share to Phillip	Share to Case	Total

Complete a schedule for each of the four plans being considered by showing how the partnership profit or loss for each year would be allocated to the partners. Round your answers to the nearest whole dollar.

Problem 11-3A **Partnership profit allocation, statement of changes in equity, and closing entries** LO2,3 e**X**cel

CHECK FIGURES: 1c. Conway: $146,400; Chan: $125,600; Scott: $88,000

Ben Conway, Ida Chan, and Clair Scott formed CCS Consulting by making capital contributions of $245,000, $280,000, and $175,000, respectively. They anticipate annual profit of $360,000 and are considering the following alternative plans of sharing profits and losses:

a. Equally;

b. In the ratio of their initial investments; or

c. Salary allowances of $110,000 to Conway, $85,000 to Chan, and $60,000 to Scott and interest allowances of 12% on initial investments, with any remaining balance shared equally.

Required

1. Prepare a schedule with the following column headings:

Profit/Loss Sharing Plan	Calculations	Share to Conway	Share to Chan	Share to Scott

Use the schedule to show how a profit of $360,000 would be distributed under each of the alternative plans being considered.

2. Prepare a statement of changes in equity showing the allocation of profit to the partners, assuming they agree to use alternative (c) and the profit actually earned for the year ended

December 31, 2017, is $360,000. During the year, Conway, Chan, and Scott withdraw $40,000, $30,000, and $20,000, respectively.

3. Prepare the December 31, 2017, journal entry to close Income Summary assuming they agree to use alternative (c) and the profit is $360,000. Also, close the withdrawals accounts.

Problem 11-4A **Admission of a partner** LO4

CHECK FIGURES: b. Dr Zeller, Capital: $6,187.50; c. Cr Zeller, Capital: $6,975.00

Zeller, Acker, and Benton are partners with capital balances as follows: Zeller, $84,000; Acker, $69,000; and Benton, $147,000. The partners share profit and losses in a 3:2:5 ratio. Dent is admitted to the partnership on May 1, 2017, with a 25% equity. Prepare general journal entries to record the entry of Dent into the partnership under each of the following unrelated assumptions:

    a. Dent invests $100,000.   **b.** Dent invests $72,500.   **c.** Dent invests $131,000.

Problem 11-5A **Partnership entries, profit allocation, admission of a partner** LO2,3,4

CHECK FIGURES: c. Cr Bow: $245,200; Cr Amri: $134,800; d. Dr Amri: $48,000

On June 1, 2017, Jill Bow and Aisha Amri formed a partnership, to open a commercial gluten-free bakery, contributing $280,000 cash and $360,000 of equipment, respectively. Also, the partnership assumed responsibility for a $40,000 note payable associated with the equipment. The partners agreed to share profits as follows: Bow is to receive an annual salary allowance of $150,000, both are to receive an annual interest allowance of 8% of their original capital investments, and any remaining profit or loss is to be shared 40/60 (to Bow and Amri, respectively). On November 20, 2017, Amri withdrew cash of $100,000. At year-end, May 31, 2018, the Income Summary account had a credit balance of $380,000. On June 1, 2018, Peter Wilems invested $120,000 and was admitted to the partnership for a 20% interest in equity.

Required

  1. Prepare journal entries for the following dates:

      a. June 1, 2017   **b.** November 20, 2017   **c.** May 31, 2018   **d.** June 1, 2018

  2. Calculate the balance in each partner's capital account immediately after the June 1, 2018, entry.

Problem 11-6A **Withdrawal of a partner** LO4

CHECK FIGURES: d. Dr Gale, Capital: $23,625; e. Cr Gale, Capital: $3,656.25

Gale, McLean, and Lux are partners of Burgers and Brew Company with capital balances as follows: Gale, $84,000; McLean, $69,000; and Lux, $147,000. The partners share profit and losses in a 3:2:5 ratio. McLean decides to withdraw from the partnership. Prepare general journal entries to record the May 1, 2017, withdrawal of McLean from the partnership under each of the following unrelated assumptions:

    a. McLean sells his interest to Freedman for $168,000 after Gale and Lux approve the entry of Freedman as a partner (where McLean receives the cash personally from Freedman).

    b. McLean gives his interest to a son-in-law, Park. Gale and Lux accept Park as a partner.

    c. McLean is paid $69,000 in partnership cash for his equity.

d. McLean is paid $132,000 in partnership cash for his equity.

e. McLean is paid $27,250 in partnership cash plus machinery that is recorded on the partnership books at $115,000 less accumulated depreciation of $83,000.

Problem 11-7A **Liquidation of a partnership** L05 e**X**cel

CHECK FIGURES: a. Cash to Lui: $79,938; b. Cash to Lui: $68,625; c. Cash to Lui: $52,375; d. Cash to Lui: $46,000

Lui, Montavo, and Johnson plan to liquidate their Premium Pool and Spa business. They have always shared profit and losses in a 1:4:5 ratio, and on the day of the liquidation their balance sheet appeared as follows:

Premium Pool and Spa Balance Sheet June 30, 2017				
Assets			**Liabilities**	
Cash		$ 68,750	Accounts payable	$130,375
Machinery......................................	$588,750		**Equity**	
Less: Accumulated depreciation....	137,500	451,250	Jim Lui .... $ 76,250	
Total assets		$520,000	Kent Montavo, capital 200,875	
			Dave Johnson, capital 112,500	
			Total equity	389,625
			Total liabilities and equity	$520,000

Required

Part 1

Under the assumption that the machinery is sold and the cash is distributed to the proper parties on June 30, 2017, complete the schedule provided below.

	Cash	Machinery (net)	Accounts Payable	Jim Lui, Capital	Kent Montavo, Capital	Dave Johnson, Capital
Account balances June 30, 2017...............................						

Show the sale, the gain or loss allocation, and the distribution of the cash in each of the following unrelated cases:

a. The machinery is sold for $488,130.

b. The machinery is sold for $375,000.

c. The machinery is sold for $212,500, and any partners with resulting deficits can and do pay in the amount of their deficits.

d. The machinery is sold for $187,500, and the partners have no assets other than those invested in the business.

Part 2

Prepare the entry to record the final distribution of cash assuming case (a) above.

Problem 11-8A Liquidation of a partnership L05

CHECK FIGURES: a. Dr Craig, Capital: $549,000; b. Dr Craig, Capital: $114,000

Trish Craig and Ted Smith have a bio-energy and consulting business and share profit and losses in a 3:1 ratio. They decide to liquidate their partnership on December 31, 2017, when the balance sheet shows the following:

Craig and Smith Consulting Balance Sheet December 31, 2017					
Assets			**Liabilities**		
Cash		$ 91,200	Accounts payable		$ 50,400
Property, plant, and equipment	$513,600		**Equity**		
Less: Accumulated depreciation	199,200	314,400	Trish Craig, capital	$244,800	
Total assets		$405,600	Ted Smith, capital	110,400	
			Total equity		355,200
			Total liabilities and equity		$405,600

Required Prepare the entries on December 31, 2017, to record the liquidation under each of the following independent assumptions:

    a. Property, plant, and equipment are sold for $720,000.

    b. Property, plant, and equipment are sold for $140,000.

Alternate Problems

Problem 11-1B Methods of allocating partnership profit L03 *eXcel*

CHECK FIGURE: c. Dr Lister, Capital: $6,000

Phung, Moier, and Lister invested $130,000, $150,000, and $120,000, respectively, into an organic farm to restaurant distribution business. During its first year, the firm earned $25,000.

Required Prepare entries to close the firm's Income Summary account as of December 31 and to allocate the profit to the partners under each of the following assumptions.

    a. The partners did not specify any special method of sharing profit.

    b. The partners agreed to share profit and losses in the ratio of their beginning investments.

    c. The partners agreed to share profit by providing annual salary allowances of $75,000 to Phung, $40,000 to Moier, and $40,000 to Lister; allowing 20% interest on the partners' beginning investments; and sharing the remainder equally.

Problem 11-2B Allocating partnership profits and losses; sequential years L03 *eXcel*

CHECK FIGURES: d. Year 1: Bosch: $(25,750); Gilbert: $110,750
d. Year 2: Bosch: $(90,750); Gilbert: $45,750
d. Year 3: Bosch: $105,750; Gilbert: $242,250

Bosch and Gilbert are in the process of forming a golf course equipment maintenance company. Bosch will contribute one-third time and Gilbert will work full time. They have discussed the following alternative plans for sharing profit and losses.

a. In the ratio of their initial investments, which they have agreed will be $140,000 for Bosch and $210,000 for Gilbert.

b. In proportion to the time devoted to the business.

c. A salary allowance of $8,000 per month to Gilbert and the balance in accordance with their initial investment ratio.

d. A $10,500 per month salary allowance to Gilbert, 15% interest on their initial investments, and the balance equally.

The partners expect the business to generate profit as follows: Year 1, $85,000 profit; Year 2, $45,000 loss; and Year 3, $348,000 profit.

Required Prepare four schedules with the following column headings:

Year	Calculations	Share to Bosch	Share to Gilbert	Total

Complete a schedule for each of the four plans being considered by showing how the partnership profit or loss for each year would be allocated to the partners. Round your answers to the nearest whole dollar.

Problem 11-3B **Partnership profit allocation, statement of changes in equity, and closing entries** LO2,3 e**X**cel

CHECK FIGURES: 1c. Jobs: $81,667; Alford: $46,667; Norris: $111,666

Jobs, Alford, and Norris formed the JAN Partnership to provide landscape design services in Edmonton, by making capital contributions of $150,000, $100,000, and $250,000, respectively on January 7, 2017. They anticipate annual profit of $240,000 and are considering the following alternative plans of sharing profit and losses:

a. Equally;

b. In the ratio of their initial investments (do not round the ratio calculations); or

c. Salary allowances of $70,000 to Jobs, $40,000 to Alford, and $90,000 to Norris; interest allowances of 10% on initial investments, with any remaining balance shared equally.

Required

1. Prepare a schedule with the following column headings:

Profit/Loss Sharing Plan	Calculations	Share to Jobs	Share to Alford	Share to Norris	Total

Use the schedule to show how a profit of $240,000 would be distributed under each of the alternative plans being considered. Round your answers to the nearest whole dollar.

2. Prepare a statement of changes in equity showing the allocation of profit to the partners, assuming they agree to use alternative (c) and the profit actually earned for the year ended December

31, 2017, is $240,000. During 2017, Jobs, Alford, and Norris withdrew $50,000, $40,000, and $60,000, respectively.

3. Prepare the December 31, 2017, journal entry to close Income Summary, assuming they agree to use alternative (c) and the profit is $240,000. Also, close the withdrawals accounts.

Problem 11-4B Admission of a partner LO4

CHECK FIGURES: b. Dr Conway, Capital: $10,800; c. Cr Conway, Capital: $22,320

Conway, Kip, and Zack are partners of Force, a local cross-fit training facility with capital balances as follows: Conway, $367,200; Kip, $122,400; and Zack, $244,800. The partners share profit and losses in a 1:2:1 ratio. Young is admitted to the partnership on November 30 with a 20% equity. Prepare general journal entries to record the entry of Young under each of the following unrelated assumptions:

    a. Young invests $183,600.

    b. Young invests $129,600.

    c. Young invests $295,200.

Problem 11-5B Partnership entries, profit allocation, withdrawal of a partner LO2,3,4

CHECK FIGURES: 1a. Cr Harris: $56,000; 1b. Cr Davis: $110,600; 1c. Cr Harris: $157,500

On November 1, 2017, Harris, Davis, and Tallis formed Restore, a home renovation business by contributing $56,000 in cash, $91,000 of equipment, and a truck worth $42,000, respectively. The partners agreed to share profits and losses as follows: Davis and Tallis were to receive an annual salary allowance of $196,000 each and any remaining profit or loss was to be shared 5:2:3. On October 31, 2018, the partnership's first year-end, the Income Summary account had a debit balance of $35,000. On November 1, 2018, Harris withdrew from the partnership and received $7,000 from the partnership.

Required
1. Prepare journal entries for the following dates:

    a. November 1, 2017

    b. October 31, 2018

    c. November 1, 2018

2. Calculate the balance in each partner's capital account immediately after the November 1, 2018, entry.

Problem 11-6B Withdrawal of a partner LO4

CHECK FIGURES: d. Dr Burke, Capital: $14,400; e. Cr Burke, Capital: $17,600

Burke, Comeau, and LeJeune are partners of Happy Feet, a music theatre production company with capital balances as follows: Burke, $244,800; Comeau, $81,600; and LeJeune, $163,200. The partners share profit/(losses) in a 1:2:1 ratio. LeJeune decides to withdraw from the partnership. Prepare general journal entries to record the November 30 withdrawal of LeJeune from the partnership under each of the following unrelated assumptions:

    a. LeJeune sells her interest to Devereau for $68,480 after Burke and Comeau approve the entry of Devereau as a partner.

    b. LeJeune gives her interest to a daughter-in-law, Shulak. Burke and Comeau accept Shulak as a partner.

c. LeJeune is paid $163,200 in partnership cash for her equity.

d. LeJeune is paid $206,400 in partnership cash for her equity.

e. LeJeune is paid $57,600 in partnership cash plus manufacturing equipment recorded on the partnership books at $124,800 less accumulated depreciation of $72,000.

Problem 11-7B **Liquidation of a partnership** L05 e**X**cel

CHECK FIGURES: a. Cash to Olive: $34,766; b. Cash to Olive: $20,790; c. Cash to Olive: $7,140; d. Cash to Olive: $0

Poppy, Sweetbean, and Olive have always shared profit and losses in a 3:1:1 ratio. They recently decided to liquidate their partnership. Just prior to the liquidation, their balance sheet appeared as follows:

Poppy, Sweetbean, and Olive Balance Sheet October 15, 2017				
Assets		**Liabilities**		
Cash..	$ 9,450	Accounts payable		$ 39,690
Equipment (net)*	166,320	**Equity**		
Total assets...	$175,770	Ernie Poppy, capital	$63,840	
		Lynn Sweetbean, capital	42,000	
		Ned Olive, capital..............................	30,240	
		Total equity....................................		136,080
		Total liabilities and equity		$175,770

*Accumulated depreciation = $40,600

Required

Part 1

Under the assumption that the equipment is sold and the cash is distributed to the proper parties on October 15, 2017, complete the schedule provided below.

	Cash	Equipment (net)	Accounts Payable	Ernie Poppy, Capital	Lynn Sweetbean, Capital	Ned Olive, Capital
Account balances October 15, 2017						

Show the sale, the gain or loss allocation, and the distribution of the cash in each of the following unrelated cases:

a. The equipment is sold for $189,000.

b. The equipment is sold for $119,070.

c. The equipment is sold for $50,820, and any partners with resulting deficits can and do pay in the amount of their deficits.

d. The equipment is sold for $38,640, and the partners have no assets other than those invested in the business.

Part 2

Prepare the entry to record the final distribution of cash assuming case (a) above.

Problem 11-8B Liquidation of a partnership L05

CHECK FIGURES: a. Dr Bjorn, Capital: $154,200; b. Dr Bjorn, Capital: $31,800

Leslie Bjorn, Jason Douglas, and Tom Pierce have an architect firm and share profit(losses) in a 3:1:1 ratio. They decide to liquidate their partnership on March 31, 2017. The balance sheet appeared as follows on the date of liquidation:

BDP Architects Balance Sheet March 31, 2017				
Assets			**Liabilities**	
Cash..		$ 47,400	Accounts payable............	$ 27,600
Property, plant, and equipment...........	$233,400		**Equity**	
Less: Accumulated depreciation	128,400	105,000	Leslie Bjorn, capital $55,200	
Total assets		$152,400	Jason Douglas, capital 63,600	
			Tom Pierce, capital.............. 6,000	
			Total equity	124,800
			Total liabilities and equity....	$152,400

Required Prepare the entries on March 31, 2017, to record the liquidation under each of the following independent assumptions:

    a. Property, plant, and equipment is sold for $270,000.

    b. Property, plant, and equipment is sold for $66,000.

Assume that any deficiencies are paid by the partners.

Analytical and Review Problems

A & R Problem 11-1 Liquidation of a partnership

Jake, Sacha, and Brianne own a tour company called Adventure Sports. The partners share profit and losses in a 1:3:4 ratio. After lengthy disagreements among the partners and several unprofitable periods, the friends decided to liquidate the partnership. Before the liquidation, the partnership balance sheet showed total assets, $238,000; total liabilities, $200,000; Jake, Capital, $8,000; Sacha, Capital, $10,000; and Brianne, Capital, $20,000. The cash proceeds from selling the assets were sufficient to repay all but $45,000 to the creditors. Calculate the loss from selling the assets, allocate the loss to the partners, and determine how much of the remaining liability should be paid by each partner.

A & R Problem 11-2 Liquidation of a limited partnership

Assume that the Jake, Sacha, and Brianne partnership of A & R Problem 11-1 is a limited partnership. Jake and Sacha are general partners and Brianne is a limited partner. How much of the remaining $45,000 liability should be paid by each partner?

A & R Problem 11-3 Profit allocation

Keith Scott and David Dawson agreed to share the annual profit or losses of their corporate law partnership as follows: If the partnership earned a profit, the first $60,000 would be allocated 40% to Scott and 60% to Dawson to reflect the time devoted to the business by each partner. Profit in excess of $60,000 would be shared equally. Also, the partners have agreed to share any losses equally.

Required

1. Prepare a schedule showing how profit of $72,000 for 2017 should be allocated to the partners.

2. Sometime later in 2018, the partners discovered that $80,000 of accounts payable had existed on December 31, 2017, but had not been recorded. These accounts payable relate to expenses incurred by the business. The partners are now trying to determine the best way to correct their accounting records, particularly their capital accounts. Dawson suggested that they make a special entry crediting $80,000 to the liability account, and debiting their capital accounts for $40,000 each. Scott, on the other hand, suggested that an entry should be made to record the accounts payable and retroactively correct the capital accounts to reflect the balance that they would have had if the expenses had been recognized in 2017. If they had been recognized, the partnership would have reported a loss of $8,000 instead of the $72,000 profit.

   a. Present the journal entry suggested by Dawson for recording the accounts payable and allocating the loss to the partners.

   b. Give the journal entry to record the accounts payable and correct the capital accounts according to Scott's suggestion. Show how you calculated the amounts presented in the entry.

3. Which suggestion do you think complies with their partnership agreement? Why?

Ethics Challenge

EC 11-1

Paul, Frank, and Basil formed Fresh, a greenhouse and garden centre business, 10 years ago, and Paul is about to retire. Paul is not experienced in financial accounting, but knows, based on the partnership agreement, that he is entitled to one-third of partnership assets upon his retirement. Total assets have a book value of $900,000 and Paul feels that he is entitled to his share. Frank and Basil are aware that the market value of the firm's net assets approximates $1,500,000. Frank and Basil plan to form a new partnership.

Required What are the financial and ethical implications of distributing $300,000 to Paul upon his retirement?

Focus on Financial Statements

FFS 11-1

CHECK FIGURES: Total current assets = $116,800; Total assets = $221,800; Total current liabilities = $24,000

Les Waruck, Kim Chau, and Leena Manta formed a partnership, WCM Sales, on January 11, 2017, by investing $68,250, $109,200, and $95,550, respectively. The partnership agreement states that profits and losses are to be shared on the basis of a salary allowance of $40,000 for Waruck, $80,000 for Chau, and $40,000 for Manta, with any remainder shared on the ratio of beginning-of-period capital balance. Following is the December 31, 2017, adjusted trial balance, in alphabetical order:

Account	Balance*	Account	Balance*
Accounts payable	14,000	Leena Manta, capital	95,550
Accounts receivable	46,000	Leena Manta, withdrawals	10,000
Accumulated amortization, patent	6,000	Les Waruck, capital	68,250
Accumulated depreciation, fixtures	3,000	Les Waruck, withdrawals	30,000
Accumulated depreciation, furniture	6,000	Merchandise inventory	22,000
Allowance for doubtful accounts	1,200	Notes payable, due 2020**	34,000
Amortization expense, patent	2,000	Patent	20,000
Bad debt expense	2,800	Prepaid rent	36,000
Cash	14,000	Rent expense	84,000
Depreciation expense, fixtures	3,000	Sales	102,000
Depreciation expense, furniture	6,000	Sales discounts	3,400
Fixtures	31,000	Unearned sales	3,000
Furniture	69,000	Wages expense	49,000
Kim Chau, capital	109,200		
Kim Chau, withdrawals	14,000		

*Assume all accounts have a normal balance.
**$7,000 is due during 2018.

Required Prepare the December 31, 2017, classified balance sheet, showing all appropriate supporting calculations.

Analysis Component:

Assuming that the assets of businesses similar to WCM Sales are financed 60% by debt and 40% by equity, does WCM Sales compare favourably or unfavourably to the industry average? What is the relationship between type of financing and risk?

FFS 11-2

Refer to the financial statements for Danier Leather and WestJet in Appendix II.

Required Answer the following questions.
1. Is Danier Leather a partnership? Explain why or why not.
2. Identify whether each of Indigo, Telus, and WestJet is a sole proprietorship, partnership, or corporation. Explain.

Critical Thinking Mini Case

Josh and Ben Shaw are brothers. They each have $75,000 to invest in a business together: Northern Canadian Extreme Adventures. They estimate that an additional $200,000 is required to get the business operating but have yet to determine how to get this additional financing.

Required Using the elements of critical thinking described on the inside front cover, comment. To get started, consider the following framework to organize your response:

- Problem:
- Goal:
- Principles:
- Facts:
- Conclusions/Consequences:

Organization and Operation of Corporations

A Look Back

Chapter 11 focused on the partnership form of organization. We described crucial characteristics of partnerships and the accounting and reporting of their important transactions.

A Look at This Chapter

This chapter emphasizes details of the corporate form of organization. The accounting concepts and procedures for equity transactions are explained. We also describe how to report and analyze profit, earnings per share, and retained earnings.

© Zigloo.ca

LEARNING OBJECTIVES

LO1 Identify characteristics of corporations and their organization.

LO2 Describe and contrast the specialized components of corporate financial statements.

LO3 Record the issuance of common and preferred shares and describe their presentation in the equity section of the balance sheet.

LO4 Describe and account for cash dividends.

LO5 Distribute dividends between common and preferred shares.

LO6 Record closing entries for a corporation.

Private Goes Modular

The word *corporation* conjures up images of Canadian giants like the Toronto-Dominion Bank, Bombardier Inc., and WestJet. These are examples of *public* corporations, which means ownership is achieved through the purchase of *publicly traded* shares (shares that are bought and sold on a stock exchange). The shareholders, or owners, can be from anywhere across Canada or around the globe. There are, however, corporations that do not trade their shares publicly, like McCain Foods Limited and Friesens; these are *private* corporations.

3twenty Solutions, specializing in the design and construction of intermodal steel building units (ISBUs), is also a private corporation. *ISBU* is the term used for a shipping container when used for building and construction. The University of Saskatchewan founders of 3twenty Solutions—Evan Willoughby, Channing McCorriston, and Bryan McCrea—founded the company in 2009, establishing its manufacturing centre and head office in Saskatoon. Old shipping containers are recyclable; they are purchased and transformed by 3twenty into modular motels perfect for relocatable mining and oil and gas camps, or converted into a site office, or some other custom solutions.

Zigloo (also a private corporation, owned and operated by Keith Dewey out of Victoria, British Columbia) is leading the way in the custom design of ISBU homes with the goal to significantly reduce the construction cost of housing while at the same time lowering our carbon footprint by reusing freight containers and saving forests.

Is the ISBU industry sustainable? According to Brett Wilson, one of Canada's most successful businesspeople and now a philanthropist, there is still plenty of room for more competitors in the ISBU industry.

Source: www.3twenty.ca

Video Links: Interview with CBC: https://www.youtube.com/watch?v=As4qiKDGuRA&app=desktop

Dragon's Den Episode: http://www.cbc.ca/dragonsden/pitches/3twenty-solutions

CRITICAL THINKING CHALLENGE Why might a company stay private? Why might a private company go public?

CHAPTER PREVIEW

There are three common types of business organizations: corporations, partnerships, and proprietorships. This chapter explains key accounting fundamentals for the corporate form of business organization. Corporations are fewest in number but, with dollar sales at least 10 times the combined sales of unincorporated companies, they are very important players in our global economy. Understanding the advantages and disadvantages of the forms of business organization was important for the owners of 3twenty Solutions and Zigloo, described in the chapter opening vignette. The chapter begins by providing general information to help us make the decision as to which form of organization best satisfies our needs. We then analyze financial statements for corporations, contrasting them with the unincorporated organizations. The basic journal entries specific to corporations are illustrated, including those related to issuing shares, issuing dividends, and closing the accounts.

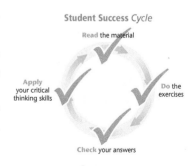

Student Success *Cycle*

Read the material

Do the exercises

Check your answers

Apply your critical thinking skills

Corporate Form of Organization

LO1   Identify characteristics of corporations and their organization.

A corporation is an entity that is created by law and is separate from its owners. It has most of the rights and privileges granted to single proprietorships. Owners of corporations are called **shareholders**. Each unit of ownership in a corporation is called a **share**. **Share capital**, also referred to as **capital stock**, is a general term referring to all types (or classes) of a corporation's shares. *Common shares* and *preferred shares*, explained in a later section, are names given to two classes of shares issued (sold) by corporations to shareholders. Corporations can be separated into *privately held* and *publicly held* corporations. A **privately held corporation** does not offer its shares for public sale and usually has few shareholders. A **publicly held corporation** offers its shares to the public through a *public sale* and can have thousands of shareholders. **Public sale** refers to trading in an organized stock market such as the Montreal, Toronto, New York, London, Shanghai, or Tokyo stock exchanges.

Characteristics of Corporations

Corporations are important because of advantages created by the unique characteristics of the corporate structure of ownership. We describe these characteristics in this section.

SEPARATE LEGAL ENTITY

A corporation is a separate legal entity that conducts its affairs with the same rights, duties, and responsibilities as a person. A corporation takes actions through its agents, who are its officers and managers.

LIMITED LIABILITY OF SHAREHOLDERS

Because a corporation is a separate legal entity, it is responsible for its own acts and its own debt. Because shareholders are not liable for either, the corporate form of organization is also known as a *limited company*. Shareholders invest in the business by contributing cash or other assets in return for ownership rights in the corporation. If the business fails, the amount contributed by shareholders is the maximum loss to the shareholders. If there are insufficient assets to pay business creditor claims, creditors have no claim on the shareholders' personal assets, an important advantage of a corporation.

OWNERSHIP RIGHTS ARE TRANSFERABLE

Ownership of a corporation is evidenced by shares that are usually easily bought or sold. The transfer of shares from one shareholder to another usually has no effect on the corporation or its operations.[1] Many corporations have thousands or even millions of their shares bought and sold daily in major stock exchanges throughout the world. For example, it is not uncommon for over 2,000,000 **Toronto-Dominion Bank** shares to trade in one day.

CONTINUOUS LIFE

A corporation's life can continue indefinitely because it is not tied to the physical lives of its owners. This means a corporation can exist as long as it continues to be successful.

SHAREHOLDERS ARE NOT CORPORATE AGENTS

A corporation acts through its agents, who are the officers or managers of the corporation. Shareholders who are not officers or managers of the corporation do not have the power to bind the corporation to contracts. This is also referred to as *lack of mutual agency*.

---

1   A transfer of ownership can create significant effects if it brings about a change in who controls the company's activities.

EXHIBIT 12.1

Summary of Advantages and Disadvantages of the Corporate Form of Organization

Advantages	Disadvantages
Limited liability of shareholders	Government regulation
Ownership rights are easily transferable	Corporate taxation
Continuous life	Separation of management and ownership
Lack of mutual agency	
Ease of capital accumulation	

EASE OF CAPITAL ACCUMULATION

Buying shares in a corporation often is attractive to investors because of the advantages of the corporate form of organization, as summarized in Exhibit 12.1. These advantages make it possible for some corporations to accumulate large amounts of capital from the total investments of many shareholders. For example, by the end of its 2014 fiscal year, Bombardier Inc., a Canadian company that manufactures aircraft and trains, had shareholders who owned 1,425,395,218 of its common shares.[2]

GOVERNMENTAL REGULATION

Corporations must meet requirements of provincial or federal incorporation laws. Single proprietorships and partnerships escape some of these regulations. Private corporations, however, are exempt from most of the security and corporate legislation reporting requirements. According to the *Canada Business Corporations Act* (CBCA), any publicly traded company with gross revenues of $10 million or assets exceeding $5 million must make public its financial statements, which have been prepared according to generally accepted accounting principles. All public corporations that are registered with one of the provincial securities bodies, depending on the province, must file annual audited financial statements within 140–170 days of their fiscal year-end. International Financial Reporting Standards (IFRS) were adopted by Canadian publicly accountable enterprises for fiscal periods beginning on or after January 1, 2011. Because financial statements include comparative figures, the prior-year financial statements must be in accordance with IFRS as well. Privately held corporations may choose to adopt either IFRS or **Private Enterprise GAAP (PE GAAP),** which simplify the accounting in areas of IFRS identified as being overly complex.

Many Canadian companies are listed on U.S. stock exchanges as well and are also required to file their annual reports with U.S. regulators. Some of these companies—such as Barrick Gold Corp., Bombardier Inc., and Lululemon Athletica Inc.—actually issue their annual reports in U.S. dollars.

CORPORATE TAXATION

Corporations are subject to the same property, payroll, and consumption taxes (PST, GST, and HST) as proprietorships and partnerships. Corporations are subject to an *additional* tax not levied on either of these two forms, however; that is, income tax expense (normally referred to as just *tax expense*).

The tax situation of a corporation is *usually* a disadvantage. But in some cases it can be an advantage to shareholders because corporate and individual tax rates are *progressive*. A **progressive tax** means higher levels of profit are taxed at higher rates and lower levels of profit are taxed at lower rates. This suggests that taxes can be saved or at least delayed if a large amount of profit is divided among two or more tax-paying entities. A business owner who has a large personal income and pays a high rate of

---

2   Annual report, Bombardier Inc., 2014.

personal tax can benefit if some of his or her income is earned by the corporation, so long as the corporation avoids paying dividends.[3]

Corporate income tax is an expense that appears on the income statement. However, income tax expense is *not* an operating expense because income tax expense is determined by government tax laws rather than by how the business operates. It is therefore reported as a separate expense, as shown in the excerpt below taken from the income statement of Loblaw Companies Limited for its year ended December 31, 2013.

(millions of dollars)	
Earnings before income taxes...	$858
Less: Income tax expense..	228
Net earnings before other items	$630

Choosing the proper form of entity for a business is crucial. Many factors should be considered, including taxes, liability, tax and fiscal year-end, ownership structure, estate planning, business risks, and earnings and property distributions. The chart below gives a summary of several important characteristics of business organizations:

	Proprietorship	Partnership	Corporation
Business entity	yes	yes	yes
Legal entity..................................	no	no	yes
Limited liability..............................	no	no	yes
Business taxed..............................	no	no	yes
One owner allowed........................	yes	no	yes

Organizing a Corporation

This section describes incorporation and treatment of organization costs.

INCORPORATION

A corporation may be created under either provincial law or federal laws. Those incorporated federally must comply with the *Canada Business Corporations Act* (CBCA). Most of the provincial laws are modelled after the federal statute. Requirements vary across provinces and from the CBCA, but essentially a legal document known as a charter, articles of incorporation, letters patent, or memo of association is completed and signed by the prospective shareholders. A corporation's charter *authorizes* the number and types (or classes[4]) of shares to be issued. **Authorized shares** are the total number of shares that a corporation is permitted to sell. When all of the legal requirements are satisfied, investors purchase the corporation's shares, meet as shareholders, and elect a board of directors. Directors are responsible for guiding a corporation's affairs.

---

3 If a shareholder receives dividends, the shareholder must include the dividend amount as income and pay income tax, except in certain situations that are better discussed in a tax course.

4 There is no limit on the number of classes of shares that can be set out in the articles of incorporation. Shares may be alphabetized by class such as *Class A* and *Class B* or may be assigned names such as *common shares* and *preferred shares*. TWC Enterprises Limited, for instance, is authorized to issue an unlimited number of each of preferred and common shares. Bombardier Inc. reported in its December 31, 2014, annual report that it is authorized to issue 12 million each of Series 2 and Series 3 preferred shares, 9.4 million Series 4 preferred shares, and 1,892 million each of Class A and Class B common shares.

ORGANIZATION COSTS

The costs of organizing a corporation are **organization costs** or **start-up costs**. They include legal fees, promoters' fees, and amounts paid to obtain a charter. Organization costs are expensed as incurred.[5]

Sometimes a corporation gives shares to promoters in exchange for their services in selling shares of the corporation. The entry to record this transaction would credit the appropriate share capital account instead of the Cash account.

MANAGEMENT OF A CORPORATION

Ultimate control of a corporation rests with its shareholders through election of the *board of directors*. Individual shareholders' rights to affect management are limited to a vote in shareholders' meetings, where each shareholder has one vote for each common share owned. This relation is shown in Exhibit 12.2.

EXHIBIT 12.2

Corporation Authority Structure

A corporation's board of directors is responsible for and has final authority for managing the corporation's activities but usually limits its actions to establishing broad policy and hiring the external auditors and corporate executive officers. It can act only as a collective body, and an individual director has no power to transact corporate business.

A group of shareholders owning or controlling votes of more than 50% of a corporation's shares can elect the board and control the corporation. However, in many corporations few shareholders actually get involved in the voting process, which means a much smaller percentage is often able to dominate the election of board members. Shareholders may delegate their voting rights to an agent by signing a document called a **proxy**.

RIGHTS OF SHAREHOLDERS

According to the *Canada Business Corporations Act*, shareholders have three basic rights: the right to vote, the right to receive dividends that have been declared, and the right to receive property of the corporation after its closure. When there is more than one class of shares, each of these three basic rights is assigned to at least one class but not necessarily to all. When a corporation has only one class of shares, those shares are identified as **common shares**. Shareholders are also entitled to receive timely reports on the corporation's financial position and results of operations. These reports take the form of financial statements and are the topic of the next section.

---

[5] IFRS 2015, IAS 38, para. 69, requires that organization costs be expensed unless they are part of property, plant, and equipment.

CHECKPOINT

1. $60,000 cash was paid for costs related to the organization of ABC Inc. Journalize the organization costs.

Do Quick Study question: QS 12-1

Corporate Financial Statements

LO2 Describe and contrast the specialized components of corporate financial statements.

The financial statements for the corporate form of organization are similar to those of unincorporated businesses. The differences all relate to *who owns* each form of business organization. We focus on these differences by comparing the assumed statements for ABC Corporation to those of a single proprietorship, Gage's Servicing.

Income Statement

The income statements in Exhibit 12.3 are identical except for income tax expense. Corporations are required by law to pay tax because they are a separate legal entity. Application of corporate tax rules can be complex. Therefore, to show how tax expense appears on the income statement for a corporation, we have simplified the calculation and assumed a 20% flat tax rate. The 20% tax rate is applied to *profit before tax* (20% × $60 = $12). The resulting tax expense of $12 is subtracted from *profit before tax* to arrive at *profit (another term for profit is income, earnings or net earnings)*. Therefore, the term *profit* for a corporation means profit after tax. Because the single proprietorship and partnership forms of business organization are not taxed (the owners are taxed), the profit for these two business organizations excludes income tax expense.

EXHIBIT 12.3

Comparison of Income Statements

ABC Corporation Income Statement For Year Ended December 31, 2017		
Revenues		$116
Operating expenses................................		40
Profit from operations.............................		$ 76
Other revenues and expenses:[6]		
Gain on sale of capital assets...............	$ 7	
Interest revenue..................................	3	
Loss on sale of capital assets	(12)	
Interest expense.................................	(14)	(16)
Profit before tax		$ 60
Income tax expense		12
Profit...		$ 48

Gage's Servicing Income Statement For Year Ended December 31, 2017		
Revenues		$116
Operating expenses		40
Profit from operations		$ 76
Other revenues and expenses:[6]		
Gain on sale of capital assets	$ 7	
Interest revenue.................................	3	
Loss on sale of capital assets	(12)	
Interest expense	(14)	(16)
Profit		$ 60

The income statements are identical except for the $12 of income tax expense.

---

6 Some companies will divide this section on their income statement between *Other Revenues and Gains* and *Other Expenses and Losses*. Flexibility is permitted in this regard.

Statement of Changes in Equity[7]

A single proprietorship prepares a statement of changes in equity to show how equity changed during the accounting period. The equity of the owners, regardless of the form of business organization, changes because of:

- Profits or losses
- Distributions of profit (known as withdrawals for a single proprietorship)
- Owner investments

A single proprietorship includes all three of these activities in one account, the owner's Capital account.

The equity of a corporation also changes because of profits or losses, distributions of profit (called *dividends*), and owner investments. However, profits or losses and dividends are recorded in the *Retained Earnings* account while shareholder (or owner) investments are recorded in a share capital account, either common shares or preferred shares. **Retained earnings** represents the profit to date that has been kept (retained) by the corporation for the purpose of reinvestment. The **statement of changes in equity for a corporation** shows how both retained earnings and share capital have changed during an accounting period, as shown in Exhibit 12.4.

EXHIBIT 12.4

Comparison of Statements of Changes in Equity for a Corporation and Proprietorship

ABC Corporation Statement of Changes in Equity For Year Ended December 31, 2017	Share Capital	Retained Earnings	Total Equity
Balance, January 1...............	$ -0-	$ -0-	$ -0-
Issuance of share capital......	500		500
Profit (loss)..........................		48	48
Dividends		(40)	(40)
Balance, December 31	$500	$ 8	$508

Gage's Servicing Statement of Changes in Equity For Year Ended December 31, 2017		
Nolan Gage, capital, January 1............		$ -0-
Add: Owner investment	$500	
Profit...	60	
Total...		$560
Less: Withdrawals..............................		40
Nolan Gage, capital, December 31		$520

Important Tip: Notice that both statements include profit (losses) and distributions of profit (called *dividends* for a corporation and *withdrawals* for a single proprietorship). Investments by the corporation's owners, called shareholders, are part of *share capital* while the investments made by the owner of the single proprietorship are included in Nolan Gage, Capital.

Balance Sheet

The balance sheets for the corporation and the single proprietorship are identical except for the equity section. The equity section for the sole proprietorship can be called *owner's equity* because the equity belongs to the one owner. The equity section can be called *shareholders' equity* for a corporation because the equity belongs to a group of owners known as shareholders. In this textbook the equity section for all types of business organizations (sole proprietorships, partnerships, and

---

7 IFRS 2015, IAS 1, para. 10 and para. 106–110.

corporations) is called *equity* for consistency in student learning. Assume the owner of the single proprietorship invested $500 into the business. This $500 investment is included as part of Nolan Gage, Capital, as shown in Exhibits 12.4 and 12.5. The shareholders of ABC Corporation also invested $500. Their investment is recorded in a share capital account, which is shown in Exhibit 12.4 and on the balance sheet as part of Equity in Exhibit 12.5.

EXHIBIT 12.5

Comparison of Balance Sheets

ABC Corporation Balance Sheet December 31, 2017		
Assets		
Cash		$148
Other assets		600
Total assets		$748
Liabilities		$240
Equity		
Share capital	$500	
Retained earnings	8	
Total equity		508
Total liabilities and equity		$748

Gage's Servicing Balance Sheet December 31, 2017	
Assets	
Cash	$160
Other assets	600
Total assets	$760
Liabilities	$240
Equity	
Nolan Gage, Capital	520
Total liabilities and equity	$760

> **Important Tip:** The equity sections for both organizations include the same transactions: profits (losses), distributions of profit, and owner investments.

In summary, the transactions that affect equity for the corporate form of organization are the same as for an unincorporated business. The difference is into which accounts the transactions are recorded. A corporation records profits (losses) and dividends in Retained Earnings and shareholder investments are recorded in a Share Capital account. How we record shareholder investments is the topic of the next section. Dividends are discussed later in the chapter.

CHECKPOINT

2. Refer to Exhibit 12.5. Explain why there is a difference of $12 between *Total liabilities and equity* on the corporate balance sheet and on the single proprietorship balance sheet.
3. Explain the difference between the income statement for a corporation and that for an unincorporated business.
4. How is the statement of changes in equity for a corporation different from the statement of changes in equity for a single proprietorship?
5. Explain the differences between equity on the balance sheets for a corporation and a single proprietorship.

Do Quick Study questions: QS 12-2, QS 12-3, QS 12-4, QS 12-5, QS 12-6, QS 12-7

Issuing Shares

When investors buy a corporation's shares, they sometimes receive a *share certificate* as proof they purchased shares. Refer to Extend Your Knowledge 12-1 for an example of a share certificate. Issuance of certificates is becoming less common. Instead, most shareholders maintain accounts with the corporation or their stockbrokers and never receive certificates. If a corporation's shares are traded on a major stock exchange, the corporation must have a *registrar* who keeps shareholder records and prepares official lists of shareholders for shareholders' meetings and dividend payments.

The selling or issuing of shares by a corporation is referred to as **equity financing** because assets are increased (financed) through shareholder (equity) investment. For instance, assume ABC Corporation issued shares to shareholders in exchange for $100,000 cash. The balance sheet prepared for ABC Corporation immediately after this transaction shows the $100,000 cash having been provided through equity.

ABC Corporation Balance Sheet December 31, 2017	
Assets	
Cash	$100,000
Total assets	$100,000
Liabilities	$ -0-
Equity	
Share capital	100,000
Total liabilities and equity	$100,000

The next section introduces us to the terminology and basic accounting for the issuance of common and preferred shares.

DECISION INSIGHT

Cara Operations raises $200 million in IPO

Cara Operations Ltd., owned by members of Canada's Phelan family and Fairfax Financial Holdings Ltd., decided to go public and sold $8.7 million subordinate voting shares for $23 each, raising $200.1 million in its initial public offering. The initial shares were purchased by banks including Bank of Nova Scotia, Bank of Montreal, and Royal Bank of Canada and will subsequently trade on the Toronto Stock Exchange under the ticker symbol CAO.

© Andrew Melbourne/Alamy Stock Photo

Cara is the owner of 837 restaurants Canada-wide with popular brands including Swiss Chalet, Harvey's, Milestones, Montana's, Kelsey's, East Side Marios, and Bier Markt. According to CBC.com, Cara's prospectus documents revealed "the chain's restaurants generated $1.7 billion in sales last year, big enough to make Cara the third-largest single restaurant owner in the country behind Tim Hortons and McDonalds."

SOURCES: http://www.theglobeandmail.com/report-on-business/swiss-chalet-owner-cara-raises-200-million-in-ipo/article23733730/; http://www.cbc.ca/m/news/business/cara-operations-owner-of-swiss-chalet-harvey-s-milestones-plans-ipo-1.2956446; http://business.financialpost.com/investing/cara-operations-ltd-to-sell-shares-at-19-to-200-in-200-million-ipo

Accounting for Shares

LO3   Record the issuance of common and preferred shares and describe their presentation in the equity section of the balance sheet.

Corporations can sell shares either *directly* or *indirectly* to shareholders at the *market value per share*. To **sell shares directly**, a corporation advertises its share issuance directly to potential buyers, which is most common with privately held corporations. To **sell shares indirectly**, a corporation pays a brokerage house (investment banker) to issue its shares. Some brokerage houses **underwrite** an indirect issuance of shares, meaning they buy the shares from the corporation and take all gains or losses from the shares' resale to shareholders.

Market value per share is the price at which a share is bought or sold. Market value is influenced by a variety of factors, including expected future earnings, dividends, growth, and other company and economic events. Market values of frequently traded shares are reported online and in daily newspapers such as The Financial Post. For example, WestJet Airlines' trading history over a three-year period ending March 2015 is illustrated in a chart format below. The first chart shows the changes in share price over three years. During that time, the market price per share has fluctuated between a low of $13.48 per share and a high of about $34.45 per share.

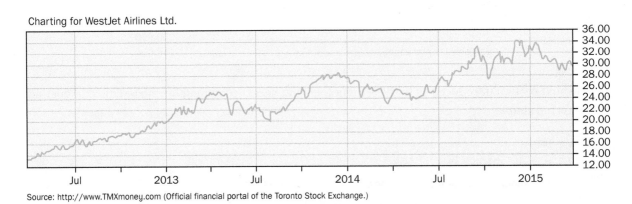

Charting for WestJet Airlines Ltd.

Source: http://www.TMXmoney.com (Official financial portal of the Toronto Stock Exchange.)

Market values of shares not actively traded are more difficult to determine. Several techniques are used to estimate the value of these and other shares but most use accounting information as an important input. *We must remember that the buying and selling of shares between investors does not impact that corporation's equity accounts.*

COMMON SHARES

Recall that if a corporation has only one class of shares, those are known as common shares. Common shares represent *residual equity*, or what is left over after creditors and other shareholders (if any) are paid when a corporation is liquidated (or closed). Common shares have certain rights, which are summarized in Exhibit 12.10.

ISSUING COMMON SHARES FOR CASH

The *Canada Business Corporations Act* (CBCA) requires that all shares be of **no par value** or nominal value. **Par value** is an arbitrary value a corporation places on each share of its share capital. Par value shares are rare in Canada and are addressed in Extend Your Knowledge 12-2.

Shares are most commonly issued in exchange for cash. For example, assume that on June 4, 2017, Dillon Snowboards Inc. was granted a charter to issue an unlimited number of both common and preferred shares. The entry to record Dillon Snowboards' immediate issuance of 30,000 common shares for $300,000 on June 5, 2017, is:

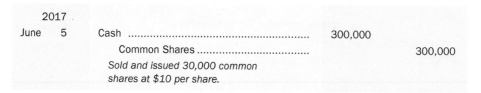

2017			
June 5	Cash	300,000	
	Common Shares		300,000
	Sold and issued 30,000 common		
	shares at $10 per share.		

Many important terms and phrases are used in the equity section of a corporate balance sheet. Exhibit 12.6 details each of these using the equity section of the balance sheet for Dillon Snowboards Inc. at June 30, 2017, assuming profit for June of $65,000 and no dividend payments.

EXHIBIT 12.6

Equity of Dillon Snowboards Inc. at June 30, 2017

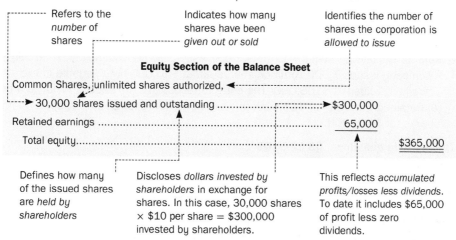

For simplicity, we will assume that **outstanding shares** (or shares held by shareholders) will be equal to the shares issued (or sold) unless otherwise noted.

ISSUING COMMON SHARES FOR NON-CASH ASSETS

A corporation can receive assets other than cash in exchange for its shares.[8] The corporation records the assets acquired at the assets' fair market values as of the date of the transaction.[9]

To illustrate, here is the entry to record Dillon Snowboards' receipt on July 2, 2017, of land valued at $105,000 in return for immediate issuance of 4,000 common shares:

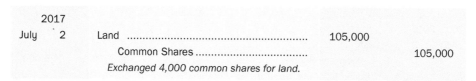

2017			
July 2	Land	105,000	
	Common Shares		105,000
	Exchanged 4,000 common shares for land.		

Exhibit 12.7 shows the equity section of the balance sheet for Dillon Snowboards at July 31, 2017, assuming profit earned during July of $82,000.

---

8 It can also assume liabilities on assets received such as a mortgage on property.

9 Fair market value is determined by the current value of the item given up. If the current value for the item being given up cannot be determined, then the fair value of the item received is used. In the example that follows, the fair market value of the shares being given up cannot be determined so the $105,000 value of the land is used.

EXHIBIT 12.7

Equity of Dillon Snowboards Inc. at July 31, 2017

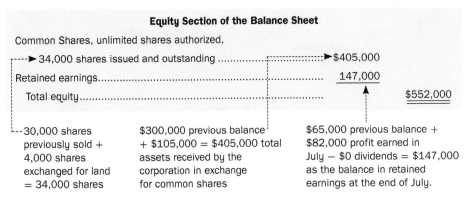

Equity Section of the Balance Sheet

Common Shares, unlimited shares authorized,

34,000 shares issued and outstanding $405,000

Retained earnings.. 147,000

Total equity... $552,000

30,000 shares previously sold + 4,000 shares exchanged for land = 34,000 shares

$300,000 previous balance + $105,000 = $405,000 total assets received by the corporation in exchange for common shares

$65,000 previous balance + $82,000 profit earned in July − $0 dividends = $147,000 as the balance in retained earnings at the end of July.

CHECKPOINT

6. Refer to Exhibit 12.7. What was the average issue price per common share at July 31, 2017?

7. A company issues 7,000 common shares and a $40,000 note payable in exchange for equipment valued at $105,000. The entry to record this transaction includes a credit to (a) Retained Earnings for $65,000; (b) Common Shares for $65,000; or (c) Common Shares for $105,000.

Do Quick Study questions: QS 12-8, QS 12-9

PREFERRED SHARES

Preferred shares have special rights that give them priority (or senior status) over common shares in one or more areas. Special rights typically include a preference for receiving dividends and for the distribution of assets if the corporation is liquidated. Because of these special rights, preferred shares are always listed before common shares in the equity section. Most preferred shares do not have the right to vote.

ISSUING PREFERRED SHARES FOR CASH

A separate account is used to record preferred shares. To illustrate, if on August 3, 2017, Dillon Snowboards issued 5,000 preferred shares with a dividend preference of $3 per share for a total of $125,000 cash, the entry is:

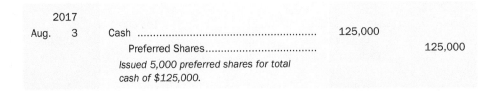

2017				
Aug.	3	Cash	125,000	
		Preferred Shares....................................		125,000
		Issued 5,000 preferred shares for total cash of $125,000.		

Issuing preferred shares for non-cash assets is treated like similar entries for common shares.

The Preferred Shares account is included as part of contributed capital. The equity section of the balance sheet at August 31, 2017, for Dillon Snowboards—assuming profit earned during August of $156,000—would appear as shown in Exhibit 12.8.

EXHIBIT 12.8

Equity With Common and Preferred Shares

When more than one class of shares has been issued, the equity section is classified by grouping the share capital accounts under the heading *contributed capital*. **Contributed capital** is the total amount of cash and other assets received by the corporation from its shareholders in exchange for common and/or preferred shares.

The notation "$3" is the dividend preference, which means preferred shareholders are entitled to dividends at the rate of $3 per year per preferred share when declared.

Equity Section of the Balance Sheet

Contributed capital:		
Preferred shares, $3, unlimited shares authorized,		
5,000 shares issued and outstanding	$125,000	
Common shares, unlimited shares authorized,		
34,000 shares issued and outstanding	405,000	
Total contributed capital...		$530,000
Retained earnings		303,000
Total equity..		$833,000

Profit of $65,000 for June + $82,000 profit for July + $156,000 profit for August − $0 dividends = $303,000 as the balance in retained earnings at August 31, 2017.

EXHIBIT 12.9

Equity on August 31, 2017, Balance Sheet

Dillon Snowboards Inc.
Balance Sheet
August 31, 2017

Assets			
Current assets:			
Cash			
Total current assets			
Property, plant, and equipment:			
Land			
Total property, plant, and equipment........................			
Total assets			$
Liabilities			
Current liabilities:			
Accounts payable...			
Total current liabilities			
Non-current liabilities:...			
Total liabilities..			
Equity			
Contributed capital:			
Preferred shares	$125,000		
Common shares...	405,000		
Total contributed capital		$530,000	
Retained earnings		303,000	
Total equity...		$833,000	
Total liabilities and equity...		$	

An *abbreviated* example of how Dillon Snowboards' equity might appear within the balance sheet at August 31, 2017, is illustrated here in Exhibit 12.9.

EXHIBIT 12.10

Summary of Rights of Preferred and Common Shareholders

Rights of Preferred Shareholders	Rights of Common Shareholders
1. No voting rights. 2. The right to receive dividends *before* the common shareholders receive a dividend. In other words, a dividend cannot be paid to common shareholders unless preferred shareholders also receive one. 3. The right to share equally *before* common shareholders in any assets that remain after creditors are paid when the corporation is liquidated. 4. The right to sell or otherwise dispose of their shares.	1. The right to vote at shareholders' meetings. 2. The right to share pro rata with other common shareholders in any dividends declared. This means each common share receives the same dividend per share. 3. The right to share equally in any assets that remain after creditors and preferred shareholders are paid when the corporation is liquidated. 4. The right to sell or otherwise dispose of their shares. 5. The right to purchase additional shares of common shares issued by the corporation in the future, called the **preemptive right**. It protects shareholders' proportionate interest in the corporation. For example, a shareholder who owns 25% of a corporation's common shares has the first opportunity to buy 25% of any new common shares issued. This enables the shareholder to maintain a 25% ownership interest if desired.

Motivation for Preferred Shares

There are several reasons for a corporation to issue preferred shares. One reason is to raise capital without sacrificing control of the corporation. For example, let's suppose the organizers of a company have $100,000 cash to invest and wish to organize a corporation needing $200,000 of capital to get off to a good start. If they sold $100,000 worth of common shares, they would have only 50% control and would need to negotiate with other shareholders in setting policies and making key decisions. If they instead issue $100,000 of the common shares to themselves and sell outsiders 1,000 shares of $8 cumulative preferred shares with no voting rights for $100,000, they retain control of the corporation.

A second reason for issuing preferred shares is to increase the return earned by common shareholders. To illustrate, let's suppose a corporation's organizers expect their new company to earn an annual profit of $24,000 on an investment of $200,000. If they sell and issue $200,000 worth of common shares, this profit produces a 12% return on the $200,000 of equity belonging to the common shareholders ($24,000/$200,000 = 0.12 or 12%). However, if they issue 1,000 shares of $8 preferred shares to outsiders for $100,000 and $100,000 of common shares to themselves, their own return increases to 16% per year, as shown in Exhibit 12.11.

EXHIBIT 12.11

Return to Common Shareholders

Net after-tax profit	$24,000
Less: Preferred dividends at $8	
(1,000 preferred shares × $8 dividends per share)	8,000
Balance to common shareholders	$16,000
Return to common shareholders ($16,000/$100,000)	16%

Common shareholders earn 16% instead of 12% because assets contributed by preferred shareholders are invested to earn $12,000 while the preferred dividend payments amount to only $8,000.

Use of preferred shares to increase return to common shareholders is an example of **financial leverage**. Whenever the dividend rate on preferred shares is less than the rate the corporation earns on the amount invested by preferred shareholders, the effect of issuing preferred shares is to increase (or *leverage*) the rate earned by common shareholders. Financial leverage also occurs when debt is issued and the interest rate paid on it is less than the rate earned from using the assets the creditors lent to the corporation.

There are other reasons for issuing preferred shares. For example, a corporation's preferred shares may appeal to some investors who believe its common shares are too risky or that the dividend rate on common shares is too low. Remember, preferred shareholders get paid before anything is paid to common shareholders upon dissolution of the corporation, reducing the risk of loss to preferred shareholders. Also, if a corporation's management wants to issue common shares but believes the current market price for common shares is too low, the corporation may issue preferred shares that are *convertible* into common shares. If and when the price of common shares increases, the preferred shareholders can *convert* their shares into common shares. *Convertible preferred shares* are discussed later in this chapter.

DECISION MAKER
Answer—End of chapter

Concert Organizer

You are in the business of organizing music concerts. You've recently decided to move away from venues targeting under 5,000 people to those targeting between 10,000 and 50,000 people. The switch in venue size demands additional funding to pay facilities rental fees and attract key performers. You decide to incorporate because of the increased risk of lawsuits and your desire to issue shares to meet funding demands. It is important to you that you keep control of the company for decisions on whom to schedule and where to host the concert. What type of share issuance best meets your needs?

CHECKPOINT

8. In what ways do preferred shares often have priority over common shares?

9. Increasing the return to common shareholders by issuing preferred shares is an example of (a) financial leverage; (b) cumulative earnings; or (c) dividends in arrears.

Do Quick Study question: QS 12-10

MID-CHAPTER DEMONSTRATION PROBLEM

Raja Inc. began operations on January 2, 2017, and immediately issued 8,000 common shares for cash of $1.50 per share. On January 3, 500 common shares were issued to promoters in exchange for their services in selling shares of the corporation; the costs were charged to Organization Expenses. The shares were valued at a total of $1,000. On January 11, 4,000 preferred shares were issued for cash of $5.00 per share.

On February 5, 10,000 common shares were issued in exchange for land valued at $24,925. On February 25, 3,000 more preferred shares were issued for total cash of $15,700.

a. Present the journal entries that the company's accountant would use to record these transactions.

b. Prepare the statement of changes in equity for the month ended February 28, 2017. Assume a loss of $10,000 was realized in January, profit earned during February was $55,000, and dividends totalling $5,000 had been declared and paid in February.

c. Prepare the equity section of the February 28, 2017, balance sheet. Raja Inc. is authorized to issue an unlimited number of preferred and common shares.

d. What was the average issue price per common share as of February 28, 2017?

e. What was the average issue price per preferred share as of February 28, 2017?

Analysis Component:

Assume Raja Inc.'s total assets were $378,750 at February 28, 2017. Rounding calculations to two decimal places, what percentage of the assets was financed by:

a. Total debt
c. Equity of preferred shareholders

b. Total equity
d. Equity of common shareholders

Solution

a.

2017				
Jan.	2	Cash	12,000	
		Common Shares		12,000
		Issued 8,000 common shares for cash; 8,000 × $1.50 = $12,000.		
	3	Organization Expenses..................................	1,000	
		Common Shares		1,000
		Issued 500 common shares for services in selling shares.		
	11	Cash	20,000	
		Preferred Shares.....................................		20,000
		Issued 4,000 preferred shares for cash; 4,000 × $5.00 = $20,000.		
Feb.	5	Land	24,925	
		Common Shares		24,925
		Issued 10,000 common shares in exchange for land.		
	25	Cash	15,700	
		Preferred Shares.....................................		15,700
		Issued 3,000 preferred shares for cash.		

b.

Raja Inc.
Statement of Changes in Equity
For Month Ended February 28, 2017

	Preferred Shares	Common Shares	Retained Earnings	Total Equity
Balance, February 1..	$20,000	$13,000	$ (10,000)	$ 23,000
Issuance of shares	15,700	24,925		40,625
Profit (loss)			55,000	55,000
Dividends..			(5,000)	(5,000)
Balance, February 28......................................	$35,700	$37,925	$ 40,000	$113,625

c.

Raja Inc. Equity Section of the Balance Sheet February 28, 2017		
Contributed capital:		
Preferred shares, unlimited shares authorized, 7,000 shares issued and outstanding..	$35,700	
Common shares, unlimited shares authorized; 18,500 shares issued and outstanding...	37,925	
Total contributed capital..		$ 73,625
Retained earnings...		40,000
Total equity		$113,625

d. $37,925/18,500$ shares $= \$2.05$ average issue price per common share

e. $35,700/7,000$ shares $= \$5.10$ average issue price per preferred share

Analysis Component:

a. $[(\$378,750 - \$113,625 = \$265,125)/\$378,750] \times 100\% = 70\%$

b. $100\% - 70\% = 30\%$ OR $\$113,625/\$378,750 \times 100\% = 30\%$

c. $\$35,700/\$378,750 \times 100\% = 9.43\%$

d. $(\$37,925 + \$40,000 = \$77,925)/\$378,750 \times 100\% = 20.57\%$

Dividends

Dividends are a distribution of earnings (also referred to as a distribution of profit). The corporation's board of directors is responsible for making decisions regarding dividends. Dividends cause retained earnings to decrease. They are paid on outstanding shares, which are the shares held by the shareholders (refer to Exhibit 12.6 to review *outstanding shares for Dillon Snowboards Inc.*). The two most common types of dividends are cash dividends and share (or stock) dividends. A share (stock) split is not a type of dividend but has a similar effect on equity as share dividends do. Share dividends and splits are discussed in Chapter 13. Cash dividends are explained in the following section.

Cash Dividends

LO4 Describe and account for cash dividends.

Generally a corporation is permitted to pay cash dividends if there are retained earnings held in the company and cash resources exist to pay shareholders. The decision to pay cash dividends rests with the board of directors and involves more than evaluating retained earnings and cash. The directors, for instance, may decide to keep the cash and invest in new techonologies, facilities, or other areas to support the growth of the corporation. Other reasons to keep the cash include meeting unexpected payments, taking advantage of opportunities as they come up, or paying off corporate debt.

Many corporations pay cash dividends to their shareholders in regular amounts at regular dates. These cash flows provide a return to investors and almost always improve the shares' market value.

ENTRIES FOR CASH DIVIDENDS

The payment of dividends involves three important dates: declaration, record, and payment.

Date of declaration is the date the directors vote to pay a dividend, creating a legal liability of the corporation to its shareholders. To illustrate, the entry to record a November 9 declaration of a $1 per share dividend by the directors of Tech Ltd. with 5,000 outstanding common shares is:

Nov.	9	Cash Dividends	5,000
		Common Dividends Payable....................		5,000
		Declared a $1 per share cash dividend on common shares.	

Cash Dividends is a temporary account that gathers information about total dividends declared during the reporting period. It is not an expense account. An alternative to using a Cash Dividends account is to debit Retained Earnings, as illustrated previously in the mid-chapter demonstration problem. The Common Dividends Payable account reflects the corporation's current liability to its common shareholders.

Date of record is the future date specified by the directors for recording the shareholders listed in the corporation's records to receive dividends. Persons who own shares on the date of record receive dividends. No journal entry is needed at the date of record.

Date of payment is the date when shareholders receive payment. If a balance sheet is prepared between the date of declaration and date of payment, Common Dividends Payable is reported as a current liability. For instance, **Telus Corporation** reported $222,000,000 of dividends payable as at December 31, 2013, and provided disclosure in note 12 of its annual report for its declared $806 million in dividends in fiscal 2013.

(a) Dividends declared

Years ended December 31 (millions except per share amounts)	2013				2012			
	Declared				Declared			
Equity share dividends	Effective	Per share*	Paid to shareholders	Total	Effective	Per share*	Paid to shareholders	Total
Quarter 1 dividend	Mar. 11, 2013	$0.32	Apr. 1, 2013	$ 209	Mar. 9, 2012	$0.290	Apr. 2, 2012	$189
Quarter 2 dividend	June. 10, 2013	0.34	July 2, 2013	222	June 8, 2012	0.305	July 3, 2012	198
Quarter 3 dividend	Sep. 10, 2013	0.34	Oct. 1, 2013	213	Sep. 10, 2012	0.305	Oct. 1, 2012	199
Quarter 4 dividend	Dec. 11, 2013	0.36	Jan 2, 2014	222	Dec. 11, 2012	0.320	Jan, 2, 2013	208
		$1.36		$ 866		$1.220		$794

On December 1, Tech Ltd.'s date of payment, the following entry is recorded:

Dec.	1	Common Dividends Payable	5,000
		Cash		5,000
		Paid cash dividend to common shareholders.	

At the end of the reporting period, the balance of Tech Ltd.'s Cash Dividends account is closed to Retained Earnings as follows:

Dec.	31	Retained Earnings	5,000
		Cash Dividends.....................................		5,000
		To close Cash Dividends account.	

> **Important Tip:** If *Retained Earnings is debited directly on the date of declaration, no closing entry is required when using this alternative approach.*

Because dividends cause retained earnings to decrease, they are subtracted on the statement of changes in equity as shown previously for ABC Corporation in Exhibit 12.4. For example, BCE Corporation Ltd.'s retained earnings were decreased by $1,938,000,000 for the year ended December 31, 2013, because of a cash dividend declared and paid to common shareholders.

The entries regarding cash dividends on preferred shares would be recorded in the same way as shown for common shares.

DEFICITS AND CASH DIVIDENDS

A corporation with a debit (abnormal) balance in Retained Earnings is said to have a **deficit**. A deficit arises when a company has cumulative losses greater than total profits earned in prior years. For example, **Nortel Networks Corporation**'s deficit at December 31, 2011, is deducted on its balance sheet as shown in Exhibit 12.12.

EXHIBIT 12.12

Nortel Networks Corporation—Deficit Illustrated

Nortel Networks Corporation Equity Section of the Balance Sheet December 31, 2011 (millions of U.S. dollars)	
Share capital	$ 35,604
Deficit	(42,406)

www.nortel.com

Note: At the time of the deficit Nortel Networks Corporation was under bankruptcy protection and has subsequently ceased operations and sold off its business units.

A corporation with a deficit is not allowed to pay a cash dividend to its shareholders in most jurisdictions. This legal restriction is designed to protect creditors of the corporation by preventing distribution of assets to shareholders at a time when the company is in financial difficulty.

Special Features of Preferred Shares

Preferred shares can have a number of special features such as being cumulative or non-cumulative, participating, callable, and convertible. These characteristics are unique to preferred shares and are discussed in this section.

Dividend Preference

In exchange for voting rights, preferred shares usually carry a **dividend preference**, which means a dividend cannot be paid to common shareholders unless preferred shareholders are paid first. The dividend preference is usually expressed as a dollar amount per share as illustrated in Exhibit 12.13.

A preference for dividends does not guarantee dividends. If the directors do not declare a dividend, neither the preferred nor the common shareholders receive one. However, if dividends are not declared on preferred shares, the undeclared dividends from prior periods plus current dividends are paid if the preferred shares have a *cumulative* feature. The feature known as cumulative and non-cumulative dividends is the topic of the next section.

EXHIBIT 12.13

Presentation of Dividend Preference

Pike Technology Ltd.
Equity Section of the Balance Sheet
April 30, 2017

Contributed capital:
  Preferred shares, $2.20, 25,000 shares authorized;
    7,000 shares issued and outstanding.................................. $ 84,000
  Common shares, unlimited shares authorized;
    80,000 shares issued and outstanding............................... 760,000
  Total contributed capital... $844,000
Retained earnings.. 49,000
Total equity $893,000

The preferred shareholders are entitled to receive $2.20 per share annually when dividends are declared.

CUMULATIVE OR NON-CUMULATIVE DIVIDEND

LO5 Distribute dividends between common and preferred shares.

Many preferred shares carry a *cumulative* dividend right. **Cumulative preferred shares** have a right to be paid both current and all prior periods' undeclared dividends before any dividend is paid to common shareholders. When preferred shares are cumulative and the directors either do not declare a dividend to preferred shareholders or declare a dividend that does not satisfy the cumulative dividend, then the unpaid dividend amount is called a **dividend in arrears.** Accumulation of dividends in arrears on cumulative preferred shares does not guarantee they will be paid. Some preferred shares are *non-cumulative.* **Non-cumulative preferred shares** have no right to prior periods' unpaid dividends if they were not declared.

To illustrate and show the difference between cumulative and non-cumulative preferred shares, refer to the assumed information regarding the shares of Pike Technology Ltd. in Exhibit 12.13.

During the year ended April 30, 2017, the first year of the corporation's operations, the directors declared and paid total cash dividends of $31,400. During the years ended April 30, 2018 and 2019, total dividends declared and paid were $0 and $110,800 respectively. Allocations of total dividends are shown in Exhibit 12.14 under two assumptions:

a. The preferred shares are non-cumulative, and

b. The preferred shares are cumulative.

With non-cumulative preferred shares, the preferred shareholders in Exhibit 12.14 never receive the $15,400 not declared for the year ended 2018. Undeclared dividends are *lost* if preferred shares are non-cumulative.

When preferred shares are cumulative, undeclared dividends are not lost because they go into arrears. In Exhibit 12.14, the $15,400 not declared in 2018 is paid during the year ended 2019 before the common shareholders receive a dividend.

EXHIBIT 12.14

Allocation of Dividends Between Preferred and Common Shares

a. If non-cumulative preferred:

	Preferred	Common	Total
Year ended 2017:			
7,000 shares × $2.20/share...............................	$15,400		
Remainder to common		$16,000	$ 31,400
Year ended 2018:...	-0-	-0-	$ -0-
Year ended 2019:			
7,000 shares × $2.20/share...............................	$15,400		
Remainder to common		$95,400	$110,800

b. If cumulative preferred:

	Preferred	Common	Total
Year ended 2017:			
7,000 shares × $2.20/share...............................	$15,400		
Remainder to common		$16,000	$ 31,400
Year ended 2018:...	-0-	-0-	$ -0-
Year ended 2019:			
Dividends in arrears = $15,400			
+ Current year dividends of $15,400	$30,800		
Remainder to common		$80,000	$110,800

FINANCIAL STATEMENT DISCLOSURE OF DIVIDENDS

A liability for a dividend does not exist until the directors declare a dividend. This means that if a preferred dividend date passes and the corporation's board fails to declare the dividend on its cumulative preferred shares, the dividend in arrears is not a liability. When preparing financial statements, the *full disclosure principle* requires the corporation to report the amount of preferred dividends in arrears as of the balance sheet date. This information is usually disclosed in a note to the financial statements.

CHECKPOINT

10. The Cash Dividends account is normally (a) reported on the balance sheet as a liability; (b) closed to Income Summary; or (c) closed to Retained Earnings.

11. What three dates are involved in the process of paying a cash dividend?

12. When does a dividend become a legal obligation of the company?

13. A corporation has issued 9,000 shares of $5 cumulative preferred shares for a total of $450,000 and 27,000 common shares for a total of $270,000. No dividends have been declared for 2015 and 2016. During 2017, the corporation declares a $288,000 dividend. The amount paid to common shareholders is (a) $198,000; (b) $153,000; or (c) $108,000.

Do Quick Study questions: QS 12-11, QS 12-12, QS 12-13

In addition to being cumulative or non-cumulative, preferred shares can have other features. This is the topic of the next section.

Other Features of Preferred Shares

PARTICIPATING OR NON-PARTICIPATING DIVIDENDS ON PREFERRED SHARES

Non-participating preferred shares have dividends limited to a maximum amount each year. This maximum is often stated as a specific dollar amount per share. Once preferred shareholders receive this amount, the common shareholders receive any and all additional dividends.

Participating preferred shares have a feature in which preferred shareholders share with common shareholders in any dividends paid in excess of the dollar amount specified for the preferred shares. This participating feature does not apply until common shareholders receive dividends in a ratio equal to the preferred shares' dividend. While many corporations are authorized to issue participating preferred shares, they are rarely issued.

CONVERTIBLE PREFERRED SHARES

Preferred shares are more attractive to investors if they carry a right to exchange preferred shares for a fixed number of common shares. **Convertible preferred shares** give holders the option of exchanging their preferred shares for common shares at a specified rate. This feature offers holders of convertible preferred shares a higher potential return. When a company prospers and its common shares increase in value, convertible preferred shareholders can share in this success by converting their preferred shares into more valuable common shares. Also, these holders benefit from increases in the value of common shares without converting their preferred shares because the preferred shares' market value is affected by changes in the value of common shares.

To illustrate the entries to record the conversion of preferred shares to common, assume that the preferred shares in Exhibit 12.15 were convertible at the rate of two common shares for each preferred share.

EXHIBIT 12.15

Presentation of Dividend Preference

Pike Technology Ltd. Equity Section of the Balance Sheet April 30, 2017		
Contributed capital:		
Preferred shares, $2.20, 25,000 shares authorized; 7,000 shares issued and outstanding..	$ 84,000	
Common shares, unlimited shares authorized; 80,000 shares issued and outstanding..	760,000	
Total contributed capital..		$844,000
Retained earnings...		49,000
Total equity		$893,000

The average issue price of the preferred shares is used as the basis of the calculation to record the conversion of 1,000 preferred shares into common shares on May 1, 2017:

2017				
May	1	Preferred Shares	12,000	
		Common Shares		12,000

*To record the conversion of preferred
shares into common; $84,000/7,000 shares
= $12/share average issue price; $12/share
× 1,000 shares = $12,000.*

This entry transfers $12,000 from the Preferred Shares account to the Common Shares account. Total equity does not change.

CALLABLE PREFERRED SHARES

Callable preferred shares, also known as **redeemable preferred shares**, give the issuing corporation the right to purchase (retire) these shares from their holders at specified future prices and dates. Many issues of preferred shares are callable. The amount paid to call and retire a preferred share is its **call price**, or *redemption value*. This amount is set at the time the shares are issued. The call price normally includes the issue price of the shares plus a premium giving holders additional return on their investment. When the issuing corporation calls and retires preferred shares, it must pay the call price *and* any dividends in arrears.

For instance, in Note 18 of its December 31, 2013, annual report, TransCanada PipeLines announced the redemption on January 27, 2014 of all four million outstanding cumulative redeemable preferred shares. Series Y at $50 per share plus accrued and unpaid dividends.

Closing Entries for Corporations

LO6   Record closing entries for a corporation.

Recall that the closing process involves closing all temporary accounts. This includes closing revenues and expenses to the Income Summary account. For the corporate form of organization, the balance in the Income Summary account is closed to Retained Earnings. To demonstrate, assume Scriver Inc. had the adjusted trial balance at December 31, 2017, as shown below. After closing all of the revenue and expense accounts, the Income Summary account would appear as shown to the right.

Acct. No.	Account	Debit	Credit
101	Cash...	$ 40,000	
106	Prepaid rent......................................	57,000	
153	Trucks...	137,000	
154	Accumulated depreciation, trucks........		$ 16,000
201	Accounts payable		20,000
307	Common shares		75,000
315	Preferred shares...............................		40,000
318	Retained earnings.............................		30,000
319	Cash dividends.................................	10,000	
401	Revenue..		238,000
611	Depreciation expense, trucks..............	35,000	
640	Rent expense	120,000	
695	Income taxes expense	20,000	
	Totals...	$419,000	$419,000

Income Summary

Dec 31/17	175,000	238,000	Dec. 31/17
		Bal.	
		63,000	Dec. 31/17

The entry to close the Income Summary account is:[10]

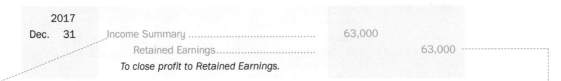

2017				
Dec.	31	Income Summary	63,000	
		Retained Earnings.............................		63,000
		To close profit to Retained Earnings.		

After posting the closing entries, the Income Summary will show a balance of $0, as illustrated in the T-account below.

Income Summary

Dec 31/17	175,000	238,000	Dec. 31/17
			Bal.
Dec. 31/17	63,000	63,000	Dec. 31/17
			Bal.
		-0-	Dec. 31/17

The final step in the closing process would be to close dividends as follows (unless Retained Earnings had been debited directly):

2017				
Dec.	31	Retained Earnings	10,000	
		Cash Dividends..................................		10,000
		To close the Cash Dividends account to		
		Retained Earnings.		

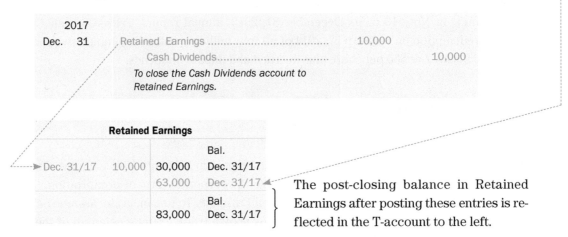

Retained Earnings

			Bal.
Dec. 31/17	10,000	30,000	Dec. 31/17
		63,000	Dec. 31/17
			Bal.
		83,000	Dec. 31/17

The post-closing balance in Retained Earnings after posting these entries is reflected in the T-account to the left.

CHECKPOINT

14. Assume Retained Earnings had a January 1, 2017, balance of $5,000. During January, dividends of $3,000 were declared but not paid and a profit of $7,000 was realized. What is the January 31, 2017, post-closing balance in Retained Earnings?

Do Quick Study questions: QS 12-14, QS 12-15, QS 12-16

---

10   If, instead, Scriver Inc. had realized a loss during the accounting period of $14,000, the balance in the Income Summary account would have been a debit after closing all revenues and expenses. The entry to close the Income Summary account in this instance would be:

2017				
Dec.	31	Retained Earnings..	14,000	
		Income Summary..		14,000
		To close loss to Retained Earnings.		

Financial Statement Analysis

Two helpful tools financial statement users can use in analyzing a public company's performance and value are Return on Common Shareholders' Equity and the Book Value per Share.

RETURN ON EQUITY

The Return on Equity ratio is a very helpful financial statement analysis tool that enables users to assess how profitable a company is from the financial position of the shareholders.

$$\text{Return on Common Shareholders' Equity} = \frac{\text{Profit} - \text{Preferred Dividends}}{\text{Average Common Shareholders' Equity}}$$

When comparing two company's performance, a higher percentage return will identify the company that has provided the greatest value to shareholders in the past year of financial performance. The financial information is presented for two Canadian banks:

Financial Information	The Toronto Dominion Bank October 31, 2014 (in millions CDN)	Royal Bank of Canada October 13, 2014 (in millions CDN)
Profit	7,783 million	$9,004 million
Preferred Dividends	143 million	213 million
Common Shareholder's Equity Total Equity − Preferred Share Equity	2014: 54,682 − 2,200 = 52,482 2013: 49875 − 3,395 = 46,480	2014: 52,640 − 4,075 = 48,565 2013: 47,665 − 4,600 = 43,065
Average Common Shareholder's Equity	$= \dfrac{52,482 + 46,480}{2}$ $= 49,481$	$= \dfrac{48,565 + 43,065}{2}$ $= 45,815$
Number of Shares Outstanding 2014	1,846.2 million	1,442,232,886
2013	1,838.9 million	1,441,055,616

Source: Above information has been taken from the Annual Financial Reports for the year ended October 31, 2014 for Toronto Dominion Bank and Royal Bank of Canada.

Presented next is the calculation of Return on Equity:

Return on Equity Calculation	The Toronto Dominion Bank	Royal Bank of Canada
Profit − Preferred Dividends (A)	7,783 million − 143 million	9,004 million − 213 million
Average Common Shareholders' Equity (B)	49,481 million	45,815 million
Return on Equity = (A)/(B)	15%	19%

Based on the above analysis, Royal Bank of Canada has a slightly higher ROE than Toronto Dominion Bank for the 2014 fiscal period.

BOOK VALUE PER SHARE

Book value per share is a common analysis tool used to perform a baseline estimate of the value of a company, in terms of a single share.

$$\text{Book Value per Share} = \frac{\text{Common Shareholders' Equity}}{\text{Average Number of Shares Outstanding}}$$

Market values of a firm's shares are typically higher than the book value, as investors take into consideration a variety of factors that go beyond reported net assets, such as revenue growth, cash flow, profitability, and anticipated future market conditions.

Book Value per Share	The Toronto Dominion Bank (TD.TO)	Royal Bank of Canada (RY.TO)
Common Shareholders' Equity End of Period (A)	52,482 million	48,565 million
Average Number of Shares Outstanding (B)	$= \dfrac{1{,}846.2 \text{ million} + 1{,}838.9 \text{ million}}{2}$ $= 1{,}842.55 \text{ million}$	$\dfrac{1{,}442 \text{ million} + 1{,}441 \text{ million}}{2}$ $= 1{,}441.5$
Book value per share = (A)/(B)	$28.48	$33.69
Market value per share on July 17, 2015	$53.03	$77.30

Source: Above information has been taken from the Annual Financial Reports for the year ended October 31, 2014 for Toronto Dominion Bank and Royal Bank of Canada.

Based on the above analysis of Book Value per Common Share, Royal Bank has a higher book value per share, indicating Royal Bank of Canada has a higher base net worth. However, the calculation above is based on the balance sheet presentation of equity. The market price per share also reflects a higher value for the Royal Bank, trading at $77.30 on July 17, 2015, compared to $53.03 for TD Bank on the same day. It is important to keep in mind that it is a base analysis of value, as several items on the balance sheet are not presented at their fair values at the end of the reporting period.

CRITICAL THINKING CHALLENGE

Refer to the Critical Thinking Challenge questions at the beginning of the chapter. Compare your answers to those suggested on Connect.

IFRS AND ASPE—THE DIFFERENCES

Difference	International Financial Reporting Standards (IFRS)	Accounting Standards for Private Enterprises (ASPE)
Statement of changes in equity	• A statement of changes in equity that presents all changes in the equity accounts is required.	• A statement of retained earnings that presents all changes to retained earnings is required. • Any changes to contributed capital are disclosed in the notes to the financial statements; a statement of changes in equity is not required.
Issuing shares for a non-cash item	• When shares are issued in exchange for a non-cash item, such as land or equipment, the transaction is recorded at the fair value of the item received. If the fair value of the item received cannot be reliably determined, the fair value of the item given up is used.	• When shares are issued in exchange for a non-cash item, the transaction is recorded using either the fair value of the item received or the fair value of the item given up, whichever is more reliable.
Authorized number of shares	• The financial statements must show both the number of shares authorized and the number of shares issued.	• The financial statements must show the number of shares issued but showing the number of shares authorized is not a requirement.

A Look Ahead

Chapter 13 focuses on corporate reporting, profit, earnings per share, and retained earnings. We explain how to calculate and present profit to shareholders and other financial statement users in financial statements.

For further study on some topics of relevance to this chapter, please see the following Extend Your Knowledge Supplements:

EYK 12-1 Example of Share Certificate

EYK 12-2 Per Value Shares

EYK 12-3 Corporate Supplement: Closing Entries Detailed

Summary

LO1 Identify characteristics of corporations and their organization. Corporations are separate legal entities and their shareholders are not liable for corporate debts. Shares issued by corporations are easily transferred between shareholders, and the life of a corporation does not end with the incapacity or death of a shareholder. A corporation acts through its agents, who are its officers and managers, not its shareholders. Corporations are regulated by the government and are subject to income taxes.

LO2 Describe and contrast the specialized components of corporate financial statements. The income statement for a corporation is similar to that of an unincorporated organization except for the inclusion of income tax expense. A corporation, like a proprietorship, reports changes in equity caused by profits (losses), distributions of profit (in the form of dividends) to its owners (shareholders), and owner (shareholder) investments on the statement of changes in equity. Accumulated profits less losses and dividends are recorded in Retained Earnings. Shareholder investments are recorded in share capital accounts, either common shares or preferred shares. An unincorporated business records these three activities in the owner's capital account. The equity section on a corporation's balance sheet can be called shareholders' equity, while on a sole proprietorship's balance sheet it can be called owner's equity.

LO3 Record the issuance of common and preferred shares and describe their presentation in the equity section of the balance sheet. When only one class of shares is issued, they are called common shares. Shares, both common and preferred, can be issued for cash or other assets. The number of shares authorized, issued, and outstanding, along with the dollar value contributed by the shareholders, is shown under the heading Contributed Capital in the equity section of the balance sheet. Preferred shares have a priority (or senior status) relative to common shares in one or more areas. The usual areas include preference as to (1) dividends and (2) assets in case of liquidation. They do not have voting rights.

LO4 Describe and account for cash dividends. The board of directors makes all decisions regarding dividends. In accounting for dividends, there are three key dates that are relevant: the date of declaration, the date of record, and the date of payment. The date of declaration is the date the liability to pay dividends is created. All shareholders holding shares as of the date of record are eligible to receive the declared dividend. The dividend payment date is when dividends are actually paid.

LO5 Distribute dividends between common and preferred shares. Preferred shareholders usually hold the right to receive dividend distributions before common shareholders. This right is known as dividend preference. When preferred shares are cumulative and in arrears, the amount in arrears must be caught up and be distributed to preferred shareholders before any dividends can be paid to common shareholders. Preferred shares can also be convertible or callable. Convertibility permits the holder to convert preferred shares to common shares. Callability permits the issuing corporation to buy preferred shares back under specified conditions.

LO6 Record closing entries for a corporation. Revenues and expenses are closed to the Income Summary account as for an unincorporated organization. The balance in Income Summary is closed to Retained Earnings. Dividends are closed to Retained Earnings, as well.

Guidance Answer to DECISION MAKER

Concert Organizer

Because you wish to maintain control of the company, you want to issue shares in a way that does not interfere with your ability to run the company the way you desire. You have two basic options: (1) different classes of common shares, or (2) common and preferred shares. Your objective in this case is to issue a class of shares to yourself that has all or a majority of the voting power. The other class of shares you issue would carry limited or no voting rights. In this way you maintain complete control and are able to raise your necessary funds.

Guidance Answers to CHECKPOINT

1.

Organization Expenses (or Various Exp.) 60,000	
Cash	60,000

2. All transactions are identical for both organizations except for the $12, which represents the income tax expense imposed on the corporation but not on the unincorporated form of organization.

3. The income statement of a corporation includes Income Tax Expense but the income statement for an unincorporated business does not. This is because a corporation must pay taxes on its profit, whereas an unincorporated business does not since it is not a separate legal entity.

4. The statement of changes in equity for a corporation includes investments by the shareholders (called *owner* in a single proprietorship) in a share capital account and profits (losses) less distributions of earnings (called *dividends* for a corporation) in a retained earnings account. The statement of changes in equity for a single proprietorship shows investments by the owner, profits (losses), and distributions of earnings (called *withdrawals* for the single proprietorship) as part of one account, the owner's capital.

5. The equity sections of the balance sheet for both the corporation and single proprietorship include investments by the shareholders or owner, and profits (losses) less dividends or withdrawals. The difference is into which accounts these activities are recorded. The corporation shows shareholder investments in a Share Capital account and profits (losses) less dividends in Retained Earnings, while a single proprietorship shows all three activities in the owner's Capital account.

6. The average issue price per common share at July 31, 2017, was $405,000/34,000 = $11.91 (rounded).

7. *b*

8. Special rights include a preference for receiving dividends and for the distribution of assets if the corporation's assets are liquidated.

9. *a*

10. *c*

11. The three dates are the date of declaration, date of record, and date of payment.

12. A dividend becomes a legal obligation of the company when it is declared by the board of directors on the date of declaration.

13. *b*

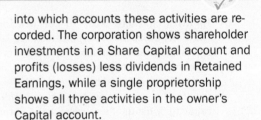

Total dividend	$288,000
To preferred shareholders	135,000*
Remainder to common shareholders	$153,000

*9,000 × $5 × 3 = $135,000

14. $5,000 − $3,000 + $7,000 = $9,000.

DEMONSTRATION PROBLEM

Barton Corporation was established on January 1, 2017 as an online retailer to distribute off-road adventure gear out of its warehouse in Banff, Alberta. Barton is authorized by its articles of incorporation to issue 100,000 shares of $10 cumulative preferred shares and an unlimited number of common shares. The following transactions relating to equity occurred during the first two years of the company's operations.

2017

Jan.	2	Issued 200,000 common shares at $12 per share.
	2	Issued 100,000 common shares in exchange for a building valued at $820,000 and merchandise inventory valued at $380,000.
	3	Paid a cash reimbursement to the company's founders for $100,000 of organization costs; the Organization Expenses account was debited.
	3	Issued 12,000 preferred shares for cash at $110 per share.
Dec.	31	The Income Summary account for 2017 had a $125,000 credit balance before being closed to Retained Earnings; no dividends were declared on either common or preferred shares.

2018

June	4	Issued 100,000 common shares for cash at $15 per share.
Dec.	10	Declared total cash dividends of $540,000 payable on January 10, 2019.
	31	The Income Summary account for 2018 had a $1 million credit balance before being closed to Retained Earnings.

Required

1. Prepare the journal entries to record these transactions.

2. Prepare statements of changes in equity for the years ended December 31, 2017 and 2018.

3. Prepare the balance sheet presentation of the liabilities and equity as at December 31, 2017 and 2018. Include appropriate notes to the financial statements (regarding any dividends in arrears).

Analysis Component:

What effect does the declaration and subsequent payment of cash dividends have on the income statement and balance sheet?

Planning the Solution

- Record journal entries for the transactions in 2017 and 2018.

- Close the accounts related to retained earnings at the end of each year.

- Prepare the statements of changes in equity for the years 2017 and 2018.

- Determine the balances for the 2017 and 2018 contributed capital accounts for the balance sheet including information about the number of shares issued.

- Prepare the equity section of the 2017 and 2018 balance sheet including a note regarding any dividends in arrears.

- Prepare an answer for the analysis component.

Solution

1.

2017				
Jan.	2	Cash	2,400,000	
		Common Shares		2,400,000
		Issued 200,000 common shares;		
		200,000 × $12.		
	2	Building	820,000	
		Merchandise Inventory.................................	380,000	
		Common Shares		1,200,000
		Issued 100,000 common shares.		
	3	Organization Exp. (or other various exp.).........	100,000	
		Cash..		100,000
		Reimbursed the founders for organization		
		costs.		
	3	Cash	1,320,000	
		Preferred Shares.................................		1,320,000
		Issued 12,000 preferred shares;		
		12,000 × $110.		
Dec.	31	Income Summary	125,000	
		Retained Earnings...............................		125,000
		Close the Income Summary account and		
		update Retained Earnings.		
	2018			
June	4	Cash	1,500,000	
		Common Shares		1,500,000
		Issued 100,000 common shares;		
		100,000 × $15.		
Dec.	10	Cash Dividends (or Retained Earnings)...........	540,000	
		Preferred Dividend Payable...................		240,000
		Common Dividend Payable		300,000
		Declared current dividends and dividends		
		in arrears to common and preferred		
		shareholders, payable on January 10, 2019;		
		Preferred = $10/share × 12,000 shares ×		
		2 years; Common = $540,000 − $240,000.		
	31	Income Summary	1,000,000	
		Retained Earnings...............................		1,000,000
		To close the Income Summary account and		
		update Retained Earnings.		
	31	Retained Earnings	540,000	
		Cash Dividends....................................		540,000
		To close to Retained Earnings the		
		*Cash Dividends.**		

*Assuming Retained Earnings was not debited on December 10, 2018.

2.

Barton Corporation				
Statement of Changes in Equity				
For Years Ended December 31, 2017 and 2018				
	Preferred Shares	**Common Shares**	**Retained Earnings**	**Total Equity**
Balance, January 1, 2017	$ -0-	$ 0-	$ 0-	$ 0-
Changes in equity for 2017				
Issuance of share capital.................................	1,320,000	3,600,000		4,920,000
Profit (loss)..			125,000	125,000
Dividends..			-0-	-0-
Balance, December 31, 2017	$1,320,000	$3,600,000	$ 125,000	$5,045,000
Changes in equity for 2018				
Issuance of share capital.................................	-0-	1,500,000		1,500,000
Profit (loss)..			1,000,000	1,000,000
Dividends..			(540,000)	(540,000)
Balance, December 31, 2018	$1,320,000	$5,100,000	$ 585,000	$7,005,000

3. Balance sheet presentations:

Barton Corporation		
Partial Balance Sheet		
As of December 31, 2018		
	2018	**2017**
Liabilities		
Preferred dividend payable...	$ 240,000	$ -0-
Common dividend payable	300,000	-0-
Equity		
Contributed capital:		
Preferred shares, $10 cumulative, 100,000 shares authorized; 12,000 shares issued and outstanding.............................	$1,320,000	$1,320,000
Common shares, unlimited shares authorized; 400,000 shares issued and outstanding in 2018; 300,000 shares issued and outstanding in 2017..	5,100,000	3,600,000
Total contributed capital...	$6,420,000	$4,920,000
Retained earnings (see Note 1)	585,000	125,000
Total equity	$7,005,000	$5,045,000

Note 1: As of December 31, 2017, there were $120,000 of dividends in arrears on the preferred shares.

Analysis Component:

The declaration and subsequent payment of cash dividends will not affect the income statement in any way. On the balance sheet, assets will decrease because cash is paid to the shareholders and equity will decrease—specifically, Retained Earnings.

Glossary

Authorized shares The total number of shares that a corporation's charter authorizes it to sell. Federally incorporated companies are authorized to issue an unlimited number.

Book value per share A common analysis tool used to perform a baseline estimate of the value of a company, calculated as common shareholders' equity divided by average shares outstanding.

Callable preferred shares Preferred shares that the issuing corporation, at its option, may retire by paying a specified amount (the call price) to the preferred shareholders plus any dividends in arrears.

Call price The amount that must be paid to call and retire a preferred share.

Capital stock See *share capital*.

Closely held corporation See *privately held corporation*.

Common shares Shares of a corporation when there is only one class of shares.

Contributed capital The total amount of cash and other assets received by the corporation from its shareholders in exchange for common and/or preferred shares.

Convertible preferred shares Preferred shares that give holders the option of exchanging their preferred shares for common shares at a specified rate.

Cumulative preferred shares Preferred shares on which undeclared dividends accumulate until they are paid; common shareholders cannot receive a dividend until all cumulative dividends have been paid.

Date of declaration The date the directors vote to pay a dividend.

Date of payment The date when shareholders receive the dividend payment.

Date of record The future date specified by the directors for identifying those shareholders listed in the corporation's records to receive dividends.

Deficit Arises when a corporation has a debit (abnormal) balance for Retained Earnings.

Dividend in arrears An unpaid dividend on cumulative preferred shares; it must be paid before any current dividends on the preferred shares and before any dividends on the common shares are paid.

Dividend preference The rate per share at which dividends are paid when declared.

Equity financing Obtaining capital, or money, by issuing shares.

Financial leverage Achieving an increased return on common shares by paying dividends on preferred shares or interest on debt at a rate that is less than the rate of return earned with the assets that were invested in the corporation by the preferred shareholders or creditors.

Market value per share The price at which shares are bought or sold.

Non-cumulative preferred shares Preferred shares on which the right to receive dividends is lost for any year that the dividends are not declared.

Non-participating preferred shares Preferred shares on which dividends are limited to a maximum amount each year.

No par value A class of shares that has not been assigned a par value by the corporate charter.

Organization costs The costs of bringing a corporation into existence, including legal fees, promoters' fees, and amounts paid to the incorporating legal jurisdiction.

Outstanding shares The number of shares held by shareholders.

Participating preferred shares Preferred shares with a feature that allows preferred shareholders to share with common shareholders in any dividends paid in excess of the percent stated on the preferred shares.

Par value An arbitrary value a corporation places on each of the corporation's shares.

Preemptive right The right to purchase additional common shares issued by the corporation in the future.

Preferred shares Shares that give their owners a priority status over common shareholders in one or more ways, such as the payment of dividends or the distribution of assets on liquidation.

Private Enterprise GAAP (PE GAAP) Generally accepted accounting principles that privately held corporations may choose to adopt over IFRS; PE GAAP simplify areas in IFRS identified as being overly complex.

Privately held corporation When a corporation offers its shares to only a few shareholders; shares are not for public sale; also called *closely held corporation*.

Progressive tax Higher levels of profit are taxed at higher rates and lower levels of profit are taxed at lower rates.

Proxy A legal document that gives an agent of a shareholder the power to exercise the voting rights of that shareholder's shares.

Publicly held corporation When a corporation offers its shares for public sale, which can result in thousands of shareholders.

Public sale Refers to trading in an organized stock market.

Redeemable preferred shares See *callable preferred shares*.

Retained earnings The cumulative profit less losses and dividends retained by a corporation.

Sell shares directly When a corporation advertises its shares' issuance directly to potential buyers. This is most common with privately held corporations.

Sell shares indirectly When a corporation pays a brokerage house (investment banker) to issue its shares.

Share One unit of ownership in a corporation.

Share capital Refers to all types (or classes) of a corporation's shares; also called *capital stock*.

Shareholder(s) The owners of a corporation.

Start-up costs See *organization costs*.

Statement of changes in equity for a corporation A financial statement that details the changes in share capital and retained earnings for the period.

Underwrite When a brokerage house buys the shares from the corporation and takes all gains or losses from their resale to shareholders.

Concept Review Questions

1. Who is responsible for directing the affairs of a corporation?

2. What are organization costs? List examples of these costs.

3. List the general rights of common shareholders.

4. What is the preemptive right of common shareholders?

5. What is the meaning of the *call price* of a share?

6. Why would an investor find convertible preferred shares attractive?

7. Refer to the financial statements for Indigo in Appendix II, looking at the consolidated statements of changes in equity. What were the total cash dividends declared and paid during the year ended March 30, 2013 and March 29, 2014?

8. Refer again to the financial statements for Indigo in Appendix II, looking at the consolidated statements of cash flows. Notice the same cash dividends paid during the year ended March 30, 2013 and March 29, 2014 as on the consolidated statements of changes in equity. What section did you find these same numbers in on the consolidated statements of cash flows?

9. Refer to the financial statements for Indigo in Appendix II, specifically Note 13. What was the amount during fiscal 2013 and 2014 of the distributed dividends per share?

10. 3Twenty Solutions in the opening vignette is a private corporation that was formed by three graduates of the University of Saskatchewan. Bombardier Inc. is an example of a Canadian public corporation. What is the main difference between a private corporation and a public corporation?

Quick Study

QS 12-1 **Characteristics of corporations** LO1

Of the following statements, which are true for the corporation form of business?

    a. Capital often is more easily accumulated than with other forms of organization.

    b. It has a limited life.

    c. Owners have unlimited liability for corporate debts.

    d. It is a separate legal entity.

    e. Ownership rights cannot be easily transferred.

QS 12-2 **Corporate financial statements** LO2

Mogul Ltd., a ski boot manufacturer, showed the following amounts for its year just ended October 31, 2017. Prepare a multi-step income statement assuming a tax rate of 25%.

Cost of goods sold	$420,000	Operating expenses	$162,000
Gain on sale of plant and equipment	4,000	Sales	982,000
Interest expense	6,200		

QS 12-3 Components of the equity section of a corporate balance sheet LO2

From the following list of selected accounts for Giant Inc., identify the equity accounts. Use "CC" for contributed capital, "RE" for retained earnings, and "X" if not an equity account.

_____ Cash		_____ Preferred shares	
_____ Common shares		_____ Retained earnings	
_____ Common dividend payable		_____ Preferred dividend payable	
_____ Deficit		_____ Preferred shares, $5 non-cumulative	

QS 12-4 Corporate financial statements LO2

Vision HR Consulting began operations on January 1, 2017. Complete the following schedule with journal entries detailing the transactions during 2017 for Vision HR Consulting under two forms of organization: as a single proprietorship (owned by Ian Smith), and as a corporation.

	FORM OF BUSINESS ORGANIZATION	
Transaction	Single Proprietorship	Corporation
Jan. 1, 2017: The owner(s) invested $10,000 into the new business		
During 2017: Revenues of $50,000 were earned; all cash		
During 2017: Expenses of $30,000 were incurred; all cash		
Dec. 15, 2017: $15,000 cash was distributed to the owner(s)		
Dec. 31, 2017, Year-End: All temporary accounts were closed – Close revenue account		
– Close expense account		
– Close income summary account to appropriate equity account(s)		
– Close withdrawal/cash dividends declared account		
Equity section on the balance sheet at December 31, 2017, after the first year of operations.	Vision HR Consulting Partial Balance Sheet December 31, 2017	Vision HR Consulting Inc. Partial Balance Sheet December 31, 2017

QS 12-5 Retained earnings LO2

Benson Inc. had a credit balance in Retained Earnings on December 31, 2017, of $48,000. During 2018, Benson recorded profit of $146,000 and declared and paid dividends of $47,000. During 2019, the company recorded a loss of $15,000. No dividends were declared or paid in 2019. Calculate the balance in Retained Earnings at December 31, 2019.

QS 12-6 Analyzing retained earnings LO2

The Retained Earnings account for Callaho Inc. is shown below:

Retained Earnings		
50,000	120,000	(Balance Jan. 1/17)
	X	
	300,000	(Balance Dec. 31/17)

1. Calculate X.
2. What does X represent?
3. What caused the debit of $50,000?

QS 12-7 Preparing a statement of changes in equity LO2

Fisher Inc. began operations on January 1, 2017. During its first year, $750,000 of common shares were issued and a loss of $28,000 was realized. In 2018, Fisher's second year of operations, an additional $125,000 of common shares were issued, profit of $148,000 was earned, and dividends of $40,000 were declared and paid. Prepare a statement of changes in equity for the year ended December 31, 2018.

QS 12-8 Issuance of common shares LO3

On February 1, Excel Corporation issued 37,500 common shares for $252,440 cash. On February 12, an additional 47,000 common shares were issued for cash of $7.25 per share. Present the entries to record these transactions and calculate the average issue price per common share.

QS 12-9 Interpreting journal entries for share issuances LO3

Each of these entries was recently recorded by a different corporation. Provide an explanation for the transaction described by each entry.

a.	Apr.	1	Cash	60,000	
			Common Shares.................................		60,000
b.	Apr.	3	Organization Expenses.................................	90,000	
			Common Shares.................................		90,000
c.	Apr.	5	Merchandise Inventory................................	90,000	
			Machinery..	130,000	
			Notes Payable.....................................		144,000
			Common Shares.................................		76,000

QS 12-10 Issuance of preferred shares in exchange for land LO3

On October 3, 2017, Synthetic Inc, a cell-phone protector company issued 4,000 of its preferred shares for cash of $15 each. On November 19 the company issued 3,400 preferred shares in exchange for land with a fair market value of $52,480.

    a. Prepare the entries for October 3 and November 19.

    b. Calculate the average issue price per preferred share.

QS 12-11 Accounting for cash dividends LO4

Prepare journal entries to record the following transactions for Desmond Corporation:

Apr.	15	Declared a $48,000 cash dividend payable to common shareholders.
June	30	Paid the dividend declared on April 15.
Dec.	31	Closed the Cash Dividends account.

QS 12-12 Dividend allocation between classes of shareholders LO5

The equity section of the Holden Ltd. balance sheet includes 75,000 shares of $0.40 cumulative preferred shares that had been issued for $375,000 and 200,000 common shares issued for a total of $720,000. Holden did not declare any dividends during the prior year and now declares and pays a $108,000 cash dividend.

a. Determine the amount distributed to each class of shareholders.

b. Repeat the calculations assuming the preferred shares were non-cumulative.

QS 12-13 Components of equity LO2,3,4,5

Reese Corporation
Partial Balance Sheet
December 31, 2017

Equity	
Contributed capital:	
Preferred shares, $0.50 cumulative; 20,000 shares authorized, issued, and outstanding..	$ 200,000
Common shares, unlimited shares authorized; 150,000 shares issued and outstanding..	750,000
Total contributed capital	$ 950,000
Retained earnings	890,000
Total equity..	$1,840,000

Explain each of the following terms included in the equity section of the partial balance sheet above:

a. $0.50 cumulative

b. Total contributed capital

c. 20,000 shares authorized

d. 150,000 shares issued and outstanding

e. Retained earnings

f. Unlimited shares authorized

QS 12-14 Statement of changes in equity, closing entries for a corporation—profit LO2,6

Peter Puck Inc. showed the following adjusted information on May 31, 2017, its second year-end:

Assets	Liabilities	Preferred Shares
120,000	40,500	7,000

Common Shares	Retained Earnings	Cash Dividends
13,000	29,000	3,500

Revenues	Expenses	Income Summary
92,000	58,000	

a. Prepare the appropriate closing entries.

b. Prepare a statement of changes in equity for the year ended May 31, 2017. No shares were issued during the second year.

QS 12-15 Statement of changes in equity, closing entries for a corporation—loss LO2,6

Morris Inc. showed the following adjusted information on November 30, 2017, its second year-end:

Assets	Liabilities	Preferred Shares
95,000	18,000	10,000

Common Shares	Retained Earnings	Cash Dividends
48,000	42,000	14,000

Revenues	Expenses	Income Summary
87,000	96,000	

a. Prepare the appropriate closing entries.

b. Prepare a statement of changes in equity for the year ended November 30, 2017. No shares were issued during the second year.

QS 12-16 Statement of changes in equity, closing entries for a corporation—loss and deficit LO2,6

Velor Ltd., a patio gas heater company, showed the following adjusted information on August 31, 2017, its second year-end:

Assets	Liabilities	Preferred Shares
75,000	23,000	10,000

Common Shares	Retained Earnings	Cash Dividends
48,000	12,000	-0-

Revenues	Expenses	Income Summary
76,000	94,000	

a. Prepare the appropriate closing entries.

b. Prepare a statement of changes in equity for the year ended August 31, 2017. No shares were issued during the second year.

QS 12-17 Book value per share LO6

Invisible Marketing Ventures had 186,000 shares outstanding on January 1, 2017, and issued an additional 24,000 shares during the year. The common shareholders' equity was $5,841,000 at the end of the year. Calculate the average number of shares outstanding and the book value per common share.

Exercises

Exercise 12-1 **Comparative entries for partnership and corporation** LO2

Surj Uppal and Parvinder Atwal began a new business on February 14 when each invested $162,500 in the company. On December 20, it was decided that $62,400 of the company's cash would be distributed equally between the owners. Two cheques for $31,200 were prepared and given to the owners on December 23. On December 31, the company reported a $124,800 profit.

Prepare two sets of journal entries to record the investments by the owners, the distribution of cash to the owners, the closing of the Income Summary account, and the withdrawals or dividends under these alternative assumptions:

a. The business is a partnership, and

b. The business is a corporation that issued 1,000 common shares.

Exercise 12-2 **Issuing shares** LO3

Prepare journal entries for each of the following selected transactions that occurred during Tio Networks Corporation's first year of operations:

	2017	
Jan.	15	Issued 2,000 common shares to the corporation's promoters in exchange for their efforts in creating it. Their efforts are estimated to be worth $31,500.
Feb.	21	15,000 common shares were issued for cash of $14 per share.
Mar.	9	6,000 preferred shares were issued for cash totalling $110,600.
Aug.	15	55,000 common shares were issued in exchange for land, building, and equipment with appraised values of $315,000, $420,000, and $112,000 respectively.

Exercise 12-3 **Share transactions, equity** LO2,3

CHECK FIGURE: b. Total equity = $236,200

Fierra Sceptre Inc. was authorized to issue 50,000 $1.50 preferred shares and 300,000 common shares. During 2017, its first year of operations, the following selected transactions occurred:

Jan.	1	5,000 of the preferred shares were issued at $12.00 per share; cash.
Feb.	5	15,000 of the common shares were issued for a total of $126,000; cash.
Mar.	20	3,000 of the common shares were given to the organizers of the corporation regarding their efforts. The shares were valued at a total of $28,800.
May	15	12,000 preferred shares and 20,000 common shares were issued at $13.20 and $9.60 respectively; cash.
Dec.	31	The Income Summary account was closed; it showed a debit balance of $329,000. December 31 is Fierra's year-end.

Required

a. Journalize the above transactions.

b. Prepare the equity section of Fierra Sceptre Inc.'s balance sheet at December 31, 2017.

c. The preferred shares are described as "*$1.50 preferred shares.*" Explain what the *$1.50* means.

Exercise 12-4 Cash dividend LO4

On March 1, the board of directors declared a cash dividend of $0.75 per common share to shareholders of record on March 10, payable March 31. There were 125,000 shares issued and outstanding on March 1 and no additional shares had been issued during the month. Record the entries for March 1, 10, and 31.

Exercise 12-5 Issuing shares LO3,4

Mainland Resources Inc. began operations on June 5, 2017. Journalize the following equity transactions that occurred during the first month of operations:

2017		
June	5	Gave 4,000 common shares to the organizers of the corporation in exchange for accounting and legal services valued at $84,500.
	15	Received $22 cash per share for the issuance of 75,000 common shares.
	16	Issued 10,000 preferred shares for cash of $39 per share.
	17	8,000 common shares were issued to a creditor who was owed $130,000.
	18	The board of directors declared a cash dividend of $19,500 on the preferred shares and $5,000 on the common shares to shareholders of record on June 20, payable July 1.
	30	150,000 common shares were issued in exchange for machinery with a fair market value of $2,600,000. The shares were actively trading on this date at $16.00 per share.
July	1	The dividends declared on June 18 were paid.

Exercise 12-6 Issuing shares; equity LO2,3,4

CHECK FIGURE: b. Total equity = $413,500

Westby Corp., a high school uniform manufacturer, was authorized to issue an unlimited number of common shares. During January 2017, its first month of operations, the following selected transactions occurred:

Jan.	1	1,000 shares were issued to the organizers of the corporation. The total value of the shares was determined to be $12,000.
	5	15,000 shares were sold to various shareholders for $13.50 each.
	15	The board of directors declared a cash dividend of $0.75 per common share to shareholders of record on January 19, payable January 31.
	20	4,000 shares were issued in exchange for land valued at $48,000. The shares were actively trading on this date at $11.50 per share.
	31	Closed the Income Summary account, which showed a credit balance of $165,000.
	31	Paid the dividends declared on January 15.

Required

a. Journalize the above transactions.

b. Prepare the equity section of Westby's balance sheet at January 31, 2017.

c. What was the average issue price per common share?

Exercise 12-7 **Retained earnings, dividend distribution** LO2,5

CHECK FIGURE: 2. $104,900

The December 31, 2017, equity section of ZoomZoom Inc.'s balance sheet appears below.

ZoomZoom Inc. Equity Section of the Balance Sheet December 31, 2017	
Contributed capital:	
Preferred shares, $3.75 cumulative,	
40,000 shares authorized and issued	$1,660,000
Preferred shares, $10 non-cumulative,	
8,000 shares authorized and issued	670,000
Common shares, 400,000 shares authorized and issued..........................	1,750,000
Total contributed capital...	$4,080,000
Retained earnings..	741,600
Total equity	$4,821,600

Required All the shares were issued on January 1, 2015 (when the corporation began operations). No dividends had been declared during the first two years of operations (2015 and 2016). During 2017, the cash dividends declared and paid totalled $613,300.

1. Calculate the amount of cash dividends paid during 2017 to each of the three classes of shares.

2. Assuming profit earned during 2017 was $1,250,000, determine the December 31, 2016, balance in retained earnings.

3. Prepare a statement of changes in equity for the year ended December 31, 2017.

Exercise 12-8 **Share transactions, distribution of dividends, equity** LO2,3,5

White Pear Inc., an organic soap manufacturer, showed the following equity information as at December 31, 2017:

White Pear Inc. Equity Section of the Balance Sheet December 31, 2017	
Contributed capital:	
Preferred shares, $3.60 non-cumulative; 100,000 shares authorized	
75,000 shares issued and outstanding...	A
Common shares; unlimited shares authorized;	
E shares issued and outstanding	B
Total contributed capital	$6,250,000
Retained earnings	C
Total equity..	D

Other information:

a. The preferred shares had sold for an average price of $36.00.

b. The common shares had sold for an average price of $14.20.

c. Retained earnings at December 31, 2016, was $192,000. During 2017, profit earned was $1,728,000. The board of directors declared a total cash dividend of $540,000.

Required Calculate A, B, C, D, and E.

Exercise 12-9 **Share transactions, distribution of dividends, equity** LO1,2,3,4,5

CHECK FIGURES: 5. $732,000; 6. $906,000

Selected T-accounts for Jade Mineral Corporation at December 31, 2017, are duplicated below.

Preferred Shares, $6 cumulative 10,000 shares authorized 8,000 shares issued	
	192,000 Dec. 31/16 Bal.
	192,000 Dec. 31/17 Bal.

Common Shares, 50,000 shares authorized 45,000 shares issued	
	540,000 Dec. 31/16 Bal.
	540,000 Dec. 31/17 Bal.

Retained Earnings	
	126,000 Dec. 31/16 Bal.
	???? Dec. 31/17 Bal.

Note: • *Dividends were not paid during 2015 or 2016. Dividends of $4.80 per common share were declared and paid for the year ended December 31, 2017.*
• *2015 was the first year of operations.*
• *All shares were issued in the first year of operations.*

Required Using the information provided, answer the following questions.

1. What is the total amount of dividends that the preferred shareholders are entitled to receive per year?

2. Are there any dividends in arrears at December 31, 2016? If yes, calculate the dividends in arrears.

3. Calculate total dividends paid during 2017 to the:

   a. Preferred shareholders.

   b. Common shareholders.

4. During 2017, the company earned profit of $408,000. Calculate the balance in the Retained Earnings account at the end of 2017.

5. Calculate Total Contributed Capital at the end of 2017.

6. Calculate Total Equity at December 31, 2017.

7. How many more preferred shares are available for issue at December 31, 2017?

8. What was the average issue price per share of the preferred shares at December 31, 2017?

Exercise 12-10 **Allocating dividends between common and cumulative preferred shares** LO5

The outstanding share capital of Sheng Inc. includes 47,000 shares of $9.60 cumulative preferred and 82,000 common shares, all issued during the first year of operations. During its first four years of operations, the corporation declared and paid the following amounts in dividends:

Year	Total Dividends Declared
2017	$ -0-
2018	480,000
2019	1,008,000
2020	480,000

Determine the total dividends paid in each year to each class of shareholders. Also determine the total dividends paid to each class over the four years.

Exercise 12-11 Allocating dividends between common and non-cumulative preferred shares LO5

Determine the total dividends paid in each year to each class of shareholders of Exercise 12-10 under the assumption that the preferred shares are non-cumulative. Also determine the total dividends paid to each class over the four years.

Exercise 12-12 Identifying characteristics of preferred shares LO5

Match each of the numbered descriptions with the characteristic of preferred shares that it best describes. Indicate your answer by writing the letter for the correct characteristic in the blank space next to each description.

A. Callable or redeemable   **D.** Non-cumulative

B. Convertible   **E.** Non-participating

C. Cumulative   **F.** Participating

_____ 1. The holders of the shares can exchange them for common shares.

_____ 2. The issuing corporation can retire the shares by paying a prearranged price.

_____ 3. The holders of the shares are entitled to receive dividends in excess of the stated rate under some conditions.

_____ 4. The holders of the shares are not entitled to receive dividends in excess of the stated rate.

_____ 5. The holders of the shares lose any dividends that are not declared.

_____ 6. The holders of the shares are entitled to receive current and all past dividends before common shareholders receive any dividends.

Exercise 12-13 Dividend allocation LO5

Cableserve Inc. has the following outstanding shares:

> 15,000 shares, $5.40 cumulative preferred
> 35,000 shares, common

During 2017, the company declared and paid $180,000 in dividends. Dividends were in arrears for the previous year (2016) only. No new shares have been issued since the first year of operations.

Required

1. What was the total amount paid to the preferred shareholders as dividends in 2017?

2. What was the total amount paid to the common shareholders as dividends in 2017?

Exercise 12-14 Closing entries for a corporation LO6

CHECK FIGURE: Retained Earnings, Dec. 31, 2017 = $129,920

Spicer Inc. showed the following alphabetized list of adjusted account balances at December 31, 2017:

Accounts Payable	$ 25,760	Income Tax Expense	$ 40,600
Accounts Receivable	39,200	Land	117,600
Accum. Deprec., Equip.	10,640	Notes Payable, due in 2020	33,600
Accum. Deprec., Warehouse	21,280	Operating Expenses	109,200
Cash	8,400	Preferred Shares	39,200
Cash Dividends	19,600	Retained Earnings	27,720
Common Shares	112,000	Revenue	271,600
Equipment	78,400	Warehouse	128,800

Required Assuming normal balances, prepare the closing entries at December 31, 2017, the company's year-end. Also, calculate the post-closing balance in Retained Earnings at December 31, 2017.

Exercise 12-15 **Analysis of equity** LO1,2,3,4,5,6

CHECK FIGURE: Total assets = $340,480

Using the information in Exercise 12-14, prepare a classified balance sheet at December 31, 2017, and then answer each of the following questions (assume that the preferred shares are non-cumulative; round percentages to the nearest whole percent):

1. What percentage of the total assets is owned by the shareholders?
2. What percentage of Spicer Inc. is equity financed?
3. What percentage of Spicer Inc. is financed by debt?
4. What percentage of the total assets is owned by the common shareholders?
5. What percentage of the assets is financed by the preferred shareholders?
6. What are the advantages to the common shareholders of issuing preferred shares over additional common shares?

Exercise 12-16 **Share transactions, distribution of dividends, equity, closing** LO1,2,3,4,5,6

CHECK FIGURE: 2. Total equity = $944,400

The equity section of the December 31, 2016, balance sheet for Delicious Alternative Desserts Inc. showed the following:

Delicious Alternative Desserts Inc. Equity Section of the Balance Sheet December 31, 2016	
Contributed capital:	
Preferred shares, $0.40 cumulative; 80,000 shares authorized; 60,000 shares issued and outstanding	$240,000
Common shares; 250,000 shares authorized; 120,000 shares issued and outstanding	192,000
Total contributed capital..	$432,000
Retained earnings...	148,000
Total equity	$580,000

During the year 2017, the company had the following transactions affecting equity accounts:

Jan.	3	Sold 20,000 common shares for a total of $34,400 cash.
Mar.	1	Sold 5,000 preferred shares at $4.80 each; cash.
June	15	Exchanged 7,000 common shares for equipment with a fair market value of $26,000. The last common share trade was dated March 15 at $4.88.
Dec.	31	Closed the Income Summary account, which showed a credit balance of $280,000.

The board of directors had not declared dividends for the past two years (2016 and 2017).

Required

1. Journalize the above transactions.

2. Prepare the equity section as at December 31, 2017.

3. How many preferred shares are available for issue at December 31, 2017?

4. How many common shares are available for issue at December 31, 2017?

Exercise 12-17 **Share transactions, dividend distribution, balance sheet, closing** LO2,3,4,5,6

CHECK FIGURES: B. Total assets = $989,400; Total equity = $892,920

Earth Star Diamonds Inc. began a potentially lucrative mining operation on October 1, 2017. It is authorized to issue 100,000 shares of $0.60 cumulative preferred shares and 500,000 common shares.

Part A

Required Prepare journal entries for each of the transactions listed.

Oct.	1	Issued for cash, 1,000 shares of the preferred shares at $4.80 each.
	10	Issued for cash, 50,000 shares of the common stock at $3.60 per share.
	15	Earth star purchased land for $186,000, paying cash of $66,000 and borrowing the balance from the bank (to be repaid in two years).
	20	15,000 preferred shares were issued today for total cash proceeds of $84,600.
	24	In addition to the declaration of the annual dividend on the preferred shares, dividends of $26,880 were declared on the common shares today, payable November 15, 2017.
	31	Revenues of $900,000 were earned during the month; all cash. Expenses, all cash, totalling $300,000 were incurred in October. Close the Income Summary and dividend accounts.

Part B

Required Based on the transactions in Part A, prepare the balance sheet as at October 31, 2017.

Exercise 12-18 **Book Value per Share** LO6

Sunray Solar Ltd is a growing company with a hot new marketing plan. On January 1, 2017, it had 127,650 shares outstanding and they issued an additional 44,500 shares during the year. The company reported $3,222,850 in common shareholders' equity in its annual report for 2017. The market value per share trading on the East-West Stock Exchange was $32.50 on February 1, 2018. Calculate the book value per share for 2017 and explain the difference between the book value per share and the market value per share.

Problems

Problem 12-1A **Corporate balance sheet preparation** LO2

CHECK FIGURES: Total assets = $550,800; Total equity = $300,600

Required Using the information from the alphabetized post-closing trial balance below, prepare a classified balance sheet for Sassy Pharmaceuticals Inc. as at March 31, 2017. *Be sure to use proper form, including all appropriate subtotals.*

Account Description	Account Balance*
Accounts payable	$ 20,400
Accounts receivable	67,200
Accumulated amortization, patent..	50,400
Accumulated depreciation, equipment	148,800
Accumulated depreciation, vehicles...	62,400
Advertising payable	3,000
Allowance for doubtful accounts	3,600
Cash..	28,800
Common shares, 100,000 shares authorized; 25,000 shares were issued at an average price of $9.60; market price per share on March 31, 2017, was $10.80	?
Equipment..	468,000
Income tax payable..	55,200
Notes payable**	144,000
Patent...	115,200
Prepaid rent	55,200
Retained earnings...	?
Unearned revenues..	27,600
Vehicles..	81,600

*Assume that all accounts have normal balances.
**$60,000 of the notes payable will be paid by March 31, 2018.

Analysis Component:

1. What percentage of the assets is financed by debt?

2. What percentage of the assets is financed by equity?

3. Assuming that 37% of the company's assets were financed by debt at March 31, 2016, has the balance sheet been strengthened over the current year? *Note: When a balance sheet is said to have been strengthened, it means, in general, that total liabilities (or risk associated with debt financing) have decreased and equity has increased.*

Problem 12-2A **Retained earnings, dividends** LO2,4 *eXcel*

The equity sections from the 2017 and 2018 balance sheets of Fab-Form Industries Inc. appeared as follows:

Fab-Form Industries Inc. Equity Section of the Balance Sheet December 31, 2017	
Contributed capital:	
Common shares, unlimited shares authorized, 96,000 shares issued and outstanding	$ 688,000
Retained earnings..	558,608
Total equity	$1,246,608

Fab-Form Industries Inc. Equity Section of the Balance Sheet December 31, 2018	
Contributed capital:	
Common shares, unlimited shares authorized, 115,200 shares issued and outstanding	$ 833,920
Retained earnings..	459,600
Total equity	$1,293,520

On March 16, June 15, September 5, and November 22, 2018, the board of directors declared $0.20 per share cash dividends on the outstanding common shares. On October 14, 2018, 19,200 additional common shares were issued.

Required Under the assumption that there were no transactions affecting retained earnings other than the ones given, determine the 2018 profit (loss) of Fab-Form Industries Inc. Show your calculations.

Problem 12-3A Convertible preferred shares LO4,5

Walking Bear Resources Inc. Equity Section of the Balance Sheet March 31, 2017	
Contributed capital:	
Preferred shares, $17 cumulative, 2,500 shares authorized, issued, and outstanding...	$ 600,000
Common shares, unlimited shares authorized,	
40,000 shares issued and outstanding	960,000
Total contributed capital...	$1,560,000
Retained earnings..	462,000
Total equity	$2,022,000

Required Refer to the equity section above. Assume that the preferred are convertible into common at a rate of eight common shares for each share of preferred. If 1,000 shares of the preferred are converted into common on April 1, 2017, prepare the entry and describe how this affects the equity section of the balance sheet (immediately after the conversion).

Analysis Component: If you are a common shareholder in this company, and the company plans to pay total cash dividends of $720,000, does it make any difference to you whether the conversion takes place before the dividend declaration? Why?

Problem 12-4A Analyzing equity, dividend allocation LO2,5

Use the information provided below to answer the following questions.

Victoria Products Inc. Equity Section of the Balance Sheet October 31, 2017	
Contributed capital:	
Preferred shares, $3.00 non-cumulative; unlimited shares authorized, A shares issued and outstanding	$ 540,000
Common shares, unlimited shares authorized, 325,000 shares issued and outstanding	B
Total contributed capital...	C
Deficit..	D
Total equity	$3,468,000

Other information:
- All of the shares were issued during the first year of operations (year ended October 31, 2016).
- The common shares were issued for an average price of $9.60 per share.
- The preferred shares were issued for an average price of $18.00 per share.
- Retained Earnings at October 31, 2016, was $384,000. No dividends had been paid for the year ended October 31, 2017.

Required

1. Calculate *A*.

2. Calculate *B*.

3. Calculate *C*.

4. Calculate *D*.

5. Calculate Profit/Loss for the year ended October 31, 2017.

6. Assume cash dividends of $120,000 were paid during the year ended October 31, 2016. Calculate the total dividends actually paid during the year ended October 31, 2016, to the:

   a. Preferred shareholders.

   b. Common shareholders.

7. Referring to your answers in Part 6 above, calculate the dividends *per share* actually received by the:

   a. Preferred shareholders.

   b. Common shareholders.

8. Are there any dividends in arrears as at October 31, 2017? If yes, calculate the amount of the arrears.

9. Explain the difference between "Retained Earnings" and "Deficit."

10. Explain the difference between "dividends in arrears" and "dividends payable."

Problem 12-5A Dividend allocation L05 e**X**cel

Garda World Security Corporation has the following shares, taken from the equity section of its balance sheet dated December 31, 2017.

Preferred shares, $4.48 non-cumulative,	
45,000 shares authorized and issued*	$2,880,000
Common shares,	
80,000 shares authorized and issued*	1,280,000

*All shares were issued during 2015.

During its first three years of operations, Garda World Security Corporation declared and paid total dividends as shown in the last column of the following schedule.

Required

Part A

Complete the following schedule by filling in the shaded areas.

1. Calculate the total dividends paid in each year to the preferred and to the common shareholders.

Year	Preferred Dividend	Common Dividend	Total Dividend
2015			$ 160,000
2016			400,000
2017			560,000
Total for three years			$1,120,000

2. Calculate the dividends paid *per share* to both the preferred and the common shares in 2017.

Part B

Repeat the requirements in Part A assuming the preferred shares are cumulative.

Analysis Component: Which shares would have a greater market value: cumulative or non-cumulative? Explain.

Problem 12-6A Share transactions, dividends, statement of changes in equity LO2,3,4,5,6

CHECK FIGURES: 2. Retained earnings, December 31, 2018 = $428,800; 3. Total equity = $859,600

The balance sheet for Umi Sustainable Seafood Inc. reported the following components of equity on December 31, 2017:

Common shares, unlimited shares authorized,	
20,000 shares issued and outstanding	$368,000
Retained earnings...	216,000
Total equity	$584,000

In 2018, Umi had the following transactions affecting shareholders and the equity accounts:

Jan.	5	The directors declared a $3.20 per share cash dividend payable on Feb. 28 to the Feb. 5 shareholders of record.
Feb.	28	Paid the dividend declared on January 5.
July	6	Sold 750 common shares at $38.40 per share.
Aug.	22	Sold 1,250 common shares at $27.20 per share.
Sept.	5	The directors declared a $3.20 per share cash dividend payable on October 28 to the October 5 shareholders of record.
Oct.	28	Paid the dividend declared on September 5.
Dec.	31	Closed the $347,200 credit balance in the Income Summary account.
	31	Closed the Cash Dividends account.

Required

1. Prepare journal entries to record the transactions and closings for 2018.

2. Prepare a statement of changes in equity for the year ended December 31, 2018.

3. Prepare the equity section of the corporation's balance sheet as of December 31, 2018.

Analysis Component: Explain the relationship between assets and retained earnings; use your answer in Part 3 above as part of the explanation.

Problem 12-7A Share transactions, statement of changes in equity, dividend distribution, closing LO2,3,4,5,6

CHECK FIGURES: 2. Retained earnings, Dec. 31, 2019 = $224,880; 3. Total equity = $1,700,880

Hammond Manufacturing Inc. was legally incorporated on January 2, 2017. Its articles of incorporation granted it the right to issue an unlimited number of common shares and 100,000 shares of $14.40 non-cumulative preferred shares. The following transactions are among those that occurred during the first three years of operations:

2017

Jan.	12	Issued 40,000 common shares at $4.80 each.
	20	Issued 6,000 common shares to promoters who provided legal services that helped to establish the company. These services had a fair value of $36,000.
	31	Issued 80,000 common shares in exchange for land, building, and equipment, which have fair market values of $360,000, $480,000, and $48,000 respectively.
Mar.	4	Purchased equipment at a cost of $8,160 cash. This was thought to be a special bargain price. It was felt that at least $10,800 would normally have had to be paid to acquire this equipment.
Dec.	31	During 2017, the company incurred a loss of $96,000. The Income Summary account was closed.

2018

| Jan. | 4 | Issued 5,000 preferred shares at $72 per share. |
| Dec. | 31 | The Income Summary account was closed. Profit for 2018 was $216,000. |

2019

Dec.	4	The company declared a cash dividend of $0.12 per share on the common shares payable on December 18 and also declared the required dividend on the preferred shares.
	18	Paid the dividends declared on December 4.
	31	Profit for the year ended December 31, 2019, was $192,000. The Income Summary and Cash Dividends accounts were closed.

Required

1. Journalize the transactions for the years 2017, 2018, and 2019.

2. Prepare the statement of changes in equity for the year ended December 31, 2019.

3. Prepare the equity section on the December 31, 2019, balance sheet.

Analysis Component: Determine the net assets of Hammond Manufacturing Inc. for 2017, 2018, and 2019. Is the trend favourable or unfavourable? Explain.

Problem 12-8A Share transactions, dividends, statement of changes in equity LO2,3,4,5,6

CHECK FIGURES: 2. Retained earnings, Dec. 31, 2018 = $1,063,300; 3. Equity, Dec. 31, 2018 = $2,666,300

The balance sheet for Tactex Controls Inc., provincially incorporated in 2015, reported the following components of equity on December 31, 2016.

Tactex Controls Inc.
Equity Section of the Balance Sheet
December 31, 2016

Contributed capital:	
Preferred shares, $2.10 cumulative, unlimited shares authorized;	
20,000 shares issued and outstanding	$ 392,000
Common shares, unlimited shares authorized;	
75,000 shares issued and outstanding.	735,000
Total contributed capital...	$1,127,000
Retained earnings...	378,000
Total equity	$1,505,000

In 2017 and 2018, the company had the following transactions affecting shareholders and the equity accounts:

2017

Jan.	1	Sold 30,000 common shares at $10.64 per share.
	5	The directors declared a total cash dividend of $231,000 payable on Feb. 28 to the Feb. 5 shareholders of record. Dividends had not been declared for the years 2015 and 2016. All of the preferred shares had been issued during 2015.
Feb.	28	Paid the dividends declared on January 5.
July	1	Sold preferred shares for a total of $156,800. The average issue price was $22.40 per share.
Dec.	31	Closed the dividend accounts along with the $576,800 credit balance in the Income Summary account.

2018

Sept.	5	The directors declared the required cash dividend on the preferred shares and a $1.40 per common share cash dividend payable on October 28 to the October 5 shareholders of record.
Oct.	28	Paid the dividends declared on September 5.
Dec.	31	Closed the Cash Dividends account along with the $543,200 credit balance in the Income Summary account.

Required

1. Prepare journal entries to record the transactions and closings for 2017 and 2018.

2. Prepare a statement of changes in equity for the year ended December 31, 2018.

3. Prepare the equity section of the company's balance sheet as of December 31, 2018.

Alternate Problems

Problem 12-1B **Corporate balance sheet preparation** LO2

CHECK FIGURES: Total assets = $6,382,000; Total equity = $5,201,200

Using the information from the alphabetized post-closing trial balance below, prepare a classified balance sheet for Malta Industries Inc. as at October 31, 2017. Be sure to use proper form, including all appropriate subtotals.

Account Description	Account Balance*
Accounts Payable	$ 221,200
Accounts Receivable	315,000
Accumulated Depreciation—Building	1,166,200
Accumulated Depreciation—Machinery..	1,068,200
Building	4,025,000
Cash...	497,000
Common shares (unlimited shares authorized; 50,000 shares issued at an average price of $44.80 per share; market price per share on October 31, 2017, $79.80)	?
Land...	1,400,000
Long-Term Notes Payable (due in 2021)..	770,000
Machinery...	2,240,000
Office Supplies...	119,000
Preferred Shares ($2.10 non-cumulative, unlimited shares authorized; 30,000 shares issued at an average price of $48 per share; market price per share on October 31, 2017, $72)...	?
Prepaid Insurance...	20,400
Retained Earnings	?
Unearned Revenue..	33,600
Wages Payable..	156,000

*Assume all accounts have normal balances.

Problem 12-2B Retained earnings, dividends LO2,4 e**X**cel

The equity sections from the 2017 and 2018 balance sheets of The Saucy Bread Company Inc. appeared as follows:

The Saucy Bread Company Inc.
Equity Section of the Balance Sheet
December 31, 2017

Contributed capital:	
Common shares, unlimited shares authorized,	
175,000 shares issued	$5,250,000
Retained earnings	1,176,432
Total equity	$6,426,432

The Saucy Bread Company Inc.
Equity Section of the Balance Sheet
December 31, 2018

Contributed capital:	
Common shares, unlimited shares authorized,	
192,500 shares issued	$5,796,000
Retained earnings	1,320,300
Total equity	$7,116,300

On February 11, May 24, August 13, and December 12, 2018, the board of directors declared $0.30 per share cash dividends on the outstanding shares. 7,500 common shares were issued on August 1, 2018, and another 10,000 were issued on November 2, 2018.

Required Under the assumption that there were no transactions affecting retained earnings other than the ones given, determine the 2018 profit of the company. Show your calculations.

Problem 12-3B Convertible preferred shares LO4,5

Jager Metal Corp.
Equity Section of the Balance Sheet
November 30, 2017

Contributed capital:	
Preferred shares, $13.20 cumulative,	
2,000 shares authorized and issued	$ 480,000
Common shares, unlimited shares authorized; 60,000 shares issued	1,440,000
Total contributed capital	$1,920,000
Retained earnings	1,008,000
Total equity	$2,928,000

Required Refer to the equity section above. Assume that the preferred shares are convertible into common at a rate of eight common shares for each share of preferred. If 1,000 shares of the preferred are converted into common shares on December 1, 2017, prepare the entry and describe how this affects the equity section of the balance sheet (immediately after the conversion).

Analysis Component: If you are a common shareholder in this company, and it plans to pay total cash dividends of $584,400, does it make a difference to you whether the conversion takes place before the dividend declaration? Why?

Problem 12-4B **Analyzing equity, dividend allocation** LO2,5

Rainchief Energy Inc. Equity Section of the Balance Sheet October 31, 2017	
Contributed capital:	
Preferred shares, $4.80 cumulative, unlimited shares authorized, 45,000 shares issued and outstanding...	A
Preferred shares, $3.00 non-cumulative, unlimited shares authorized, B shares issued and outstanding:	2,280,000
Common shares, unlimited shares authorized, 265,000 shares issued and outstanding...	C
Total contributed capital	D
Retained earnings..	E
Total equity	F

Required

1. Calculate *A* assuming an average issue price of $12 per share.

2. Calculate *B* assuming an average issue price of $60 per share.

3. Calculate *C* assuming the average issue price was $3.00 per share.

4. Calculate *D*.

5. Calculate *E* assuming that Rainchief Energy Inc. showed profit/losses for the years ended October 31, 2014, 2015, 2016, and 2017, of $1,500,000, $1,050,000, $780,000, and $(1,320,000) respectively. Dividends totalling $720,000 were declared and paid during the year ended October 31, 2014. No other dividends have been declared to date.

6. Calculate *F*.

7. Calculate any dividends in arrears as at October 31, 2017 (all of the shares were issued early in 2014).

Problem 12-5B **Dividend allocation** LO5   e**X**cel

Kangaroo Media Inc. has issued and outstanding a total of 40,000 shares of $7.20 preferred shares and 120,000 of common shares. The company began operations and issued both classes of shares on January 1, 2016.

Required

1. Calculate the total dividends to be paid to each group of shareholders in each year by completing the following chart. Assume that the preferred shares are cumulative.

Year	Dividends Declared and Paid	Preferred Dividends	Common Dividends
2016	$360,000		
2017	60,000		
2018	150,000		
2019	900,000		

2. Calculate the total dividends to be paid to each group of shareholders in each year by completing the following chart. Assume that the preferred shares are non-cumulative.

Year	Dividends Declared and Paid	Preferred Dividends	Common Dividends
2016	$360,000		
2017	60,000		
2018	150,000		
2019	900,000		

Problem 12-6B Share transactions, statement of changes in equity, dividend distribution, closing LO2,3,4,5,6

CHECK FIGURES: 2. Retained earnings, December 31 = $699,600; 3. Total equity = $1,318,800

The balance sheet for QuickStream Inc. reported the following components of equity on December 31, 2017:

Common shares, unlimited shares authorized, 100,000 shares issued and outstanding	$ 480,000
Retained earnings..	648,000
Total equity	$1,128,000

The company completed these transactions during 2018:

Mar.	2	The directors declared a $0.90 per share cash dividend payable on March 31 to the March 15 shareholders of record.
	31	Paid the dividend declared on March 2.
Nov.	11	Issued 12,000 common shares at $7.80 per share.
	25	Issued 8,000 common shares at $5.70 per share.
Dec.	1	The directors declared a $1.50 per share cash dividend payable on January 2, 2019, to the December 10 shareholders of record.
	31	Closed the $321,600 credit balance in the Income Summary account to Retained Earnings.
	31	Closed the Cash Dividends account.

Required

1. Prepare general journal entries to record the transactions and closings for 2018.

2. Prepare a statement of changes in equity for the year ended December 31, 2018.

3. Prepare the equity section of the company's balance sheet as of December 31, 2018.

Analysis Component: How much of QuickStream's assets are financed by the common shareholders at December 31, 2018? Explain what other sources of financing are available.

Problem 12-7B Share transactions, statement of changes in equity, dividend distribution, closing LO2,3,4,5,6

CHECK FIGURES: 2. Retained earnings, December 31, 2017 = $399,480; 3. Total equity = $4,203,480

Labtech Pharmacy Inc. is authorized to issue an unlimited number of common shares and 100,000 shares of $24 non-cumulative preferred. The company completed the following transactions:

2015		
Feb.	5	Issued 70,000 common shares at $24 for cash.
	28	Gave the corporation's promoters 3,750 common shares for their services in organizing the corporation. The directors valued the services at $96,000.
Mar.	3	Issued 44,000 common shares in exchange for the following assets with the indicated reliable market values: land, $192,000; buildings, $504,000; and machinery, $372,000.
Dec.	31	Closed the Income Summary account. A $64,800 loss was incurred.
2016		
Jan.	28	Issued for cash 4,000 preferred shares at $240 per share.
Dec.	31	Closed the Income Summary account. A $235,200 profit was earned.
2017		
Jan.	1	The board of directors declared a $24 per share cash dividend to preferred shares and $0.48 per share cash dividend to outstanding common shares, payable on February 5 to the January 24 shareholders of record.
Feb.	5	Paid the previously declared dividends.
Dec.	31	Closed the Cash Dividends and Income Summary accounts. A $381,600 profit was earned.

Required

1. Prepare general journal entries to record the transactions.

2. Prepare a statement of changes in equity for the year ended December 31, 2017.

3. Prepare the equity section of the balance sheet as of the close of business on December 31, 2017.

Analysis Component: Calculate the net assets of Labtech Inc. for 2015, 2016, and 2017. Is the trend favourable or unfavourable? Explain.

Problem 12-8B Share transactions, dividends, statement of changes in equity LO2,3,4,5,6

CHECK FIGURES: 2. Retained earnings, Dec. 31, 2017 = $754,500; 3. Equity, Dec. 31, 2017 = $4,345,500

Pace Oil & Gas Corp. began operations in 2015. Its balance sheet reported the following components of equity on December 31, 2015.

Pace Oil & Gas Corp. Equity Section of the Balance Sheet December 31, 2015	
Contributed capital:	
Preferred shares, $1.80 non-cumulative, unlimited shares authorized; 25,000 shares issued and outstanding................................	$ 780,000
Common shares, unlimited shares authorized; 162,500 shares issued and outstanding..	1,755,000
Total contributed capital..	$2,535,000
Retained earnings...	681,000
Total equity	$3,216,000

The corporation completed these transactions during 2016 and 2017:

2016

Jan.	1	Sold 50,000 common shares at $11.40 per share.
	5	The directors declared the first cash dividend totalling $191,250 payable on Feb. 28 to the Feb. 5 shareholders of record.
Feb.	28	Paid the dividends declared on January 5.
July	1	Issued preferred shares for a total of $486,000. The average issue price was $32.40 per share.
Dec.	31	Closed the dividend accounts along with the Income Summary account, which reflected profit earned during 2016 of $768,000.

2017

Sept.	5	The directors declared a $1.80 cash dividend per preferred share and a $0.90 per common share cash dividend payable on October 28 to the October 5 shareholders of record.
Oct.	28	Paid the dividends declared on September 5.
Dec.	31	Closed the dividend accounts along with the $240,000 debit balance in the Income Summary account.

Required

1. Prepare journal entries to record the transactions and closings for 2016 and 2017.

2. Prepare the statement of changes in equity for the year ended December 31, 2017.

3. Prepare the equity section of the company's balance sheet as of December 31, 2017.

Analytical and Review Problems

A & R 12-1

Fargo Inc. showed the following profit statement information for its first three years of operations:

For the Years Ended December 31			
	2018	2017	2016
Net Sales..	$5,000,000	$4,000,000	$3,000,000
Cost of Goods Sold..................................	3,000,000	2,400,000	1,650,000
Operating Expenses................................	1,400,000	1,300,000	900,000
Other Revenues (Expenses)....................	(200,000)	(220,000)	50,000
Income Tax Expense	80,000	16,000	100,000

Partial information regarding Fargo's equity for the past three years follows:

	Dec. 31, 2018	Dec. 31, 2017	Dec. 31, 2016
Contributed capital:			
Preferred shares, $2 non-cumulative; 100,000 shares authorized; 20,000* shares issued and outstanding	$400,000	$400,000	$400,000
Common shares, 500,000 shares authorized; 100,000* shares issued and outstanding	550,000	550,000	550,000
Total contributed capital..	?	?	?
Retained earnings**...	?	?	?
Total equity	?	?	?

*Issued on January 1, 2016.

**Cash dividends of $100,000 were declared and paid for the year ended Dec. 31, 2016. Dividends were not declared for the years ended Dec. 31, 2017, or Dec. 31, 2018.

Required
1. Calculate Gross Profit, Operating Profit, Profit Before Tax, and Profit for the years ended December 31, 2016, 2017, and 2018.

2. Calculate Contributed Capital as at December 31, 2016, 2017, and 2018.

3. Calculate Retained Earnings as at December 31, 2016, 2017, and 2018.

4. Calculate Total Equity as at December 31, 2016, 2017, and 2018.

Analysis Component: Assume total liabilities in 2018, 2017, and 2016 were $1,123,200, $936,000, and $900,000, respectively. Identify whether the balance sheet has been strengthened from 2016 to 2018. Explain what this means.

Ethics Challenge

EC 12-1

Jack and Bill are partners in a computer software company. They developed a word processing program that is remarkably similar to a Corel product. Jack telephones Bill at home one evening and says, "We should convert our partnership into a corporation before we launch this new word processing software. Let's withdraw most of our assets from the business before forming a corporate entity. If we are sued by Corel, our liability will be limited to our business assets." Bill feels a little uneasy and replies, "Let's meet tomorrow to discuss this matter."

Required Explain why Bill might be feeling uneasy.

Focus on Financial Statements

FFS 12-1

CHECK FIGURES: Total equity = $337,000; Total current assets = $58,800; Total assets = $520,400

Barry Bowtie incorporated his business under the name BowTie Fishing Expeditions Corp. on March 1, 2017. It was authorized to issue 30,000 $2 cumulative preferred shares and an unlimited number of common shares. During March, the following equity transactions occurred:

   a. 50,000 common shares were issued for cash of $3 per share.

   b. 10,000 preferred shares were issued for $5,000 cash plus equipment with a fair market value of $37,000.

   c. The corporation reported profit for the month of $190,000.

   d. Total cash dividends of $45,000 were declared payable on April 15 to shareholders of record on March 31.

Required Using the information provided in (a) through (d) plus the following March 31, 2017, selected account balances[1], prepare the statement of changes in equity for the month ended March 31, 2017, along with the March 31, 2017, balance sheet:

Accounts Payable	$17,000	Cash	15,000
Accounts Receivable	36,000	Customer Deposits	28,000
Accumulated Amortization, Patent	2,000	Equipment	140,000
Accumulated Depreciation, Building	12,000	Estimated Warranty Liabilities	3,400
Accumulated Depreciation,		Furniture	75,000
Equipment	2,000	Land	105,000
Accumulated Depreciation, Furniture	5,000	Notes Payable[2]	90,000
Allowance for Doubtful Accounts	1,200	Patent	14,000
Building	$148,600	Prepaid Rent	9,000

[1] This list of accounts is incomplete; you will have to add several accounts based on the information provided in (a) through (d).
[2] The note payable is due in principal installments of $30,000 beginning March 1, 2018.

Analysis Component: Use your financial statements prepared above to answer each of the following questions (round percentages to the nearest whole percent):

1. What percentage of the total assets is equity financed?

2. What percentage of the total assets is financed by debt?

3. Assume that 30% of BowTie Fishing (the previous proprietorship) was financed by debt at March 31, 2016. Has the risk associated with debt financing increased or decreased from 2016 to 2017? Explain.

4. What percentage of the total assets is owned by the common shareholders?

5. What percentage of the assets is financed by the preferred shareholders?

FFS 12-2

Barrick Gold Corporation is a Canadian company with its head office in Toronto, Ontario. It mines gold and precious metals around the world. Barrick's shares trade on the New York and Toronto stock exchanges. The equity section of its December 31, 2014, balance sheet, along with Section 28(a) of the notes to the financial statements, showed the following:

Barrick Gold Corporation

(in millions of United States dollars)	December 31, 2014	December 31, 2013
Equity		
Capital stock (note 30)	$ 20,864	$20,869
Retained earnings (deficit)	(10,739)	(7,581)

28. Capital Stock

a)   Common Shares

The authorized capital stock includes an unlimited number of common shares (2014–issued 1,164,669,608 common shares; 2013–issued 1,164,652,426 common shares); 10,000,000 First preferred shares Series A (issued nil); 10,000,000 Series B (issued nil); 1 Series C (issued nil) and 15,000,000 Second preferred shares Series A (issued nil).

Dividends

In 2014, Barrick declared and paid dividends in US dollars totalling $0.20 per share and in 2013, $0.50 per share.

Required Using the information provided above, answer the following questions.

1. Calculate the total dividends declared and paid in 2014 and 2013 by Barrick Gold.

2. What are dividends? Be sure to include as part of your answer the effect of dividends on equity.

3. How many common shares does Barrick Gold have available for issue at December 31, 2014?

4. How many preferred shares did Barrick Gold have issued at December 31, 2014?

5. Barrick reported a deficit of $10,739 million at December 31, 2014. Explain what that means.

Critical Thinking Mini Case

Jones Inc. needs $100,000 to finance the purchase of new equipment. The finance manager is considering two options:

1. Borrowing the funds over a five-year term and paying interest at the rate of 6% per year, or

2. Issuing 6,000 shares of $1 cumulative preferred shares.

The equipment is estimated to have a life of five years and no residual value. Profit before interest expense and tax is expected to be $80,000. The tax rate is assumed to be 25%.

Required Using the elements of critical thinking described on the inside front cover, respond. Consider the following subheadings to organize your response, and provide calculations with your facts on the different costs to borrow versus issue preferred shares.

- Problem
- Goal
- Principles
- Facts
- Conclusions

Corporate Reporting: Profit, Earnings Per Share, and Retained Earnings

A Look Back

Chapter 12 focused on corporate equity transactions, including stock issuances and dividends.

A Look at This Chapter

In this chapter we investigate how to report and analyze profit, earnings per share, and retained earnings.

© Guynamedjames/Dreamstime.com/GetStock.com

LEARNING OBJECTIVES

LO1   Describe and account for share dividends and share splits.

LO2   Describe and account for retirement of shares.

LO3   Calculate earnings per share and describe its use.

LO4   Explain the form and content of a corporate income statement with continuing and discontinued operations and earnings per share.

LO5   Explain restricted retained earnings and accounting changes.

Apple Inc.'s Ascent: From Tech Startup to a Stock Split of 7:1

Apple is the largest U.S. corporation in terms of market capitalization[1] and is one of the world's largest companies in terms of total revenue, reaching $182.8 billion in fiscal 2014.

Apple began with the invention of its first computer, "Apple 1." The company was founded by friends Steve Jobs and Steve Wozniak who met at the Homebrew Computer Club. The club enabled computer hobbyists to meet and exchange concepts and components with other young techies in a California garage. It was at the club that Wozniak demonstrated his design of the first computer with a typewriter-style keyboard and ability to connect to a TV for viewing. According to MacWorld UK, Jobs saw the computer, understood its brilliance, and "sold his VW microbus to fund its production." Wozniak constructed each computer by hand and Jobs priced the Apple 1 at $666.66. The pair got a major order from Byte Shop in Mountain View California for 50 computers at a price of $500 each. Like many young entrepreneurs, they faced a key challenge, cash flow. They needed sufficient funds to buy the parts needed to fulfill the order. After being turned down by a local bank they managed to negotiate with the manager at Cramer Electronics to extend them 30 days of credit on the sale of the parts.

The risk the pair took on was not being able to meeting the Byte Shop order within their 30-day obligation to Cramer Electronics. Family and friends helped put together the parts at a kitchen table. The delivered Apple 1 had no keyboard or television and needed to be manually programmed to transmit data. Upon receiving the primitive product the Byte Shop manager was "reluctant to pay but Jobs stared him down, and he agreed to take delivery" and pay for the goods. Overall, Apple sold 200 Apple 1 computers in its first year and a half in business.

In 1997 Apple Inc. neared bankruptcy. *Business Insider* calls Apple "the greatest corporate comeback story of all time." Jobs, the company's founder and key visionary, had left Apple in 1985 after a power struggle with the company CEO at the time, John Scully. Three CEOs had come and gone in a decade and with mounting losses, the company was struggling to survive. In an effort to save the company, Jobs agreed to take an interim position and lead a major restructuring program.

Under Jobs' leadership and incredible vision, Apple reinvented itself and began to market itself as the market leader in industrial design and innovation. The company's continued innovation has led to the following consumer products: Apple Pay, iPhone, iPad, iPad mini, iPod, and the newest edition to its product line, the Apple Watch.

In June 2014 Apple made the decision to do a stock split of 7:1 to bring the per unit share price down and become more accessible for the individual investor. The stock split resulted in the stock going from over $645.57 per share to a more accessible $92.44. Investors who owned Apple prior to the split now have 7 times more stock at a lower price, maintaining the overall value of Apple stock in their portfolio. Below is Apple's monthly share performance from its

---

1   Market capitalization is a measure of business value based on share price multiplied by the number of shares outstanding. It signifies the market's assessment of stock value and is a moving target as it changes with the changes in stock price. Apple grew from $3 billion in 1997 to a record market capitalization of $775 billion in February 2015, making it worth more than double the market cap of any other U.S. publicly traded company.

initial public offering on December 12, 1980, to December 31, 2014, adjusted for stock splits and dividend payouts, as presented by Dividend.com:

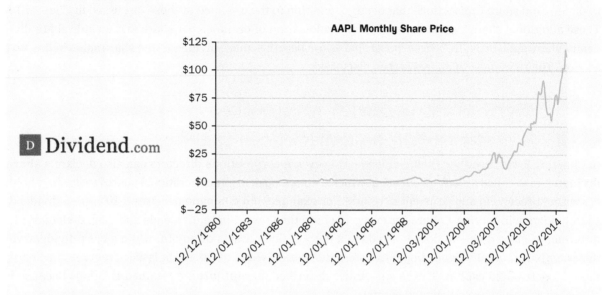

AAPL Monthly Share Price

Source: This is an original chart owned by Dividend.com, and is found online here: http://www.dividend.com/dividend-education/the-complete-history-of-apple-aapl/.

Video Link: http://news.yahoo.com/5-things-know-apples-stock-split-043335990.html

> **CRITICAL THINKING CHALLENGE** What factors, other than the repurchase of shares, cause earnings per share to increase or decrease?

CHAPTER PREVIEW

This chapter begins by describing share transactions that affect the calculation of an important ratio, earnings per share, which is included directly on the corporate income statement. Earnings per share is described in more detail in the second section of the chapter. Corporations constantly evaluate their performance and make decisions to keep pace with changes in their global marketplace. This ongoing process often results in activities that include profit-related transactions that go beyond a company's continuing, normal operations. The income statement needs to provide useful information to help users understand both current and past transactions, and to predict future performance. The third section of this chapter focuses on the reporting of additional profit information. The final section highlights important items affecting retained earnings and outlines presentation considerations for the statement of changes in equity. Understanding these topics helps us read, interpret, and use financial statements for decision making, and helps shareholders, suppliers, and banks when they evaluate the performance of companies like Apple Inc., as described in the opening article.

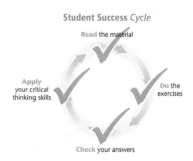

Student Success *Cycle*

Read the material

Apply your critical thinking skills

Do the exercises

Check your answers

Additional Share Transactions

In order to discuss completely the earnings per share calculation explained later in this chapter, we need to understand share transactions that occur in addition to the issuance of those discussed in Chapter 12. These additional share transactions affect the calculation of earnings per share and include share dividends, share splits, and the retirement of shares. We describe share dividends and share splits in the next section. The retirement of shares is then discussed.

Share Dividends

LO1 Describe and account for share dividends and share splits.

In Chapter 12, we described cash dividends. However, a corporation's directors can also declare a **share dividend**, also called a *stock dividend*, in which a company distributes additional shares to its shareholders without receiving any payment in return. For example, if a company declares a 10% stock dividend, shareholders will receive 1 share for every 10 share they own. Share dividends and cash dividends are different: A share dividend does not reduce a corporation's assets or equity, while a cash dividend reduces both. A share dividend simply transfers the market value of the stock issued from retained earnings to contributed capital. This is sometimes described as *capitalizing* retained earnings because it increases a company's contributed capital.

REASONS FOR SHARE DIVIDENDS

If share dividends do not affect assets or total equity, then why declare and distribute them? Key reasons for issuing share dividends include the following:

1. Directors are said to use share dividends to keep the market price of the shares affordable. For example, if a profitable corporation grows but does not pay cash dividends, the price of its common shares continues to increase. The price of such shares may become so high that it discourages some investors from buying them. When a corporation declares a share dividend, it increases the number of outstanding shares and lowers the market price of its shares.

2. Issuing share dividends conserves cash for business expansion that might lead to positive returns on shareholder investment.

3. A share dividend provides evidence of management's confidence that the company is doing well.

ENTRIES FOR SHARE DIVIDENDS

To illustrate share dividends, we use the equity section of the December 31, 2017, balance sheet for X-Quest Ltd., shown in Exhibit 13.1, just *before* the company's declaration of a share dividend.

EXHIBIT 13.1

Equity Before the Share Dividend

Contributed capital:	
Common shares, unlimited shares authorized,	
10,000 shares issued and outstanding	$108,000
Retained earnings	35,000
Total equity	$143,000

Let's assume the directors of X-Quest Ltd. declare a 10% share dividend on December 31, 2017. This share dividend of 1,000 shares, calculated as 10% of its 10,000 *outstanding* shares, is to be distributed on January 20 to the shareholders of record on January 15. The *Canada Business Corporations Act* requires that the value to be assigned to a share dividend be *equal to the market value of the shares on the date of declaration*. Since the market price of X-Quest's shares on December 31 is $15 per share, the dividend declaration is recorded as:

Dec. 31	Retained Earnings	15,000		*or*	Dec. 31	Share Dividends	15,000
	Common Share Dividends					Common Share Dividends	
	Distributable..................		15,000			Distributable..................	15,000
	To record declaration of a					*To record declaration of a*	
	share dividend of 1,000					*share dividend of 1,000*	
	common shares.					*common shares.*	

The debit is recorded in the temporary (contra equity) account called Share Dividends. This account serves the same purpose as the Cash Dividends account. As shown above, an alternative entry is to debit Retained Earnings directly to eliminate the need to close the Share Dividends account at the end of the accounting period. The $15,000 credit is an increase to a contributed capital account called Common Share Dividends Distributable. This account balance exists only until the shares are actually issued.

A share dividend is *never a liability* because shareholders will be given shares in the future; shareholders receiving a share dividend are *not* owed any assets. Share dividends affect equity accounts only. The equity section of X-Quest's December 31, 2017, balance sheet immediately *after* the declaration of the share dividend appears in Exhibit 13.2.

EXHIBIT 13.2

Equity After Declaring a Share Dividend

Contributed capital:	
Common shares, unlimited shares authorized,	
10,000 shares issued and outstanding	$108,000
Common share dividends distributable, 1,000 shares...................................	15,000
Total contributed capital..	$123,000
Retained earnings..	20,000
Total equity	$143,000

As part of the year-end closing process, X-Quest Ltd. closes the Share Dividends account to Retained Earnings with the following entry:

Dec.	31	Retained Earnings	15,000	
		Share Dividends.....................................		15,000
		To close the Share Dividends account.		

Note that if Retained Earnings had been debited on the date of declaration instead of Share Dividends, the above closing entry would not be required. No entry is made on the date of record for a share dividend. On January 20, the date of distribution,[2] X-Quest distributes the new shares to shareholders and records this with the entry:

Jan.	20	Common Share Dividends Distributable..........	15,000	
		Common Shares		15,000
		To record distribution of a 1,000-share common share dividend.		

The combined effect of these two share dividend entries is to transfer (or capitalize) $15,000 of retained earnings to contributed capital. Share dividends have no effect on *total* equity as shown in Exhibit 13.3. Nor do they affect the percentage of the company owned by individual shareholders.

EXHIBIT 13.3

Equity Before and After Distribution of Share Dividend

	Dec. 31, 2017, Before Declaration of Share Dividend	Jan. 20, 2018, After Declaration of Share Dividend
Contributed capital:		
Common shares, unlimited shares authorized,		
Dec. 31, 2017: 10,000 shares issued and outstanding......................	$108,000	
Jan. 20, 2018: 11,000 shares issued and outstanding		$123,000
Retained earnings..	35,000	20,000
Total equity	$143,000	$143,000

Share Splits

A **share split** is the distribution of additional shares to shareholders according to their percentage of ownership. When a share split occurs, the corporation calls in its outstanding shares and issues more than one new share in exchange for each old share.[3] Splits can be done in any ratio including two-for-one (expressed as 2:1), three-for-one (expressed as 3:1), or higher. There are no journal entries for a share split but note disclosure is required and should state the number of shares distributed. For example:

> Note 6: As a result of a two-for-one share split declared by the board of directors, the company issued an additional 200,000 common shares on July 1, 2017.

To illustrate the effect of a share split on equity, assume the information in Exhibit 13.4 for Halogen Inc. at December 31, 2017, immediately prior to the declaration of a share split. Halogen Inc.'s board of

---

[2] For a share dividend, additional shares are issued (no cash is paid). Therefore, January 20 is referred to as the date of distribution and not the date of payment.

[3] To reduce administrative cost, most splits are done by issuing new certificates to shareholders for the additional shares they are entitled to receive. The shareholders keep the old certificates.

EXHIBIT 13.4

Equity for Halogen Inc. Before and After Share Split

	Dec. 31, 2017 Before Share Split	Jan. 4, 2018 After Share Split
Contributed capital:		
Common shares, unlimited shares authorized,		
Dec. 31, 2017: 20,000 shares issued and outstanding......................	$240,000	
Jan. 4, 2018: 60,000 shares issued and outstanding		$240,000
Retained earnings...	90,000	90,000
Total equity	$330,000	$330,000

directors declared a 3:1 share split on December 31, 2017, to be issued on January 4, 2018. Notice that the share split simply replaces the 20,000 shares issued on December 31, 2017, with 60,000 shares on January 4, 2018. A share split does not affect individual shareholders' percentage of ownership. The Contributed Capital and Retained Earnings accounts are unchanged by a split. The only effect of a share split on the accounts is a change in the number of common shares. However, the market will respond by reducing the market value of the shares in proportion to the share split. For example, if Halogen Inc.'s shares were trading on December 31, 2017, for $21 per share, the market value would be reduced to about $7 ($21 ÷ 3) per share after the share split.

Presented below is a one-year history for the shares of Apple Inc. highlighting the stock split on June 9, 2014. The benefit of a stock split is that it makes the stock more affordable by increasing the number of shares outstanding and lowering the market price of the shares. As highlighted in the chapter opening vignette, as a result of the 7:1 stock split, Apple's stock price dropped from $645.57 to a more affordable $92.44.

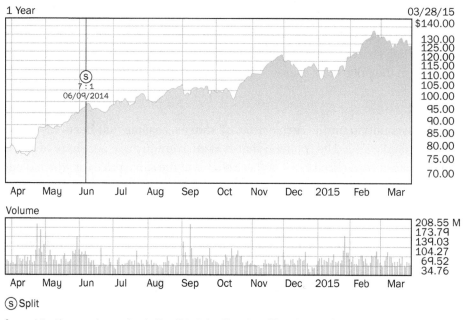

Source: http://www.nasdaq.com/symbol/aapl/stock-chart?intraday=off&timeframe=1y&splits=on&earnings=off&moving average=None&lowerstudy=volume&comparison=off&index=&drilldown=off

A **reverse share split** is the opposite of a share split. It increases both the market value per share and the issued value per share. It does this by specifying the ratio to be less than one-to-one, such as one-for-two. This means shareholders end up with fewer shares after a reverse share split.

CHECKPOINT

1. Which of the following statements is correct?
   a. A share split increases the market value per share.
   b. Share dividends and share splits have the same effect on the total assets and retained earnings of the issuing corporation.
   c. A share dividend does not transfer corporate assets to the shareholders but does require that retained earnings be capitalized.
2. What distinguishes a share dividend from a share split?
3. What amount of retained earnings is capitalized for a share dividend?

Do Quick Study questions: QS 13-1, QS 13-2

Repurchase of Shares

LO2 Describe and account for retirement of shares.

Under the *Canada Business Corporations Act*, a corporation may repurchase shares of its own outstanding share capital. Shares can be repurchased and then retired; this is referred to as a retirement or **cancelling of shares**.

For example, Note 7 of Apple Inc.'s 2014 annual report states that as of September 27, 2014, Apple has repurchased and cancelled 67.9 billion shares since 2013.

Retiring shares reduces the number of issued shares. Purchases and retirements of shares are allowed under the *Canada Business Corporations Act* only if they do not jeopardize the interests of creditors and shareholders and are therefore limited by the balance of retained earnings. Corporations buy back their own shares for several reasons: they can repurchase shares to avoid a hostile takeover by an investor, or they can buy shares to maintain a strong or stable market. By buying shares, management shows its confidence in the price of its shares.

RETIRING SHARES

To demonstrate the accounting for the **retirement of shares**, assume that Beats Electronics, a subsidiary of Apple Inc. originally issued its common shares at an average price per share of $12.[4] If, on May 1, the corporation purchased and retired 1,000 of these shares at the same price for which they were issued, the entry would be:

May	1	Common Shares...	12,000	
		Cash...		12,000
		Purchased and retired 1,000 common		
		shares equal to the average issue price;		
		$12 × 1,000 shares.		

---

4 Shares are often issued at different amounts per share. Therefore, when retiring shares, the average issue price per share is used to determine the amount to be debited to the share capital account. Average issue price per share is equal to Total share capital ÷ Total number of shares issued.

If, on June 1, Beats Electronics retires 500 common shares, paying $11, which is less than the $12 average issue price, the entry would be:

June	1	Common Shares..	6,000	
		Cash...		5,500
		Contributed Capital from Retirement of Common Shares		500
		Purchased and retired 500 common shares at less than the average issue price; $12 × 500 shares = $6,000; $11 × 500 shares = $5,500.		

The Contributed Capital from Retirement of Common Shares account is reported as a separate item in the contributed capital section of equity. *No gain is ever reported from the retirement of shares.* Why? Because the repurchase of shares affects balance sheet accounts, specifically equity accounts, not income statement accounts. When shares are repurchased, the transaction is between shareholders and the corporation (balance sheet); it is not an operating activity (income statement).

Now assume that on July 5 Beats Electronics pays $15 to retire 2,000 common shares, which is *more than* the average issue price of $12. The entry would be:

July	5	Common Shares..	24,000	
		Contributed Capital from Retirement of Common Shares.....................................	500	
		Retained Earnings	5,500	
		Cash...		30,000
		Purchased and retired 2,000 common shares at more than the average issue price; $12 × 2,000 shares = $24,000; $15 × 2,000 shares = $30,000.		

When shares are retired at a price *greater* than their average issue price, Retained Earnings is debited for the excess paid over the purchase price. However, if there is a balance in the Contributed Capital from Retirement account, this account must be debited *first* to the extent of its balance.

A corporation may also repurchase shares with the intent to reissue them. This is referred to as a *treasury share* transaction. Treasury share transactions are discussed in more detail in a more advanced course in Intermediate Accounting.

Now that we understand share dividends, share splits, and the retirement of shares, we are ready to explore earnings per share, the topic of the next section.

 **CHECKPOINT**

4. If shares are retired and cancelled, what is the effect on the number of shares outstanding?

Do Quick Study questions: QS 13-3, QS 13-4

MID-CHAPTER DEMONSTRATION PROBLEM

Air Travel Inc. showed the following in its equity section on the August 31, 2017, balance sheet:

Contributed capital:

Common shares, unlimited shares authorized,	
10,000 shares issued and outstanding*	$150,000
Retained earnings...	80,000
Total equity	$230,000

*All of the common shares had been issued for an average price of $15.00 per share calculated as $150,000 ÷ 10,000 shares.

Part 1

On September 3, 2017, Air's board of directors declared a 20% share dividend to shareholders of record on September 17 to be distributed on September 24. The share price on each of these dates was:

Date	Market Price Per Share
Sept. 3, 2017	$15.20
17, 2017	15.25
24, 2017	12.30

Several months later, the board declared a two-for-one share split effective June 12, 2018.

Required

    a. Prepare the journal entries, if applicable, for September 3, 17, and 24, along with June 12.

    b. Prepare a comparative equity section immediately before and after the share dividend, similar to Exhibit 13.3. Assume no other changes to retained earnings.

    c. Prepare a comparative equity section immediately before and after the share split, similar to Exhibit 13.4.

Part 2

Required

Assuming the information for Air Travel Inc. only at August 31, 2017, record the following entries:

    a. On September 16, 2017, Air Travel repurchased and retired 500 of its common shares, paying $15.00 per share.

    b. Air repurchased and retired 1,000 of its shares on November 5, 2017, paying $14.50 per share.

    c. Air paid $16.20 per share on July 14, 2018, to repurchase and retire 1,000 of its shares.

Analysis Component:

Explain how the effects of a share dividend on the balance sheet differ from and are similar to those of a share split.

Solution

Part 1

a.

2017				
Sept.	3	Share Dividends	30,400	
		Common Share Dividends Distributable......................................		30,400
		Declared a 20% share dividend; *10,000 × 20% = 2,000 shares;* *2,000 shares × $15.20/share = $30,400.*		
	17	No entry.		
	24	Common Share Dividends Distributable..........	30,400	
		Common Shares		30,400
		Distributed 2,000 shares regarding the share dividend declared on September 3.		
2018				
June	12	No entry.		
		Note disclosure is required stating that an additional 12,000 shares are to be distributed as a result of the two-for-one share split.		

b.

	Before Share Dividend	After Share Dividend
Contributed capital:		
Common shares, unlimited shares authorized,		
Before share dividend: 10,000 shares issued and outstanding	$150,000	
After share dividend: 12,000 shares issued and outstanding.............		$180,400
Retained earnings...	80,000	49,600
Total equity	$230,000	$230,000

c.

	Before Share Split	After Share Split
Contributed capital:		
Common shares, unlimited shares authorized,		
Before share split: 12,000 shares issued and outstanding.	$180,400	
After share split: 24,000 shares issued and outstanding...................		$180,400
Retained earnings...	49,600	49,600
Total equity	$230,000	$230,000

Part 2

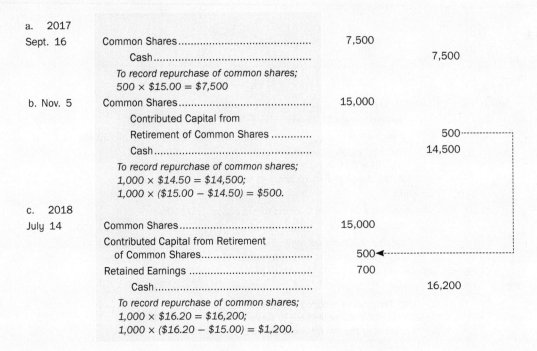

a.   2017
Sept. 16   Common Shares   7,500
          Cash   7,500
          To record repurchase of common shares;
          500 × $15.00 = $7,500

b. Nov. 5   Common Shares   15,000
          Contributed Capital from
          Retirement of Common Shares   500
          Cash   14,500
          To record repurchase of common shares;
          1,000 × $14.50 = $14,500;
          1,000 × ($15.00 − $14.50) = $500.

c.   2018
July 14   Common Shares   15,000
          Contributed Capital from Retirement
          of Common Shares   500
          Retained Earnings   700
          Cash   16,200
          To record repurchase of common shares;
          1,000 × $16.20 = $16,200;
          1,000 × ($16.20 − $15.00) = $1,200.

Analysis Component:

A share dividend affects the balance sheet differently than a share split does in that the share dividend transfers equity from Retained Earnings to the Share Capital account; a share split does not affect any dollar amounts. A share dividend and split are similar in that assets and liabilities and total equity are not affected. However, both do cause the total number of shares outstanding to increase.

Financial Statement Presentation and Analysis

Earnings Per Share (EPS)

LO3 Calculate earnings per share and describe its use.

Earnings per share, commonly abbreviated as **EPS**, is the amount of profit earned by each share of a company's outstanding common shares. Earnings per share information is included on the face of the income statement in accordance with accounting standards. Earnings per share is useful because it reports a company's earnings in terms of a single common share. The earnings per share formula is shown in Exhibit 13.5.

EXHIBIT 13.5

Earnings Per Share Formula

$$\text{Earnings per share} = \frac{\text{Profit} - \text{Preferred dividends}}{\text{Weighted-average common shares}}$$

> **Important Tip:** It should be noted that *only dividends actually declared in the current year are subtracted from profit in the Earnings Per Share formula.* The exception is when preferred shares are cumulative, in which case annual dividends are deducted regardless of whether they have been declared or not. Dividends in arrears are not adjusted for when calculating earnings per share.

EARNINGS PER SHARE WHEN THERE IS NO CHANGE IN COMMON SHARES OUTSTANDING

Consider Lescon Inc., with shares issued as shown in the equity section of its December 31, 2017, balance sheet in Exhibit 13.6.

EXHIBIT 13.6

Equity of Lescon Inc. at December 31, 2017

Contributed capital:
Common shares, unlimited shares authorized,
500,000 shares issued and outstanding $6,500,000
Retained earnings.. 480,000
Total equity $6,980,000

Exhibit 13.7 illustrates the earnings per share presentation for Lescon Inc. for the year ended December 31, 2017, calculated as $750,000/500,000 shares = $1.50.

EXHIBIT 13.7

Income Statement with Earnings Per Share Information

Lescon Inc.
Income Statement
For Year Ended December 31, 2017

Sales	$8,500,000
Cost of goods sold	4,600,000
Profit	$ 750,000
Earnings per common share	$1.50

Danier Leather reported a loss per share of $2.00 for the year ended June 28, 2014, as shown on its income statement found in Appendix II. **WestJet** reported earnings per share of $2.22 for the year ended December 31, 2014.

When common shares outstanding are constant throughout the year, the calculation of earnings per share is straightforward because the denominator of the ratio, weighted-average common shares outstanding, is equal to the reported number of shares outstanding. The next section demonstrates the calculation of earnings per share when the number of shares outstanding *changes* during the year.

EARNINGS PER SHARE WHEN THERE ARE CHANGES IN COMMON SHARES OUTSTANDING

The number of shares outstanding can change because of:

- The issuance of additional shares,
- Share dividends,
- Share splits, and/or
- The retirement of shares

We consider the effect of each on the denominator of the earnings per share calculation.

When Shares Are Sold or Purchased in the Period

When a company sells or repurchases shares during the year, the denominator of the earnings per share formula must equal the *weighted-average number of outstanding shares*. The idea behind this calculation is to measure the average amount of earnings to the average number of shares outstanding during the year. Why do we need a weighted-average calculation? To illustrate, assume you have $100 to invest in a 12% savings account at the bank. What is the earning power of your investment? The earning power is dependent on how long the money is in the savings account. If you deposit the money on January 1, 2017, the interest income earned by December 31, 2017, is $12 ($100 × 12%). If the money is invested on December 1, 2017, $1 ($100 × 12% × 1/12) of earnings would be realized by December 31, 2017. The earning power of an investment is greater the longer the funds are invested. Shares represent investments made by shareholders in the corporation. The longer those investments are in the company, the greater their potential impact on earnings.

Assume Lescon Inc. reported profit of $880,000 for the year ended December 31, 2018. During 2018, Lescon issued 50,000 preferred and 40,000 additional common shares and retired 30,000 common shares, as shown in the equity section of Lescon's December 31, 2018, balance sheet in Exhibit 13.8. Dividends were declared on the preferred shares only.

EXHIBIT 13.8

Equity of Lescon Inc. at December 31, 2018

Contributed capital:	
Preferred shares, $5 cumulative, unlimited shares authorized,	
50,000 shares issued and outstanding	$1,000,000
Common shares, unlimited shares authorized,	
510,000 shares issued and outstanding*	7,200,000
Total contributed capital	$8,200,000
Retained earnings	1,110,000
Total equity	$9,310,000

* 500,000 shares were issued and outstanding on January 1, 2018; 40,000 common shares were issued on April 1, 2018; 30,000 common shares were repurchased and retired on November 1, 2018.

To calculate the weighted-average number of shares outstanding, we need to determine the number of months that each group of common shares was outstanding during the year. Exhibit 13.9 shows us how to calculate Lescon's weighted-average number of shares outstanding for the year 2018.

EXHIBIT 13.9

Calculating Weighted-Average Number of Shares Outstanding

Time Period	Outstanding Shares	Fraction of Year Outstanding	Weighted Average
January–March	500,000	× 3/12	= 125,000
April–October	540,000	× 7/12	= 315,000
November–December	510,000	× 2/12	= 85,000
Weighted-average outstanding shares			525,000

We can then calculate Lescon's earnings per share for the year ended December 31, 2018, as:

$$\text{Earnings per share} = \frac{\$880,000 \text{ profit} - \$250,000 \text{ preferred dividends declared*}}{525,000}$$

$$= \$1.20$$

*Note: Because the preferred shares are cumulative, the annual dividends of $250,000 would be subtracted even if the dividends had not been declared.

Lescon reports the $1.20 earnings per share number on the face of its December 31, 2018, income statement, similar to that shown in Exhibit 13.7.

Share Dividends or Splits in the Period

The number of outstanding shares is also affected by a share split or share dividend. Earnings for the year are spread over a larger number of shares as a result of a share dividend or share split. This affects our calculation of the weighted-average number of shares outstanding. We handle a share split or share dividend by restating the number of shares outstanding during the year to reflect the share split or dividend *as if it had occurred at the beginning of the year.*

To illustrate, let's assume Lescon declared a two-for-one share split effective December 1, 2018. The calculations in Exhibit 13.9 would change as shown in Exhibit 13.10. Notice that the only change in calculating weighted-average shares outstanding is the additional multiplication. This shows the split as if it had occurred at the beginning of the year. The December outstanding shares already reflect the split and do not require any adjustment.

EXHIBIT 13.10

Calculating Weighted-Average Number of Shares Outstanding with Share Split

Time Period	Outstanding Shares	Effect of Split	Fraction of Year	Weighted Average
January–March	500,000	× 2	× 3/12	= 250,000
April–October	540,000	× 2	× 7/12	= 630,000
November	510,000	× 2	× 1/12	= 85,000
December	1,020,000	× 1	× 1/12	= 85,000
Weighted-average outstanding shares				1,050,000

Lescon's earnings per share for the year 2015 under the assumption of the two-for-one share split is:

$$\text{Earnings per share} = \frac{\$880,000 \text{ profit} - \$250,000 \text{ preferred dividends declared}}{1,050,000}$$

$$= \$0.60$$

Exhibit 13.11 shows the calculation of weighted-average shares outstanding if the two-for-one share split had instead been a 10% share dividend. The December outstanding shares already reflect the share dividend and do not require any adjustment.

EXHIBIT 13.11

Calculating Weighted-Average Number of Shares with Share Dividend

Time Period	Outstanding Shares	Effect of Share Dividend	Fraction of Year	Weighted Average
January–March	500,000	× 1.10	× 3/12	= 137,500
April–October	540,000	× 1.10	× 7/12	= 346,500
November	510,000	× 1.10	× 1/12	= 46,750
December	561,000	× 1	× 1/12	= 46,750
Weighted-average outstanding shares				577,500

Earnings per share under the assumption of the 10% share dividend would be:

$$\text{Earnings per share} = \frac{\$880{,}000 \text{ profit} - \$250{,}000 \text{ preferred dividends declared}}{577{,}500}$$

$$= \$1.09^*$$

*Rounded to two decimal places

CHECKPOINT

5. During 2017, FDI reports profit of $250,000 and pays $70,000 in current-year preferred dividends. On January 1, 2017, the company had 25,000 outstanding common shares and retired 5,000 shares on July 1, 2017. The 2017 earnings per share value is (a) $8; (b) $9; or (c) $10.
6. In addition to the facts in Checkpoint 5, assume a 3:1 share split occurred on August 1, 2017. The 2017 weighted-average number of common shares outstanding is: (a) 60,000; (b) 117,500; or (c) 67,500.
7. How are share splits and share dividends treated in calculating the weighted-average number of outstanding common shares?

Do Quick Study questions: QS 13-5, QS 13-6, QS 13-7, QS 13-8, QS 13-9, QS 13-10

The next section discusses some additional profit reporting issues and how they affect the income statement.

Dividend Payout Ratio

LO4 Explain the form and content of a corporate income statement with continuing and discontinued operations and earnings per share.

The **dividend payout ratio** outlines how much of the company's earnings are paid out in dividends. The ratio assesses the company's payout of dividends in relation to its earnings. External users can determine if the dividend payments paid out are sustainable and make sense given the industry. Cash dividends redirect company resources from reinvesting earnings in the business to ensure the long-run viability and growth of a company. If dividend payouts are too high in relation to earnings, they may not be in the best interests of investors interested in long-run viability and growth opportunities. Dividend payout is calculated as follows:

$$\text{Dividend payout ratio} = \frac{\text{annual dividends per share}}{\text{earnings per share}}$$

The analysis below demonstrates **Telus Corporation** has a relatively stable dividend payout policy with 66% in 2014 and 67% in 2013. A 66% payout ratio indicates that a significant portion of profits is being paid to shareholders with the remaining 34% of earnings being reinvested in the business for future growth initiatives. High-payout ratios are appealing to investors, who are earning profit on their equity investment; however, it is important to ensure that the company is investing a sufficient amount of resources into sustaining its business for the future.

	2014	2013
Dividends per Share[5] (A)	$1.52	$1.36
Earnings per Share[6] (B)	$2.31	$2.02
Dividend Payout Ratio = (A)/(B)	66%	67%

Reporting Profit Information

The basic corporate income statement of Exhibit 13.12 shows the revenues, expenses, and profit generated by the Maxo Corporations's **continuing operations**. Prior chapters have explained the nature of the items and measures included in profit from these continuing operations.

EXHIBIT 13.12

Corporate Income Statement Showing Continuing Operations

Maxo Corporation
Income Statement
For Year Ended December 31, 2017

Sales		$100	
Cost of goods sold		40	
Gross profit		$ 60	
Operating expenses		18	
Profit from operations		$ 42	Continuing Operations
Other revenues and expenses:[7]			
Gain on sale of plant and equipment	$ 4		
Interest income	3		
Loss on sale of plant and equipment	(7)		
Interest expense	(2)	(2)	
Profit before tax		$ 40	
Income tax expense		10	
Profit		$ 30	

---

5 As disclosed in Note 12 of Telus Corporation's 2014 Annual Report.

6 2014 Annual Report.

7 Some companies will divide this section on the income statement between Other Revenues and Gains and Other Expenses and Losses. Flexibility is permitted in this regard.

When a company's activities include profit-related transactions that are not part of a company's continuing, normal operations, the income statement needs to be expanded to include different sections to provide more useful information to users. The most important of these additional sections include Discontinued Operations and Earnings per Share. Discontinued operations will be discussed in this section. Earnings per share was described in detail in the previous section. Exhibit 13.13 shows the additional income statement items as reported for Warkworth Art Co. for its year ended December 31, 2017.

EXHIBIT 13.13

Expanded Income Statement for a Corporation with Discontinued Operations

Warkworth Art Co.
Income Statement
For Year Ended December 31, 2017

Net sales	$8,440,000	
Cost of goods sold	5,950,000	
Gross profit..	$2,490,000	
Operating expenses...	570,000	
Operating profit	$1,920,000	① Continuing operations
Other revenues and expenses:		
Investment income	100,000	
Loss on relocating storage facility	(145,000)	
Profit from continuing operations before		
income tax...	$1,875,000	
Income tax expense	397,000	
Profit from continuing operations	$1,478,000	
Discontinued operations:		
Profit from discontinued operation [Note 18]		
A (net of $66,000 tax benefit).......................................	266,000	② Discontinued operations
Profit	$1,744,000	
Earnings per common share (200,000		
outstanding shares):		
Profit from continuing operations	$ 7.39	
Profit from discontinued operations...................................	1.33	
Profit (earnings per share)...	$ 8.72	③ Earnings per share
Note 18 Disclosure:		

Discontinued operations:		
Earnings from discontinued Profit from operating		
Division A (net of $180,000 income taxes).........................	$ 420,000	
Loss on disposal of Division A (net of		
$66,000 tax benefit)	(154,000)	266,000
A (net of $66,000 tax benefit)		

Many companies have several different lines of business or operating *segments* that deal with different groups of customers. A **segment of a business** is a part of a company's operations that serves a particular line of business or class of customers and is of interest to users of financial statements. For instance, Loblaw Companies Ltd.'s 2014 annual report discloses the following Reportable Operating

Segments: Retail Segment, Financial Services Segment and Choice Properties Segment. In its March 31, 2014, statements, **Lions Gate Entertainment** reports its operations in two business segments in Note 17 of its annual report:

17. Segment Information

Accounting guidance requires the Company to make certain disclosures about each reportable segment. The Company's reportable segments are determined based on the distinct nature of their operations and each segment is a strategic business unit that offers different products and services and is managed separately. The Company has two reportable business segments as of March 31, 2014: Motion Pictures and Television Production.

DISCONTINUED OPERATIONS

When an operating segment of the business is discontinued, a **discontinued operation** results and two items must be reported as a combined figure in a separate section of the income statement[8] with additional disclosure provided in the financial statement notes:

1. The profit or loss from selling or closing down a segment, and
2. The profit from operating the discontinued segment prior to its disposal.

The income tax effects of each are also reported net of tax separate from continuing operations as shown in Section 2 of Exhibit 13.13. When an amount is shown **net of tax**, it means that it has been adjusted for the income tax effect. The income tax effect can be an additional expense or a benefit (reduction of total tax expense). For example, in the case of the $420,000 reported in Section 2 as the *Profit from operating Division A*, it is *net of $180,000 income tax expense*. This means that the gross profit (or before-tax amount) was $600,000 ($420,000 net amount + $180,000 income tax expense). For the *Loss on disposal of Division A*, the $154,000 is reported net of a *$66,000 tax benefit*. Because a loss reduces profit, it also reduces income tax expense—therefore, a tax *benefit* results.

The purpose of reporting discontinued operations separately is to clearly isolate the results of discontinued operations from continuing operations. Additional information regarding the transaction must be disclosed in the notes to the financial statements.

Comprehensive Income

Comprehensive income is equal to profit plus *other comprehensive income*. Exhibit 13.14 shows the income statement for **Canadian Tire Corporation**'s fiscal year ending January 3, 2015.[9] Notice how the *profit*, called *net income* by Canadian Tire., is taken from the income statement in Exhibit 13.14, and added to *other comprehensive income* in Exhibit 13.15 to arrive at *total comprehensive income*.

---

8 IFRS 2015, IFRS 5, para. 33.

9 Diluted earnings per share presented in Exhibit 13.14 is an intermediate accounting topic that is beyond the scope of this course.

EXHIBIT 13.14

Canadian Tire Corporation's Consolidated Income Statement for the Year Ended January 3, 2015

Consolidated Statements of Income For the Years Ended (C$ in millions, except per share amounts)	January 3, 2015	December 28, 2013
Revenue (Note 30)	$ 12,462.9	$ 11,785.6
Cost of producing revenue (Note 31)	(8,416.9)	(8,063.3)
Gross margin	4,046.0	3,722.3
Other income (expense)	11.0	(3.0)
Selling, general and administrative expenses (Note 32)	(3,052.9)	(2,828.9)
Net finance costs (Note 33)	(108.9)	(105.8)
Change in fair value of redeemable financial instrument (Note 35)	(17.0)	–
Income before income taxes	878.2	784.6
Income taxes (Note 18)	(238.9)	(220.2)
Net income	$ 639.3	$ 564.4
Net income attributable to:		
Owners of Canadian Tire Corporation	$ 604.0	$ 561.2
Non-controlling interests (Note 17)	35.3	3.2
	$ 639.3	$ 564.4
Basic earnings per share attributable to owners of Canadian Tire Corporation	$ 7.65	$ 6.96
Diluted earnings per share attributable to owners of Canadian Tire Corporation	$ 7.59	$ 6.91
Weighted average number of Common and Class A Non-Voting Shares outstanding:		
Basic	78,960,025	80,652,472
Diluted	79,612,957	81,180,863

The related notes form an integral part of these consolidated financial statements.

Source: Canadian Tire Corporation. Annual Report 2014, page 64.

Other Comprehensive Income is an account that includes gains and losses that are not part of profit but affect equity. Other comprehensive income is detailed on the **statement of comprehensive income**. An example of a statement of comprehensive income is shown in Exhibit 13.15 from Canadian Tire Corporation's January 3, 2015, financial statements.

 **CHECKPOINT**

8. Identify the three major sections of the income statement that are potentially reported.

Do Quick Study question: QS 13-11

EXHIBIT 13.15

Canadian Tire Corporation's Consolidated Statement of Comprehensive Income for the Year Ended January 3, 2015

Consolidated Statements of Comprehensive Income For the Years Ended (C$ in millions)		
	January 3, 2015	December 26 2013
Net income	**$639.3**	$564.4
Other Comprehensive income		
Items that may be reclassified subsequently to net income:		
Cash flow hedges:		
Gains, net of tax of $40.4 (2013 – $30.0)..	**114.0**	83.1
Reclassification of gains to non-financial assets, net of tax of $27.2 (2013 – $12.2)...	**(77.5)**	(33.7)
Reclassification of gains to income, net of tax of $0.6 (2013 – $0.1)........................	**(1.5)**	(0.4)
Available-for-sale financial assets:		
(Losses) gains, net of tax of $0.1 (2013 – $nil)	**(0.1)**	–
Reclassification of gains to income, net of tax of $nil (2013 – $nil).........................	**(0.1)**	0.1
Item that will not be reclassified subsequently to net income:		
Actuarial (losses) gains, net of tax of $4.7 (2013 – $3.6)..	**(13.2)**	10.0
Other comprehensive income..	**21.6**	59.1
Other comprehensive income attributable to:		
Owners of Canadian Tire Corporation	**$ 21.5**	$ 59.1
Non-controlling interests	**0.1**	–
	$ 21.6	$ 59.1
Comprehensive income	**$660.9**	$623.5
Comprehensive income attributable to:		
Owners of Canadian Tire Corporation	**$625.5**	$620.3
Non-controlling interests	**35.4**	3.2
	$660.9	$623.5

The related notes form an integral part of these consolidated financial statements.

Source: Canadian Tire Corporation. Annual Report 2014, page 65.

Retained Earnings

LO5 Explain restricted retained earnings and accounting changes.

Recall that the Retained Earnings account changes over the accounting period and these changes are detailed on the statement of changes in equity. Retained earnings are part of the shareholders' claim on the company's net assets. A common error is to think that retained earnings represent cash. Retained earnings are not cash. Retained earnings do not imply that there is a certain amount of cash available to pay shareholders, nor any other asset. They simply describe how much of the assets are owned by the shareholders as a result of earnings that have been *retained* for the purpose of reinvestment.

The next section describes important items affecting retained earnings. It also explains how we include these as part of the financial statements.

Restricted Retained Earnings

To protect creditors' interests in assets of a corporation, incorporating acts sometimes place *restrictions* on retained earnings. **Restrictions** are limits that identify how much of the retained earnings balance is not available for dividends or the repurchase of shares. Restrictions must be disclosed on the balance sheet or the statement of changes in equity, or in the notes to the financial statements.[10] There are three kinds of restrictions:

1. *Statutory restrictions* are imposed by a regulatory body. For example, dividends are limited to the balance of retained earnings.

2. *Contractual restrictions* occur when certain contracts, such as loan agreements, restrict retained earnings such that the payment of dividends is limited to a certain amount or percentage of retained earnings.

3. *Voluntary restrictions* are placed on retained earnings by a corporation's directors to limit dividends because of a special need for cash, such as for the purchase of new facilities.

Accounting Changes

Another issue that can affect retained earnings is that of accounting changes. There are three types of accounting changes but only two have the potential to affect retained earnings. Exhibit 13.16 summarizes accounting changes and their appropriate treatment:

EXHIBIT 13.16

Guidelines for the Treatment of Accounting Changes[11]

Accounting Change	Accounting Treatment
1. Change in Accounting Policy	– Retrospective restatement of financial statements, where practicable, results in adjustment to prior-period, current and future financial statements, – Only permitted if they are required based on a change in the IFRS standards or if the change results in more reliable and more relevant information – Disclosure requiring description of change and effect on financial statements,
2. Correction of Error(s) in Prior Financial Statements	– New policy or corrected amount is reported in current year's operating results, and – Usually charged or credited (net of tax) to opening balance of Retained Earnings.[12]
3. Change in Estimate	Accounted for in period of change and future period financial statements (prospectively).

---

10 IFRS 2015, IAS 1, para. 79(v).

11 IFRS 2015, IAS 8.

12 IFRS 2015, IAS 8, para 26 and 42. Usually the retrospective adjustment resulting from a change in accounting policy is made to retained earnings. The retrospective correction of an error requires the restatement of comparative amounts for prior periods where practicable.

1. CHANGE IN ACCOUNTING POLICY

A *change in accounting policy* occurs if, for example, a company changes from FIFO to the weighted-average method for calculating the cost of sales and merchandise inventory. A change in accounting policy is represented by a change from an existing accounting policy to an alternative one. The consistency principle of the IFRS framework requires a company to continue applying the same accounting policies once they are chosen to ensure financial statements are comparable from one accounting period to the next. A company can change from one acceptable accounting policy to another as long as the change improves the usefulness of information in its financial statements or if it is required as a result of an updated IFRS standard. The accounting treatment for a change in accounting policy is noted in Exhibit 13.16.

2. CORRECTION OF ERROR(S) IN PRIOR FINANCIAL STATEMENTS

Sometimes errors occur. For instance, assume Globe Inc. makes an error in a 2017 journal entry for the purchase of land by incorrectly debiting an expense account for $240,000. This error was discovered in 2018 and requires correction as per the guidelines outlined in Exhibit 13.16. The entry to record the correction is:

2018				
Dec. 31	Land...		240,000	
	Income Tax Payable*			
	($240,000 × 25%)			60,000
	Retained Earnings................................			180,000
	To adjust for error in 2017 journal entry			
	that expensed the purchase of land.			

*Note: Income taxes payable is adjusted as the 2017 financial statements reported income too low due to the incorrect recognition of the purchase of land as an expense. Calculated based on an assumed flat tax rate of 25% for simplicity.

To correct the error, the 2017 financial statements are restated, appropriate note disclosure is included explaining the error, and retained earnings are restated as per Exhibit 13.17. There is no effect on the current year's operating results in this particular instance.

EXHIBIT 13.17

Presentation of Accounting Changes on the Statement of Changes in Equity

Globe Inc. Statement of Changes in Equity For Year Ended December 31, 2018	Common Shares	Retained Earnings	Total Equity
Balance, January 1..	$1,750,000	$ 56,000	$1,806,000
Issuance of common shares..................................	125,000		125,000
Correction of error — cost of land incorrectly expensed (net of $60,000 tax expense)...............................		180,000	180,000
Profit (loss)		148,000	148,000
Dividends...		(40,000)	(40,000)
Balance, December 31...	$1,875,000	$344,000	$2,219,000

CHANGE IN ESTIMATE

Many items reported in financial statements are based on estimates. Future events are certain to reveal that some of these estimates were inaccurate even when based on the best data available at the time.

Because these inaccuracies are not the result of mistakes, they are considered to be **changes in accounting estimates** and *not* accounting errors.

The accounting treatment for a change in estimate involves adjusting the estimate in the current period and in future financial statements. For example, if the estimated useful life of a PPE item changed because of new information, this would be identified as a change in estimate. Examples of changes in estimates are provided below:

Examples of Changes in Estimate	Examples of Changes in Accounting Policies
Allowance for Doubtful Accounts provision is increased to 6% of Accounts Receivable from 5% of Accounts Receivable in prior year	Inventory costing switches from FIFO to weighted average
Estimate of useful life of PPE item changes from 10 years to 6 years	Valuation method selected to assess inventory valuation
Estimated warranty liability is increased from 3% of sales to 5% of sales based on issues with a new product line	Depreciation policy over cost allocation of property, plant, and equipment
Adjustments for contingencies relating to expectations over expected payouts relating to litigation	Corporate policy over classifying repairs and maintenance costs.

CHECKPOINT

9. A company that has used FIFO for the past 15 years decides to switch to moving weighted average. Which of the following statements describes the effect of this event on past years' profit?
   a. The cumulative effect is reported as an adjustment to ending retained earnings for the prior period.
   b. The cumulative effect is ignored, as it is a change in an accounting estimate.
   c. The cumulative effect is reported only on the current year's income statement.

Do Quick Study questions: QS 13-12, QS 13-13

CRITICAL THINKING CHALLENGE

Refer to the Critical Thinking Challenge questions at the beginning of the chapter. Compare your answers to those suggested on Connect.

IFRS AND ASPE—THE DIFFERENCES

Difference	International Financial Reporting Standards (IFRS)	Accounting Standards for Private Enterprises (ASPE)
Comprehensive income	• Disclosure of comprehensive income is required.	• The disclosure of comprehensive profit is not required.
Earnings per share	• Earnings per share presentation is required.	• Earnings per share presentation is not required.
Accounting Changes	• Change in accounting policy can be made only if it is to conform to a change in GAAP or if the change results in more reliable and relevant disclosure.	• Changes in accounting policy are permitted in specific areas such as accounting for R&D costs or an accounting policy change over accounting for income taxes.

A Look Ahead

Chapter 14 The next chapter describes the accounting for and analysis of bonds and notes. We explain their characteristics, payment patterns, interest computations, retirement, and reporting requirements.

Summary

LO1 Describe and account for share dividends and share splits. Both a share dividend and a share split divide a company's outstanding shares into smaller pieces. The total value of the company is unchanged, but the price of each new share is smaller. Share dividends and share splits do not transfer any of the corporation's assets to shareholders and do not affect assets, total equity, or the equity attributed to each shareholder. Share dividends are recorded by capitalizing retained earnings equal to the market value of the distributed shares. Share splits are not recorded with journal entries but do require note disclosure.

LO2 Describe and account for retirement of shares. When a corporation purchases its own previously issued outstanding shares for the purpose of retirement, the share capital account is debited based on the original issue price. If the amount paid by the corporation is less than the original issue price, the excess is credited to the Contributed Capital from Retirement of Shares account. If the amount paid is greater than the original issue price, Contributed Capital from Retirement of Shares is debited to the extent a credit balance exists in that account and any remaining amount is debited to Retained Earnings.

LO3 Calculate earnings per share and describe its use. Corporations calculate earnings per share by dividing profit less any preferred dividends by the weighted-average number of outstanding common shares.

LO4 Explain the form and content of a corporate income statement with continuing and discontinued operations and earnings per share. Corporate income statements are similar to those for proprietorships and partnerships except for the inclusion of income taxes. The income statement consists of three potential sections: (1) continuing operations, (2) discontinued operations, and (3) earnings per share. Comprehensive income, which is equal to profit plus other comprehensive income, is detailed on the statement of comprehensive income.

LO5 Explain restricted retained earnings and accounting changes. Retained earnings are sometimes restricted to limit dividends and reacquisition of shares or to protect creditors. Corporations may voluntarily restrict retained earnings as a means of informing shareholders why dividends are not larger. Accounting changes that affect retained earnings of prior years include (1) change in accounting policy/procedure, and (2) correction of an error. A change in accounting estimate, also a type of accounting change, does not affect retained earnings of prior years.

Guidance Answers to CHECKPOINT

1. *c*

2. A share dividend increases the number of shares issued and outstanding and requires a journal entry to transfer (or capitalize) a portion of retained earnings to contributed capital. A share split does not involve a journal entry and simply increases the number of shares issued and outstanding.

3. Retained earnings equal to the market value of the distributable shares should be capitalized.

4. The number of shares outstanding is reduced by the number of shares retired and cancelled.

5. *a*

Calculations: ($250,000 − $70,000)/ 22,500* = $8.00

Time Period	Outstanding Shares	Fraction of Year Outstanding	Weighted Average
January–June	25,000	× 6/12	= 12,500
July–December...............	20,000	× 6/12	= 10,000
Weighted-average outstanding shares......			22,500

6. *c*

Calculations:

Time Period	Outstanding Shares	Effect of Split	Fraction of Year	Weighted Average
January–June..............	25,000	× 3	× 6/12	= 37,500
July............................	20,000	× 3	× 1/12	= 5,000
August–December.......	60,000	× 1	× 5/12	= 25,000
Weighted-average outstanding shares ..				67,500

7. The number of shares previously outstanding is retroactively restated to reflect the share split or share dividend as if it had occurred at the beginning of the year.

8. The three major sections are Profit from Continuing Operations, Discontinued Operations, and Earnings Per Share.

9. *a*

DEMONSTRATION PROBLEM

Raxx Ltd. began 2017 with the following balances in its shareholders' equity accounts:

Common shares, unlimited shares authorized, 500,000 shares issued and outstanding	$3,000,000
Retained earnings	2,500,000

The following share-related transactions occurred during the year:

Date	Transaction
March 1	Issued at $20 per share 100,000 $2.50 non-cumulative preferred shares with an unlimited number authorized.
May 1	Issued 50,000 common shares at $15 per share.
Sept. 1	Repurchased and retired 150,000 common shares at $16 per share.
Nov. 30	Declared and distributed a 3:1 share split on the common shares.

Required

a. Calculate the weighted-average number of shares outstanding using the information above.

b. Using the information provided, prepare an income statement for 2017 similar to Exhibit 13.13:

Cumulative effect of a change in depreciation method (net of $26,000 tax benefit)	$ (136,500)
Operating expenses (related to continuing operations)	(2,072,500)
Gain on disposal of discontinued operations' assets (net of $8,600 tax expense)	37,500
Investment income on sale of investment in shares	400,000
Loss from operating discontinued operations (net of $40,000 tax benefit)	(182,500)
Income taxes on profit from continuing operations	(660,000)
Revenues	5,375,000
Loss from sale of plant assets*	(650,000)

*The assets were items of equipment replaced with new technology.

Analysis Component: Why are gains/losses and other income shown separately on the income statement?

Planning the Solution

- Based on the shares outstanding at the beginning of the year and the transactions during the year, calculate the weighted-average number of outstanding shares for the year.
- Calculate earnings per share.
- Assign each of the listed items to an appropriate income statement category.
- Prepare an income statement similar to Exhibit 13.13, including separate sections for continued operations, discontinued operations, and earnings per share.
- Answer the analysis component.

Solution

a. Calculate the weighted-average number of outstanding shares:

Time Period	Outstanding Shares	Effect of Split	Fraction of Year	Weighted Average
January–April...	500,000	× 3	× 4/12	= 500,000
May–August...	550,000	× 3	× 4/12	= 550,000
September–November.............................	400,000	× 3	× 3/12	= 300,000
December	1,200,000	× 1	× 1/12	= 100,000
Weighted-average outstanding shares				1,450,000

b. Prepare an income statement for 2017:

Raxx Ltd. **Income Statement** **For Year Ended December 31, 2017**		
Revenues...		$5,375,000
Operating expenses		2,072,500
Profit from operations		$3,302,500
Other revenues and expenses:		
Investment income	$ 400,000	
Loss from sale of plant assets	(650,000)	(250,000)
Profit from continuing operations before tax		$3,052,500
Income tax expense...		660,000
Profit from continuing operations		$2,392,500
Discontinued operations:		
Loss from discontinued operations (net of $31,400 tax)		(145,000)
Profit		$2,247,500
Earnings per share		
(1,450,000 average shares outstanding):		
Profit from continuing operations		$ 1.65[1]
Loss from discontinued operation		(0.10)[2]
Profit		$ 1.55

[1]$2,392,500/1,450,000 = $ 1.65
[2]$(145,000)/1,450,000 = $(0.10)

857

> **Analysis Component:** Gains/losses and other income is shown separately on the income statement to ensure users can interpret performance based on operating activities. Including gains/losses as part of revenues/operating expenses could distort analyses.

Glossary

Cancelling of shares See *retirement of shares.*

Changes in accounting estimates Corrections to previous estimates or predictions about future events and outcomes, such as residual values and the useful lives of operating assets; the changes are accounted for in the current and future periods.

Comprehensive income Equals *profit* plus *other comprehensive income.*

Continuing operations That section of an income statement that shows the revenues, expenses, and profit generated by the company's day-to-day operating activities.

Discontinued operation When a company with operations in different segments sells a segment, the sold segment is known as a discontinued operation.

Dividend payout ratio Analyzes much of the company's earnings are paid out in dividends. The ratio assesses the company's payout of dividends in relation to its earnings.

Earnings per share The amount of profit earned by each share of a company's outstanding common shares; commonly abbreviated as *EPS.* Calculated with the formula (Profit − Preferred dividends) ÷ Weighted-average common shares.

EPS See *earnings per share.*

Net of tax An amount reported net of tax means the income tax expense (benefit) has already been subtracted.

Other Comprehensive Income An account that includes gains and losses that are not part of profit but affect equity. An unrealized gain or loss on available-for-sale investments is an example of an *other comprehensive income* item.

Restrictions Legal or contractual or voluntary limitations that cause a portion of the retained earnings balance not to be available for dividends or the repurchase of shares. No journal entry is required but note disclosure is necessary.

Retirement of shares Occurs when a corporation repurchases and cancels its own shares.

Reverse share split An act by a corporation to call in its shares and replace each share with less than one new share; reverse splits are opposite of share splits as they increase both the market value per share and the book value per share.

Segment of a business A component of a company's operations that serves a particular line of business or class of customers and that has assets, activities, and financial results of operations that can be distinguished from other parts of the business.

Share dividend A corporation's distribution of its own shares to its shareholders without receiving any payment in return. Also called a *stock dividend.*

Share split An act by a corporation to call in its shares and replace each share with more than one new share; a share split will decrease the market value per share and also the book value per share.

Statement of comprehensive income The statement that details comprehensive income.

Concept Review Questions

1. What is the difference between a share dividend and a share split?

2. What effects does declaring a share dividend have on the corporation's assets, liabilities, and total equity? What effects does the distribution of the shares have?

3. Refer to the financial statements for Indigo in Appendix II. The balance in share capital at March 30, 2013, was 25,297,389 shares. What is the balance as of March 29, 2014? What caused the change in share capital from 2013 to 2014?

4. How are earnings per share results calculated for a corporation with a simple capital structure?

5. Refer to the financial statements for Danier Leather in Appendix II. Did basic EPS increase or decrease from 2013 to 2014?

6. Refer to the financial statements for WestJet in Appendix II. In both 2013 and 2014 the balance of shares issued and outstanding was reduced. What caused the balance of the account to go down? And, what had shares been issued for?

7. After taking five years' straight-line depreciation expense for an asset that was expected to have an eight-year useful life, a company decided that the asset would last another six years. Is this decision a change in accounting policy? How would the financial statements describe this change?

8. The chapter opening vignette highlighted Apple Inc.'s 7:1 stock split. What is the key reason executives at Apple would decide to provide shareholders with seven shares of stock for each common share held?

Quick Study

QS 13-1 Accounting for a share dividend LO1

Information taken from Jamestown Corp.'s balance sheet as of April 1, 2017, follows:

Common shares, 375,000 shares authorized,	
150,000 shares issued and outstanding	$1,102,500
Retained earnings...	633,000

On April 1, Jamestown declares and distributes a 10% share dividend. The market value of the shares on this date is $25. Prepare the equity section for Jamestown immediately following the share dividend (assume all dividends are debited directly to Retained Earnings).

QS 13-2 Share split LO1

Vector Gaming Ltd. showed the following equity account balances on December 31, 2017:

Common shares, 100,000 shares authorized;	
28,000 shares issued and outstanding	$476,000
Retained earnings	85,000

On January 2, 2018, Vector declared and distributed a 3:1 share split. Prepare a comparative equity section immediately before and after the share split similar to Exhibit 13.4.

QS 13-3 Repurchase and retirement of shares LO2

On September 2, Garrett Corporation purchased and retired 2,000 of its own shares for $18,000. The shares had been issued at an average price of $5. Prepare the September 2 entry for the purchase and retirement of the shares (assuming this is the first retirement ever recorded by Garrett).

QS 13-4 Repurchase and retirement of shares LO2

Outdoor Equipment Inc. had 180,000 common shares issued and outstanding as at December 31, 2017. The shares had been issued for $9.80 each. On September 12, 2018, Outdoor repurchased and retired 40,000 of these shares at $9.10 each, the first retirement ever recorded by Outdoor. Outdoor also repurchased and retired 20,000 shares at $11.40 on December 17, 2018. Record the entries on September 12 and December 17.

QS 13-5 Earnings per share LO3

Nelson Corp. earned profit of $450,000. The number of common shares outstanding all year long was 200,000 and preferred shareholders received a dividend totalling $10,000. Calculate the earnings per share for Nelson Corp.

QS 13-6 Earnings per share L03

Bellevue Ltd. reported profit of $860,000 for its year ended December 31, 2017. Calculate earnings per share given the following additional information at December 31, 2017:

Preferred shares, $2 cumulative, 50,000 shares authorized;	
26,000 shares issued and outstanding	$286,000
Common shares, 300,000 shares authorized,	
160,000 shares issued and outstanding*	544,000
Retained earnings**...	180,000

*There was no change in the outstanding shares during the year.
**Dividends totalling $100,000 were declared during 2017. There were no dividends in arrears.

QS 13-7 Weighted average shares outstanding L03 eXcel

On January 1, Harmon Corp. had 100,000 common shares outstanding. On February 1, Harmon Corp. issued 40,000 additional common shares. On June 1, another 80,000 common shares were issued. Calculate Harmon Corp.'s weighted-average shares outstanding. Round calculations to the nearest whole share.

QS 13-8 Weighted-average common shares outstanding—share dividend L03 eXcel

On January 1, Harrell Corp. had 75,000 common shares issued and outstanding. On April 1, it issued 24,000 additional shares and on June 1, declared and distributed a 20% share dividend. Calculate Harrell's weighted-average outstanding shares for the year.

QS 13-9 Weighted-average common shares outstanding—share split L03 eXcel

On January 1, Star Corp. had 50,000 common shares issued and outstanding. On April 1, it issued 4,000 additional shares and on June 5, declared and distributed a two-for-one share split. Calculate Star's weighted-average outstanding shares for the year.

QS 13-10 Weighted-average common shares outstanding—repurchase L03 eXcel

On January 1, 2017, Winston Mining Corp. had 580,000 common shares issued and outstanding. On April 30, it issued an additional 220,000 shares and on October 1 it repurchased and cancelled 100,000 shares. Calculate Winston's weighted-average shares outstanding for the year ended December 31, 2017. Round calculations to the nearest whole share.

QS 13-11 Income statement categories L04

Using the numbers to represent each section of a comprehensive income statement, identify where each of items (a) through (k) should be reported:

1. Continuing operations
2. Discontinued operations
3. Earnings per share

a. Gain on sale of Division E _____		**g.** Cost of goods sold	_____
b. Operating expenses _____		**h.** Loss from operating Division E	_____
c. Loss on sale of equipment _____		**i.** Income tax expense	_____
d. Interest income _____		**j.** Gain on sale of warehouse	_____
e. Depreciation expense _____		**k.** Interest expense	_____
f. Earnings per share _____			

QS 13-12 **Accounting for estimate changes and error adjustments** LO5

Answer the questions about each of the following items related to a company's activities for the year:

a. After using an expected useful life of seven years and no residual value to depreciate its office equipment over the preceding three years, the company decided early this year that the equipment would last only two more years. How should the effects of this decision be reported in the current financial statements?

b. An account receivable in the amount of $180,000 was written off two years ago. It was recovered this year. The president believes this should be reported as an error. How should the proceeds be reported in the current year's financial statements?

QS 13-13 **Accounting changes** LO5

Barton Inc. changed the method of calculating depreciation on its equipment from straight-line to double-declining-balance during 2017. The cumulative effect of the change is an additional expense of $46,000 related to prior years. The tax benefit is $13,000. Record the entry on December 31, 2017.

Exercises

Exercise 13-1 **Share dividends** LO1

CHECK FIGURE: 2. Retained earnings = $810,000

Arcus Development Inc.'s equity section on the December 31, 2016, balance sheet showed the following information:

Common shares, unlimited shares authorized,	
150,000 shares issued and outstanding	$1,480,000
Retained earnings..	380,000

On January 15, 2017, the company's board of directors declared a 5% share dividend to the shareholders of record on January 20 to be distributed on January 30. The market prices of the shares on January 15, 20, and 30 were $12.00, $10.80, and $11.40, respectively.

Required
1. Prepare the required entries for January 15, 20, and 30.
2. Prepare the equity section on the January 31, 2017, balance sheet, assuming profit earned during January 2017 was $520,000.

Analysis Component: What effect did the share dividend have on the market price of Arcus's shares and why?

Exercise 13-2 **Share dividends** LO1

CHECK FIGURE: 3. Total equity = $10,697,800

Pacifica Papers Inc. needed to conserve cash so, instead of a cash dividend, the board of directors declared a 15% common share dividend on June 30, 2017, distributable on July 15, 2017. Because performance during 2017 was better than expected, the company's board of directors declared a $0.40 per share cash dividend on November 15, 2017, payable on December 1, 2017, to shareholders of record on November 30, 2017. The equity section of Pacifica's December 31, 2016, balance sheet showed:

Common shares, unlimited shares authorized, 650,000 shares issued and outstanding	$6,240,000
Retained earnings	2,400,000

Required

1. Journalize the declaration of the share dividend. The market prices of the shares were $16.00 on June 30, 2017, and $17.60 on July 15, 2017.

2. Journalize the declaration of the cash dividend.

3. Prepare the equity section of the balance sheet at December 31, 2017, assuming profit earned during the year was $2,356,800.

Exercise 13-3 Share splits LO1

CHECK FIGURE: 2. Retained earnings = $300,000

Bandara Gold Inc.'s equity section on the October 31, 2017, balance sheet showed the following information:

Common shares, unlimited shares authorized, 500,000 shares issued and outstanding	$900,000
Retained earnings	112,500

On November 15, 2017, Bandara's board of directors declared a 3:1 share split to the shareholders of record on November 20 to be distributed on November 29. The market prices of the shares on November 15, 20, and 29 were $2.25, $0.72, and $0.78, respectively.

Required

1. Prepare the required entries for November 15, 20, and 29.

2. Prepare the equity section on the November 30, 2017, balance sheet, assuming profit earned during November 2017 was $187,500.

Analysis Component: What effect did the share split have on the market price of Bandara's shares and why?

Exercise 13-4 Share dividends and splits LO1

CHECK FIGURE: 2. Total equity = $25,526,400

On March 1, 2017, VisionTech Inc.'s board of directors declared a 5% share dividend when the market price per share was $10.00. On November 15, 2017, the board of directors declared a 4:1 share split. The equity section of the company's December 31, 2016, balance sheet showed:

Common shares; 20,000,000 shares authorized; 2,500,000 shares issued and outstanding	$15,600,000
Retained earnings	5,142,400

Required

1. Prepare a statement of changes in equity for the year ended December 31, 2017, assuming profit earned during the year was $4,784,000.

2. Prepare the equity section of the December 31, 2017, balance sheet.

Exercise 13-5 Share dividend, share split, equity section of balance sheet LO1

CHECK FIGURE: Equity Dec. 31, 2017 = $3,836,480

CarFind Inc. showed the following equity information at December 31, 2016.

Common shares, unlimited shares authorized;	
4,000,000 shares issued and outstanding	$1,004,480
Retained earnings	1,312,000

On April 1, 2017, 200,000 common shares were issued at $0.60 per share. On June 1, the board of directors declared a 15% share dividend to shareholders of record on June 15; the distribution date was July 1. The market prices of the shares on June 1, June 15, and July 1 were $2.08, $1.76, and $1.96, respectively. On December 11, the board of directors declared a 2:1 share split to shareholders of record on December 15; the distribution date was December 20. Profit earned during the year was $1,400,000.

Required Prepare the company's equity section on the December 31, 2017, balance sheet.

Analysis Component: What are the benefits to CarFind Inc. of declaring a share dividend as opposed to a cash dividend?

Exercise 13-6 Retirement of shares LO2

CHECK FIGURE: c. Dr Common Shares: 5,400

Information taken from Nanotec Security Inc.'s January 31, 2017, balance sheet follows:

Common shares, 600,000 shares authorized,	
30,000 shares issued and outstanding	$405,000
Retained earnings	79,350

On February 1, 2017, the company repurchased and retired 400 common shares (the first retirement the company has recorded).

Required Prepare general journal entries to record the repurchase and retirement under each of the following independent assumptions.

The shares were repurchased for:

   a. $9.00 per share   **b.** $13.50 per share   **c.** $18.00 per share

Exercise 13-7 Share split, retirement of shares LO1,2

CHECK FIGURE: 2. Retained earnings, Dec. 31, 2017 = $2,168,000

The Data Group Inc. had the following balances in its equity accounts at December 31, 2016:

Common shares, unlimited shares authorized;	
200,000 shares issued and outstanding	$2,400,000
Retained earnings	400,000

During 2017, the following equity transactions occurred:

Apr.	15	Repurchased and retired 15,000 common shares at $10.40 per share.
May	1	Repurchased and retired 25,000 common shares at $13.60 per share.
Nov.	1	The board of directors declared a 2:1 share split effective on this date.

Required

1. Prepare journal entries to account for the transactions during 2017 (assuming the retirements were the first ever recorded by The Data Group Inc.).

2. Prepare the company's equity section on the December 31, 2017, balance sheet, assuming a loss for the year of $136,000.

Analysis Component: What does a share repurchase and retirement accomplish for Data Group Inc.?

Exercise 13-8 Share dividends, share splits, retirements, equity section of balance sheet LO1,2

CHECK FIGURE: Equity, Dec. 31, 2017 = $7,264,000

Mady Entertainment Inc. showed the following equity account balances on the December 31, 2016, balance sheet:

Common shares, unlimited authorized shares, 680,000 shares issued and outstanding	$5,440,000
Retained earnings	2,880,000

During 2017, the following selected transactions occurred:

Apr.	1	Repurchased and retired 280,000 common shares at $8.40 per share; this is the first retirement recorded by Mady.
June	1	Declared a 2:1 share split to shareholders of record on June 12, distributable June 30.
Dec.	1	Declared a 10% share dividend to shareholders of record on December 10, distributable December 20. The market prices of the shares on December 1, December 10, and December 20 were $4.40, $3.84, and $4.16 respectively.
	20	Distributed the share dividend declared December 1.
	31	Closed the credit balance of $1,296,000 in the Income Summary account.

Required

a. Journalize the transactions above (assuming the retirements were the first ever recorded by Mady Entertainment Inc.).

b. Prepare the equity section on the December 31, 2017, balance sheet.

Exercise 13-9 Reporting earnings per share LO3,4

CHECK FIGURE: EPS = $0.60

Earlyrain Inc.'s 2017 income statement, excluding the earnings per share portion of the statement, was as follows:

Revenues..		$380,000
Expenses:		
Depreciation	$ 41,520	
Income taxes	52,080	
Other expenses..	164,000	257,600
Profit from continuing operations		$122,400
Loss from operating discontinued business segment		
(net of $18,800 tax benefit)..	$ 44,800	
Loss on sale of business segment		
(net of $7,520 tax benefit)...	17,600	(62,400)
Profit		$ 60,000

The weighted-average number of common shares outstanding during the year was 100,000. Present the earnings per share portion of the 2017 income statement (round EPS calculations to two decimal places).

Exercise 13-10 **Weighted-average shares outstanding and earnings per share** L03

CHECK FIGURE: Weighted-average outstanding shares = 86,000

Liberty Ventures Inc. reported $209,840 profit in 2017 and declared preferred dividends of $34,400. The following changes in common shares outstanding occurred during the year:

Jan.	1	60,000 common shares were outstanding.
June	30	Sold 20,000 common shares.
Sept.	1	Declared and issued a 20% common share dividend.
Nov.	2	Sold 12,000 common shares.

Calculate the weighted-average number of common shares outstanding during the year and earnings per share. (Round EPS calculations to two decimal places.)

Exercise 13-11 **Weighted-average shares outstanding and earnings per share** L03 eXcel

CHECK FIGURE: Weighted-average outstanding shares = 93,000

Horticultural Products Inc. reported $889,800 profit in 2017 and declared preferred dividends of $79,800. The following changes in common shares outstanding occurred during the year.

Jan.	1	60,000 common shares were outstanding.
Mar.	1	Declared and issued a 30% common share dividend.
Aug.	1	Sold 20,000 common shares.
Nov.	1	Sold 40,000 common shares.

Calculate the weighted-average number of common shares outstanding during the year and earnings per share. Round calculations to two decimal places.

Analysis Component: What is the effect of a share dividend on earnings per share?

Exercise 13-12 **Weighted-average shares outstanding and earnings per share** L03

CHECK FIGURE: b. Weighted-average outstanding shares = 433,500

Kiwi Charter Corp. reported $1,612,530 of profit for 2017. On November 2, 2017, it declared and paid the annual preferred dividends of $234,000. On January 1, 2017, Kiwi had 80,000 and 270,000 outstanding preferred and common shares, respectively. The following transactions changed the number of shares outstanding during the year:

Feb.	1	Declared and issued a 10% common share dividend.
Apr.	30	Sold 180,000 common shares for cash.
May	1	Sold 50,000 preferred shares for cash.
Oct.	31	Sold 99,000 common shares for cash.

   a. What is the amount of profit available for distribution to the common shareholders?

   b. What is the weighted-average number of common shares for the year?

   c. What is the earnings per share for the year?

Analysis Component: Did the sale of preferred shares on May 1, 2017, affect the basic earnings per common share?

Exercise 13-13 Weighted-average shares outstanding and earnings per share L03 eXcel

CHECK FIGURE: c. EPS = $2.63

A company reported $576,000 of profit for 2017. It also declared $78,000 of dividends on preferred shares for the same year. At the beginning of 2017, the company had 50,000 outstanding common shares. These three events changed the number of outstanding shares during the year:

June	1	Sold 30,000 common shares for cash.
Aug.	31	Purchased and retired 13,000 common shares.
Oct.	1	Completed a three-for-one share split.

   a. What is the amount of profit available for distribution to the common shareholders?

   b. What is the weighted-average number of common shares for the year?

   c. What is the earnings per share for the year? Round calculations to two decimal places.

Analysis Component: What is the effect of a share split on earnings per share?

Exercise 13-14 Income statement categories L04

CHECK FIGURE: Profit = $212,146

The following list of items was extracted from the December 31, 2017, trial balance of Future Products Corp. Using the information contained in this listing, prepare the company's multiple-step income statement for 2017. You need not complete the earnings per share calculations.

	Debit	Credit
Salaries expense	$ 73,370	
Income tax expense (continuing operations)	102,498	
Loss from operating Division C (net of $11,220 tax benefit)	26,400	
Sales		$770, 264
Total effect on prior years' profit of change from declining-balance to straight-line depreciation (net of $10,560 tax)		35,640
Gain on provincial condemnation of land owned by Future		102,080
Depreciation expense	68,310	
Gain on sale of Division C (net of $21,670 tax)		72,600
Cost of goods sold	462,220	

Exercise 13-15 Classifying profit items not related to continuing operations LO4

In preparing the annual financial statements for Jade Oil Inc., the correct manner of reporting the following items was not clear to the company's employees. Explain where each of the following items should appear in the financial statements.

   a. After depreciating office equipment for three years based on an expected useful life of eight years, the company decided this year that the office equipment should last seven more years. As a result, the depreciation for the current year is $8,000 instead of $10,000.

   b. This year, the accounting department of the company discovered that an installment payment on the five-year note payable had been charged entirely to interest expense last year. The after-tax effect of the charge to interest expense was $15,400.

   c. The company keeps its repair trucks for several years before disposing of the old trucks and buying new trucks. On June 1 of this year, for the first time in 10 years, it sold old trucks for a gain of $19,900. New trucks were purchased in August of the same year.

Exercise 13-16 Income statement categories LO4

During 2017, GlenTel Inc. sold its interest in a chain of wholesale outlets. This sale took the company out of the wholesaling business completely. The company still operates its retail outlets. Following is a lettered list of sections of an income statement:

   a. Profit or loss from continuing operations

   b. Profit or loss from operating a discontinued operation

   c. Profit or loss from disposing of a discontinued operation

Indicate where each of the eight profit-related items for the company would appear on the 2017 income statement by writing the letter of the appropriate section in the blank beside each item.

		Debit	Credit
_____	1. Depreciation expense	$157,500	
_____	2. Gain on sale of wholesale operation (net of $135,000 income taxes)		$ 405,000
_____	3. Loss from operating wholesale operation (net of $111,000 tax benefit)	333,000	
_____	4. Salaries expense	324,000	
_____	5. Sales		1,620,000
_____	6. Gain on expropriation of company property		264,000
_____	7. Cost of goods sold	828,000	
_____	8. Income taxes expense	190,200	

Exercise 13-17 Income statement presentation LO4

CHECK FIGURE: Profit from continuing operations (after tax) = $384,300

Use the data for GlenTel Inc. in Exercise 13-16 to present a multiple-step income statement for 2017. You need not complete the earnings per share calculations.

Exercise 13-18 **Statement of changes in equity** LO5

CHECK FIGURE: a. Total equity = $1,053,600

Ice Industries Inc. showed the following equity account balances at December 31, 2016:

Common shares, unlimited shares authorized,	
70,000 shares issued and outstanding	$816,000
Retained earnings	112,800

The company issued long-term debt during 2017 that requires a retained earnings restriction of $72,000. Share dividends declared but not distributed during 2017 totalled 7,000 shares capitalized for a total of $84,000.

    a. Prepare a statement of changes in equity for the year ended December 31, 2017, assuming profit earned during the year was $124,800.

    b. What is the maximum amount of dividends that the company can declare during 2018?

Exercise 13-19 **Accounting for a change in accounting policy** LO5

Holt Developments Ltd. put an asset in service on January 1, 2015. Its cost was $270,000, its predicted service life was six years, and its expected residual value was $27,000. The company decided to use double-declining-balance depreciation. After consulting with the company's auditors, management decided to change to straight-line depreciation in 2017, without changing either the original service life or residual value.

Required Explain how and where this change should be accounted for.

Exercise 13-20 **Accounting changes** LO5

CHECK FIGURE: Total equity = $2,381,280

Selected information regarding the accounts of Infinity Minerals Corp. follows:

Common shares, unlimited authorized, 50,000 shares	
issued and outstanding, December 31, 2016	$1,074,000
Common dividends declared and paid during 2017	120,000
Cumulative effect of change in accounting estimate	
(net of $7,200 tax)	(33,600)
Profit for the year ended December 31, 2017	342,000
Preferred dividends declared and paid during 2017	72,000
Preferred shares, $4.80 non-cumulative, 15,000 shares	
authorized, issued, and outstanding, December 31, 2016	450,000
Retained earnings, December 31, 2016 (as originally reported)	588,000

Prepare a statement of changes in equity for the year ended December 31, 2017, assuming 7,000 common shares were issued during 2017 at an average price of $21.84 per share and that no preferred shares were issued in 2017.

Problems

Problem 13-1A **Earnings per share calculations and presentation** LO1,2,3,4 e**X**cel

CHECK FIGURES: Weighted-average outstanding shares: 2. a. 35,364; b. 44,880; c. 171,720

Note: Problem 13-1B covers LO1, 3 with no retirement of shares.

Except for the earnings per share statistics, the 2018, 2017, and 2016 income statements for Ace Group Inc. were originally presented as follows:

	2018	2017	2016
Sales	$998,900	$687,040	$466,855
Costs and expenses	323,570	?	?
Profit from continuing operations	?	?	309,435
Gain (loss) on discontinued operations	(107,325)	80,410	?
Profit (loss)	?	$532,950	$153,244

Information on Common Shares for Ace Group Inc.*

Shares outstanding on December 31, 2015	28,800
Purchase and retirement of shares on March 1, 2016	− 2,880
Sale of shares on June 1, 2016	+12,480
Share dividend of 5% on August 1, 2016	+ ?
Shares outstanding on December 31, 2016	?
Sale of shares on February 1, 2017	+ 5,760
Purchase and retirement of shares on July 1, 2017	− 1,440
Shares outstanding on December 31, 2017	?
Sale of shares on March 1, 2018	+16,560
Purchase and retirement of shares on September 1, 2018	− 3,600
Share split of 3:1 on October 1, 2018	+ ?
Shares outstanding on December 31, 2018	?

*No preferred shares have been issued.

Required

1. Calculate the 11 missing amounts.

2. Calculate the weighted-average number of common shares outstanding during:

   a. 2016   **b.** 2017   **c.** 2018.

3. Rounding calculations to two decimal places, prepare the earnings per share income statement presentations for:

   a. 2016   **b.** 2017   **c.** 2018.

Analysis Component: *Profit from continuing operations* increased from 2017 to 2018 yet there was a decrease in the earnings per share calculated for this amount for the same years. Explain.

Problem 13-2A Earnings per share LO1,3

Range Energy Corp.'s financial statements for the current year ended December 31, 2017, have been completed and submitted to you for review. The equity account balances a year ago, at December 31, 2016, are as follows:

Preferred shares, $4.20 non-cumulative, 10,000 shares authorized, issued, and outstanding	$ 748,050
Common shares, unlimited shares authorized, 120,000 shares issued and outstanding	1,420,350
Retained earnings	675,795

The only share transactions during 2017 were the declaration and distribution of a 24,000 common share dividend on July 1 and the issuance of 12,000 common shares for cash on October 31. The company's 2017 profit was $620,880. A cash dividend on the preferred shares was declared on December 1, but was not paid as of December 31. Earnings per share for 2017 were calculated as follows:

$$\frac{\text{Profit}}{\text{Common shares outstanding on Dec. 31, 2014}} = \frac{\$620{,}880}{156{,}000} = \$3.98$$

Required

1. Explain what is wrong with the earnings per share calculation, indicating what corrections should be made to both the numerator and the denominator. Round calculations to two decimal places.

2. Explain how your answer to requirement 1 would be different if there had not been a cash dividend declaration to preferred shares and if the share dividend had taken place on January 2, 2017.

Problem 13-3A Dividends, retirement, statement of changes in equity LO1,2,5

CHECK FIGURES: 2. Dec. 31, 2017 Retained Earnings = $642,720; Total equity = $1,512,600

Note: Problem 13-3B covers LO1, 5 with no retirement of shares.

Zen Aerospace Corporation reported the following equity account balances on December 31, 2016:

Preferred shares, $3.60 cumulative, unlimited shares authorized	$ -0-
Common shares, unlimited shares authorized,	
20,000 shares issued and outstanding	552,000
Retained Earnings	324,000

In 2017, the company had the following transactions affecting shareholders and the shareholders' equity accounts:

Jan.	1	Purchased and retired 2,000 common shares at $36 per share.
	14	The directors declared a 10% share dividend distributable on February 5 to the January 30 shareholders of record. The shares were trading at $45.60 per share.
	30	Date of record regarding the 10% share dividend.
Feb.	5	Date of distribution regarding the 10% share dividend.
July	6	Sold 5,000 preferred shares at $60 per share.
Sept.	5	The directors declared a total cash dividend of $48,000 payable on October 5 to the September 20 shareholders of record.
Oct.	5	The cash dividend declared on September 5 was paid.
Dec.	31	Closed the $465,600 credit balance in the Profit Summary account to Retained Earnings.
	31	Closed the dividend accounts.

Required

1. Prepare journal entries to record the transactions and closings for 2017 (assume the retirements were the first ever recorded by Zen Aerospace).

2. Prepare the statement of changes in equity for the year ended December 31, 2017.

Problem 13-4A Presenting items in an income statement LO4

CHECK FIGURE: Profit = $575,820

The following table shows the balances from various accounts in the adjusted trial balance for UniLink Telecom Corp. as of December 31, 2017:

	Debit	Credit
a. Interest income		$ 28,800
b. Depreciation expense, equipment	$ 86,400	
c. Loss on sale of office equipment...	59,400	
d. Accounts payable		100,800
e. Other operating expenses	234,000	
f. Accumulated depreciation, equipment		176,400
g. Gain from settling a lawsuit..		100,800
h. Cumulative effect of change in accounting principle (pre-tax)		151,200
i. Accumulated depreciation, buildings		392,400
j. Loss from operating a discontinued operation (pre-tax).........................	46,800	
k. Gain on expropriation of land and building by government		68,400
l. Sales...		2,329,200
m. Depreciation expense, buildings	129,600	
n. Correction of overstatement of prior year's sales (pre-tax)	36,000	
o. Gain on sale of discontinued operation's assets (pre-tax)......................		79,200
p. Loss from settling a lawsuit	57,600	
q. Income taxes expense	?	
r. Cost of goods sold	1,170,000	

Required

1. Assuming that the company's income tax rate is 30%, what are the tax effects and after-tax measures of the items labelled as pre-tax?

2. Prepare a multi-step income statement for the year ended December 31, 2017.

Problem 13-5A **Income statement** LO4,5

CHECK FIGURE: Profit = $537,600

The income statement for Weatherford International Inc.'s year ended December 31, 2017, was prepared by an inexperienced bookkeeper. As the new accountant, your immediate priority is to correct the statement. All amounts included in the statement are before tax (assume a rate of 30%). The company had 100,000 common shares issued and outstanding throughout the year, as well as 20,000 shares of $1.20 cumulative preferred shares issued and outstanding. Retained earnings at December 31, 2016, were $328,800.

Weatherford International Inc. Income Statement December 31, 2017		
Revenues:		
Sales	$1,152,000	
Gain on sale of equipment...	14,400	
Interest income	6,720	
Gain on sale of plant...	141,600	
Operating profit on discontinued operation...........................	29,040	$1,343,760
Expenses:		
Cost of goods sold...	$ 348,000	
Selling and administrative expenses	180,000	
Sales discounts..	11,760	
Loss on sale of discontinued operation	36,000	
Dividends..	120,000	695,760
Profit...		$ 648,000
Earnings per share		$ 6.48

Required Prepare a corrected income statement, including earnings per share information. Round earnings per share calculations to the nearest whole cent.

Problem 13-6A Dividends, statement of changes in equity LO1,5

CHECK FIGURES: Retained earnings, Dec. 31, 2017 = $382,060; Total equity = $872,895

Kaye Biotech Inc. had the following equity account balances at December 31, 2016:

Preferred shares, $2.45, non-cumulative,	
Authorized: 20,000 shares	
ˊIssued and outstanding: 5,000 shares	$ 35,000
Common shares,	
Authorized: Unlimited	
Issued and outstanding: 85,000 shares	287,695
Retained earnings..	40,600

On February 1, 2017, 5,000 preferred shares were issued at $7.70 each. The board of directors declared and paid the annual cash dividend on the preferred shares on June 30, 2017, and a 12% common share dividend was declared and distributed on the same day when the market price per common share was $4.20. On October 1, 2017, 20,000 common shares were issued at $4.34 each. Profit earned during 2017 was $408,800.

Required Using the information provided, prepare the statement of changes in equity for the year ended December 31, 2017.

Problem 13-7A Retirement of shares, retained earnings analysis LO1,2,5

CHECK FIGURE: 1. Outstanding shares Oct. 5 = 22,200

Note: Problem 13-7B covers LO1, 5 with no retirement of shares.

The equity section from the December 31, 2017 and 2018, balance sheets of Westburne Corporation appeared as follows:

	2018	2017
Contributed capital:		
Common shares, 50,000 shares authorized; 22,200 and		
20,000 shares issued and outstanding, respectively	$486,920	$392,000
Retained earnings	560,000	448,000

The following transactions occurred during 2018 (assume the retirements were the first ever recorded by Westburne):

Jan.	5	A $1.40 per share cash dividend was declared, and the date of record was five days later.
Mar.	20	1,500 common shares were repurchased and retired at $19.60 per share.
Apr.	5	A $1.40 per share cash dividend was declared, and the date of record was five days later.
July	5	A $1.40 per share cash dividend was declared, and the date of record was five days later.
	31	A 20% share dividend was declared when the market value was $33.60 per share.
Aug.	14	The share dividend was issued.
Oct.	5	A $1.40 per share cash dividend was declared, and the date of record was five days later.

Required

1. How many shares were outstanding on each of the cash dividend dates?

2. How much profit did the company earn during 2018?

Alternate Problems

Problem 13-1B **Earnings per share calculations and presentation** LO1,3,4

CHECK FIGURES: Weighted-average outstanding shares: 2. a. 27,300; b. 40,800; c. 92,000

The original income statements for ZoomMed, Inc., presented the following information when they were first published in 2016, 2017, and 2018:

	2018	2017	2013
Sales	$400,000	$300,000	$250,000
Expenses	?	215,000	?
Profit from continuing operations	?	?	90,000
Gain (loss) on discontinued segment	(37,125)	14,100	(26,145)
Profit	$ 92,875	?	?

The company also experienced some changes in the number of outstanding common shares over the three years through the following activities:[1]

Outstanding shares on December 31, 2015	20,000
2016	
Issued shares on July 1	+ 2,000
Issued shares on September 30	+ 7,000
20% share dividend on December 1	?
Outstanding shares on December 31, 2016	?
2017	
Issued shares on March 31	+ 8,000
Outstanding shares on December 31, 2017	?
2018	
Issued shares on July 1	+ 6,400
2:1 split on November 1	?
Outstanding shares on December 31, 2018	?

[1]No preferred shares have been issued.

Required

1. Calculate the 11 missing amounts.

2. Calculate the weighted-average number of common shares outstanding during:

    a. 2016   **b.** 2017   **c.** 2018

3. Rounding calculations to two decimal places, prepare the earnings per share income statement presentations for:

    a. 2016   **b.** 2017   **c.** 2018

Problem 13-2B **Earnings per share** LO1,3

Tropical Vacation Inc. has tentatively prepared its financial statements for the year ended December 31, 2017, and has submitted them to you for review. The equity account balances at December 31, 2017, are as follows:

Preferred shares, $2 cumulative, 30,000 shares authorized,	
18,000 shares issued and outstanding	$416,080
Common shares, unlimited shares authorized;	
132,000 shares issued and outstanding	622,272
Retained earnings	796,960

The company's 2017 profit was $480,000 and no cash dividends were declared. The only share transaction that occurred during the year was the issuance of 24,000 common shares on March 31, 2017. Earnings per share for 2017 were calculated as follows:

$$\frac{\text{Profit}}{\text{Common plus preferred shares outstanding on Dec. 31}} = \frac{\$480,000}{132,000 + 18,000} = \$3.20$$

Required

1. Explain what is wrong with the earnings per share calculation, indicating what corrections should be made to both the numerator and the denominator.

2. Explain how your answer to requirement 1 could be different if the preferred shares were not cumulative and if the issuance of 24,000 shares had been a share dividend.

Problem 13-3B **Dividends, share dividend, share split, statement of changes in equity** LO1,5

CHECK FIGURE: 2. Dec. 31, 2017 Retained earnings = $1,565,600

The equity accounts for Kalimantan Corp. showed the following balances on December 31, 2016:

Preferred shares, $2 non-cumulative, unlimited shares authorized	$ -0-
Common shares, unlimited shares authorized, 100,000 shares issued and outstanding	640,000
Retained earnings..	864,000

The company completed these transactions during 2017:

Jan.	10	Issued 20,000 common shares at $9.60 cash per share.
	15	The directors declared a 10% share dividend to the January 30 shareholders of record, distributable on February 15. The market price of the shares on January 15 was $9.80.
Feb.	15	Distributed the share dividend.
Mar.	2	The directors declared a $1.20 per share cash dividend payable on March 31 to the March 15 shareholders of record.
	31	Paid the dividend declared on March 2.
Apr.	10	The directors announced a 3:1 share split to the April 20 shareholders of record. The shares were trading just prior to the announcement at $10.00 per share.
Nov.	11	Issued 12,000 preferred shares at $20.00 per share.
Dec.	1	The board of directors declared total dividends of $182,400 payable December 15, 2017.
	15	Paid the dividends declared on December 1.
	31	Closed the $1,160,000 credit balance in the Profit Summary account.
	31	Closed the Cash Dividends account.

Required

1. Prepare general journal entries to record the transactions and closings for 2017.

2. Prepare the statement of changes in equity for the year ended December 31, 2017.

Problem 13-4B **Presenting items in an income statement** LO4 eXcel

CHECK FIGURE: Profit = $204,000

The following table shows the balances from various accounts in the adjusted trial balance for Decoma International Corp. as of December 31, 2017:

	Debit	Credit
a. Accumulated depreciation, buildings		$ 160,000
b. Interest income		8,000
c. Cumulative effect of change in accounting policy (pre-tax)		36,800
d. Sales		1,056,000
e. Income taxes expense	$?	
f. Loss on condemnation of property	25,600	
g. Accumulated depreciation, equipment		88,000
h. Other operating expenses	131,200	
i. Depreciation expense, equipment	40,000	
j. Loss from settling a lawsuit	14,400	
k. Gain from settling a lawsuit		27,200
l. Loss on sale of office equipment	9,600	
m. Loss from operating a discontinued operation (pre-tax)	48,000	
n. Depreciation expense, buildings	62,400	
o. Correction of overstatement of prior year's expense (pre-tax)		19,200
p. Cost of goods sold	416,000	
q. Loss on sale of discontinued operation's assets (pre-tax)	72,000	
r. Accounts payable		52,800

Required

1. Assuming that the company's income tax rate is 25%, what are the tax effects and after-tax measures of the items labelled as pre-tax?

2. Prepare a multi-step income statement for the year ended December 31, 2017.

Problem 13-5B **Income statement** LO3,4,5

CHECK FIGURE: Profit = $576,600

After returning from vacation, the accountant of Online Hearing Inc. was dismayed to discover that the income statement for the year ended December 31, 2017, was prepared incorrectly. All amounts included in the statement are before tax (assume a rate of 40%). The company had 200,000 common shares issued and outstanding throughout the year as well as 70,000 $1.00 cumulative preferred shares. Dividends had not been paid for the past two years (2015 and 2016). Retained earnings at December 31, 2016, were $171,000.

Online Hearing Inc. Income Statement December 31, 2017		
Revenues:		
Sales	$900,000	
Gain on sale of discontinued operation (pre-tax)	120,000	
Accumulated depreciation, equipment...	22,500	
Operating profit on discontinued operation (pre-tax)	318,000	$1,360,500
Expenses:		
Cost of goods sold...	$240,000	
Selling and administrative expenses..	90,000	
Sales returns and allowances	7,000	
Loss on disposal of plant assets (pre-tax)..	40,000	
Dividends	47,500	424,500
Profit..		$ 936,000
Earnings per share		$ 4.68

Required Prepare a corrected income statement, using a multi-step format, including earnings per share information. Round all earnings per share calculations to the nearest whole cent.

Problem 13-6B Dividends, statement of changes in equity LO1,5

CHECK FIGURES: Retained earnings, Dec. 31, 2017 = $294,600; Total equity = $2,362,440

Venir Exchange Corp. had the following equity account balances at December 31, 2016:

Preferred shares, $0.60, cumulative, Authorized: 100,000 shares	
Issued and outstanding: 45,000 shares	$ 432,000
Common shares, Authorized: Unlimited	
Issued and outstanding: 300,000 shares	1,077,840
Retained earnings..	261,600

On November 1, 2017, the board of directors declared and paid the current year's cash dividend on the preferred shares plus the two years of dividends in arrears. On the same day, a 10% common share dividend was declared and distributed; the market price per common share was $4.20. On December 1, 2017, 100,000 common shares were issued at $4.32. Profit earned during 2017 was $240,000.

Required Using the information provided, prepare the statement of changes in equity for the year ended December 31, 2017.

Problem 13-7B Retained earnings analysis LO1,5

CHECK FIGURE: 1. Outstanding shares Nov. 15, 2017 = 18,900

The equity sections from the December 31, 2016 and 2017, balance sheets of Synergy Acquisition Corporation appeared as follows:

	2017	2016
Contributed capital:		
Common shares, unlimited shares authorized, 18,900 and		
8,500 shares issued and outstanding, respectively............................	$268,920	$240,000
Retained earnings...	480,000	162,000
Total equity	$748,920	$402,000

The following occurred during 2017:

Feb.	15	A $0.48 per share cash dividend was declared, and the date of record was five days later.
Mar.	2	500 common shares were issued at $27.60 per share.
May	15	A $0.48 per share cash dividend was declared, and the date of record was five days later.
Aug.	15	A 2:1 share split was declared and distributed to shareholders of record five days later.
Oct.	4	A 5% share dividend was declared when the market value was $16.80 per share.
	20	The dividend shares were issued.
Nov.	15	A $0.48 per share cash dividend was declared, and the date of record was five days later.

Required

1. How many shares were outstanding on each of the cash dividend dates?

2. How much profit did the company earn during 2017?

Analytical and Review Problem

A & R 13-1

CHECK FIGURES: Profit = $33,500; Retained earnings, Dec. 31, 2017 = $48,000

The following adjusted trial balance information (with accounts in alphabetical order) for Willis Tour Co. Inc. as at December 31, 2017, was made available after its second year of operations:

Account	Debit	Credit
Accounts Payable		$ 2,500
Accumulated Depreciation, Office Equipment...............................		8,000
Cash...	$ 17,500	
Common Shares, 20,000 authorized; 10,000 issued and outstanding		12,500
Dividends Payable		4,500
Gain on Expropriation of Land and Building.................................		25,000
Income Tax Expense	12,000	
Income Tax Payable		2,000
Loss on Sale of Office Equipment...	13,500	
Notes Payable (due in 18 months)..		8,500
Office Equipment...	56,000	
Operating Expenses...	195,500	
Preferred Shares, $0.25 non-cumulative; 5,000 shares authorized; 2,000 shares issued and outstanding		10,000
Prepaid Rent	22,500	
Retained Earnings		14,500
Ticket Sales		229,500
Totals	$317,000	$317,000

Required The dividends declared by Willis in the amount of $4,500 during the year ended December 31, 2017, were debited directly to retained earnings. Prepare an income statement (in multi-step format), and a classified balance sheet for Willis Tour Co. Inc. using the information provided. Include the appropriate presentation for earnings per share.

Ethics Challenge

EC 13-1

JenStar's management team has decided that its income statement would be more useful if depreciation were calculated using the straight-line method instead of the double-declining-balance method. This change in accounting policy adds $156,000 to income in the current year. As the auditor of the company, you are reviewing the decision to make the change in accounting policy. You review the equipment in question and realize that it is a piece of high-tech equipment and the risk of obsolescence in the near future is relatively high. You are also aware that all members of top management receive year-end bonuses based on profit.

Required As an auditor in this situation, would you support the change in policy or ask management to continue using the straight-line method? Justify your response.

Focus on Financial Statements

FFS 13-1

CHECK FIGURES: 1. Profit = $393,400; 2. Total assets = $2,851,250; Total equity = $2,614,650

LR Enterprises Inc. had the following equity account balances at December 31, 2016:

Preferred shares, $1.75, non-cumulative, Authorized: 100,000 shares	
Issued and outstanding: 45,000 shares	$ 675,000
Common shares, Authorized: Unlimited	
Issued and outstanding: 800,000 shares	1,320,000
Retained earnings	645,000

Sales during 2017 totalled $1,560,000 and operating expenses were $998,000. Assume that income tax is accrued at year-end at the rate of 30% of annual operating profit. On March 1, 2017, 200,000 of the common shares were repurchased at $1.70 each and then cancelled. The board of directors declared and paid the annual cash dividend on the preferred shares on December 1 and an 8% common share dividend was declared and distributed on the same day when the market price per common share was $1.80.

Required

Preparation Component:

Use the information provided to prepare:

1. An income statement for the year ended December 31, 2017, including appropriate earnings per share information.

2. A classified balance sheet at December 31, 2017, assuming the following adjusted account balances: Cash, $168,000; Accounts Receivable, $102,000; Allowance for Doubtful Accounts, $3,500; Prepaid Insurance, $36,000; Land, $1,000,000; Building, $500,000; Accumulated Depreciation, Building, $241,000; Machinery, $1,909,600; Accumulated Depreciation, Machinery, $653,850; Furniture, $78,000; Accumulated Depreciation, Furniture, $44,000; Accounts Payable, $41,000; Notes Payable (due March 2019), $27,000.

Analysis Component:

3. What percentage of the assets is financed by debt?

4. What percentage of the assets is financed by equity?

FFS 13-2

Refer to the financial statements in Appendix II.

Part 1

Required Answer the following questions regarding Danier Leather.

    a. Did retained earnings increase or decrease from June 29, 2013, to June 28, 2014?

    b. A review of the statement of changes in equity shows a share repurchase during the year ended June 28, 2014. Explain what a share repurchase is.

    c. Prepare the entry that might have been recorded regarding the share repurchase.

Part 2

Required Answer the following questions regarding Westjet.

    a. A review of Westjet's statement of changes in equity for the year ending December 31, 2014 shows that it repurchased shares originally recorded at $6,751,000 with a resulting $32,680,000 reduction in retained earnings. Were these shares repurchased for more or less than what they were originally issued for? Reconstruct the possible journal entry regarding this repurchase.

    b. Westjet does not show a balance in contributed surplus at December 31, 2014. Why is there no balance? Explain what might create a balance in the future.

Critical Thinking Mini Case

CanaCo showed the following equity on its December 31, 2017, balance sheet:

Contributed capital	
Preferred shares, $2 non-cumulative Authorized: 50,000	
Issued and outstanding: 0	$ -0-
Common shares	
Authorized: Unlimited Issued and outstanding: 50,000...	6,800,000
Total contributed capital..	$ 6,800,000
Retained earnings	3,800,000
Total equity	$10,600,000

The shareholders of CanaCo expressed concerns to the board of directors at the recent annual meeting that the market price of their shares has not changed significantly over the past 18 months, yet the company is very profitable. Profit for each of the past three years has been $1,800,000, $2,300,000, and $3,500,000, respectively. Cash dividends were paid in each of these years equal to 50% of profit.

Required Using the elements of critical thinking described on the inside front cover, comment. Consider the following sub-headings to organize your response, and try to really think about the complexity of share prices. What really will affect share prices?

- Problem

- Goal

- Principles

- Facts

- Conclusions

Bonds and Long-Term Notes Payable

A Look Back

In Chapters 12 and 13 we learned that companies can get funds through equity financing by issuing shares and increasing retained earnings through profitable operations. We also explained how to account for issuing dividends, share splits, and share repurchases. Lastly, we analyzed how financial statements present earnings per share, changes in accounting policies, and presentation considerations for the income statement report and analyze profit, earnings per share, and retained earnings.

A Look at This Chapter

This chapter describes the accounting for and analysis of bonds and notes. We explain their characteristics, payment patterns, interest computations, retirement, and reporting requirements.

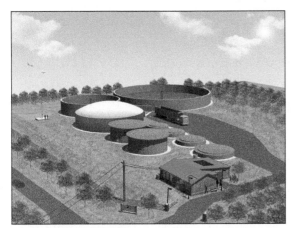

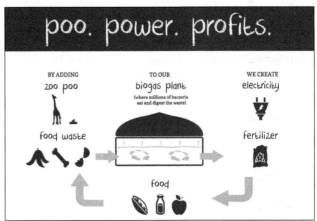

Photos: Courtesy of ZooShare

LEARNING OBJECTIVES

LO1	Compare bond versus share financing.
LO2	Explain the types of bonds and their issuing procedures.
LO3	Prepare entries to record bonds issued at par.
LO4	Determine the price of a bond.
LO5	Prepare entries to record bonds issued at a discount.
LO6	Prepare entries to record bonds issued at a premium.
LO7	Record the retirement of bonds.
LO8	Explain and record notes.
LO9	Prepare entries to record lease liabilities.
LO10	Calculate and interpret the debt to equity ratio.

Zooshare Cooperative Turns Waste into Resources

ZooShare is a non-profit renewable energy cooperative and North America's first zoo-based biogas energy plant. The cooperative has plans to convert 3,000 tonnes of animal manure and 14,000 tonnes of inedible food waste from local grocery stores to renewable power for the Ontario power grid. The project not only provides power to local residents, but also reduces greenhouse gas emissions equivalent to removing 2,100 cars off the road, and returns nutrients to the soil by generating a high quality fertilizer.

The plant is expected to begin operations early in 2016. According to the Executive Director of ZooShare, Daniel Bida, CFA, the plant receives animal waste from the Metro Toronto Zoo and the food waste from a large local grocery chain. "Undigested food waste contains more energy than animal waste, and contributes to 95% of the energy produced from the plant." The grocery retailer has installed mills to grind the food waste and has built underground reservoirs to contain the liquefied food waste, minimizing odours and providing ease of transport. Trucks arrive to vacuum up the liquid and transport it to the ZooShare power facility. It is then mixed with the zoo animal waste and is heated to 38 degrees Celsius, producing a mixture of "methane and carbon dioxide that is fed into a gas powered engine that generates electrical current and a solid matter that can be used as an organic fertilizer for crops".

ZooShare has a solid strategy to draw an estimated $1.3 million of revenue per year from the project in three key ways:

1. Selling 4.1 kWh per year to the Ontario Power Grid based on a 20 year fixed feed in price contract with the Ontario Power Authority, which subsequently merged with the Independent Electric System Operator (IESO). The plant will produce enough power to service approximately 250 homes. As a cooperative, ZooShare is able to earn 1 cent per kWh more on its sale of energy than if it was not a cooperative.

2. Charging grocers fees per tonne of waste received.

3. Selling the organic fertilizer byproduct.

Greenbonds are corporate or government bonds that are focused on environmentally sustainable causes. When the biogas cooperative looked into raising funds to finance the project, it opted to raise funds via green bonds. According to Bida, ZooShare adopted a "community grass-roots approach to fundraising," visiting farmers' markets, trade shows, and green conferences and relied on word-of-mouth advertising to sell its member bonds.

The first group of ZooShare members purchased Founders' Club bonds, and consisted of 27 individuals investing a total of $506,000. The Founders Club bonds also have a more senior security position over subsequent bond issuances. The term of the bonds is three years from the date of drawdown and they pay out accrued principal and interest upon maturity, August 2016. If ZooShare is unable to make the payment on time, the members will continue to accrue interest until the principal of the bond is returned to the bondholder. Bida refers to this as "patient capital." This initial investment is being used to do all the development work relating to getting the project up and running and obtaining the required approvals.

To compensate Founders' Club members for taking on higher risk in the development phase, ZooShare offered a higher interest rate. Investments of $10,000–49,999 received an 11.5% annual return, investments of $50,000–$99,000 received 12%, and investments greater than $100,000 received 12.5%.

The next $2.2 million was raised through community bonds and will be used for the construction phase. With an investment of a minimum of $500, the bonds offer a return of 7% per year over a 7-year term. After servicing its 7% per year commitment to the $2.2 million in outstanding community bonds, the cooperative is mandated to reinvest further earnings into biogas projects and education programs aimed at shifting the way people think about their waste.

Sources: https://zooshare.ca/about-zooshare, accessed March 20, 2015; interview with Executive Director of ZooShare Daniel Bida, CFA, April 6, 2015.

Video Links: Youtube presentations by zooshare: https://youtu.be/HuCUiKjEKnU; https://youtu.be/3_pUry72pvY

CRITICAL THINKING CHALLENGE Why would ZooShare consider pursuing a public bond offering in lieu of obtaining a bank loan or other investors?

CHAPTER PREVIEW

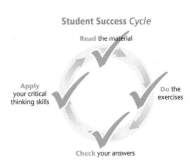

Chapter 14 investigates a major source of corporate funds—debt financing through the issuance of bonds and long-term debt facilities. Companies and governments issue bonds as an alternative source of financing outside equity share issuances for operating activities. In return for cash received, bonds promise to repay the amount borrowed plus interest. The ZooShare bonds highlighted in the chapter opening vignette offer 7% to their bondholders for a 7-year term. This chapter explains the basics of bonds and the accounting for their issuance and retirement. We explain how present value concepts affect bonds' accounting and reporting. We describe the accounting treatment for long-term notes and instalment notes. Understanding how liabilities can be used to the advantage of a company, if well managed, is an important goal of this chapter.

Basics of Bonds

A **bond** is a written promise to pay an amount identified as the *par value* of the bond along with interest at a stated annual rate. A bond is a liability to the borrowing or issuing corporation. The **par value** of the bond, also called the *face amount* or *face value*, is paid at a specified future date known as the *maturity date of the bond*. The total amount of interest paid each year is determined by multiplying the par value of the bond by the bond's stated rate of interest. The **stated interest rate**—sometimes called the **contract rate, nominal rate**, or **coupon rate**—is quoted as an *annual rate*. Interest can be paid annually, monthly, or for some other fraction of the year. For example, let's suppose a company issues a $1,000 bond with a contract interest rate of 8% to be paid semiannually. For this bond, the annual interest of $80 (= 8% × $1,000) is paid in two semiannual payments of $40 each. The document that specifies the issuer's name, the bond's par value, the contract interest rate, and the maturity date is called a **bond certificate**. An example bond certificate for ABC Company Inc. is presented on the next page.

Advantages of Bonds

LO1   Compare bond versus share financing.

There are three main advantages of bond financing over share financing:

1. *Bonds do not affect shareholder control.* Shares reflect an ownership right in the corporation, and affect equity. A *bondholder* lends the company money, which increases liabilities on the issuing corporation's balance sheet, but enables current shareholders to maintain control.

2. *Interest on bonds is tax deductible.* Bond interest is tax deductible, but dividends to shareholders are not. To illustrate the importance of this, let's assume a company that pays tax at the rate of 40% issued $1,000,000 of bonds that pay interest at 10%. Interest expense will be $100,000 (= $1,000,000 × 10%). Because interest expense is tax deductible, the company's income tax expense will be reduced by the amount of the interest expense times the tax rate or $40,000 (= $100,000 × 40%). Because the corporation saves $40,000 in taxes, the true cost (or after-tax cost) of borrowing is $60,000 (= $100,000 interest expense less $40,000 tax saving). If the same amount of money were raised by issuing shares instead of bonds, the $100,000 paid out as dividends is the true cost of capital, as it is a return of equity to the shareholders and does not represent an expense.

Issuing Company

Interest Rate

Maturity Date

Principal Amount

Certificate Number
0001

$2,000,000.00

ABC COMPANY INC.
(incorporated under
the laws of Canada)

CUSIP TO FOLLOW

6.0% Debentures

ABC Company Inc. (the "Company"), for value received, hereby promises to pay to the registered holder (the "Holder"), John Doe on February 28, 2019, or on such earlier date as the principal amount hereof may become payable in accordance with the conditions herein set out and with the provisions of the Trust Indenture hereinafter mentioned, on presentation and surrender of this Debenture, the sum of $ 2,000,000.00 in lawful money of Canada, at the office of the Trustee at Anytown, Saskatchewan, and to pay interest thereon from and including the date of issue at the Interest Rate, payable after as well as before maturity and after as well as before default judgment, with interest on amounts in default at the same rate, on each interest payment date.

As interest becomes due on this Debenture, (excepting interest payable at maturity which may be paid upon presentation and surrender of such Debentures for payment at the offices of the Trustee in Anytown), the Fund shall cause to be sent by prepaid first class mail a cheque for such interest (less any tax required by law to be withheld therefrom) payable to the order of the Holder and addressed to him at his last address appearing on the register, unless the Holder otherwise directs. In the case of joint Holders the cheque shall be payable to/or issued to the order of all such joint Holders and addressed to them at the last address appearing on the register, unless such joint Holders otherwise direct. If more than one address appears on the register in respect of such joint Holders, the cheque shall be made to the first address so appearing. In the event of non-receipt of any cheque for interest by the Holder, the Fund will cause to be issued a replacement cheque for like amount upon being furnished with such evidence of non-receipt as it shall reasonably require and upon being indemnified to its satisfaction, acting reasonably.

This Debenture is one of the Debentures in lawful money of Canada issued under a Trust Indenture (herein referred to as the "Trust Indenture") dated as of February 28, 2017, made between the Company and XYZ Trust Company, as Trustee. The aggregate principal amount of Debentures which may be authorized under the Trust Indenture is $40,000,000. Reference is made hereby to the Trust Indenture and any instruments supplemental thereto for a statement and description of the terms and conditions upon which this Debenture is issued and the rights and remedies of the Holders of the Debentures, the Fund and the Trustee with respect thereto, all to the same effect as if the provisions of the Trust Indenture and of any instruments supplemental thereto were herein set forth, to all of which provisions the registered Holder of this Debenture, by acceptance hereof assents.

The Debentures are issuable as fully registered Debentures in denominations of One Thousand ($1,000) Dollars and integral multiples thereof only. Upon compliance with the provisions of the Trust Indenture, Debentures of any authorized denominations may be exchanged for an equal aggregate principal amount of Debentures in any other authorized denomination or denominations.

All Debentures issued under the Trust Indenture rank equally and rateably without priority or preference.

The Debenture may only be transferred upon compliance with the conditions prescribed in the Trust Indenture on one of the registers to be kept at the principal office of the Trustee in Anytown and at such other place or places (if any) and/or by such other registrar or registrars (if any) as the Fund with the approval of the Trustee may designate, by the registered holder hereof or his executors or administrators or other legal representatives, or his or their attorney duly appointed by an instrument in writing in form and execution satisfactory to the Trustee and/or other registrar may prescribe, and then, only if such transfer shall have been duly entered on one of the appropriate registers or noted on this Debenture by a proper registrar.

The Trust Indenture contains provisions making binding upon all Holders of Debentures outstanding thereunder resolutions passed at meetings of such Holders held in accordance with such provisions and instruments in writing signed by the Holders of a specified percentage of the principal amount of the Debentures outstanding.

This Debenture shall not become obligatory for any purpose until it shall have been certified by the Trustee for the time being under the Trust Indenture

Unless otherwise defined, all initially capitalized terms used herein shall have the meaning ascribed to such terms in the Trust Indenture.

IN WITNESS WHEREOF ABC Company has caused this Debenture to be signed by its duly authorized officers as of the 28th day of February, 2017.

ABC Company Inc.

By   By

Trustee   Trustee

3. *Bonds can increase return on equity.* **Return on equity** is profit available to common share-holders divided by common shareholders' equity.[1] When a company earns a higher return through effective management of the borrowed funds than it is paying in interest, it increases its return on equity. This process is called **financial leverage.**

To illustrate the effect on return on equity, let's look at Magnum Skates Corp. Magnum's income before tax is $100,000 per year and the company has no interest expense. It has $1 million in equity, and is planning a $500,000 expansion to meet increasing demand for its product. Magnum predicts the $500,000 expansion will provide $125,000 in additional profit before paying any interest and tax. Magnum is considering three plans:

- Plan A is not to expand.
- Plan B is to expand, and raise $500,000 from issuing shares.
- Plan C is to sell $500,000 worth of bonds paying 10% annual interest, or $50,000.

Exhibit 14.1 shows us how these three plans affect Magnum's profit, equity, and return on equity (Profit ÷ Equity).

EXHIBIT 14.1

Financing With Bonds or Shares

	Plan A: Do Not Expand	Plan B: Increase Equity	Plan C: Issue Bonds
Profit before interest expense and tax.....................................	$ 100,000	$ 225,000	$ 225,000
Interest expense...	—	—	(50,000)
Profit before tax...	$ 100,000	$ 225,000	$ 175,000
Equity..	$1,000,000	$1,500,000	$1,000,000
Return on equity (Profit ÷ Equity)	**10.0%**	**15.0%**	**17.5%**

Analysis of these plans shows that the corporation will earn a higher return on equity if it expands. The preferred plan of expansion is to issue bonds. Why? Even though the projected profit before tax under Plan C of $175,000 is smaller than the $225,000 under Plan B, the return on equity is larger because of less shareholder investment. This is an important example of financial leverage and proves a general rule: Return on equity increases when the expected rate of return from the new assets is greater than the rate of interest on the bonds. Issuing bonds also allows the current owners to remain in control.

Disadvantages of Bonds

There are two main disadvantages of bond financing over share financing.

1. *Bonds require payment of both annual interest and par value at maturity.* Bond payments can be a burden when a company's profit is low. Shares, on the other hand, do not require payment of dividends because they are declared at the discretion of the board of directors.

---

1 Ratios are discussed in more detail in Chapter 17.

> **2.** *Bonds can decrease return on equity.* When a company earns a lower return with its management of the borrowed funds than it is paying in interest, it decreases its return on equity. This is a risk of bond financing and is more likely to arise when a company has periods of low profit.

A company must weigh the risks of these disadvantages against the advantages of bond financing when deciding how to finance operations.

Types of Bonds

LO2 Explain the types of bonds and their issuing procedures.

Bonds appear on the balance sheets of companies such as **Bell Canada**, **Canadian Tire Corp. Ltd.**, **Loblaw Companies Ltd.**, **Rogers Communications Inc.**, and **Suncor Energy Inc.** We describe the more common kinds of bonds in this section.

SECURED AND UNSECURED BONDS

Secured bonds have specific assets of the issuing company pledged (or *mortgaged*) as *collateral* (a guarantee). This arrangement gives bondholders added protection if the issuing company fails to pay interest or par value. In the event of non-payment, secured bondholders can demand that the secured assets be sold and the proceeds be used to pay the bond obligation.

Unsecured bonds, also called **debentures**, are supported by the issuer's general credit standing. Because debentures are unsecured, a company generally must be financially strong to issue debentures successfully at a favourable rate of interest.

TERM AND SERIAL BONDS

Term bonds make up a bond issue that becomes due at a single specified date. **Serial bonds** comprise a bond issue whose component parts mature at several different dates (in series). For instance, $1 million of serial bonds might mature at the rate of $100,000 each year from Year 6 until all the bonds are fully repaid in Year 15.

REGISTERED BONDS AND BEARER BONDS

Bonds issued in the names and addresses of their owners are **registered bonds**. The issuing company makes bond payments by sending cheques to these registered owners.

Bonds payable to the person who holds them (the *bearer*) are called **bearer bonds**, or *unregistered bonds*. Since there may be no record of sales or exchanges, the holder of a bearer bond is presumed to be its rightful owner. As a result, lost or stolen bearer bonds are difficult to replace. Bearer bonds are now uncommon.

Many bearer bonds are also **coupon bonds**. This term reflects interest coupons that are attached to these bonds. Each coupon matures on a specific interest payment date. The owner detaches each coupon when it matures and presents it to a bank or broker for collection.

CONVERTIBLE AND CALLABLE BONDS

Bondholders can exchange **convertible bonds** for a fixed number of the issuing company's common shares. Convertible bonds offer bondholders the potential to participate in future increases in the shares' market value. If the shares do not appreciate and the bonds are not converted, bondholders continue to receive periodic interest and will receive the par value when the bond matures. In most cases, the bondholders decide whether and when to convert the bonds to shares. **Callable** or **redeemable bonds** have an option under which they can be retired at a stated dollar amount prior to maturity. In the case of callable bonds, the issuer has the option of retiring them; in the case of redeemable bonds, it is the purchaser who has the option of retiring them. The callable bond can be an advantage for a corporation that has sufficient cash flow to repay the bonds and wants to eliminate the annual interest expense.

A summary of types of bonds and their features is presented in Exhibit 14.2.

EXHIBIT 14.2

Summary of Bond Features

Types of Bonds	Explanation
1. Secured or Unsecured	
a. Secured	a. Assets are pledged as a guarantee of payment by the issuing company.
b. Unsecured (called debentures)	b. Backed not by specific assets but only by the earning capacity and credit reputation of the issuer.
2. Term and Serial	
a. Term	a. Principal of all bonds is due in a lump sum at a specified single date.
b. Serial	b. Principal is due in instalments at several different dates.
3. Registered and Bearer	
a. Registered	a. Bonds issued registered in the names of the buyers. Ownership records are kept up to date.
b. Bearer	b. Bonds payable to the person who possesses them. No records are kept for change of ownership. Many are coupon bonds, meaning that interest is paid to the holder of attached coupons.
4. Convertible, Callable, Redeemable	
a. Convertible	a. Bonds that allow the buyer to exchange the bond for common shares at a fixed ratio.
b. Callable	b. Bonds that may be called for early retirement at the option of the issuing corporation.
c. Redeemable	c. Bonds that may be retired early at the option of the purchaser.

Bond Issuing Procedures

Issuing company bonds usually requires approval by both the board of directors and shareholders and is governed by provincial and federal laws that require registration with a securities commission. Registration with the securities commission requires that it be informed of the number of bonds authorized, their par value, and the contract interest rate. Bonds are typically issued in par value units of $1,000 or $5,000.

The legal document (contract) identifying the rights and obligations of both the bondholders and the issuer is called the **bond indenture**. The issuing company normally sells the bonds to an investment firm such as **BMO Nesbitt Burns**, called an *underwriter*, which resells them to the public or directly to investors. The bondholders' interests are represented and protected by a *trustee* who monitors the issue to ensure it complies with the obligations in the bond indenture. Most trustees are large banks or trust companies.

As a current example of a bond issuance, **Telus Corporation** raised $1.2 billion in September 2014 through the issuance of two corporate bonds:

1) $800 million of 10-year notes with 3.75 per cent interest rate, priced at $99.775 per $100 principal amount for an effective yield of 3.77 per cent per year, maturing on January 17, 2025

2) $400 million of 30-year notes with 4.75 per cent interest rate, priced at $99.291 per $100 principal amount for an effective yield of 4.795 per cent per year, maturing on January 17, 2045.

Source: http://about.telus.com/community/english/news_centre/news_releases/blog/2014/09/10/telus-offering-12-billion-in-new-debt-notes

Bond Trading

The offering of bonds to the public for sale is called a bond issuance, or *floating an issue*. Subsequent to the initial bond issuance by corporations, they are subsequently traded through decentralized, over-the-counter markets between banks and investment dealers. There isn't an active market as is the case with corporate shares. As a result, market data on bond pricing can be difficult to obtain in real time.

DECISION INSIGHT

Perimeter Markets Inc. provides electronic trading services for institutional investors, investment dealers, and other brokers. Through its website www.Canadianfixedincome.ca, it posts selected up-to-date market information on bond pricing as well as information on closing prices for government, provincial and corporate fixed income instruments (bonds).

Sample pricing for the 10 year Telus Corporate Bond Issuance above on April 23, 2015, obtained from Perimeter Markets is presented below:

	Coupon	**Effective Maturity**	**Price**	**Yield**
Telus Corp.	3.750	2025-Jan-17	106.11	3.02

SOURCES: http://www.pfin.ca, accessed April 2015; http://www.pfin.ca/canadianfixedincome/Default.aspx, accessed April 2015; http://thomsonreuters.com/en/press-releases/2015/06/tr-expands-coverage-of-canada-fixed-income-market.html, accessed July 2015.

Because bonds are exchanged in the market, they have a market value (price). For convenience, bond market values are expressed as a percentage of their par (face) value. For example, a company's bonds might be trading at 103½, which means they can be bought or sold for 103.5% of their par value. For example, if their par value is $1,000, their market price would be $1,035. Bonds that trade above par value are said to trade at a **premium**. Bonds trading below par value trade at a **discount**. For instance, if a company's bonds are trading at 95, they can be bought or sold at 95% of their par value.

The **market rate of interest**, or **effective interest rate**, is the amount of interest borrowers are willing to pay and lenders are willing to earn for a particular bond given its risk level, also known as **bond yield**. The effective interest is impacted by the risk level of the bond and the stated coupon rate of interest that the bond is paying, taking into consideration the time value of money, and determines the price the bond is issued for or the price paid for the bond. When the contract rate and market rate are equal, the bonds sell at their par value, or 100%. When the contract rate does not equal the market rate, the bonds sell at either above or below their par values (greater or less than 100%) as detailed in Exhibit 14.3.

EXHIBIT 14.3

Relation Between Bond Issue Price, Contract Rate, and Market Rate

Coupon/Contract rate is:		Bond sells:	
Above market rate	⇒	At a premium	(> 100% of face value)
Equal to market rate	⇒	At par value	(= 100% of face value)
Below market rate	⇒	At a discount	(< 100% of face value)

For example, assuming a 6% contract rate (or *bond interest* rate, also commonly known as the *coupon rate*), a $1,000 face value bond would sell as follows given various market interest rates:

Contract rate is 6%:		Bond sells:	
If the market rate is 4%	⇒	At a premium	(e.g., 101%* or $1,010)
If the market rate is 6%	⇒	At par value	(e.g., 100% or $1,000)
If the market rate is 7%	⇒	At a discount	(e.g., 98%* or $980)

*Assumed

CHECKPOINT

1. Unsecured bonds supported only by the issuer's general credit standing are called (a) serial bonds; (b) debentures; (c) registered bonds; (d) convertible bonds; (e) bearer bonds.
2. How do you calculate the amount of interest a bond issuer pays each year?
3. When the contract interest rate is above the market interest rate, do bonds sell at a premium or a discount? Do purchasers pay more or less than the par value of the bonds?

Do Quick Study questions: QS 14-1, QS 14-2, QS 14-3

Accounting for Bonds

Issuing Basic Bonds—Par Value Bonds

LO3 Prepare entries to record bonds issued at par.

This section explains accounting for basic bond issuances at par. We first show the accounting for bonds issued on the stated date and in the next section we expand the example to show how to account for bonds that are issued between interest dates. Later in the chapter we will explain accounting for bonds issued below par and above par.

To illustrate an issuance of bonds at par value, let's suppose **Second Cup** decides to open a series of new coffee shops located in prime downtown locations. In order to assist in financing the expansion, the company issues $800,000 of 9%, 20-year bonds. The bonds are dated January 1, 2017, and are due in 20 years on January 1, 2037. They pay interest semiannually each June 30 and December 31. If all bonds are sold at their par value, Second Cup would record this entry to account for the initial sale of the bonds:

2017					
Jan.	1	Cash	800,000	
		Bonds Payable		800,000
		Sold bonds at par.		

This entry reflects increases in the Second Cup's cash and non-current liabilities.

Six months later, the first semiannual interest payment is made, and Second Cup records the payment as:

	2017			
	June	30	Bond Interest Expense	36,000	
			Cash		36,000
			Paid semiannual interest on bonds;		
			9% × $800,000 × 6/12.		

Barnes pays and records the semiannual interest every six months until the bonds mature.

When the bonds mature 20 years later, Second Cup would record its payment of the maturity value with this entry:

	2037			
	Jan.	1	Bonds Payable	800,000	
			Cash		800,000
			Paid bonds at maturity.		

Issuing Bonds Between Interest Dates

Many bonds are sold on an interest payment date. When a company sells its bonds on a date other than an interest payment date, the purchasers pay the issuer the purchase price plus any interest accrued since the prior interest payment date. This accrued interest is then repaid to the bondholders by the issuing corporation on the next interest date.

To illustrate, let's suppose that **Lululemon Athletica Inc.** has $100,000 of 9% bonds available for sale on January 1. Interest is payable semiannually on each June 30 and December 31. If the bonds are sold at par on March 1, two months after the original issue date of January 1, the issuer collects two months' interest from the buyer at the time of the sale. This amount is $1,500 (= $100,000 × 9% × 2/12) as shown in Exhibit 14.4.

EXHIBIT 14.4

Accruing Interest Between Interest Dates

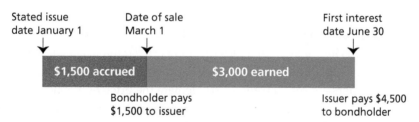

Lululemon Athletica's entry to record the sale of its bonds on March 1 is:

Mar.	1	Cash	101,500	
		Interest Payable[2]		1,500
		Bonds Payable		100,000
		Sold $100,000 of bonds at par with two		
		months' accrued interest.		

Liabilities for interest payable and the bonds are recorded in separate accounts.

---

2 When selling bonds between interest dates, Interest Expense could be credited instead of Interest Payable.

When the June 30 semiannual interest date arrives, Lululemon Athletica Inc. pays a full six months' interest of $4,500 (= $100,000 × 9% × 6/12) to the bondholder. This payment includes the four months' interest of $3,000 earned by the bondholder from March 1 to June 30 plus the repayment of two months' accrued interest collected by Lululemon when the bonds were sold, as shown in Exhibit 14.4.

Lululemon's entry to record this first interest payment is:

June	30	Interest Payable	1,500	
		Bond Interest Expense	3,000	
		Cash		4,500
		Paid semiannual interest on the bonds.		

The practice of collecting and then repaying accrued interest with the first interest payment is done to simplify the bond issuer's administrative efforts. To understand this, suppose Lululemon sold bonds on 20 different dates between the original issue date and the first interest payment date. If Lululemon did not collect accrued interest from buyers, it would need to pay 20 different amounts of cash to various bond-holders on the first interest payment date. The extra recordkeeping this would involve is avoided by having each buyer pay accrued interest at the time of purchase. Issuers then pay interest of equal amounts to all purchasers, regardless of when the bonds were purchased.

CHECKPOINT

4. Assume the City of Oakville issued a $200,000, 7%, five-year bond dated on November 1, 2017. Interest is paid quarterly beginning February 1, 2018. What is the total amount of interest paid on February 1, 2018?

Do Quick Study questions: QS 14-4, QS 14-5

Bond Pricing

 Determine the price of a bond.

Prices for bonds that are traded on an organized exchange are published in newspapers and available through online services. This information includes the bond price (called *quote*), its contract rate, and its market rate (called *yield*). Only a fraction of bonds outstanding are actually traded on an organized exchange, however; many others are rarely traded. To calculate the price of a bond, we need to apply present value concepts. This can be done using special bond pricing tables or through calculating the present value of a bond's cash flows. The *market* interest rate is used to find the present value of a bond. The *contract* interest rate is used to calculate the cash interest payments produced by the bond. This section explains how we use *present value concepts* to price a *discount bond* and a *premium bond*.

Present Value of a Discount Bond

The issue price of a bond is found by calculating the present value of the bond's future cash payments. To illustrate, Fila Corp. announces an offer to issue bonds with a $100,000 par value, an 8% annual contract rate with interest payable *semiannually*, and a three-year life. The market rate for Fila's bonds is 10%, meaning the bonds will sell at a discount since the contract rate (8%) is less than the market rate (10%).[3]

---

3 The difference between the contract rate and the market rate of interest on a new bond issue is usually a fraction of a percent. However, here we use a difference of 2% to emphasize the effects.

When calculating the present value of the Fila bond, we work with semiannual compounding periods because the time between interest payments is six months. This means the annual market rate of 10% is equal to a semiannual rate of 5% and the three-year life of the bonds is equal to six semiannual periods.

The two steps involved in calculating the issue price are to find the present values of the:

1. $100,000 maturity payment
2. Six interest payments of $4,000 each (= $100,000 × 8% × 6/12)

These present values can be determined by using present value functions found on business calculators,[4] by keying in present value formulas on basic calculators that have a power key, by using the present value function in an Excel worksheet,[5] or by using present value tables. Appendix 14A lists two present value tables for those who choose not to use calculators to find the present value factors. Table 14A.1 is used to calculate the present value of the single $100,000 maturity payment, and Table 14A.2 is used to calculate the present value of the $4,000 series of equal interest payments that form an *annuity*. An **annuity** is a series of equal payments occurring at equal time intervals.

The bond price is calculated as the present value of the principal plus the present value of the cash interest payments. The present value is found by multiplying the cash flow amounts by the corresponding table values as shown in Exhibit 14.5.

EXHIBIT 14.5

Calculating Fila's Bond Price

Cash Flow	Table	Table Value	Amount	Present Value
$100,000 par value..	14A.1	0.7462	$100,000	$74,620
$4,000 interest payments	14A.2	5.0757	4,000	20,303*
Issue price of bond				**$94,923**[6]

*Rounded to the nearest whole dollar.

This analysis shows that if 5% is the semiannual market rate for Fila bonds, the maximum price that buyers will pay (and the minimum price the issuer will accept) is $94,923. At this price the cash flow for the Fila bonds will provide investors a 5% semiannual rate of return (or 10% annual return) on the $94,923 they have lent Fila.

Present Value of a Premium Bond

For illustration purposes, assume that the Metro Toronto Zoo issues bonds to fund a new panda exhibit with a $50,000 par value, a 14% annual contract rate with interest payable *annually*, and a four-year life. The market rate for the Metro Toronto Zoo bonds is 12% on the issue date, meaning the bonds will sell at a premium because the contract rate (14%) is greater than the market rate (12%). This means buyers of these bonds will bid up the market price until the yield equals the market rate. We estimate the issue price

---

4 Many inexpensive calculators provide present value functions for easy calculation of bond prices. Extend Your Knowledge 14-2 provides a present value tutorial using a Sharp EL 738C calculator.

5 Extend Your Knowledge 14-3 provides a tutorial with supporting exercises to reinforce the use of the present value function in Excel.

6 Because of rounding, the present value tables will often result in a slightly different bond price than using the present value function on a calculator. In this case, a calculator would indicate a bond price of $94,924.

of the Metro Toronto Zoo bonds by using the market rate to calculate the present value of its future cash flows. Recall that the Fila bond paid interest semiannually, every six months. In contrast, interest is paid annually on the the Metro Toronto Zoo bonds. Therefore, when calculating the present value of the the Metro Toronto Zoo bond, we work with *annual* compounding periods because 12 months or one year is the time between interest payments.

The two-step process for calculating the issue price of a bond sold at a premium is the same as shown previously for a discount and is summarized in Exhibit 14.6.

EXHIBIT 14.6

Calculating the Metro Toronto Zoo Bond Price

Cash Flow	Table	Table Value	Amount	Present Value
$50,000 par value	15B.1	0.6355	$50,000	$31,775
$7,000 interest payments	15B.2	3.0373	7,000	21,261*
Issue price of bond				**$53,036**[7]

*Rounded to the nearest whole dollar.

This analysis shows that if 12% is the annual market rate for The Metro Toronto Zoo bonds, the maximum price that buyers will pay (also the minimum price the issuer will accept) is $53,036.

CHECKPOINT

5. Using the tables in Appendix 14A, calculate the present value of a 9%, $400,000 bond with a three-year term issued when the market rate of interest was 8%. Interest is paid quarterly.

Do Quick Study questions: QS 14-6, QS 14-7

Issuing Bonds at a Discount

LO5 Prepare entries to record bonds issued at a discount.

A **discount on bonds payable** occurs when a company issues bonds with a contract rate less than the market rate. This means the issue price is less than the bonds' par value (or < 100%).

To illustrate, let's assume that the Fila bonds discussed earlier are issued on December 31, 2017, at the discounted price of $94,923 (94.923% of par value). Fila records the bond issue as follows:

	2017			
	Dec. 31	Cash..	94,923	
		Discount on Bonds Payable..........................	5,077	
		Bonds Payable.......................................		100,000
		Sold bonds at a discount on the original issue date.		

---

7   Using the present value function on a calculator would result in a bond price of $53,037.

These bonds obligate the issuer to pay out two different future cash flows:

1. $100,000 face amount at the end of the bonds' three-year life, and
2. $4,000 interest (8% × $100,000 × 6/12) at the end of each six-month interest period of the bonds' three-year life

The pattern of cash flows for Fila's bonds is shown in Exhibit 14.7.

EXHIBIT 14.7

Cash Flows of Fila's Bonds

These bonds are reported in the Long-Term Liability section of the issuer's December 31, 2017, balance sheet, as shown in Exhibit 14.8.

EXHIBIT 14.8

Balance Sheet Presentation of Bond Discount

Non-current liabilities:
Bonds payable, 8%, due December 31, 2020... $100,000
Less: Discount on bonds payable... **5,077** $94,923

The discount is deducted from the par value of the bonds to produce the **carrying** *(or book)* **value** of the bonds payable. Discount on Bonds Payable is a *contra liability account.* The book or carrying value of the bonds at the date of issue is always equal to the cash price of the bonds. You will learn in the next section that the carrying value of bonds issued at a discount or premium changes over the life of the bond issue.

Amortizing a Bond Discount

The issuer (Fila) received $94,923 for its bonds and will pay bondholders the $100,000 face amount after three years plus interest payments totalling $24,000 (= $4,000 × 6 interest payments). Because the $5,077 discount is eventually paid to bondholders at maturity, it is part of the cost of using the $94,923 for three years. The upper portion of Exhibit 14.9 shows that the total interest cost of $29,077 is the difference between the total amount repaid to bondholders ($124,000) and the amount borrowed from bondholders ($94,923). Alternatively, we can calculate total bond interest expense as the sum of the interest payments and the bond discount. This alternative calculation is shown in the lower portion of Exhibit 14.9.

Accounting for Fila's bonds must include two procedures:

1. Allocating the total bond interest expense of $29,077 across the six six-month periods in the bonds' life, and
2. Updating the carrying value of the bonds at each balance sheet date.

EXHIBIT 14.9

Total Bond Interest Expense for Bonds Issued at a Discount

Amount repaid:

Six interest payments of $4,000	$ 24,000
Par value at maturity	100,000
Total repaid to bondholders	$124,000
Less: Amount borrowed from bondholders	94,923
Total bond interest expense	$ 29,077

Alternative Calculation

Six payments of $4,000	$ 24,000
Add: Discount	5,077
Total bond interest expense	$ 29,077

To allocate the total bond interest expense over the life of the bonds, known as amortizing the bond discount, the effective interest method is used.[8] The effective interest amortization method reduces the discount on the bonds over the life of the bonds.

EFFECTIVE INTEREST METHOD AMORTIZATION

The **effective interest method** allocates bond interest expense over the life of the bonds in a way that yields a constant rate of interest. *This constant rate of interest is the market rate at the issue date.* The effect of selling bonds at a premium or discount is that the issuer incurs the prevailing market rate of interest at issuance and not the contract rate.

Important Tip: Bond interest expense for the current period is found by multiplying the balance of the liability at the end of the last period by the bonds' original market interest rate.

To apply the effective interest method to Fila's bonds for the period ending June 30, 2018, we multiply the $94,923 balance of the liability by the 5% original market rate. This gives us a total bond interest expense of $4,746.[9] Although Fila incurs a $4,746 bond interest expense in the first period, it pays only $4,000. The $746 unpaid interest in the first period is part of the amount to be repaid when the bond becomes due ($5,077 discount + $94,923 issue price = $100,000 total face amount to be paid at maturity). An amortization table can be constructed to help us keep track of interest allocation and the balances of bond-related accounts. Exhibit 14.10 shows an amortization table for the Fila bonds.

The amortization table in Exhibit 14.10 shows how the balance of the discount (Column D) is amortized by the effective interest method until it reaches zero. The bonds' carrying value changes each period until it equals par value at maturity.

The issuer records bond interest expense and updates the balance of the bond liability for each semi-annual cash payment with this entry:

2018			
June 30	Bond Interest Expense	4,746	
	Discount on Bonds Payable		746
	Cash		4,000
	To record six months' interest and discount amortization.		

8 IFRS 2015, IFRS 9, para. 4.2.1.

9 For simplicity, all calculations are rounded to the nearest whole dollar. Do the same when solving the exercises and problems at the end of the chapter.

EXHIBIT 14.10

Effective Interest Amortization of Bond Discount

Period Ending	(A) Cash Interest Paid $100,000 × 4%	(B) Period Interest Expense E × 5%	(C) Discount Amort. B − A	(D) Unamortized Discount	(E) Carrying Value $100,000 − (D)
Dec. 31/17				$5,077	$ 94,923
Jun. 30/18	$ 4,000	$ 4,746[1]	$ 746	4,331	95,669
Dec. 31/18	4,000	4,783[2]	783	3,548	96,452
Jun. 30/19	4,000	4,823	823	2,725	97,275
Dec. 31/19	4,000	4,864	864	1,861	98,139
Jun. 30/20	4,000	4,907	907	954	99,046
Dec. 31/20	4,000	4,954[3]	954	-0-	100,000
	$24,000	$29,077	$5,077		

[1] $94,923 × 0.05 = $4,746
[2] $95,669 × 0.05 = $4,783
[3] Adjusted for rounding.

Column (A) is the bonds' par value ($100,000) multiplied by the semiannual contract rate (4%).

Column (B) is the bonds' prior period carrying value multiplied by the semiannual market rate (5%).

Column (C) is the difference between bond interest expense and interest paid, or [(B) − (A)].

Column (D) is the prior period's unamortized discount less the current period's discount amortization.

Column (E) is the bonds' par value less unamortized discount, or [$100,000 − (D)].

The $746 credit to the Discount on Bonds Payable account increases the bonds' carrying value as shown in Exhibit 14.10. This increase occurs because we decrease the balance of the Discount on Bonds Payable (contra) account, which is subtracted from the Bonds Payable account. Exhibit 14.10 shows this pattern of decreases in the Discount on Bonds Payable account (the unamortized discount in Column D), along with the increases in the bonds' carrying value (Column E). Total bond interest expense is $29,077, comprising $24,000 of semiannual cash interest payments and $5,077 of the original discount below par value.

We use the numbers in Exhibit 14.10 to journalize entries throughout the three-year life of the bonds. We can also use information in this exhibit to prepare comparative balance sheet information. For example, we prepare the bonds payable section of non-current liabilities for 2019 and 2018 as shown in Exhibit 14.11. Note that the carrying value of the bonds payable increases as the discount on bonds payable gets smaller.

EXHIBIT 14.11

Balance Sheet Presentation of Bond Discount

	Dec. 31, 2019	Dec. 31, 2018
Non-current liabilities:		
Bonds payable, 8%, due December 31, 2020	$100,000	$100,000
Less: Discount on bonds payable	1,861	3,548
Carrying value	$ 98,139	$ 96,452

CHECKPOINT

Use this information to answer Checkpoint questions 6, 7, and 8: Five-year, 6% bonds with a $100,000 par value are issued at a price of $91,893. Interest is paid semiannually, and the market rate is 8% on the issue date.

6. Are these bonds issued at a discount or a premium? Explain why.

7. What is the issuer's journal entry to record the sale?

8. What is the amount of bond interest expense recorded at the first semiannual cash payment using the effective interest method?

Do Quick Study questions: QS 14-8, QS 14-9

Issuing Bonds at a Premium

LO6 Prepare entries to record bonds issued at a premium.

When bonds carry a contract rate greater than the market rate, the bonds sell at a price greater than par value (or > 100%). The difference between par and market value is the **premium on bonds**. Buyers bid up the price of bonds above the bonds' par value until it reaches a level yielding the market rate.

To illustrate, let's assume that the Metro Toronto Zoo bonds discussed earlier are issued on December 31, 2017, at 106.072 (106.072% of par value), which amounts to $53,036. The Metro Toronto Zoo records the bond issue with this entry:

2017				
Dec. 31	Cash...	53,036		
	Premium on Bonds Payable		3,036	
	Bonds Payable..		50,000	
	Sold bonds at a premium on the original issue date.			

The Metro Toronto Zoo's bonds obligate it to pay out two different future cash flows:

1. $50,000 face amount at the end of the bonds' four-year life.

2. $7,000 (= 14% × $50,000) at the end of each annual interest period of the bonds' four-year life.

The pattern of cash flows for the Metro Toronto Zoo bonds is shown in Exhibit 14.12.

EXHIBIT 14.12

Cash Flows of the Metro Toronto Zoo Bonds

These bonds are reported in the non-current liability section of the issuer's December 31, 2017, balance sheet, as shown in Exhibit 14.13.

EXHIBIT 14.13

Balance Sheet Presentation of Bond Premium

Non-current liabilities:		
Bonds payable, 14%, due December 31, 2021...	$50,000	
Add: Premium on bonds payable	**3,036**	$53,036

The premium is added to the par value of the bonds to produce the carrying (book) value of the bonds payable. Premium on Bonds Payable is an adjunct (also called accretion) liability account.

Amortizing a Bond Premium

The issuer (The Metro Toronto Zoo) receives $53,036 for its bonds and will pay bondholders the $50,000 face amount after four years have passed plus interest payments totalling $28,000. Because the $3,036 premium is not repaid to bondholders at maturity, it reduces the expense of using the $53,036 for four years.

The upper portion of Exhibit 14.14 shows that total bond interest expense of $24,964 is the difference between the total amount repaid to bondholders ($78,000) and the amount borrowed from bondholders ($53,036). Alternatively, we can calculate total bond interest expense as the sum of the interest payments less the bond premium. The premium is subtracted because it will not be paid to the bondholders when the bonds mature. This alternative calculation is shown in the lower portion of Exhibit 14.14. Total bond interest expense is allocated over the four annual periods with the effective interest method.

EXHIBIT 14.14

Total Bond Interest Expense for Bonds Issued at a Premium

Amount repaid:	
Four interest payments of $7,000	$28,000
Par value at maturity	50,000
Total repaid to bondholders	$78,000
Less: Amount borrowed from bondholders	53,036
Total bond interest expense	$24,964
Alternative Calculation	
Four payments of $7,000	$28,000
Less: Premium	3,036
Total interest expense	$24,964

EFFECTIVE INTEREST METHOD AMORTIZATION

Exhibit 14.15 presents an amortization table using the effective interest method for the The Metro Toronto Zoo bonds.

The amount of cash paid (Column A) is larger than bond interest expense (Column B) because the cash payment is based on the higher 14% contract rate.

The effect of premium amortization on the bond interest expense and the bond liability is seen in the journal entry on December 31, 2018, when the issuer makes the first interest payment:

2018			
Dec. 31	Bond Interest Expense	6,364	
	Premium on Bonds Payable	636	
	Cash		7,000
	To record annual interest and premium amortization.		

Similar entries are recorded at each payment date until the bonds mature at the end of 2021. The effective interest method yields decreasing amounts of bond interest expense and increasing amounts of premium amortization over the bonds' life.

EXHIBIT 14.15

Effective Interest Amortization of Bond Premium

Period Ending	(A) Cash Interest Paid $50,000 × 14%	(B) Period Interest Expense (E) × 12%	(C) Premium Amort. (A) − (B)	(D) Unamortized Premium	(E) Carrying Value $50,000 + (D)
Dec. 31/17............................				$3,036	$53,036
Dec. 31/18............................	$ 7,000	$ 6,364[1]	$ 636	2,400	52,400
Dec. 31/19............................	7,000	6,288[2]	712	1,688	51,688
Dec. 31/20............................	7,000	6,203	797	891	50,891
Dec. 31/21............................	7,000	6,109[3]	891	-0-	50,000
Totals	$28,000	$24,964	$3,036		

[1] $53,036 × 0.12 = $6,364
[2] $52,400 × 0.12 = $6,288
[3] Adjusted for rounding.

Column (A) is the bonds' par value ($50,000) multiplied by the annual contract rate (14%).

Column (B) is the bonds' prior period carrying value multiplied by the annual market rate (12%).

Column (C) is the difference between interest paid and bond interest expense, or [(A) − (B)].

Column (D) is the prior period's unamortized premium less the current period's premium amortization.

Column (E) is the bonds' par value plus unamortized premium, or [$50,000 + (D)].

CHECKPOINT

9. When the period interest expense is increasing over the term of a bond, is this reflective of the amortization of a bond premium or discount?

Do Quick Study questions: QS 14-10, QS 14-11

Summary of Bond Discount and Premium Behaviour

The Fila and the Metro Toronto Zoo bond examples have shown that bond discounts and premiums behave in opposite ways over the term of a bond and therefore affect the bond's carrying value differently. The graphs presented in Exhibit 14.16 summarize these behaviour patterns.

Accruing Bond Interest Expense

If a bond's interest period does not coincide with the issuing company's accounting period, an adjusting entry is necessary to recognize bond interest expense accruing since the most recent interest payment.

To illustrate, let's assume that the Metro Toronto Zoo bonds described in Exhibit 14.15 were issued on December 31, 2017. If the Metro Toronto Zoo's year-end is April 30, four months of bond interest and premium amortization accrue (from December 31, 2017, to April 30, 2018). An adjusting entry is needed to capture:

1. Four months of interest equal to $2,121 (= $6,364 from Column B of Exhibit 14.15 × 4/12), and

2. Four months of premium amortization equal to $212 (= $636 from Column C of Exhibit 14.15 × 4/12).

EXHIBIT 14.16

Graphic Comparison of Bond Discount and Premium Behaviour

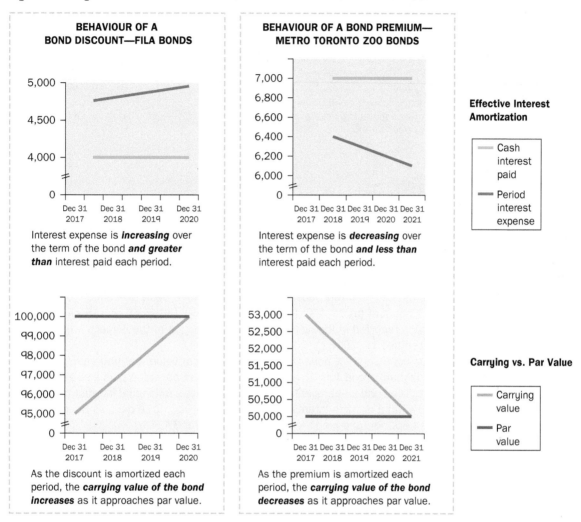

The resulting interest payable is $2,333, the sum of the $2,121 interest expense and $212 premium amortization (also calculated as $7,000 from Column A of Exhibit 14.15 × 4/12). We record these effects with this adjusting entry:

2018				
Apr.	30	Bond Interest Expense	2,121	
		Premium on Bonds Payable...........................	212	
		Interest Payable......................................		2,333
		To record four months' accrued interest and premium amortization.		

Similar entries are made on each April 30 year-end throughout the three-year life of the bonds.

When the $7,000 cash payment occurs on the December 31, 2018, interest date, the journal entry recognizes the bond interest expense and amortization for May through December, a total of eight months.

It must also eliminate the interest payable liability created by the April 30 adjusting entry. In this case we make the following entry to record payment on December 31, 2018:

	2018			
Dec.	31	Interest Payable	2,333	
		Bond Interest Expense ($6,364 × 8/12)........	4,243	
		Premium on Bonds Payable ($636 × 8/12) ...		424
		Cash..		7,000
		To record eight months' interest and amortization and eliminate the accrued interest liability.		

CHECKPOINT

Use this information to solve Checkpoint questions 10, 11, and 12: On December 31, 2017, a company issued 16%, 10-year bonds with a par value of $100,000. Interest is paid on June 30 and December 31. The bonds are sold at an issue price of $110,592 to yield a 14% annual market rate.

10. Are these bonds issued at a discount or a premium? Explain why.

11. Using the effective interest method of allocating bond interest expense, the issuer records the second interest payment (on December 31, 2018) with a debit to Premium on Bonds Payable in the amount of (a) $7,470; (b) $7,741; (c) $259; (d) $530; or (e) $277.

12. How are the bonds reported in the non-current liability section of the issuer's balance sheet as of December 31, 2018?

13. On May 1, a company sells 9% bonds with a $500,000 par value that pay semiannual interest on each January 1 and July 1. The bonds are sold at par value plus interest accrued since January 1. The bond issuer's entry to record the first semiannual interest payment on July 1 includes (a) a debit to Interest Payable for $15,000; (b) a debit to Bond Interest Expense for $22,500; or (c) a credit to Interest Payable for $7,500.

Do Quick Study questions: QS 14-12, QS 14-13

Bond Retirements

LO7 Record the retirement of bonds.

This section describes the retirement of bonds (1) at maturity, (2) before maturity, and (3) by converting them to shares.

Bond Retirement at Maturity

The carrying value of bonds at maturity will always equal their par value. Both Exhibits 14.10 (a discount) and 14.15 (a premium) show that the carrying value of these bonds at the end of their life equals the bonds' par value.

The entry to record the retirement of the Metro Toronto Zoo bonds in Exhibit 14.15 at maturity, assuming interest is already paid and recorded, is:

	2021			
Dec.	31	Bonds Payable	50,000	
		Cash..		50,000
		To record retirement of bonds at maturity.		

Bond Retirement Before Maturity

Companies sometimes wish to retire some or all of their bonds prior to maturity. For instance, if interest rates decline significantly, a company may wish to replace old high-interest paying bonds with new low-interest bonds. Two common ways of retiring bonds before maturity are to:

1. Exercise a call option, or
2. Purchase them on the open market

In the first instance, a company can reserve the right to retire bonds early by issuing callable bonds. This means the bond indenture gives the issuing company an option to call the bonds before they mature by paying the par value plus a *call premium* to the bondholders. In the second case, the issuer retires bonds by repurchasing them on the open market at their current price. When there is a difference between the bonds' carrying value and the amount paid in a bond retirement transaction, the issuer records a gain or loss equal to the difference. Any unrecorded discount or premium up to the date of the call must be recorded to bring the carrying value of the bond up to date.

To illustrate bond retirement before maturity, let's assume a company has issued callable bonds with a par value of $100,000. The call option requires the issuer to pay a call premium of $3,000 to bondholders in addition to the par value. Immediately after the June 30, 2017, interest payment, the bonds have a carrying value of $104,500. On July 1, 2017, the issuer calls these bonds and pays $103,000 to bondholders. The issuer recognizes a $1,500 gain from the difference between the bonds' carrying value of $104,500 and the retirement price of $103,000. The entry to record this bond retirement is:

July	1	Bonds Payable	100,000	
		Premium on Bonds Payable...........................	4,500	
		Gain on Retirement of Bonds		1,500
		Cash..		103,000
		To record retirement of bonds before maturity.		

A company generally must call all of its bonds when it exercises a call option. But a company can retire as many or as few bonds as it desires through open market transactions. If it retires less than the entire set of bonds, it recognizes a gain or loss for the difference between the carrying value of those bonds retired and the amount paid to acquire them.

Bond Retirement by Conversion to Shares

Convertible bonds are those that give bondholders the right to convert their bonds to a specified number of common shares. When conversion occurs, the carrying value of bonds is transferred from non-current liability accounts to contributed capital accounts and no gain or loss is recorded.

To illustrate, on January 1 the $100,000 par value bonds of Converse Corp., with a carrying value of $100,000, are converted to 15,000 common shares. The entry to record this conversion is:

Jan.	1	Bonds Payable	100,000	
		Common Shares		100,000
		To record retirement of bonds by conversion into common shares.		

Notice that the market prices of the bonds and shares have no bearing on this entry. Any related bond discount or premium must also be removed. For example if there had been a $4,000 balance in Discount on Bonds Payable, it must be credited as shown in the following entry:

Jan.	1	Bonds Payable	100,000	
		Discount on Bonds Payable		4,000
		Common Shares		96,000
		To record retirement of bonds by conversion into common shares.		

CHECKPOINT

14. Six years ago, a company issued $500,000 of 6%, eight-year bonds at a price of 95. The current carrying value is $493,750. The company retired 50% of the bonds by buying them on the open market at a price of 102½. What is the amount of gain or loss on retirement of these bonds?

Do Quick Study questions: QS 14-14, QS 14-15

MID-CHAPTER DEMONSTRATION PROBLEM

On February 1, 2017, Enviro-Engineering Inc. has available for issue a $416,000, 5%, two-year bond. Interest is to be paid quarterly beginning May 1, 2017.

Required

Part 1

Calculate the issue price of the bonds assuming a market interest rate of:

    a. 5%   b. 4%   c. 8%

Part 2

Assuming the bonds were issued on April 1, 2017, at a market interest rate of 5%, prepare the entries for the following dates:

    a. April 1, 2017 (date of issue)   b. May 1, 2017 (interest payment date)

Part 3

Assuming the bonds were issued on Feb. 1, 2017, at a market interest rate of 4%:

    a. Prepare an amortization schedule using the effective interest method.

    b. Record the entries for the following dates:

        i. February 1, 2017 (date of issue)

        ii. May 1, 2017 (interest payment date)

        iii. May 31, 2017 (Enviro's year-end)

Part 4

Assuming the bonds were issued on February 1, 2017, at a market interest rate of 8%:

    a. Prepare an amortization schedule using the effective interest method.

    b. Record the entries for the following dates:
        i. February 1, 2017 (date of issue)
       ii. May 1, 2017 (interest payment date)
      iii. May 31, 2017 (Enviro's year-end)

Part 5

Assume the bonds issued in Part 4 were retired on August 1, 2018, for cash of $410,500. Record the retirement (assume the August 1 interest payment had been journalized).

Analysis Component:

When bonds sell at a premium, the total interest expense related to the bond is reduced. Explain.

Planning the Solution

- Calculate the issue price of the bonds using the PV tables in Appendix 14A or a calculator.

- Record the journal entries for bonds issued at par (market interest rate of 5%).

- Using the effective interest method, prepare an amortization schedule for bonds issued at a premium (market rate of 4%).

- Using the effective interest amortization schedule, record the journal entries for bonds issued at a premium.

- Using the effective interest method, prepare an amortization schedule for bonds issued at a discount (market interest rate of 8%).

- Using the effective interest amortization schedule, record the journal entries for bonds issued at a discount.

- Record the retirement of the bonds.

- Answer the analysis component.

Solution

Part 1

    a. $416,000

    b.

PV of face amount (Table 14A.1).................	$416,000	×	0.9235	=	$384,176
PV of interest annuity (Table 14A.2)............	$ 5,200[1]	×	7.6517	=	39,789
					$423,965[2]

[1]$416,000 × 5% × 3/12 = $5,200
[2]Using the present value function on a calculator would result in a bond price of $423,958.

    c.

PV of face amount (Table 14A.1).................	$416,000	×	0.8535	=	$355,056
PV of interest annuity (Table 14A.2)............	$ 5,200[1]	×	7.3255	=	38,093
					$393,149[2]

[1]$416,000 × 5% × 3/12 = $5,200
[2]Using the present value function on a calculator would result in a bond price of $393,144.

Part 2—Issued at a market interest rate of 5% (par).

a.

	2017				
	April	1	Cash	419,467	
			Interest Payable		
			($416,000 × 5% × 2/12)......................		3,467
			Bonds Payable..		416,000

b.

	May	1	Interest Payable	3,467	
			Bond Interest Expense		
			($416,000 × 5% × 1/12)............................	1,733	
			Cash		5,200

Part 3—Issued at a market interest rate of 4% (premium).

a.

Period Ending	(A) Cash Interest Paid $416,000 × 5% × 3/12	(B) Period Interest Expense (E) × 4% × 3/12	(C) Premium Amort. (A) − (B)	(D) Unamortized Premium	(E) Carrying Value $416,000 + (D)
Feb. 1/17				$ 7,965	$423,965
May 1/17	$ 5,200	$ 4,240	$ 960	7,005	423,005
Aug. 1/17	5,200	4,230	970	6,035	422,035
Nov. 1/17	5,200	4,220	980	5,055	421,055
Feb. 1/18	5,200	4,211	989	4,066	420,066
May 1/18	5,200	4,201	999	3,067	419,067
Aug. 1/18	5,200	4,191	1,009	2,058	418,058
Nov. 1/18	5,200	4,181	1,019	1,039	417,039
Feb. 1/19	5,200	4,161*	1,039	-0-	416,000
Totals	$41,600	$33,635	$7,965		

*Adjusted for rounding.

b.

	2017				
i.	Feb.	1	Cash...	423,965	
			Premium on Bonds Payable		7,965
			Bonds Payable.................................		416,000
ii.	May	1	Bond Interest Expense	4,240	
			Premium on Bonds Payable....................	960	
			Cash		5,200
iii.	May	31	Bond Interest Expense ($4,230 × 1/3)....	1,410	
			Premium on Bonds Payable ($970 × 1/3)	323	
			Interest Payable ($5,200 × 1/3)		1,733

Part 4—Issued at a market interest rate of 8% (discount).

a.

Period Ending	(A) Cash Interest Paid $416,000 × 5% × 3/12	(B) Period Interest Expense (E) × 8% × 3/12	(C) Discount Amort. (B) – (A)	(D) Unamortized Discount	(E) Carrying Value $416,000 – (D)
Feb. 1/17				$22,851	$393,149
May 1/17	$ 5,200	$ 7,863	$ 2,663	20,188	395,812
Aug. 1/17	5,200	7,916	2,716	17,472	398,528
Nov. 1/17	5,200	7,971	2,771	14,701	401,299
Feb. 1/18	5,200	8,026	2,826	11,875	404,125
May 1/18	5,200	8,083	2,883	8,992	407,008
Aug. 1/18	5,200	8,140	2,940	6,052	409,948
Nov. 1/18	5,200	8,199	2,999	3,053	412,947
Feb. 1/19	5,200	8,253*	3,053	-0-	416,000
Totals	$41,600	$64,451	$22,851		

*Adjusted for rounding.

b.

```
        2017
i   Feb.  1   Cash.....................................   393,149
                Discount on Bonds Payable....................    22,851
                  Bonds Payable...............................            416,000
ii.  May   1   Bond Interest Expense .........................     7,863
                  Discount on Bonds Payable ............             2,663
                  Cash ...........................................             5,200
iii. May  31   Bond Interest Expense ($7,916 × 1/3)....     2,639
                Discount on Bonds Payable
                  ($2,716 × 1/3)..........................                906*
                Interest Payable ($5,200 × 1/3) ......                1,733
```

*Adjusted for rounding.

Part 5

```
        2018
Aug.   1   Bonds Payable .............................................   416,000
           Loss on Retirement of Bonds .......................       552
             Discount on Bonds Payable ...................                6,052
             Cash....................................................            410,500
           To record retirement of bonds prior to maturity.
```

Analysis Component:

Cash greater than the face value of the bond is received by the issuing corporation when it sells bonds at a premium. However, when the bond matures, only the face value of the bond is repaid to the bondholders. The excess cash received reduces the interest expense associated with the bond. This is accomplished by amortizing the bond premium against bond interest expense over the term of the bond.

Long-Term Notes Payable

Like bonds, companies issue notes payable to finance operations. But, unlike signing a bond, signing a note payable is typically a transaction with a single lender such as a bank, insurance company, or pension fund. A note is initially measured and recorded at its selling or issue price. Over the life of a note, the amount of interest expense allocated to each period is calculated by multiplying the interest rate of the note by the beginning-of-period balance of the note.

Interest-Bearing Notes

LO8   Explain and record notes.

Let's assume Chipotle buys on January 2, 2017, equipment with a fair market value of $45,000 by issuing an 8%, three-year note with a face value of $45,000 to the equipment seller. The company records the purchase with this entry:

2017			
Jan. 2	Equipment...	45,000	
	Notes Payable		45,000
	Issued a $45,000, three-year, 8% note		
	payable for equipment.		

The company (note issuer) reports annual interest expense equal to the original interest rate times each year's beginning balance of the note over the life of the note. Exhibit 14.17 shows this interest expense calculation and allocation.

EXHIBIT 14.17

Interest-Bearing Note—Interest Paid at Maturity

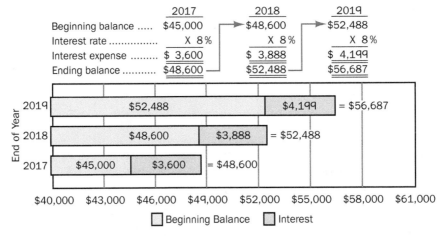

Interest is calculated by multiplying each year's beginning balance by the original 8% interest rate. Interest is then added to the beginning balance to calculate the ending balance. A period's ending balance becomes next period's beginning balance. Because the balance grows by compounding, the amount of interest allocated to each year increases over the life of the note. The final ending balance of $56,687 equals the original $45,000 borrowed plus total interest of $11,687.[10] A note like this one that

---

10   Using the present value/future value functions on a calculator will yield the same results.

delays interest payments is more common for lower-risk companies that wish to delay cash payments until some later period. It is often backed with assets as collateral.

 **CHECKPOINT**

15. On January 1, 2017, a company signs a $6,000 three-year note payable bearing 6% annual interest. The original principal and all interest is paid on December 31, 2016. Interest is compounded annually. How much interest is allocated to year 2018? (a) $0; (b) $360; (c) $381.60; (d) $741.60.

Do Quick Study question: QS 14-16

Instalment Notes

An **instalment note** is an obligation requiring a series of periodic payments to the lender. Instalment notes are common for franchises and other businesses where costs are large and the owner desires to spread these costs over several periods. For example, in Note 10 of its financial statements, WestJet reports the instalment details regarding loans totalling $790,751,000 at December 31, 2014 as illustrated below:

10. Long-term debt

	2014	2013
Term loans—purchased aircraft[i]	343,056	510,764
Term loans—purchased aircraft[ii]	218,425	238,964
Term loans—purchased aircraft[iii]	229,270	128,667
Senior unsecured notes[iv]	397,912	–
Ending balance	1,188,663	878,395
Current portion	(159,843)	(189,191)
Long term portion	1,028,820	689,204

To illustrate, let's assume Strike Inc., a bowling alley operator, borrows $60,000 from a bank to purchase AMF and Brunswick bowling equipment. Strike Inc. signs an 8% instalment note with the bank requiring three annual payments and records the note's issuance as:

2016			
Dec. 31	Cash	60,000	
	Notes Payable		60,000
	Borrowed $60,000 by signing an 8% instalment note.		

Payments on an instalment note normally include the interest expense accruing to the date of the payment plus a portion of the amount borrowed (the *principal*). Generally, we can identify two types of payment patterns:

1. Accrued interest plus equal principal payments, and
2. Equal payments.

The remainder of this section describes these two patterns and how we account for them.

ACCRUED INTEREST PLUS EQUAL PRINCIPAL PAYMENTS

This payment pattern creates cash flows that decrease in size over the life of the note. This decrease occurs because each payment reduces the note's principal balance, yielding less interest expense for the next period.

To illustrate, let's assume the $60,000, 8% note signed by Strike Inc. requires it to make three payments, one at the end of each year, equal to *accrued interest plus $20,000 of principal*. Exhibit 14.18 describes these payments, interest, and changes in the balance of this note.

This table shows that total interest expense is $9,600 and total principal is $60,000. This means total cash payments are $69,600. Notice the decreasing total payment pattern, decreasing accrued interest, and constant principal payments of $20,000.

EXHIBIT 14.18

Instalment Note—Accrued Interest Plus Equal Principal Payments

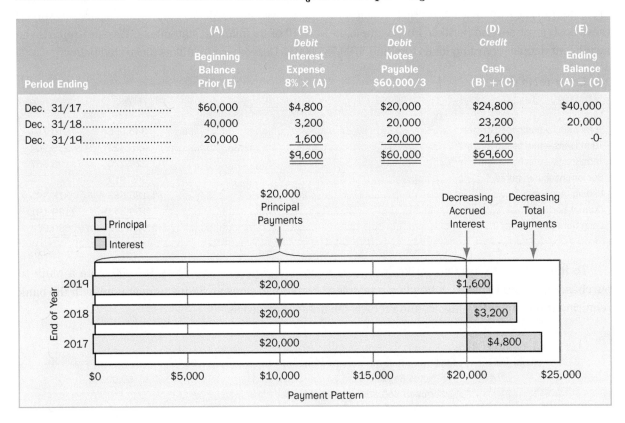

Period Ending	(A) Beginning Balance Prior (E)	(B) Debit Interest Expense 8% × (A)	(C) Debit Notes Payable $60,000/3	(D) Credit Cash (B) + (C)	(E) Ending Balance (A) − (C)
Dec. 31/17	$60,000	$4,800	$20,000	$24,800	$40,000
Dec. 31/18	40,000	3,200	20,000	23,200	20,000
Dec. 31/19	20,000	1,600	20,000	21,600	-0-
		$9,600	$60,000	$69,600	

Strike Inc. (borrower) records the effects of the first payment with this entry:

	2017			
Dec.	31	Interest Expense	4,800	
		Notes Payable	20,000	
		Cash		24,800
		To record first instalment payment.		

After all three payments are recorded, the balance of the Notes Payable account is zero.

EQUAL TOTAL PAYMENTS

Instalment notes that require the borrower to make a series of equal payments consist of changing amounts of interest and principal.

To illustrate, let's assume the previous $60,000 note requires Strike Inc. to make three equal total payments, one at the end of each year. Table 14A.2 is used to calculate the series of three payments equal to the present value of the $60,000 note at 8% interest. We go to Row 3 of the table and go across to the 8% column, where the table value is 2.5771. We solve for the payment by dividing $60,000 by 2.5771. The resulting $23,282 payment includes both interest and principal. Exhibit 14.19 shows that while all three payments are equal, the accrued interest decreases each year because the principal balance of the note is declining. As the amount of interest decreases each year, the amount applied to the principal increases.

EXHIBIT 14.19

Instalment Note—Equal Total Payments

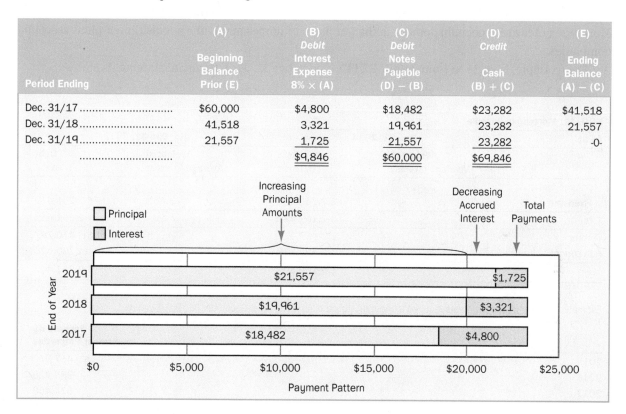

Period Ending	(A) Beginning Balance Prior (E)	(B) Debit Interest Expense 8% × (A)	(C) Debit Notes Payable (D) − (B)	(D) Credit Cash (B) + (C)	(E) Ending Balance (A) − (C)
Dec. 31/17	$60,000	$4,800	$18,482	$23,282	$41,518
Dec. 31/18	41,518	3,321	19,961	23,282	21,557
Dec. 31/19	21,557	1,725	21,557	23,282	-0-
		$9,846	$60,000	$69,846	

The amounts in Exhibit 14.19 are used to show how we record the journal entry for the first payment toward this note:

2017			
Dec. 31	Interest Expense	4,800	
	Notes Payable	18,482	
	Cash		23,282
	To record first instalment payment.		

The borrower records similar entries for each of the remaining payments. After three years, the Notes Payable account balance is zero.

It is interesting to compare the two payment patterns graphed in Exhibits 14.18 and 14.19. The series of equal total payments leads to a greater amount of interest expense over the life of the note. This is because the first three payments in Exhibit 14.19 are smaller and do not reduce the principal as quickly as the first three payments in Exhibit 14.18.

Mortgage Notes

A **mortgage** is a legal agreement that helps protect a lender if a borrower fails to make the required payments on bonds or notes. A mortgage gives the lender the right to be paid out of the cash proceeds from the sale of a borrower's specific assets identified in the mortgage. A separate legal document, called a *mortgage contract*, describes the terms of a mortgage.

Mortgage notes include a mortgage contract pledging title to specific assets as security for the note. This contract usually requires the borrower to pay all property taxes on the mortgaged assets, to maintain them properly, and to carry adequate insurance against fire and other types of losses. These requirements are designed to keep the property from losing value and avoid diminishing the lender's security. Mortgage notes are especially popular in the purchase of homes and in the acquisition of plant assets by companies.

For example, Note 11 to **Boardwalk REIT**'s December 31, 2014, financial statements states:

NOTE 11: Mortgages Payable

As at	Dec 31, 2014		Dec 31, 2013	
	Weighted Average Interest	**Debt Balance**	**Weighted Average Interest**	**Debt Balance**
Mortgage payable				
Fixed rate	3.34%	$ 2,169,499	3.46%	$ 2,261,412
Total		2,169,499		2,261,412
Current		$ 467,320		$ 470,787
Non-current		1,702,179		1,790,625
		$ 2,169,499		$ 2,261,412

Estimated future principal payments required to meet mortgage obligations as at December 31, 2014, are as follows:

	Secured By Investment Properties
2015	$ 467,320
2016	294,423
2017	324,468
2018	186,376
2019	385,137
Subsequent	585,906
	2,243,630
Unamortized deferred financing costs	(74,188)
Unamortized mark-to-market adjustment	57
	$ 2,169,499

Accounting for mortgage notes and bonds is essentially the same as accounting for unsecured notes and bonds. The primary difference is that the mortgage agreement needs to be disclosed to users of financial statements.

CHECKPOINT

16. Which of the following is true for an instalment note requiring a series of equal payments?
   a. Payments consist of an increasing amount of interest and a decreasing amount of principal.
   b. Payments consist of changing amounts of principal, but the interest portion remains constant.
   c. Payments consist of a decreasing amount of interest and an increasing amount of principal.

17. How is the interest portion of an instalment note payment calculated?

18. When a borrower records a periodic interest payment on an instalment note, how are the balance sheet and income statement affected?

Do Quick Study question: QS 14-17

Lease Liabilities

Leasing is an alternative to purchasing an asset and, in certain situations, is reported like a liability on the balance sheet. A company can lease an asset by agreeing to make a series of rental payments to the property owner, called the *lessor*. Because a lease gives the asset's user (called the *lessee*) exclusive control over the asset the lessee can use it to earn revenues. A lease creates a liability if it has essentially the same characteristics as a purchase of an asset on credit. The following section illustrates basic accounting for leases.

Lease Liabilities

LO9 Prepare entries to record lease liabilities.

There are two types of leases: operating leases and finance leases. An **operating lease** is a short-term lease that does not require the lessee to record the right to use the property as an asset or to record any liability for the future lease payments. An operating lease is a form of off-balance-sheet financing. The lessee has an obligation to make future lease payments but is not required to report this liability on the balance sheet. Note disclosure of the future commitments of the lease agreement is all that is required. Accounting for operating leases is relatively uncomplicated. No recognition is given to the signing of an operating lease. The term of an operating lease is only a portion of the asset's operating life. Therefore, the leased asset remains on the books of the lessor because the lessor retains all the risks of ownership.

ACCOUNTING FOR OPERATING LEASES

To illustrate accounting for an operating lease, assume that Tammy Company leases a new luxury crossover vehicle, Audi Q 5 while at a conference in Maui from Marvin Travel Company. The cost of the short-term rental contract is $3,000 and is required to be paid upfront on the day of pick up, February 1, 2017.

Books of Tammy Company (The Lessee)

Feb.	1	Rent Expense...	3,000	
		Cash...		3,000
		Paid rental fee for February.		

Books of Marvin Company (The Lessor)

Feb.	1	Cash..	3,000	
		Rental Revenue....................................		3,000
		Received rental fee for February.		

ACCOUNTING FOR FINANCE LEASES

A finance lease arrangement is a type of lease agreement that results in the lessee having substantially all the benefits and risks of owning the underlying asset. A lease is required to be classified and accounted for as a **finance lease** if the lease terms meet any of the following criteria:[11]

- The present value of the minimum lease payments covers substantially all of the fair value of the property at the inception of the lease.
- The lease term covers the majority of the asset's economic life.
- Ownership transfers to the lessee at the end of the lease term because of a condition of the lease or because the lease has a bargain purchase option allowing the lessee to purchase the asset at less than the fair market value.
- The leased asset is specific to the needs of the lessee and without significant changes would not be of use to another company.

The lessee must report both a leased asset and a lease liability if the lease qualifies as a finance lease. A finance lease is a lease agreement transferring the risks and benefits associated with ownership to the lessee. This type of lease spans a number of years and creates a non-current liability that is paid off in a series of payments. A finance lease is the economic equivalent of a purchase with financing arrangements.

When a finance lease is entered into, the lessee records a leased asset and depreciates it over its useful life. The corresponding interest portion of the lease liability is allocated (amortized) to interest expense over the years of the lease. This interest allocation process is the same as that for notes payable.

In summary, with a finance lease both an asset and a liability are reported on the balance sheet of the lessee and both interest expense and depreciation expense are reported on the income statement. With an operating lease, the lessee reports rent expense on the income statement; there is nothing to be shown on the balance sheet for an operating lease.

To illustrate accounting for a finance lease, assume that Tammy Company leases a piece of snow removal equipment from Marvin Company at $3,000 per year for four years beginning January 2, 2017, with payments due at the end of each year. The economic life of the equipment is expected to be 4 years, which qualifies the lease as a finance lease. An 8% interest rate is assumed and the lease qualifies as a finance lease. Tammy Company must record the asset at $9,936, the present value of the lease payments ($3,000 payment times the present value of an annuity factor of 3.3121).

Books of Tammy Company (The Lessee)

2017				
Jan.	2	Leased Equipment...	9,936	
		Lease Liability		9,936
		To recognize leased asset and related liability.		

---

[11] IFRS 2015, IAS 17, para. 4, 8.

Tammy Company recognizes two expenses related to this equipment. The first expense is depreciation of the leased asset over the asset's useful life:

Dec.	31	Depreciation Expense	2,484	
		Accumulated Depreciation,		
		Leased Asset...		2,484
		To recognize leased asset and related liability		
		($9,936 ÷ 4 years); assuming straight-line		
		depreciation and a zero residual value.		

The second expense to be recognized is the interest expense on the lease liability. A portion of each $3,000 payment is interest expense and the remainder is a reduction of the lease liability:

(A) year	(B) Lease Liability at Start of Year	(C) Payment	(D) Interest Expense (B) × (0.08)	(E) Reduction in Lease Liability (C) − (D)	(F) Lease Liability at End of Year (B) − (E)
2017......................................	9,936	3,000	795	2,205	7,731
2018......................................	7,731	3,000	618	2,382	5,349
2019......................................	5,349	3,000	428	2,572	2,777
2020......................................	2,777	3,000	223*	2,777	-0-

*Adjusted for rounding.

The entry to record the lease payment at the end of 2017 is:

Dec.	31	Lease Liability...	2,205	
		Interest Expense..	795	
		Cash..		3,000
		To record annual payment of the lease.		

The balance sheet presentation of the leased asset at the end of 2017 for Tammy Company is as follows:

Assets:		
Equipment...	$9,936	
Less: Accumulated depreciation..	2,484	$7,452
Liabilities:		
Current liabilities:		
Lease liability—current portion...		$2,382
Non-current liabilities:		
Lease liability..		$5,349

Books of Marvin Company (The Lessor)

The lessor, Marvin Company, treats this type of a lease as both a sale of an asset and as a Lease Receivable. Accounting for a financing lease for a lessor is a topic that is covered in a subsequent accounting course.

 **CHECKPOINT**

19. Why does a finance type lease require the lessee to capitalize and depreciate the underlying asset and treat the related debt as a loan arrangement?

Do Quick Study question: QS 14-18

Financial Statement Analysis

Debt to Equity Ratio

LO10 Calculate and interpret the debt to equity ratio.

The **debt to equity ratio** is a financial statement analysis tool that enables users to evaluate the relative riskiness of a company compared to others in its industry. Debt includes both current and non-current liabilities. Equity includes both funds raised through share issuances and retained earnings from previous years' of profit. A higher debt to equity ratio signals to users that a company is more highly leveraged and is considered to be more risky, as debt usually corresponds with required principle and interest payments consuming valuable cash flow of the company. If debt repayments are missed or unable to be met, the risk relates to the potential for the creditors to sell assets to meet debt obligations. This could have significant consequences for the company, as several missed payments could lead the company to bankruptcy. If a business finds that its debt to equity ratio is rising, eventually it could be a symptom of a potential future cash flow problem, especially if the business is not experiencing a corresponding growth in revenue/market share.

Debt to equity ratio is calculated as follows:

$$\text{Debt to Equity Ratio} = \frac{\text{Total Liabilities}}{\text{Total Equity}}$$

Certain industries typically have higher debt to equity ratios than others. The financial services sector typically has the highest debt to equity ratios. Customers that have balances with the bank are reported as a liability for the bank, as the bank has an obligation to provide the resources at the customers' request. For example, the Toronto Dominion Bank and Royal Bank of Canada both have debt to equity ratios of over 16 in 2014.

The debt to equity ratios for **BCE Inc.** and Telus Inc. are analyzed below:

	BCE Inc. (in millions)		Telus Inc. (in millions)	
	2014	2013	2014	2013
Total Debt (A)...	31,058	29,134	15,763	13,551
Total Equity (B)	15,239	16,250	7,454	8,015
Debt to Equity (= A/B)...	2.04	1.79	2.11	1.69

The above ratios indicate that both BCE Inc. and Telus Inc. are highly leveraged, having approximately double the amount of debt compared to equity funding from shareholders in 2014. Both companies increased their debt loads and experienced a decrease in equity in 2014 over 2013. It is also important to keep in mind that a certain level of debt is healthy and certain industries tend to support higher levels of debt.

 **CHECKPOINT**

20. Why is a high debt to equity ratio an area of concern for investors?

Do Quick Study question: QS 14-19

CRITICAL THINKING CHALLENGE

Refer to the Critical Thinking Challenge question at the beginning of the chapter. Compare your answer to that suggested on Connect.

IFRS AND ASPE—THE DIFFERENCES

Difference	International Financial Reporting Standards (IFRS)	Accounting Standards for Private Enterprises (ASPE)
Bonds	• The effective interest method is used to amortize bond premiums/discounts.	• The same except that other methods are permitted provided the results are not materially different from the effective interest method.
Leases	• There is more professional judgment to apply in assessing the IFRS criteria as no specific numeric thresholds are established. • A lease is determined to be a finance type lease if the lease term is for the majority of the economic life of the asset. • A lease is determined to be a finance type lease if the PV of the minimum lease payments covers substantially all of the fair value of the asset at the inception of the lease.	• Under ASPE, finance leases are referred to as capital leases. • Numeric thresholds are assigned to assess whether the lease is a capital or operating lease: • If the length of the lease is equal to 75% or more of the life of the asset, it meets the criteria to be classified as a capital lease. • IF the PV of the minimum lease payments is equal to 90% or more of the fair value of the asset, it is to be recorded as a capital lease.

A Look Ahead

Chapter 15 focuses on how to classify, account for, and report investments in both debt and equity securities, identifying the difference between strategic and non-strategic investments.

For further study on some topics of relevance to this chapter, please see the following Extend Your Knowledge supplements:

EYK 14-1 Present Value (PV) Tutorial
EYK 14-2 PV Tutorial Using Calculator
EYK 14-3 PV Tutorial Using Excel
EYK 14-4 PV Tables

Summary

LO1 Compare bond versus share financing. Bond financing is used to fund business activities. Advantages of bond financing versus common shares include (1) no effect on shareholders' control, (2) tax savings, and (3) increased earnings due to financial leverage. Disadvantages include (1) required interest and principal payments, and (2) decreased earnings when operations turn less profitable.

LO2 Explain the types of bonds and their issuing procedures. An issuer's bonds usually are sold to many investors. Certain bonds are secured by the issuer's assets (also referred to as asset-backed

debt instruments), while other bonds, called *debentures,* are unsecured. Serial bonds mature at different points in time while term bonds mature together. Registered bonds have each bondholder's name and address recorded by the issuing company, while bearer bonds are payable to the person who holds the bonds. Convertible bonds are exchangeable by bondholders for the issuing company's shares. Callable bonds can be retired by the issuer at a set price. Bonds are often issued by an underwriter, and a bond certificate is evidence of the issuer's obligation.

LO3 Prepare entries to record bonds issued at par. When bonds are issued at par, Cash is debited and Bonds Payable is credited for the bonds' par value. At the bonds' interest payment dates, Bond Interest Expense is debited and Cash is credited for an amount equal to the bonds' par value multiplied by the bonds' contract rate. The cash paid to bondholders on semiannual interest payment dates is calculated as one-half of the result of multiplying the par value of the bonds by their contract rate.

LO4 Determine the price of a bond. The price of a bond is determined by summing the present values of two amounts: (1) the present value of the interest payments (an annuity), and (2) the present value of the face value of the bond that is received at the bond's maturity date. Both amounts are discounted to present value using the market rate of interest.

LO5 Prepare entries to record bonds issued at a discount. Bonds are issued at a discount when the contract rate is less than the market rate. This is the same as saying the issue (selling) price is less than par. When this occurs, the issuer records a credit to Bonds Payable (at par) and debits both to Discount on Bonds Payable and to Cash. The amount of bond interest expense assigned to each period is calculated using the effective interest method. Bond interest expense using the effective interest method equals the bonds' beginning-of-period carrying value multiplied by the original market rate at time of issuance.

LO6 Prepare entries to record bonds issued at a premium. Bonds are issued at a premium when the contract rate is higher than the market rate. This means that the issue (selling) price is greater than par. When this occurs, the issuer records a debit to Cash and credits to both Premium on Bonds Payable and Bonds Payable (at par). The amount of bond interest expense assigned to each period is calculated using the effective interest method. The balance of the Premium on Bonds Payable is allocated to reduce bond interest expense over the life of the bonds.

LO7 Record the retirement of bonds. Bonds are retired at maturity with a debit to Bonds Payable and a credit to Cash for the par value of the bonds. Bonds can be retired early by the issuer by exercising a call option or by purchases on the open market. The issuer recognizes a gain or loss for the difference between the amount paid out and the bonds' carrying value. Alternatively, bondholders can retire bonds early by exercising a conversion feature on convertible bonds.

LO8 Explain and record notes. Notes can require repayment of principal and interest (1) at the end of a period of time, or (2) gradually over a period of time in either equal or unequal amounts. Notes repaid over a period of time are called instalment notes and usually follow one of two payment patterns: (1) decreasing payments of interest plus equal amounts of principal, or (2) equal total payments. Interest is allocated to each period in a note's life by multiplying its carrying value by its interest rate.

LO9 Prepare entries to record lease liabilities. Lease liabilities are one type of non-current liability often used as an alternative to purchase assets. Finance leases are recorded as assets and liabilities. Other leases, called *operating leases*, are recorded as rent expense when the asset is leased.

LO10 Calculate and interpret the debt to equity ratio. The debt to equity ratio gives investors and other users a glimpse at the overall debt burden of a company compared to its total equity.

Guidance Answers to CHECKPOINT

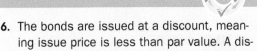

1. *b*

2. Multiply the par value of the bonds by the contract rate of interest.

3. The bonds sell at a premium, and the purchasers pay more than the par value of the bonds.

4. $200,000 \times 7\% \times 3/12 = \$3,500$

5.

$400,000	× 0.7885 =	$ 315,400
$9,000 interest payments	× 10.5753 =	95,178[1]
Issue price of bond		**$410,578[2]**

[1]Rounded to the nearest whole dollar
[2]Using the present value function on a calculator would result in a bond price of $410,575.

6. The bonds are issued at a discount, meaning issue price is less than par value. A discount occurs because the bonds' contract rate is less than their market rate.

7.

Cash	91,893	
Discount on Bonds Payable	8,107	
Bonds Payable		100,000

8. $3,676 (Beginning balance of $91,893 times 4% market interest rate.)

9. Bond discount

10. The bonds are issued at a premium, meaning issue price is greater than par value. A premium occurs because the bonds' contract rate is greater than their market rate.

11. e. (On June 30, 2018: $110,592 × 7% = $7,741 bond interest expense; $8,000 − $7,741 = $259 premium amortization; $110,592 − $259 = $110,333 ending balance. On Dec. 31, 2018: $110,333 × 7% = $7,723 bond interest expense; $8,000 − $7,723 = $277 premium amortization.)

12.

Bonds payable, 16%, due December 31, 2027.......	$100,000	
Add: Premium on bonds payable	10,056*	$110,056

* Beginning premium balance of $10,592 less $259 and $277 amortized on June 30, 2018, and Dec. 31, 2018.

13. a

14. $9,375 loss (Difference between repurchase price of $256,250 [50% of ($500,000 × 102.5%)] and carrying value of $246,875 [50% of $493,750].)

15. c [$6,000 + ($6,000 × 0.06)] × 0.06 = $381.60

16. c

17. The interest portion of an instalment payment equals the beginning balance for the period multiplied by the original interest rate.

18. On the balance sheet, the balances of the liability and cash are decreased. On the income statement, interest expense is increased.

19. The terms of the lease arrangement signals that the lessee essentially has ownership of the asset over the majority of its life and the lease arrangement functions as a debt financing arrangement. Recording the associated asset on the balance sheet and the lease obligation as debt better mirrors the economic reality of the transaction.

20. Debt financing requires fixed payments of principal and interest absorbing valuable cash flow of a company. If a debt payment cannot be repaid, debtors can require a company to liquidate assets, triggering bankruptcy.

DEMONSTRATION PROBLEM

The Modern Tile Corp. patented and successfully test-marketed a new product. However, to expand its ability to produce and market the product, the company needed to raise $800,000 of additional financing. On January 1, 2017, the company borrowed the money under these arrangements:

a. Modern Tile signed a $400,000, 10% instalment note that will be repaid with five equal annual instalments. The payments will be made on December 31 of 2017 through 2021.

b. Modern Tile issued five-year bonds with a par value of $400,000. The bonds have a 10% annual contract rate and pay interest on June 30 and December 31. The annual market interest rate for the bonds was 8% on January 1, 2017.

Required

1. For the instalment note, prepare an amortization table and present the entry for the first payment.

2. For the bonds:

   (a) Calculate the issue price of the bonds

   (b) Present the January 1, 2017, entry to record issuing the bonds

   (c) Prepare an amortization table using the effective interest method

   (d) Present the June 30, 2017, entry to record the first payment of interest

Analysis Component:

The principal, the rate of interest being paid by Modern Tile Corp., and the term are all the same for both the instalment note and the bond. Explain the difference in the total interest expense incurred for both liabilities.

Planning the Solution

- For the instalment note, divide the borrowed amount by the annuity table factor for 10% and five payments (or use a calculator). Prepare a table similar to Exhibit 14.19 and use the numbers in the table to prepare the required entries.
- For the bonds, calculate the issue price by using the market rate to find the present values of the bonds' cash flows (use a calculator or tables found in Appendix 14A). Then, use this result to record issuing the bonds. Next, develop an amortization table like Exhibit 14.15, and use it to get the numbers that you need for the journal entry.
- Answer the analysis component.

Solution

Part 1

Period Ending	(A) Beginning Balance	(B) *Debit* Interest Expense	+	(C) *Debit* Notes Payable	=	(D) *Credit* Ending Cash[1, 2]	(E) Balance
2017...................................	$400,000	$ 40,000		$ 65,519		$105,519	$334,481
2018...................................	334,481	33,448		72,071		105,519	262,410
2019...................................	262,410	26,241		79,278		105,519	183,132
2020...................................	183,132	18,313		87,206		105,519	95,926
2021...................................	95,926	9,593		95,926		105,519	-0-
Total..................................		$127,595		$400,000		$527,595	

[1]$400,000 ÷ 3.7908 = $105,519

[2]Using the present value function on a calculator would yield the same result.

	2017			
	Dec. 31	Interest Expense..	40,000	
		Notes Payable..	65,519	
		Cash..		105,519
		To record first instalment payment.		

Part 2

a.

PV of face amount (Table 14A.1).......................	$400,000 × 0.6756 = $270,240
PV of interest annuity (Table 14A.2).................	$ 20,000[1] × 8.1109 = 162,218
	$432,458[2]

[1]$400,000 × 10% × 6/12 = $20,000
[2]Using the present value function on a calculator would result in a bond price of $432,444.

b.

	2017			
Jan.	1	Cash	432,458	
		Premium on Bonds Payable		32,458
		Bonds Payable.......................................		400,000
		Sold bonds at a premium.		

c.

Period Ending	(A) Cash Interest Paid $400,000 × 10% × 6/12	(B) Period Interest Expense (E) × 8% × 6/12	(C) Premium Amort. (A) – (B)	(D) Unamortized Premium	(E) Carrying Value $400,000 + (D)
Jan. 1/17				$32,458	$432,458
June 30/17	$ 20,000	$ 17,298	$ 2,702	29,756	429,756
Dec. 31/17	20,000	17,190	2,810	26,946	426,946
June 30/18	20,000	17,078	2,922	24,024	424,024
Dec. 31/18	20,000	16,961	3,039	20,985	420,985
June 30/19	20,000	16,839	3,161	17,824	417,824
Dec. 31/19	20,000	16,713	3,287	14,537	414,537
June 30/20	20,000	16,581	3,419	11,118	411,118
Dec. 31/20	20,000	16,445	3,555	7,563	407,563
June 30/21	20,000	16,303	3,697	3,866	403,866
Dec. 31/21	20,000	16,134*	3,866	0	400,000
	$200,000	$167,542	$32,458		

*Adjusted for rounding

d.

	2017			
June	30	Bond Interest Expense	17,298	
		Premium on Bonds Payable..........................	2,702	
		Cash		20,000
		Paid semiannual interest on the bonds.		

Analysis Component:

The total interest expense on the instalment note was $127,595 and for the bond $135,084 (= $167,542 – $32,458). The bond has a higher total interest expense because only interest (no principal) is paid on each of the payment dates; the payments on the instalment note are blended, part principal and part interest. It should be noted that part of the higher interest realized on the bond was offset by the premium received at the time of sale (a reduction of $32,458).

PV Tables

Note that printable versions of the PV tables are available online in EYK 14-4.

TABLE 14A.1

Present Value of 1 Due in *n* Periods

Periods	1%	2%	3%	4%	5%	6%	7%	8%	9%	10%	12%	15%
1	0.9901	0.9804	0.9709	0.9615	0.9524	0.9434	0.9346	0.9259	0.9174	0.9091	0.8929	0.8696
2	0.9803	0.9612	0.9426	0.9246	0.9070	0.8900	0.8734	0.8573	0.8417	0.8264	0.7972	0.7561
3	0.9706	0.9423	0.9151	0.8890	0.8638	0.8396	0.8163	0.7938	0.7722	0.7513	0.7118	0.6575
4	0.9610	0.9238	0.8885	0.8548	0.8227	0.7921	0.7629	0.7350	0.7084	0.6830	0.6355	0.5718
5	0.9515	0.9057	0.8626	0.8219	0.7835	0.7473	0.7130	0.6806	0.6499	0.6209	0.5674	0.4972
6	0.9420	0.8880	0.8375	0.7903	0.7462	0.7050	0.6663	0.6302	0.5963	0.5645	0.5066	0.4323
7	0.9327	0.8706	0.8131	0.7599	0.7107	0.6651	0.6227	0.5835	0.5470	0.5132	0.4523	0.3759
8	0.9235	0.8535	0.7894	0.7307	0.6768	0.6274	0.5820	0.5403	0.5019	0.4665	0.4039	0.3269
9	0.9143	0.8368	0.7664	0.7026	0.6446	0.5919	0.5439	0.5002	0.4604	0.4241	0.3606	0.2843
10	0.9053	0.8203	0.7441	0.6756	0.6139	0.5584	0.5083	0.4632	0.4224	0.3855	0.3220	0.2472
11	0.8963	0.8043	0.7224	0.6496	0.5847	0.5268	0.4751	0.4289	0.3875	0.3505	0.2875	0.2149
12	0.8874	0.7885	0.7014	0.6246	0.5568	0.4970	0.4440	0.3971	0.3555	0.3186	0.2567	0.1869
13	0.8787	0.7730	0.6810	0.6006	0.5303	0.4688	0.4150	0.3677	0.3262	0.2897	0.2292	0.1625
14	0.8700	0.7579	0.6611	0.5775	0.5051	0.4423	0.3878	0.3405	0.2992	0.2633	0.2046	0.1413
15	0.8613	0.7430	0.6419	0.5553	0.4810	0.4173	0.3624	0.3152	0.2745	0.2394	0.1827	0.1229
16	0.8528	0.7284	0.6232	0.5339	0.4581	0.3936	0.3387	0.2919	0.2519	0.2176	0.1631	0.1069
17	0.8444	0.7142	0.6050	0.5134	0.4363	0.3714	0.3166	0.2703	0.2311	0.1978	0.1456	0.0929
18	0.8360	0.7002	0.5874	0.4936	0.4155	0.3503	0.2959	0.2502	0.2120	0.1799	0.1300	0.0808
19	0.8277	0.6864	0.5703	0.4746	0.3957	0.3305	0.2765	0.2317	0.1945	0.1635	0.1161	0.0703
20	0.8195	0.6730	0.5537	0.4564	0.3769	0.3118	0.2584	0.2145	0.1784	0.1486	0.1037	0.0611
25	0.7798	0.6095	0.4776	0.3751	0.2953	0.2330	0.1842	0.1460	0.1160	0.0923	0.0588	0.0304
30	0.7419	0.5521	0.4120	0.3083	0.2314	0.1741	0.1314	0.0994	0.0754	0.0573	0.0334	0.0151
35	0.7059	0.5000	0.3554	0.2534	0.1813	0.1301	0.0937	0.0676	0.0490	0.0356	0.0189	0.0075
40	0.6717	0.4529	0.3066	0.2083	0.1420	0.0972	0.0668	0.0460	0.0318	0.0221	0.0107	0.0037

TABLE 14A.2

Present Value of an Annuity of 1 Period

Periods	1%	2%	3%	4%	5%	6%	7%	8%	9%	10%	12%	15%
1	0.9901	0.9804	0.9709	0.9615	0.9524	0.9434	0.9346	0.9259	0.9174	0.9091	0.8929	0.8696
2	1.9704	1.9416	1.9135	1.8861	1.8594	1.8334	1.8080	1.7833	1.7591	1.7355	1.6901	1.6257
3	2.9410	2.8839	2.8286	2.7751	2.7232	2.6730	2.6243	2.5771	2.5313	2.4869	2.4018	2.2832
4	3.9020	3.8077	3.7171	3.6299	3.5460	3.4651	3.3872	3.3121	3.2397	3.1699	3.0373	2.8550
5	4.8534	4.7135	4.5797	4.4518	4.3295	4.2124	4.1002	3.9927	3.8897	3.7908	3.6048	3.3522
6	5.7955	5.6014	5.4172	5.2421	5.0757	4.9173	4.7665	4.6229	4.4859	4.3553	4.1114	3.7845
7	6.7282	6.4720	6.2303	6.0021	5.7864	5.5824	5.3893	5.2064	5.0330	4.8684	4.5638	4.1604
8	7.6517	7.3255	7.0197	6.7327	6.4632	6.2098	5.9713	5.7466	5.5348	5.3349	4.9676	4.4873
9	8.5660	8.1622	7.7861	7.4353	7.1078	6.8017	6.5152	6.2469	5.9952	5.7590	5.3282	4.7716

TABLE 14A.2

Present Value of an Annuity of 1 Period *(continued)*

Periods	1%	2%	3%	4%	5%	6%	7%	8%	9%	10%	12%	15%
10	9.4713	8.9826	8.5302	8.1109	7.7217	7.3601	7.0236	6.7101	6.4177	6.1446	5.6502	5.0188
11	10.3676	9.7868	9.2526	8.7605	8.3064	7.8869	7.4987	7.1390	6.8052	6.4951	5.9377	5.2337
12	11.2551	10.5753	9.9540	9.3851	8.8633	8.3838	7.9427	7.5361	7.1607	6.8137	6.1944	5.4206
13	12.1337	11.3484	10.6350	9.9856	9.3936	8.8527	8.3577	7.9038	7.4869	7.1034	6.4235	5.5831
14	13.0037	12.1062	11.2961	10.5631	9.8986	9.2950	8.7455	8.2442	7.7862	7.3667	6.6282	5.7245
15	13.8651	12.8493	11.9379	11.1184	10.3797	9.7122	9.1079	8.5595	8.0607	7.6061	6.8109	5.8474
16	14.7179	13.5777	12.5611	11.6523	10.8378	10.1059	9.4466	8.8514	8.3126	7.8237	6.9740	5.9542
17	15.5623	14.2919	13.1661	12.1657	11.2741	10.4773	9.7632	9.1216	8.5436	8.0216	7.1196	6.0472
18	16.3983	14.9920	13.7535	12.6593	11.6896	10.8276	10.0591	9.3719	8.7556	8.2014	7.2497	6.1280
19	17.2260	15.6785	14.3238	13.1339	12.0853	11.1581	10.3356	9.6036	8.9501	8.3649	7.3658	6.1982
20	18.0456	16.3514	14.8775	13.5903	12.4622	11.4699	10.5940	9.8181	9.1285	8.5136	7.4694	6.2593
25	22.0232	19.5235	17.4131	15.6221	14.0939	12.7834	11.6536	10.6748	9.8226	9.0770	7.8431	6.4641
30	25.8077	22.3965	19.6004	17.2920	15.3725	13.7648	12.4090	11.2578	10.2737	9.4269	8.0552	6.5660
35	29.4086	24.9986	21.4872	18.6646	16.3742	14.4982	12.9477	11.6546	10.5668	9.6442	8.1755	6.6166
40	32.8347	27.3555	23.1148	19.7928	17.1591	15.0463	13.3317	11.9246	10.7574	9.7791	8.2438	6.6418

Glossary

Annuity A series of equal payments occurring at equal time intervals.

Bearer bonds Bonds that are made payable to the person who holds them (called the bearer); also called *unregistered bonds*.

Bond A written promise to pay an amount identified as the par value of the bond along with interest at a stated annual amount; usually issued in denominations of $1,000.

Bond certificate A document containing information about the bond, such as the issuer's name, the bond's par value, the contract interest rate, and the maturity date.

Bond indenture The contract between the bond issuer and the bondholders; it identifies the rights and obligations of the parties.

Bond yield See *market rate of interest.*

Callable bonds Bonds that give the issuer an option of retiring them at a stated dollar amount prior to maturity.

Carrying value The net amount at which bonds are reflected on the balance sheet; equals the par value of the bonds less any unamortized discount or plus any unamortized premium; also called the *book value* of the bonds.

Contract rate The interest rate specified in the bond indenture; it is multiplied by the par value of the bonds to determine the amount of interest to be paid each year;

also called the *coupon rate*, the *stated rate,* or the *nominal rate.*

Convertible bonds Bonds that can be exchanged by the bondholders for a fixed number of shares of the issuing company's common shares.

Coupon bonds Bonds that have interest coupons attached to their certificates; the bondholders detach the coupons when they mature and present them to a bank or broker for collection.

Coupon rate See *contract rate.*

Debt to equity ratio A financial statement analysis ratio calculated by dividing total debt obligations of a company as determined by their balance sheet category of "total debt" divided by the "total equity" of a company.

Debentures See *unsecured bonds.*

Discount Bonds trading below par value.

Discount on bonds payable The difference between the par value of a bond and its lower issue price; arises when the contract rate is lower than the market rate.

Effective interest method Allocates interest expense over the life of the bonds in a way that yields a constant rate of interest; interest expense for a period is found by multiplying the balance of the liability at the beginning of the period by the bonds' original market rate.

Effective interest rate See *market rate of interest.*

Finance lease A lease that gives the lessee the risks and benefits normally associated with ownership.

Financial leverage When a company earns a higher return with borrowed funds than it is paying in interest, the result is an increase in return on equity.

Instalment note An obligation requiring a series of periodic payments to the lender.

Market rate of interest The interest rate that borrowers are willing to pay and that lenders are willing to earn for a particular bond given its risk level and the length of time to maturity. Also called the *effective interest rate and bond yield*.

Mortgage A legal agreement that protects a lender by giving the lender the right to be paid out of the cash proceeds from the sale of the borrower's specific assets identified in the mortgage.

Nominal rate *See contract rate.*

Operating lease A short-term lease that does not require the lessee to record the right to use the property as an asset or to record any liability for future lease payments.

Par value of a bond The amount that the bond issuer agrees to pay at maturity and the amount on which interest payments are based; also called *the face amount* or *face value*.

Premium Bonds that trade above par value.

Premium on bonds The difference between the par value of a bond and its higher issue price; arises when the contract rate is higher than the market rate.

Redeemable bonds Bonds that give the purchaser an option of retiring them at a stated dollar amount prior to maturity.

Registered bonds Bonds owned by investors whose names and addresses are recorded by the issuing company; the interest payments are made with cheques to the registered owners.

Return on equity A ratio calculated as profit available to common shareholders divided by common shareholders' equity; measures how much profit is being generated for the common shareholders by their investment.

Secured bonds Bonds that have specific assets of the issuing company pledged as collateral.

Serial bonds Bonds that mature at different dates with the result that the entire debt is repaid gradually over a number of years.

Stated interest rate *See contract rate.*

Term bonds Bonds that are scheduled for payment (mature) at a single specified date.

Unsecured bonds Bonds that are backed by the issuer's general credit standing; unsecured bonds are almost always more risky than secured bonds; also called *debentures*.

Concept Review Questions

1. What is the difference between notes payable and bonds payable?

2. What is the primary difference between a share and a bond?

3. What is the main advantage of issuing bonds instead of issuing shares to investors?

4. What is a bond indenture? What provisions are usually included in an indenture?

5. What obligation do issuing corporations have to bondholders?

6. Refer to the annual report for **Indigo** presented in Appendix II. Where are the details regarding the composition of the $227,000 March 29, 2014, balance in long-term debt?

7. What are the contract and market interest rates for bonds?

8. What factors affect the market interest rates for bonds?

9. If you know the par value of bonds, the contract rate, and the market interest rate, how can you estimate the market value of the bonds?

10. What is the cash price of a $2,000 bond that is sold at 98¼? What is the cash price of a $6,000 bond that is sold at 101½?

11. Why does a company that issues bonds between interest dates collect accrued interest from the bonds' purchasers?

12. Describe two alternative payment patterns for instalment notes.

13. Refer to the annual report for Indigo presented in Appendix II. In June 2013 the company cancelled its revolving line of credit. Why did the company do this?

14. How would a lease create an asset and a liability for the lessee?

15. The initial ZooShare community bond offering highlighted in the chapter opening vignette offered investors a 11.5–12.5% return. Why would the initial ZooShare bond offering provide investors with such an attractive return at such a high interest rate?

Note: When solving the exercises and problems:
1. Round all dollar amounts to the nearest whole dollar, and
2. Assume that none of the companies uses reversing entries.

Quick Study

QS 14-1 Calculating bond interest LO1

A $15,000 bond with a contract interest rate of 6% was issued on March 1, 2017. Calculate the cash paid on the first interest payment date if interest is paid:

a. annually   **c.** quarterly

b. semiannually   **d.** monthly

QS 14-2 Bond financing LO1

Curtis Ltd. issued $100,000 of 8% bonds at face value on October 1, 2017. Interest is paid each March 31 and September 30. If Curtis's tax rate is 40%, what is the annual after-tax borrowing cost (a) in percentage terms and (b) in dollars?

QS 14-3 Bond terms and identifications LO2

Match the following terms and phrases by entering the letter of the phrase that best describes each term in the blank next to the term.

_____ Serial bonds   _____ Secured bonds

_____ Convertible bonds   _____ Debentures

_____ Registered bonds   _____ Bond indenture

_____ Bearer bonds

   a. Issuer records the bondholders' names and addresses.

   b. Unsecured; backed only by the issuer's general credit standing.

   c. Varying maturity dates.

   d. Identifies the rights and responsibilities of the issuer and bondholders.

   e. Can be exchanged for shares of the issuer's common shares.

   f. Unregistered; interest is paid to the person who possesses them.

   g. Specific assets of the issuer are mortgaged as collateral.

QS 14-4 Issuance of bond at par, recording interest payment and accrual LO3

On March 1, 2017, JenStar Hydroponics Inc. issued at par an $80,000, 6%, three-year bond. Interest is to be paid quarterly beginning May 31, 2017. JenStar's year-end is July 31. A partial payment schedule is shown below:

Period Ending	Cash Interest Paid*	Carrying Value
Mar. 1/17		$80,000
May 31/17	$ 1,200	80,000
Aug. 31/17	1,200	80,000
Aug. 31/19	1,200	80,000
Nov. 30/19	1,200	80,000
Feb. 28/20	1,200	80,000
Total	$14,400	

*$80,000 × 6% × 3/12

    a. Record the issuance of the bond on March 1, 2017.

    b. Record the payment of interest on May 31, 2017.

    c. Record the accrual of bond interest on July 31, 2017, JenStar's year-end, and the subsequent payment of interest on August 31, 2017.

QS 14-5 Issue of bonds at par between interest dates L03

Purity Vegetable Corp. issued $200,000 of 6% bonds on November 1, 2017, at par value. The bonds were dated October 1, 2017, and pay interest each April 1 and October 1. Record the issue of the bonds on November 1, 2017.

QS 14-6 Calculating the price of a bond using PV tables (or business calculator PV function) L04

On August 1, 2017, Billboard Inc. issued $520,000 of 10%, seven-year bonds. Interest is to be paid semiannually. Calculate the issue price of the bonds if the market interest rate was:

    a. 12%   **b.** 10%   **c.** 14%

QS 14-7 Calculating the price of a bond using business calculator PV function L04

On February 1, 2017, Swiss Travel Corp. issued $750,000 of 11%, eight-year bonds. Interest is to be paid quarterly. Calculate the issue price of the bonds if the market interest rate was:

    a. 6%   **b.** 11%   **c.** 13%

QS 14-8 Issuance of bonds at a discount, payment of interest L05

Bellevue Marketing Corp. issued $600,000 of 6%, four-year bonds for $579,224 on July 1, 2017, the day the bonds were dated. The market interest rate on this date was 7%. Interest is paid quarterly beginning October 1, 2017. Bellevue uses the effective interest method to amortize bond discounts and premiums. Record the issuance of the bonds and the first payment of interest.

QS 14-9 Bond transactions—discount L05

Alberta Industries Ltd. issued 10%, 10-year bonds with a par value of $200,000 and semiannual interest payments. On the issue date, the annual market rate of interest for the bonds was 12%, and the selling price was $177,059. The effective interest method is used to allocate the interest.

    a. What is the total amount of bond interest expense that will be recognized over the life of the bonds?

    b. What is the total bond interest expense recorded on the first interest payment date?

QS 14-10 Issuance of bonds at a premium, payment of interest L06

Maier Investment Corporation issued $700,000 of 6%, six-year bonds for $735,902 on July 1, 2017, the day the bonds were dated. The market interest rate was 5%. Interest is paid semiannually beginning December 31, 2017. Maier uses the effective interest method to amortize bond discounts and premiums. Record the issuance of the bonds and the first payment of interest.

QS 14-11 Bond transactions—premium L06

Dawson Limited issued 12%, 10-year bonds with a par value of $60,000 and semiannual interest payments. On the issue date, the annual market rate of interest for the bonds was 10%, and they sold for $67,478. The effective interest method is used to allocate the interest.

    a. What is the total amount of bond interest expense that will be recognized over the life of the bonds?

    b. What is the amount of bond interest expense recorded on the first interest payment date?

QS 14-12 Issuance of bond at discount, recording interest payment and accrual LO5

Bonanza Graphics Inc. issued a $200,000, 8%, three-year bond on November 1, 2017, for cash of $194,792. Interest is to be paid quarterly. The annual market rate of interest is 9%. Assume a year-end of December 31. The amortization schedule, using the effective interest method, is shown below:

Period Ending	(A) Cash Interest Paid $200,000 × 8% × 3/12	(B) Period Interest Expense (E) × 9% × 3/12	(C) Discount Amort. (B) − (A)	(D) Unamortized Discount	(E) Carrying Value $200,000 − (D)
Nov. 1/17				$5,208	$194,792
Feb. 1/18	$ 4,000	$ 4,383	$ 383	4,825	195,175
Aug. 1/20	4,000	4,478	478	492	199,508
Nov. 1/20	4,000	4,492*	492	-0-	200,000
Totals	$48,000	$53,208	$5,208		

*Adjusted for rounding.

a. Record the issuance of the bond on November 1, 2017.

b. Record the accrual of bond interest at year-end, December 31, 2017, and the subsequent payment on February 1, 2018.

QS 14-13 Issuance of bond at premium, accrual, and payment of interest LO6

Henderson Armour Inc. issued a $652,000, 14% 10-year bond on October 1, 2017, for cash of $697,701. Interest is to be paid quarterly. The annual market rate of interest is 12.75%. Assume a year-end of February 28. A partial amortization schedule, using the effective interest method, is shown below.

Period Ending	(A) Cash Interest Paid $652,000 × 14% × 3/12	(B) Period Interest Expense (E) × 12.75% × 3/12	(C) Premium Amort. (A) − (B)	(D) Unamortized Premium	(E) Carrying Value $652,000 + (D)
Oct. 1/17				$45,701	$697,701
Jan. 1/18	$ 22,820	$ 22,239	$ 581	45,120	697,120
Apr. 1/18	22,820	22,221	599	44,521	696,521
July 1/18	22,820	22,202	618	43,903	695,903
Oct. 1/27	22,820	20,845	1,975	-0-	652,000
Totals	$912,800	$867,099	$45,701		

a. Record the issuance of the bond on October 1, 2017.

b. Record the accrual of bond interest and premium amortization on February 28, 2018, the year-end, and the subsequent payment of interest on April 1, 2018.

QS 14-14 Retiring bonds before maturity LO7

On July 1, 2017, Lester Shoes Ltd. exercises a $4,000 call option on its outstanding bonds, which have a carrying value of $206,000 and par value of $200,000. Lester exercises the call option immediately after the semiannual interest is paid on June 30, 2017. Record the journal entry to show the retirement of the bonds.

QS 14-15 Bond retirement by share conversion LO7

On January 1, 2017, the $1,000,000 par value bonds of Sinclair Corporation with a carrying value of $950,000 are converted to 500,000 common shares. Journalize the conversion of the bonds.

QS 14-16 Calculating the amount due on an interest-bearing note LO8

On January 1, 2017, the Pareto Company borrowed $80,000 in exchange for an interest-bearing note. The note plus interest compounded at an annual rate of 8% is due on December 31, 2019. Calculate the amount that Pareto will pay on the due date.

QS 14-17 Installment note with equal payments LO8

Calvin Corp. borrowed $80,000 from a bank and signed an instalment note that calls for five annual payments of equal size, with the first payment due one year after the note was signed. Use Table 14A.2 or a calculator to calculate the size of the annual payment for each of the following annual interest rates:

   a. 5%   **b.** 7%   **c.** 10%

QS 14-18 Leasing explanation LO9

Explain the difference between an operating lease and a financing lease.

QS 14-19 Calculate debt to equity ratio LO10

   a. Calculate the debt to equity ratio for 2016 and 2017, for the following 3 separate companies.

   b. Comment on whether the ratio for each has improved or weakend from a risk perspective.

	Fab Form Industries		Recycle Resources		Outdoor Adventure Company	
	2017	2016	2017	2016	2017	2016
Total Debt (A)	2,306,225	2,522,364	4,4141,368	4,437,345	1,137,720	1,021,295
Total Equity (B)	1,246,608	1,293,520	2,556,400	2,689,300	875,169	928,450

Exercises

Exercise 14-1 Bonds issued at par LO3

On January 1, 2017, British Software Ltd. issued $450,000 of 20-year, 8% bonds that pay interest semiannually on June 30 and December 31. The bonds were sold to investors at their par value.

   a. How much interest will British pay to the holders of these bonds every six months?

   b. Show the journal entries that British would make to record:

      1. the issuance of the bonds on January 1, 2017;

      2. the first interest payment on June 30, 2017; and

      3. the second interest payment on December 31, 2017.

Exercise 14-2 Bonds issued at par between interest dates LO3

On March 1, 2017, Jagger Metal Corp. issued 8% bonds dated January 1, 2017. The bonds have a $900,000 par value, mature in 20 years, and pay interest semiannually on June 30 and December 31. The bonds were sold to investors at their par value plus the two months' interest that had accrued since the original issue date.

   a. How much accrued interest was paid to Jagger by the purchasers of these bonds on March 1, 2017?

    b. Show the journal entries that Jagger would make to record:
   1. the issuance of the bonds on March 1, 2017;
   2. the first interest payment on June 30, 2017; and
   3. the second interest payment on December 31, 2017.

Exercise 14-3 **Bonds issued at par between interest dates** LO3

Xtra-Gold Corporation had a $1,200,000, 5% bond available for issue on September 1, 2017. Interest is to be paid quarterly beginning November 30. All of the bonds were issued at par on October 1. Prepare the appropriate entries for:

    a. October 1, 2017

    b. November 30, 2017

    c. December 31, 2017 (Xtra-Gold's year-end)

    d. February 28, 2018

Exercise 14-4 **Bonds issued at par between interest dates** LO3

Omni Film Corporation had a $1,250,000, 7% bond available for issue on April 1. Interest is to be paid on the last day of each month. On April 14 and 25, bonds with a face value of $890,000 and $360,000, respectively, were issued at par. Record the entries for April 14, 25, and 30.

Exercise 14-5 **Calculating the issue price using business calculator PV function** LO4

CHECK FIGURE: c. $871,551

On October 1, 2017, Eastern Timber Inc. has available for issue $840,000 bonds due in four years. Interest at the rate of 4% is to be paid quarterly. Calculate the issue price if the market interest rate is:

    a. 5%   **b.** 4%   **c.** 3%

Exercise 14-6 **Calculating the issue price using business calculator PV function** LO4

CHECK FIGURE: a. $3,302,437

Chinook Inc. has available for issue a $3,200,000 bond due in eight years. Interest at the rate of 6% is to be paid semiannually. Calculate the issue price if the market interest rate is:

    a. 5.5%   **b.** 6%   **c.** 6.75%

Exercise 14-7 **Calculating the present value of a bond and recording the issuance** LO4,5

CHECK FIGURE: e. Discount = $46,110 (PV tables) or $46,117 (calculator)

Mindsetta Music Inc. issued bonds on March 1, 2017, with a par value of $300,000. The bonds mature in 15 years and pay 8% annual interest in two semiannual payments. On the issue date, the annual market rate of interest for the bonds turned out to be 10%.

    a. What is the size of the semiannual interest payment for these bonds?

    b. How many semiannual interest payments will be made on these bonds over their life?

    c. Use the information about the interest rates to decide whether the bonds were issued at par, at a discount, or at a premium.

    d. Estimate the market value of the bonds as of the date they were issued.

    e. Present the journal entry that would be made to record the bonds' issuance.

Exercise 14-8 Allocation of interest for bonds sold at a discount LO5

CHECK FIGURE: b. Total interest expense = $26,169

Huskey Mining Corporation issued bonds with a par value of $90,000 on January 1, 2017. The annual contract rate on the bonds is 8%, and the interest is paid semiannually. The bonds mature after three years. The annual market interest rate at the date of issuance was 10%, and the bonds were sold for $85,431.

    a. What is the amount of the original discount on these bonds?

    b. How much total bond interest expense will be recognized over the life of these bonds?

    c. Present an amortization table for these bonds; use the effective interest method of allocating the interest and amortizing the discount.

Exercise 14-9 Amortization table and accrued interest LO5

CHECK FIGURE: a. Total interest expense = $303,836

SweetFish Corp. issued bonds with a par value of $820,000 and a five-year life on May 1, 2017. The contract interest rate is 7%. The bonds pay interest on October 31 and April 30. They were issued at a price of $803,164 when the market interest rate was 7.5%. SweetFish Corp.'s year-end is December 31.

    a. Prepare an amortization table for these bonds that covers their entire life. Use the effective interest method of allocating interest.

    b. Show the journal entries that the issuer would make to record the entries on October 31, 2017; December 31, 2017; and April 30, 2018.

Exercise 14-10 Amortization of bond discount LO5

CHECK FIGURE: a. $726,256 (PV tables) or $726,247 (calculator)

On November 1, 2017, Yardley Distributors Inc. issued a $740,000, 5%, two-year bond. Interest is to be paid semiannually each May 1 and November 1.

Required

    a. Calculate the issue price of the bond assuming a market interest rate of 6% on the date of the bond issue.

    b. Using the effective interest method, prepare an amortization schedule similar to Exhibit 14.10.

Exercise 14-11 Amortization of bond discount LO5

CHECK FIGURES: a. $644,605 (PV tables) or $644,597 (calculator); b. Total interest expense = $368,595 (PV tables) or $368,603 (calculator)

On October 1, 2017, Dejour Energy Inc. issued a $680,000, 7%, seven-year bond. Interest is to be paid annually each October 1.

Required

    a. Calculate the issue price of the bond assuming a market interest rate of 8% on the date of the bond issue.

    b. Using the effective interest method, prepare an amortization schedule similar to Exhibit 14.10.

Exercise 14-12 **Recording bonds issued at a discount** LO5

Refer to the amortization schedule prepared in Exercise 14.11. Dejour Energy Inc. has a November 30 year-end.

Required

Part 1

Record the following entries:

    a. Issuance of the bonds on October 1, 2017,

    b. Adjusting entry to accrue bond interest and discount amortization on November 30, 2017,

    c. Payment of interest on October 1, 2018.

Part 2

Show how the bond will appear on the balance sheet under non-current liabilities at November 30, 2021.

Exercise 14-13 **Journal entries for bond issuances** LO5,6

CHECK FIGURE: b. Premium = $24,000

On January 1, 2017, Ultra Vision Corp. issued $1,200,000 of 20-year 8% bonds that pay interest semiannually on June 30 and December 31. Assume the bonds were sold at (1) 98; and (2) 102. Journalize the issuance of the bonds at 98 and 102.

Exercise 14-14 **Calculating the present value of a bond and recording the issuance** LO4,6

CHECK FIGURE: e. Cash = $179,402

Point North Inc. issued bonds on September 1, 2017, with a par value of $150,000. The bonds mature in 15 years and pay 8% annual interest in two semiannual payments. On the issue date, the annual market rate of interest for the bonds turned out to be 6%.

    a. What is the semiannual interest payment for these bonds?

    b. How many semiannual interest payments will be made on these bonds over their life?

    c. Use the information about the interest rates to decide whether the bonds were issued at par, at a discount, or at a premium.

    d. Calculate the issue price of the bonds on September 1, 2017.

    e. Present the journal entry that would be made to record the bonds' issuance.

Exercise 14-15 **Allocation of interest for bonds sold at a premium** LO6

CHECK FIGURE: b. Total interest expense = $247,394

Tahoe Tent Ltd. issued bonds with a par value of $800,000 on January 1, 2017. The annual contract rate on the bonds was 12%, and the interest is paid semiannually. The bonds mature after three years. The annual market interest rate at the date of issuance was 10%, and the bonds were sold for $840,606.

    a. What is the amount of the original premium on these bonds?

    b. How much total bond interest expense will be recognized over the life of these bonds?

    c. Present an amortization table for these bonds (similar to Exhibit 14.15); use the effective interest method of allocating the interest and amortizing the premium.

Exercise 14-16 Amortization of bond premium LO6

CHECK FIGURES: a. $1,583,802 (PV tables) or $1,583,736 (calculator); b. Total interest expense = $651,198 (PV tables) or $651,264 (calculator)

On October 1, 2017, Ross Wind Energy Inc. issued a $1,500,000, 7%, seven-year bond. Interest is to be paid annually each October 1.

Required

    a. Calculate the issue price of the bond assuming a market interest rate of 6% on the date of the bond issue.

    b. Using the effective interest method, prepare an amortization schedule similar to Exhibit 14.15.

Exercise 14-17 Recording bonds issued at a premium LO6

Refer to the amortization schedule prepared in Exercise 14-16. Assume a November 30 year-end.

Required

Part 1

Record the following entries:

    a. Issuance of the bonds on October 1, 2017

    b. Adjusting entry to accrue bond interest and premium amortization on November 30, 2017

    c. Payment of interest on October 1, 2018

Part 2

Show how the bond will appear on the balance sheet under non-current liabilities at November 30, 2021.

Exercise 14-18 Amortization of bond premium LO4,6

CHECK FIGURES: a. $836,811 (PV tables) or $836,796 (calculator); b. Total interest expense: $280,689 (PV tables) or $280,704 (calculator)

On October 1, 2017, Best Biopharma Inc. issued a $750,000, 7%, seven-year bond. Interest is to be paid annually each October 1.

Required

    a. Calculate the issue price of the bond assuming a market interest rate of 5%.

    b. Prepare an amortization schedule similar to Exhibit 14.15 using the effective interest method.

Exercise 14-19 Recording bonds issued at a premium LO6

Refer to the amortization schedule prepared in Exercise 14-18. Assume a November 30 year-end.

Required

Part 1

Record the following entries:

    a. Issuance of the bonds on October 1, 2017

    b. Adjusting entry to accrue bond interest and premium amortization on November 30, 2017

    c. Payment of interest on October 1, 2018

Part 2

Show how the bond will appear on the balance sheet under non-current liabilities at November 30, 2022.

Exercise 14-20 Retiring bonds for cash LO7

CHECK FIGURE: c. Loss = $3,400

Solar Energy Inc. issued a $900,000, 5%, five-year bond on October 1, 2017. Interest is paid annually each October 1. Solar's year-end is December 31.

Required Using the amortization schedule provided below, record the entry to retire the bonds on October 1, 2020, for cash of:

a. $881,000   b. $883,500   c. $886,900

Period Ending	Cash Interest Paid	Period Interest Expense	Discount Amort.	Unamortized Discount	Carrying Value
Oct. 1/17				$37,911	$862,089
Oct. 1/18	$ 45,000	$ 51,725	$ 6,725	31,186	868,814
Oct. 1/19	45,000	52,129	7,129	24,057	875,943
Oct. 1/20	45,000	52,557	7,557	16,500	883,500
Oct. 1/21	45,000	53,010	8,010	8,490	891,510
Oct. 1/22	45,000	53,490	8,490	-0-	900,000
	$225,000	$262,911	$37,911		

Exercise 14-21 Conversion of bonds payable LO7

Computalog Inc. showed the following on its December 31, 2017, balance sheet:

Bonds payable, convertible $4,000,000
Less: Unamortized discount 14,400 $3,985,600

Required

1. Assuming the bonds are convertible into 400,000 common shares, journalize the conversion on January 1, 2018, when the market value per common share was $10.25.

2. How will the conversion of bonds into common shares affect the elements of the balance sheet (assets, liabilities, equity)?

Exercise 14-22 Conversion of bonds payable LO7

Trilium Gold Inc.'s December 31, 2017, adjusted trial balance shows the following:

Account Description	Balance*
Bonds payable, convertible	$1,050,000
Premium on bonds payable	14,000

*Assume normal balances.

Required

1. What is the carrying value of the bonds on December 31, 2017?

2. The bonds were converted into 105,000 common shares on January 1, 2018. Journalize the entry assuming the market value per common share on this date was $9.10.

Exercise 14-23 Installment note with payments of accrued interest and equal amounts of principal LO8

CHECK FIGURE: b. Total interest expense = $11,250

On December 31, 2017, Sack Port Ventures Inc. borrowed $90,000 by signing a four-year, 5% instalment note. The note requires annual payments of accrued interest and equal amounts of principal on December 31 of each year from 2018 through 2021.

    a. How much principal will be included in each of the four payments?

    b. Prepare an amortization table for this instalment note like the one presented in Exhibit 14.18.

Exercise 14-24 Journal entries for an instalment note with payments of accrued interest and equal amounts of principal LO8

Use the data in Exercise 14-23 to prepare journal entries that Sack Port Ventures Inc. would make to record the loan on December 31, 2017, and the four payments starting on December 31, 2018, through the final payment on December 31, 2021.

Exercise 14-25 Installment note with equal payments LO8

CHECK FIGURE: b. Total interest expense = $12,804

On December 31, 2017, KEC Environmental Corp. borrowed $100,000 by signing a four-year, 5% instalment note. The note requires four equal payments of accrued interest and principal on December 31 of each year from 2018 through 2021.

    a. Calculate the size of each of the four equal payments.

    b. Prepare an amortization table for this instalment note like the one presented in Exhibit 14.19.

Exercise 14-26 Journal entries for an instalment note with equal payments LO8

Use the data in Exercise 14-25 to prepare journal entries that KEC Environmental Corp. would make to record the loan on December 31, 2017, and the four payments starting on December 31, 2018, through the final payment on December 31, 2021.

Exercise 14-27 Liabilities from leasing LO9

CHECK FIGURES: a. $27,294; c. $2,729 interest

On December 31, 2017, a day when the available interest rate was 10%, Valcent Products Inc. leased equipment with an eight-year life. The contract called for a $7,200 annual lease payment at the end of each of the next five years, with the equipment becoming the property of the lessee at the end of that period. Prepare entries to record (a) the leasing of the equipment, (b) depreciation expense for 2018 assuming straight-line and a zero residual value, (c) the December 31, 2018, lease payment, including the recognition of interest expense on the lease liability on December 31, 2018, and (d) an amortization schedule for the lease liability.

Exercise 14-28 Calculate debt to equity ratio LO10

For Solar Industries and its related, but separate financing company, Solar Financing Corp, calculate the debt to equity ratio for 2016 and 2017. Explain why there are such significant differences in the ratios.

	Solar Industries (in millions)		Solar Financing Corp (in millions)	
	2017	2016	2017	2016
Total Debt (A)	42,850	36,700	88,760	76,452
Total Equity (B)..............................	20,502	23,955	8,470	7,454

Problems

Problem 14-1A **Calculating bond prices and recording issuance with journal entries** LO3,5,6

CHECK FIGURES: 1a. $275,712; 2a. $240,000; 3a. $210,091

Quetzal Energy Inc. issued bonds on January 1, 2017, that pay interest semiannually on June 30 and December 31. The par value of the bonds is $240,000, the annual contract rate is 8%, and the bonds mature in 10 years.

Required For each of these three situations, (a) determine the issue price of the bonds and (b) show the journal entry that would record the issuance, assuming the market interest rate at the date of issuance was

1. 6%

2. 8%

3. 10%

Problem 14-2A **Allocating bond interest and amortizing a bond discount** LO4,5   e**X**cel

CHECK FIGURE: 1. $139,469 (PV tables) or $139,470 (calculator)

Banjo Education Corp. issued a 4%, $150,000 bond that pays interest semiannually each June 30 and December 31. The date of issuance was January 1, 2017. The bonds mature after four years. The market interest rate was 6%. Banjo Education Corp.'s year-end is December 31.

Required

Preparation Component:

1. Calculate the issue price of the bond.

2. Prepare a general journal entry to record the issuance of the bonds.

3. Determine the total bond interest expense that will be recognized over the life of these bonds.

4. Prepare the first two years of an amortization table based on the effective interest method.

5. Present the journal entries Banjo would make to record the first two interest payments.

Analysis Component: Now assume that the market interest rate on January 1, 2017, was 3% instead of 6%. Without presenting any specific numbers, describe how this change would affect the amounts presented on Banjo's financial statements.

Problem 14-3A **Amortization of bond discount—using business calculator PV function** LO4,5   e**X**cel

CHECK FIGURES: a. $526,929 b. Total interest expense = $207,471

On June 1, 2017, JetCom Inventors Inc. issued a $540,000 12%, three-year bond. Interest is to be paid semiannually beginning December 1, 2017.

Required

    a. Calculate the issue price of the bond assuming a market interest rate of 13%.

    b. Using the effective interest method, prepare an amortization schedule similar to Exhibit 14.10.

Problem 14-4A **Recording bonds issued at a discount** LO5

CHECK FIGURES: 1a. Cash = $526,929; 1b. Cash = $32,400

Refer to the amortization schedule prepared in Problem 14-3A. Assume JetCom Inc. has a January 31 year-end.

Required

Part 1

Record the following entries:

    a. Issuance of the bonds on June 1, 2017

    b. Payment of interest on December 1, 2017

    c. Adjusting entry to accrue bond interest and discount amortization on January 31, 2018

    d. Payment of interest on June 1, 2018

Part 2

Show how the bonds will appear on the balance sheet under non-current liabilities at January 31, 2019.

Problem 14-5A Bond premium amortization and finding the present value of remaining cash flows LO6 e**X**cel

CHECK FIGURE: 2. Total interest expense = $182,185

Calculations Marketing Inc. issued 8.5% bonds with a par value of $450,000 and a five-year life on January 1, 2017, for $459,125. The bonds pay interest on June 30 and December 31. The market interest rate was 8% on the original issue date.

Required

1. Calculate the total bond interest expense over the life of the bonds.

2. Prepare an amortization table using the effective interest method similar to Exhibit 14.15.

3. Show the journal entries that Calculations Marketing Inc. would make to record the first two interest payments assuming a December 31 year-end.

4. Use the original market interest rate to calculate the present value of the remaining cash flows for these bonds as of December 31, 2019. Compare your answer with the amount shown on the amortization table as the balance for that date and explain your findings.

Problem 14-6A Bonds issued at a premium and discount (using business calculator PV function) LO4,5,6 e**X**cel

CHECK FIGURES: 1a. = $615,986; 2a. = $592,200

On March 1, 2017, Quinto Mining Inc. issued a $600,000, 8%, three-year bond. Interest is payable semiannually beginning September 1, 2017.

Required

Part 1

    a. Calculate the bond issue price assuming a market interest rate of 7% on the date of issue.

    b. Using the effective interest method, prepare an amortization schedule.

    c. Record the entry for the issuance of the bond on March 1, the adjusting entry to accrue bond interest and related amortization on April 30, 2017, Quinto's year-end, and the payment of interest on September 1, 2017.

Part 2

    a. Calculate the bond issue price assuming a market interest rate of 8.5% on the date of issue.

    b. Using the effective interest method, prepare an amortization schedule.

    c. Record the entries for the issuance of the bond on March 1; the adjusting entry to accrue bond interest and related amortization on April 30, 2017, Quinto's year-end; and the payment of interest on September 1, 2017.

    d. Record the entries for the retirement of 30% of the bonds at 102, on September 1, 2017, after the interest payment.

Problem 14-7A **Recording bonds** LO5,6,7

Mahalo Boat Adventure Inc. has a July 31 year-end. It showed the following partial amortization schedules regarding two bond issues:

Bond Issue A

Period Ending	(A) Cash Interest Paid $680,000 × 9% × 6/12	(B) Period Interest Expense (E) × 8% × 6/12	(C) Amort. (A) − (B)	(D) Unamortized Balance	(E) Carrying Value $680,000 ÷ (D)
June 1/17				$43,042	$723,042
Dec. 1/17	$ 30,600	$ 28,922	$ 1,678	41,364	721,364
Dec. 1/23	30,600	27,913	2,687	15,137	695,137
June 1/24	30,600	27,805	2,795	12,342	692,342
Dec. 1/24	30,600	27,694	2,906	9,436	689,436
June 1/25	30,600	27,577	3,023	6,413	686,413
Dec. 1/25	30,600	27,457	3,143	3,270	683,270
June 1/26	30,600	27,330	3,270	-0-	680,000
Totals	**$550,800**	**$507,758**	**$43,042**		

Bond Issue B

Period Ending	(A) Cash Interest Paid $540,000 × 8% × 3/12	(B) Period Interest Expense (E) × 8.5% × 3/12	(C) Amort. (A) − (B)	(D) Unamortized Balance	(E) Carrying Value $540,000 − (D)
Apr. 1/15				$18,067	$521,933
Jul. 1/15	$ 10,800	$ 11,091	$ 291	17,776	522,224
Apr. 1/23	10,800	11,359	559	4,918	535,082
Jul. 1/23	10,800	11,370	570	4,348	535,652
Oct. 1/23	10,800	11,383	583	3,765	536,235
Jan. 1/24	10,800	11,395	595	3,170	536,830
Apr. 1/24	10,800	11,408	608	2,562	537,438
Jul. 1/24	10,800	11,421	621	1,941	538,059
Oct. 1/24	10,800	11,434	634	1,307	538,693
Jan. 1/25	10,800	11,447	647	660	539,340
Apr. 1/25	10,800	11,460*	660	-0-	540,000
Totals	**$432,000**	**$450,067**	**$18,067**		

*Adjusted for rounding

Required Answer the following for each bond issue:

    a. Were the bonds issued at a premium and/or discount?

    b. Journalize the issuance of bond issue A and B on June 1, 2017, and April 1, 2015, respectively.

    c. What is the contract interest rate for each bond issue?

    d. Interest of how much is paid how often for each bond issue?

    e. What is the term of each bond issue?

    f. Show how each of the bonds would appear on the balance sheet under non-current liabilities at July 31, 2023.

    g. Calculate the total bond interest expense that would appear on the income statement for the year ended July 31, 2024.

    h. Independent of (a) through (g), assume both bond issues were retired on December 1, 2024, at 97. Record the entries.

Problem 14-8A Installment notes LO8 e**X**cel

CHECK FIGURE: 2. Total interest expense = $31,696

On November 30, 2017, Calla Resources Ltd. borrowed $100,000 from a bank by signing a four-year instalment note bearing interest at 12%. The terms of the note require equal payments each year on November 30, starting November 30, 2018.

Required

1. Calculate the size of each instalment payment.

2. Complete an instalment note amortization schedule for this note similar to Exhibit 14.19.

3. Present the journal entries that Calla would make to record accrued interest as of December 31, 2017 (the end of the annual reporting period), and the first payment on the note.

4. Now assume that the note does not require equal payments but does require four payments that include accrued interest and an equal amount of principal in each payment. Complete an instalment note amortization schedule for this note similar to Exhibit 14.18. Present the journal entries that Calla would make to record accrued interest as of December 31, 2017 (the end of the annual reporting period), and the first payment on the note.

Problem 14-9A Lease liabilities LO9

CHECK FIGURE: 2. Total interest expense = $28,880

Laporte Engineering Company leased a machine on January 1, 2017, under a contract calling for four annual payments of $30,000 on December 31, 2017 through 2020. The machine becomes the property of the lessee after the fourth payment. The machine was predicted to have a service life of six years and no residual value, and the interest rate available to Laporte Engineering was 12% on the day the lease was signed. The machine was delivered on January 10, 2017, and was immediately placed in service.

Required

1. Determine the initial net liability created by the lease and the cost of the leased asset.

2. Prepare a table showing the calculation of the amount of interest expense allocated to each year the lease is in effect and the carrying amount of the liability at the end of each of those years.

3. Prepare the entry to record the leasing of the machine.

4. Prepare entries that would be made on December 31, 2018, to record the annual depreciation on a straight-line basis, and the recording of the lease payment. Also show how the machine and the lease liability should appear on the December 31, 2018, balance sheet.

Alternate Problems

Problem 14-1B **Calculating bond prices and recording issuance with journal entries** LO3,5,6

CHECK FIGURES: 1a. $113,592; 2a. $100,000; 3a. $88,530

Goth Inc. issued a group of bonds on January 1, 2017, that pay interest semiannually on June 30 and December 31. The par value of the bonds is $100,000, the annual contract rate is 10%, and the bonds mature in 10 years.

Required For each of these three situations, (a) determine the issue price of the bonds, and (b) show the journal entry that would record the issuance, assuming the market interest rate at the date of issuance was:

1. 8%   **2.** 10%   **3.** 12%

Problem 14-2B **Allocating interest and amortizing a bond discount (using business calculator PV function)** LO4,5 e**X**cel

CHECK FIGURE: 1. Cash = $922,428

Wind-Electric Corp. issued $940,000 of bonds that pay 9.7% annual interest with two semiannual payments. The date of issuance was January 1, 2017, and the interest is paid on June 30 and December 31. The bonds mature after 10 years and were issued at the price of $922,428. The market interest rate was 10% and the company uses the effective interest method of amortization.

Required

1. Show how the bond price was determined and prepare a general journal entry to record the issuance of the bonds.

2. Determine the total bond interest expense that will be recognized over the life of these bonds.

3. Prepare the first two lines of an amortization table based on the effective interest method.

4. Present the journal entries that Wind-Electric Corp. would make to record the first two interest payments.

Problem 14-3B **Amortization of bond premium—using business calculator PV function** LO4,6 e**X**cel

CHECK FIGURES: a. $418,089; b. Total interest expense = $221,911

On September 1, 2017, Messner Corp. issued a $400,000, 15%, four-year bond. Interest is payable semiannually beginning March 1, 2018.

Required

    a. Calculate the bond issue price assuming a market interest rate of 13.5% on the date of issue.

    b. Using the effective interest method, prepare an amortization schedule similar to Exhibit 14.15.

Problem 14-4B Recording bonds issued at a premium LO6

CHECK FIGURES: 1a. Cash = $418,089; 1c. Cash = $30,000

Refer to the amortization schedule prepared in Problem 14-3B. Assume a January 31 year-end.

Required

Part 1

Record the following entries:

    a. Issuance of the bonds on September 1, 2017

    b. Adjusting entry to accrue bond interest and premium amortization on January 31, 2018

    c. Payment of interest on March 1, 2018

Part 2

Show how the bond will appear on the balance sheet under non-current liabilities at January 31, 2020.

Problem 14-5B Bond discount amortization and finding the present value of remaining cash flows using business calculator PV function LO4,5 eXcel

CHECK FIGURE: 2. Total interest expense = $298,903

Westgate Motor Homes Inc. issued bonds with a par value of $680,000 and a five-year life on January 1, 2017. The bonds pay interest on June 30 and December 31. The contract interest rate is 8%. The market interest rate was 9% on the original issue date.

Required

1. Calculate the issue price and the total bond interest expense over the life of the bonds.

2. Prepare an amortization table using the effective interest method similar to Exhibit 14.10.

3. Show the journal entries that Westgate would make to record the first two interest payments. Assume a December 31 year-end.

4. Use the original market interest rate to calculate the present value of the remaining cash flows for these bonds as of December 31, 2019. Compare your answer with the amount shown on the amortization table as the balance for that date, and explain your findings.

Problem 14-6B Bonds issued at a discount and premium using business calculator PV function LO4,5,6 eXcel

CHECK FIGURES: 1a. $883,157; 2a. $908,561

On February 1, 2017, Fireside Corp. issued a $900,000, 5%, two-year bond. Interest is payable quarterly each May 1, August 1, November 1, and February 1.

Required

Part 1

    a. Calculate the bond issue price assuming a market interest rate of 6% on the date of issue.

    b. Using the effective interest method, prepare an amortization schedule.

  c. Record the entry for the issuance of the bond on February 1; the adjusting entry to accrue bond interest and related amortization on March 31, 2017, Fireside Corp.'s year-end; and the payment of interest on May 1, 2017.

  d. Record the entry for the retirement of the shares at 101, on February 1, 2018, one year early, and after the interest payment.

Part 2

  a. Calculate the bond issue price assuming a market interest rate of 4.5% on the date of issue.

  b. Using the effective interest method, prepare an amortization schedule.

  c. Record the entries for the issuance of the bond on February 1; the adjusting entry to accrue bond interest and related amortization on March 31, 2017, Fireside Corp.'s year-end; and the payment of interest on May 1, 2017.

Problem 14-7B Recording bonds LO5,6,7

Dimensional Media Inc. has a December 31 year-end. It showed the following partial amortization schedules regarding its two bond issues:

Bond Issue 1

Period Ending	Cash Interest Paid	Period Interest Expense	Amortization	Unamortized Balance	Carrying Value
Sept. 1/18.........................				$26,571	$623,429
Dec. 1/18.........................	$ 11,375	$ 12,469	$ 1,094	25,477	624,523
Dec. 1/22.........................	11,375	12,876	1,501	4,685	645,315
Mar. 1/23.........................	11,375	12,906	1,531	3,154	646,846
June 1/23.........................	11,375	12,937	1,562	1,592	648,408
Sept. 1/23.........................	11,375	12,967*	1,592	-0-	650,000
Totals.................................	$227,500	$254,071	$26,571		

*Adjusted for rounding.

Bond Issue 2

Period Ending	Cash Interest Paid	Period Interest Expense	Amortization	Unamortized Balance	Carrying Value
May 1/17.........................				$20,763	$800,763
Nov. 1/17.........................	$ 42,900	$ 42,040	$ 860	19,903	799,903
May 1/18.........................	42,900	41,995	905	18,998	798,998
Nov. 1/22.........................	42,900	41,465	1,435	8,384	788,384
May 1/23.........................	42,900	41,390	1,510	6,874	786,874
Nov. 1/23.........................	42,900	41,311	1,589	5,285	785,285
May 1/24.........................	42,900	41,227	1,673	3,612	783,612
Nov. 1/24.........................	42,900	41,140	1,760	1,852	781,852
May 1/25.........................	42,900	41,048*	1,852	-0-	780,000
Totals.................................	$686,400	$665,637	$20,763		

*Adjusted for rounding.

Required Answer the following for each bond issue:

    a. Were the bonds issued at a premium and/or discount?

    b. Journalize the issuance of bond issue 1 and 2 on September 1, 2018, and May 1, 2017, respectively.

    c. What is the contract interest rate for each bond issue?

    d. What was the market interest rate at issuance for each bond?

    e. Interest of how much is paid how often for each bond issue?

    f. What is the term of each bond issue?

    g. Show how each of the bonds would appear on the balance sheet at December 31, 2022.

    h. Calculate the total bond interest expense that would appear on the income statement for the year ended December 31, 2023.

    i. Independent of (a) through (h), assume both bond issues were retired on December 1, 2022, at 101. Record the entries.

Problem 14-8B **Installment notes** LO8 e**X**cel

CHECK FIGURE: 2. Total interest expense = $135,896

On May 31, 2017, Iceflow Technologies Inc. borrowed $400,000 from a bank by signing a four-year instalment note bearing interest at 14%. The terms of the note require equal semiannual payments each year beginning on November 30, 2017.

Required

1. Calculate the size of each instalment payment.

2. Complete an instalment note amortization schedule for this note similar to Exhibit 14.19.

3. Present the journal entries that Iceflow Technologies would make to record the first payment on the note, the accrued interest as of December 31, 2017 (the end of the annual reporting period), and the second payment on the note.

4. Now assume that the note does not require equal payments but does require eight payments that include accrued interest and an equal amount of principal in each payment. Complete an instalment note amortization schedule for this note similar to Exhibit 14.18. Present the journal entries that Iceflow would make to record the first payment on the note and the accrued interest as of December 31, 2017 (the end of the annual reporting period).

Problem 14-9B **Lease liabilities** LO9

CHECK FIGURE: 2. Total interest expense = $90,845

Peerless Carpet Corp. leased a machine on January 1, 2017, under a contract calling for six annual payments of $60,000 on December 31, 2017 through 2022. The machine becomes the property of the lessee after the sixth payment. The machine was predicted to have a service life of seven years and no residual value, and the interest rate available to Peerless for equipment loans was 9% on the day the lease was signed. The machine was delivered on January 8, 2017, and was immediately placed in service.

Required

1. Determine the initial net liability created by the lease and the cost of the leased asset.

2. Prepare a table showing the calculation of the amount of interest expense allocated to each year the lease is in effect and the carrying amount of the liability at the end of each of those years.

3. Prepare the entry to record the leasing of the machine.

4. Prepare entries that would be made on December 31, 2018, to record the annual depreciation on a straight-line basis, and the recording of the lease payment. Also show how the machine and the lease liability should appear on the December 31, 2018, balance sheet.

Ethics Challenge

EC 14-1

A few years ago, politicians needed a new headquarters building for their municipal government. The price tag for the building approached $24 million. The politicians felt that the voters were unlikely to approve a bond issue to raise money for the headquarters since approving the bond issue would cause taxes to increase. The politicians opted for a different approach. They had a bank issue $24 million worth of securities to pay for the construction of the building. The municipality then agreed to make a yearly lease payment (comprising repayment of principal and interest) to repay the obligation. Unlike conventional municipal bonds, the lease payments are not binding obligations on the municipal government and, therefore, no voter approval is required.

Required

1. Do you think the actions of the politicians and the investment bankers were ethical in this situation?

2. How does the security issued to pay for the building compare in riskiness to a regular municipal bond issued by a municipal government?

Focus on Financial Statements

FFS 14-1

ZedCon Inc. intends to raise $10,000,000 for the purpose of expanding operations internationally. Two options are available:

- Plan 1: Issue $10,000,000 of 5% bonds payable due in 2027, or
- Plan 2: Issue 100,000 common shares at $100 per share.

The expansion is expected to generate additional annual profit before interest and tax of $800,000. ZedCon's tax rate is 35%. The assumed adjusted trial balance at December 31, 2018, one year after the expansion under each of Plan 1 and Plan 2, is shown below:

Account	Balance* Plan 1	Balance* Plan 2
Accounts payable	$ 33,000	$ 33,000
Accounts receivable	48,000	48,000
Accumulated depreciation, buildings	78,000	78,000
Accumulated depreciation, equipment	202,000	202,000
Accumulated depreciation, international assets	100,000	100,000
Additional profit as a result of expansion	800,000	800,000
Allowance for doubtful accounts	5,200	5,200
Bad debt expense	3,200	3,200
Bonds payable	10,000,000	-0-
Buildings	150,000	150,000
Cash	312,800	812,800
Cash dividends	92,000	92,000
Cash over/short	100	100
Common shares (1,000 shares issued and outstanding)**	100,000	–
Common shares (101,000 shares issued and outstanding)**	–	10,100,000
Cost of goods sold	48,000	48,000
Delivery expense	700	700
Depreciation expense	127,000	127,000
Dividends payable	31,000	31,000
Equipment	273,000	273,000
Revenue	1,050,000	1,050,000
Income tax expense	?	?
Income tax payable	?	?
Interest expense	506,100	6,100
Interest receivable	300	300
Interest income	800	800
International property, plant, and equipment assets	10,000,000	10,000,000
Land	32,000	32,000
Merchandise inventory	32,000	32,000
Mortgage payable ($14,000 due in 2019)	60,000	60,000
Notes receivable, due October 2022	14,000	14,000
Patent	7,000	7,000
Petty cash	800	800
Retained earnings	25,600	25,600
Salaries expense	916,000	916,000
Sales	59,000	59,000
Sales discounts	1,400	1,400
Unearned revenue	19,000	19,000

*Assume normal account balances.
**Assume all shares were outstanding for the entire year.

Required

Preparation Component:

1. Prepare a single-step income statement for 2018 (showing salaries expense, depreciation expense, cost of goods sold, interest expense, and other expenses) and a classified balance sheet at December 31, 2018, assuming:

    a. Plan 1, and then   b. Plan 2.

Analysis Component: Which financing plan should ZedCon Inc. choose assuming its goal is to:

  a. Maximize earnings per share, or

  b. Maximize profit.

Explain your answers showing any relevant calculations (rounded to the nearest whole cent).

FFS 14-2

Required Answer the following questions by referring to the 2014 financial statements for each of **Danier** and WestJet in Appendix II.

1. How much of Danier's total assets are financed by debt? by equity?

2. How much long-term debt does WestJet report on its balance sheet?

3. How much of WestJet's total assets are financed by debt? by equity?

4. Which of the two companies has the stronger balance sheet?* Is it reasonable to compare these two balance sheets? Why or why not?

*When a balance sheet is said to have been strengthened, it means, in general, that total liabilities (or risk associated with debt financing) have decreased and equity has increased.

Critical Thinking Mini Case

5-Star Adventures Inc. financed its $1,000,000 expansion by issuing on January 1, 2017, a 5%, 10-year bond dated the same day with annual interest payments to be made each December 31. The market interest rate at the time of issue was 7%. Assume that you are the chief financial officer of 5-Star Adventures. At the December 31, 2018, board meeting, a draft set of financial statements was presented for the board's review and a major shareholder immediately said: "The $1,000,000 bond payable is reported on the December 31, 2018, draft balance sheet as $869,695 and the income statement reports bond interest expense of $50,000. In Note 7 to the financial statements it indicates that total interest expense to be recognized over the 10-year term on this bond is $500,000. This doesn't make sense to me."

Required Using the elements of critical thinking described on the inside front cover, respond. Consider the following subheadings to organize your response, and include an amortization table to show the total interest expense.

- Problem
- Goal
- Principles
- Facts
- Conclusions

Accounting for Debt and Share Investments

A Look Back

Chapter 14 investigated the issues around recognition and measurement of non-current liabilities, including accounting treatment over corporate bonds.

A Look at This Chapter

This chapter focuses on the recording and reporting of corporate investments in debt and shares.

Photo Courtesy of The Farmery

LEARNING OBJECTIVES

LO1 Describe and explain the purpose of debt and share investments.

LO2 Identify and describe the investment classifications.

LO3 Account for and report non-strategic investments.

LO4 Account for investments in associates.

LO5 Describe the accounting for business combinations.

The Farmery—Grown from the Ground Up

Two restaurateurs and brothers from Manitoba, Chris and Lawrence Warwaruk, have a big dream to turn their family farm into the first Canadian estate brewery.

Their partnership story goes back to the late 1990s when the family farm was facing bankruptcy. The two brothers moved to Winnipeg to assess their future and decided to start a high-end four-star restaurant called LuxSole. With the profits, the brothers purchased a family farm in their hometown community two hours north of Winnipeg. Ten years later they opened Luxalune Gastropub in Winnipeg, a pub with over 100 beer varieties.

Over beer one night, according to Chris, they had an "aha moment." Why not make their own beer? Why not sell their own beer? With a passion for their farm-to-glass initiative, the brothers decided to close LuxSole to focus on the Farmery Brewery and developed the motto "grown from the ground up." The brothers wanted to go back to their farming roots and utilize the family farmland to grow barley and establish hop yards to make their own craft beer, Farmery.

When *Dragons' Den* was holding auditions in Winnipeg, Lawrence's wife suggested they take the Farmery concept to the show. Realizing the opportunity and great timing, they scrambled to get their beer and marketing together. On hearing of the Farmery's audition, the Winnipeg Free Press did a one-page feature article on the brewery, providing free marketing and credibility to their concept. How would the Dragons respond? With overwhelming support. The Dragons loved both the product concept and the beer's outstanding flavour. The business-savvy entrepreneurs asked the Dragons for $200,000 for a 20% stake in Farmery Inc. In their presentation to the Dragons, the brothers estimated they would reach sales of $150,000 in the first few months and expected to hit $1.5 million in revenue within a year.

The Farmery brothers preferred not to give up equity at such an early phase of the business. After suggesting to the Dragons that they would prefer a royalty arrangement, they received two solid offers:

1) Jim Treliving asked for a 7% royalty on the $200,000 investment.
2) David Chilton and Arlene Dickinson offered a 6% royalty on the $200,000 investment.

The business partners were not only looking for an investment, but also wanted to select the investors who would provide valuable advice and guidance to take their craft brewery to the next level. Although both proposals were attractive, they opted for the 6% royalty on the $200,000 investment based on their perceived better fit with Chilton and Dickinson.

The brewery experienced strong sales in the next few months over its first summer and, to avoid committing to a lifelong royalty arrangement, the brothers decided to build the company themselves, using a model of self-financed, calculated growth, rather than accepting money from the Dragons. Chilton graciously offered to continue to mentor the brothers without a financial stake in the business because he believed in the brothers and their product.

Besides the mentorship opportunity, according to Chris, each time the *Dragons' Den* episode airs, they see their website traffic go through the roof. The brothers value the marketing the show has provided them: "It gives us the extra edge needed for the consumer to pause and recognize the brand and our "homegrown" vision, encouraging them to consider purchasing our product." Domestic and imported beer markets are falling; the growth is in craft breweries as consumers are opting to purchase higher quality beer in smaller quantities than in the past. The brothers plan to stay cautious as the company expands so their brand message is clear and to ensure the business is able to meet cash flow and inventory needs. They have now launched in Saskatchewan and Alberta and are continuing their calculated expansion plans across the country.

Chris and Lawrence process their home-grown ingredients for the beer in an Ontario facility, paying shipping charges and a manufacturing premium to have it processed externally. They are now working on the next phase—to build a destination brewery on the family farm. Using an estate brewery model, they want to attract people to the farm to enable customers to experience the farm-to-bottle initiative. They advise future entrepreneurs, "If you have a passion and a dream, just stick to it, fight for it, and never give up. If something knocks you down get up and get back to it."

Sources: www.farmery.ca; Interview with Chris Warwick, May 15, 2015.

Video Links: CBC Interview on LuxSole: https://www.youtube.com/watch?v=__AO8vkzT70
Dragons' Den Episode: https://www.youtube.com/watch?v=y5ZWRAXHSJ0

How would a corporation, such as Arlene Dickinson's investment company, account for investment income when purchasing shares in a new start-up company, as is often featured on *Dragons' Den*?

CHAPTER PREVIEW

This chapter focuses on the recording and reporting of investments in debt and shares. Many companies have investments in the form of debt and shares issued by other companies. Our understanding of the topics in this chapter is important to our ability to read and interpret financial statements.

Purpose of Debt and Share Investments

LO1 Describe and explain the purpose of debt and share investments.

Corporations frequently purchase debt and shares of other corporations. These are called **intercorporate investments**. A **debt investment** (or **debt security**) such as a bond represents an amount owed and arises when one company lends money to another. A share investment (or equity security) represents one company's purchase of the shares of another company. The company that purchases as an investment the debt or shares of another is called the **investor**, and the company whose debt (i.e., bonds) or shares (common or preferred) are being purchased is called the **investee**. For instance, if you own shares in WestJet, then you are the investor and WestJet is the investee. The Dragons featured on CBC's *Dragons' Den* have investment companies that hold equity investments in numerous start-up companies.

Investments are made in other corporations for various reasons. Examples include:

Non-Strategic Investments

- To earn greater interest or dividend income on available excess cash than can be earned by leaving the cash in a typical bank account
- To earn investment income over the original purchase price on the eventual sale of purchased shares
- To earn interest on debt held for its contract life.

Strategic Investments

- To participate in new markets or new technologies
- To build a favourable business relationship, generally with a major customer or supplier
- To achieve non-controlling interest with the investee by acquiring enough shares to be influential to the investee's operating, financing, and investing decisions
- To acquire a controlling interest in the investee

An investor who has made a **non-strategic investment** cannot significantly influence or control the operations of the investee company. A **strategic investment** has occurred when the investee is controlled by the investor (known as a *business combination*), is significantly influenced by the investor (known as an *investment in an associate*), or is in a joint arrangement with the investor. In order to account for investments, we must understand how equity and debt investments are classified. This is the topic of the next section.

946

Classification of Investments

Non-strategic investments are of two types: debt investments and share investments. A company with excess cash arising from, for example, seasonal sales fluctuations may wish to earn a higher return than might be realized by holding the cash in a bank account. If the company's excess cash is available for a short period of time, it will typically invest in debt investments with low risk and high liquidity that generate interest income. For example, **Loblaw Companies Limited**'s December 28, 2013, balance sheet showed current investments of $290 million also consisting mostly of secure government-backed instruments. **Equity investments** are not popular as temporary because they can have greater risk than debt investments. For example, if the shares decrease in value when the company needs to liquidate the investment, a loss would be incurred.

If a company has cash available for a longer-term investment, both debt and equity investments may be considered. For example, **PMC-Sierra Inc.**'s is a semi-conductor and cloud data centre solutions innovator from Burnaby, BC. PMC-Sierra's December 27, 2014, balance sheet has $162.1 million in investments in securities with the specific note disclosure shown in Exhibit 15.1. PMC-Sierra's financial statements have been prepared in accordance with US GAAP and are presented for comparison purposes only. The term "available for sale investments" is no longer used under IFRS. Non-strategic investments are classified on the balance sheet as current investments or non-current (long-term) investments depending on how long the investment is expected to be held:

EXHIBIT 15.1

Example Disclosure for Investment in Securities

NOTE 7. INVESTMENT SECURITIES

At December 27, 2014, the Company had investments in securities of $162.1 million (December 28, 2013 – $128.9 million) comprised of money market funds, United States Treasury and Government Agency notes, Federal Deposit Insurance Corporation insured corporate notes, United States State and Municipal Securities, foreign government and agency notes, and corporate bonds and notes.

The Company's available for sale investments, by investment type, as classified on the consolidated balance sheets consist of the following as at December 27, 2014 and December 28, 2013:

(in thousands)	December 27, 2014			
	Amortized Cost	Gross Unrealized Gains*	Gross Unrealized Losses*	Fair Value
Cash equivalents:				
Money market funds	$ 8,729	$ —	$ —	$ 8,729
Total cash equivalents	8,729	—	—	8,729
Short-term investments:				
Corporate bonds and notes	43,777	498	(16)	44,259
US treasury and government agency notes	1,010	79	—	1,089
Foreign government and agency notes	501	36	—	537
Total short-term investments	45,288	613	(16)	45,885
Long-term investment securities:				
Corporate bonds and notes	61,357	28	(213)	61,172
US treasury and government agency notes	38,650	7	(76)	38,581
Foreign government and agency notes	7,563	1	(39)	7,525
US states and municipal securities	230	1	—	231
Total long-term investment securities	107,800	37	(328)	107,509
Total	$161,817	$650	$(344)	$162,123

- Gross unrealized gains include accrued interest on investments of $0.6 million, which are detailed in the Consolidated Statement of Operations. The remainder of the gross unrealized gains and losses are included [on] the Consolidated Balance Sheet as Accumulated other comprehensive income (loss).

SOURCE: PMC-Sierra. investor.pmcs.com

Strategic investments include the following three categories: *investments in associates, business combinations*, and *joint arrangements*. **Investments in associates** occur when the investor can significantly influence the strategic operating, investing, and/or financing policies of the investee. The presumed rule for determining **significant influence** is that it exists if 20% to 50% of the investee's voting shares are held by the investor. This is a *general* rule because an owner with 40% ownership could have no influence if all of the other shares were held by one owner. A **business combination** exists when the investor owns sufficient shares to control the investee's strategic operating, investing, and financing policies without the cooperation of others. Again, the *general* rule is that control exists when more than 50% of the voting shares are owned by a single investor. **Indigo Books** has a 50% equity investment in Calendar Club as disclosed in note 20 of its financial statements for the year ended March 29, 2014, shown in Exhibit 15.2.

EXHIBIT 15.2

Example Disclosure for an Investment in Associate

20. EQUITY INVESTMENT

The Company holds a 50% equity ownership in its associate, Calendar Club, to sell calendars, games, and gifts through seasonal kiosks and year-round stores in Canada. The Company uses the equity method of accounting to record Calendar Club results. In fiscal 2014, the Company received $1.2 million (2013 – $1.3 million) of distributions from Calendar Club.

The following tables represent financial information for Calendar Club along with the Company's shares therein:

	Total			Company's share		
(thousands of Canadian dollars)	March 29, 2014	March 30, 2013	April 1, 2012	March 29, 2014	March 30, 2013	April 1, 2012
Cash and cash equivalents	1,185	2,278	1,766	593	1,139	883
Total current assets	2,565	3,316	2,798	1,283	1,658	1,399
Total long-term assets	658	831	1,071	329	416	536
Total current liabilities	2,027	2,212	1,948	1,014	1,106	974

	Total		Company's share	
(thousands of Canadian dollars)	52-week period ended March 29, 2014	52-week period ended March 30, 2013	52-week period ended March 29, 2014	52-week period ended March 30, 2013
Revenue	31,003	30,543	15,502	15,272
Expenses	(29,425)	(27,914)	(14,713)	(13,957)
Net earnings	1,578	2,629	789	1,315

SOURCE: www.indigo.ca/en-ca/investor-relations/corporate-documents

---

The accounting for non-strategic and strategic investments is described in the remainder of the chapter.

 **CHECKPOINT**

1. What is the main difference between non-strategic and strategic investments?
2. How are debt investments different from equity investments?
3. Explain why the 20% to 50% rule to determine significant influence does not always hold true.

Do Quick Study questions: QS 15-1, QS 15-2

Accounting for Debt and Share Investments

Accounting for Non-Strategic Investments

LO3 Account for and report non-strategic investments.

This section explains the basics of accounting for non-strategic investments in both equity and debt securities.

Accounting for Equity Investments (Non-Strategic)

Recall that the main distinguishing feature of non-strategic equity investments is that the investor's intent is to generate profit primarily through short-term changes in fair values; the receipt of dividend income is secondary. The investor initially records non-strategic equity investments using the *fair value through profit and loss method.*[1]

- *Accounting for Initial Acquisition.* The **fair value through profit and loss method** requires that the initial purchase of non-strategic equity investments be recorded as the purchase cost. Any transaction costs, such as brokerage fees or commissions[2] are expensed directly to profit as transaction fees.

  For example, on June 2, 2017, TechCom purchased 300 Cameco Corporation common shares at $50 per share plus a $50 commission. TechCom intends to hold these shares for six to twelve months for the purpose of realizing a gain in share price fluctuation. The entry to record this purchase is:

2017				
June	2	Investment—Cameco.....................................	15,000	
		Transaction fees...	50	
		Cash..		15,050
		Purchased shares to be held as actively traded *investment; $50 × 300 shares =* *$15,000 + $50 = $15,050.*		

- *Accounting for Dividends Received.* Dividends received from investments are credited to an income statement account—Dividend Income, increasing current-period profit.

  Assume that on December 12, TechCom received a $0.40 cash dividend per share on its Cameco share investment. This dividend is credited to a revenue account as follows:

Dec.	12	Cash..	120	
		Dividend Income		120
		$0.40 × 300 shares.		

- *Accounting for Fair Value Adjustments at Period-End.* After recording the purchase, fair values must be assessed at the end of each reporting period. To calculate these **fair value adjustments**, any increases (decreases) in fair values are added to (deducted from) the investment account. Any gain (or loss) should be recognized as investment income (loss) in profit in the period in which it arises.

---

1 IFRS 2015, IFRS 9, para. 4.1.1–4.1.4.

2 IFRS 2015, IFRS 9, para. 5.1.1.

To demonstrate, assume that TechCom's investment in the Cameco shares had a fair value, on December 31, 2017, of $53. The unadjusted balance and fair value at December 31, 2017, of TechCom's investment can be summarized as follows:

	Unadjusted Balance	Fair Value	Difference
Cameco shares	$15,000	$15,900*	$900

*$53 × 300 shares = $15,900

The entry to record the year-end fair value adjustment is:

Dec.	31	Investment—Cameco.....................................	900	
		Investment Income.................................		900
		To record the investment income related to the end of period fair value adjustment. resulting from adjustment of investment to fair value.		

Because the Cameco shares increased in value, the increase is added or debited to the *Investment—Cameco* account. The result is that the Investment account will reflect December 31, 2017, fair values on the current assets section balance sheet. The net difference of the fair value adjustment is a gain of $900 that is recorded on the income statement.

On the December 31, 2017, balance sheet, TechCom would report the adjusted balance of the investment account as shown below.

Current assets:
Investment.. $15,900

Investors can obtain real-time fair values and historical price data for share and debt investments from a number of online sources such as ca.finance.yahoo.com, theglobeandmail.com, msn.com, or the Financial Post. Spin Master Corp, an international children's entertainment company, was founded over 20 years ago by two childhood friends, Ronnen Harary and Anton Rabie, shortly after graduating from University of Western Ontario. Its popular brands include Air Hogs and Bakugan, and the current children's hit TV program *Paw Patrol*. On July 30, 2015, the company issued shares under an initial public offering on the Toronto Stock Exchange under the ticker symbol TOY. The following stock history at market close Friday, July 31, 2015, a day after the company's initial public share offering, is shown in Exhibit 15.3.

Sale of Marketable Securities. Upon sale of the securities, the investment is removed from its investment account at its most recent period-end cost and the income or loss on the sale of the investment is recorded in the current-period income statement as is illustrated below.

To demonstrate the entries for the sale of actively traded equity investments, assume that on January 14, 2018, TechCom sold 200 of its Cameco shares at $52 per share and paid a commission of $90. The entry to record this is:

2018				
Jan.	14	Cash...	10,310	
		Transaction Fee	90	
		Investment Income (Loss)	200	
		Investment—Cameco		10,600
		$52 × 200 shares = $10,400 − $90 = $10,310; $15,900 × 200/300 = $10,600.		

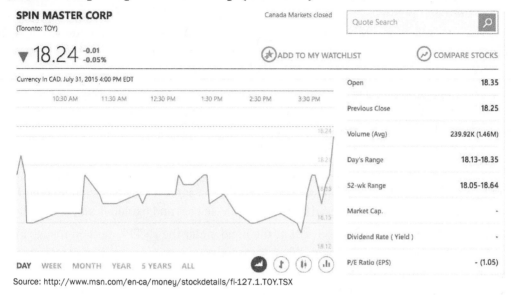

EXHIBIT 15.3

Stock Quote Example: Spin Master Corp (TSX:TOY)

Source: http://www.msn.com/en-ca/money/stockdetails/fi-127.1.TOY.TSX

Recall that the balance in *Investment—Cameco* was adjusted to $15,900 on December 31, 2017 (originally recorded at $15,000 plus fair value adjustment of $900 = $15,900). Since TechCom sold 200 of the total 300 shares, the related amounts must be removed from the accounting records. To do this, we credit *Investment—Cameco* for the proportion of the $15,900 balance sold.[3]

CHECKPOINT

4. Explain how transaction costs such as brokerage fees and commissions are accounted for regarding non-strategic equity investments.

5. How are investment income and losses upon fair value testing of actively traded investments at year-end accounted for?

Do Quick Study questions: QS 15-3, QS 15-4, QS 15-5, QS 15-6

Accounting for Debt Investments

Debt investments classified as non-strategic investments are recorded in one of three key ways, which is dependent on the business objective for holding the debt instrument:

> **1.** Debt instruments held with the business objective of collecting principal and interest payments while holding the debt for its contract life are measured using the **amortized cost method** described below. Transaction costs under amortized cost method are included in the initial cost of the investment.

---

3 An alternative calculation would be to take the $15,900 total balance and divide by 300 total shares to get an average per share of $53.00 × 200 shares sold = $10,600.

> **2.** Debt instruments held with the business objective of collecting principal and interest payments and selling the debt instruments as financial assets are recorded as **fair value through other comprehensive income** (unless irrevocably designated at FVTPL under specific conditions). This method is summarized briefly in Exhibit 15.7 and is covered more extensively in future courses in intermediate accounting. Transaction costs under this approach are added to the acquisition cost.
>
> **3.** Debt instruments held to be traded on the active market are recorded using the fair value through profit and loss method (FVTPL) illustrated in the next section. Under the fair value method, transaction costs are expensed in the current period as transaction fees.

FAIR VALUE THROUGH PROFIT AND LOSS (FVTPL) METHOD

The fair value through profit and loss method (FVTPL) is the same as the fair value method described earlier where the initial purchase is recorded as the purchase cost and excludes any transaction costs.[4]

- *Acquisition of Bond.* The acquisition cost of the bond under the FVTPL method results in a debit to the corresponding investment account. When transaction fees are incurred, we record a debit to the Transaction Fees account and a credit to Cash.

    To demonstrate, assume TechCom Company paid $29,500, plus a $120 transaction fee to buy Power Corp. 7% bonds payable with a $30,000 par value on September 1, 2017. The bonds pay interest semiannually on August 31 and February 28, and will mature on February 28, 2021. TechCom intends to trade these bonds within the next six to nine months; therefore, they are current investments as opposed to non-current investments. The entry to record this purchase is:

2017			
Sept. 1	Investment—Power Corp.	29,500	
	Transaction Fees	120	
	Cash		29,620
	Purchased bonds to be held as actively traded investments.		

- *Period-End Accrual of Interest.* At year-end, the interest earned from the acquisition date to the period-end date must be accrued with a debit to Interest Receivable and a credit to Interest Income (or debit to Investment Income (Loss) in the case of a decrease in fair value).

    On December 31, 2017, at the end of its accounting period, TechCom accrues interest receivable on the Power Corp. bond in the following entry:

Dec. 31	Interest Receivable	700	
	Interest Income		700
	$30,000 × 7% × 4/12.		

- *Period-End Fair Value Adjustment.* At the end of the reporting period, under the FVTPL method, the bond must be assessed for fair value. Any investment income or loss arising from the fair value test would be recorded on the income statement and the **carrying value** of the bond would be adjusted.

---

4   IFRS 2015, IFRS 9, para. 5.1.1. Note: The FVTPL is irrevocable once designated at initial recognition and can be selected only if doing so significantly reduces a measurement or recognition inconsistency.

On December 31, 2017, at the end of the day, the Power Corp. bond was trading for $29,600.

Investment—Power Corp.	100	
Investment Income		100

Receipt of Interest Income. Under the FVTPL method, interest income received on the bond is recorded as a debit to cash, a credit to interest receivable for the interest portion previously accrued at period-end, and the interest earned after period-end is credited to investment income.

On February 28, if TechCom Company has the Power Corp. bonds in its investment portfolio it will receive its first semiannual interest payment. Under the FVTPL method, the interest is recorded as follows:

Feb.	28	Cash	1,050	
		Interest Receivable		700
		Interest Income		350
		$30,000 × 7% × 6/12.		

AMORTIZED COST METHOD

Purchases of debt investments using the *amortized cost method* are recorded based on the present value of future cash flows discounted using the effective interest method.[5] The effective interest method was described in detail in Chapter 14. The amortized cost method records investments at cost and interest income is recorded as time passes, including any premium or discount amortization. Under the amortized cost method, transaction fees are added to the acquisition cost of the investment.

To demonstrate, assume that on January 1, 2017, Music City paid $28,477, including transaction fees to buy an 8%, three-year, Crystal Records Inc. $30,000 par value bond when the market interest rate was 10%. Interest is paid semiannually each June 30 and December 31. The amortization for this bond is shown in Exhibit 15.4. The entry to record the purchase is:

2017				
Jan.	1	Investment—Crystal Records Inc.	28,477	
		Cash		28,477
		Purchased a bond at a discount to be held for the duration of the bond's life.		

After initial recognition, an entity must measure debt investments at amortized cost using the effective interest method.[6] Therefore, on June 30, 2017, the first interest receipt date, Music City would record:

June	30	Cash	1,200	
		Investment—Crystal Records Inc.	224	
		Interest Income		1,424
		Recorded receipt of interest and amortization of bond discount using the effective interest method; $30,000 × 8% × 6/12 = $1,200; $28,477 × 10% × 6/12 = $1,424.		

The calculation of the $224 discount amortization is based on the amortization schedule using the effective interest method shown in Exhibit 15.4.[7]

---

5 IFRS 2015, IFRS 9, para. 5.4.1.
6 IFRS 2015, IFRS 9, para 4.1.2 and 5.2.1.
7 To review the concepts and calculations involved regarding bond premiums and discounts, refer to Chapter 14.

EXHIBIT 15.4

Amortization Schedule Using Effective Interest Method—Crystal Records Inc. Bond

Period Ending	Cash Interest Received	Period Interest Income	Discount Amort.	Unamortized Discount	Carrying Value
Jan. 1/17				$1,523	$28,477
June 30/17..........................	$1,200	$1,424	$ 224	1,299	28,701
Dec. 31/17..........................	1,200	1,435	235	1,064	28,936
June 30/18..........................	1,200	1,447	247	817	29,183
Dec. 31/18..........................	1,200	1,459	259	558	29,442
June 30/19..........................	1,200	1,472	272	286	29,714
Dec. 31/19..........................	1,200	1,486	286	-0-	30,000
Totals	$7,200	$8,723	$1,523		

Notice that because the bond was purchased at a discount, the discount amortization on each interest receipt date is added or debited to the investment account.

Music City would have reported its investment in the Crystal Records Inc. bond on its December 31, 2017, balance sheet as a non-current asset:

Investment at amortized cost $28,936

This will cause the balance in the investment account to approach face value until maturity.

At maturity, the entries recorded by Music City would be:

2019			
Dec. 31	Cash..	1,200	
	Investment—Crystal Records Inc.	286	
	Investment Income (Loss).......................		1,486
	Recorded receipt of interest and amortization of bond discount using the effective interest method; $30,000 × 8% × 6/12 = $1,200; $29,714 × 10% × 6/12 = $1,486.		

and

Dec. 31	Cash..	30,000	
	Investment—Crystal Records Inc.		30,000
	Record collection of cash resulting from maturity of investment in bond.		

If there is evidence that the debt investment is impaired, the investment must be reduced to the fair value with the amount of the loss recognized on the income statement. The calculation of the loss is beyond the scope of this chapter.[8] If in a future period the value of the investment increases, the previously recognized fair value loss is to be reversed.[9]

Recall that the distinguishing feature of debt investments held for their contract life is that *they are generally held for the purpose of collecting payments of principal and interest.* Therefore, they would

---

8 IFRS 2015, IFRS 9, para. 5.5.1
9 IFRS 2015, IFRS 9, para. 5.5.8.

not normally be sold prior to maturity so fluctuations in value resulting in temporary investment income and losses are a non-issue for these investments. If these investments are sold prior to maturity, any investment income or losses realized would be recorded in the manner described for equity investments.

CHECKPOINT

6. How is the recording of debt investments using the amortized cost method different from the FVTPL method?

Do Quick Study questions: QS 15-7, QS 15-8, QS 15-9, QS 15-10

MID-CHAPTER DEMONSTRATION PROBLEM

The following transactions relate to Copper Company's investment activities during 2017 and 2018. Copper Company did not own any debt or share investments prior to 2017.

2017

Jan.	1	Purchased a 5%, three-year, $60,000 IBM bond paying $61,680, which includes transaction costs; the market interest rate is 4%. Interest is paid semiannually each June 30 and December 31. The bond will be held to maturity.
June	30	Received semiannual interest on IBM bond.
Oct.	2	Purchased 2,000 shares of M&T as an investment for $60,000 cash plus a transaction fee of $75.
	17	Purchased 1,000 shares of Four Seasons Hotels for $40,000 cash plus transaction fees of $30 to be held as an actively traded investment.
Nov.	30	Received $3,000 cash dividend from MT&T.
Dec.	15	Received $1,400 cash dividend from Four Seasons.
	17	Sold the MT&T shares at $33 per share.
	31	Received semiannual interest on IBM bond.
	31	Fair values for the investments are Four Seasons Hotels, $45,000; and IBM, $61,142.

2018

Mar.	1	Purchased 7,000 shares of Violet Inc. common shares at $11 per share plus a transaction fee of $80 with the intention for these shares to be actively traded.
June	30	Received semiannual interest on IBM bond.
Aug.	17	Sold the Four Seasons shares for $52,000 cash.
Dec.	31	Received semiannual interest on IBM bond.
	31	Fair values for the investments are Violet Inc., $69,000; and IBM, $60,582.

Required

Show the appropriate journal entries that describe these transactions.

Planning the Solution

- Prepare an amortization schedule using the effective interest method for the IBM bond.
- Account for the investments in MT&T, Four Seasons Hotels, and Violet as non-strategic investments using the fair value method. Management expects to hold the investments for the short term to take advantage of temporary fluctuations in their market values.
- Account for the investment in the IBM bond using the amortized cost method and assume the bond is to be held for the duration of their contract life.

Solution

Amortization schedule for IBM bond:

Period Ending	Cash Interest Received	Period Interest income	Premium Amort.	Unamortized Premium	Carrying Value
Jan. 1/17				$1,680	$61,680
June 30/17	$1,500	$1,234	$ 266	1,414	61,414
Dec. 31/17	1,500	1,228	272	1,142	61,142
June 30/18	1,500	1,223	277	865	60,865
Dec. 31/18	1,500	1,217	283	582	60,582
June 30/19	1,500	1,212	288	294	60,294
Dec. 31/19	1,500	1,206	294	-0-	60,000
Totals	$9,000	$7,320	$1,680		

Journal entries:

2017				
Jan.	1	Investment—IBM Bond	61,680	
		Cash		61,680
		Purchased bonds to hold for the duration of their contract life.		
June	30	Cash...	1,500	
		Investment—IBM Bond..........................		266
		Interest Income......................................		1,234
		$60,000 × 5% × 6/12 = $1,500;		
		$61,680 × 4% × 6/12 = $1,234.		
Oct.	2	Investment—MT&T Shares	60,000	
		Transaction fees...	75	
		Cash...		60,075
		Purchased shares as an investment.		
	17	Investment—Four Seasons Shares..	40,000	
		Transaction fees..	30	
		Cash...		40,030
		Purchased shares as an investment.		
Nov.	30	Cash...	3,000	
		Dividend Income		3,000
		Received dividends on MT&T shares.		
Dec.	15	Cash...	1,400	
		Dividend Income		1,400
		Received dividends on Four Seasons shares.		
	17	Cash...	66,000	
		Investment—MT&T Shares		60,000
		Investment Income (Loss)......................		6,000
		$33 × 2,000 = $66,000.		
	31	Cash...	1,500	
		Investment—IBM Bond..........................		272
		Interest Income......................................		1,228
		$60,000 × 5% × 6/12 = $1,500;		
		$61,414 × 4% × 6/12 = $1,228.		
	31	Investment—Four Seasons Shares	5,000	
		Investment Income (Loss)......................		5,000
		$45,000 − $40,000 = $5,000.		

	2018			
Mar.	1	Investment—Violet Shares	77,000	
		Transaction fees.......................................	80	
		Cash..		77,080
		($11 × 7,000) + $80 = $77,080.		
June	30	Cash...	1,500	
		Investment—IBM Bond.........................		277
		Interest Income..................................		1,223
		$60,000 × 5% × 6/12 = $1,500;		
		$61,142 × 4% × 6/12 = $1,223.		
Aug.	17	Cash...	52,000	
		Investment—Four Seasons Shares..........		45,000
		Investment Income (Loss)......................		7,000
		To record sale of investment in shares.		
Dec.	31	Cash...	1,500	
		IBM Bond		283
		Interest Income..................................		1,217
		$60,000 × 5% × 6/12 = $1,500;		
		$60,865 × 4% × 6/12 = $1,217.		
	31	Investment Income (Loss)	8,000	
		Violet Shares.....................................		8,000
		$77,000 − $69,000 = $8,000.		

DECISION INSIGHT

The Ponzi Scheme: An Unexpected Risk of Investing

Reasonably sophisticated investors understand that there are risks associated with debt and share investments, broadly, that expected returns might not be realized and, depending on the type of investment, a portion of the principal might even be under threat. Despite warnings from law enforcement agencies and regulatory bodies—that if it sounds too good to be true, it probably is—a significant number of investors continue to suffer severe negative consequences because of an unexpected investment risk . . . the risk of fraud! In 2009, Bernard Madoff, a 71-year-old former non-executive chairman of the NASDAQ stock exchange, was sentenced in a U.S. court to 150 years in prison, the maximum allowed, for defrauding clients of more than $10 billion in a Ponzi scheme. In 2010, an unlicensed Canadian financial advisor, Earl Jones, was sentenced to 11 years in prison after pleading guilty to defrauding clients of

© Timothy A. Clary/Staff/Getty Images

$50 million in another elaborate Ponzi scheme. Then, in 2011, Andre Lewis was charged in connection with a suspected Toronto-based Ponzi scheme involving the loss of at least $2.3 million.

A Ponzi scheme, named for American con man Charles Ponzi, is a scam that pays initial investors returns out of the investments of subsequent investors. For example, Client A invests $100,000 and is promised a high return, say, 20%. Client B later invests $50,000. Client A is paid 20% out of Client B's $50,000. Client C then invests $150,000 and Client A and Client B are paid their returns out of Client C's investment. Often, because clients are so pleased with their return, they reinvest that money, despite having received no physical cash but only statements about the fictitious growth of their investment.

Accounting for Investments in Associates

LO4 Account for investments in associates.

Investments in associates result when it is determined that investors that hold 20% to 50% of an investee's voting shares have significant influence. The **equity method** of accounting and reporting is used for long-term share investments with significant influence.[10] Under the equity method, shares are recorded at cost when they are purchased.[11, 12] To illustrate, Micron Company purchased 3,000 shares (30%) of OPT common shares for a total cost of $70,650 on January 1, 2017. The entry to record this purchase on Micron's books is:

2017				
Jan.	1	Investment in Associate—OPT	70,650	
		Cash		70,650
		Purchased 3,000 shares.		

Under the equity method, the investor records its share of the investee's earnings and dividends. This means that when OPT closes its books and reports profit of $20,000 for 2017, Micron records its 30% share of those earnings in its investment account as:

Dec.	31	Investment in Associate—OPT	6,000	
		Investment Income (Loss)		6,000
		To record 30% equity in investee's		
		earnings of $20,000.		

The debit reflects the increase in Micron's equity in OPT caused by OPT's $20,000 increase in equity through profit. Micron must debit the investment account for its proportionate share in the associate's equity (OPT's profit). The credit shows the source of the increase in the investment account.

If the investee incurs a loss instead of a profit, the investor records its share of the loss and reduces (credits) its investment account.

The receipt of cash dividends is not recorded as revenue when using the equity method because the investor has already recorded its share of the earnings reported by the investee. When the investee pays dividends its retained earnings are reduced by the amount of the dividend. The investee's equity is reduced and therefore the investment of the investor must also be reduced. Dividends received from an investee change the form of the investor's asset from a shares investment to cash. This means dividends reduce the balance of the investment account, but increase cash. To illustrate, OPT declared and paid $10,000 in cash dividends on its common shares. Micron's entry to record its 30% share of these dividends received on January 9, 2018, is:

2018				
Jan.	9	Cash	3,000	
		Investment in Associate—OPT		3,000
		To record receipt of 30% of $10,000		
		dividend paid by OPT.		

The book value of an investment in equity securities when using the equity method is equal to the cost of the investment plus the investor's equity in the undistributed earnings of the investee. Once we record the above transactions for Micron, its investment account appears as in Exhibit 15.5.

---

[10] Note that in situations where there is a large number of small share holdings, significant influence is possible for an investor that owns less than 20% of the investee. Also, an investor may not be able to exert significant influence with a shareholding of greater than 20% if another shareholder owns a 51% block of shares in the investee.

[11] IFRS 2015, IAS 28, (Revised), para. 10, 16.

[12] A simplified approach to demonstrate the equity method is used here. The complexities are left to a more advanced course.

EXHIBIT 15.5

Investment in Associate—OPT Common Shares Ledger Account

Date	Explanation	Debit	Credit	Balance
2017				
Jan. 1	Investment in OPT	70,650		70,650
Dec. 31	Share of earnings	6,000		76,650
2018				
Jan. 9	Share of dividends		3,000	73,650

If a balance sheet were prepared on this date, Micron would normally report its investment in OPT on the balance sheet after total current assets but before property, plant, and equipment items. Any investment income would be reported on the income statement as shown in the bottom section of Exhibit 15.6.

EXHIBIT 15.6

Statement Presentation of Non-current Significant Influence Investment and Investment Income

Partial Balance Sheet	
Assets	
Total current assets..	$ XXX,XXX
Investment in associate...	73,650
Property, plant, and equipment	XXX,XXX
Total assets	$X,XX,XXX
Partial Income Statement	
Profit from operations	$XXX,XXX
Other revenues and expenses:	
Investment Income (Loss)..	6,000

RECORDING THE SALE OF AN EQUITY INVESTMENT

When an investment in equity securities is sold, the investment income or loss is calculated by comparing proceeds from the sale with the book value of the investment on the date of sale. Care should be taken to ensure that the investment account is brought up to date in terms of earnings and dividends before recording the sale. If Micron sells its OPT shares for $80,000 on January 10, 2018, the entry to record the sale is:

Jan. 10	Cash...	80,000	
	Investment in Associate—OPT		73,650
	Investment Income (Loss).......................		6,350
	Sold 3,000 shares for $80,000.		

CHECKPOINT

7. Optix Inc. owns 50,000 of the 140,000 shares issued and outstanding of Alliance Corp. Does this represent significant influence? Explain why or why not.

Do Quick Study questions: QS 15-11, QS 15-12

Accounting for Investment in Subsidiaries: Business Combinations

LO5 Describe the accounting for business combinations.

A business combination occurs when an investor with a long-term share investment that represents more than 50% of the investee's voting shares has *control* over the investee. **Control** is more than influence. The controlling investor can dominate all other shareholders in electing the corporation's board of directors and has control over the investee corporation's management. The controlling corporation (investor) is known as the **parent company** and the company whose shares are held by the parent is referred to as a **subsidiary** (investee).

A company owning all the outstanding shares of a subsidiary can take over the subsidiary's assets, cancel the subsidiary's shares, and merge the subsidiary into the parent company, creating potential financial, legal, and tax advantages.

When a business operates as a parent company with subsidiaries, separate accounting records are maintained by each entity. From a legal viewpoint, the parent and each subsidiary are still separate entities with all the rights, duties, and responsibilities of individual companies. However, investors in the parent company are indirect investors in the subsidiaries. To evaluate their investments, parent company investors must consider the financial status and operations of the subsidiaries as well as the parent. This information is provided in *consolidated financial statements*.

Consolidated financial statements show the financial position, results of operations, and cash flows of all companies under the parent's control, including all subsidiaries. These statements are prepared as if the company were organized as one entity. The parent uses the equity method in its accounts, but the investment account is *not* reported on the parent's consolidated financial statements. Instead, the individual assets and liabilities of the parent and its subsidiaries are combined on one balance sheet. The amount of equity in the subsidiary that is not owned by the parent is presented under the equity item "non-controlling interest."[13] Their revenues and expenses also are combined on one income statement and their cash flows are combined on one statement of cash flows. The detailed procedures for preparing consolidated financial statements are included in advanced courses.

 **CHECKPOINT**

8. Food Etc. purchased 80,000 of the 80,000 common shares issued and outstanding of Ellai Inc. This would be classified as what type of investment by Food Etc.?
   a. Investment in associate
   b. Business combination
   c. Non-current investment
   d. None of the above

SUMMARY: ACCOUNTING FOR DEBT AND SHARE INVESTMENTS

Recall that many investments can be classified as either current or non-current depending on management's intent and ability to convert them into cash in the future. Exhibit 15.7 outlines the key types of investments (both strategic and non-strategic), the accounting treatment required under IFRS, and the financial statement presentation considerations for each category. It is important to note that management's initial classification of investments in securities can be changed only if it changes its business model for managing financial assets.[14] FVTPL stands for fair value through profit and loss, meaning that the security is adjusted at the balance sheet date to its current fair value with the investment income/losses reported in current-period profit.

---

13   2015 IFRS, IFRS 10 para. B86, and para. 22.
14   IFRS 2015, IFRS 9, para. 4.9

EXHIBIT 15.7

Accounting for Investments Summary Chart

NON-STRATEGIC INVESTMENTS <20% ownership with no power over financial and operating policy decisions [15]	Investments held where investor's intent is to generate profit through flow of income or temporary changes in value		
Types:	**Description/Intent**	**Accounting Treatment**	**Financial Statement Presentation**

FVTPL Category of Investments	Equity investments that trade in an active market
	
	 Or debt investments where business objective of holding debt investments is to actively trade
		Initially recorded at cost with transaction fees booked as a current-period expense:
		 Dr. Investment
		 Dr. Transaction fees
		   Cr. Cash
		 Measured at fair value at end of period:
		 Dr. Investment
		   Cr. Investment Income (Loss) or
		 Dr. Investment Income (Loss)
		   Cr. Investment
		 Dividends (Interest):
		 Dr. Cash
		   Cr. Dividend (Interest) Income
			If expected to be sold within 12 months or primarily held for trading or it's a cash equivalent, classify investment as a current asset; otherwise, classify as non-current

FVTOCI Category of Investments	Debt investments where business objective is **both** held for collecting contractual cash flows **and** selling assets unless irrevocably designated as above FVTPL category of investments.	Initially recorded at cost including any transaction fees incurred:
		 Dr. Investment (OCI)
		   Cr. Cash
		 Measured at fair value at end of period:
		 Dr. Investment (OCI)
		   Cr. Unrealized Gain (OCI)
		 Note: Measured at FVTOCI (unless specially designated at FV through profit under certain criteria)
		 Interest (Dividend) payments:
		 Dr. Cash
		   Cr. Interest (Dividend) Income
		 Note: On sale of the instrument, cumulative investment income or loss that had been booked to OCI in previous years is reclassified to current-period income statement
			Classify investment as current asset

Cost/Amortized Cost Category of Investments	Debt investments where the business model is to hold investments to maturity	Initially recorded at cost
		 Dr. Investment
		   Cr. Cash
		 Subsequently measured at **amortized cost** with interest income reported on current-period income statement
		 Dr. Cash
		 Dr. Investment
		   Cr. Interest Income
		 to record receipt of interest and amortization of bond
			Classify investment as non-current asset

(continue)

---

15 IFRS 2015, IAS 28(2011), para. 6.

EXHIBIT 15.7

Accounting for Investments Summary Chart—*continued*

STRATEGIC INVESTMENTS	Management has the power to participate in:		
Types:	**Description/Intent**	**Accounting Treatment**	**Financial Statement Presentation**
Associate with significant Influence: Equity Method 20–50% ownership/ ability to influence financial and operating policy decisions [16]	Holds 20% or more of the shares of an investee but does not have complete control over the investee.	Recognized at cost on acquisition. Measurement at end of period: Dr Investment in Associates Cr. Investment Income Based on investor/s share of the associate's earnings Dividends: Dr. Cash Cr. Investment in Associates Reduces share of investment, as it reflects a return of capital from investment	Classified as an investment in associate, as a non-current asset
Control: Business Combination >50% ownership/ power to independently influence financial and operating decisions	Controlling corporation—either owns more than 50% of the shares or has the ability to influence the investee's activities to influence its returns on its investment in the investee.	Consolidated financial statements—individual assets and liabilities of the parent and subsidiary are combined on the balance sheet. Amount of equity in subsidiary that is not owned by the parent company is reported as non-controlling interest and is presented between total liabilities and equity Revenues and expenses are combined on the income statement Cash flows are combined on statement of cash flows	Presented as combined statements with additional disclosure details on subsidiary's operations

IFRS AND ASPE—THE DIFFERENCES

Difference	International Financial Reporting Standards (IFRS)	Accounting Standards for Private Enterprises (ASPE)
Recording of non-strategic investments	• Amortized cost is used to record debt investments where business model is to hold investments to maturity unless FVTPL is designated • Fair value is used for equity investments and for debt instruments where the the business objective for holding the debt investments is to actively trade • Where business objective is to both actively trade and collect contractual cash flows of debt investments, investment is measured at FVTOCI	• Initial measurement of both debt and equity investments is at fair value; there is no option for FVTPL • Subsequent measurement of debt investments is at amortized cost and for equity investments fair value is used
Investments in associates	• Equity method must be used	• May use cost, equity, or fair value method depending on situation
Consolidation	• Required	• Choice of consolidation, equity, cost, or fair value depending on situation

---

16 IFRS 2015, IAS 28(2011), para. 6.

A Look Ahead

Chapter 16 focuses on reporting and analyzing cash inflows and cash outflows. We emphasize how to prepare and interpret the statement of cash flows.

Summary

LO1 Describe and explain the purpose of debt and share investments. Debt investments (or debt securities) reflect a creditor relationship and include investments in notes, bonds, and certificates of deposit. Debt investments are issued by governments, companies, and individuals. Share investments (or equity securities) reflect an ownership relationship and include shares issued by corporations. Investments can be non-strategic or strategic in nature.

LO2 Identify and describe the investment classifications. Non-strategic investments include debt or equity investments where no control or influence exists. Strategic investments include investments in associates, business combinations, and joint arrangements. Investments in associates have significant influence, which generally exists when the investor owns 20% to 50% of the investee's shares. Investors in a business combination have control, which exists when more than 50% of the investee's shares are owned by the investor, in general. Joint arrangements are contractual investments as opposed to an investment in shares or debt securities.

LO3 Account for and report non-strategic investments. Non-strategic equity investments are intended to be held to generate profit from changes in fair value and they are recorded using the fair value method. Non-strategic debt investments are typically held to maturity, in which case the amortized cost method is used to record them; if held for the near term, the fair value through profit and loss (FVTPL) method is used.

LO4 Account for investments in associates. The equity method is used when an investor has a significant influence over an investee. This usually occurs when an investor owns 20% or more of the investee's voting shares, but not exceeding 50%. Under the equity method, the investor records its share of the investee's earnings with a debit to the investment account and a credit to a revenue account. Dividends received reduce the investment account balance and the investor debits its share of annual earnings (credits its share of losses) to the investment account.

LO5 Describe the accounting for business combinations. In a business combination, the investor owns more than 50% of another company's voting shares and controls the investee. The investor's financial reports are prepared on a consolidated basis as if the company were organized as one entity. The individual financial statements of the parent and its subsidiaries are combined into one balance sheet, one income statement, and one statement of cash flows.

Guidance Answers to CHECKPOINT

1. Investors in non-strategic investments cannot significantly influence or control the operations of the investee company, while investors in strategic investments can.

2. Equity investments are investments in shares, while debt investments are the purchase of debt instruments.

3. The *20% to 50% rule* to determine significant influence does not always hold true because an investor could hold 10% of the shares and be able to exert significant influence if all other investors have very small percentage holdings and, conversely, a 30% holding may not have significant influence if another investor has 60%.

4. Transaction costs such as brokerage fees and commissions are debited to an expense account—Transaction Fees—regarding the purchase and sale of non-strategic equity investments.

5. At year-end, investment income (losses) upon fair value testing of non-strategic share investments are credited (debited) to Investment Income (Loss) account that appears on

the income statement and debited (credited) to the investment account, which adjusts it to its fair value on the balance sheet.

6. The FVTPL method assumes the investment will be held for the near term, while the amortized cost method assumes the investment will be held with the expectation to collect contractual cash flows of principal and interest over the term of the investment.

7. Optix's ownership in Alliance Corp. represents a 35.7% interest, which qualifies as significant influence and therefore as an investment in an associate.

8. b.

DEMONSTRATION PROBLEM

Forestry Inc. has excess cash and has decided to utilize excess resources to begin investing in debt and shares. The following investment transactions occurred during 2017. Prepare the journal entries.

2017		
Jan.	1	Purchased 5,000 Lindel Inc. common shares for $320,000 cash. These shares represent 35% of Lindel's outstanding shares.
Oct.	2	Purchased 12,000 LG common shares paying cash of $3.50 per share. Forestry Inc. plans to hold the shares for less than a year.
	15	Purchased 50,000 Wall Corp. shares for $24,925 cash. Forestry Inc. will sell the shares after Wall Corp. declares and pays dividends in January 2018.
Nov.	30	Received a cash dividend of $3.50 per share from Lindel Inc.
Dec.	15	Received $0.40 cash dividend per share from LG.
	31	Lindel Inc. reported a profit of $820,000 for the year ended December 31, 2017.
	31	Fair values per share for the investments are Lindel Inc., $65; LG, $3.45; and Wall Corp. $0.50.
2018		
Jan.	5	Wall Corp. declared dividends of $0.10 per share to the January 18 shareholders of record payable on January 25.
	25	Forestry Inc. received the Wall Corp. dividend.
Feb.	10	Sold the Wall Corp. shares for $24,800 cash.
Mar.	1	Sold 8,000 of the LG common shares at $3.75 per share.
May	2	Purchased 16,000 of the 40,000 issued and outstanding Delta Corp. common shares for $38 cash per share.
Aug.	1	Purchased a $150,000, 7%, five-year BCE Inc. bond paying cash of $146,966. Interest is paid annually each July 31. The market interest rate is 7.5%. Forestry Inc. plans to hold the bond until July 31, 2019.

Analysis Component:

The sale of the Wall Corp. shares on February 10, 2018, resulted in a loss. Does this indicate that this was a poor investment decision? Explain, using calculations as appropriate.

Planning the Solution

• Account for the equity investment in Lindel Inc. and Delta Corp. using the equity method.

• Account for the investments in LG, Wall Corp., and BCE Inc. using the fair value method, making sure to apply fair value adjustments at year-end as appropriate.

• Answer the analysis component question.

Solution

Journal entries:

2017				
Jan.	1	Investment in Associate—Lindel Inc.		
		Shares	320,000	
		Cash		320,000
		To record purchase of 35% interest for $320,000.		
Oct.	2	Investment—LG Shares	42,000	
		Cash		42,000
		12,000 × $3.50 = $42,000.		
	15	Investment—Wall Corp.		
		Shares	24,925	
		Cash		24,925
		Purchased shares as a non-strategic investment.		
Nov.	30	Cash	17,500	
		Investment in Associate—Lindel Inc.		17,500
		5,000 × $3.50 = $17,500.		
Dec.	15	Cash	4,800	
		Dividend Income		4,800
		12,000 × $0.40 = $4,800.		
	31	Investment in Associate—Lindel Inc.		
		Shares	287,000	
		Investment Income (Loss)—Lindel Inc.		287,000
		To record 35% share of investee's $820,000 profit; $820,000 × 35% = $287,000.		
	31	Investment Income (Loss)	525	
		Investment—Wall Corp Shares	75	
		Investment—LG Shares		600
		To apply fair value adjustment at year-end as per the following calculations:		

	Unadjusted Balance	Fair Value	Difference
LG Shares	$42,000	$41,400*	$(600)
Wall Corp.	24,925	25,000**	75
Investment Income (loss)	$66,925	$66,400	$(525)

*12,000 × 3.45 = 41,400
**50,000 × 0.50 = 25,000

2018				
Jan.	5	No entry		
	25	Cash..	5,000	
		Dividend Income		5,000
		50,000 × $0.10 = $5,000.		
Feb.	10	Cash..	24,800	
		Investment Income (Loss)	200	
		Investment—Wall Corp.		25,000
		To record the sale of investment in Wall Corp.		
Mar.	1	Cash..	30,000	
		Investment—LG Shares..........................		27,600
		Investment Income (Loss).......................		2,400
		8,000 × $3.75 = $30,000;		
		$41,400/12,000 = $3.45;		
		$3.45 × 8,000 = $27,600.		
May	2	Investment in Associate—Delta Corp.	608,000	
		Cash		608,000
		To record purchase of 40% interest for		
		$608,000; 16,000/40,000 = 0.40 × 100%		
		= 40%; 16,000 × $38 = $608,000.		
Aug.	1	Investment—BCE Inc. Bond..........................	146,966	
		Cash		146,966
		Purchased bond as an actively traded		
		investment.		

Analysis Component:

The sale of the Wall Corp. shares on February 10, 2018, did result in a loss; however, this was not a poor investment decision because the investment generated a cash inflow of $4,875 over the investment period (calculated as $24,925 cash paid initially plus $5,000 dividends received plus $24,800 cash proceeds from sale).

Glossary

Amortized cost method Business model is to hold the investments to maturity. Initially recorded at cost and subsequently accounted for *by recording the receipt of interest and the amortization of bond discount using the effective interest method*

Business combination The investor owns sufficient shares to control the investee's strategic operating, investing, and financing policies without the cooperation of others.

Carrying value The amount that a specific asset or liability is reported on the balance sheet at the end of the accounting period. Also referred to as *book value*.

Consolidated financial statements Financial statements that show the results of all operations under the parent's control, including those of any subsidiaries; assets and liabilities of all affiliated companies are combined on a single balance sheet, revenues and

expenses are combined on a single income statement, and cash flows are combined on a single statement of cash flows as if the business were in fact a single company.

Control When an investor can dominate all other shareholders in electing the corporation's board of directors and has control over the investee corporation's financial and operating policy decisions, generally by holding more than 50% of the investee's voting shares.

Debt investment Represents an amount owed; arises when one company lends money to another, such as in the case of a bond. Also called *debt security*.

Debt security See *debt investment*.

Equity method An accounting method used for long-term investments when the investor has significant influence over the investee; the investment account is initially debited for cost and then is increased to reflect the investor's share of the investee's earnings and decreased to reflect the investor's receipt of dividends paid by the investee.

Equity investment Represents one company's purchase of the shares in another company. Also called *share investment or equity security*.

Fair value adjustment Investment income (or loss) recorded at the end of the accounting period based on the fluctuations in the market price of the underlying securities; it is recorded to adjust investments to their fair market value, although no transaction has occurred.

Fair value method Refer to *fair value through profit and loss method* (FVTPL).

Fair value through other comprehensive income Debt instruments held with the business objective of collecting principal and interest payments and selling the debt instruments as financial assets.

Fair value through profit and loss method (FVTPL) An accounting method for recording non-strategic investments that is the standard approach for accounting for equity investments unless an irrevocable election is made for subsequent changes in fair value to go to other comprehensive income. Also referred to as the fair value method.

Intercorporate investments Debt and shares of one corporation purchased by another corporation.

Investee The company whose debt or shares are being purchased.

Investments in associates Situations in which the investor can significantly influence the financial and operating policies of the investee, generally holding more than 20% of the shares and less than 50% of the outstanding shares.

Investor The company that purchases as an investment the debt or shares of another.

Non-strategic investment An investment in which the investor cannot significantly influence or control the operations of the investee company.

Parent company A corporation that owns a controlling interest in another corporation (more than 50% of the voting shares is required).

Significant influence See *investments in associates*.

Strategic investment An investment through which the investor has the power to influence financial and operating policy decisions over the investee.

Subsidiary A corporation that is controlled by another corporation (the parent) because the parent owns more than 50% of the subsidiary's voting shares.

Concept Review Questions

1. Identify the classes for debt and share investments.
2. What is the difference between an equity investment and a debt investment?
3. How is interest recognized on debt investments that are expected to be held for their contract life?
4. When non-strategic investments are accounted for using the fair value method, when should investment income be recognized?
5. When non-strategic debt investments are accounted for using the amortized cost method, when should interest income be recognized?
6. In accounting for common share investments, when should the equity method be used?
7. When share investments are accounted for using the equity method, when should investment income be recognized? What accounts are debited and credited?
8. Using the equity method, dividends received are not recorded as profit. Explain why this is true.
9. Under what circumstances would a company prepare consolidated financial statements?
10. Start-up companies such as the Farmery highlighted in the chapter opening vignette, often have challenges raising sufficient capital. From the issuing company perspective, what are the advantages and disadvantages, including costs and key considerations of pursuing the following forms of capital to finance future expansion?
    a) Issuing $1,000,000 in corporate bonds at a 14% rate of interest.
    b) Finding an equity partner to contribute a $1,000,000 in exchange for a 25% equity stake in the corporation, and having a significant influence on the strategic direction of the business.
    c) Issuing 100,000 corporate shares on the Toronto Stock Exchange at a price of $10 per share.

Quick Study

QS 15-1 Share vs. debt investments LO1

ABC Inc. had the following selected transactions during the year. Identify whether each of 1 through 8 represents an equity investment (E), investment in a debt security (D), or neither (N) from ABC Inc.'s perspective. If you answer N, explain.

1. _____ Purchased 5,000 shares of Douglas Inc. to be held for about 30 days.

2. _____ Purchased at par a $100,000, 5% five-year bond; interest is payable quarterly and the bond will be held until maturity.

3. _____ Purchased 50,000 of the 80,000 authorized shares of Dolby Inc.

4. _____ Purchased equipment costing $140,000 by issuing shares.

5. _____ Purchased land costing $289,000 by borrowing $200,000 from the bank and issuing shares for the balance.

6. _____ Signed a contract with two other organizations regarding a project to develop and market a new computer program; each investor has a 1/3 share in the project costs and revenues.

7. _____ Purchased 80,000 Inco shares to be held for several years; Inco has over 5 million shares issued and outstanding.

8. _____ Purchased 3,000 Perdu shares, representing a 25% ownership interest.

QS 15-2 Classification of investments LO2

Refer to QS 15-1. Identify how each investment would be classified from ABC Inc.'s perspective: non-strategic (N), investment in associate (I), business combination (B), joint arrangement (J), or not applicable (NA).

QS 15-3 Equity investments—non-strategic LO3

On May 2, 2017, Sysco Industries Inc. acquired 1,200 common shares of Computer Web Corp. at $40.50 per share. Sysco's intent is to sell the shares within eight to ten months. On August 7, Sysco received dividends of $0.50 per share regarding the Computer Web investment. Record the entries on May 2 and August 7.

QS 15-4 Fair value adjustment—non-strategic LO3

Dynamic Express Inc. prepared the summary shown below regarding its investments on December 31, 2017, its year-end. Prepare the appropriate entry on December 31, 2017, to record the fair value adjustment.

Non-Strategic Investments	Unadjusted Balance at Dec. 31/17	Fair Values at Dec. 31/17
Zelco shares	$102,000	$ 98,000
IMC shares	540,000	547,000
Petra shares	96,000	48,000

QS 15-5 Fair value adjustment—non-strategic LO3

Wind Industries had selected unadjusted balances as shown below at year-end. A search on the Internet showed fair values on December 31, 2017, of: CashCo, $18; Wells, $0.70. Prepare the appropriate entry on December 31, 2017, to record the valuation adjustment.

Non-strategic Investments	Unadjusted Balance at Dec. 31/17
CashCo shares (21,250 shares)..	$340,000
Wells shares (45,000 shares)	34,000

QS 15-6 Balance sheet presentation—non-strategic investments LO3

Refer to the information in QS 15-5. Show how the investments will be presented on the December 31, 2017, balance sheet.

QS 15-7 Debt investments—non-strategic LO3

On February 1, 2017, Snappy Printing Inc. purchased 4% Telus bonds with a face value of $5,000 at 98 as a non-strategic investment. Interest is paid quarterly beginning May 1, 2017. The bonds mature February 1, 2027. Record the entries on February 1 and May 1 using the amortized cost method. Assume the market interest rate is 4.25%.

QS 15-8 Debt investments—premium LO3

On January 1, 2017, Gordon Activewear purchased a 12%, $40,000 Telus bond with a three-year term for $42,030. Interest is to be paid semiannually each June 30 and December 31. Gordon is planning to hold the bond until maturity. Record the entries on January 1, 2017, June 30, 2017, and December 31, 2019, using the amortization schedule provided below.

Period Ending	Cash Interest Received	Period Interest Income	Premium Amort.	Unamortized Premium	Carrying Value
Jan. 1/17..				$2,030	$42,030
June 30/17..	$ 2,400	$ 2,102	$ 298	1,732	41,732
Dec. 31/17..	2,400	2,087	313	1,419	41,419
June 30/18..	2,400	2,071	329	1,090	41,090
Dec. 31/18..	2,400	2,055	345	745	40,745
June 30/19..	2,400	2,037	363	382	40,382
Dec. 31/19..	2,400	2,018	382	-0-	40,000
Totals	$14,400	$12,370	$2,030		

QS 15-9 Debt investments—discount LO3

On January 1, 2017, Nickle Entertainment Inc. purchased a 4%, $50,000 Imax bond for $46,490. Interest is to be paid semiannually each June 30 and December 31. Nickle Inc. is planning to hold the bond until maturity. Record the entries on January 1, 2017, and June 30, 2017, based on the partial amortization schedule shown below.

Period Ending	Cash Interest Received	Period Interest Income	Discount Amort.	Unamortized Discount	Carrying Value
Jan. 1/17..				$3,510	$46,490
June 30/17..	$1,000	$1,395	$395	3,115	46,885
Dec. 31/17..	1,000	1,407	407	2,708	47,292

QS 15-10 Balance sheet presentation—debt investments LO3

Refer to the information in QS 15-9. Show how the investment will be presented on the December 31, 2017, balance sheet, assuming the carrying value reflected the fair value.

QS 15-11 Investment in associate—equity method LO4

On January 2, 2017, Nassau Travel Corp. paid $500,000 cash to acquire 10,000 of Suffolk Corporation's 40,000 outstanding common shares. Assume that Nassau has significant influence over Suffolk as a result. On October 12, 2017, Suffolk Corp. paid a $100,000 dividend and on December 31, 2017, it reported profit of $400,000 for 2017. Prepare Nassau's entries on January 2, October 12, and December 31.

QS 15-12 Investment in associate—equity method LO4

On January 2, 2017, Bella Software Corp. paid cash of $1,200,000 to acquire 704,000 of Domino Inc.'s 3,200,000 outstanding common shares. Assume that Bella has significant influence over Domino as a result. On March 15, 2017, Domino paid dividends of $0.20 per common share and on December 31, 2017, it reported a loss of $1,675,000 for 2017. Prepare Bella's entries on January 2, March 15, and December 31.

Exercises

Exercise 15-1 Non-strategic investments LO3

CHECK FIGURE: Dec. 31, 2017 Fair value adjustment to profit = $7,500

Prepare entries to record the following non-strategic investment transactions of Ace Investment Corporation.

2017		
Mar.	1	Paid $60,980 to purchase a $60,000 two-year, 7% bond payable of Chrystal Corporation dated March 1. Interest is paid quarterly beginning June 1. Management intends to hold the bonds for the duration of their contract life.
Apr.	16	Bought 2,000 common shares of Windsor Motors at $25.50.
May	2	Paid $38,968 to purchase a five-year, 4.5%, $40,000 bond payable of Bates Corporation. Interest is paid annually each April 30.
June	1	Received a cheque from Chrystal Corporation regarding quarterly interest.
Aug.	1	Windsor Motors' board of directors declared a dividend of $0.75 per share to shareholders of record on August 10, payable August 15.
	15	Received the Windsor Motors dividend.
Sept.	1	Received a cheque from Chrystal Corporation regarding quarterly interest.
	17	Purchased 25,000 Delta Inc. common shares at $3.20.
Oct.	20	Sold the Windsor Motors shares at $31.00.
Dec.	1	Received a cheque from Chrystal Corporation regarding quarterly interest.
	1	Sold the Chrystal Corporation bond at 101.
	31	Accrued interest on the Bates bond. The fair value of the equity security on this date was Delta, $3.50. The carrying value equalled the fair value for the Bates bond.
2018		
Apr.	30	Received a cheque from Bates Corporation regarding annual interest.

Analysis Component If the fair value adjusting entry on December 31, 2017, were not recorded, what would the effect be on the income statement and balance sheet? Based on your understanding of GAAP, would it be better or worse to omit an investment loss than investment income? Explain.

Exercise 15-2 **Non-strategic investments** LO3

CHECK FIGURE: Dec. 31, 2017 Investment loss = $35,150

Prepare entries to record the following non-strategic investment transactions of Wiki Garden Tool Inc.. Assume each bond acquired is purchased with the intention to actively trade.

2017

Feb.	1	Paid $120,000, plus $200 in transaction fees to purchase a $124,000 four-year, 3% bond payable of Capital Inc. dated Feb. 1. Interest is paid semiannually beginning August 1.
Mar.	29	Bought 100,000 common shares of Regina Inc. for a total of $85,600, plus paid an extra $500 for transaction fees.
May	7	Regina Inc.'s board of directors declared a total dividend of $525,000 regarding the total 3,500,000 shares issued and outstanding. The date of record is May 30, payable June 15.
June	1	Paid $139,000 including $500 in transaction fees to purchase a five-year, 6%, $136,000 bond payable of Yates Corporation. Interest is paid annually each May 30.
	15	Received a cheque regarding the dividends declared on May 7.
Aug.	1	Received a cheque from Capital Inc. regarding semiannual interest.
	1	Sold the Capital Inc. bond at 98.
	17	Purchased 75,000 Tech Inc. common shares at $6.00 plus $400 in transaction fees.
Dec.	1	Sold 75,000 of the Regina Inc. shares at $0.95 and incurred $250 in transaction fees.
	31	Accrued interest on the Yates bond. Fair values of the equity securities on this date were Regina, $0.95; Tech Inc., $5.50. Assume that the carrying value of the Yates bond was equal to its fair value.

2018

May	30	Received a cheque from Yates Corporation regarding annual interest.

Analysis Component: How would the financial statements have been affected differently if the dividends received on June 15 were from a significant influence investment or investment in associate as opposed to a non-strategic investment?

Exercise 15-3 **Fair value adjustments at year-end** LO3

CHECK FIGURE: Dec. 31, 2017 Investment loss = $2,650

Pacific Fishing Inc.'s non-strategic investments as of December 31, 2017, are as follows:

	Cost	Fair Value
RIM common shares	$17,600	$19,450
Northern Electric common shares	42,750	42,050
Imperial Oil common shares	25,200	24,250
Inco Limited common shares	34,800	31,950

Pacific Fishing Inc. had no investments prior to 2017.

Required

1. Prepare the fair value adjustment at December 31, 2017, based on the information provided.

2. Illustrate how the investments will be reported on the December 31, 2017, balance sheet.

Exercise 15-4 **Fair value adjustments at year-end** LO3

CHECK FIGURES: 2. Dec. 31, 2017 = $22,000; Dec. 31, 2018 = $27,350

The cost and fair value of non-strategic investments of International Journalist Corporation on December 31, 2017, and December 31, 2018, are as follows:

	Cost	Fair Value
On December 31, 2017	$23,500	$22,000
On December 31, 2018	26,500	27,350

Required

1. Prepare the fair value adjustment at December 31, 2017, and December 31, 2018, based on the information provided.

2. Illustrate how the non-strategic investments will be reported on the December 31, 2017, and December 31, 2018, balance sheets.

Exercise 15-5 Non-strategic investments L03

CHECK FIGURE: 3. Dec. 31, 2017 = $196,128

Following are the non-strategic investment transactions of Corona Inc.:

2017

Jan.	1	Purchased for $78,141 an 8%, $75,000 bond that matures in 10 years from Hanna Corporation when the market interest rate was 7.4%. Interest is paid semiannually beginning June 30, 2017.
June	30	Received interest on the Hanna bond.
July	1	Paid $118,047 for a Trust Inc. bond with a par value of $120,000 and a five-year term. The bond pays interest quarterly beginning September 30, 2017, at the annual rate of 7.8%; the market interest rate on the date of purchase was 8.2%.
Sept.	30	Received interest on the Trust bond.
Dec.	31	Received interest on the Hanna and Trust bonds.
	31	The fair values of the bonds on this date equalled the fair values.

Required

1. For each of the bond investments, prepare an amortization schedule showing only 2017 and 2018.

2. Prepare the entries to record the transactions described above.

3. Show how the investments would be reported on Corona's December 31, 2017, balance sheet.

Exercise 15-6 Non-strategic investments L03

CHECK FIGURE: 2. Jan. 14, 2018, Investment loss = $4,200

George's Mortgage Inc. engaged in the following non-strategic investment transactions during 2017:

2017

Jan.	1	Purchased for $406,894 a 6%, $400,000 Jarvis Corp. bond that matures in five years when the market interest rate was 5.6%. Interest is paid semiannually beginning June 30, 2017. George's Inc. plans to hold this investment until maturity.
Mar.	1	Bought 6,000 shares of Medley Corp., paying $32.50 per share.
May	7	Received dividends of $0.90 per share on the Medley Corp. shares.
June	1	Paid $316,000 for 21,000 shares of Zhang common shares.
June	30	Received interest on the Jarvis bond.
Aug.	1	Sold the Medley Corp. shares for $32.75 per share.
Dec.	31	Received interest on the Jarvis bond.
Dec.	31	The fair value of the Zhang shares on this date was $14.80 per share. Assume the fair value of the bonds equalled the carrying value.
2018		
Jan.	14	Sold the Zhang shares for $14.60.

Required

1. Prepare an amortization schedule for the Jarvis bond showing only 2017 and 2018.

2. Prepare the entries to record the transactions described above.

3. Show how the investments would be reported on George's December 31, 2017, balance sheet.

Exercise 15-7 Share investment transactions; equity method LO4

CHECK FIGURE: Dec. 31, 2018: Loss = $8,360

The following events are for Toronto Investment Inc.:

2017

Jan. 14 Purchased 18,000 shares of Queen's Inc. common shares for $156,900. Queen's has 90,000 common shares outstanding and has acknowledged the fact that its policies will be significantly influenced by Toronto.

Oct. 1 Queen's declared and paid a cash dividend of $2.60 per share.

Dec. 31 Queen's announced that profit for the year amounted to $650,000.

2018

April 1 Queen's declared and paid a cash dividend of $2.70 per share.

Dec. 31 Queen's announced that profit for the year amounted to $733,100.

31 Toronto sold 6,000 shares of Queen's for $104,320.

Required Prepare general journal entries to record each transaction. Round *per share* calculations to two decimal places.

Problems

Problem 15-1A Non-strategic investments LO2,3

CHECK FIGURE: 2. Feb. 16, 2018, Investment Income = $2,475

Landers Inc. had the following transactions involving non-strategic investments during 2017.

2017

Apr. 1 Paid $100,000 to buy a 90-day term deposit, $100,000 principal amount, 5%, dated April 1.

12 Purchased 3,000 common shares of Drifter Ltd. at $22.25.

June 9 Purchased 1,800 common shares of Power Corp. at $49.50.

20 Purchased 700 common shares of Westburne Ltd. at $15.75.

July 1 Purchased for $67,412 a 7%, $65,000 Littleton Inc. bond that matures in eight years when the market interest rate was 6.4%. Interest is paid semiannually beginning December 31, 2017. Landers Inc. plans to hold this investment until maturity.

3 Received a cheque for the principal and accrued interest on the term deposit that matured on June 30.

15 Received a $0.95 per share cash dividend on the Drifter common shares.

28 Sold 1,500 of the Drifter common shares at $26.00.

Sept. 1 Received a $2.10 per share cash dividend on the Power Corp. common shares.

Dec. 15 Received a $1.35 per share cash dividend on the remaining Drifter Ltd. common shares owned.

31 Received the interest on the Littleton bond.

31 The fair values of Landers Inc.'s investments on this date were Drifter shares, $24.60; Power Corp. shares, $42.35; Westburne shares, $16.05. Assume the fair value and the carrying value of the Littleton bond were equal.

2018

Feb. 16 Sold the remaining Drifter shares at $26.25.

Required

1. Prepare an amortization schedule for the Littleton bond showing only 2017 and 2018.

2. Prepare journal entries to record the preceding transactions.

3. Show how Landers Inc.'s investments will appear on its December 31, 2017, balance sheet.

Analysis Component: How is the investment income recorded on the Drifter shares on December 31, 2017, different from the investment income from the sale of shares recorded on February 16, 2018?

Problem 15-2A Non-strategic investments LO2,3

CHECK FIGURE: Dec. 31, 2017, Investment loss = $704

Safety Development Corporation had relatively large idle cash balances and invested them as follows in securities to be held as non-strategic investments:

2017

Feb.	7	Purchased 2,200 common shares of Royal Bank at $26.50, plus $500 in transaction fees.
	19	Purchased 1,200 common shares of Imperial Oil at $51.75, and paid $250 in transaction fees.
Apr.	1	Paid $88,258 plus $500 in transaction fees for a 6.8%, four-year, $90,000 Minco Inc. bond that pays interest quarterly beginning June 30. The market rate of interest on this date was 7.2%. Sellers Corporation plans to hold this investment until for the duration of the bond's contract life.
May	26	Purchased 2,000 common shares of BCE at $13.38, plus $200 in transaction fees.
June	1	Received a $0.25 per share cash dividend on the Royal Bank common shares.
	17	Sold 1,200 Royal Bank common shares at $27.00.
	30	Received interest on the Minco Inc. bond.
Aug.	5	Received a $0.50 per share cash dividend on the Imperial Oil common shares.
Sept.	1	Received a $0.275 per share cash dividend on the remaining Royal Bank common shares.
	30	Received interest on the Minco Inc. bond.
Dec.	31	Received interest on the Minco Inc. bond.

On December 31, 2017, the fair values of the investments held by Safety Development Corporation were: Royal Bank, $27.50; Imperial Oil, $50.13; and BCE, $13.50. Assume the fair value and carrying value of the Minco Inc. bond were equal.

Required

1. Prepare an amortization schedule for the Minco Inc. bond showing only 2017.

2. Prepare journal entries to record the investment activity including the appropriate fair value adjustment on December 31.

3. Show how the investments will be reported on the December 31, 2017, balance sheet.

Analysis Component: If the fair value adjustment is not recorded by Safety Development Corporation, what is the impact on the financial statements?

Problem 15-3A Non-strategic investments LO3

CHECK FIGURE: 3. $241,343

On January 1, 2017, Liu Corporation paid $241,960 to acquire bonds of Singh Investment Corp with a par value of $240,000. The annual contract rate on the bonds is 6% and interest is paid semiannually on June 30 and December 31. The bonds mature after three years. The market rate of interest was 5.7%. Liu Corporation intends to hold the bonds until maturity.

Required

1. Prepare an amortization schedule for the investment showing only 2017.

2. Prepare Liu's entries to record (a) the purchase of the bonds, (b) the receipt of the first two interest payments.

3. Show how the investment will appear on the December 31, 2017, balance sheet.

Problem 15-4A Non-strategic investments and investment in associate LO3,4

CHECK FIGURE: Dec. 30, 2017, Investment Income = $15,000

Johnson Inc.'s non-strategic investment portfolio at December 31, 2016, consisted of the following:

Debt and Equity Investments*	Cost	Fair Value
10,000 Xavier Corporation common shares...	$163,500	$145,000
1,250 Young Inc. common shares..	65,000	62,000
120,000 Zed Corp. common shares...	40,000	35,600

*The fair value adjustments were recorded on December 31, 2016.

Johnson had no other debt and equity investments at December 31, 2016, other than those shown above. During 2017, Johnson engaged in the following transactions:

2017

Jan.	17	Sold 750 common shares of Young Inc. for $36,000. Johnson Inc. planned to hold these shares for less than one year.
Mar.	3	Purchased 5,000 common shares of Allen Corp. for $300,000. The shares represent a 30% ownership in Allen Corp.
June	7	Received dividends from Allen Corp. at the rate of $2.50 per share.
Aug.	14	Sold the remaining Young Inc. shares at $31.50.
Nov.	28	Purchased a 5% ownership in Davis Corp. by acquiring 10,000 common shares at a total of $89,000. Johnson Inc. will sell these shares in six to nine months.
Dec.	30	Sold 10,000 shares of Xavier Corporation for $160,000.
Dec.	31	Allen Corp. announced a net profit of $280,000 for the year.

Required Journalize the above transactions.

Analysis Component: Assume the Allen Corp. shares were sold on January 16, 2018, for $364,000. Calculate the investment income or loss and explain the impact on the financial statements.

Problem 15-5A **Accounting for share investments** LO4

CHECK FIGURE: 2. Carrying value per share, $14.15

Hamilton Ltd. was organized on January 2, 2017. The following investment transactions and events occurred during the following months:

2017

Jan.	6	Hamilton paid $575,500 for 50,000 shares (20%) of Wong Inc. outstanding common shares.
Apr.	30	Wong declared and paid a cash dividend of $1.10 per share.
Dec.	31	Wong announced that its profit for 2017 was $480,000. Fair value of the shares was $11.80 per share.

2018

Oct.	15	Wong declared and paid a cash dividend of $0.70 per share.
Dec.	31	Wong announced that its profit for 2018 was $630,000. Fair value of the shares was $12.18 per share.

2019

Jan.	5	Hamilton sold all of its investment in Wong for $682,000 cash.

Assume that Hamilton has a significant influence over Wong with its 20% share.

Required

1. Give the entries to record the preceding transactions in Hamilton's books.

2. Calculate the carrying value per share of Hamilton's investment as reflected in the investment account on January 4, 2019.

3. Calculate the change in Hamilton's equity from January 2, 2017, through January 5, 2019, resulting from its investment in Wong.

Alternate Problems

Problem 15-1B **Non-strategic investments** LO2,3

CHECK FIGURE: 2. Feb. 16, 2018, Investment Income = $100

Huang Hardware Inc. had the following transactions involving non-strategic investments during 2017:

2017

Feb.	1	Paid $70,000 to buy a 60-day term deposit, $70,000 principal amount, 6.23%, dated Feb. 1.
	21	Purchased 6,000 common shares of Hilton Ltd. at $11.25.
Apr.	2	Received a cheque for the principal and accrued interest on the term deposit that matured today.
	15	Purchased 8,200 common shares of Elder Corp. at $9.75.
	20	Purchased 14,000 common shares of Venture Ltd. at $3.40.
July	1	Purchased for $67,069 a 6.8%, $68,000 Barker Inc. bond that matures in four years when the market interest rate was 7.2%. Interest is paid semiannually beginning December 31, 2017. Huang Inc. plans to hold this investment until maturity.
	15	Received a $0.30 per share cash dividend on the Hilton common shares.
	28	Sold 4,000 of the Hilton common shares at $11.15.
Dec.	1	Received a $0.30 per share cash dividend on the remaining Hilton common shares owned.
	31	Received the interest on the Barker bond.
	31	The fair values of Huang Inc.'s investments on this date were Hilton shares, $12.60; Elder shares, $10.30; Venture shares, $3.20. Assume the fair value and carrying value of the Barker bond were equal.

2018

Feb.	16	Sold the remaining Hilton shares at $12.65 less a transaction fee of $200.

Required

1. Prepare an amortization schedule for the Barker bond showing only 2017 and 2018.

2. Prepare journal entries to record the preceding transactions.

3. Show how Huang Hardware Inc.'s investments will appear on its December 31, 2017, balance sheet.

Analysis Component: Huang Hardware Inc. purchased the Barker Inc. bond for less than face value. Explain why.

Problem 15-2B **Non-strategic investments** LO2,3

CHECK FIGURE: Dec. 31, 2017, Investment loss = $8,000

Thornhill Corporation has excess cash resulting from extremely successful operations. It has decided to invest this cash in debt and equity securities as follows to be held as non-strategic investments:

2017

Jan.	18	Purchased 16,000 common shares of Logitech at $1.40, plus $500 in transaction fees.
Feb.	27	Purchased 500 common shares of Gordon Activewear at $103.00, plus paid $100 transaction fees.
Apr.	26	Purchased 1,000 common shares of Winston at $18.00, plus an additional $250 in transaction fees.
	30	Received a $0.10 per share cash dividend on the Logitech common shares.
June	4	Sold 10,000 Logitech common shares at $1.15, less a transaction fee of $250.
July	1	Paid $142,933, which included $500 in transaction fees, for a 7.2%, five-year, $140,000 Sharp Inc. bond that pays interest semiannually beginning December 31. The market rate of interest on this date was 6.7%. Thornhill Corporation plans to hold this investment until maturity.
	17	Received a $7.25 per share cash dividend on the Gordon Activewear shares.
Sept.	1	Received a $0.10 per share cash dividend on the remaining Logitech shares.
Dec.	31	Received interest on the Sharp Inc. bond.

2018

Feb.	6	Sold the remaining Logitech shares at $0.85, less a transaction fee of $150.
June	30	Received interest on the Sharp Inc. bond.

On December 31, 2017, the fair values of the investments held by Thornhill Corporation were Logitech, $0.90; Gordon Activewear, $101.00; and Winston, $14.00. Assume the fair value and carrying value of the Sharp bond were equal.

Required

1. Prepare an amortization schedule for 2017 and 2018 regarding the Sharp Inc. bond.

2. Prepare journal entries to record the investment activity, including the fair value adjustment on December 31, 2017.

3. Show how the investments will be reported on the December 31, 2017, balance sheet.

Analysis Component: If the December 31, 2017, fair value adjustment on the Logitech shares were not recorded by Thornhill Corporation, would the February 6, 2018, journal entry be affected? Explain.

Problem 15-3B **Non-strategic investments** LO3

CHECK FIGURE: 3. $852,440

On April 1, 2017, Joe Lite Corporation paid $851,560 to acquire bonds of Santos Electric Inc. with a par value of $860,000. The annual contract rate on the bonds is 6.5% and interest is paid quarterly beginning June 30, 2017. The bonds mature in six years. The market rate of interest at the time of purchase was 6.7%. Joe Lite Corporation plans to hold the bonds until they mature.

Required

1. Prepare an amortization schedule for the investment showing only 2017.

2. Prepare Joe Lite's entries to record (a) the purchase of the bonds, and (b) the receipt of the first three interest payments.

3. Show how the investment will appear on the December 31, 2017, balance sheet.

Problem 15-4B **Non-strategic investments and investment in associate** LO3,4

CHECK FIGURE: Dec. 30, 2017, Investment loss = $10,000

Irving Inc.'s non-strategic investment portfolio at December 31, 2016, consisted of the following:

Debt and Equity Investments*	Cost	Fair Value
50,000 Cumber Corporation common shares	$138,000	$145,000
18,000 Olds Inc. common shares...	124,200	118,900
45,000 Waters Corp. common shares...	265,500	261,000

*The fair value adjustments were recorded on December 31, 2016.

Irving Inc. had no other debt and equity investments at December 31, 2016, other than those shown above. During 2017, Irving engaged in the following transactions:

2017

Feb.	2	Sold 45,000 of the Cumber Corporation shares for $2.48 per share.
June	27	Purchased 280,000 common shares of King Corp. for $540,000. The shares represent a 38% ownership in King Corp.
	30	Received dividends of $0.45 per share from King Corp.
July	3	Sold the remaining Cumber Corporation shares for $14,680.
Aug.	7	Purchased a 15% ownership in Amber Corp. by acquiring 45,000 common shares at $14.50 per share. Irving Inc. plans to sell these shares in six to nine months.
Dec.	30	Sold 25,000 shares of Waters Corp. for $5.40 per share.
	31	King Corp. announced a loss of $40,000 for the year.

Required

1. Calculate the total fair value adjustment that was recorded on December 31, 2016.

2. Journalize the 2017 transactions as detailed above.

Problem 15-5B Accounting for share investments LO4

CHECK FIGURE: 2. Carrying value per share, $19.63

River Outdoor Supply Corporation (River Corp.) was organized on January 2, 2017. River Corp. issued 50,000 common shares for $250,000 on that date. The following investment transactions and events subsequently occurred:

2017

Jan.	12	River Corp. acquired 12,000 shares of Turner Ltd. at a cost of $250,000. This investment represented 24% of Turner's outstanding shares.
Mar.	31	Turner Ltd. declared and paid a cash dividend of $1.00 per share.
Dec.	31	Turner Ltd. announced that its profit for 2017 was $125,000.

2018

Aug.	15	Turner Ltd. declared and paid a cash dividend of $0.80 per share.
Dec.	31	Turner Ltd. announced that its loss for 2018 was $95,000.

2019

Jan.	6	River Corp. sold all of its investment in Turner Ltd. for $230,000 cash.

Assume that River Corp. has significant influence over Turner Ltd. with its 24% share.

Required

1. Give the entries to record the preceding transactions in River Corp.'s books.

2. Calculate the carrying value per share of River Corp.'s investment as reflected in the investment account on January 1, 2019.

3. Calculate the change in River Corp.'s equity from January 12, 2017, through January 6, 2019, resulting from its investment in Turner Ltd.

Analytical and Review Problem

A & R 15-1

On January 1, 2017, Holiday Resorts Ltd. purchased 30% of Chapman Ltd.'s outstanding common shares. The balance in Holiday Ltd.'s Investment in Chapman Ltd. account was $500,000 as of December 31, 2018. The following information is available for years 2017 and 2018 for Chapman Ltd.:

	Profit	Dividends Paid
2017	$300,000	$100,000
2018	$400,000	$100,000

Required Calculate the purchase price paid by Holiday Ltd. for Chapman Ltd. shares on January 1, 2017.

Ethics Challenge

EC 15-1

Jack Phelps is the controller for Jayhawk Corporation. Jayhawk has a corporate policy of investing idle cash in non-strategic investments. About 18 months ago, the company had significant amounts of idle cash and invested in 16%, 10-year Delta Inc. bonds. Management's intent was to hold the bonds for the duration of the contract life. Jack is preparing the year-end financial statements. In accounting for investments, he knows he must review the fair values of his equity investments and assess bonds held under the amortized cost method for impairment. Since the bonds were purchased, Delta Inc.'s success has declined significantly and there have been recent media discussions that indicate Delta Inc. may be heading into bankrupcty. Jack earns a bonus each year that is calculated as a percentage of the profit of the corporation.

Required

1. Will Jack's bonus be affected in any way by a year-end impairment adjustment of the Delta Inc. bonds?

2. What criteria should Jack consider when reviewing whether the bonds are impaired?

3. Are there any likely checks in the corporation to review how Jack has treated the bonds for year-end?

Focus on Financial Statements

FFS 15-1

Delta Corporation showed the following adjusted trial balance at its year-end, December 31, 2017:

Delta Corporation Adjusted Trial Balance December 31, 2017 (000s)	
Account	**Balance[1]**
Accounts payable	96
Accounts receivable	71
Accumulated depreciation—equipment	76
Allowance for doubtful accounts	8
Cash	70
Cash dividends	40
Common shares	100
Cost of goods sold	395
Earnings from investment in Tildon Inc.[2]	40
Equipment	101
Income taxes payable	7
Income tax expense	52
Interest expense	5
Investment income	136
Investment in Tildon Inc. shares[2]	238
Investment—Apple Inc. bonds, due 2027	56
Merchandise inventory	28
Notes payable, due March 2022	74
Operating expenses	218
Preferred shares	44
Prepaid rent	6
Retained earnings	82
Sales	620
Investment—Cornerstone Inc. shares	15
Unearned revenue	12

[1]Assume all balances are normal.
[2]Delta owns 36% of the outstanding shares of Tildon Inc.

Required Using the information provided, prepare a single-step income statement and a classified balance sheet, in thousands.

Analysis Component: Explain the impact on the financial statements if a non-strategic equity investment was listed instead as a strategic equity investment.

FFS 15-2

Canadian Tire, a major Canadian retailer, reported the following in its January 3, 2015, financial statements:

	January 3, 2015
Current investments...	$289.1 million
Non-current investments	176.0 million

No other investments were reported.

Required

1. On which financial statement would the above information have appeared?

2. Are the investments described above non-strategic or strategic? Explain why or why not.

3. Describe what types of investments might be included in each of the categories above.

Critical Thinking Mini Case

You are the chair of the board of CT Inc., a Canadian-based multinational corporation, which has excess cash totalling $75 million. The company is interested in investing some or all of this in Delmar Corp., one of CT's key suppliers. The following statements are available for your review.

Delmar Corp. Income Statement For Year Ended November 30, 2017 (millions of $)		
Sales..		$500
Cost of goods sold		190
Gross profit...		$310
Operating expenses:.............................		
Depreciation expense[3]......................	$ 50	
Other expenses...............................	170	
Total operating expenses		220
Profit from operations		$ 90
Income tax expense.............................		10
Profit		$ 80

Delmar Corp. Comparative Balance Sheet Information November 30 (millions of $)	2017	2016
Cash..	$ 15	$ 5
Accounts receivable (net)	46	10
Inventory...	80	75
Prepaid rent	30	15
Property, plant and equipment (net).......	300	350
Accounts payable	40	22
Accrued liabilities.................................	35	50
Income tax payable.............................	7	2
Common shares[1]................................	150	150
Retained earnings[2]	239	231

[1]There were 25 million common shares issued and outstanding; no new shares were issued during 2016 or 2017. Fair value on November 30, 2017: $8.50 per share.

[2]Dividends totalling $72 million were declared and paid during 2017.

[3]Delmar Inc. uses straight-line depreciation; no PPE have been purchased or sold since start-up.

Required Using the elements of critical thinking described on the inside front cover, detail the Problem, Goal, Principles, Facts, and a Conclusion for this situation. A bond amortization schedule may be helpful with the analysis.

Reporting and Analyzing Cash Flows

A Look Back

Chapter 15 analyzed accounting treatment on the recording and reporting of corporate investments in debt and shares.

A Look at This Chapter

This chapter focuses on reporting and analyzing cash inflows and cash outflows. We emphasize how to prepare and interpret the statement of cash flows.

Photo Courtesy of Butter Avenue

LEARNING OBJECTIVES

LO1 Explain the purpose and importance of cash flow information.

LO2 Distinguish among operating, investing, and financing activities.

LO3 Identify and disclose non-cash investing and financing activities.

LO4 Describe and prepare the statement of cash flows.

LO5 Calculate cash flows from operating activities using the indirect method.

LO6 Determine cash flows from both investing and financing activities.

LO7 Calculate cash flows from operating activities using the direct method.

Cash Flow Analysis Critical to Strategic Growth

Calvin and Tina Su are two siblings who have a taste for success. The partners launched Butter Avenue, an elegant patisserie/café in Toronto that specializes in French macarons, a colourful, small, delicate, meringue-based confectionary. Each sibling brings a different skillset to the partnership, enabling them to establish a strong product with a committed customer base, experiencing steady growth since its launch in 2011. In establishing their business, effective cash flow management has been critical to Butter Avenue's continued growth and success.

Tina is a French-trained pastry chef with a passion for perfection. She worked at several bakeries in France and trained at Le Cordon Bleu's Institute in Ottawa. The idea of opening a bakery sprang from her experiments with recipes for French macarons at home, serving her creations to her brother Calvin and his friends. Calvin had been searching for a business opportunity for several years, and he immediately knew her product was a winner. Together, they took the leap and opened up a Facebook page and an online shop to test the market. Relying on the power of social media, they started to get online orders and courageously decided to take the leap and open up a location in a high-end neighbourhood on Yonge Street in Toronto. According to Calvin, the Butter Avenue brand is built on the foundation of "Japanese perfection with a focus on Scandinavian style."

Tina designs many varieties of French macarons, and creates exceptional flavours of cookies and cakes artistically topped with her famous macarons. As head chef, she has trained several sous chefs and bakers, most of whom bring with them impressive experience and credentials from Canada's top cooking schools. With a background in economics and experience in business, Calvin focuses his efforts on corporate sales and organizes pop-up shops in partnership with brands such as Tommy Hilfiger, Jimmy Choo, and Holt Renfrew. Butter Avenue's Yonge Street location has enabled the company to network with local executives and establish product distribution in the designer retailer market. Because Calvin believes that "having different investors with different interests and goals can cause difficulties in enabling expansion," he recommends to "if at all possible, self-finance your business to avoid potential conflict and obstacles." In establishing a new business, "Planning is so important. You need to know your clientele, your product and marketing strategy and plan ahead.... Analyze performance against the plan regularly."

The sibling duo discovered that entrepreneurs face great challenges as they are stretched to make decisions in previously unchartered territory, such as selections over the interior design of their shops, branding, and packaging design. Having a keen understanding of each others' strengths and weaknesses and an impressive relationship rooted in trust and respect enables the siblings to focus on the best interests of the business as their main priority. Calvin receives monthly financial reports from his accountant. With his accountant, they then analyze actual performance compared to the budget and assess the impact to cash flow. He advises future entrepreneurs "it helps to have a professional you can rely on to understand the numbers." Butter Avenue's success in their first two years led them to launch a second location on Queen Street West in downtown Toronto. What has been the key to their success thus far? In Calvin's words, "consistency, hard work, and strategic networking."

Sources: http://www.theglobeandmail.com/report-on-business/small-business/starting-out/siblings-find-sweet-success-as-macaron-makers/article21352212/
http://www.aznmodern.com/2014/10/10/butter-avenue-opens-one-hippest-places-earth/; Interview with Calvin Su, dated March 10, 2015.

Video Link: https://www.facebook.com/ButterAvenueCo

| CRITICAL THINKING CHALLENGE | How does debt financing affect cash flow? How does equity financing affect cash flow? What effect does debt versus equity financing have on the strength of the balance sheet? |

CHAPTER PREVIEW

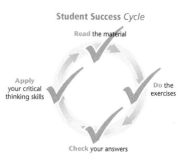

Student Success *Cycle*

Profitability is a primary goal of most managers, but it is not the only goal. Companies such as Butter Avenue, featured in the chapter opening vignette, cannot achieve or maintain profits without careful management of cash. Managers and other users of information pay close attention to a company's cash position and the transactions affecting cash. Information about these transactions is reported in the statement of cash flows. This chapter explains how we prepare, analyze, and interpret a statement of cash flows using both the indirect method, which is entrenched in practice, and the direct method, which is recommended by the International Accounting Standards Board.[1] The chapter also discusses the importance of cash flow information for predicting future performance and making managerial decisions. Developing cash flow strategies based upon an understanding of the statement of cash flows is especially important for a new growing business, as is made clear by Butter Avenue in the chapter opening vignette.

Basics of Cash Flow Reporting

This section describes the basics of cash flow reporting, including its purpose, measurement, classification, format, and preparation.

Purpose of the Statement of Cash Flows

LO1 Explain the purpose and importance of cash flow information.

The purpose of the **statement of cash flows** is to report detailed information about the major cash receipts (inflows) and cash payments (outflows) during a period. This includes separately identifying the cash flows related to operating, investing, and financing activities.

The statement of cash flows helps financial statement users evaluate the liquidity and solvency of an enterprise and assess the enterprise's ability to generate cash from internal sources, to repay its liabilities, and to reinvest and make distributions to owners.

We can examine balance sheets at the beginning and end of a year to determine by how much cash has changed, but the statement of cash flows gives the details about individual cash flows that help users answer questions such as:

- How does a company obtain its cash?
- Where does a company spend its cash?
- What is the reason behind the changes to the cash balance over the period?

The statement of cash flows addresses these important questions by summarizing, classifying, and reporting a company's periodic cash inflows and outflows; it is an analytical tool used to assess, evaluate, and analyze performance for decision making.

---

1 IFRS 2015, IAS 7, para. 18–19.

Importance of Cash Flows

Information about cash flows, and inflows and outflows, can influence decision makers in important ways. For instance, we look more favourably at a company that is financing its expenditures with cash from operations than at one that does it by selling its property, plant, and equipment. Information about cash flows helps users decide whether a company has enough cash to:

- Pay its existing debts as they mature
- Meet unexpected obligations
- Pursue unexpected opportunities
- Plan day-to-day operating activities
- Make long-term investment decisions.

There are many striking examples of how careful analysis and management of cash flows has led to improved financial stability. There are examples of the opposite as well. Nortel Networks, a former Canadian telecommunications giant, went bankrupt, despite having over $US10 billion in annual revenues in its last three years of operation (2007–2009), proving that strategic management over cash flow is critical for continued operational success.

Measuring Cash Flows

The statement of cash flows details the difference between the beginning and ending balances of cash and *cash equivalents*. While we continue to use the terms *cash flows* and *statement of cash flows*, we must remember that both terms refer to cash and cash equivalents.

A **cash equivalent**[2] is an investment that must:

1. Be readily convertible to a known amount of cash
2. Have a maturity of three months or less from its date of acquisition.

Bank overdrafts repayable on demand may be included in the cash and cash equivalent balance.[3] Share investments are normally not included as cash equivalents because their values are subject to risk of changes in market prices. Classifying short-term, highly liquid investments as cash equivalents is based on the idea that companies make these investments to earn a return on idle cash balances, yet they can be converted into cash quickly.

 **DECISION INSIGHT**

Top 10 Cash Flow Management Tips:

1. Work ahead to forecast future cash demands.
2. Review sales and expenses regularly to ensure expected cash shortfalls are easier to manage through financing alternatives before a cash shortfall arrives.
3. Encourage customers to pay early by offering a variety of payment options including taking advantage of technology such as the use of square credit card reader, accepting debit cards, credit cards, or wire transfers.

---

2   IFRS 2015, IAS 7, para. 7, defines cash equivalents as investments that must be "readily convertible to known amounts of cash and be subject to an insignificant risk of changes in value. Therefore, an investment normally qualifies as a cash equivalent only when it has a short maturity of, say, three months or less from the date of acquisition."

3   IFRS 2015, IAS 7, para. 8.

4. Ask customers for an upfront deposit to help finance inventory costs.
5. Ensure excess cash reserves are managed through strategic short-term investments.
6. Develop a product/service marketing plan that encourages repeat customers or customer referrals and encourage sales during slower seasons.
7. Hire an accounts receivable clerk to focus on collections of overdue accounts and have a formal process in place to assess creditworthiness of new customers.
8. Establish good relationships with suppliers and work to lengthen credit term if possible with suppliers.
9. Invest in an ERP system to help manage inventory levels and ensure inventory stores match forecasted demand.
10. Question expenditures, especially those with recurring charges. Ensure each significant or recurring expense you commit to is in the best long-term interests of the company.

SOURCES: https://youinc.com/content/money/ideas-to-improve-cash-flow; http://www.entrepreneur.com/article/66008; http://smallbizla.org/2014/10-tips-to-know-about-managing-your-business-cash-flow/; http://smallbizla.org/2009/10-tips-for-improving-your-cash-flow/

Classifying Cash Flows

LO2   Distinguish among operating, investing, and financing activities.

All individual cash receipts and payments (except cash paid/received for the purchase/sale of cash equivalents) are classified and reported on the statement as operating, investing, or financing activities. A net cash inflow (source) occurs when the receipts in a category exceed the payments. A net cash outflow (use) occurs when the payments in a category exceed receipts.

OPERATING ACTIVITIES

Operating activities are the principal revenue-producing activities of the entity.[4] They include the cash effects of transactions that determine profit. But not all items in profit, such as gains and losses, are operating activities. We discuss these exceptions later in the chapter.

Examples of **operating activities** are the production and purchase of merchandise, the sale of goods and services to customers, and administrative expenses of the business. Changes in current assets and current liabilities are normally the result of operating activities. Exhibit 16.1 lists the more common cash inflows and outflows from operating activities.

EXHIBIT 16.1

Cash Flows From Operating Activities

Cash Inflows	Cash Outflows
From customers' cash sales	To employees for salaries and wages
From collection on credit sales	To suppliers for goods and services
From cash dividends received[5]	To governments for taxes and fines
From borrowers for interest earned[5]	To lenders for interest paid[5]
From suppliers for refunds	To customers for refunds issued
From lawsuit settlements received	To charities for donations paid

---

4   IFRS 2015, IAS 7, para. 6.

INVESTING ACTIVITIES

Investing activities include:

a. Purchase and sale of property, plant, and equipment
b. Purchase and sale of investments, other than cash equivalents
c. Lending and collecting on loans (receivables).

Changes in non-current assets are normally caused by investing activities. Exhibit 16.2 lists examples of cash flows from investing activities. Proceeds from collecting the principal amounts of loans deserve special attention. If the loan results from sales to customers, its cash receipts are classified as operating activities whether short term or long term. But if the loan results from a loan to another party, then its cash receipts from collecting the principal of the note are classified as an investing activity.

EXHIBIT 16.2

Cash Flows From Investing Activities[5]

Cash Inflows	Cash Outflows
From selling capital assets	To purchase capital assets
From selling equity investments	To purchase equity investments
From selling debt investments	To purchase debt investments
From collecting principal on loans	To provide loans to a third party
From selling (discounting) of loans	

FINANCING ACTIVITIES

Financing activities are those that affect a company's owners and creditors. They include (a) obtaining cash from issuing debt and repaying the amounts borrowed, and (b) obtaining cash from or distributing cash to owners. Transactions with creditors that affect profit are classified as operating activities. For example, interest expense on a company's debt is classified as an operating rather than a financing activity because interest is deducted as an expense in calculating profit. Also, cash payments to settle credit purchases of merchandise, whether on account or by note, are operating activities because they are more related to a company's ongoing operations. Changes in long-term debt and equity and short-term debt not involving operating activities are normally a result of financing activities. Exhibit 16.3 lists examples of cash flows from financing activities.

EXHIBIT 16.3

Cash Flows From Financing Activities

Cash Inflows	Cash Outflows
From issuing its own shares	To pay cash dividends to shareholders[6]
From issuing bonds and notes	To repurchase shares
From issuing and current and non-current liabilities	To repay cash loans to lenders
	To pay withdrawals by owners

---

5 IFRS 2015, IAS 7, para. 33, states that interest paid/received and dividends received are usually classified as operating cash flows but may be included under financing/investing activities, respectively. For consistency in presentation, this textbook will show interest paid/received and dividends received as operating cash flows.

6 IFRS 2015, IAS 7, para. 34, states that dividends paid may be classified as a financing cash flow but may be included under operating activities. For consistency in presentation, this textbook will show dividends paid as a financing cash flow.

Non-Cash Investing and Financing Activities

LO3 Identify and disclose non-cash investing and financing activities.

Companies sometimes enter into direct exchange transactions in which non-current balance sheet items are exchanged but cash is not affected. Yet because of their importance and the full disclosure principle, these important non-cash investing and financing activities are disclosed in a note to the statement of cash flows.[7] One example of such a transaction is the purchase of non-current assets by giving a long-term note payable. Exhibit 16.4 lists some transactions that are disclosed as non-cash investing and financing activities.

EXHIBIT 16.4

Examples of Non-Cash Investing and Financing Activities

- Retirement of debt by issuing shares
- Conversion of preferred shares to common shares
- Purchase of a long-term asset by issuing a note payable
- Exchange of non-cash assets for other non-cash assets
- Purchase of non-cash assets by issuing shares or debt
- Declaration and issuance of a share dividend

To illustrate, let's assume Burton Company purchases machinery for $12,000 by paying cash of $5,000 and trading in old machinery with a market value of $7,000. The statement of cash flows reports only the $5,000 cash outflow for the purchase of machinery. This means the $12,000 investing transaction is only partially described in the body of the statement of cash flows. Yet this information is potentially important to users in that it changes the makeup of assets.

Companies disclose non-cash investing and financing activities not reported in the body of the statement of cash flows in either (1) a note, or (2) a separate schedule attached to the statement. In the case of Burton Company, it could either describe the transaction in a note or include a small schedule at the bottom of its statement that lists the $12,000 asset investment along with financing of $5,000 and a $7,000 trade-in of old machinery.

DECISION MAKER

Answer—End of chapter

Community Activist

You are a community activist trying to raise public awareness of pollution emitted by a local manufacturer. The manufacturer complains about the high costs of pollution controls and points to its recent $4 million annual loss as evidence. But you also know its net cash flows were a positive $8 million this past year. How are these results possible?

---

[7] IFRS 2015, IAS 7, para. 43–44.

Format of the Statement of Cash Flows

LO4 Describe and prepare the statement of cash flows.

Accounting standards require companies to include a statement of cash flows in a complete set of financial statements. **Brick Brewing Company Ltd.**'s cash flow statement from its Annual Report for the year ended January 31, 2014 is presented below:

STATEMENTS OF CASH FLOWS
Years ended January 31, 2014 and 2013

	Notes	January 31, 2014	January 31, 2013
			[Revised-note 27]
Operating activities			
Net income		$ 525,199	$ 351,033
Adjustments for:			
Income tax expense	11	201,476	234,000
Finance costs	10	692,156	666,579
Depreciation and amortization of property, plant and equipment and intangibles	12,13	2,995,060	2,570,596
Loss (gain) on disposal of property, plant and equipment		(29,331)	22,660
Share-based payments	17	194,588	167,646
Change in non-cash working capital related to operations		(979,470)	(903,726)
Less:			
Interest paid		(595,734)	(581,843)
Cash provided by operating activities		**3,003,944**	2,526,945
Investing activities			
Purchase of property, plant and equipment	12	(2,982,916)	(3,917,277)
Proceeds from sale of property, plant and equipment	12	206,500	5,260
Purchase of intangible assets	13	(503,772)	(468,121)
Cash used in investing activities		**(3,280,188)**	(4,380,138)
Financing activities			
Increase/(decrease) in bank indebtedness	22	(620,036)	297,709
Decrease in obligation under financial lease		—	(24,650)
Issuance of long-term debt	20	1,578,543	1,834,938
Repayment of long-term debt	20	(3,515,157)	(1,452,525)
Issuance of shares	17	30,781	16,938
Proceeds from warrants, net	17	2,802,113	1,180,783
Cash provided by financing activities		**276,244**	1,853,193
Net increase/(decrease) in cash		**—**	—
Cash, beginning of period		**—**	—
Cash, end of period		**$ —**	$ —

The accompanying notes are an integral part of these financial statements.
SOURCE: http://www.brickbeer.com/sites/brick_corporate/files/2013_annual_report.pdf

Notice that cash at the end of the period is reported as zero. This is due to the fact that Brick Brewing Ltd. is in a negative cash position, meaning the company is operating under a bank line of credit. This is referred to as "bank indebtedness" and is presented as a current liability in the amount of $1,694,178 on its January 31, 2014 balance sheet. The decrease in bank indebtedness of $620,036 is reported under financing activities on the statement of cash flows. For more example cash flow statements, refer to the partial financial statements for **Indigo**, **Telus**, **WestJet** and **Danier** in Appendix II.

Exhibit 16.5 shows us the usual format that reports cash inflows and cash outflows from three activities: operating, investing, and financing. The statement explains how transactions affect the beginning-of-period cash (and cash equivalents) balance to produce its end-of-period balance.

EXHIBIT 16.5

Format of the Statement of Cash Flows

Company Name Statement of Cash Flows Period Covered	
Cash flows from operating activities:	
[List of individual inflows and outflows]	
Net cash inflow (outflow) from operating activities	$ ###
Cash flows from investing activities:	
[List of individual inflows and outflows]	
Net cash inflow (outflow) from investing activities..	###
Cash flows from financing activities:	
[List of individual inflows and outflows]	
Net cash inflow (outflow) from financing activities	###
Net increase (decrease) in cash (and cash equivalents)...	$ ###
Cash (and cash equivalents) balance at beginning of period	###
Cash (and cash equivalents) balance at end of period	$ ###
Note disclosure of *non-cash investing and financing transactions,* for example, "Note 4. During the year the company purchased new equipment by issuing bonds."	

CHECKPOINT

1. Does a statement of cash flows disclose payments of cash to purchase cash equivalents? Does it disclose receipts of cash from selling cash equivalents?
2. Identify the categories of cash flows reported separately on the statement of cash flows.
3. Identify the category for each of the following cash flow activities: (a) purchase of equipment for cash; (b) payment of wages; (c) issuance of common shares for cash; (d) receipt of cash dividends from share investment; (e) collection of cash from customers; (f) issuance of bonds for cash.

Do Quick Study questions: QS 16-1, QS 16-2, QS 16-3, QS 16-4

Preparing the Statement of Cash Flows

The information we need to prepare a statement of cash flows comes from:

- Comparative balance sheets at the beginning and end of the period
- An income statement for the period
- A careful analysis of additional information

Preparation of a statement of cash flows involves five steps:

1. Calculate the net increase or decrease in cash and cash equivalents.
2. Calculate and report net cash inflows (outflows) from operating activities using either the
   a. Indirect method or   b. Direct method.
3. Calculate and report net cash inflows (outflows) from investing activities.
4. Calculate and report net cash inflows (outflows) from financing activities.
5. Calculate net cash flow by combining net cash inflows (outflows) from operating, investing, and financing activities and then prove it by adding it to the beginning cash balance to show it equals the ending cash balance.

Non-cash investing and financing activities are disclosed in a note to the statement or in a separate schedule to the statement, as shown at the bottom of Exhibit 16.5.

The remaining sections of this chapter explain these important steps in preparing the statement of cash flows using the 2017 income statement of Gelato Corp. along with its December 31, 2016 and 2017, balance sheets shown in Exhibit 16.6. Our objective with the statement of cash flows is to explain the increase or decrease in cash during 2017.

EXHIBIT 16.6

Financial Statements

In addition to providing its income statement and comparative balance sheet, Gelato Corp. also discloses additional information about year 2017 transactions:

a. All accounts payable balances result from merchandise purchases.

b. Equipment costing $70,000 is purchased by paying $10,000 cash and issuing $60,000 of bonds payable.

c. Equipment with an original cost of $30,000 and accumulated depreciation of $12,000 is sold for $12,000 cash. This yields a $6,000 loss.

d. Proceeds from issuing 3,000 common shares are $15,000.

e. Paid $18,000 to retire bonds with a book value of $34,000. This yields a $16,000 gain from bond retirement.

f. Cash dividends of $14,000 are declared and paid.

Gelato Corp.
Income Statement
For Year Ended December 31, 2017

Sales...		$ 590,000
Cost of goods sold	$300,000	
Wages and other operating expenses..........................	216,000	
Interest expense..	7,000	
Income taxes expense	15,000	
Depreciation expense..	24,000	(562,000)
Loss on sale of equipment		(6,000)
Gain on retirement of bonds		16,000
Profit		$ 38,000

Gelato Corp.
Balance Sheet
December 31, 2017 and 2016

	2017	2016
Assets		
Current assets:		
Cash	$ 17,000	$ 12,000
Accounts receivable...	60,000	40,000
Merchandise inventory...	84,000	70,000
Prepaid expenses..	6,000	4,000
Total current assets..	$167,000	$126,000
Non-current assets		
Property, plant, and equipment	$250,000	$210,000
Less: Accumulated depreciation...............................	(60,000)	(48,000)
Total assets	$357,000	$288,000
Liabilities		
Current liabilities:		
Accounts payable..	$ 35,000	$ 40,000
Interest payable..	3,000	4,000
Income taxes payable..	22,000	12,000
Total current liabilities..	$ 60,000	$ 56,000
Non-current liabilities		
Bonds payable	90,000	64,000
Total liabilities	$150,000	$120,000
Equity		
Contributed capital:		
Common shares..	$ 95,000	$ 80,000
Retained earnings...	112,000	88,000
Total equity	207,000	168,000
Total liabilities and equity.......................................	$357,000	$288,000

1. Calculate the Net Increase or Decrease in Cash

The increase or decrease in cash equals the current end of period's cash balance minus the prior period's end of period cash balance. This is the *bottom line* figure for the statement of cash flows and is a helpful check on the accuracy of our work. To illustrate, the summarized cash account of Gelato Corp. in Exhibit 16.7 shows a net increase in cash of $5,000 for the year ended December 31, 2017 ($17,000 balance, Dec. 31, 2017, less the $12,000 balance, Dec. 31, 2016).

EXHIBIT 16.7

Summarized Cash Account

Summarized Cash Account			
Balance, Dec. 31/16	12,000		
Receipts from customers	570,000	319,000	Payments for merchandise
Proceeds from sale of equipment	12,000		Payments for wages and
Proceeds from share issuance	15,000	218,000	operating expenses
		8,000	Interest payments
		5,000	Tax payments
		10,000	Payment for equipment
		18,000	Payments to retire bonds
		14,000	Dividend payments
Balance, Dec. 31/17	17,000		

2. Calculate and Report Net Cash Inflows (Outflows) From Operating Activities

On the income statement, profit is calculated using accrual basis accounting. Accrual basis accounting recognizes revenues when earned and expenses when incurred. But revenues and expenses do not necessarily coincide with the receipt and payment of cash. Both the *indirect* and *direct* methods convert accrual-based profit to the same amount of cash provided by operating activities. IFRS 2015, IAS 7, encourages the use of the direct method because it provides greater detail regarding operating cash flows.

The **indirect method** calculates the net cash inflows (outflows) from operating activities by *adjusting accrual to a cash basis.* The indirect method reports the necessary adjustments to reconcile profit to net cash inflows (outflows) from operating activities.

The **direct method** separately lists *each major item of operating cash receipts* (such as cash received from customers) and each major item of operating cash payments (such as cash paid for merchandise). The cash payments are subtracted from cash receipts to determine the net cash inflows (outflows) from operating activities. The operating activities section is a restatement of profit from an accrual basis (as reported on the income statement) to a cash basis.

Although the direct method is encouraged[8] (it is *not required*), *most companies prefer the indirect format because it reconciles profit or loss to cash flows and clearly presents non-cash operating items such as depreciation and gains/losses.* We begin by illustrating the indirect method in this chapter by preparing the operating activities section of the statement of cash flows for Gelato Corporation. The direct method, which is the preferred method of accounting standard setters, will be covered later in the chapter. Exhibit 16.14 provides a summary of both the indirect and direct methods.

---

8 IFRS 2015, IAS 7, para. 18–19.

Indirect Method of Reporting Operating Cash Flows

LO5 Calculate cash flows from operating activities using the indirect method.

We draw on the financial statements of Gelato Corp. in Exhibit 16.6 to illustrate application of the indirect method. The indirect method of reporting begins with profit of $38,000 for Gelato Corp. and then adjusts it to get net cash inflows (outflows) from operating activities. Exhibit 16.8 highlights the results of the indirect method of reporting operating cash flows for Gelato Corp. The net cash inflows from operating activities are $20,000.

> **Important Tip:** *The amount of net cash inflows for operating activities is the same as that for the direct method of reporting operating cash flows detailed later in the chapter (see Exhibit 16.9).*

The two methods always yield the same net cash inflows (outflows) from operating activities. Only the calculations and presentation are different.

EXHIBIT 16.8

Statement of Cash Flows—Indirect Method of Reporting Operating Cash Flows

Gelato Corp. Statement of Cash Flows For Year Ended December 31, 2017			
Cash flows from operating activities:			
Profit		$ 38,000	
Adjustments to reconcile profit to net cash provided by operating activities:			
Increase in accounts receivable		(20,000)	
Increase in merchandise inventory		(14,000)	
Increase in prepaid expenses		(2,000)	
Decrease in accounts payable		(5,000)	
Decrease in interest payable		(1,000)	
Increase in income taxes payable		10,000	
Depreciation expense		24,000	
Loss on sale of equipment		6,000	
Gain on retirement of bonds		(16,000)	
Net cash inflow from operating activities			$20,000
Cash flows from investing activities:			
Cash received from sale of equipment		$ 12,000	
Cash paid for purchase of equipment		(10,000)	
Net cash inflow from investing activities			2,000
Cash flows from financing activities:			
Cash received from issuing shares		$ 15,000	
Cash paid to retire bonds		(18,000)	
Cash paid for dividends		(14,000)	
Net cash outflow from financing activities			(17,000)
Net increase in cash			$ 5,000
Cash balance at beginning of 2017			12,000
Cash balance at end of 2017			$17,000

The indirect method adjusts profit for three types of adjustments:

1. Adjustments for changes in non-cash current assets and current liabilities relating to operating activities.

2. Adjustments to income statement items involving operating activities that do not affect cash inflows or outflows during the period.

3. Adjustments to eliminate gains and losses resulting from investing and financing activities (those not part of operating activities).

This section describes each of these three types of adjustments in applying the indirect method.

ADJUSTMENTS FOR CHANGES IN NON-CASH CURRENT ASSETS

Changes in non-cash current assets are normally the result of operating activities. Under the indirect method for reporting operating cash flows:

> *Decreases in non-cash current assets are added to profit.*

> *Increases in non-cash current assets are subtracted from profit.*

To demonstrate, we now look at the individual non-cash current assets of Gelato as shown in Exhibit 16.6.

Accounts Receivable   Accounts Receivable of Gelato *increased* $20,000 in the period, from a beginning balance of $40,000 to an ending balance of $60,000. This increase implies Gelato collected less cash than its reported sales amount for this period. It also means some of these sales were in the form of accounts receivable, leaving Accounts Receivable with an increase. This lesser amount of cash collections compared with sales is reflected in the Accounts Receivable account as shown here:

Accounts Receivable			
Balance, Dec. 31/16	40,000		
Sales, 2017	590,000	570,000	= Collections
Balance, Dec. 31/17	60,000		

This $20,000 increase in Accounts Receivable is subtracted from profit as part of our adjustments to get net cash inflows from operating activities. Subtracting it adjusts sales to the cash receipts amount, as it represents cash sales not yet collected from customers.

Merchandise Inventory   Merchandise Inventory *increased* $14,000 in the period, from a beginning balance of $70,000 to an ending balance of $84,000. This increase implies Gelato had a greater amount of cash purchases than goods sold this period. This greater amount of cash purchases ended up in the form of inventory, resulting in an inventory increase. This greater amount of cash purchases compared to the amount subtracted from profit as cost of goods sold is reflected in the Merchandise Inventory account increase:

Merchandise Inventory			
Balance, Dec. 31/16	70,000		
Purchases =	314,000	300,000	Cost of goods sold
Balance, Dec. 31/17	84,000		

The $14,000 increase in inventory is subtracted from profit because extra cash was spent on inventory.

Prepaid Expenses   Prepaid Expenses *increased* $2,000 in the period, from a beginning balance of $4,000 to an ending balance of $6,000. This increase implies Gelato's cash payments exceeded its operating expenses incurred this period. These larger cash payments ended up increasing the amount of prepaid expenses. This is reflected in the Prepaid Expenses account:

Prepaid Expenses			
Balance, Dec. 31/16	4,000		
Payments =	218,000		Wages and other
		216,000	operating expenses
Balance, Dec. 31/17	6,000		

This $2,000 increase in prepaid expenses is subtracted from profit, as the additional cash was spent by the organization but not reflected in profit.

ADJUSTMENTS FOR CHANGES IN CURRENT LIABILITIES

Changes in current liabilities are normally the result of operating activities. Under the indirect method for reporting operating cash flows:

> *Increases in current liabilities are added to profit.*

> *Decreases in current liabilities are subtracted from profit.*

To demonstrate, we now analyze the individual current liabilities of Gelato as shown in Exhibit 16.6.

Accounts Payable   Accounts Payable of Gelato *decreased* $5,000 in the period, from a beginning balance of $40,000 to an ending balance of $35,000. This decrease implies its cash payments exceeded its merchandise purchases by $5,000 for the period. This larger amount for cash payments compared to purchases is reflected in the Accounts Payable account:

Accounts Payable			
		40,000	Balance, Dec. 31/16
Payments =	319,000	314,000	Purchases
		35,000	Balance, Dec. 31/17

The $5,000 decrease in Accounts Payable is subtracted from profit. Accounts Payable decreased over the prior year, therefore the amount is taken out of profit, as cash was spent by the organization to pay off its suppliers.

Interest Payable   Interest Payable *decreased* $1,000 in the period, from a beginning balance of $4,000 to an ending balance of $3,000. This decrease indicates cash payments for interest exceeded interest expense as reported on the income statement for the period by $1,000. This larger cash payment compared to the reported interest expense is reflected in the Interest Payable account:

Interest Payable			
		4,000	Balance, Dec. 31/16
Interest paid =	8,000	7,000	Interest expense
		3,000	Balance, Dec. 31/17

The $1,000 decrease in Interest Payable is subtracted from profit as it represents an additional use of current period cash flow.

Income Taxes Payable   Income Taxes Payable *increased* $10,000 in the period, from a beginning balance of $12,000 to an ending balance of $22,000. This increase implies the amount owed for income taxes exceeded the cash payments for the period by $10,000. This smaller cash payment compared to income taxes owed is reflected in the Income Taxes Payable account:

Income Taxes Payable			
		12,000	Balance, Dec. 31/16
Income taxes paid =	5,000	15,000	Income taxes expense
		22,000	Balance, Dec. 31/17

The $10,000 increase in income taxes payable is added to profit, as actual cash flow spent on interest is lower than interest expense as reported under accrual accounting on the income statement.

ADJUSTMENTS FOR OPERATING ITEMS NOT PROVIDING OR USING CASH

The income statement usually includes certain expenses that do not reflect cash outflows in the period. Examples are depreciation of plant and equipment assets, amortization of intangible assets, amortization of bond discount, and bad debts expense. The indirect method for reporting operating cash flows requires that:

> *Expenses with no cash outflows are added back to profit.*

To see this logic, recall that items such as depreciation and bad debts are recorded with debits to expense accounts and credits to non-cash accounts. There is no cash effect in these entries. Yet because items such as depreciation expense are proper deductions in calculating accrual-based profit, we need to add them back to profit when calculating net cash flows from operations. Adding them back cancels their deductions.

Similarly, when profit includes revenues that do not reflect cash inflows in the period, the indirect method for reporting operating cash flows requires that:

> *Revenues with no cash inflows are subtracted from profit.*

For example, a sale on credit is recorded as a debit to Accounts Receivable and a credit to Sales. This transaction increases profit yet there is no cash inflow. Therefore, we need to subtract transactions with no cash inflows from accrual-based profit to determine the actual cash generated from (or used in) operating activities.

We now look at the individual operating items of Gelato that fit this category and do not provide or use cash.

Depreciation   Depreciation expense is the only operating item for Gelato that does not affect cash flows in the period. Our discussion indicates that we must add $24,000 depreciation expense back to profit as part of our adjustments to get net cash inflows from operating activities.

ADJUSTMENTS FOR NON-OPERATING ITEMS

The income statement sometimes includes losses that are not part of operating activities. Examples are a loss from the sale of property, plant, and equipment assets and a loss from retirement of a bond payable. Under the indirect method for reporting operating cash flows:

> **Non-operating losses are added back to profit, as they reflect financing or investing activities.**

To see the logic, consider items such as the sale of equipment and bond retirement. We record these transactions by recognizing the cash, removing equipment or bond accounts, and recognizing the loss or gain. The cash received or paid is not part of operating activities but is recorded under either investing or financing activities. There is no operating cash flow effect. But because the non-operating loss is a deduction in calculating accrual-based profit, we need to add it back to profit when calculating the net cash flow effect from operations. *Adding the loss back to profit cancels the deduction.*

Similarly, when profit includes other income/gains that are not part of operating activities, under the indirect method for reporting operating cash flows:

> **Non-operating income/gains are subtracted from profit.**

These profit adjustments are part of calculations to get net cash provided by operating activities. We now look at the individual non-operating items of Gelato.

Loss on Sale of Equipment   Gelato reports a $6,000 loss on the sale of equipment in its income statement. This loss is a proper deduction in calculating profit, but it is *not part of operating activities.* Instead, *a sale of equipment is part of investing activities.* This means the $6,000 non-operating loss is added back to profit as part of our adjustments to get net cash inflows from operating activities. Adding it back cancels the recorded loss. Earlier in the chapter we explained how the cash inflow from the equipment sale was reported in investing activities.

Gain on Retirement of Bonds   There is a $16,000 gain on retirement of bonds reported in the income statement of Gelato. This gain is properly included in profit, but it is *not part of operating activities.* This means the $16,000 non-operating gain is subtracted from profit as part of our adjustments to get net cash inflows from operating activities. Subtracting it cancels the recorded gain. Earlier in the chapter we describe how the cash outflow to retire the bond was reported in financing activities.

While the calculations in determining net cash inflows (outflows) from operating activities are different for the indirect and direct methods, the results are identical. Both methods yield the same $20,000 figure for net cash inflows (outflows) from operating activities; see Exhibits 16.8 (indirect method) and 16.9 (direct method). An approach used to prepare a statement of cash flows is a detailed T-account analysis. A spreadsheet can also be used to organize information needed to prepare a statement of cash flows. Both of these alternatives are described on Connect.

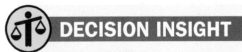

DECISION INSIGHT

Cash or Profit

The difference between profit and operating cash flows can be large. For example, **Loblaw Companies Ltd.** reported a profit of $630 million for the year ended December 28, 2013, but operating cash flows were $1,491 million.

CHECKPOINT

4. Is the direct or indirect method of reporting operating cash flows more informative? Explain. Which method is more common in practice?

5. Determine the net cash inflows (outflows) from operating activities using the following data:

Profit	$74,900
Decrease in accounts receivable.....................	4,600
Increase in inventory................................	11,700
Decrease in accounts payable........................	1,000
Loss on sale of equipment	3,400
Payment of dividends................................	21,500

6. Why are expenses such as depreciation added to profit when cash flow from operating activities is calculated by the indirect method?

7. A company reports profit of $15,000 that includes a $3,000 gain on the sale of land. Why is this gain subtracted from profit in calculating cash flow from operating activities using the indirect method?

Do Quick Study questions: QS 16-5, QS 16-6, QS 16-7, QS 16-8

MID-CHAPTER DEMONSTRATION PROBLEM

Mitchell Corporation Comparative Balance Sheet Information

	December 31	
Assets	**2017**	**2016**
Cash...	$ 15,000	$ 20,000
Accounts receivable	23,000	25,000
Merchandise inventory......................	37,000	34,000
Prepaid expenses	6,000	8,000
Investments	39,000	40,000
Property, plant, and equipment	191,000	170,000
Accumulated depreciation	(31,000)	(25,000)
Total assets	$280,000	$272,000
Liabilities and Equity		
Accounts payable	$ 38,000	$ 30,000
Accrued liabilities............................	68,000	65,000
Bonds payable	100,000	90,000
Common shares	40,000	37,000
Retained earnings............................	34,000	50,000
Total liabilities and equity.................	$280,000	$272,000

Mitchell Corporation Income Statement For Year Ended December 31, 2017

Sales..	$250,000
Cost of goods sold	165,000
Gross profit.....................................	$ 85,000
Operating expenses...........................	40,000
Operating profit before taxes	$ 45,000
Investment income	8,000
Profit before taxes.............................	$ 53,000
Income taxes....................................	14,800
Profit	$ 38,200

Additional information:

a. Depreciation expense of $6,000 is included in operating expenses.

b. There were no gains or losses other than the $8,000 gain on sale of investment reported on the income statement.

Required

Prepare the operating activities section of the statement of cash flows for the year ended December 31, 2017, using the indirect method.

Analysis Component:

What is the significance of *profit* versus *net cash inflow from operations*?

Solution

Profit	$38,200
Adjustments:	
Depreciation	$ 6,000
Gain on sale of investment	(8,000)
Decrease in accounts receivable[1]	2,000
Increase in merchandise inventory[2]	(3,000)
Decrease in prepaid expenses[3]	2,000
Increase in accounts payable[4]	8,000
Increase in accrued liabilities[5]	3,000
Net cash inflow from operations	$48,200

[1]$23,000 − $25,000 = $2,000 decrease
[2]$37,000 − $34,000 = $3,000 increase
[3]$6,000 − $8,000 = $2,000 decrease
[4]$38,000 − $30,000 = $8,000 increase
[5]$68,000 − $65,000 = $3,000 increase

Analysis Component:

The *profit* comes from the income statement, which is prepared using accrual accounting; transactions are recorded when they occur regardless of whether cash is received or paid. For example, a credit sale increases profit but does not affect cash. The *net cash inflow from operations* represents the actual cash generated from operating activities; it is the accrual basis profit adjusted to a cash basis profit.

3. Cash Flows From Investing Activities

LO6   Determine cash flows from both investing and financing activities.

The third major step in preparing the statement of cash flows is to calculate and report net cash flows from investing activities. We normally do this by identifying changes in all non-current asset accounts. Changes in these accounts are then analyzed using available information to determine their effect, if any, on cash. Results of this analysis are reported in the investing activities section of the statement.

> **Important Tip:** *Reporting of investing activities is identical under the direct method and indirect method.*

Investing activities include transactions such as those listed in Exhibit 16.2. Information to calculate cash flows from investing activities is usually taken from beginning and ending balance sheets and from the income statement. Information provided earlier in the chapter about the transactions of Gelato reveals it both purchased and sold equipment during the period. Both transactions are investing activities.

We use a three-step process in determining net cash inflows (outflows) from investing activities:

1. Identify changes in investing-related accounts.
2. Explain these changes using reconstruction analysis.
3. Report cash flow effects.

PROPERTY, PLANT, AND EQUIPMENT (PPE) TRANSACTIONS

For equipment, we need to deal with both the equipment account and its related accumulated depreciation account. Comparative balance sheet information for these accounts is in Exhibit 16.6. The *first step* reveals a $40,000 increase in equipment from $210,000 to $250,000, and a $12,000 increase in accumulated depreciation from $48,000 to $60,000. We need to explain these changes.

The *second step* begins by reviewing ledger accounts and any additional information at our disposal. An equipment account is affected by both purchases and sales of equipment. An accumulated depreciation account is increased by depreciation and reduced by removing accumulated depreciation on asset disposals. Items (b) and (c) from the additional information reported with Exhibit 16.6 for Gelato are relevant for these accounts. To explain changes in these accounts and to help us understand the cash flow effects, we prepare *reconstructed entries*. A reconstructed entry is our reproduction of an entry from a transaction; *it is not the actual entry made by the preparer.* Item (b) reports that Gelato purchased equipment costing $70,000 by issuing $60,000 in bonds payable to the seller and paying $10,000 in cash. The reconstructed entry for our analysis of item (b) is:

Equipment	70,000	
Bonds Payable		60,000
Cash		**10,000**

This entry reveals a $10,000 cash outflow for assets purchased. It also reveals a non-cash investing and financing transaction involving $60,000 bonds given up for $60,000 of equipment.

Item (c) reports that Gelato sold equipment costing $30,000 (with $12,000 of accumulated depreciation) for cash received of $12,000, resulting in a loss of $6,000. The reconstructed entry for item (c) is:

Cash	**12,000**	
Accumulated Depreciation	12,000	
Loss on Sale of Equipment	6,000	
Equipment		30,000

This entry reveals a $12,000 cash inflow for equipment sold. The $6,000 loss is calculated by comparing the equipment's book value to the cash received, and does not reflect any cash inflow or outflow.

We can also reconstruct the entry for depreciation expense using information from the income statement:

Depreciation Expense	24,000	
Accumulated Depreciation		24,000

This entry shows that depreciation expense results in no cash flow effects.

These reconstructed entries are reflected in the ledger accounts for both equipment and accumulated depreciation.

Equipment			
Balance, Dec. 31/16	210,000		
Purchases	70,000	30,000	Sale
Balance, Dec. 31/17	250,000		

Accumulated Depreciation, Equipment			
		48,000	Balance, Dec. 31/16
Sale	12,000	24,000	Deprec. expense
		60,000	Balance, Dec. 31/17

In performing an actual cash flow analysis we have the entire ledger and additional information at our disposal. Here, for brevity, we are given the additional information for reconstructing accounts and verifying that our analysis of the investing-related accounts is complete.

The *third step* is to make the necessary disclosures on the statement of cash flows. Disclosure of the two cash flow effects in the investing section of the statement appears as (also see Exhibit 16.8):

Gelato Corp.
Statement of Cash Flows
For Year Ended December 31, 2017

Cash flows from investing activities:

Cash received from sale of equipment	$ 12,000
Cash paid for purchase of equipment	(10,000)

Note: Non-cash investing and financing activity
During the period equipment was acquired with issuance of $60,000 of bonds.

The $60,000 portion of the purchase described in item (b) and financed by issuance of bonds is a non-cash investing and financing activity and can be reported in a note to the statement as shown above.

We have now reconstructed these accounts by explaining how the beginning balances of both accounts are affected by purchases, sales, and depreciation in yielding their ending balances.

 **CHECKPOINT**

8. Equipment costing $80,000 with accumulated depreciation of $30,000 is sold at a loss of $10,000. What is the cash receipt from the sale? In what category of the statement of cash flows is it reported?

Do Quick Study questions: QS 16-9, QS 16-10

4. Cash Flows From Financing Activities

The *fourth step* in preparing the statement of cash flows is to calculate and report net cash flows from financing activities. We normally do this by identifying changes in all notes payable (current and non-current), non-current liabilities, and equity accounts. These accounts include Long-Term Debt, Notes Payable, Bonds Payable, Owner's Capital, Common Shares, and Retained Earnings. Changes in these accounts are then analyzed using available information to determine their effect, if any, on cash. Results of this analysis are reported in the financing activities section of the statement.

> **Important Tip:** *Reporting of financing activities is identical under the direct method and indirect method.*

Financing activities include those described in Exhibit 16.3. Information provided about the transactions of Gelato reveals four transactions involving financing activities. We already analyzed one of these, the $60,000 issuance of bonds payable to purchase equipment as a non-cash investing and financing activity. The remaining three transactions are retirement of bonds, issuance of common shares, and payment of cash dividends. We again use a three-step process in determining net cash inflows (outflows) from financing activities:

1. Identify changes in financing-related accounts

2. Explain these changes using reconstruction analysis

3. Report cash flow effects

BONDS PAYABLE TRANSACTIONS

Comparative balance sheet information from Exhibit 16.6 for bonds payable is our starting point. The *first step* reveals an increase in bonds payable from $64,000 to $90,000. We need to explain this change.

The *second step* is to review the Bonds Payable ledger account and any additional information available. Item (e) is relevant to bonds payable and reports that bonds with a carrying value of $34,000 are retired for $18,000 cash, resulting in a $16,000 gain. The reconstructed entry for our analysis of item (e) is:

Bonds Payable	34,000	
Gain on Retirement of Debt		16,000
Cash		**18,000**

This entry reveals an $18,000 cash outflow for retirement of bonds. It also shows a $16,000 gain from comparing the bonds payable carrying value with the cash received. This gain does not reflect any cash inflow or outflow.

Item (b) also involves bonds payable. It reports that Gelato purchased equipment costing $70,000 by issuing $60,000 in bonds payable to the seller and paying $10,000 in cash. We already reconstructed its entry for our analysis of investing activities. Recall it increased bonds payable by $60,000 and is reported as a non-cash investing and financing transaction. These reconstructed entries are reflected in the ledger account for bonds payable:

Bonds Payable

		64,000	Balance, Dec. 31/16
Retired bonds	34,000	60,000	Issued bonds
		90,000	Balance, Dec. 31/17

The *third step* is to make the necessary disclosures on the statement of cash flows. Disclosure of the cash flow effect from the bond retirement in the financing section of the statement appears as (also see Exhibit 16.8):

Gelato Corp.
Statement of Cash Flows
For Year Ended December 31, 2017

Cash flows from financing activities:
Cash paid to retire bonds .... (18,000)

COMMON SHARES TRANSACTIONS

We use comparative balance sheet information from Exhibit 16.6 for the *first step* in analyzing the Common Shares account. This reveals an increase in common shares from $80,000 to $95,000. We need to explain this change.

Our *second step* is to review the Common Shares ledger account and any additional information available. Item (d) reports that it issued 3,000 common shares for $5 per share. The reconstructed entry for our analysis of item (d) is:

Cash	**15,000**	
Common shares		15,000

This entry reveals a $15,000 cash inflow from the issuance of shares. This reconstructed entry is reflected in the ledger account for common shares:

Common Shares

	80,000	Balance, Dec. 31/16
	15,000	Issued shares
	95,000	Balance, Dec. 31/17

The *third step* is to make the necessary disclosure on the statement of cash flows. Disclosure of the cash flow effect from share issuance in the financing section of the statement appears as (also see Exhibit 16.8):

Gelato Corp.
Statement of Cash Flows
For Year Ended December 31, 2017

Cash flows from financing activities:
Cash received from issuing shares $15,000

RETAINED EARNINGS TRANSACTIONS

The *first step* in analyzing the Retained Earnings account is to review comparative balance sheet information from Exhibit 16.6. We need to explain the increase in retained earnings from $88,000 to $112,000.

Our *second step* is to analyze the Retained Earnings account and any additional information available. Item (f) reports that cash dividends of $14,000 were paid. The reconstructed entry for our analysis of item (f) is:

Retained Earnings	14,000			Cash Dividends	14,000	
Cash		14,000	OR	Cash		14,000

This entry reveals a $14,000 cash outflow to pay cash dividends.[9] We must also remember that retained earnings are affected by profit from the income statement. Profit was already dealt with under the operating section of the statement of cash flows. This reconstruction analysis is reflected in the ledger account for retained earnings:

Retained Earnings

		88,000	Balance, Dec. 31/16
Cash dividend	14,000	38,000	Profit
		112,000	Balance, Dec. 31/17

The *third step* is to make the necessary disclosure on the statement of cash flows. Disclosure of the cash flow effect from the cash dividend appears in the financing section of the statement as (also see Exhibit 16.8):

Gelato Corp.
Statement of Cash Flows
For Year Ended December 31, 2017

Cash flows from financing activities:
Cash paid for dividends .... (14,000)

---

9 *Share dividends* are a non-cash activity.

5. Proving Cash Balances

We have now explained all of the cash inflows and outflows of Gelato, along with one non-cash investing and financing transaction. Our analysis has reconciled changes in all non-cash balance sheet accounts. The fifth and final step in preparing the statement is to report the beginning and ending cash balances and prove the net change in cash as explained by operating, investing, and financing net cash flows. This step is highlighted below for Gelato:

Gelato Corp.
Statement of Cash Flows
For Year Ended December 31, 2017

Cash flows from operating activities:

Cash flows from financing activities:

Cash received from issuing shares	$ 15,000	
Cash paid to retire bonds	(18,000)	
Cash paid for dividends	(14,000)	
Net cash outflow from financing activities		(17,000)
Net increase in cash		$ 5,000
Cash balance at beginning of 2017		12,000
Cash balance at end of 2017		$ 17,000

The statement shows that the $5,000 net increase in cash from $12,000 at the beginning of the period to $17,000 at the end is reconciled by net cash flows from operating ($20,000 inflow), investing ($2,000 inflow), and financing ($17,000 outflow) activities.

CHECKPOINT

9. Identify which of the following represent financing activities:
  a. Paid $1,000 of interest on the bank loan.
  b. Purchased $25,000 of equipment by paying cash of $25,000.
  c. Issued a $75,000 bond payable.
  d. Issued $50,000 of common shares in exchange for land valued at $50,000.
  e. Made a $10,000 payment on the bank loan.

Do Quick Study questions: QS 16-11, QS 16-12, QS 16-13, QS 16-14

DECISION MAKER   Answer—End of chapter

Reporter

You are a newspaper reporter covering a workers' strike. Management grants you an interview and complains about recent losses and negative cash flows. They show you income statement numbers revealing a recent $600,000 loss that included a $930,000 loss from the sale of machinery. They also show you the company's total net cash outflow of $550,000, which included net cash outflows of $850,000 for investing activities and $350,000 for financing activities. What is your initial reaction to management's complaints?

Cash Flows From Operating Activities—Direct Method

LO7 Calculate cash flows from operating activities using the direct method.

We calculate cash flows from operating activities under the direct method by adjusting accrual-based income statement items to a cash basis. The usual approach is to adjust income statement accounts related to operating activities for changes in their related balance sheet accounts:

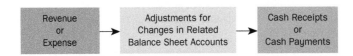

The direct and indirect statements of cash flows are identical except for how the $20,000 net cash inflow from operations is calculated.

In preparing the operating section for Gelato Corp. using the direct method as highlighted in Exhibit 16.9, we first look at its cash receipts and then its cash payments, drawing on the income statement and balance sheets in Exhibit 16.6.

EXHIBIT 16.9

Statement of Cash Flows—Direct Method of Reporting Operating Cash Flows

Gelato Corp. Statement of Cash Flows For Year Ended December 31, 2017		
Cash flows from operating activities:		
Cash received from customers	$ 570,000	
Cash paid for merchandise	(319,000)	
Cash paid for wages and other operating expenses	(218,000)	
Cash paid for interest	(8,000)	
Cash paid for taxes	(5,000)	
Net cash inflow from operating activities................................		$ 20,000
Cash flows from investing activities:		
Cash received from sale of equipment.....................................	$ 12,000	
Cash paid for purchase of equipment	(10,000)	
Net cash inflow from investing activities.................................		2,000
Cash flows from financing activities:		
Cash received from issuing shares...	$ 15,000	
Cash paid to retire bonds..	(18,000)	
Cash paid for dividends	(14,000)	
Net cash outflow from financing activities		(17,000)
Net increase in cash...		$ 5,000
Cash balance at beginning of 2017		12,000
Cash balance at end of 2017		$ 17,000
Note: Non-cash investing and financing activity		
During the period equipment was acquired with issuance of $60,000 of bonds.		

OPERATING CASH RECEIPTS

Exhibit 16.6 and the additional information from Gelato identify only one potential cash receipt—that of sales to customers. This section starts with sales from the income statement and adjusts it as necessary to give us cash received from customers.

Cash Received From Customers   If all sales are for cash, the amount of cash received from customers is equal to sales. But when sales are on account, we must adjust the amount of sales revenue for the change in Accounts Receivable. For example, an increase in Accounts Receivable must be deducted from sales because sales revenue relating to Accounts Receivable has been recorded for which the cash has not yet been received. This is shown in Exhibit 16.10.

EXHIBIT 16.10

Formula to Calculate Cash Received From Customers—Direct Method

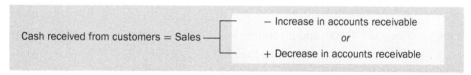

It is often helpful to use *account analysis* for this purpose. To illustrate, the T-account below reconstructs the cash receipts and payments. The balance sheet in Exhibit 16.6 shows that the beginning balance is $40,000 and the ending balance is $60,000. The income statement shows sales of $590,000.

Accounts Receivable

Balance, Dec. 31/16	40,000		
Sales	590,000	570,000 = Collections	
Balance, Dec. 31/17	60,000		

Cash receipts from customers are $570,000, calculated as $40,000 + $590,000 − [collections] = $60,000. As summarized in Exhibit 16.10, this calculation can be rearranged to express cash received as equal to sales of $590,000 less a $20,000 increase in accounts receivable.

The statement of cash flows for Gelato Corp. in Exhibit 16.9 reports the $570,000 cash received from customers as a cash inflow from operating activities.

Other Cash Receipts   While cash receipts of Gelato are limited to collections from customers, we sometimes see other types of cash receipts involving rent, interest, and dividends. We calculate cash received from these items by subtracting an increase or adding a decrease in the related receivable.

OPERATING CASH PAYMENTS

Exhibit 16.6 and the additional information from Gelato identify four operating expenses. We analyze each of these expenses to calculate its operating cash payment for the statement of cash flows.

Cash Paid for Merchandise   We calculate cash paid for merchandise by analyzing both cost of goods sold and merchandise inventory. When the balances of Merchandise Inventory and Accounts Payable change, we must adjust cost of goods sold for changes in both of these accounts to calculate cash paid for merchandise. This adjustment has two steps. First, we use the change in the balance of Merchandise Inventory along with the amount of cost of goods sold to calculate cost of purchases for the period. An increase in inventory implies that we bought more than was sold and we add the increase in inventory to cost of goods sold to calculate cost of purchases. A decrease in inventory implies that we bought less than was sold and we subtract the decrease in inventory from cost of goods sold to calculate cost of purchases.

The second step uses the change in the balance of Accounts Payable along with the amount of cost of purchases to calculate cash paid for merchandise. A decrease in Accounts Payable implies that we paid for more goods than were acquired this period and we add the Accounts Payable change to cost of purchases to calculate cash paid for merchandise. An increase in Accounts Payable implies that we paid for less than the amount of goods acquired, and we subtract the Accounts Payable change from purchases to calculate cash paid for merchandise.

First, we use account analysis of merchandise inventory to calculate cost of purchases. We do this by reconstructing the Merchandise Inventory account:

Merchandise Inventory

Balance, Dec. 31/16	70,000		
Purchases = 314,000		300,000	Cost of goods sold
Balance, Dec. 31/17	84,000		

The beginning balance is $70,000, and its ending balance is $84,000. The income statement shows cost of goods sold is $300,000. We can then determine the cost of purchases as $314,000 (equal to cost of goods sold of $300,000 plus the $14,000 increase in inventory).

Our second step is to calculate cash paid for merchandise by adjusting purchases for the change in accounts payable. Reconstructing Accounts Payable:

Accounts Payable

		40,000	Balance, Dec. 31/16
Payments = 319,000		314,000	Purchases
		35,000	Balance, Dec. 31/17

This account shows us that its beginning balance of $40,000 plus purchases of $314,000 minus an ending balance of $35,000 gives us cash paid of $319,000 (or $40,000 + $314,000 − [purchases] = $35,000). Alternatively, we can express cash paid for merchandise as equal to purchases of $314,000 plus the $5,000 decrease in accounts payable.

We summarize the two-step adjustment to cost of goods sold to calculate cash paid for merchandise in Exhibit 16.11.

EXHIBIT 16.11

Two Steps to Calculate Cash Paid for Merchandise—Direct Method

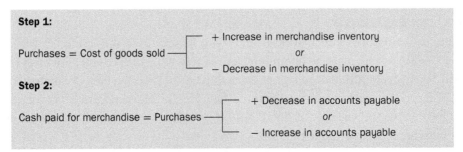

Exhibit 16.9 shows that the $319,000 cash paid by Gelato for merchandise is reported on the statement of cash flows as a cash outflow for operating activities.

Cash Paid for Wages and Operating Expenses (Excluding Depreciation and Other Non-Cash Expenses)   The income statement of Gelato shows wages and other operating expenses of $216,000 (see Exhibit 16.6). To calculate cash paid for wages and other operating expenses, we adjust this amount for changes in their related balance sheet accounts.

We begin by looking for prepaid expenses and accrued liabilities relating to wages and other operating expenses in the beginning and ending balance sheets of Gelato in Exhibit 16.6. These balance sheets show that Gelato has prepaid expenses but no accrued liabilities. This means its adjustment to this expense item is limited to the change in prepaid expenses. The amount of adjustment is calculated by assuming all cash paid for wages and other operating expenses is initially debited to Prepaid Expenses. This assumption allows us to reconstruct the Prepaid Expenses account:

Prepaid Expenses			
Balance, Dec. 31/16	4,000		
Payments = 218,000		216,000	Wages and other operating expenses
Balance, Dec. 31/17	6,000		

This account shows that prepaid expenses increased by $2,000 in the period. This means cash paid for wages and other operating expenses exceeded the reported expense by $2,000. Alternatively, we can express cash paid for wages and other operating expenses of Gelato as equal to its expenses of $216,000 plus the $2,000 increase in prepaid expenses for total payments of 218,000.

Exhibit 16.12 summarizes the adjustments to wages (including salaries) and other operating expenses. While the balance sheet of Gelato did not report accrued liabilities, we add these to the exhibit to explain the adjustment to cash when they do exist. If accrued liabilities decrease, it implies we paid for more goods or services than received this period, and we must add the change in accrued liabilities to the expense amount to get cash paid for these goods or services. If accrued liabilities increase, it implies we paid less than was acquired and we must subtract the change in accrued liabilities from the expense amount to get cash paid.

EXHIBIT 16.12

Formula to Calculate Cash Paid for Wages and Operating Expenses—Direct Method

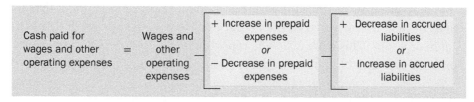

Cash Paid for Both Interest and Income Taxes   Our analysis for calculating operating cash flows for interest and taxes is similar to that for operating expenses. Both require adjustments to the amounts on the income statement for changes in their related balance sheet accounts.

We begin with the income statement of Gelato showing interest expense of $7,000 and income taxes expense of $15,000. To calculate the cash paid, we adjust interest expense for the change in interest payable and we adjust income taxes expense for the change in income taxes payable. These calculations involve reconstructing both liability accounts:

Interest Payable					Income Taxes Payable		
	4,000	Balance, Dec. 31/16				12,000	Balance, Dec. 31/16
Interest paid = 8,000	7,000	Interest expense		Income taxes paid = 5,000		15,000	Income tax expense
	3,000	Balance, Dec. 31/17				22,000	Balance, Dec. 31/17

These accounts reveal cash paid for interest of $8,000 and cash paid for income taxes of $5,000. The formulas to calculate these amounts are shown in Exhibit 16.13.

Formulas to Calculate Cash Paid for Both Interest and Taxes—Direct Method

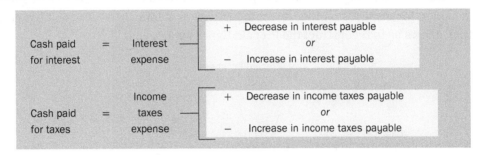

Both of these cash payments are reported as operating cash outflows on the statement of cash flows for Gelato in Exhibit 16.9.

ANALYSIS OF OTHER OPERATING EXPENSES

Gelato reports three other operating expenses on its income statement: $24,000 of depreciation, a $6,000 loss on sale of equipment, and a $16,000 gain on retirement of debt. We consider each of these for its potential cash effects.

Depreciation Expense   Depreciation expense for Gelato is $24,000. It is known as a non-cash expense because there are no cash flows associated with depreciation. Depreciation expense is an allocation of the depreciable cost of plant and equipment assets. The cash outflow associated with purchasing plant and equipment is reported as part of investing activities when it is paid. This means depreciation expense is never reported on a statement of cash flows using the direct method.

Loss on Sale of Assets   Sales of assets frequently results in gains and losses reported as part of profit. But the amount of recorded gain or loss does not reflect cash flows in these transactions. Asset sales result in cash inflow equal to the actual cash received, regardless of whether the asset was sold at a gain or a loss. This cash inflow is reported under investing activities. This means the loss or gain on a sale of assets is never reported on a statement of cash flows using the direct method.

Gain on Retirement of Bonds   Retirements of bonds usually yield gains and losses reported as part of profit. But the amount of recorded gain or loss does not reflect cash flows in these transactions. Bond retirement results in cash outflow equal to the actual amount paid to settle the bond, regardless of whether the bond was retired at a gain or loss. This cash outflow is reported under financing activities. This means the loss or gain from retirement of a bond is never reported on a statement of cash flows using the direct method.

DIRECT METHOD FORMAT OF OPERATING ACTIVITIES SECTION

Exhibit 16.9 shows the statement of cash flows for Gelato using the direct method. Major items of cash inflows and cash outflows are listed separately in the operating activities section. The format requires that operating cash outflows be subtracted from operating cash inflows to get net cash inflows (outflows) from operating activities.

CHECKPOINT

10. Net sales in a period are $590,000, beginning accounts receivable are $120,000, and ending accounts receivable are $90,000. What amount is collected from customers in the period?

11. The Merchandise Inventory account balance decreases in a period from a beginning balance of $32,000 to an ending balance of $28,000. Cost of goods sold for the period is $168,000. If the Accounts Payable balance increases $2,400 in the period, what is the amount of cash paid for merchandise?

12. Reported wages and other operating expenses incurred total $112,000. At the end of the prior year, prepaid expenses totalled $1,200, and this year the balance is $4,200. The current balance sheet shows wages payable of $5,600, whereas last year's did not show any accrued liabilities. How much is paid for wages and other operating expenses this year?

Do Quick Study questions: QS 16-15, QS 16-16, QS 16-17, QS 16-18, QS 16-19

DEMONSTRATION PROBLEM—DIRECT METHOD

Mitchell Corporation Comparative Balance Sheet Information

	December 31	
Assets	**2017**	**2016**
Cash......................................	$ 15,000	$ 20,000
Accounts receivable.........................	23,000	25,000
Merchandise inventory.....................	37,000	34,000
Prepaid expenses	6,000	8,000
Investments	39,000	40,000
Equipment.....................................	191,000	170,000
Accumulated depreciation	(31,000)	(25,000)
Total assets	$280,000	$272,000
Liabilities and Equity		
Accounts payable	$ 38,000	$ 30,000
Accrued liabilities............................	68,000	65,000
Bonds payable	100,000	90,000
Common shares	40,000	37,000
Retained earnings...........................	34,000	50,000
Total liabilities and equity.................	$280,000	$272,000

Mitchell Corporation Income Statement For Year Ended December 31, 2017

Sales...	$250,000
Cost of goods sold	165,000
Gross profit......................................	$ 85,000
Operating expenses............................	40,000
Operating profit before taxes................	$ 45,000
Investment income	8,000
Profit before taxes..............................	$ 53,000
Income taxes.....................................	14,800
Profit	$ 38,200

Required

a. Calculate sales adjusted to a cash basis.

b. Calculate cost of goods sold adjusted to a cash basis.

c. How much cash was paid for operating expenses?

d. How much cash was provided by operating activities?

Solution

a.	Sales revenue reported per income statement	$ 250,000	
	Adjustments to cash basis:		
	Decrease in accounts receivable	2,000	(source of cash)
	Sales adjusted to a cash basis	$ 252,000	
b.	Cost of goods sold per income statement	$ 165,000	
	Adjustments to cash basis:		
	Increase in inventory	3,000	(use of cash)
	Increase in accounts payable	(8,000)	(source of cash)
	Cost of goods sold adjusted to a cash basis	$ 160,000	
c.	Operating expenses per income statement	$ 40,000	
	Adjustments to a cash basis:		
	Decrease in prepaid expenses	(2,000)	(non-cash expense)
	Increase in accrued liabilities	(3,000)	(increase in expense not using cash)
	Depreciation	(6,000)	(non-cash expense)
	Cash paid for operating expenses	$ 29,000	
d.	Sales adjusted to a cash basis	$ 252,000	
	Less: Cost of goods sold adjusted to a cash basis	(160,000)	
	Cash paid for operating expenses	(29,000)	
	Cash paid for income tax	(14,800)	
	Cash inflow from operating activities	$ 48,200	

As noted in the chapter, the preparation of the statement of cash flows involves five steps (recall that the indirect versus direct method affects step 2 only):

1. Calculate the net increase or decrease in cash.
2. Calculate and report net cash inflows (outflows) from operating activities. This was detailed in the first part of the last chapter segment on the direct method of presenting the statement of cash flows. To verify that the net cash inflows (outflows) from operating activities are the same for both the indirect and direct methods, compare Exhibits 16.8 (indirect) and 16.9 (direct).

Since the following steps will be the same regardless of method, detailed explanations will not be repeated here.

3. Calculate and report net cash inflows (outflows) from investing activities.
4. Calculate and report net cash inflows (outflows) from financing activities.
5. Calculate net cash flow by combining net cash inflows (outflows) from operating, investing, and financing activities and then prove it by adding it to the beginning cash balance to show it equals the ending cash balance.

Upon completion of step 5, the statement of cash flows using the direct method will appear as shown in Exhibit 16.9.

Summary of Reporting and Analyzing Cash Flows

Understanding cash flow statements is critical for businesses to both maintain successful operations and make effective decisions in growing the business. Exhibit 16.14 is an effective tool to summarize the key differences and similarities between the indirect and direct methods of preparing the statement of cash flows.

EXHIBIT 16.14

Cash Flow Statement Summary

	INDIRECT METHOD	DIRECT METHOD
A **CASH FLOWS FROM OPERATING ACTIVITIES**	**Profit** **Adjustments to reconcile Profit to Net Cash provided by operating activities:** **Changes in non-cash current assets:** +(−) Decrease (Increase) in A/R +(−) Decrease (Increase) in Inventory +(−) Decrease (Increase) in Prepaid Assets **Changes in current liabilities:** +(−) Increase (Decrease) in A/P +(−) Increase (Decrease) in Interest Payable +(−) Increase (Decrease) in Taxes Payable +(−) Increase (Decrease) in Other Payables **Adjust for financing or investing activities that impacted the income statement:** + Expenses with no cash outflow (such as depreciation) +(−) Non-Operating Loss (Gain) such as on sale of equipment and *losses (gains)* on sale of investment	**Cash receipts from customer:** = Sales +(−) Decrease (Increase) in A/R **Cash paid for merchandise:** = COGS +(−) Increase (Decrease) in Inventory +(−) Decrease (Increase) in Accounts Payable **Cash paid for wages and operating expenses:** = Wages and operating expenses +(−) Increase (Decrease) in prepaid expenses +(−) Decrease (Increase) in accrued liabilities **Cash paid for interest:** = Interest expense +(−) Decrease (Increase) in interest payable **Cash paid for taxes:** = Income tax expense +(−) Decrease (Increase) in income taxes payable
	Net Cash Inflow from Operating Activities	Net Cash Inflow from Operating Activities
B **CASH FLOWS FROM INVESTING ACTIVITIES**	+ Cash received from sale of PPE − Cash paid for purchase of PPE + Cash received from sale of investments − Cash paid on sale of investments + Cash collected on principal repayments from loans provided to a third party − Cash paid to provide loans to a third party **Net Cash Inflow (Outflow) from investing activities**	**SAME AS INDIRECT METHOD**
C **CASH FLOWS FROM FINANCING ACTIVITIES**	+ Cash received from issuing shares/bonds − Cash paid to retire shares/debt − Cash paid for dividends − Cash paid to repay loans to lenders − Cash withdrawals by owners **Net Cash Inflow (Outflow) from financing activities**	**SAME AS INDIRECT METHOD**
NET INCREASE IN CASH AND CASH EQUIVALENTS **CASH AND CASH EQUIVALENTS BEGINNING OF PERIOD** **CASH AND CASH EQUIVALENTS AT END OF PERIOD**		= A + B + C + END OF PRIOR YEAR CASH CURRENT PERIOD CASH FLOW

Important Tip: After completing the cash flow statement, confirm that the calculation of cash and cash equivalents at the end of period equals the end-of-period cash balance reported on the balance sheet.

CRITICAL THINKING CHALLENGE

Refer to the Critical Thinking Challenge questions at the beginning of the chapter. Compare your answers to those suggested on Connect.

IFRS AND ASPE—THE DIFFERENCES

Difference	International Financial Reporting Standards (IFRS)	Accounting Standards for Private Enterprises (ASPE)
Classification of interest and dividends received	• Operating or investing activity; must be done consistently from period to period	• Operating activity
Classification of interest and dividends paid	• Operating or financing activity; must be done consistently from period to period	• Interest paid is an operating activity • Dividends paid are a financing activity

A Look Ahead

Chapter 17 reviews tools available for analyzing financial statements to assess corporate performance and analyze management effectiveness.

For further study on some topics of relevance to this chapter, please see the following Extend Your Knowledge supplements:

EYK 16-1 Using T-Accounts to Prepare a Statement of Cash Flows (Direct Method)

EYK 16-2 Using a Spreadsheet to Prepare a Statement of Cash Flows

Summary

LO1 Explain the purpose and importance of cash flow information. The main purpose of the statement of cash flows is to report the major cash receipts and cash payments for a period. This includes identifying cash flows as relating to operating, investing, or financing activities. Many business decisions involve evaluating cash flows. Users' evaluations include focusing on the transactions that cause cash inflows (outflows).

LO2 Distinguish among operating, investing, and financing activities. Operating activities include the cash effects of transactions and events that determine profit. Investing activities include (a) purchase and sale of non-current assets, (b) purchase and sale of short-term investments other than cash equivalents, and (c) lending and collecting on loans. Financing activities include (a) getting cash from issuing debt and repaying the amounts borrowed, and (b) getting cash from or distributing cash to owners and giving owners a return on investment.

LO3 Identify and disclose non-cash investing and financing activities. For external reporting, a company must supplement its statement of cash flows with a description of its non-cash investing and financing activities. These activities are disclosed either in a note to the statement or in a separate schedule usually reported at the bottom of the statement.

LO4 Describe and prepare the statement of cash flows. The statement of cash flows reports cash inflows and outflows in one of three categories: operating, investing, or financing activities. Preparation of a statement of cash flows involves five steps: (1) calculate the net increase or decrease in cash, (2) calculate net cash inflows (outflows) from operating activities, (3) calculate net cash inflows (outflows) from investing activities, (4) calculate net cash inflows (outflows) from financing activities; and (5) report the beginning and ending cash balances and prove the change is explained by operating, investing, and financing net cash flows. Non-cash investing and financing activities are disclosed either in a note or in a separate schedule to the statement.

LO5 Calculate cash flows from operating activities using the indirect method. The indirect method for reporting net cash inflows (outflows) from operating activities starts with profit and then adjusts it for three items: (1) changes in non-cash current assets and current liabilities related to operating activities, (2) revenues and expenses not creating cash inflows (outflows), and (3) gains and losses from investing and financing activities.

LO6 Determine cash flows from both investing and financing activities. Cash flows from both investing and financing activities are determined by identifying the cash flow effects of transactions affecting each balance sheet account related to these activities.

LO7 Calculate cash flows from operating activities using the direct method. The direct method

for reporting net cash inflows (outflows) from operating activities, encouraged in IAS 7, involves separately listing the major classes of operating cash inflows and outflows. The operating cash outflows are then subtracted from operating cash inflows to get the net inflow or outflow from operating activities.

Guidance Answers to DECISION MAKER

Community Activist

There could be several explanations for an increase in net cash flows when a loss is reported. Possibilities include (1) early recognition of expenses relative to revenues generated (research and development), (2) valuable long-term cash sales contracts not yet recognized in profit, (3) issuances of debt or shares to finance expansion, (4) selling of assets, (5) delayed cash payments, and (6) prepayment on sales. Your analysis of this manufacturer needs to focus on the components of both profit and net cash flows, and their implications for future performance.

Reporter

Your initial course of action is to verify management's claims about poor performance. A $600,000 loss along with a $550,000 decrease in net cash flows seemingly supports its claim. But closer scrutiny reveals a different picture. You calculate its cash flow from operating activities at a positive $650,000, calculated as [X] − $850,000 − $350,000 = $(550,000) net cash outflow.

You note also that profit before the loss from the sale of machinery is a positive $330,000, calculated as [?] − $930,000 = $(600,000). This is powerful information to open discussions. A serious and directed discussion is likely to reveal a far more positive picture of this company's financial performance.

Cash flow from operating activities calculated as:

$$X - 850,000 - 350,000 = (550,000)$$
$$X = 850,000 + 350,000 - 550,000$$
$$X = 650,000$$

Guidance Answers to CHECKPOINT

1. No. The statement of cash flows reports changes in the sum of cash plus cash equivalents. It does not report transfers between cash and cash equivalents.

2. The three categories of cash inflows and outflows are operating activities, investing activities, and financing activities.

3. **a.** Investing
   b. Operating
   c. Financing
   d. Operating
   e. Operating
   f. Financing

4. The direct method is more informative because it separately lists each major item of operating cash receipts and each major item of operating cash payments. The indirect method is used most often.

5. $74,900 + $4,600 − $11,700 − $1,000 + $3,400 = $70,200

6. In the calculation of profit, expenses such as depreciation are subtracted because these expenses do not require current cash outflows. Therefore, adding these expenses back to profit eliminates non-cash items from the profit number, converting it to a cash basis.

7. In the process of reconciling profit to net cash inflows (outflows) from operating activities, a gain on the sale of land is subtracted from profit because a sale of land is not an operating activity; it is an investing activity.

8. $80,000 − $30,000 − $10,000 = $40,000

   The $40,000 cash receipt is reported as an investing activity.

9. c, e

10. $590,000 + ($120,000 − $90,000) = $620,000

11. $168,000 − ($32,000 − $28,000) − $2,400 = $161,600

12. $112,000 + ($4,200 − $1,200) − $5,600 = $109,400

DEMONSTRATION PROBLEM—PART A: INDIRECT METHOD

Sunset Cove Ice Cream Inc.'s balance sheet information, income statement, and additional information follow.

Sunset Cove Ice Cream Inc. Comparative Balance Sheet Information		
	December 31	
	2017	2016
Cash...	$ 43,050	$ 23,925
Accounts receivable....................	34,125	39,825
Merchandise inventory................	156,000	146,475
Prepaid expenses	3,600	1,650
Equipment.................................	135,825	146,700
Accumulated depreciation	61,950	47,550
Accounts payable	31,475	33,750
Dividends payable	-0-	4,500
Bonds payable	10,000	37,500
Common shares	208,750	168,750
Retained earnings......................	60,425	66,525

Sunset Cove Ice Cream Inc. Income Statement For Year Ended December 31, 2017		
Sales...		$ 380,850
Cost of goods sold	$222,300	
Other operating expenses	134,850	
Depreciation expense.................	25,500	(382,650)
Loss on sale of equipment		(3,300)
Loss		$ 5,100

¹See (a) of the additional information below.
²See (b) and (c) of the additional information below.
³See (d) of the additional information below.

Additional information:

a. Equipment costing $21,375 was sold for cash.

b. The change in the balance of Accumulated Depreciation resulted from depreciation expense and from the sale of equipment.

c. Equipment was purchased for cash.

d. The change in the balance of Retained Earnings resulted from dividend declarations and the loss.

Required

Prepare a statement of cash flows using the indirect method for the year ended December 31, 2017.

Analysis Component:

Explain why the statement of cash flows reports a $5,500 cash outflow regarding dividends, yet dividends actually declared during 2017 were $1,000.

Planning the Solution

- Prepare a blank statement of cash flows with sections for operating, investing, and financing activities using the indirect method format.

- Under the operating activities section, enter the loss from the income statement and include adjustments regarding depreciation expense, loss on sale of equipment, and changes in current assets and current liabilities (except dividends payable—recall that cash dividend payments are financing activities).

- To calculate the cash received from the sale of equipment and the cash paid for the purchase of equipment, refer to the additional information. Use T-accounts for Equipment and Accumulated Depreciation to help chart the effects of the sale and purchase of the equipment; reconstructing the journal entries for the sale and purchase is also helpful in determining the cash received/paid.

- Calculate the effect of dividends and loss on the change in Retained Earnings. Use T-accounts for Dividends Payable and Retained Earnings to help chart the effects of the dividends declared, dividends paid, and loss; reconstructing the journal entries for dividends declared and dividends paid is also helpful.

- Calculate the effect of the change in Bonds Payable and Common Shares.

- Total each section of the statement, determine the total change in cash, and add the beginning balance to get the ending balance.

- Answer the analysis component.

Solution

1. Calculations regarding the adjustments for changes in:
   a. Current assets (except cash and cash equivalents):
      - Accounts receivable: $34,125 − $39,825 = $5,700 decrease
      - Merchandise inventory: $156,000 − $146,475 = $9,525 increase
      - Prepaid expenses: $3,600 − $1,650 = $1,950 increase
   b. Current liabilities (except dividends payable):
      - Accounts payable: $31,475 − $33,750 = $2,275 decrease

2. To calculate the cash received/paid for the sale/purchase of equipment, it is helpful to use T-accounts and reconstruct journal entries as follows:

Equipment				Accumulated Depreciation, Equipment			
Dec. 31, 2016 Bal.	146,700					47,550	Dec. 31, 2016 Bal.
Purchase (calculated)	(?)	21,375	Sale (given)	Sale (calculated)	(?)	25,500	Deprec. Expense (given)
Dec. 31, 2017 Bal.	135,825					61,950	Dec. 31, 2017 Bal.

Accumulated Depreciation, Equipment[1]	11,100
Cash[4]	(?) = 6,975 to statement of cash flows
Loss on sale of equipment[2]	3,300
Equipment[3]	21,375
Reconstructed entry recording the sale of equipment.	

[1]Calculated from T-account: $47,550 + $25,500 − x = $61,950; x = $11,100.
[2]Given in the income statement.
[3]Given in (a) of the additional information.
[4]$21,375 − $11,100 − $3,300 = $6,975.

Equipment[5]	10,500
Cash..	(?) = 10,500 to statement of cash flows
Reconstructed entry recording the purchase of equipment	

[5]Calculated from T-account: $146,700 − $21,375 + x = $135,825; x = $10,500.

3. Calculations regarding the:
   a. Declaration, and

Retained Earnings[1]	1,000
Dividends Payable..	1,000
Reconstructed entry recording the declaration of dividends.	

[1]Calculated from T-account: $66,525 + $5,100 − x = $60,425; x = $1,000.

Dividends Payable				Retained Earnings			
		4,500	Dec. 31, 2016 Bal.			66,525	Dec. 31, 2016 Bal.
Dividends Paid	(?)	1,000	Dividends Declared (from Retained Earnings)	Loss	5,100		
		-0-	Dec. 31, 2017 Bal.	Dividends Declared (calculated)	(?)		
						60,425	Dec. 31, 2017 Bal.

   b. Payment of dividends:

Dividends Payable[2]	5,500
Cash...	(?) = 5,500 to statement of cash flows
Reconstructed entry recording the payment of dividends.	

[2]Calculated from T-account: $4,500 + $1,000 − x = $0; x = $5,500.

4. Calculations regarding the payment of bonds and issuance of common shares.
   - Bonds payable: $10,000 − $37,500 = $27,500 decrease
   - Common shares: $208,750 − $168,750 = $40,000 increase

Sunset Cove Ice Cream Inc.
Statement of Cash Flows
For Year Ended December 31, 2017

Cash flows from operating activities:

Loss	$ (5,100)	
Adjustments:		
Depreciation	25,500	
Loss on sale of equipment	3,300	
Decrease in accounts receivable[1(a)]	5,700	
Increase in merchandise inventory[1(a)]	(9,525)	
Increase in prepaid expenses[1(a)]	(1,950)	
Decrease in accounts payable[1(b)]	(2,275)	
Net cash inflow from operations		$15,650
Cash flows from investing activities:		
Cash received from sale of equipment[2]	$ 6,975	
Cash paid for equipment[2]	(10,500)	
Net cash outflow from investing activities		(3,525)
Cash flows from financing activities:		
Cash paid for dividends[3]	$ (5,500)	
Cash paid to retire bonds payable[4]	(27,500)	
Cash received from issuing common shares[4]	40,000	
Net cash inflow from financing activities		7,000
Net increase in cash		$19,125
Cash balance at beginning of year		23,925
Cash balance at end of year		$43,050

[1(a)]Calculation from the solution, part 1(a)
[1(b)]Calculation from the solution, part 1(b)
[2]Calculation from the solution, part 2
[3]Calculation from the solution, part 3(b)
[4]Calculation from the solution, part 4

Note to Student: Remember that the statement of cash flows explains the change in the Cash account balance from one period to the next.

Sunset Cove Ice Cream Inc.
Comparative Balance Sheet Information

	December 31	
Assets	**2017**	**2016**
Cash	$ 43,050	$ 23,925
Accounts receivable	34,125	39,825
Merchandise inventory	156,000	146,475
Prepaid expenses	3,600	1,650
Equipment	135,825	146,700
Accumulated depreciation	(61,950)	(47,550)
Total assets	$310,650	$311,025
Liabilities and Equity		
Accounts payable	$ 31,475	$ 33,750
Dividends payable	-0-	4,500
Bonds payable	10,000	37,500
Common shares	208,750	168,750
Retained earnings	60,425	66,525
Total liabilities and equity	$310,650	$311,025

Analysis Component:

Sunset Cove's 2017 statement of cash flows reports a $5,500 cash outflow regarding dividends even though dividends declared in 2017 were $1,000. This is because there was a $4,500 balance in Dividends Payable representing unpaid dividends declared in the previous year. An analysis of Dividends Payable showed that the $4,500 unpaid balance from 2013 plus the $1,000 of dividends declared in 2017 were paid during 2017; this resulted in a total cash outflow of $5,500.

DEMONSTRATION PROBLEM—PART B: DIRECT METHOD

Sunset Cove Ice Cream Inc.'s balance sheet information, income statement, and additional information follow.

Sunset Cove Ice Cream Inc. Income Statement For Year Ended December 31, 2017		
Sales[1].....................................		$ 380,850
Cost of goods sold[2]..................	$222,300	
Other operating expenses[3].........	134,850	
Depreciation expense.................	25,500	(382,650)
Loss on sale of equipment.........		(3,300)
Loss.....................................		$ 5,100

[1]See (a) of the additional information below.
[2]See (b) and (c) of the additional information below.
[3]See (d) of the additional information below.

Sunset Cove Ice Cream Inc. Comparative Balance Sheet Information		
	December 31	
	2017	2016
Cash...	$ 43,050	$ 23,925
Accounts receivable	34,125	39,825
Merchandise inventory...............	156,000	146,475
Prepaid expenses	3,600	1,650
Equipment.................................	135,825	146,700
Accumulated depreciation	61,950	47,550
Accounts payable	31,475	33,750
Dividends payable	-0-	4,500
Bonds payable	10,000	37,500
Common shares	208,750	168,750
Retained earnings......................	60,425	66,525

Additional information:

a. All sales were made on credit.

b. All merchandise purchases were on credit.

c. Accounts Payable balances resulted from merchandise purchases.

d. Prepaid expenses relate to other operating expenses.

e. Equipment costing $21,375 was sold for cash.

f. Equipment was purchased for cash.

g. The change in the balance of Accumulated Depreciation resulted from depreciation expense and from the sale of equipment.

h. The change in the balance of Retained Earnings resulted from dividend declarations and the loss.

Required

Prepare a statement of cash flows using the direct method for the year ended 2017.

Planning the Solution

- Prepare a blank statement of cash flows with sections for operating, investing, and financing activities using the direct method format.
- Calculate cash received from customers, cash paid for merchandise, and cash paid for other operating expenses and taxes as illustrated in the chapter.
- The preparation of the investing and financing sections of the statement of cash flows is identical regardless of whether the direct or indirect method of preparing the operating activities section of the statement of cash flows is used. Since the Demonstration Problem earlier in the chapter is identical to this one, refer to it for the calculations regarding investing and financing activities.
- Total each section of the statement, determine the total change in cash, and add the beginning balance to get the ending balance.

Solution

Calculations:

1.

Sales	$380,850
Add decrease in accounts receivable	5,700
Cash received from customers	$386,550

2.

Cost of goods sold	$222,300
Plus increase in merchandise inventory	9,525
Purchases	$231,825
Plus decrease in accounts payable	2,275
Cash paid for merchandise	$234,100

3.

Other operating expenses	$134,850
Plus increase in prepaid expenses	1,950
Cash paid for other operating expenses	$136,800

Direct Method

Sunset Cove Ice Cream Inc.
Statement of Cash Flows
For Year Ended December 31, 2017

Cash flows from operating activities:

Cash received from customers[1]	$ 386,550	
Cash paid for merchandise[2]	(234,100)	
Cash paid for other operating expenses[3]	(136,800)	
Net cash inflow from operations		$15,650
Cash flows from investing activities:		
Cash received from sale of equipment*	$ 6,975	
Cash paid for equipment*	(10,500)	
Net cash outflow from investing activities		(3,525)
Cash flows from financing activities:		
Cash paid for dividends*	$ (5,500)	
Cash paid to retire bonds payable*	(27,500)	
Cash received from issuing common shares*	40,000	
Net cash inflow from financing activities		7,000
Net increase in cash		$19,125
Cash balance at beginning of year		23,925
Cash balance at end of year		$43,050

*Refer to the Demonstration Problem for the calculations.
[1]Calculation from the solution, part 1.
[2]Calculation from the solution, part 2.
[3]Calculation from the solution, part 3.

REMINDER:

The direct and indirect statements of cash flows are identical for both investing and financing activities. The only difference is how the $15,650 net cash inflow from operations is calculated.

Indirect Method
(copied here from Demonstration Problem)

Sunset Cove Ice Cream Inc.
Statement of Cash Flows
For Year Ended December 31, 2017

Cash flows from operating activities:

Loss	$ (5,100)	
Adjustments:		
Depreciation	25,500	
Loss on sale of equipment	3,300	
Decrease in accounts receivable	5,700	
Increase in merchandise inventory	(9,525)	
Increase in prepaid expenses	(1,950)	
Decrease in accounts payable	(2,275)	
Net cash inflow from operations		$15,650
Cash flows from investing activities:		
Cash received from sale of equipment	$ 6,975	
Cash paid for equipment	(10,500)	
Net cash outflow from investing activities		(3,525)
Cash flows from financing activities:		
Cash paid for dividends	$ (5,500)	
Cash paid to retire bonds payable	(27,500)	
Cash received from issuing common shares	40,000	
Net cash inflow from financing activities		7,000
Net increase in cash		$19,125
Cash balance at beginning of year		23,925
Cash balance at end of year		$43,050

Glossary

Cash equivalent An investment that must be readily convertible to a known amount of cash, and have a maturity of three months or less from its date of acquisition.

Direct method A calculation of the net cash inflows (outflows) from operating activities that lists the major classes of operating cash receipts, such as receipts from customers, and subtracts the major classes of operating cash disbursements, such as cash paid for merchandise. This method is encouraged by IFRS in IAS 7.

Financing activities Transactions with a company's owners and creditors that include getting cash from issuing debt and repaying the amounts borrowed, and getting cash from or distributing cash to owners and giving owners a return on investments.

Indirect method A calculation that starts with profit or loss and then adjusts this figure by adding and subtracting items that are necessary to yield net cash inflows or outflows from operating activities.

Investing activities The acquisition and disposal of non-current assets and other investments that are not classified as cash equivalents.

Operating activities The principal revenue-producing activities that are not investing or financing activities. Operating activities involve the production or purchase of merchandise and the sale of goods and services to customers, including expenditures related to administering the business.

Statement of cash flows A financial statement that reports the cash inflows and outflows for an accounting period, and that classifies those cash flows as operating activities, investing activities, and financing activities.

Concept Review Questions

1. What is the purpose of a statement of cash flows?

2. What are cash equivalents and why are they included with cash when preparing a statement of cash flows?

3. Describe the direct method of reporting cash flows from operating activities.

4. Describe the indirect method of reporting cash flows from operating activities.

5. If a company reports a profit for the year, is it possible for the company to show a net cash outflow from operating activities? Explain your answer.

6. Refer to WestJet's statement of cash flows shown in Appendix II.

   (a) Which method was used to calculate net cash provided by operating activities?

   (b) WestJet has two off balance sheet arrangements. What are they?

7. Explain why non-cash expenses and losses are added to profit in calculating cash provided by operating activities using the indirect method.

8. Is depreciation an outflow of cash? Explain.

9. On June 3, a company borrowed $50,000 by giving its bank a 60-day, interest-bearing note. On the June 30 statement of cash flows, where should this item be reported?

10. What are some examples of items reported on a statement of cash flows as investing activities?

11. A company purchases land for $100,000, paying $20,000 cash and borrowing the remainder on a long-term note payable. How should this transaction be reported on a statement of cash flows?

12. What are some examples of items reported on a statement of cash flows as financing activities?

13. Refer to Indigo's statement of cash flows shown in Appendix II. What activities composed Indigo's two largest cash outflows from financing activities for the fiscal year ended 2014?

14. Refer to Danier Leather's balance sheet shown in Appendix II. First, find the Cash balances on June 29, 2013, and June 28, 2014, and calculate the change in Cash. Next, refer to Danier's statement of cash flows, page 42 and identify the change in Cash reported for the year ended June 28, 2014. Explain the relationship between Danier's Cash account reported on the balance sheet and the change in Cash reported on its statement of cash flows.

15. Refer to Danier Leather's statement of cash flows shown in Appendix II. What activity comprised the largest investing activity resulting in cash outflows for the year ended 2014?

16. When a statement of cash flows is prepared by the direct method, what are some examples of items reported as cash flows from operating activities?

17. Explain how sales are converted from an accrual basis to a cash basis for use in the direct method.

18. Explain how cost of goods sold is converted from an accrual basis to a cash basis for use in the direct method.

19. The chapter opening vignette indicated that Calvin Su follows the cash flow of his business very closely. Why do you think it is imperative for business owners to strictly manage their cash resources?

Quick Study

QS 16-1 Classifying transactions by activity L02

Classify the following cash flows as operating, investing, or financing activities:

1. Paid interest on outstanding bonds.
2. Received interest on investment.
3. Issued common shares for cash.
4. Paid dividends.
5. Paid property taxes on the company offices.
6. Received payments from customers.
7. Collected proceeds from sale of long-term investments.
8. Paid wages.
9. Purchased merchandise for cash.
10. Sold delivery equipment at a loss.

QS 16-2 Classifying transactions by activity L02

Classify each of the following transactions as operating, financing, or investing activities, or none of these classifications, and state whether it is an inflow or outflow of cash.

1. The Corporation's outstanding bonds were retired.
2. Land was sold at a gain.
3. The Corporation's outstanding preferred shares were converted into common shares.
4. Machinery was purchased by giving a long-term note to the seller.
5. Additional common shares were issued for cash.
6. Dividends were received on shares of another company held as an investment.
7. Paid utilities expense.
8. A share dividend was declared and issued on the corporation's outstanding common shares.

QS 16-3 Classifying transactions by activity L02

Classify each of the following events as operating, financing, or investing activities and give a reason for your choice.

1. Change in Accounts Receivable.
2. Change in Equipment account.
3. Change in Accumulated Depreciation.
4. Change in Accrued Wages.
5. Change in Bonds Payable.
6. Proceeds from sale of land.

QS 16-4 Identifying non-cash transactions L03

Identify which of the following are non-cash financing and investing transactions.

1. Long-term bonds were retired by issuing common shares.
2. Recorded depreciation expense on the building.
3. A 3:2 share split was declared.
4. A cash dividend was declared and paid.

5. Merchandise was sold on credit.

6. Property, plant, and equipment items were acquired by borrowing from the bank.

7. Borrowed cash from the bank and signed a long-term note payable.

8. Property taxes owed to the city were accrued.

QS 16-5 Calculating cash from operating activities (indirect method) LO5

Using the indirect method, calculate the cash inflow or outflow from operating activities, using the following information:

Denman Inc. Comparative Balance Sheet Information	December 31	
	2017	2016
Cash	$ 10	$ 25
Accounts receivable (net)	28	36
Merchandise inventory	49	22
Prepaid rent	5	4
Office supplies	3	4
Property, plant, and equipment (net)*	120	145
Accounts payable	18	20
Unearned revenue	7	2
Common shares	90	90
Retained earnings**	100	124

*No property, plant, and equipment items were purchased or sold during 2017.
**No dividends were declared or paid during 2017.

QS 16-6 Calculating cash flows from operating activities (indirect method) LO5

Using the indirect method, calculate the cash inflow or outflow from operating activities using the following information:

Willaby Inc. Comparative Balance Sheet Information	December 31	
	2017	2016
Cash	$ 50	$ 35
Accounts receivable (net)	46	20
Merchandise inventory	30	33
Prepaid rent	7	9
Property, plant, and equipment (net)*	260	265
Accounts payable	59	52
Accrued liabilities	16	20
Common shares	90	90
Retained earnings**	228	200

*No property, plant, and equipment items were purchased or sold during 2017.
**No dividends were declared or paid during 2017.

QS 16-7 Calculating cash flows from operating activities (indirect method) LO5

The following information for 2017 is extracted from Hartfield Limited, owner of a retail store:

Profit	$24,500
Accounts receivable decrease	1,000
Inventory increase	1,500
Depreciation expense	5,000
Wages payable increase	900

Calculate the cash inflow or outflow from operating activities.

QS 16-8 Calculating cash flows from operating activities (indirect method) LO5

The following information for 2017 relates to Day Cycle Manufacturing Corp.:

Profit	$49,000
Inventory decrease	3,000
Depreciation expense	6,000
Accounts payable decrease	900
Income taxes payable increase	1,200
Loss on sale of plant and equipment	1,000

Calculate the cash inflow or outflow from operating activities.

QS 16-9 Calculating cash from investing activities LO6

Refer to the information below for Douglas Cement Inc.

a. Calculate the cash paid for equipment purchased during 2017.

b. Calculate the cash proceeds for equipment sold during 2017.

Douglas Cement Inc. Comparative Balance Sheet Information		
	December 31	
	2017	**2016**
Cash	$ 20	$ 5
Accounts receivable (net)	50	20
Equipment[1]	328	300
Accumulated depreciation	100	95
Long-term investments[2]	90	120
Accounts payable	59	52
Accrued liabilities	16	20
Common shares	90	90
Retained earnings[3]	223	188

[1] Equipment costing $150 was sold during 2017; equipment was purchased during 2017.

[2] Long-term investments sold at a profit during 2017.

[3] Profit for 2017 included a $30 loss on sale of equipment and a $10 profit on sale of long-term investments; depreciation expense recorded during 2017 totalled $20.

QS 16-10 **Calculating cash from investing activities** L06

Refer to the information below for Morningside Environmental Inc. Calculate the:

    a. Cash paid for the purchase of the franchise during 2017.

    b. Cash proceeds for equipment sold during 2017.

    c. Change in cash and cash equivalents during 2017.

Morningside Environmental Inc. Comparative Balance Sheet Information		
	December 31	
	2017	**2016**
Cash	$ 25	$ 5
Cash equivalents	25	30
Accounts receivable (net)	46	20
Equipment[1]	260	265
Accumulated depreciation	80	90
Franchise (net)	20	0
Accounts payable	59	52
Common shares	90	90
Retained earnings[2]	147	88

[1] Equipment was sold during 2017; equipment was purchased for $70 cash.

[2] Profit for 2017 included depreciation expense of $30, $5 amortization expense, and a gain on sale of equipment of $35.

QS 16-11 **Calculating cash from financing activities** L06

Refer to the following information for Lighting Inc.

    a. What caused the change in common shares during 2017? Calculate the change.

    b. What caused the change in notes payable? Calculate the change.

    c. Were dividends paid during 2017? If so, calculate.

Lighting Inc. Comparative Balance Sheet Information		
	December 31	
	2017	**2016**
Cash	$ 25	$ 5
Accounts receivable (net)	46	20
Plant and equipment (net)	245	245
Franchise (net)	15	0
Accounts payable	59	52
Notes payable, long-term	15	40
Common shares	110	90
Retained earnings[1]	147	88

[1]Profit for 2017 was $80.

QS 16-12 Calculating cash from financing activities LO6

Refer to the information below for CakePops Inc.

    a. Calculate the profit or loss for 2017.

    b. What caused common shares to change during 2017? Show your calculations.

    c. What caused the change in notes payable during 2017?

    d. Do share dividends affect the statement of cash flows? Explain your answer.

CakePops Inc.
Comparative Balance Sheet Information

	December 31 2017	December 31 2016
Cash	$ 25	$ 5
Accounts receivable (net)	15	20
Machinery (net)	300	262
Franchise (net)	20	0
Accounts payable	65	52
Notes payable, long-term	70	30
Common shares	160	90
Retained earnings[1]	65	115

[1]$10 of share dividends were declared and distributed during 2017.

QS 16-13 Preparing the statement of cash flows (indirect method) LO4,5,6

Use the following information to prepare a statement of cash flows for the year ended March 31, 2017, using the indirect method.

Parker Consulting
Income Statement
For Year Ended March 31, 2017

Sales		$340
Operating expenses:		
Depreciation expense	$ 25	
Other expenses	300	
Total operating expenses		325
Profit (loss)		$ 15

Parker Consulting
Comparative Balance Sheet Information

	March 31 2017	March 31 2016
Cash	$ 40	$ 5
Accounts receivable (net)	85	40
Office supplies	15	22
Prepaid rent	30	0
Equipment*	180	160
Accum. deprec., equipment	70	45
Accounts payable	25	30
Unearned revenue	20	12
Common shares	190	80
Retained earnings**	45	60

*The change in Equipment was caused by a $20 purchase.
**$30 of dividends were paid during 2017.

QS 16-14 Preparing the statement of cash flows (indirect method) LO4,5,6

Use the following information to prepare a statement of cash flows for the year ended October 31, 2017, using the indirect method.

Sugar Bakery Inc.
Income Statement
For Year Ended October 31, 2017

Sales...		$140
Operating expenses:		
Depreciation expense	$ 5	
Other expenses.......................	139	
Total operating expenses		144
Profit (loss)		$ (4)

Sugar Bakery Inc.
Comparative Balance Sheet Information

	October 31	
	2017	**2016**
Cash...	$25	$35
Accounts receivable (net)	40	45
Merchandise inventory...............	15	6
Machinery (net)*	75	25
Accounts payable	6	2
Accrued liabilities........................	2	5
Long-term notes payable.............	40	50
Common shares	95	38
Retained earnings**....................	12	16

* $55 of machinery was purchased during 2017; there were no sales of machinery.

**No dividends were declared or paid during 2017.

QS 16-15 Calculating cash paid for other expenses (direct method) LO7

Organic Gardening Ltd. had operating expenses of $968,000 during 2017. Accrued liabilities at the beginning of the year were $27,000, and were $36,000 at the end of the year. Assuming all debits and credits to accrued liabilities are related to operating expenses, what was the total cash paid for operating expenses during 2017?

QS 16-16 Calculating cash flows from operating activities (direct method) LO7

Middleton Supplies Inc. had sales revenue of $805,000 during 2017. Accounts receivable at the beginning of the year were $20,000 but were $24,000 at the end of the year. How much cash was collected from customers during 2017?

QS 16-17 Calculating cash flows from operating activities (direct method) LO7

Drum Holdings Inc. collected $737,000 cash from customers during 2017. If beginning accounts receivable were $41,000 and credit sales totalled $705,000, what was the balance in ending accounts receivable?

QS 16-18 Calculating cash from operating activities (direct method) LO7

Use the following information to answer questions (a) through (c) below.

Drinkwater Inc.
Income Statement
For Year Ended June 30, 2017

Sales		$234,000
Cost of goods sold		156,000
Gross profit		$ 78,000
Operating expenses:		
Depreciation expense	$19,300	
Other expenses	28,500	
Total operating expense		47,800
Profit from operations		$ 30,200
Income taxes		12,300
Profit		$ 17,900

Drinkwater Inc.
Comparative Balance Sheet Information

	June 30	
	2017	**2016**
Cash..	$ 42,900	$17,500
Accounts receivable (net)	26,000	21,000
Inventory..................................	43,400	48,400
Prepaid expenses	3,200	2,600
Furniture	55,000	60,000
Accumulated depreciation	9,000	5,000
Accounts payable	8,000	11,000
Wages payable..........................	5,000	3,000
Income taxes payable................	1,200	1,800
Notes payable (long-term)	15,000	35,000
Common shares	115,000	90,000
Retained earnings......................	17,300	3,700

a. How much cash was received from customers during 2017?

b. How much cash was paid for merchandise during 2017?

c. How much cash was paid for operating expenses during 2017?

QS 16-19 **Calculating cash from operating activities (direct method)** LO7

Use the following information to answer questions (a) through (e) below.

Skate Corp. Income Statement For Year Ended November 30, 2017		
Sales..		$500
Cost of goods sold		190
Gross profit		$310
Operating expenses:		
Depreciation expense	$ 20	
Other expenses	200	
Total operating expenses		220
Profit from operations		$ 90
Income tax expense...................		10
Profit		$ 80

Skate Corp. Comparative Balance Sheet Information		
	November 30	
	2017	**2016**
Cash	$ 25	$ 5
Accounts receivable (net)	46	20
Inventory	80	95
Prepaid rent	30	15
Equipment (net)	300	320
Accounts payable	40	22
Accrued liabilities	35	50
Income tax payable	7	2
Common shares	100	100
Retained earnings	299	281

a. How much cash was received from customers during 2017?

b. How much cash was paid for merchandise during 2017?

c. How much cash was paid for operating expenses during 2017?

d. How much cash was paid for income taxes during 2017?

e. Calculate the cash inflows (outflows) from operating activities using the direct method.

Exercises

Exercise 16-1 **Classifying transactions on statement of cash flows (indirect method)** LO5

The following transactions occurred during the year. Assuming that the company uses the indirect method of reporting cash provided by operating activities, indicate the proper accounting treatment for each transaction listed below by placing an X in the appropriate column.

	Statement of Cash Flows			Note Describing Non-Cash Investing and Financing Activities	Not Reported on Statement or in Footnote
	Operating Activities	Investing Activities	Financing Activities		
a. Land was purchased by issuing common shares.					
b. Recorded depreciation expense.					
c. Income tax payable increased by 15% from prior year.					
d. Declared and paid a cash dividend					
e. Paid cash to purchase merchandise inventory.					
f. Sold equipment at a loss.					
g. Accounts receivable decreased during the year.					

Exercise 16-2 Making adjustments to derive cash flow from operating activities (indirect method) LO5

	Adjust by	
	Adding	Subtracting
1. Changes in non-cash current assets:		
a. Increases	_____	_____
b. Decreases	_____	_____
2. Changes in current liabilities		
a. Increases	_____	_____
b. Decreases	_____	_____
3. Depreciation of plant and equipment	_____	_____
4. Amortization of intangible assets	_____	_____
5. Interest expense:		
a. Bond premium amortized	_____	_____
b. Bond discount amortized	_____	_____
6. Sale of non-current asset:		
a. Gain	_____	_____
b. Loss	_____	_____

Indicate by an X in the appropriate column whether an item is added or subtracted to derive cash flow from operating activities.

Exercise 16-3 Calculating cash flows from operating activities (indirect method) LO5

CHECK FIGURE: 1. Net cash inflow from operating activities = $324,800

The account balances for the non-cash current assets and current liabilities of Peartree Software Inc. are as follows:

	December 31	
	2017	2016
Accounts receivable	$126,000	$103,600
Inventory..	89,600	117,600
Prepaid expenses	53,200	47,600
Totals	$268,800	$268,800
Accounts payable	$ 84,000	$ 64,400
Salaries payable...	25,200	36,400
Interest payable	47,600	39,200
Totals	$156,800	$140,000

During 2017, Peartree Software Inc. reported depreciation expense of $56,000. All purchases and sales are on account. Profit for 2017 was $252,000.

Required

1. Prepare the operating activities section of the statement of cash flows using the indirect method.

2. Explain why cash flows from operating activities are different from profit.

Exercise 16-4 Calculating cash flows from operating activities (indirect method) LO5

CHECK FIGURE: 1. Net cash inflow from operating activities = $375,040

Green Forest Corp.'s 2017 income statement showed the following: profit, $291,200; depreciation expense, building, $36,000; depreciation expense, equipment, $6,560; and gain on sale of equipment,

$5,600. An examination of the company's current assets and current liabilities showed that the following changes occurred because of operating activities: accounts receivable decreased $14,480; merchandise inventory decreased $41,600; prepaid expenses increased $2,960; accounts payable decreased $7,360; and other current payables increased $1,120. Use the indirect method to calculate the cash flow from operating activities.

Exercise 16-5 Analyzing cash inflows and outflows LO1,5,6

(in thousands)	Fraser	Singh	Travis
Cash inflow (outflow) from operating activities	$ 64,000	$ 56,000	$ (27,200)
Cash inflow (outflow) from investing activities:			
Proceeds from sale of plant and equipment		28,800	
Purchase of plant and equipment	(30,400)	(28,000)	
Cash inflow (outflow) from financing activities:			
Proceeds from issuance of debt		26,400	
Repayment of debt	(5,600)		
Net increase (decrease) in cash	28,000	28,000	28,000
Average assets	640,000	520,000	320,000

Required Which of the three competing corporations is in the strongest relative position as indicated by their comparative statements of cash flows?

Exercise 16-6 Calculating cash flows from operating activities (indirect method) LO5

CHECK FIGURE: Net cash inflow from operating activities = $360

Use the following income statement and information about changes in non-cash current assets and current liabilities to present the cash flows from operating activities using the indirect method:

Kelly Gold Inc.
Income Statement
For Year Ended May 31, 2017

Sales	$2,850
Cost of goods sold	1,440
Gross profit	$1,410
Operating expenses:	
Depreciation expense	$ 225
Other expenses	1,140
Total operating expenses	1,365
Loss on sale of long-term investment	90
Profit (loss) from operations	$ (45)
Income tax expense	-0-
Profit (loss)	$ (45)

Changes in current asset and current liability accounts during the year were as follows:

Accounts receivable	$135 decrease
Inventory	54 increase
Prepaid insurance	6 increase
Accounts payable	30 increase
Accrued liabilities	15 decrease

Exercise 16-7 Preparing the statement of cash flows (indirect method) LO2,5,6

CHECK FIGURE: Net cash inflow from operating activities = $166,752

Required Use the Western Environmental Inc. information given below to prepare a statement of cash flows for the year ended June 30, 2017, using the indirect method.

a. A note is retired at carrying value.

b. The only changes affecting retained earnings during 2017 are profit and cash dividends paid.

    c. New equipment is acquired during 2017 for $70,320.

    d. The profit on sale of equipment costing $58,320 during 2017 is $2,400.

    e. Prepaid expenses and wages expense affect other expenses on the income statement.

    f. All sales and purchases of merchandise were on credit.

Western Environmental Inc.
Income Statement
For Year Ended June 30, 2017

Sales...		$786,000
Cost of goods sold		478,800
Gross profit.................................		$307,200
Operating expenses:		
Depreciation expense	$70,320	
Other expenses......................	80,400	
Total operating expenses		150,720
Profit from operations		$156,480
Gain on sale of equipment		2,400
Profit before taxes		$158,880
Income taxes.............................		54,768
Profit		$104,112

Western Environmental Inc.
Comparative Balance Sheet Information

	June 30	
	2017	**2016**
Cash...	$ 90,960	$ 42,000
Accounts receivable (net)	96,000	74,400
Inventory....................................	80,160	116,160
Prepaid expenses	6,480	6,240
Equipment..................................	156,000	144,000
Accumulated depreciation	33,600	12,000
Accounts payable	31,200	38,400
Wages payable...........................	8,400	19,200
Income taxes payable................	2,880	4,320
Notes payable (long-term)	48,000	84,000
Common shares	276,000	216,000
Retained earnings......................	29,520	8,880

Exercise 16-8 **Calculating cash flows from operating activities (direct method)** LO7

Refer to the information about Western Environmental Inc. presented in Exercise 16-7. Use the direct method and prepare a statement of cash flows.

Exercise 16-9 **Classifying transactions on the statement of cash flows (direct method)** LO7

The following occurred during the year. Assuming that the company uses the direct method of reporting cash provided by operating activities, indicate the proper accounting treatment for each item by placing an X in the appropriate column.

	Statement of Cash Flows			Note Describing Non-Cash Investing and Financing Activities	Not Reported on Statement or in Footnote
	Operating Activities	Investing Activities	Financing Activities		
a. Long-term bonds payable were retired by issuing common shares.	_____	_____	_____	_____	_____
b. Surplus merchandise inventory was sold for cash.	_____	_____	_____	_____	_____
c. Borrowed cash from the bank by signing a nine-month note payable	_____	_____	_____	_____	_____
d. Paid cash to purchase a patent.	_____	_____	_____	_____	_____
e. A six-month note receivable was accepted in exchange for a building that had been used in operations	_____	_____	_____	_____	_____
f. Recorded depreciation expense on all plant and equipment.	_____	_____	_____	_____	_____
g. A cash dividend that was declared in a previous period was paid in the current period.	_____	_____	_____	_____	_____

Exercise 16-10 Calculating cash flows (direct method) LO7

In each of the following cases, use the information provided about the 2017 operations of Prestige Water Corp. to calculate the indicated cash flow:

Case A: Calculate cash received from customers:

Sales revenue	$306,000
Accounts receivable, January 1	15,120
Accounts receivable, December 31	20,880

Case B: Calculate cash paid for insurance:

Insurance expense	$ 41,040
Prepaid insurance, January 1	6,840
Prepaid insurance, December 31	10,260

Case C: Calculate cash paid for salaries:

Salaries expense	$122,400
Salaries payable, January 1	7,560
Salaries payable, December 31	9,000

Exercise 16-11 Calculating cash flows (direct method) LO7

In each of the following cases, use the information provided about the 2017 operations of Yellow Fish Inc. to calculate the indicated cash flow:

Case A: Calculate cash paid for rent:

Rent expense	$ 24,480
Rent payable, January 1	5,280
Rent payable, December 31	4,320

Case B: Calculate cash received from interest:

Interest income	$ 81,600
Interest receivable, January 1	7,200
Interest receivable, December 31	8,640

Case C: Calculate cash paid for merchandise:

Cost of goods sold	$422,400
Merchandise inventory, January 1	127,680
Accounts payable, January 1	54,240
Merchandise inventory, December 31	105,120
Accounts payable, December 31	67,200

Exercise 16-12 Calculating cash flows from operating activities (direct and indirect methods) LO5,7

CHECK FIGURE: Net cash inflow from operating activities = $140,064

Use the following income statement and information about changes in non-cash current assets and current liabilities to present the cash flows from operating activities using the direct method:

Opal Resources Corp. Income Statement For Year Ended December 31, 2017		
Sales		$484,800
Cost of goods sold		237,600
Gross profit from sales		$247,200
Operating expenses:		
Salaries expense	$66,276	
Depreciation expense	11,520	
Rent expense	9,760	
Amortization expense, patents	1,440	
Utilities expense	5,100	
Total operating expenses		94,096
Income on sale of equipment		1,920
Profit from operations		$155,024
Income taxes		3,200
Profit		$151,824

Changes in current asset and current liability accounts during the year were as follows:

Accounts receivable	$10,800 increase
Merchandise inventory	7,200 increase
Accounts payable	3,600 decrease
Salaries payable	1,200 decrease

Analysis Component: Use the information above to present the cash flows from operating activities using the indirect method. Explain the differences and similarities between the direct and indirect methods.

Exercise 16-13 Organizing the statement of cash flows and supporting footnote (direct method) L07

CHECK FIGURE: Net cash inflow from operating activities = $121,875

Rosetta Inc.'s records contain the following information about the 2017 cash flows.

Cash and cash equivalents balance, December 31, 2016	$ 37,500
Cash and cash equivalents balance, December 31, 2017	84,375
Cash received as interest	3,750
Cash paid for salaries	26,250
Bonds payable retired by issuing common shares (there was no gain or loss on the retirement)	281,250
Cash paid to retire long-term notes payable	91,875
Cash received from sale of equipment	37,500
Cash borrowed on six-month note payable	37,500
Land purchased and financed by long-term note payable	159,375
Cash paid for store equipment	35,625
Cash dividends paid	22,500
Cash paid for income taxes	30,000
Cash received from customers	363,750
Cash paid for merchandise	189,375
Depreciation expense	108,750

Required Prepare a statement of cash flows using the direct method and a note describing non-cash investing and financing activities.

Exercise 16-14 **Preparing the statement of cash flows (direct method)** LO7

CHECK FIGURE: Net cash inflow from operating activities = $151,040

The summarized journal entries below show the total debits and credits to the Zebra Corporation's Cash account during 2017.

Required Use the information to prepare a statement of cash flows for 2017. The cash flow from operating activities should be presented according to the direct method. In the statement, identify the entry that records each item of cash flow. Assume that the beginning balance of cash was $13,320.

Analysis Component: Consult the statement of cash flows you have just prepared and answer the following questions:

a. Of the three activity sections (operating, investing, or financing), which section shows the largest cash flow for the year 2017?

b. What was the purpose of the largest investing cash outflow in 2017?

c. Were the proceeds larger from issuing debt or equity in 2017?

d. Did the corporation have a net cash inflow or outflow from borrowing activity in 2017?

a.	Cash..	144,000	
	Common Shares		144,000
	Issued common shares for cash.		
b.	Cash..	240,000	
	Notes Payable		240,000
	Borrowed cash with a note payable.		
c.	Merchandise Inventory.................................	48,000	
	Cash		48,000
	Purchased merchandise for cash.		
d.	Accounts Payable	120,000	
	Cash		120,000
	Paid for credit purchases of merchandise.		
e.	Wages Expense	60,000	
	Cash		60,000
	Paid wages to employees.		
f.	Rent Expense	42,000	
	Cash		42,000
	Paid rent for buildings.		
g.	Cash..	300,000	
	Sales		300,000
	Made cash sales to customers.		
h.	Cash..	180,000	
	Accounts Receivable		180,000
	Collected accounts from credit customers.		
i.	Machinery..	213,600	
	Cash		213,600
	Purchased machinery for cash.		
j.	Long-Term Investments	216,000	
	Cash		216,000
	Purchased long-term investments for cash.		
k.	Interest Expense......................................	21,600	
	Notes Payable	38,400	
	Cash		60,000
	Paid notes and accrued interest.		

l.	Cash...	10,640	
	Dividend income		10,640
	Collected dividends from investments.		
m.	Cash...	21,000	
	Loss on Investments....................................	3,000	
	Investments..		24,000
	Sold investments for cash.		
n.	Cash...	72,000	
	Accumulated Depreciation, Machinery............	42,000	
	Machinery		96,000
	Gain on Sale of Machinery......................		18,000
	Sold machinery for cash.		
o.	Common Dividend Payable	51,000	
	Cash...		51,000
	Paid cash dividends to shareholders.		
p.	Income Taxes Payable..................................	48,000	
	Cash...		48,000
	Paid income taxes owed for the year.		
q.	Common Shares..	22,800	
	Cash...		22,800
	Purchased and retired common shares for cash.		

Problems

Problem 16-1A **Preparing the statement of cash flows (indirect method)** LO5,6

CHECK FIGURE: Net cash inflow from operating activities = $67,200

LAG Network Inc.'s balance sheet and income statement are as follows:

LAG Network Inc. Income Statement For Year Ended December 31, 2017		
Sales		$929,600
Cost of goods sold		557,200
Gross profit		$372,400
Operating expenses:		
Depreciation expense	$ 25,200	
Other expenses	233,800	
Total operating expenses		259,000
Profit from operations		$113,400
Income taxes		19,600
Profit		$ 93,800

LAG Network Inc. Comparative Balance Sheet Information		
	December 31	
Assets	**2017**	**2016**
Cash..	$ 81,200	$ 54,600
Accounts receivable	43,400	37,800
Merchandise inventory................	284,200	249,200
Equipment..................................	155,400	138,600
Accumulated depreciation	(72,800)	(47,600)
Total assets	$491,400	$432,600
Liabilities and Equity		
Accounts payable	$ 32,200	$ 44,800
Income taxes payable	12,600	11,200
Common shares	364,000	336,000
Retained earnings.......................	82,600	40,600
Total liabilities and equity.............	$491,400	$432,600

Additional information regarding LAG Network Inc.'s activities during 2017:

a. Equipment is purchased for $16,800 cash.

b. 11,200 common shares are issued for cash at $2.50 per share.

c. Declared and paid $51,800 of cash dividends during the year.

Required Prepare a statement of cash flows for 2017 that reports the cash inflows and outflows from operating activities according to the indirect method. Show your supporting calculations.

Analysis Component: Assume that LAG Network Inc. had a loss instead of a profit. Does a loss mean that there will always be a cash outflow from operating activities on the statement of cash flows?

Problem 16-2A Preparing the statement of cash flows (direct method) LO7

CHECK FIGURE: Net cash outflow from financing activities = $23,800

Refer to the information in Problem 16-1A. Other information regarding LAG Network Inc.:

a. All sales are credit sales.

b. All credits to accounts receivable are receipts from customers.

c. All purchases of merchandise are on credit.

d. All debits to accounts payable result from payments for merchandise.

e. Other operating expenses are cash expenses.

f. The only decrease in income taxes payable is for payment of taxes.

Required Prepare a statement of cash flows for 2017 using the direct method to report cash inflows and outflows from operating activities.

Problem 16-3A Preparing the statement of cash flows (indirect method) LO5,6

CHECK FIGURE: Cash inflow from operating activities = $37,800

Union Brake Inc.'s comparative balance sheet information at December 31, 2017 and 2016, and its income statement for the year ended December 31, 2017, are as follows:

Union Brake Inc.
Income Statement
December 31, 2017

Sales		864,000
Cost of goods sold		576,000
Gross profit		288,000
Operating expenses	132,720	
Depreciation expense	41,280	174,000
Operating Profit		114,000
Loss on sale of equipment	3,840	
Investment income	11,520	
Profit before taxes		121,680
Income taxes		18,000
Profit		103,680

Union Brake Inc.
Balance Sheet Information

	December 31 2017	2016	Net Change
Cash	$ 48,000	$ 24,960	$ 23,040
Cash equivalents	17,280	9,600	7,680
Accounts receivable	88,320	37,440	50,880
Inventory	114,240	83,520	30,720
Investment	-0-	17,280	(17,280)
Land	76,800	76,800	-0-
Building and equipment	444,480	456,000	(11,520)
Accumulated depreciation	118,080	96,960	21,120
Accounts payable	19,920	37,800	(17,880)
Dividends payable	1,200	600	600
Bonds payable	24,000	-0-	24,000
Preferred shares	81,600	81,600	-0-
Common shares	406,080	406,080	-0-
Retained earnings	138,240	82,560	55,680

During 2017, the following transactions occurred:

1. Purchased equipment for $19,200 cash.

2. Sold the investment on January 1, 2017, for $28,800.

3. Sold equipment for $6,720 cash that had originally cost $30,720 and had $20,160 of accumulated depreciation.

4. Issued $24,000 of bonds payable at face value.

Required

1. How much cash was paid in dividends?

2. Prepare a statement of cash flows for Union Brake for the year ended December 31, 2017, using the indirect method.

Analysis Component: The net increase in cash during 2017 for Union Brake was $30,720. Briefly explain what caused this change using the statement of cash flows prepared in part 2 above.

Problem 16-4A Preparing the statement of cash flows (direct method) LO7

CHECK FIGURE: Cash inflow from investing activities = $16,320

Required Refer to the information in Problem 16-3A. Prepare a statement of cash flows for 2017 using the direct method to report cash inflows and outflows from operating activities.

Other information:

    a. All sales are credit sales.

    b. All credits to accounts receivable in the period are receipts from customers.

    c. All purchases of merchandise are on credit.

    d. All debits to accounts payable in the period result from payments for merchandise.

    e. Other operating expenses are cash expenses.

    f. Income taxes are cash expenses.

Problem 16-5A Preparing the statement of cash flows (indirect method) LO5,6

CHECK FIGURE: Net cash inflow from operating activities = $74,760

ICE Drilling Inc.'s balance sheet information and income statement are as follows:

ICE Drilling Inc. Income Statement For Year Ended December 31, 2017		
Sales..		1,111,600
Cost of goods sold		560,000
Gross profit................................		551,600
Operating expenses:		
Depreciation expense	$ 42,000	
Other expenses.....................	305,760	
Total operating expenses		347,760
Profit from operations		203,840
Loss on sale of equipment		11,480.0
Profit before taxes		192,360
Income taxes............................		27,160
Profit		165,200

ICE Drilling Inc. Comparative Balance Sheet Information		
	December 31	
	2017	**2016**
Cash...	$120,680	$171,640
Accounts receivable	145,600	111,160
Merchandise inventory.................	613,200	565,600
Prepaid expenses	12,040	14,000
Equipment....................................	357,280	246,400
Accumulated depreciation	77,560	98,560
Accounts payable	197,400	261,240
Current notes payable..................	22,400	14,000
Notes payable.............................	210,000	120,400
Common shares	450,800	350,000
Retained earnings........................	290,640	264,600

Additional information regarding ICE Drilling's activities during 2017:

1. Loss on sale of equipment is $11,480.

2. Paid $70,280 to reduce a long-term note payable.

3. Equipment costing $105,000, with accumulated depreciation of $63,000, is sold for cash.

4. Equipment costing $215,880 is purchased by paying cash of $56,000 and signing a long-term note payable for the balance.

5. Borrowed $8,400 by signing a short-term note payable.

6. Issued 5,600 common shares for cash at $18 per share.

7. Declared and paid cash dividends of $139,160.

Required Prepare a statement of cash flows for 2017 that reports the cash inflows and outflows from operating activities according to the indirect method. Show your supporting calculations. Also prepare a note describing non-cash investing and financing activities.

Analysis Component: Merchandise Inventory, Prepaid Expenses, Notes Payable, and Common Shares are some of the accounts that changed during 2017. Explain what transactions likely caused each of these accounts to increase and/or decrease.

Problem 16-6A Preparing the statement of cash flows (direct method) LO7

CHECK FIGURE: Net cash outflow from investing activities = $25,480

Required Refer to the information in Problem 16-5A. Prepare a statement of cash flows for 2017 using the direct method to report cash inflows and outflows from operating activities.

Other information:

    a. All sales are credit sales.

    b. All credits to accounts receivable in the period are receipts from customers.

    c. Purchases of merchandise are on credit.

    d. All debits to accounts payable in the period result from payments for merchandise.

    e. The only decrease in income taxes payable is for payment of taxes.

    f. The other expenses are paid in advance and are initially debited to Prepaid Expenses.

Problem 16-7A Preparing the statement of cash flows (indirect method) LO5,6

CHECK FIGURE: Net cash outflows from investing activities = $160 (thousand)

Paddleboard Inc. began operations on January 1, 2016. Its post-closing trial balance at December 31, 2016 and 2017, is shown below along with some other information.

Paddleboard Inc. Income Statement For Year Ended December 31, 2017 (000s)		
Revenues:		
Sales.....................................		3,784
Cost of goods sold................		1,536
Gross Profit.............................		2,248
Expenses:		
Other expenses......................	880	
Depreciation expense............	80	
Total operating expenses.......		880
Profit from operations...............		1,368
Income tax expense...............		288
Profit		1,080

Paddleboard Inc. Post-Closing Trial Balance (000s)		
	December 31	
Account	2017	2016
Cash..	$2,880	$1,840
Receivables.....................................	2,800	2,080
Merchandise inventory.....................	2,560	3,040
Property, plant, and equipment	3,040	2,720
Accumulated depreciation	1,920	1,840
Investments	2,080	2,240
Accounts payable	1,920	1,440
Accrued liabilities.............................	320	480
Bonds payable	2,240	2,400
Common shares	3,040	2,720
Retained earnings............................	3,920	3,040

Other information regarding Paddleboard Inc. and its activities during 2017:

1. Assume all accounts have normal balances.

2. Cash dividends were declared and paid during the year.

3. There were no sales of property, plant, and equipment assets during the year.

4. Investments were sold for cash at their original cost.

Required Using the information provided, prepare a statement of cash flows (applying the *indirect* method) for the year ended December 31, 2017.

Analysis Component:

      a. Paddleboard Inc. experienced an increase in cash during 2017. Does this necessarily represent a favourable situation? Explain why or why not.

      b. Explain the causes of change in Paddleboard Inc.'s cash situation during 2017.

Problem 16-8A **Preparing the statement of cash flows (direct method)** LO7

CHECK FIGURE: Net cash inflow from operating activities = $1,160 (thousand)

Required Refer to the information in Problem 16-7A. Prepare a statement of cash flows for 2017 using the direct method to report cash inflows and outflows from operating activities.

    Other information:

      a. All accounts payable balances result from merchandise purchases.

      b. All sales are credit sales.

      c. All credits to accounts receivable are receipts from customers.

      d. All debits to accounts payable result from payments for merchandise.

      e. All other expenses are cash expenses.

Problem 16-9A **Preparing the statement of cash flows (indirect method)** LO5,6

CHECK FIGURE: Net cash inflows from financing activities = $900 (thousand)

Lock & Key Inc. began operations on January 1, 2016. Its post-closing trial balance at December 31, 2016 and 2017, is shown below along with some other information.

Lock & Key Inc.
Income Statement
For Year Ended December 31, 2017 (000s)

Revenues:		
Sales.....................................		3,300
Cost of goods sold................		2,520
Gross Profit.............................		780
Expenses:		
Other expenses.....................	660	
Depreciation expense............	240	
Total expenses......................		3,420
Loss		$ 120

Lock & Key Inc.
Post-Closing Trial Balance (000s)

Account	December 31 2017	December 31 2016
Cash...	$2,160	$1,260
Receivables....................................	2,100	1,440
Merchandise inventory.....................	2,040	2,280
Property, plant, and equipment	3,720	3,960
Accumulated depreciation	1,440	1,380
Accounts payable	1,440	1,080
Accrued liabilities.............................	240	360
Bonds payable	1,680	1,800
Common shares	3,084	2,040
Retained earnings............................	2,136	2,280

Other information regarding Lock & Key Inc. and its activities during 2017:

1. Assume all accounts have normal balances.

2. Cash dividends were declared and paid during the year.

3. Equipment was sold for cash equal to its book value.

Required Using the information provided, prepare a statement of cash flows (applying the *indirect* method) for the year ended December 31, 2017.

Analysis Component: Assume that the investing activities section of the statement of cash flows showed a net cash outflow of $14 thousand. What could this represent? Is a net cash outflow from investing activities necessarily favourable or unfavourable? Explain.

Problem 16-10A **Preparing the statement of cash flows (direct method)** LO7

CHECK FIGURE: Net cash outflow from operating activities = $60 (thousand)

Required Refer to the information in Problem 16-9A. Prepare a statement of cash flows for 2017 using the direct method to report cash inflows and outflows from operating activities.

Other information:

a. All accounts payable balances result from merchandise purchases.

b. All sales are credit sales.

c. All credits to accounts receivable are receipts from customers.

d. All debits to accounts payable result from payments for merchandise.

e. All other expenses are cash expenses.

Problem 16-11A **Preparing the statement of cash flows (indirect method)** LO5,6

CHECK FIGURE: Net cash outflow from investing activities = $8,000

Sunny Technologies Inc. began operations on January 1, 2016. Its post-closing trial balance at December 31, 2016, and 2017, is shown below along with some other information.

Sunny Technologies Inc.
Income Statement
For Year Ended December 31, 2017

Revenues:		
Sales		627,200
Cost of goods sold		483,200
Gross Profit		144,000
Expenses and other:		
Other expenses	155,200	
Depreciation expense	25,600	
Total operating expenses		180,800
Operating Profit (Loss)		(36,800)
Loss on sales of plant assets		20,800
Profit (Loss)		(57,600)

Sunny Technologies Inc.
Post-Closing Trial Balance

Account	December 31 2017	2016
Cash	$ 62,400	$ 76,800
Receivables	41,600	30,400
Merchandise inventory	27,200	35,200
Property, plant, and equipment	230,400	190,400
Accumulated depreciation	64,000	52,800
Accounts payable	49,600	62,400
Accrued liabilities	11,200	6,400
Notes payable	97,600	40,000
Common shares	49,600	8,000
Retained earnings	89,600	163,200

Other information regarding Sunny and its activities during 2017:

1. Assume all accounts have normal balances.

2. Cash dividends were declared and paid during the year.

3. Plant assets were sold during the year.

4. Plant assets worth $99,200 were purchased during the year by paying cash of $32,000 and issuing a long-term note payable for the balance.

Required Using the information provided, prepare a statement of cash flows (applying the *indirect* method) for the year ended December 31, 2017.

Analysis Component:

   a. The Cash account balance for Sunny Technologies Inc. decreased during 2017. Is this necessarily an unfavourable situation? Explain why or why not.

   b. Explain the causes of change in Sunny's cash situation during 2017.

Problem 16-12A Preparing the statement of cash flows (direct method) L07

CHECK FIGURE: Net cash outflow from operating activities = $22,400

Required Refer to the information in Problem 16-11A. Prepare a statement of cash flows for 2017 using the direct method to report cash inflows and outflows from operating activities.

   Other information:

   a. All accounts payable balances result from merchandise purchases.

   b. All sales are credit sales.

   c. All credits to accounts receivable are receipts from customers.

   d. All debits to accounts payable result from payments for merchandise.

   e. All debits and credits to accrued liabilities result from other expenses.

Alternate Problems

Problem 16-1B Preparing the statement of cash flows (indirect method) L05,6   e**X**cel

CHECK FIGURE: Net cash inflow from operating activities = $168,168

MED Supplies Inc., a software retailer, recently completed its 2017 operations. The following information is available:

MED Supplies Inc. Income Statement For Year Ended December 31, 2017		
Sales...		$1,365,840
Cost of goods sold		624,960
Gross profit...............................		$ 740,880
Operating expenses:		
Depreciation expense	$ 39,648	
Other expenses.....................	402,696	
Total operating expenses		442,344
Profit from operations		$ 298,536
Income taxes...........................		100,464
Profit		$ 198,072

MED Supplies Inc. Comparative Balance Sheet Information		
	December 31	
	2017	2016
Cash...	$120,792	$ 71,232
Accounts receivable	43,512	52,080
Merchandise inventory.................	392,784	313,320
Equipment...................................	236,208	171,360
Accumulated depreciation	108,192	68,544
Accounts payable	86,184	79,800
Income taxes payable	10,080	15,120
Common shares	463,680	369,600
Retained earnings........................	125,160	74,928

Additional information regarding MED Supplies Inc.'s activities during 2017:

1. Equipment was purchased for $64,848 cash.

2. Issued 3,360 common shares for cash at $28 per share.

3. Declared and paid $147,840 of cash dividends during the year.

Required Prepare a statement of cash flows for 2017 that reports the cash inflows and outflows from operating activities according to the indirect method. Show your supporting calculations.

Analysis Component: The net increase in cash during 2017 for MED Supplies Inc. was $49,560. Briefly explain what caused this change using the statement of cash flows prepared above.

Problem 16-2B **Preparing the statement of cash flows (direct method)** LO7

CHECK FIGURE: Net cash outflow from financing activities = $53,760

Required Refer to the information in Problem 16-1B. Prepare a statement of cash flows for 2017 using the direct method to report cash inflows and outflows from operating activities.

Other information:

- **a.** All sales were credit sales.
- **b.** All credits to accounts receivable in the period were receipts from customers.
- **c.** Purchases of merchandise were on credit.
- **d.** All debits to accounts payable were from payments for merchandise.
- **e.** The other operating expenses were cash expenses.
- **f.** The decrease in income taxes payable was for payment of taxes.

Problem 16-3B **Calculating cash flows (indirect method)** LO5,6

CHECK FIGURE: Cash inflow from operating activities = $22,800

Burrow Mining Inc.'s comparative balance sheet information at December 31, 2017, and 2016, and its income statement for the year ended December 31, 2017, are as follows:

Burrow Mining Inc. Income Statement Year Ended December 31, 2017		
Sales.....................................		504,000
Cost of goods sold..................		336,000
Gross profit............................		168,000
Operating expenses................	77,920	
Depreciation expense..............	24,080	102,000
Profit from Operations.............		66,000
Loss on sale of equipment.......		2,240
Investment income..................		6,720
Profit before Taxes..................		70,480
Income taxes..........................		10,000
Profit		60,480

Burrow Mining Inc. Comparative Balance Sheet Information			
	December 31		Net
	2017	2016	Change
Cash.................................	$ 28,000	$ 14,560	$ 13,440
Cash equivalents..............	10,080	5,600	4,480
Accounts receivable..........	51,520	21,840	29,680
Inventory..........................	66,640	48,720	17,920
Non-current investment......	-0-	10,080	(10,080)
Land.................................	44,800	44,800	-0-
Building and equipment......	259,280	266,000	(6,720)
Accumulated depreciation ...	68,880	56,560	12,320
Accounts payable..............	11,920	21,600	(9,680)
Dividends payable	400	800	(400)
Bonds payable	14,000	-0-	14,000
Preferred shares................	47,600	47,600	-0-
Common shares	236,880	236,880	-0-
Retained earnings..............	80,640	48,160	32,480

During 2017, the following transactions occurred:

1. Issued $14,000 of bonds payable at face value.
2. Sold the non-current investment on January 1, 2017, for $16,800.
3. Sold equipment for $3,920 cash that had originally cost $17,920 and had $11,760 of accumulated depreciation.
4. Purchased equipment for $11,200 cash.

Required

    a. How much was paid in dividends during 2017?

    b. Prepare a statement of cash flows for Burrow Mining Inc. for the year ended December 31, 2017, using the indirect method.

Analysis Component: Accounts Receivable increased from $21,840 to $51,520 in 2017. What transactions cause this account to change? Accounts Payable decreased during 2017. What causes this account to change?

Problem 16-4B Preparing the statement of cash flows (direct method) LO7

CHECK FIGURE: Cash inflow from investing activities = $9,520

Required Refer to the information in Problem 16-3B. Prepare a statement of cash flows for 2017 using the direct method to report cash inflows and outflows from operating activities.

    Other information:

    a. All sales are credit sales.

    b. All credits to accounts receivable are receipts from customers.

    c. All purchases of merchandise are on credit.

    d. All debits to accounts payable result from payments for merchandise.

    e. Other operating expenses are cash expenses.

    f. Income taxes are cash expenses.

Problem 16-5B Preparing the statement of cash flows (indirect method) LO5,6

CHECK FIGURE: Net cash inflow from operating activities = $141,267

Triple Flip Inc., a sporting goods retailer, recently completed its 2017 operations. Triple Flip Inc.'s balance sheet information and income statement follow.

Triple Flip Inc. Income Statement For Year Ended December 31, 2017		
Sales.....................................		1,061,340
Cost of goods sold		573,300
Gross profit............................		488,040
Operating expenses:		
Depreciation expense	35,868	
Other expenses....................	384,993	
Total operating expenses		420,861
Profit from operations		67,179
Loss on sale of equipment		2,058
Profit before Taxes...................		65,121
Income taxes..........................		9,261
Profit		55,860

Triple Flip Inc. Comparative Balance Sheet Information		
	December 31	
	2017	**2016**
Cash..	$133,770	$ 70,119
Accounts receivable	72,618	88,935
Merchandise inventory..................	445,410	480,396
Prepaid expenses	16,758	18,816
Equipment...................................	272,685	211,680
Accumulated depreciation	106,575	91,140
Accounts payable	115,101	120,981
Current notes payable..................	16,905	11,025
Notes payable.............................	110,250	80,850
Common shares	473,340	441,000
Retained earnings........................	119,070	124,950

Additional information regarding Triple Flip Inc.'s activities during 2017:

1. Loss on sale of equipment is $2,058.

2. Equipment costing $49,980 is sold for $27,489.

3. Equipment is purchased by paying cash of $37,485 and signing a long-term note payable for the balance.

4. Borrowed $5,880 by signing a short-term note payable.

5. Reduced a long-term note payable by making a payment.

6. Issued 2,940 common shares for cash at $11 per share.

7. Declared and paid cash dividends.

Required Prepare a statement of cash flows for 2017 that reports the cash inflows and outflows from operating activities according to the indirect method. Show your supporting calculations. Also prepare a note describing non-cash investing and financing activities.

Analysis Component: Using the information from the statement of cash flows just prepared for Triple Flip Inc., identify the accrual basis profit and the cash basis profit for 2017. Explain why there is a difference between the two amounts.

Problem 16-6B **Preparing the statement of cash flows (direct method)** LO7

CHECK FIGURE: Net cash outflow from financing activities = $67,620

Required Refer to the information in Problem 16-5B. Prepare a statement of cash flows for 2017 using the direct method to report cash inflows and outflows from operating activities.

   Other information:

   a. All sales were credit sales.

   b. All credits to accounts receivable in the period were receipts from customers.

   c. Purchases of merchandise were on credit.

   d. All debits to accounts payable in the period resulted from payments for merchandise.

   e. The other expenses were paid in advance and were initially debited to Prepaid Expenses.

Problem 16-7B **Preparing the statement of cash flows (indirect method)** LO5,6

CHECK FIGURE: Net cash inflow from financing activities = $840 (million)

Zhang Systems Inc. began operations on January 1, 2016. Its post-closing trial balance at December 31, 2016, and 2017, is shown below along with some other information.

Zhang Systems Inc. Income Statement For Year Ended December 31, 2017 (millions of dollars)		
Revenues:		
Sales....................................		26,700
Cost of goods sold................		19,500
Gross Profit............................		7,200
Expenses:		
Other expenses.....................	7,050	
Depreciation expense	1,350	
Total expenses......................		8,400
Profit (Loss)		(1,200)

Zhang Systems Inc. Post-Closing Trial Balance (millions of dollars)		
	December 31	
Account	**2017**	**2016**
Cash...	$ 54	$ 129
Receivables.......................................	276	372
Merchandise inventory......................	408	261
Property, plant, and equipment	6,900	8,976
Accumulated depreciation	3,699	4,125
Non-current investments	1,560	309
Accounts payable	318	405
Accrued liabilities.............................	141	117
Bonds payable	1,200	600
Common shares	2,700	2,100
Retained earnings............................	1,140	2,700

Other information regarding Zhang Systems Inc. and its activities during 2017:

1. Assume all accounts have normal balances.

2. Cash dividends were declared and paid during the year.

3. Plant assets were sold for cash equal to book value during the year.

Required Using the information provided, prepare a statement of cash flows (applying the *indirect* method) for the year ended December 31, 2017.

Analysis Component: The net decrease in cash during 2017 for Zhang Systems Inc. was $75 million. Briefly explain what caused this change using the statement of cash flows prepared above.

Problem 16-8B Preparing the statement of cash flows (direct method) LO7

CHECK FIGURE: Net cash inflow from operating activities = $36 (million)

Required Refer to the information in Problem 16-7B. Prepare a statement of cash flows for 2017 using the direct method to report cash inflows and outflows from operating activities.

Other information:

    a. All accounts payable balances result from merchandise purchases.

    b. All sales are credit sales.

    c. All credits to accounts receivable are receipts from customers.

    d. All debits to accounts payable result from payments for merchandise.

    e. All other expenses are cash expenses.

Problem 16-9B Preparing the statement of cash flows (indirect method) LO5,6

CHECK FIGURE: Net cash inflow from investing activities = $85 (million)

Clear Strategy Corp., a strategic marketing consulting firm, began operations on January 1, 2016. Its post-closing trial balance at December 31, 2016, and 2017, is shown below along with some other information.

Clear Strategy Corp.
Income Statement
For Year Ended December 31, 2017 (millions)

Revenues:		
Consulting revenue		8,750
Expenses:		
Salaries expense	4,700	
Other expenses	1,600	
Depreciation expense	400	
Total expenses		6,700
Profit from Operations		2,050
Income tax expense		350
Profit		1,700

Clear Strategy Corp.
Post-Closing Trial Balance (millions)

Account	2017	2016
Cash	$ 485	$ 75
Receivables	500	350
Prepaid insurance	60	20
Land	1,240	1,240
Equipment	535	745
Accumulated depreciation	360	85
Accounts payable	155	70
Salaries payable	20	45
Income tax payable	85	250
Notes payable	175	1,655
Common shares	800	200
Retained earnings	1,225	125

Other information regarding Clear Strategy Corp. and its activities during 2017:

1. Assume all accounts have normal balances.

2. Share dividends were declared and issued during the year.

3. Equipment was sold for cash equal to its book value.

Required Using the information provided, prepare a statement of cash flows (applying the *indirect* method) for the year ended December 31, 2017.

Analysis Component: Clear Strategy Corp.'s comparative post-closing trial balance shows that Receivables, Prepaid Insurance, Accumulated Depreciation, Accounts Payable, Common Shares, and Retained Earnings increased during 2017, while Equipment, Salaries Payable, Income Tax Payable, and Notes Payable decreased during the same period. Explain what most likely caused the changes in these accounts.

Problem 16-10B Preparing the statement of cash flows (direct method) LO7

CHECK FIGURE: Net cash inflow from operating activities = $1,805 (million)

Required Refer to the information in Problem 16-9B. Prepare a statement of cash flows for 2017 using the direct method to report cash inflows and outflows from operating activities.

Other information:

    a. All accounts payable balances result from other expenses.

    b. All consulting revenue is done on credit.

    c. All credits to accounts receivable are receipts from customers.

    d. All debits to accounts payable result from payments for other expenses.

Problem 16-11B Preparing the statement of cash flows (indirect method) LO5,6

CHECK FIGURE: Net cash inflow from investing activities = $16,000

Country Feed Inc., a Saskatchwan-based farm and ranch livestock feed distributor, began operations on January 1, 2016. Its post-closing trial balance at December 31, 2016 and 2017, is shown below along with some other information.

Country Feed Inc.
Income Statement
For Year Ended December 31, 2017

Revenues:		
Sales.....................................		513,600
Cost of goods sold		343,600
Gross Profit.............................		170,000
Expenses and other:		
Other expenses.....................	167,600	
Depreciation expense	18,000	
Total expenses and other.......		185,600
Operating Profit (Loss)		(15,600)
Gain on sale of plant assets ..		8,000
Profit (Loss)		(7,600)

Country Feed Inc.
Post-Closing Trial Balance

Account	December 31	
	2017	2016
Cash...	$ 63,200	$ 65,200
Receivables...................................	121,600	128,400
Merchandise inventory	43,200	38,800
Property, plant, and equipment	298,400	272,400
Accumulated depreciation	167,600	165,600
Accounts payable	78,800	78,000
Accrued liabilities............................	5,600	7,200
Notes payable................................	115,200	75,200
Common shares	80,000	80,000
Retained earnings............................	79,200	98,800

Other information regarding Country Feed Inc. and its activities during 2017:

    1. Assume all accounts have normal balances.

    2. Cash dividends were declared and paid during the year.

    3. Plant assets worth $70,000 were purchased during the year by paying cash of $20,000 and issuing a long-term note payable for the balance.

    4. Plant assets were sold during the year.

Required Using the information provided, prepare a statement of cash flows (applying the *indirect* method) for the year ended December 31, 2017.

Analysis Component: Country Feed Inc.'s income statement showed a *loss* of $7,600 for the year ended December 31, 2017, yet the statement of cash flows shows net cash *inflows* from operating activities of $4,000 for the same period. Explain what this difference means.

Problem 16-12B Preparing the statement of cash flows (direct method) L07

CHECK FIGURE: Net cash outflow from financing activities = $22,000

Required Refer to the information in Problem 16-11B. Prepare a statement of cash flows for 2017 using the direct method to report cash inflows and outflows from operating activities.

Other information:

    a. All accounts payable balances result from merchandise purchases.

    b. All sales are credit sales.

    c. All credits to accounts receivable are receipts from customers.

    d. All debits to accounts payable result from payments for merchandise.

    e. All debits and credits to accrued liabilities result from other expenses.

Analytical and Review Problems

A & R 16-1 (Indirect method)

Jacobson Manufacturing Corporation earned $84,000 in profit during 2017. Machinery was sold for $116,000 and a $24,000 loss on the sale was recorded. Machinery purchases totalled $330,000 including a July purchase for which an $80,000 promissory note was issued. Bonds were retired at their face value, and the issuance of new common shares produced an infusion of cash. Jacobson's comparative balance sheets were as follows:

Jacobson Corporation Comparative Balance Sheet Information (in thousands)		
	December 31	
Assets	**2017**	**2016**
Cash..	$ 104	$ 84
Accounts receivable	196	222
Merchandise inventory...	324	310
Machinery..	1,350	1,260
Accumulated depreciation	(190)	(210)
Total assets	$1,784	$1,666
Liabilities and Equity		
Accounts payable	$ 238	$ 286
Notes payable..	272	210
Dividends payable	32	20
Bonds payable	228	320
Common shares	700	560
Retained earnings..	314	270
Total liabilities and equity...................................	$1,784	$1,666

1. What was Jacobson's depreciation expense in 2017?

2. What was the amount of cash flow from operating activities?

3. What was the amount of cash flow from investing activities?

4. What was the amount of dividends declared? paid?

5. By what amount would you expect the total inflows of cash to differ from the total outflows of cash?

6. What was the amount of cash flow from financing activities?

A & R 16-2 (Indirect method)

The data below refers to Money Ltd. for the year ended December 31, 2017.

Required For each item, identify both the dollar amount and its classification—that is, whether it would appear as a positive or a negative adjustment to profit in the calculation of cash flow from operations (using the *indirect method*), or as some other inflow or outflow of cash.

1. Declared a $15,000 cash dividend; paid $12,000 during the year.

2. Sold, for $90,000 cash, land that had cost $75,000 two years earlier.

3. Sold for cash 2,000 shares for $6 a share.

4. Bought machinery for $24,000 in exchange for a note due in 18 months.

5. Bought a computer that had a fair value of $35,000 by giving in exchange real estate that had cost $15,000 in an earlier period.

6. Equipment depreciation, $18,000.

7. Issued for cash on December 31, 2017, a $250,000 10-year, 10% bond at an $18,000 discount.

8. Bought its own shares for $7,500 and immediately cancelled them.

9. Paid a lawyer $6,200 for services performed, billed, and recorded correctly in 2016.

10. Reported profit of $63,000 for the year ended December 31, 2017.

A & R 16-3 (Direct method)

Swiss Farm Inc.'s 2017 statement of cash flows appeared as follows:

Cash flows from operating activities:		
Profit		$111,100
Accounts receivable increase	$(14,700)	
Inventory decrease	47,600	
Prepaid expense increase	(4,600)	
Accounts payable decrease	(16,300)	
Income taxes payable increase	4,400	
Depreciation expense	12,000	
Loss on disposal of equipment	13,400	
Gain on bond retirement	(7,700)	34,100
Net cash inflows from operating activities		$145,200
Cash flows from investing activities:		
Receipt from sale of office equipment	$ 5,100	
Purchase of store equipment	(33,000)	
Net cash outflows from investing activities		(27,900)
Cash flows from financing activities:		
Payment to retire bonds payable	$(42,300)	
Payment of dividends	(30,000)	
Net cash outflows from financing activities		(72,300)
Net increase in cash		$ 45,000
Cash balance at December 31, 2016		45,400
Cash balance at December 31, 2017		$ 90,400

Swiss Farm Inc.'s balance sheet information is as follows:

	December 31 2017	December 31 2016		December 31 2017	December 31 2016
Cash.....................................	$ 90,400	$ 45,400	Accounts payable......................	$ 58,500	$ 74,800
Accounts receivable	114,900	100,200	Income taxes payable................	10,900	6,500
Merchandise inventory....................	212,700	260,300	Dividends payable......................	-0-	7,500
Prepaid expenses	9,000	4,400	Bonds payable...........................	-0-	50,000
Equipment....................................	99,100	108,600	Common shares........................	300,000	300,000
Accumulated depreciation	18,200	30,200	Retained earnings	138,500	49,900

An examination of the company's statements and accounts showed:

a. All accounts have normal balances.

b. All sales were made on credit.

c. All merchandise purchases were on credit.

d. Accounts payable balances resulted from merchandise purchases.

e. Prepaid expenses relate to other operating expenses.

f. Equipment that cost $42,500 and was depreciated $24,000 was sold for cash.

g. Equipment was purchased for cash.

h. The change in the balance of Accumulated Depreciation resulted from depreciation expense and from the sale of equipment.

i. The change in the balance of Retained Earnings resulted from dividend declarations and profit.

j. Cash receipts from customers were $772,800.

k. Cash payments for merchandise inventory amounted to $425,400.

l. Cash payments for other operating expenses were $169,800.

m. Income taxes paid were $32,400.

Required Prepare Swiss Farm's single-step income statement for 2017. Show supporting calculations.

A & R 16-4 (Indirect method)

The following items include the 2017 and 2016 balance sheet information and the 2017 income statement of the Clear Water Corporation. Additional information about the company's 2017 transactions is presented after the financial statements.

Clear Water Corporation Comparative Balance Sheet Information		
	December 31	
	2017	2016
Cash and cash equivalents............	$ 1,000	$ 800
Accounts receivable	4,500	3,100
Merchandise inventory..................	19,000	16,000
Prepaid expenses	700	600
Investment in land	10,000	12,000
Land...	9,000	4,000
Buildings......................................	60,000	60,000
Accumulated depreciation, buildings.................................	38,000	36,000
Equipment....................................	21,000	16,000
Accumulated depreciation, equipment	6,000	4,000
Notes payable..............................	5,000	3,500
Accounts payable	9,000	10,000
Other accrued liabilities................	5,300	4,200
Interest payable	400	300
Taxes payable	300	500
Bonds payable, due in 2019	25,000	22,000
Common shares	16,000	14,000
Retained earnings........................	20,200	18,000

Clear Water Corporation Income Statement For Year Ended December 31, 2017		
Revenues:		
Sales.....................................		120,000
Cost of goods sold		50,000
Gross Profit.............................		70,000
Operating Expenses		
Other expenses....................	54,800	
Depreciation expense, buildings	2,000	
Depreciation expense, equipment.......................	4,000	
Total operating expenses		60,800
Profit from Operations..............		9,200
Interest income.....................		900
Interest expense		2,000
Gain on sale of long-term investment		3,000
Loss on sale of equipment.....		600
Profit before Taxes...................		10,500
Income tax expense..............		2,500
Profit		8,000

Additional information:

1. Received $5,000 from the sale of the land investment that originally cost $2,000.

2. Received $400 cash from the First National Bank on December 31, 2017, as interest income.

3. Sold old equipment for $1,400. The old equipment originally cost $4,000 and had accumulated depreciation of $2,000.

4. Purchased land costing $5,000 on December 31, 2017, in exchange for a note payable. Both principal and interest are due on June 30, 2018.

5. Purchased new equipment for $9,000 cash.

6. Paid $3,500 of notes payable.

7. Sold additional bonds payable at par of $3,000 on January 1, 2017.

8. Issued 1,000 common shares for cash at $2 per share.

9. Declared and paid a $5,800 cash dividend on October 1, 2017.

Required Prepare a statement of cash flows for Clear Water Corporation using the indirect method.

Ethics Challenge

EC 16-1

Wendy Cramer is working late on a Friday night in preparation for a meeting with her banker early Monday morning. Her business is just finishing its fourth year. In Year 1, the business experienced negative cash flows from operations. In Years 2 and 3, cash flows from operations turned positive. Unfortunately, her inventory costs rose significantly in Year 4 and her profit will probably be down about 25% after this year's adjusting entries. Wendy is hoping to secure a line of credit from her banker, which will be a nice financing buffer. From prior experience with her banker, she knows that a focus of Monday's meeting will be cash flows from operations. The banker will scrutinize the cash flow numbers for Years 1 through 4 and will want a projected number for Year 5. Wendy knows that a steady upward progression of cash flows in Years 1 through 4 will really help her case for securing the line of credit. Wendy decides to use her discretion as owner of the business and proposes several adjusting entries and business actions that will help turn her cash flow number in Year 4 from negative to positive.

Required

1. Identify two possible entries or business actions Wendy might use to improve the cash flow from operations number on the statement of cash flows for Year 4.

2. Comment on the ethics and possible consequences of Wendy's decision to propose the adjustments/actions for Year 4.

Focus on Financial Statements

FFS 16-1

CHECK FIGURES: Current assets = $160; Total assets = $246; Current liabilities = $27; Cash inflow from operating activities = $7

Wong Corporation began operations on January 1, 2016. Its adjusted trial balance at December 31, 2016, and 2017, is shown below along with some other information.

Wong Corporation Adjusted Trial Balance (000s)		
	December 31	
Account	**2017**	**2016**
Accounts payable	$ 21	$ 32
Accounts receivable	96	100
Accumulated depreciation, equipment	21	52
Accumulated depreciation, machinery	15	36
Allowance for doubtful accounts	6	12
Cash..	70	98
Cash dividends...	20	20
Common shares	108	98
Depreciation expense, equipment.................................	7	7
Depreciation expense, machinery	4	4
Equipment...	88	110
Income tax expense...	10	19
Machinery...	34	64
Notes payable; long term[1]..	8	25
Other expenses (including losses).................................	373	200
Preferred shares..	30	30
Retained earnings..	79	13
Revenues (including gains)..	410	316
Unearned revenue..	4	8

[1]$2,000 of the notes payable will be paid during 2018.

Other information regarding Wong Corporation and its activities during 2017:

    a. Assume all accounts have normal balances.

    b. Equipment was purchased for $26,000 cash after selling old equipment for $8,000 cash.

    c. Common shares were issued for cash.

    d. Cash dividends were declared and paid.

    e. Machinery was sold for cash of $10,000.

    f. All revenues and other expenses were on credit.

Required Using the information provided, prepare a statement of changes in equity and a statement of cash flows (applying the *indirect* or *direct* method)* for the year ended December 31, 2017, plus a classified balance sheet at December 31, 2017.

Note to Instructor: *Solutions are available for both the indirect and direct methods.*

Analysis Component: Refer to the statement of cash flows just prepared. Explain how it was possible for Wong Corporation to purchase $26 (thousand) of new equipment and pay $20 (thousand) dividends given that the company's income was only $16 (thousand).

FFS 16-2

Part 1

Required Refer to WestJet's statement of cash flows in Appendix II at the end of the textbook and answer the following questions.

    a. Identify WestJet's largest cash outflow during 2014.

    b. What was the largest cash inflow during 2014?

    c. Under the operating section of the statement of cash flows, WestJet shows an *increase in non-cash working capital* of $88,410 (thousand). What is *non-cash working capital*?

    d. Compare the *Cash and cash equivalents, end of year* for 2014 as it appears on the statement of cash flows to the *Cash and cash equivalents* balance that appears on the December 31, 2014, balance sheet. Are these amounts the same or different? Explain.

Part 2

Required Refer to the statements of cash flows for each of Indigo and Telus in Appendix II and answer the following questions.

    a. Indigo reported a loss of $(30,999,000) on its 2014 statement of cash flows, and cash flows used in operations of $(17,265,000)—a decrease of $47,658,000 compared with 2013. Telus shows the opposite on its statement of cash flows where the profit for the year ended December 31, 2014, was reported as $1,425,000,000 with cash flows from operations of $3,407,000,000—an increase of $161,000,000 from 2013. Does this comparison indicate that there is something wrong with Indigo's cash flows from operating activities?

    b. Indigo showed $10,240,000 was the cash used by financing activities for the year ended March 29, 2014, while Telus showed cash used of $15,000,000 for the year ended December 31, 2014. Compare and contrast these companies' use of cash for financing activities.

Critical Thinking Mini Case

A major shareholder of Systems Unlimited Inc., Phil Wang, is perplexed. The 2017 income statement showed a healthy profit of $280 thousand. Yet, when Linda Lewis, the bank manager and a friend of Phil's, called to let him know that the bank had just reviewed the March 31, 2017, statements, she had said, "Phil, I just wanted to give you a heads-up. We're extremely concerned about the message your 2017 statement of cash flows is sending. We may have to call in the secured loan unless the new company manager, Martha Shewart, has some reasonable explanations. I'm phoning her next."

When asked, Martha Shewart says, "That's correct, Linda. We sold some of the unsecured manufacturing equipment. It cost $245 thousand and we got $150 thousand. No, it didn't go for book value; we incurred a loss of $50 thousand ... where on the income statement? It's in *Other expenses*. Don't worry, Linda, a friend of mine, Ronald Trump, is going to sell us cheaper equipment. It's on order. I signed the contract and it will be delivered in April." After the conversation, Martha Shewart slams the phone down and thinks, "I own 20% of the shares in this company; how *dare* anybody question my actions?!"

Systems Unlimited Inc. Comparative Balance Sheet Information March 31 (thousands)		
	2017	**2016**
Cash..	$ 30	$ 75
Accounts receivable (net)	490	50
Inventory..	244	80
Property, plant, and equipment (net).....	100	305
Accounts payable	40	22
Income tax payable..............................	14	2
Bank loan payable (secured)	120	0
Common shares	390	390
Retained earnings................................	300	96

Systems Unlimited Inc. Income Statement For Year Ended March 31, 2017 (thousands)		
Sales..		$1,400
Cost of goods sold		950
Gross profit..............................		$ 450
Operating expenses:		
Depreciation expense	$ 5	
Other expenses.....................	115	
Total operating expenses		120
Profit from operations		$ 330
Income tax expense..................		50
Profit		$ 280

Required

1. Prepare a statement of cash flows (applying the *indirect* or *direct* method)* for the year ended March 31, 2017.

2. Using the elements of critical thinking described on the inside front cover, identify and discuss the problem, goal, facts, and conclusion, while keeping in mind that it is best not to jump to conclusions.

***Note to Instructor:** Solutions are available for both the indirect and direct methods.*

Analyzing Financial Statements

A Look Back

The previous chapter focused on reporting and analyzing cash inflows and cash outflows. We emphasized how to prepare and interpret the statement of cash flows.

A Look at This Chapter

In this chapter we review several financial statement analysis tools to assess corporate performance and analyze management effectiveness.

© Richard Levine/Alamy Stock Photo

LEARNING OBJECTIVES

LO1 Describe financial statement analysis and identify its focus, standards of comparison, and tools.

LO2 Describe and apply methods of horizontal analysis.

LO3 Describe and apply methods of vertical analysis.

LO4 Describe and apply ratio analysis.

Lululemon's Story of Incredible Growth

In 1998, after attending the first commercial yoga class in Vancouver, BC., Dennis "Chip" Wilson identified a big opportunity to develop athletic apparel with design features and flexibility that yoga demanded. Wilson has a strong history of entrepreneurship, having founded the popular ski surf and snowboard company Westbeach Snowboard Ltd. in 1979. To pursue his next big business venture, Wilson opened a design studio in the Kitsilano Beach area of Vancouver and set out to establish the high-end brand Lululemon Athletica Inc.

On July 27, 2007, the company raised $328 million in an IPO at a share price of $18. Since then the company has experienced incredible growth as it continues to develop internationally. By February 2015, Lululemon's retail footprint included 211 stores in the United States, 57 stores in Canada, 26 stores in Australia, five in New Zealand, two in the United Kingdom, and one in Singapore. According to its 2013 annual report, Lululemon identifies premium locations to position itself effectively as "an integral part of its community." The company's success is evidenced through an astonishing 50% compound annual growth rate in net revenue, growing from $40.7 million in its 2004 fiscal year to $1.6 billion in 2013, and reaching an impressive $1.8 billion in net revenue in 2014.

Lululemon Athletica Inc. was ranked the most profitable clothing company in North America by *Apparel Magazine* in a study released in July 2014, with profit margins of nearly 18%. The company has a distinctive strategy over inventory management that keeps customers excited about its products and enables the company to achieve generous gross margins in excess of 50%. Lululemon has developed a community-based strategy that it believes is key to the success of its brand development and guest loyalty. The company does not rely on the impressive customer data management tools used by many competitors. According to the *Wall Street Journal*, "it doesn't use focus groups, website visits or the industry staple—customer-relationship management software" to manage sales as many of the top retailers do. Instead, a former CEO, spent 'hours each week in Lululemon stores observing how customers shop, listening to their complaints, and then using the feedback to tweak product and stores.' Employees are trained to pay attention to customers, listen carefully to their complaints, and "the clothes-folding tables on the sales floor [are strategically placed] near the fitting rooms rather than in a back room so that workers can overhear complaints."

Lululemon's billionaire founder announced on February 2, 2015, he was stepping down from the board, and is excited to work with his wife, Shannon and his son, JJ, on their next entrepreneurial adventure, developing a new clothing line of street clothes called Kit&Ace.

Source: http://finance.yahoo.com/q/co?s=LULU+Competitors

Video Links: https://www.youtube.com/watch?v=O6MANRD70Jk (Chip Wilson interview)

https://www.youtube.com/watch?v=tUFUpsIKsCQ (Kit & Ace clothing)

Sources: www.lululemon.com; http://www.retail-insider.com/retail-insider/2014/7/lululemon; http://online.wsj.com/news/articles/SB10001424052702303812904577295882632723066; http://investor.lululemon.com/events.cfm; http://www.forbes.com/sites/clareoconnor/2013/12/10/lululemon-hires-ceo-from-toms-shoes-as-billionaire-founder-chip-wilson-resigns/; http://www.businessinsider.com/lululemon-founder-chip-wilson-resigns-2015-2; Lululemon Annual Report, February 2, 2014; Lululemon Annual Report, February 1, 2015

 CRITICAL THINKING CHALLENGE What is another name for the return on capital ratio? Explain what it means and why a corporation like Lululemon Athletica Inc. would want to maximize it.

CHAPTER PREVIEW

This chapter shows us how to use the information in financial statements to evaluate the financial performance and management effectiveness for a variety of companies. We describe the purpose of analysis, its basic building blocks, the information available, standards for comparisons, and tools of analysis. Three major analysis tools are emphasized—horizontal analysis, vertical analysis, and ratio analysis. We illustrate the application of each of these tools using Naturalgym.com, an online industrial playground equipment manufacturer's financial statements. Understanding how to interpret financial statement analysis tools enables companies to make effective resource allocation decisions and enables investors to make wise investment decisions.

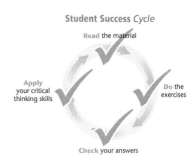

Basics of Analysis

LO1 Describe financial statement analysis and identify its focus, standards of comparison, and tools.

Financial statement analysis is the application of analytical tools to general-purpose financial statements and related data for making business decisions. It involves transforming data into useful information. Financial statement analysis reduces our reliance on hunches, guesses, and intuition. It reduces our uncertainty in decision making as an external financial statement user. However, it does not lessen the need for expert judgment. Instead, it provides us with an effective and systematic basis for asking questions, finding answers, and making business decisions. Additional research on industry reports, management forecasts, and competitive framework should also be assessed.

Macro environmental analysis incorporates factors such as the political, economic, social, and technological issues impacting the business (PEST Analysis) and is effective in understanding the industry landscape.[1] A SWOT analysis investigates the internal corporate strengths and weaknesses against external opportunities and threats. Porter's Five Forces is another industry analysis tool designed to conduct an analysis from a more global perspective.[2] This chapter focuses on the variety of tools used for financial statement analysis, its information sources, the use of comparisons, and some issues in calculations.

Purpose of Analysis

The purpose of financial statement analysis is to help users make better business decisions. These users include decision makers both internal and external to the company.

Internal users of accounting information are those individuals involved in managing and operating the company. The purpose of financial statement analysis for these users is to provide information helpful in improving the company's efficiency or effectiveness in providing products or services.

External users of accounting information are *not* directly involved in running the company. External users rely on financial statement analysis to make better and more informed decisions in pursuing their own goals.

We can identify many examples of how financial statement analysis is used. Shareholders and creditors assess future company prospects for investing and lending decisions. A board of directors analyzes financial statements in monitoring management's decisions. Employees and unions use financial statements in labour negotiations. Suppliers use financial statements in establishing credit terms. Customers analyze financial

---

1 For additional information on a comprehensive PEST/PESTLE analysis, refer to http://pestleanalysis.com/pest-analysis, accessed April 12, 2015.

2 For an example of the model applied, Forbes presents an analysis of Facebook using Porter's Five Forces at VIDEO LINK: http://www.forbes.com/sites/greatspeculations/2014/11/28/facebook-through-the-lens-of-porters-five-forces/

statements in deciding whether to establish supply relationships. Public utilities set customer rates by analyzing financial statements. Auditors use financial statements in assessing the "fair presentation" of their clients' financial statement numbers. And analyst services such as *Dun & Bradstreet*, *Moody's*, and *Standard & Poor's* use financial statements in making buy–sell recommendations and setting credit ratings.

The common goal of all these users is to evaluate company performance. This includes evaluation of (1) past and current performance, (2) current financial position, and (3) future performance and risk.

Four Key Building Blocks of Financial Statement Analysis

Financial statement analysis focuses on one or more elements of a company's financial condition or performance. Our analysis emphasizes four areas of inquiry—with varying degrees of importance. The four key areas of financial statement analysis are summarized in the following box and illustrated in detail throughout the chapter.

> - *Liquidity and Efficiency*—ability to meet current obligations and to generate revenues efficiently.
> - *Solvency*—ability to generate future revenues and meet long-term obligations.
> - *Profitability*—ability to provide financial rewards sufficient to attract and retain financing.
> - *Market*—ability to generate positive market expectations.

Information for Analysis

We explained how decision makers need to analyze financial statements. Some of these people, such as managers and a few regulatory agencies, are able to receive special financial reports prepared to meet their needs. But most must rely on general-purpose financial statements that companies publish periodically. **General-purpose financial statements** include the (1) income statement, (2) balance sheet, (3) statement of changes in equity, and (4) statement of cash flows, accompanied by notes related to all four statements.

General-purpose financial statements are part of **financial reporting**. Financial reporting refers to the communication of relevant financial information to decision makers. It not only includes financial statements, but also involves information from filings with the securities commissions, news releases, minutes of shareholders' meetings, forecasts, management letters, auditors' reports, and analyses published in annual reports. Financial reporting broadly refers to useful information for decision makers to make investment, credit, and other decisions. It should help users assess the amounts, timing, and uncertainty of future cash inflows and outflows.

Standards for Comparisons

When calculating and interpreting analysis measures as part of our financial statement analysis, we need to decide whether these measures suggest good, bad, or average performance. To make these judgments, we need standards for comparison, which can include:

- *Intracompany* The company under analysis provides standards for comparisons based on prior performance and relationships between its financial items.
- *Competitor (or intercompany)* One or more direct competitors of the company under analysis can provide standards for comparison. Care must be exercised, however, in making comparisons with other firms to allow for the financial statement effects that are due to different accounting methods (i.e., different inventory costing systems or different depreciation methods).
- *Industry* Industry statistics can provide standards of comparison. Published industry statistics are available from several services such as Dun & Bradstreet, Standard & Poor's, and Moody's.
- *Guidelines (rules of thumb)* General standards of comparison can develop from past experiences.

All of these standards of comparison are useful when properly applied. Yet analysis measures taken from a selected competitor or group of competitors are often the best standards of comparison. Also, intracompany and industry measures are important parts of all analyses. Guidelines or rules of thumb should be applied with care, and then only if they seem reasonable in light of past experience and industry norms.

CHECKPOINT

1. Who are the intended users of general-purpose financial statements?
2. What statements are usually included in general-purpose financial statements published by corporations?
3. Which of the following are least useful as a basis for comparison when analyzing ratios and turnovers? (a) companies operating in a different economy; (b) past experience; (c) rule-of-thumb standards; (d) averages within a trade or industry.
4. What basis of comparison for ratios is usually best?

Do Quick Study questions: QS 17-1, QS 17-2

Tools of Analysis

There are several tools of financial statement analysis. Three of the most common tools are:

- *Horizontal analysis* Comparison of a company's financial condition and performance across time.
- *Vertical analysis* Comparison of a company's financial condition and performance to a base amount.
- *Ratio analysis* Determination of key relationships among financial statement items.

The remainder of this chapter describes these tools of analysis and how we apply them.

Horizontal Analysis

LO2 Describe and apply methods of horizontal analysis.

Horizontal analysis is a tool to evaluate the important relationships and changes between the items in financial statements *across time.*[3] **Comparative financial statements** show financial amounts in side-by-side columns on a single statement and facilitate the comparison of amounts for two or more successive periods. For instance, IFRS and ASPE standards require companies to provide prior-year comparative information for the current reporting period. You can see an example of this through examining the financial statement information for WestJet, Danier, Telus and Indigo presented in Appendix II, as each provides prior-year comparative statements reporting two consecutive years of financial performance.

This section explains how we calculate dollar changes and percentage changes in comparative statements and illustrates their application to the financial statements of Natural Play Corp. Natural Play is an online industrial playground equipment manufacturer that markets its safe, durable, nature-inspired play structures to daycares, schools and municipalities (www.naturalplay.com). Upon completion of his Industrial Design Engineering program in Zurich, Switzerland, entrepreneur Jax Wilco started the company in 2010. After moving to Canada and exploring Montreal, he noticed that the design of children's playgrounds often stood out from their environment in parks and saw the need for a product that drew on children's imaginations and creativity, while blending into their natural setting. Since its inception Natural Play has continued to grow and to fund its international growth; the company pursued its first initial public offering in 2014.

---

3 The term *horizontal analysis* arises from the left-to-right (or right-to-left) movement of our eyes as we review comparative financial statements across time.

CALCULATION OF DOLLAR CHANGES AND PERCENTAGE CHANGES

When analyzing a set of financial statements, it is helpful to investigate four key issues:

1. Large dollar changes
2. Large percentage changes
3. Unusual line items
4. Unexpected relationships

Comparing financial statements over relatively short time periods—two to three years—is often done by analyzing changes. A change analysis usually includes an analysis of absolute dollar amount changes as well as percentage changes for each financial statement line item. Both analyses provide useful information since small dollar changes can sometimes yield large percentage changes that can be of material significance. A 50% change in long-term debt can draw attention to a new debt obligation incurred by the company. A 20% increase in accounts receivable with a corresponding 5% increase in revenue can signal weakening customer credit. Other changes can be large in terms of dollar impacts, but not be significant to the company's operations as a whole. For instance, a $5,000,000 increase in revenue is only 1% of $500,000,000. A 50% change from a base figure of $100 is less important than the same percentage change from a base amount of $100,000 in the same statement. Reference to dollar amounts is necessary to retain a proper perspective and for assessing the importance of changes.

We calculate the *dollar change* for a financial statement item as:

$$\text{Dollar change} = \text{Analysis period amount} - \text{Base period amount}$$

Analysis period represents the point or period of time for the financial statements under analysis, and *base period* is the point or period of time for the financial statements used for comparison purposes. We commonly use the prior year as the base period. Budgeted amounts are also used as a base-period amount to assess actual performance with anticipated performance.

We calculate the *percentage change* by dividing the dollar change by the base period amount, and then multiplying this quantity by 100%:

$$\text{Percentage change} = \frac{\text{Analysis period amount} - \text{Base period amount}}{\text{Base period amount}} \times 100\%$$

or

$$\text{Current-year percentage change} = \frac{\text{Current period amount} - \text{Prior period amount}}{\text{Prior period amount}} \times 100\%$$

While we can always calculate a dollar change, we must be aware of a few issues to be aware of in working with percentage changes. To illustrate, let's look at four separate cases in the chart below:

Case	Base Period	Analysis Period	Change Analysis Dollar	Change Analysis Percent
A	$ (4,500)	$ 1,500	$ 6,000	—
B	2,000	(1,000)	(3,000)	—
C	—	8,000	8,000	—
D	10,000	-0-	(10,000)	(100%)

When a negative amount appears in the base period and a positive amount in the analysis period (or vice versa), we cannot calculate a meaningful percentage change—see cases A and B. Also, when there is no value in the base period, no percentage change is identifiable—see case C. Finally, when an item has a value in the base period and is zero in the next period, the decrease is 100 percent—see case D. Case C and D highlight potential missing line items or new line items in the current year and percentage change analysis is helpful in drawing our attention to the change.

We commonly round percentages and ratios to one or two decimal places, but there is no uniform practice on this matter. Here we are focusing on highlighting big picture issues, so calculations should not be so excessively detailed that important relationships are hidden in a crowd of decimal places.

COMPARATIVE BALANCE SHEET

One of the most useful comparative statements is the comparative balance sheet. It consists of amounts from two or more balance sheet dates arranged side by side. The usefulness of comparative financial statements is often improved by also showing each item's dollar change and percentage change. This type of presentation highlights large dollar and percentage changes for decision makers. Exhibit 17.1 shows the comparative balance sheet for Natural Play Corp.

Our analysis of comparative financial statements begins by focusing on items that show large dollar or percentage changes. We then try to identify the reasons for these changes and, if possible, determine whether they are favourable or unfavourable. We also follow up on items with small changes when we expected the changes to be large.

Regarding Natural Play's comparative balance sheet, its first line item, "Cash and investments (current)" in Exhibit 17.1 stands out and shows a $28.6 million increase (50.2%). To a large extent, this increase may be explained by the increase in two other items: the $21.2 million increase in common shares and the $32.5 million increase in retained earnings.

EXHIBIT 17.1

Comparative Balance Sheet

Natural Play Corporation
Balance Sheet
November 30, 2017, and November 30, 2016

(in thousands)	2017	2016	Amount of Increase or (Decrease) in 2017	Percentage of Increase or (Decrease) in 2017
Assets				
Current assets:				
Cash and investments (current)	$ 85,618	$ 57,000	$28,618	50.2
Accounts receivable				
Trade	50,586	36,327	14,259	39.3
Other	2,264	2,185	79	3.6
Inventory	13,417	7,361	6,056	82.3
Prepaid expenses	1,348	812	536	66.0
Total current assets	$153,233	$103,685	$49,548	47.8
Property, plant, and equipment (net)	38,189	28,605	9,584	33.5
Total assets	$191,422	$132,290	$59,132	44.7
Liabilities				
Current liabilities:				
Accounts payable	$ 8,487	$ 5,391	$ 3,096	57.4
Accrued liabilities	10,722	6,073	4,649	76.6
Income taxes payable	4,930	7,400	(2,470)	(33.4)
Total current liabilities	$ 24,139	$ 18,864	$ 5,275	28.0
Long-term debt	2,330	2,192	138	6.3
Total liabilities	$ 26,469	$ 21,056	$ 5,413	25.7
Equity				
Common shares	$ 89,732	$ 68,516	$21,216	31.0
Retained earnings	75,221	42,718	32,503	76.1
Total equity	$164,953	$111,234	$53,719	48.3
Total liabilities and equity	$191,422	$132,290	$59,132	44.7

Note that Natural Play's liabilities increased by $5.4 million. In light of this, the $28.6 million increase in cash and current investments might appear to be an excessive investment in highly liquid assets that usually earn a low return. However, the company's very strong and liquid financial position indicates an outstanding ability to respond to new opportunities such as the acquisition of other companies funding the set-up of distribution centres to facilitate their mandate of international expansion.

COMPARATIVE INCOME STATEMENT

A comparative income statement is prepared similarly to the comparative balance sheet. Amounts for two or more periods are placed side-by-side, with additional columns for dollar and percentage changes. Exhibit 17.2 shows Natural Play's comparative income statement.

EXHIBIT 17.2

Comparative Income Statements

Natural Play Corporation Income Statement For Years Ended November 30, 2017 and 2016				
(in thousands)	2017	2016	Amount of Increase or (Decrease) in 2017	Percentage of Increase or (Decrease) in 2017
Net sales	$164,313	$105,027	$59,286	56.4
Cost of goods sold	35,940	24,310	11,630	47.8
Gross profit	$128,373	$ 80,717	$47,656	59.0
Expenses:				
Advertising	34,390	20,579	13,811	67.1
Selling, general and administrative	30,833	18,005	12,828	71.2
Research and development	10,888	6,256	4,632	74.0
Depreciation	6,137	4,079	2,058	50.5
Loss (gain) on foreign exchange	1,546	(480)	2,026	—
Total expenses:	$ 83,794	$ 48,439	$35,355	73.0
Profit from continuing operations	$ 44,579	$ 32,278	$12,301	38.1
Interest income	2,959	2,482	477	19.2
Less: Interest expense	98	93	5	5.4
Profit from continuing operations before income taxes	$ 47,440	$ 34,667	$12,773	36.8
Income taxes	14,937	13,814	1,123	8.1
Profit	$ 32,503	$ 20,853	$11,650	55.9

All of the income statement items (except foreign exchange) reflect the company's rapid growth. Especially note the large $13.8 million or 67.1% increase in advertising. This suggests the company's focus on international brand development and represents a strong response to competition in the playground equipment industry. Although the dollar increase in interest profit was only $0.5 million, this amounted to a 19.2% increase. This is consistent with the increase in cash and current investments reported in the balance sheet.

 **DECISION INSIGHT**

Putting Financial Statement Analysis Tools to Use

Today's accounting software packages and database management systems can produce outputs with horizontal, vertical, and ratio analyses. These analyses can include a graphical depiction of financial relationships. The key is being able to use this information properly and effectively for business decision making. External investors that rely on financial statements can draw on a number of externally prepared reports by investment analysts, industry analysts, media reports, and various online financial statement analytical tools; however, again the ability to critically analyze and objectively evaluate the information is critical for investors to make wise decisions.

Trend Analysis

Trend analysis, also called *trend percent analysis* or *index number trend analysis*, is used to reveal patterns in data covering successive periods. This method of analysis is a variation on the use of percentage changes for horizontal analysis. The difference is that trend analysis does not subtract the base period amount in the numerator. To calculate trend percentages we need to:

1. Select a *base period* and assign each item for the base period statement a weight of 100%.
2. Express financial numbers from other periods as a percentage of the base period number.

$$\text{Trend percentage} = \frac{\text{Analysis period amount}}{\text{Base period amount}} \times 100\%$$

To illustrate trend analysis, we use selected financial data of Natural Play as shown in Exhibit 17.3.

EXHIBIT 17.3

Revenues and Expenses

	2017	2016	2015	2014	2013
Net sales	$164,313	$105,027	$67,515	$52,242	$29,230
Cost of goods sold	35,940	24,310	19,459	7,735	6,015
Gross profit	$128,373	$ 80,717	$48,056	$44,507	$23,215

We select 2013 as the base period and calculate the trend percent for each year and each item by dividing each year's dollar amount by its 2013 dollar amount. For instance, the revenue trend percent for 2016 is 359.3%, calculated as $105,027 ÷ $29,230 × 100%. The trend percentages for the data from Exhibit 17.3 are shown in Exhibit 17.4.

EXHIBIT 17.4

Trend Percentages of Revenues and Expenses

	2017	2016	2015	2014	2013
Net sales	562.1%	359.3%	231.0%	178.7%	100%
Cost of goods sold	597.5	404.2	323.5	128.6	100
Gross profit	553.0	347.7	207.0	191.7	100

EXHIBIT 17.5

Trend Percentage Lines for Revenues and Selected Expenses

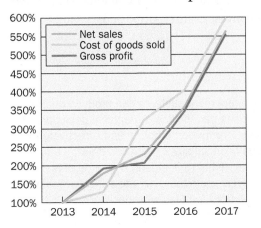

Exhibit 17.5 presents the trend percentages from Exhibit 17.4 in a *line graph*. A line graph can help us identify trends and detect changes in direction or magnitude. For example, note that the gross profit line was bending upward from 2013 to 2014 but was essentially flat from 2014 to 2015. The gross profit increased at a lower rate from 2014 to 2015 but was parallel to the net sales line from 2014 to 2017.

The line graph in Exhibit 17.5 also helps us understand the relationships between items. For example, the graph in Exhibit 17.5 shows that for 2014 through 2017, cost of goods sold increased at a rate that was somewhat more than the increase in net sales. Further, the differing trends in these two items had a clear effect on the percentage changes in gross profit. That is, gross profit increased each year at a somewhat slower rate than net sales.

Trend analysis of financial statement items also can include comparisons of relationships between items on different financial statements. For instance, Exhibit 17.6 shows a comparison of Natural Play's total assets and revenues.

EXHIBIT 17.6

Revenues and Total Assets Data

	2017	2013	Trend Percent (2017 vs 2013)
Net sales	$164.3	$29.2	562.7%
Total assets (fiscal year-end)	191.4	41.9	456.8

The rate of increase in total assets was not quite as large as the increase in revenues. Is this change favourable? We cannot say for sure. It might suggest that the company is able to use assets more efficiently than in earlier years. On the other hand, it might mean that the company may realize slower growth in future years. Monitoring this relation is important to see if Natural Play can continue to achieve high revenue growth. An important part of financial analysis is identifying questions and areas of concern such as these. Financial statement analysis often leads the analyst to ask questions, without providing one clear answer. These concerns often direct us to important factors bearing on the future of the company, highlighting both risks and potential opportunities.

CHECKPOINT

5. Analyze the following information for Lighting.com, an online direct-to-designer lighting store (expressed in millions of dollars) and identify whether the trend in accounts receivable is favourable or unfavourable when compared to the trend in net sales.

	2017	2016	2015
Net sales	$50.0	$40.0	$39.0
Accounts receivable	13.0	8.8	7.8

Do Quick Study questions: QS 17-3, QS 17-4

Vertical (or Common-Size) Analysis

LO3 Describe and apply methods of vertical analysis.

Vertical (or common-size) analysis is a tool to evaluate individual financial statement items or groups of items in terms of a specific base amount. We usually define a key aggregate figure as the base, and the base amount is commonly defined as 100%. For instance, an income statement's base is usually revenue and a balance sheet's base is a usually total asset. This section explains vertical analysis and applies it to Natural Play's statements.[4]

Common-Size Statements

The comparative statements in Exhibits 17.1 and 17.2 show how each item has changed over time, but they do not emphasize the relative importance of each item. We use **common-size financial statements** to reveal

---

4 The term *vertical analysis* arises from the up–down (or down–up) movement of our eyes as we review common-size financial statements.

changes in the relative importance of each financial statement item. A *common-size percentage* is measured by taking each individual financial statement amount under analysis and dividing it by its base amount:

$$\text{Common-size percentage} = \frac{\text{Analysis amount}}{\text{Base amount}} \times 100\%$$

COMMON-SIZE BALANCE SHEET

Common-size statements express each item as a percentage of a *base amount*. Common-size analysis enables an analyst to pay close attention to financial statement line items that are increasing or decreasing at a different pace than the growth of the company as a whole. The base amount for a common-size balance sheet is usually total assets. It is assigned a value of 100%. This also implies that the total amount of liabilities plus equity equals 100% since this amount equals total assets. Next, we calculate a common-size percent for each asset, liability, and equity item where the base amount is total assets as illustrated for Natural Play in Exhibit 17.7.

EXHIBIT 17.7

Common-Size Comparative Balance Sheet

Natural Play Corporation
Balance Sheet
November 30, 2017, and November 30, 2016

(in thousands)	2017	2016	Common-Size Percentages 2017	2016
Assets				
Current assets:				
Cash and investments (current)	$ 85,618	$ 57,000	44.7	43.1
Accounts receivable				
Trade	50,586	36,327	26.4	27.4
Other	2,264	2,185	1.2	1.7
Inventory	13,417	7,361	7.0	5.6
Prepaid expenses	1,348	812	0.7	0.6
Total current assets	$153,233	$103,685	80.0	78.4
Property, plant, and equipment (net)	38,189	28,605	20.0	21.6
Total assets	$191,422	$132,290	100.0	100.0
Liabilities				
Current liabilities:				
Accounts payable	$ 8,487	$ 5,391	4.4	4.1
Accrued liabilities	10,722	6,073	5.6	4.6
Income taxes payable	4,930	7,400	2.6	5.6
Total current liabilities	$ 24,139	$ 18,864	12.6	14.3
Long-term debt	2,330	2,192	1.2	1.6
Total liabilities	$ 26,469	$ 21,056	13.8	15.9
Equity				
Common shares, 60,000 shares issued and outstanding	$ 89,732	$ 68,516	46.9	51.8
Retained earnings	75,221	42,718	39.3	32.3
Total equity	$164,953	$111,234	86.2	84.1
Total liabilities and equity	$191,422	$132,290	100.0	100.0

COMMON-SIZE INCOME STATEMENT

Our analysis also usually benefits from an examination of a common-size income statement. The amount of net sales is the base amount and it is assigned a value of 100%. Each common-size income statement item appears as a percentage of revenues. Analyzing differences in common size percentages from one year to the next on the income statement can highlight problems with overall cost management.

Exhibit 17.8 shows the comparative income statement for 2017 and 2016.

EXHIBIT 17.8

Common-Size Comparative Income Statement

Natural Play Corporation **Income Statement** **For Years Ended November 30, 2017 and 2016**				
			Common-Size Percentages	
(in thousands)	**2017**	**2016**	**2017**	**2016**
Net sales	$164,313	$105,027	100.0	100.0
Cost of goods sold	35,940	24,310	21.9	23.1
Gross profit from sales	$128,373	$ 80,717	78.1	76.9
Expenses:				
Advertising	34,390	20,579	20.9	19.6
Selling, general, and administrative	30,833	18,005	18.8	17.1
Research and development	10,888	6,256	6.6	6.0
Depreciation	6,137	4,079	3.7	3.9
Loss (gain) on foreign exchange	1,546	(480)	0.9	(0.5)
Total expenses	$ 83,794	$ 48,439	51.0	46.1
Profit from continuing operations	44,579	32,278	27.1	30.7
Interest income	2,959	2,482	1.8	2.4
Less: Interest expense..	98	93	0.1	0.1
Profit from continuing operations				
before income taxes	$ 47,440	$ 34,667	28.8	33.0
Income taxes...	14,937	13,814	9.0	13.2
Profit	$ 32,503	$ 20,853	19.8	19.8
Earnings per share..	$ 0.63	$ 0.45		
Weighted-average shares outstanding	51,768	46,146		

One of the advantages of calculating common-size percentages for successive income statements is in helping us uncover potentially important changes in a company's expenses. For Natural Play, the relative size of each expense changed very little from 2016 to 2017. Evidence of no changes is also valuable information for our analysis.

Common-Size Graphics

An income statement readily lends itself to common-size graphical analysis. Revenues affect nearly every item in an income statement. It is also usually helpful for our analysis to know what portion of revenues various geographical regions take up. For example, Exhibit 17.9, based on assumed data for

Natural Play Corporation, uses a pie chart to highlight the contribution of revenue by geographical region.

Common-size financial statements are useful in comparing different companies because the focus is changed from dollars (which can vary significantly between companies of different sizes) to percentages (which are always expressed as X out of 100; the base is constant). Common-size statements do not reflect the relative sizes of companies under analysis but a comparison of a company's common-size statements with competitors' or industry common-size statistics alerts us to differences that should be explored and explained.

EXHIBIT 17.9

Common-Size Graphic of Natural Play's Sales by Geographic Region

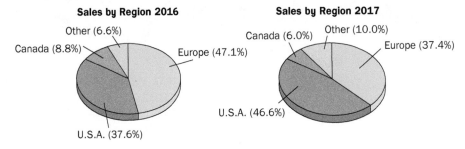

Sales by Region 2016
Other (6.6%)
Canada (8.8%)
Europe (47.1%)
U.S.A. (37.6%)

Sales by Region 2017
Canada (6.0%) Other (10.0%)
Europe (37.4%)
U.S.A. (46.6%)

 **CHECKPOINT**

6. On common-size comparative statements, which of the following is true? (a) Each item is expressed as a percentage of a base amount, (b) Total assets are assigned a value of 100%, (c) Amounts from two or more successive periods are placed side-by-side, (d) All of the above are true.
7. What is the difference between the percentages shown on a comparative income statement and those shown on a common-size comparative income statement?
8. Trend percentages are (a) shown on the comparative income statement and the comparative balance sheet; (b) shown on common-size comparative statements; or (c) also called index numbers.

Do Quick Study questions: QS 17-5, QS 17-6

MID-CHAPTER DEMONSTRATION PROBLEM

Use the financial statements of Exterior Play Inc., a playground equipment manufacturer located in Seattle, Washington to satisfy the following requirements:

1. Prepare a comparative income statement showing the percentage increases or decreases for 2017 over 2016.
2. Prepare a common-size comparative balance sheet for 2017 and 2016

Exterior Play Inc.
Income Statement
For Years Ended December 31, 2017 and 2016

	2017	2016
Net sales	$2,486,000	$2,075,000
Cost of goods sold	1,523,000	1,222,000
Gross profit from sales	$ 963,000	$ 853,000
Operating expenses:		
Advertising expense	$ 145,000	$ 100,000
Sales salaries expense	240,000	280,000
Office salaries expense	165,000	200,000
Insurance expense	100,000	45,000
Supplies expense	26,000	35,000
Depreciation expense	85,000	75,000
Miscellaneous expenses	17,000	15,000
Total operating expenses	$ 778,000	$ 750,000
Operating profit	$ 185,000	$ 103,000
Less interest expense	44,000	46,000
Profit before taxes	$ 141,000	$ 57,000
Income taxes	47,000	19,000
Profit	$ 94,000	$ 38,000
Earnings per share	$ 0.99	$ 0.40

Exterior Play Inc.
Balance Sheet
December 31, 2017

	2017	2016
Assets		
Current assets:		
Cash	$ 79,000	$ 42,000
Investments	65,000	96,000
Accounts receivable (net)	120,000	100,000
Inventory	250,000	265,000
Total current assets	$ 514,000	$ 503,000
Property, plant, and equipment:		
Land	$ 100,000	$ 100,000
Store equipment (net)	400,000	350,000
Office equipment (net)	45,000	50,000
Buildings (net)	625,000	675,000
Total property, plant, and equipment	$1,170,000	$1,175,000
Total assets	$1,684,000	$1,678,000
Liabilities		
Current liabilities:		
Accounts payable	$ 164,000	$ 190,000
Current notes payable	75,000	90,000
Taxes payable	26,000	12,000
Total current liabilities	$ 265,000	$ 292,000
Non-current liabilities:		
Notes payable (secured by mortgage on building and land)	400,000	420,000
Total liabilities	$ 665,000	$ 712,000
Equity		
Contributed capital:		
Common shares	$ 475,000	$ 475,000
Retained earnings	544,000	491,000
Total equity	$1,019,000	$ 966,000
Total liabilities and equity	$1,684,000	$1,678,000

Analysis Component:

Advertising expense increased by 45%. Would you think this is acceptable given your review of the financial statements? Explain.

Planning the Solution

- Set up a four-column income statement; enter the 2017 and 2016 amounts in the first two columns and then enter the dollar change in the third column and the percentage change from 2016 in the fourth column.

- Set up a four-column balance sheet; enter the 2017 and 2016 amounts in the first two columns and then calculate and enter the amount of each item as a percentage of total assets.

- Answer the analysis component.

Solution

1.

Exterior Play Inc.
Income Statement
For Years Ended December 31, 2017 and 2016

	2017	2016	Increase (Decrease) in 2017	
			Amount	Percent
Net sales	$2,486,000	$2,075,000	$411,000	19.8%
Cost of goods sold	1,523,000	1,222,000	301,000	24.6
Gross profit from sales	$ 963,000	$ 853,000	$110,000	12.9
Operating expenses:				
Advertising expense	$ 145,000	$ 100,000	$ 45,000	45.0
Sales salaries expense	240,000	280,000	(40,000)	(14.3)
Office salaries expense	165,000	200,000	(35,000)	(17.5)
Insurance expense	100,000	45,000	55,000	122.2
Supplies expense	26,000	35,000	(9,000)	(25.7)
Depreciation expense	85,000	75,000	10,000	13.3
Other operating expenses	17,000	15,000	2,000	13.3
Total operating expenses	$ 778,000	$ 750,000	$ 28,000	3.7
Operating profit	$ 185,000	$ 103,000	$ 82,000	79.6
Less interest expense	44,000	46,000	(2,000)	(4.3)
Profit before taxes	$ 141,000	$ 57,000	$ 84,000	147.4
Income taxes	47,000	19,000	28,000	147.4
Profit	$ 94,000	$ 38,000	$ 56,000	147.4
Earnings per share	$ 0.99	$ 0.40	$ 0.59	147.5

2.

	2017	2016	Common-Size Percentages 2017*	Common-Size Percentages 2016*
Exterior Play Inc. Balance Sheet December 31, 2017				
Assets				
Current assets:				
Cash	$ 79,000	$ 42,000	4.7%	2.5%
investments	65,000	96,000	3.9	5.7
Accounts receivable (net)	120,000	100,000	7.1	6.0
Inventory	250,000	265,000	14.8	15.8
Total current assets.................................	$ 514,000	$ 503,000	30.5	30.0
Property, plant, and equipment:				
Land..	$ 100,000	$ 100,000	5.9	6.0
Store equipment (net)...............................	400,000	350,000	23.8	20.9
Office equipment (net)	45,000	50,000	2.7	3.0
Buildings (net)...	625,000	675,000	37.1	40.2
Total property, plant, and equipment	$1,170,000	$1,175,000	69.5	70.0
Total assets	$1,684,000	$1,678,000	100.0	100.0
Liabilities				
Current liabilities:				
Accounts payable.....................................	$ 164,000	$ 190,000	9.7	11.3
Current notes payable	75,000	90,000	4.5	5.4
Taxes payable...	26,000	12,000	1.5	0.7
Total current liabilities.............................	$ 265,000	$ 292,000	15.7	17.4
Non-current liabilities:				
Notes payable (secured by mortgage on building and land)	400,000	420,000	23.8	25.0
Total liabilities	$ 665,000	$ 712,000	39.5	42.4
Equity				
Contributed capital:				
Common shares..	$ 475,000	$ 475,000	28.2	28.3
Retained earnings.....................................	544,000	491,000	32.3	29.3
Total equity	$1,019,000	$ 966,000	60.5	57.6
Total liabilities and equity........................	$1,684,000	$1,678,000	100.0	100.0

*Columns may not add due to rounding.

Analysis Component:

Assuming the advertising was effective, this appears to be reasonable given that a $45,000 increase in Precision's advertising helped to increase net sales by $411,000 ($9.13 of additional net sales per $1 of additional advertising). However, it appears that the marginal utility of each additional advertising dollar spent is decreasing given that net sales were $2,075,000 with an advertising expenditure of $100,000 ($20.75 of net sales per $1 of advertising).

Ratio Analysis

LO4 Describe and apply ratio analysis.

Ratios are among the most popular and widely used tools of financial analysis. They provide us with clues and symptoms of underlying conditions. Ratios, properly interpreted, identify areas requiring further investigation. A ratio can help us uncover conditions and trends that are difficult to detect by inspecting individual components making up the ratio. Usefulness of ratios depends on how skilfully we interpret them, and interpretation is the most challenging aspect of **ratio analysis**.

A ratio shows a mathematical relationship between two quantities. It can be expressed as a percentage, a rate, or a proportion. For instance, a change in an account balance from $100 to $250 can be expressed as (1) 250%, (2) 2.5 times, or (3) 2.5 to 1 (or 2.5:1).

This section describes an important set of financial ratios and demonstrates how to apply them. The selected ratios are organized into the four building blocks of financial statement analysis: (1) liquidity and efficiency, (2) solvency, (3) profitability, and (4) market. Many of these ratios have been explained previously at relevant points in prior chapters.

Liquidity and Efficiency

Liquidity refers to the availability of resources to meet short-term cash requirements. A company's short-term liquidity is affected by the timing of cash inflows and outflows along with its prospects for future performance. **Efficiency** refers to how well a company uses its assets. Efficiency is usually measured relative to how much revenue is generated for a certain level of assets. Inefficient use of assets can cause liquidity problems.

Both liquidity and efficiency are important and complementary in our analysis. If a company fails to meet its current obligations, its continued existence is doubtful. Viewed in this light, all other measures of analysis are of secondary importance. While accounting measurements assume indefinite existence of the company (going concern principle), our analysis must always assess the validity of this assumption using liquidity measures.

For users, a lack of liquidity often precedes lower profitability and financial hardships. It can foretell a loss of owner control or loss of investment. When the owner(s) of a proprietorship and certain partnerships possess unlimited liability, a lack of liquidity endangers their personal assets. To creditors of a company, lack of liquidity can cause delays in collecting interest and principal payments or the loss of amounts due them. A company's customers and suppliers of goods and services are affected by short-term liquidity problems. Implications include a company's inability to execute contracts and potential damage to important customer and supplier relationships, and inability to meet debt obligations can result in insolvency. This section describes and illustrates ratios relevant to assessing liquidity and efficiency.

WORKING CAPITAL AND CURRENT RATIO

The amount of current assets less current liabilities is called **working capital** or *net working capital*. A company needs an adequate amount of working capital to meet current debts, carry sufficient inventories, and take advantage of cash discounts. A company that runs low on working capital is less likely to meet current obligations or continue operating.

When evaluating a company's working capital, we must look beyond the dollar amount of current assets less current liabilities. We also need to consider the relationship between the amounts of current assets and current liabilities. The *current ratio* describes a company's ability to pay its current obligations. The current ratio relates current assets to current liabilities as follows:

$$\text{Current ratio} = \frac{\text{Current assets}}{\text{Current liabilities}}$$

Drawing on information in Exhibit 17.1, Natural Play's working capital amounts and current ratios for both 2017 and 2016 are shown in Exhibit 17.10.

EXHIBIT 17.10

Working Capital and Current Ratio

(in thousands)	Nov. 30, 2017	Nov. 30, 2016
Current assets	$ 153,233	$103,685
Current liabilities	24,139	18,864
Working capital	$129,094	$ 84,821
Current ratio:		
$153,233/$24,139	6.35 to 1	
$103,685/$18,864		5.50 to 1

A high current ratio suggests a strong liquidity position. A high ratio means a company should be able to meet its current obligations. But a company also can have a current ratio that is *too high*. An excessively high ratio means the company has invested too much in current assets compared to its current obligations. Since current assets do not normally generate much additional revenue, an excessive investment in current assets is not an efficient use of funds. For example, it could indicate a problematic buildup of inventory.

Many users apply a guideline of 2 to 1 for the current ratio in helping evaluate the debt-paying ability of a company. A company with a 2 to 1 or higher current ratio is generally thought to be a good credit risk in the short run. But this analysis is only one step in our process of assessing a company's debt-paying ability. We also need to analyze at least three additional factors:

1. Type of business
2. Composition of current assets
3. Turnover rate of current asset components

TYPE OF BUSINESS

The type of business a company operates affects our assessment of its current ratio. A service company that grants little or no credit and carries no inventories other than supplies can probably operate on a current ratio of less than 1 to 1 if its revenues generate enough cash to pay its current liabilities on time. WestJet has a relatively low current ratio for fiscal 2014 of 1.29 to 1, calculated as its current assets of $1,730,326,000 divided by its current liabilities of $1,338,301,000 (refer to WestJet's financial statements in Appendix II). A company selling high-priced clothing or furniture requires a higher ratio. This is because of difficulties in judging customer demand and other factors. For instance, if demand falls, this company's inventory may not generate as much cash as expected. A company facing these risks should maintain a current ratio of more than 2 to 1 to protect its creditors. For example, Danier Leather's current ratio at June 28, 2014, was 3.70 to 1, calculated as its current assets of $39,970,000 divided by its current liabilities of $10,790,000 (refer to Danier's financial statements in Appendix II).

The importance of the type of business to our analysis implies that an evaluation of a company's current ratio should include a comparison with ratios of other successful companies in the same industry. Sample industry average ratios for companies in a business similar to Natural Play's are shown in Exhibit 17.11. To demonstrate how ratios might be interpreted, we will compare the ratios calculated for Natural Play in the following pages against the assumed industry average ratios provided in Exhibit 17.11. In comparing the industry average current ratio of 1.6:1 to Natural Play's current ratio of 6.35:1, it appears that Natural Play is in a better position to meet its current obligations than its competitors are. However, recall the discussion earlier that an excessively high ratio means that Natural Play may have too much invested in current assets, which are generally non-productive. Another important part of our analysis is to observe how the current ratio changes over time. We must also recognize that the current ratio is affected by a company's accounting methods, especially choice of inventory method. For instance, a company using moving weighted average tends to report a smaller amount of current assets than if it uses FIFO when costs are rising. These factors should be considered before we decide whether a given current ratio is adequate.

EXHIBIT 17.11

2017 Playground Equipment Industry Average Ratios

Current ratio	1.6:1	Times interest earned	50 times
Quick ratio	1.1:1	Profit margin	14%
Accounts receivable turnover	16 times	Gross profit ratio	18%
Days' sales uncollected	21 days	Return on total assets	20%
Inventory turnover	5 times	Return on common shareholders' equity	32.7%
Days' sales in inventory	70 days	Book value per common share	$8.63
Total asset turnover	2.3 times	Book value per preferred share	$15.00
Accounts payable turnover	4 times	Earnings per share	$1.79
Debt ratio	35%	Price–earnings per share	18.2
Equity ratio	65%	Dividend yield	$0.35
Pledged assets to secured liabilities	1.4:1		

COMPOSITION OF CURRENT ASSETS

The composition of a company's current assets is important to our evaluation of short-term liquidity. For instance, cash, cash equivalents, and short-term investments are more liquid than accounts and notes receivable. Also, current receivables normally are more liquid than inventory. We know cash can be used to pay current debts immediately. But items such as accounts receivable and inventory must be converted into cash before payments can be made. An excessive amount of receivables and inventory lessens a company's ability to pay current liabilities. One way to take account of the composition of current assets is to evaluate the quick ratio. We discuss this in the next section.

 DECISION MAKER Answer—End of chapter

Banker

You are a banker, and a company calls on you for a one-year, $200,000 loan to finance an expansion. This company's current ratio is 4:1 with current assets of $160,000. Key competitors carry a current ratio of about 1.9:1. Using this information, do you approve the loan application? Does your decision change if the application is for a 10-year loan and they have yet to commence operations?

QUICK RATIO

The *quick ratio*, also called the *acid-test ratio*, is a more rigorous test of a company's ability to pay its current debts. The terminology came from the way miners test whether their findings were gold nuggets. Miners would put the nugget in acid and if it maintained its consistency it was determined to be gold. If the material corroded in acid it was another type of base metal.[5] In a similar sense, if a company passes

---

5 http://www.goldfeverprospecting.com/howtotestgold.html

the acid test ratio, the company has the stability to meet its current obligations. This ratio focuses on current asset composition. Inventory and prepaid expenses are excluded and only quick assets are included. Quick assets are cash, investments (current), accounts receivable, and notes receivable. These are the most liquid types of current assets. We calculate the quick ratio as:

$$\text{Quick ratio} = \frac{\text{Cash} + \text{Investments (current)} + \text{Net current receivables}}{\text{Current liabilities}}$$

Using the information in Exhibit 17.1, we calculate Natural Play's quick ratios as shown in Exhibit 17.12.

EXHIBIT 17.12

Quick Ratio

(in thousands)	Nov. 30, 2017	Nov. 30, 2016
Cash and investments (current)	$ 85,618	$57,000
Accounts receivable, trade	50,586	36,327
Total quick assets	$136,204	$93,327
Current liabilities	$ 24,139	$18,864
Quick ratio:		
$136,204/$24,139	5.64 to 1	
$93,327/$18,864		4.95 to 1

A common rule of thumb for an acceptable quick ratio is 1 to 1. It is important to assess what the acceptable range for the industry is. Similar to our analysis of the current ratio, we need to consider other factors. For instance, the working capital requirements of a company are affected by how frequently the company converts its current assets into cash. This implies that our analysis of the company's short-term liquidity should also include analysis of receivables and inventories. We look at these analyses next.

ACCOUNTS RECEIVABLE TURNOVER

We can measure how frequently a company converts its receivables into cash by calculating *accounts receivable turnover*. This is calculated as:

$$\text{Accounts receivable turnover} = \frac{\text{Net sales}}{\text{Average net accounts receivable}}$$

Accounts receivable turnover is more precise if credit sales are used for the numerator. Net sales (or revenues) are usually used by external users because information about credit sales is typically not reported.

While this ratio is called accounts receivable turnover, current notes receivable from customers are normally included in the denominator amount along with accounts receivable.

Average accounts receivable is estimated by averaging the beginning and the ending receivables for the period. If the beginning and ending receivables do not represent the amount normally on hand, an average of quarterly or monthly receivables may be used if available. Ending accounts receivable is sometimes substituted for the average balance in calculating accounts receivable turnover. This is acceptable if the difference between these figures is insignificant. Also, some users prefer using gross accounts receivable (before subtracting the allowance for doubtful accounts). However, this information may not be available, as some companies report only the net amount of accounts receivable.

Natural Play's 2017 accounts receivable turnover is calculated as:

$$\frac{\$164{,}313}{(\$50{,}586 + \$36{,}327)/2} = 3.78 \text{ times}^*$$

*This can be expressed in days by dividing 365 by the turnover, e.g., 365 ÷ 3.78 = 96.56 days on average to collect accounts receivable.

If accounts receivable are collected quickly, then accounts receivable turnover is high. A high turnover is favourable because it means the company does not have a large amount of resources tied up in accounts receivable. An accounts receivable turnover can be too high, as it can signal an issue with credit terms being so restrictive that they negatively affect sales volume. Natural Play's accounts receivable turnover of 3.78 times per year is unfavourable in comparison to the industry average of 16 times per year. The average playground equipment manufacturer is able to collect its receivables more than four times faster than Natural Play does.

DAYS' SALES UNCOLLECTED

We already described how accounts receivable turnover could be used to evaluate how frequently a company collects its accounts. Another measure of this activity is *days' sales uncollected* defined as:

$$\text{Days' sales uncollected} = \frac{\text{Accounts receivable}}{\text{Net sales}} \times 365$$

This formula places accounts receivable in the numerator with sales in the denominator. Any current notes receivable from customers are also normally included in the numerator.

We illustrate this ratio's application by using Natural Play's information in Exhibits 17.1 and 17.2. The days' sales uncollected figure on November 30, 2017, is:

$$\frac{\$50{,}586}{\$164{,}313} \times 365 = 112.4 \text{ days}$$

Days' sales uncollected is more meaningful if we know the company's credit terms. A rough guideline is that days' sales uncollected should not exceed one and one-third times the days in its: (a) credit period, if discounts are not offered; or (b) discount period, if discounts are offered.

Natural Play's days' sales uncollected of 112.4 days is unfavourable when compared to the industry average of 21 days. This means that Natural Play has more cash tied up in receivables than its competitors do, reflecting a less efficient use of assets.

INVENTORY TURNOVER

Working capital (current assets minus current liabilities) requirements are affected by how long a company holds inventory before selling it. One measure of this effect is the *turnover*. It provides a measure of a firm's liquidity and how quickly it can convert inventory to cash. Inventory turnover is defined as:

$$\text{Inventory turnover} = \frac{\text{Cost of goods sold}}{\text{Average inventory}}$$

Using the inventory and cost of goods sold information in Exhibits 17.1 and 17.2, we calculate Natural Play's inventory turnover for 2017 as:

$$\frac{\$35{,}940}{(\$13{,}417 + \$7{,}361)/2} = 3.46 \text{ times}^*$$

*This can be expressed in days by dividing 365 by the turnover, e.g., 365 ÷ 3.46 = 105.49 days on average to sell inventory.

Average inventory is estimated by averaging the beginning and the ending inventories for the period. If the beginning and ending inventories do not represent the amount normally on hand, an average of quarterly or monthly inventories may be used if available.

> **Important Tip:** An important tip is a high turnover ratio is typically better; however it is important to assess prior-year comparatives and competitors in the industry to ensure resources are utilized efficiently.

A company with a high turnover requires a smaller investment in inventory than one producing the same sales with a lower turnover. Inventory turnover can be too high if a company keeps such a small inventory on hand that it restricts sales volume.

Natural Play's inventory turnover of 3.46 times is unfavourable when compared to the industry average of 5 times. This comparison indicates that Natural Play sells its inventory more slowly than its competitors do.

DAYS' SALES IN INVENTORY

Days' sales in inventory is a useful measure in evaluating the liquidity of a company's inventory. Days' sales in inventory is linked to inventory in a similar manner as days' sales uncollected is linked to receivables. Days' sales in inventory is calculated as:

$$\text{Days' sales in inventory} = \frac{\text{Ending inventory}}{\text{Cost of goods sold}} \times 365$$

Applying this formula to Natural Play's 2017 financial statements, we calculate days' sales in inventory as:

$$\frac{\$13,417}{\$35,940} \times 365 = 136.3 \text{ days}$$

If the products in Natural Play's inventory are in demand by customers, this formula estimates that its inventory will be converted into receivables (or cash) in 136.3 days. If all of Natural Play's sales are credit sales, the conversion of inventory to receivables in 136.3 days plus the conversion of receivables to cash in 112.4 days suggest that inventory will be converted to cash in about 248.7 days (= 136.3 + 112.4).

Rule of thumb: a lower day's sales in inventory is better. A business selling perishables such as meat or produce, days' sales in inventory would be very low (1 or 2 days) as compared to a retailer selling slower-moving inventory such as jewellery.

Natural Play's days' sales in inventory of 136.3 days is unfavourable when compared to the industry average of 70 days. This means that Natural Play has more cash tied up in inventory than its competitors do.

TOTAL ASSET TURNOVER

Total asset turnover describes the ability of a company to use its assets to generate sales. This ratio is calculated as:

$$\text{Total asset turnover} = \frac{\text{Net sales (or revenues)}}{\text{Average total assets}}$$

In calculating Natural Play's total asset turnover for 2017, we follow the usual practice of averaging total assets at the beginning and the end of the year. Taking the information from Exhibits 17.1 and 17.2, this calculation is:

$$\frac{\$164,313}{(\$191,422 + \$132,290)/2} = 1.015 \text{ times}$$

Rule of thumb: the higher the asset turnover, the better the company is managing its cash resources. Natural Play's total asset turnover of 1.015 times is unfavourable in comparison to the industry average of 2.3 times. This means that Natural Play uses its assets less efficiently to generate sales than its competitors in the playground equipment industry do.

ACCOUNTS PAYABLE TURNOVER

The *accounts payable turnover* describes how much time it takes for a company to meet its obligations to its suppliers. In other words, it is a liquidity measure that shows how quickly management is paying trade credit. It is calculated as:

$$\text{Accounts payable turnover} = \frac{\text{Cost of goods sold}}{\text{Average accounts payable}}$$

In calculating Natural Play's accounts payable turnover for 2017, we average accounts payable by adding the beginning and the end of the year amounts and dividing by 2. Taking the information from Exhibits 17.1 and 17.2, we calculate the ratio as:

$$\frac{\$35,940}{(\$8,487 + \$5,391)/2} = 5.179 \text{ times}^*$$

*This can expressed in days by dividing 365 by the turnover, e.g., 365 ÷ 5.179 = 70.48 days on average to pay trade creditors.

Natural Play's accounts payable turnover of 5.179 times is favourable in comparison to the industry average of 4 times. It appears that Natural Play manages its payments to suppliers well. However, because average accounts payable is used in this ratio, it would be possible for a company to wait until the end of the year to pay suppliers for the purpose of manipulating this ratio in its favour. Rule of thumb: typically, a company that manages its payables well has an accounts payable turnover ratio above 6 times or below 60 days. It is important to evaluate supplier payment terms and typical early payment discounts offered in the firm's specific industry. A low accounts payable turnover may reflect an aggressive payment policy by the company; this means that payments are intentionally slowed to minimize potential borrowing and resulting interest costs.

 **CHECKPOINT**

9. The following information is from the December 31, 2017, balance sheet of Westfield Sports Corp.: cash, $820,000; accounts receivable, $240,000; inventories, $470,000; PPE assets, $910,000; accounts payable, $350,000; and income taxes payable, $180,000. Calculate the (a) current ratio, and (b) quick ratio.
10. On December 31, 2017, Westfield Sports Corp. (in Checkpoint 9) had accounts receivable of $290,000 and inventories of $530,000. During 2017, net sales amounted to $2,500,000 and cost of goods sold was $750,000. Calculate the (a) accounts receivable turnover, (b) days' sales uncollected, (c) inventory turnover, and (d) days' sales in inventory.

Do Quick Study questions: QS 17-7 to QS 17-14

Solvency

Solvency refers to a company's long-run financial viability and its ability to cover long-term obligations. All business activities of a company—financing, investing, and operating—affect a company's solvency. One of the most important components of solvency analysis is the composition of a company's **capital structure**, its sources of financing: shares and/or debt.

Analyzing solvency of a company is different from analyzing short-term liquidity. Analysis of solvency is long term and uses less precise but more encompassing measures. Analysis of capital structure is one key in evaluating solvency. Capital structure ranges from relatively permanent share capital to more risky short-term financing. Assets represent secondary sources of security for lenders ranging from loans secured by specific assets to the assets available as general security to unsecured creditors. There are different risks associated with different assets and financing sources.

This section describes tools of solvency analysis. Our analysis is concerned with a company's ability to meet its obligations and provide security to its creditors *over the long run*. Indicators of this ability include *debt* and *equity* ratios, the relation between *pledged assets* and *secured liabilities*, and the company's capacity to earn sufficient profit to pay *fixed interest charges*.

DEBT AND EQUITY RATIOS

One element of solvency analysis is to assess the portion of a company's assets contributed by its owners and the portion contributed by creditors. This relation is reflected in the debt ratio. The debt ratio expresses total liabilities as a percentage of total assets. The equity ratio provides complementary information by expressing total equity as a percentage of total assets.

$$\text{Debt ratio} = \frac{\text{Total liabilities}}{\text{Total assets}} \times 100\%$$

$$\text{Equity ratio} = \frac{\text{Total Equity}}{\text{Total assets}} \times 100\%$$

Natural Play's debt and equity ratios are calculated as:

	Nov. 30, 2017	Ratios	
Total liabilities	$ 26,469	13.8%	[Debt Ratio]
Total equity	164,953	86.2	[Equity Ratio]
Total liabilities and equity	$191,422	100.0%	

Natural Play's financial statements reflect very little debt, 13.8%, compared to the average for its competitors of 35%. The company has only one non-current liability and, at the end of 2017, its liabilities provide only 13.8% of the total assets. Rule of thumb: a company is considered less risky if its capital structure (equity and long-term debt) comprises more equity compared to debt. One source of this increased risk is the required payments under debt contracts for interest and principal amounts. Another factor is the amount of financing provided by shareholders. The greater the shareholder financing, the more losses a company can absorb through its shareholders before the remaining assets become inadequate to satisfy the claims of creditors.

From the shareholders' point of view, including debt in the capital structure of a company is desirable so long as risk is not too great. If a company earns a return on borrowed capital that is higher than the cost of borrowing, the difference represents increased profit to shareholders. Because debt can have the effect of increasing the return to shareholders, the inclusion of debt is sometimes described as *financial leverage*. We say that a firm is highly leveraged if a large portion of the company's assets is financed by debt. For example, **Air Canada**, voted best airline in North America for the fifth year in a row, exercises a high degree of financial leverage with a debt ratio of 111% (calculated as $11,781 million ÷ $10,640 million × 100%) at December 31, 2014. In contrast, The **Second Cup Ltd.** had a debt ratio of 53.24% (calculated as $28,455 thousand ÷ $53,449 thousand × 100%) at December 27, 2014.

PLEDGED ASSETS TO SECURED LIABILITIES

The ratio of pledged assets to secured liabilities is used to evaluate the risk faced by secured creditors of companies failing to meet their principle and interest payments. This ratio also is relevant to unsecured creditors. The ratio is calculated as:

$$\text{Pledged assets to secured liabilities} = \frac{\text{Book value of pledged assets}}{\text{Book value of secured liabilities}}$$

The information needed to calculate this ratio is not usually reported in published financial statements. This means that people who have the ability to obtain information directly from the company (such as bankers and certain lenders) primarily use the ratio.

A generally agreed minimum value for this ratio is about 2 to 1. But the ratio needs careful interpretation because it is based on the *book value* of pledged assets. Book values are used for simplicity purposes and are not intended to reflect amounts to be received for assets in the event of liquidation. Also, the long-term earning ability of a company with pledged assets may be more important than the value of its pledged assets. Creditors prefer that a debtor be able to pay with cash generated by operating activities rather than with cash obtained by liquidating assets.

TIMES INTEREST EARNED

The *times interest earned* ratio is used to reflect the riskiness of repayments with interest to creditors. The amount of profit before the deduction of interest charges and income taxes is the amount available to pay interest charges. We calculate this ratio as:

$$\text{Times interest earned} = \frac{\text{Income before interest and income taxes}}{\text{Interest expense}}$$

Natural Play's times interest earned ratio for 2017 is calculated as:

$$\frac{\$44,579 = \$2,959}{\$98} = 485 \text{ times}$$

The larger this ratio, the less risky is the company for lenders. A guideline for this ratio is that creditors are reasonably safe if the company earns its fixed interest charges two or more times each year.

Natural Play's times interest earned of 485 times is significantly greater than the industry average of 50 times. This means that Natural Play's lenders face little or no risk in terms of collecting the interest owed to them.

 **CHECKPOINT**

11. Which ratio best reflects the ability of a company to meet immediate interest payments? (a) Debt ratio; (b) equity ratio; (c) times interest earned; (d) pledged assets to secured liabilities.

Do Quick Study questions: QS 17-15, QS 17-16

Profitability

We are especially interested in the ability of a company to use its assets efficiently to produce profits (and positive cash flows). **Profitability** refers to a company's ability to generate an adequate return on invested capital. Return is judged by assessing earnings relative to the level and sources of financing. Profitability is also relevant to solvency.

PROFIT MARGIN

The operating efficiency and profitability of a company can be expressed in two components. The first is the company's *profit margin*. The profit margin reflects a company's ability to earn a profit from sales. Profit margin gives an indication of how sensitive profit is to changes in either prices or costs. It is measured by expressing profit as a percentage of revenues (*sales* and *revenues* are similar terms). We can use the information in Exhibit 17.2 to calculate Natural Play's 2017 profit margin as:

$$\text{Profit margin} = \frac{\text{Profit}}{\text{Net sales (or revenues)}} \times 100\% = \frac{\$32,503}{\$164,313} \times 100\% = 19.8\%$$

An improved profit margin could be due to more efficient operations resulting in lower cost of goods sold and reduced expenses. It could also be due to higher prices received for products sold. However, a strong profit margin is important, but companies should also consider the importance of investing in long-term growth opportunities. For example, a firm can reduce either advertising expenses or research and development costs as a percentage of sales, resulting in higher profit for the current year, but perhaps also resulting in reduced future sales and profits.

As a rule of thumb, the higher the profit margin the better. To evaluate the profit margin of a company, we must consider the industry in which it operates. For instance, a publishing company might be expected to have a profit margin of between 10% and 15%, while a retail supermarket might have a normal profit margin of 1% or 2%.

Natural Play's profit margin of 19.8% is favourable in comparison to the 14% industry average. This means that Natural Play earns more profit per $1 of sales than its competitors in the playground equipment industry.

The second component of operating efficiency is *total asset turnover*. We described this ratio earlier in this section. Both profit margin and total asset turnover make up the two basic components of operating efficiency. These ratios also reflect on management performance since managers are ultimately responsible for operating efficiency. The next section explains how we use both measures in analyzing return on total assets.

GROSS PROFIT RATIO

Gross profit, also called **gross margin**, is the relation between sales and cost of goods sold. A merchandising company needs sufficient gross profit to cover operating expenses or it will likely fail. To help us focus on gross profit, users often calculate a gross profit ratio. As a rule of thumb, the higher the gross profit ratio, the better a company is at managing its inventory and sales to customers. The gross profit ratio, or gross margin ratio, is defined as:

$$\text{Gross profit ratio} = \frac{\text{Gross profit from sales}}{\text{Net sales}} \times 100\%$$

The gross profit ratios of Natural Play for the years 2017 and 2016 were:

	2017	2016
Net sales	$164,313	$105,027
Cost of goods sold	35,940	24,310
Gross profit from sales	$128,373	$ 80,717
Gross profit ratio	78.13%	76.85%
Calculated as	($128,373/$164,313) × 100%	($80,717/$105,027) × 100%

This ratio represents the gross profit in each dollar of sales. For example, the calculations above show that Natural Play's gross profit ratio in 2016 was 76.85%. This means that each $1 of net sales yielded 76.85¢ in gross profit to cover all other expenses. The calculations above show that Natural Play's gross profit ratio increased from 2016 to 2017, reflecting a favourable trend. Natural Play's gross profit ratio of 78.13% for 2017 is very favourable in comparison to the industry average gross profit ratio of 18%.

RETURN ON TOTAL ASSETS

The two basic components of operating efficiency—profit margin and total asset turnover—are used to calculate a summary measure, *return on total assets*, calculated as:

$$\text{Return on total assets} = \frac{\text{Profit}}{\text{Average total assets}} \times 100\%$$

Natural Play's 2017 return on total assets is:

$$\frac{\$32,503}{(\$191,422 + \$132,290)/2} \times 100\% = 20.1\%$$

Natural Play's 20.1% return on total assets is marginally favourable compared to the industry average of 20%. But we need to evaluate the trend in the rate of return earned by the company in recent years and make comparisons with alternative investment opportunities before reaching a conclusion.

The following calculation shows the relationship between profit margin, total asset turnover, and return on total assets:

$$\text{Profit margin} \times \text{Total asset turnover} = \text{Return on total assets}$$

or

$$\left(\frac{\text{Profit}}{\text{Net sales (or revenues)}} \times 100\%\right) \times \frac{\text{Net sales (or revenues)}}{\text{Average total assets}} = \frac{\text{Profit}}{\text{Average total assets}} \times 100\%$$

Notice that both profit margin and total asset turnover contribute to overall operating efficiency, as measured by return on total assets. Rule of thumb: the higher the return on total assets, the better a company is able to manage their resources to generate profit. If we apply this formula to Natural Play we get:

$$19.8\% \times 1.015 = 20.1\%$$

RETURN ON COMMON SHAREHOLDERS' EQUITY

Perhaps the most important goal in operating a company is to earn profit for its owners. The *return on common shareholders' equity* measures the success of a company in reaching this goal. We calculate this return measure as:

$$\text{Return on common shareholders' equity} = \frac{\text{Profit} - \text{Preferred dividends}}{\text{Average common shareholders' equity}} \times 100\%$$

Recall from Exhibit 17.1 that Natural Play did not have any preferred shares outstanding. As a result we determine Natural Play's return as follows:

$$\frac{\$32,503 - \$0}{(\$164,953 + \$111,234)/2} \times 100\% = 23.5\%$$

In the numerator, the dividends on cumulative preferred shares must be subtracted whether they are declared or are in arrears. If preferred shares are non-cumulative, the dividends are subtracted only if declared. Rule of thumb: the higher the return on equity, the better the company is generating profit for the owners of the company. Natural Play's return on common shareholders' equity of 23.5% is unfavourable when compared to the industry average of 32.7%. This indicates that Natural Play's competitors are earning more profit for their owners than Natural Play is.

BOOK VALUE PER SHARE

Book value can be calculated per common share and per preferred share. Book value per common share is the recorded amount of equity applicable to common shares divided by the number of common shares outstanding.

$$\text{Book value per common share} = \frac{\text{Equity applicable to common shares}}{\text{Number of common shares outstanding}}$$

Natural Play has no preferred shares, so we calculate only book value per common share. For November 30, 2017, this ratio is calculated as:

$$\frac{\$164{,}953}{60{,}000} = \$2.75 \text{ book value per common share}$$

This ratio attempts to reflect what each share would be worth if Natural Play were to be liquidated at amounts reported on the balance sheet at November 30, 2017. The book value can be used as the starting point in share valuation methods or for merger negotiations. It is important to note that book values are used as a rough estimate. Actual asset values can deviate substantially from reported book values in the event of a liquidation.

To calculate book value when both common and preferred shares are outstanding, we must first allocate total equity between these two kinds of shares. The book value per preferred share is calculated first, and its calculation is:

$$\text{Book value per preferred share} = \frac{\text{Equity applicable to preferred shares*}}{\text{Number of preferred shares outstanding}}$$

*Stated another way, the numerator could be described as: Call price of preferred shares plus dividends in arrears or, if there is no call price, then: Paid-in capital from preferred shares plus dividends in arrears.

The equity applicable to preferred shares equals the preferred shares' call price (or average paid-in amount if the preferred shares are not callable) plus any cumulative dividends in arrears. The remaining equity is the portion applicable to common shares.

EARNINGS PER SHARE

Earnings per share was introduced in Chapter 13. Natural Play's earnings per share figure was given in Exhibit 17.8. It was calculated as:

$$\text{Earnings per share} = \frac{\text{Profit} - \text{Preferred dividends}}{\text{Weighted-average common shares outstanding}}$$

$$\frac{\$32{,}503 - \$0}{51{,}768} = \$0.63 \text{ per share}$$

Natural Play's earnings per share value of $0.63 is unfavourable in comparison to the industry average of $1.79. This shows that Natural Play has realized less earning power per share than its competitors.

Market

Market measures are useful when analyzing corporations having publicly traded shares. These market measures use share price in their calculation. Share price reflects what the market (public) expectations are for the company. This includes both the return and risk characteristics of a company as currently perceived by the market.

PRICE–EARNINGS RATIO

The *price–earnings ratio* is the most widely quoted measure of company performance. It measures how investors judge the company's future performance and is calculated as:

$$\text{Price--earnings ratio} = \frac{\text{Market price per share}}{\text{Earnings per share}}$$

Predicted earnings per share for the next period is often used in the denominator of this calculation. Reported earnings per share for the most recent period is also commonly used. In both cases, the ratio is an indicator of the future growth of and risk related to a company's earnings as perceived by investors who establish the market price of the shares.

The market price of Natural Play's common shares during 2017 ranged from a low of $14.50 to a high of $23.25. Natural Play's management reported that it did not expect 2018 revenue growth rates to be as high as those for 2017. Management also indicated that operating expenses as a percentage of revenues might increase. Nevertheless, the price–earnings ratios in 2017 are much higher than many companies'. Using Natural Play's $0.63 earnings per share that was reported at the end of 2017, we calculate its price–earnings ratios using both the low and high share prices:

$$\text{Low: } \frac{\$14.50}{\$0.63} = 23.0 \qquad \text{High: } \frac{\$23.25}{\$0.63} = 36.9$$

Natural Play's ratios, which are higher than the industry average of 18.2, reflect the expectation of investors that the company will continue to grow at a faster rate than its competitors.

DIVIDEND YIELD

We use *dividend yield* as a means of comparing the dividend-paying performance of different investment alternatives. Dividend yield is calculated as:

$$\text{Dividend yield} = \frac{\text{Annual dividends per share}}{\text{Market price per share}} \times 100\%$$

A low dividend yield is neither bad nor good by itself. Some companies decide not to declare dividends because they prefer to reinvest the cash. Natural Play, for instance, does not pay cash dividends on its common shares, but its competitors pay $0.35 per common share on average.

 **CHECKPOINT**

12. Which ratio measures the success of a company in earning profit for its owners? (a) Profit margin; (b) Return on common shareholders' equity; (c) Price–earnings ratio; (d) Dividend yield.

13. If a company has net sales of $8,500,000, profit of $945,000, and total asset turnover of 1.8 times, what is its return on total assets?

Do Quick Study questions: QS 17-17 to QS 17-24

Summary of Ratios

This chapter has presented a variety of ratios that measure liquidity and efficiency, solvency, profitability, and market performance. One purpose of ratio analysis is to provide a standard against which actual performance can be compared. Standards of comparison were discussed earlier in the chapter and may include:

- *Ratios of other firms in the same industry.* Air Canada's profit margin, for example, can be compared to WestJet's.
- *Past performance.* Danier Leather, for example, can compare the current year's profit in relation to sales with that of its past years.
- *Budgeted performance.* BCE can compare various ratios based on actual performance with expected ratios that were budgeted.
- *Subjective standards.* General standards of comparison can develop from past experience. Examples are a 2 to 1 level for the current ratio or 1 to 1 for the quick ratio. These guidelines, or rules of thumb, must be carefully applied since context is often crucial.

However, all of the foregoing comparison measures involve elements of that challenge direct comparability. For example, firms in the same industry may use different accounting methods or one company may be much older than another, making it difficult to compare the costs of assets. Another limitation is that management may engage in year-end transactions that temporarily improve certain ratios. This is an unethical activity called *window dressing*.

A ratio that is significantly higher or lower than standard merely indicates that something may be wrong and should be investigated, but ratios do not provide definitive answers. Ratio analysis is based on current or past performance, but a user may be more interested in future performance. Any conclusions are therefore tentative and must be interpreted in the light of future expectations. Ratio analysis is, however, the beginning of a process of financial analysis and can help describe the financial condition of a company and help a user piece together a story about the relative strength and future potential financial health.

Exhibit 17.13 provides a summary that matches ratios with who generally uses them based on the primary interests of the users.

EXHIBIT 17.13

Matching Ratios to User Needs

User	Primary Interest	Key Ratios Emphasized
Short-term creditor	Assess ability of firm to meet cash commitments in the near term	Liquidity and efficiency ratios
Long-term creditor	Assess both short-term and long-term ability to meet cash commitments of interest payments and debt repayment schedules	Solvency ratios
Investor	Assess the firm's ability to make profits, pay dividends, and realize share price increases	Profitability ratios and market ratios

Exhibit 17.14 presents a summary of the major financial statement analysis ratios illustrated in this chapter and throughout the book. This summary includes each ratio's title, formula, and common use.

EXHIBIT 17.14

Financial Statement Analysis Ratios

Ratio	Formula	Measure of:
Liquidity and Efficiency		
Current ratio	$= \dfrac{\text{Current assets}}{\text{Current liabilities}}$	Current debt-paying ability
Quick ratio	$= \dfrac{\text{Cash + Investments (Current) + Net current receivables}}{\text{Current liabilities}}$	Immediate current debt-paying ability
Accounts receivable turnover*	$= \dfrac{\text{Net sales}}{\text{Average net accounts receivable}}$	Liquidity and efficiency of collection
Days' sales uncollected	$= \dfrac{\text{Accounts receivable}}{\text{Net sales}} \times 365$	Liquidity of receivables
Inventory turnover*	$= \dfrac{\text{Cost of goods sold}}{\text{Average inventory}}$	Liquidity and efficiency of inventory
Days' sales in inventory	$= \dfrac{\text{Ending inventory}}{\text{Cost of goods sold}} \times 365$	Liquidity of inventory
Total asset turnover	$= \dfrac{\text{Net sales (or revenues)}}{\text{Average total assets}}$	Efficiency of assets in producing sales
Accounts payable turnover*	$= \dfrac{\text{Cost of goods sold}}{\text{Average accounts payable}}$	Efficiency in paying trade creditors
Solvency		
Debt ratio	$= \dfrac{\text{Total liabilities}}{\text{Total assets}} \times 100\%$	Creditor financing and leverage
Equity ratio	$= \dfrac{\text{Total equity}}{\text{Total assets}} \times 100\%$	Owner financing
Pledged assets to secured liabilities	$= \dfrac{\text{Book value of pledged assets}}{\text{Book value of secured liabilities}}$	Protection to secured creditors
Times interest earned	$= \dfrac{\text{Income before interest and taxes}}{\text{Interest expense}}$	Protection in meeting interest payments
Profitability		
Profit margin	$= \dfrac{\text{Profit}}{\text{Net sales (or revenues)}} \times 100\%$	Profit in each sales dollar
Gross profit ratio	$= \dfrac{\text{Gross profit from sales}}{\text{Net sales}} \times 100\%$	Gross profit in each sales dollar
Return on total assets	$= \dfrac{\text{Profit}}{\text{Average total assets}} \times 100\%$	Overall profitability of assets
Return on common shareholders' equity	$= \dfrac{\text{Profit} - \text{Preferred dividends}}{\text{Average common shareholders' equity}} \times 100\%$	Profitability of owner's investment
Book value per common share	$= \dfrac{\text{Equity applicable to common shares}}{\text{Number of common shares outstanding}}$	Liquidation at reported amounts
Book value per preferred share	$= \dfrac{\text{Equity applicable to preferred shares}}{\text{Number of preferred shares outstanding}}$	Liquidation at reported amounts
Earnings per share	$= \dfrac{\text{Profit} - \text{Preferred dividends}}{\text{Weighted-average common shares outstanding}}$	Profit on each common share
Market		
Price–earnings ratio	$= \dfrac{\text{Market price per share}}{\text{Earnings per share}}$	Market value based on earnings
Dividend yield	$= \dfrac{\text{Annual dividends per share}}{\text{Market price per share}} \times 100\%$	Cash return to each share

*These ratios can also be expressed in terms of days by dividing them into 365. For example, 365 ÷ Accounts receivable turnover = How many days on average it takes to collect receivables.

CRITICAL THINKING CHALLENGE

Refer to the Critical Thinking Challenge questions at the beginning of the chapter. Compare your answers to those suggested on Connect.

IFRS AND ASPE—THE DIFFERENCES

Difference	International Financial Reporting Standards (IFRS)	Accounting Standards for Private Enterprises (ASPE)
Earnings per share	• It is required that this ratio be reported on the income statement or statement of comprehensive income.	• This ratio is not required to be reported.

For further study on some topics of relevance to this chapter, please see the following Extend Your Knowledge supplements:

EYK 17-1 Financial Statement Analysis Ratios

Summary

LO1 Describe financial statement analysis and identify its focus, standards of comparison, and tools. The purpose of financial statement analysis is to help users make better business decisions using the tools of horizontal, vertical, and ratio analysis to evaluate (1) past and current performance, (2) current financial position, and (3) future performance and risk. The four building blocks of analysis are (1) liquidity and efficiency—ability to meet current obligations and generate revenues efficiently; (2) solvency—ability to generate future revenues and meet long-term obligations; (3) profitability—ability to provide financial rewards sufficient to attract and retain financing; and (4) market—ability to generate positive market expectations. To make conclusions from analysis we need standards for comparisons including (1) intracompany; (2) competitor; (3) industry; and (4) guidelines (rules of thumb).

LO2 Describe and apply methods of horizontal analysis. Horizontal analysis is a tool to evaluate changes in financial statement data across time. Two important tools of horizontal analysis are comparative statements and trend analysis. Comparative statements show amounts for two or more successive periods, often with changes disclosed in both absolute and percentage terms. Trend analysis is used to reveal important changes occurring from one period to the next.

LO3 Describe and apply methods of vertical analysis. In common-size statements, each item is expressed as a percentage of a base amount. The base amount for the balance sheet is usually total assets, and the base amount for the income statement is usually net sales. Vertical analysis is a tool to evaluate each financial statement item or group of items in terms of a specific base amount. This base amount is commonly defined as 100%. Two important tools of vertical analysis are common-size statements and graphical analyses.

LO4 Describe and apply ratio analysis. Ratio analysis provides clues and symptoms of underlying conditions. Ratios, properly interpreted, identify areas requiring further investigation. A ratio expresses a mathematical relation between two quantities; examples are a percentage, a rate, or a proportion. Selected ratios are organized into the building blocks of analysis: (1) liquidity and efficiency, (2) solvency, (3) profitability, and (4) market.

Guidance Answer to DECISION MAKER

Banker

Your decision on the loan application is positive for at least two reasons. First, the current ratio suggests a strong ability to meet current obligations. Second, current assets of $160,000 and a current ratio of 4:1 imply current liabilities of $40,000 (one quarter of current assets) and a working capital excess of $120,000. This working capital excess is 60% of the loan amount. However, if the application is for a 10-year loan, our decision is less optimistic. While the current ratio and working capital suggest a good safety margin, there are indications of inefficiency in operations. In particular, a 4:1 current ratio is more than double its competitors' ratio. This is characteristic of inefficient asset use.

Guidance Answers to CHECKPOINT

1. General-purpose financial statements are intended for the large variety of users who are interested in receiving financial information about a business but who do not have the ability to require the company to prepare specialized financial reports designed to meet their specific interests.

2. General-purpose financial statements include the income statement, balance sheet, statement of changes in equity, and statement of cash flows, plus notes related to the statements.

3. *a*

4. Data from one or more direct competitors of the company under analysis are usually preferred for developing standards for comparison.

5. Accounts receivable are increasing at a faster rate than sales, which is an unfavourable trend.

	2017	%	2016	%	2015	%
Sales.........	$50.0	128.2	$40.0	102.6	$39.0	100
Accounts receivable ..	13.0	166.7	8.8	112.8	7.8	100

6. *d*

7. Percentages on a comparative income statement show the increase or decrease in each item from one period to the next. On a common-size comparative income statement, each item is shown as a percentage of net sales for a specific period.

8. *c*

9. **a.**

$$\frac{(\$820,000 + \$240,000 + \$470,000)}{(\$350,000 + \$180,000)} = 2.9 \text{ to } 1$$

b. $\dfrac{(\$820,000 + \$240,000)}{(\$350,000 + \$180,000)} = 2 \text{ to } 1$

10. **a.** $2,500,000/[(\$290,000 + \$240,000)/2]$ = 9.43 times

   b. ($240,000/$2,500,000) × 365 = 35 days

   c. $750,000/[(\$530,000 + \$470,000)/2]$ = 1.5 times

   d. ($470,000/$750,000) × 365 = 228.7 days

11. *c*

12. *b*

13.

Profit margin	×	Total asset turnover	=	Return on total assets

   [($945,000/$8,500,000) × 100%] × 1.8 = 20%

DEMONSTRATION PROBLEM

Use the financial statements of Exterior Play Inc., a playground equipment manufacturer previously analyzed in the mid-chapter demonstration problem, to calculate and identify the appropriate building block of financial statement analysis for the following ratios as of December 31, 2017:

a. Current ratio

b. Quick ratio

c. Accounts receivable turnover

d. Days' sales uncollected

e. Inventory turnover

f. Debt ratio

g. Pledged assets to secured liabilities

h. Times interest earned

i. Profit margin

j. Total asset turnover

k. Return on total assets

l. Return on common shareholders' equity

Analysis Component:

Indicate whether each of the ratios calculated above for Exterior Play Inc. compares favourably (F) or unfavourably (U) to the industry average ratios in Exhibit 17.11.

Exterior Play Inc. Comparative Income Statement For Years Ended December 31, 2017 and 2016	2017	2016
Net sales.............................	$2,486,000	$2,075,000
Cost of goods sold...............	1,523,000	1,222,000
Gross profit from sales.........	$ 963,000	$ 853,000
Operating expenses:		
Advertising expense...........	$ 145,000	$ 100,000
Sales salaries expense	240,000	280,000
Office salaries expense......	165,000	200,000
Insurance expense.............	100,000	45,000
Supplies expense	26,000	35,000
Depreciation expense.........	85,000	75,000
Miscellaneous expenses	17,000	15,000
Total operating expenses....	$ 778,000	$ 750,000
Operating income.................	$ 185,000	$ 103,000
Less interest expense........	44,000	46,000
Profit before taxes...............	$ 141,000	$ 57,000
Income taxes.......................	47,000	19,000
Profit...................................	$ 94,000	$ 38,000
Earnings per share	$ 0.99	$ 0.40

Exterior Play Inc. Comparative Balance Sheet December 31	2017	2016
Assets		
Current assets:		
Cash.................................	$ 79,000	$ 42,000
Investments	65,000	96,000
Accounts receivable (net)....	120,000	100,000
Inventory..........................	250,000	265,000
Total current assets	$ 514,000	$ 503,000
Property, plant, and equipment:		
Land	$ 100,000	$ 100,000
Store equipment (net)	400,000	350,000
Office equipment (net)	45,000	50,000
Buildings (net)	625,000	675,000
Total property, plant, and equipment........................	$1,170,000	$1,175,000
Total assets.........................	$1,684,000	$1,678,000
Liabilities		
Current liabilities:		
Accounts payable	$ 164,000	$ 190,000
Current notes payable........	75,000	90,000
Taxes payable	26,000	12,000
Total current liabilities........	$ 265,000	$ 292,000
Non-current liabilities:		
Notes payable (secured by mortgage on building and land)..........................	400,000	420,000
Total liabilities......................	$ 665,000	$ 712,000
Equity		
Contributed capital:		
Common shares	$ 475,000	$ 475,000
Retained earnings	544,000	491,000
Total equity..........................	$1,019,000	$ 966,000
Total liabilities and equity	$ 1,684,000	$ 1,678,000

Planning the Solution

- Calculate the given ratios using the provided numbers; be sure to calculate the average amounts where appropriate.
- Answer the analysis component.

Solution

Ratios for 2017:

a. Current ratio: $514,000/$265,000 = 1.9 to 1 (Liquidity and Efficiency)

b. Quick ratio: ($79,000 + $65,000 + $120,000)/$265,000 = 1.0 to 1 (Liquidity and Efficiency)

c. Average receivables: ($120,000 + $100,000)/2 = $110,000

   Accounts receivable turnover: $2,486,000/$110,000 = 22.6 times (Liquidity and Efficiency)

d. Days' sales uncollected: ($120,000/$2,486,000) × 365 = 17.6 days (Liquidity and Efficiency)

e. Average inventory: ($250,000 + $265,000)/2 = $257,500

   Inventory turnover: $1,523,000/$257,500 = 5.9 times (Liquidity and Efficiency)

f. Debt ratio: $665,000/$1,684,000 × 100% = 39.5% (Solvency)

g. Pledged assets to secured liabilities: ($625,000 + $100,000)/$400,000 = 1.8 to 1 (Solvency)

h. Times interest earned: $185,000/$44,000 = 4.2 times (Solvency)

i. Profit margin: $94,000/$2,486,000 × 100% = 3.8% (Profitability)

j. Average total assets: ($1,684,000 + $1,678,000)/2 = $1,681,000

   Total asset turnover: $2,486,000/$1,681,000 = 1.48 times (Liquidity and Efficiency)

k. Return on total assets: $94,000/$1,681,000 × 100% = 5.6%, or 3.8% × 1.48 = 5.6% (Profitability)

l. Average total equity: ($1,019,000 + $966,000)/2 = $992,500

   Return on common shareholders' equity: $94,000/$992,500 × 100% = 9.5% (Profitability)

Analysis Component:

	Exterior Play Inc.	Industry Average	F/U
Current ratio	1.9:1	1.6:1	F
Quick ratio	1.0:1	1.1:1	U
Accounts receivable turnover	22.6 times	16 times	F
Days' sales uncollected	17.6 days	21 days	F
Inventory turnover	5.9 times	5 times	F
Debt ratio	39.5%	35%	U
Pledged assets to secured liabilities	1.8:1	1.4:1	F
Times interest earned	4.2 times	50 times	U
Profit margin	3.8%	14%	U
Total asset turnover	1.48 times	2.3 times	U
Return on total assets	5.6%	20%	U
Return on common shareholders' equity	9.5%	32.7%	U

Glossary

Capital structure A company's source of financing: shares and/or debt.

Common-size analysis See *vertical analysis*.

Common-size financial statements Statements in which each amount is expressed as a percentage of a base amount. In the balance sheet, the amount of total assets is usually selected as the base amount and is expressed as 100%. In the income statement, revenue is usually selected as the base amount.

Comparative financial statements Financial statements with data for two or more successive accounting periods placed in side-by-side columns, often with changes shown in dollar amounts and percentages.

Efficiency A company's productivity in using its assets; usually measured relative to how much revenue is generated for a certain level of assets.

Financial reporting The process of communicating information that is relevant to investors, creditors, and others in making investment, credit, and other decisions.

Financial statement analysis The application of analytical tools to general-purpose financial statements and related data for making business decisions.

General-purpose financial statements Statements published periodically for use by a wide variety of interested parties; include the income statement, balance sheet, statement of changes in equity, statement of cash flows, and notes related to the statements.

Gross margin See *gross profit*.

Gross profit The relation between sales and cost of goods sold.

Horizontal analysis A tool to evaluate changes in financial statement data across time.

Liquidity The availability of resources to meet up coming cash requirements.

Profitability A company's ability to generate an adequate return on invested capital.

Ratio analysis Determination of key relationships among financial statement items.

Solvency A company's long-run financial viability and its ability to cover long-term obligations.

Vertical analysis The analysis of each financial statement item or group of items in terms of a specific base amount; the base amount is commonly defined as 100% and is usually revenue on the income statement and total assets on the balance sheet. Also called *common-size analysis*.

Working capital Current assets minus current liabilities. Also known as *net working capital*.

Concept Review Questions

1. Explain the difference between financial reporting and financial statements.

2. What is the difference between comparative financial statements and common-size comparative statements?

3. Which items are usually assigned a value of 100% on a common-size comparative balance sheet and a common-size comparative income statement?

4. Why is working capital given special attention in the process of analyzing balance sheets?

5. What are three factors that would influence your decision as to whether a company's current ratio is good or bad?

6. Suggest several reasons that a 2 to 1 current ratio may not be adequate for a particular company.

7. Which assets are included in calculating the quick ratio?

8. Which two short-term liquidity ratios measure how frequently a company collects its accounts?

9. Which two terms are used to describe the difference between current assets and current liabilities?

10. Which two ratios are the basic components in measuring a company's operating efficiency? Which ratio summarizes these two components?

11. What does a relatively high accounts receivable turnover indicate about a company's short-term liquidity?

12. What is the significance of the inventory of days' sales uncollected?

13. What information does the inventory turnover provide about a company's short-term liquidity?

14. Why is the capital structure of a company, as measured by debt and equity ratios, of importance to financial statement analysts?

15. Why must the ratio of pledged assets to secured liabilities be interpreted with caution?

16. Why would a company's return on total assets be different from its return on common shareholders' equity?

17. What ratios would you calculate for the purpose of evaluating management performance?

18. Refer to the financial statements in Appendix II for WestJet and calculate the percentage change in total revenues from 2013 to 2014.

19. Refer to the financial statements in Appendix II for WestJet and calculate the percentage change in marketing, general, and administrative expenses from 2013 to 2014.

20. Refer to the financial statements in Appendix II for Danier Leather and calculate the percentage change in revenue from June 29, 2013, to June 28, 2014.

21. Refer to the financial statements in Appendix II for Danier Leather and calculate the percentage change in non-current liabilities from June 29, 2013, to June 28, 2014.

22. In the chapter opening vignette, it was mentioned that Lululemon Athletica had above-industry margins. Why should investors be concerned with gross margins? What information do gross margins provide versus looking at operating margins alone?

Quick Study

QS 17-1 Financial reporting LO1

Which of the following items are means of accomplishing the objective of financial reporting but are not included within general-purpose financial statements? (a) Income statements, (b) company news releases, (c) balance sheets, (d) certain reports filed with the Canada Revenue Agency, (e) statements of cash flows, (f) management discussions and analyses of financial performance.

QS 17-2 Comparing ratios LO1

What are four possible bases of comparison you can use when analyzing financial statement ratios? Which of these is generally considered to be the most useful? Which one is least likely to provide a good basis for comparison?

QS 17-3 Reporting percentage changes LO2

Where possible, calculate percentage of increase and decrease for the following accounts of Craft Brewery Ltd.:

	2017	2016
Current non-strategic investments	$203,000	$154,000
Accounts receivable	30,888	35,200
Notes payable	25,000	-0-

QS 17-4 Calculating trend percentages LO2

Calculate trend percentages for the following items using 2013 as the base year. Then, state whether the situation shown by the trends appears to be *favourable* or *unfavourable*.

	2017	2016	2015	2014	2013
Sales	$377,600	$362,400	$338,240	$314,080	$302,000
Cost of goods sold	172,720	164,560	155,040	142,800	136,000
Accounts receivable	25,400	24,400	23,200	21,600	20,000

QS 17-5 Common-size income statement LO3

Express the following income statement information in common-size percentages and assess whether the situation is *favourable* or *unfavourable*.

Waterford Corporation Income Statement For Years Ended December 31, 2017 and 2016		
	2017	2016
Sales	$1,056,000	$735,000
Cost of goods sold	633,600	382,200
Gross profit from sales	$ 422,400	$352,800
Operating expenses	237,600	148,470
Profit	$ 184,800	$204,330

QS 17-6 Common-size balance sheet LO3

Carmon Cupcake Inc.'s December 31 balance sheets included the following data:

	2017	2016	2015
Cash..	$ 51,800	$ 70,310	$ 73,600
Accounts receivable, net	186,800	125,940	98,400
Inventory..	223,000	165,000	106,000
Prepaid expenses	19,400	18,750	8,000
Plant and equipment, net	555,000	510,000	459,000
Total assets	$1,036,000	$890,000	$745,000
Accounts payable	$ 257,800	$150,500	$ 98,500
Long-term notes payable secured by mortgages on plant assets	195,000	205,000	165,000
Common shares (32,500 shares issued)..........	325,000	325,000	325,000
Retained earnings..	258,200	209,500	156,500
Total liabilities and equity................................	$1,036,000	$890,000	$745,000

Required Express the balance sheets in common-size percentages. Round calculations to two decimal places.

QS 17-7 Working capital and current ratio LO4

Accounts payable...................................	$10,000	Non-current portion notes payable	$20,000
Accounts receivable................................	15,000	Office supplies	3,800
Buildings	42,000	Prepaid insurance	2,500
Cash	4,000	Unearned revenue...	1,000
Current portion of notes payable...........	7,000	Wages payable	3,000

Using the information above, calculate the:

   a. Working capital

   b. Current ratio

Round calculations to two decimal places.

   c. What is the difference between working capital and the current ratio?

   d. Assuming this company's current ratio was 1.12:1 in the last accounting period, does the result of the calculation in part (b) above represent a favourable or unfavourable change?

QS 17-8 Quick ratio LO4

   a. Using the information in QS 17-7, calculate the quick ratio.

   b. At the end of the last accounting period, this company's quick ratio was 0.82:1. Has the change in the quick ratio been favourable or unfavourable?

QS 17-9 Accounts receivable turnover LO4

The following data are taken from the comparative balance sheets of Duncan Data Storage Company. Calculate the accounts receivable turnover for 2017 and 2016 (round to two decimal places). Is the change favourable or unfavourable? Explain why. Compare Duncan's turnover to the industry average turnover for 2017 of 4.2.

	2017	2016	2015
Net sales	$754,200	$810,600	$876,000
Accounts receivable	152,900	133,700	121,000

CHAPTER 17 Analyzing Financial Statements

QS 17-10 Days' sales uncollected LO4

Calculate and interpret the days' sales uncollected for 2017 and 2016 based on the following selected information for Lumbar Cushions Company (round to two decimal places):

	2017	2016
Accounts receivable	$ 220,000	$ 160,000
Net sales	2,380,000	1,450,000

QS 17-11 Inventory turnover LO4

Livingston Lumber Company begins the year with $200,000 of goods in inventory. At year-end, the amount in inventory has increased to $230,000. Cost of goods sold for the year is $1,600,000. Calculate Livingston's inventory turnover (round calculations to two decimal places). Assuming an industry average inventory turnover of 4, what is your assessment of Livingston's inventory management?

QS 17-12 Days' sales in inventory LO4

	Company A	Company B	Company C
Ending inventory	$ 20,000	$ 75,000	$ 140,000
Cost of goods sold	345,000	540,000	2,100,000

a. Calculate the days' sales in inventory for each company (round to two decimal places).

b. Which company will take the longest to sell its current balance in inventory?

QS 17-13 Calculating total asset turnover LO4

Outdoor Play Inc. reported the following facts in its 2017 annual report: net sales of $9,683 million for 2016 and $9,050 million for 2017; total end-of-year assets of $10,690 million for 2016 and $13,435 million for 2017. Calculate the total asset turnover for 2017 and identify whether it compares favourably or unfavourably with the industry average in Exhibit 17.11.

QS 17-14 Accounts payable turnover LO4

Family Co manufactures books. It buys significant quantities of supplies from various vendors in order to make its quality products. Calculate Family's accounts payable turnover for 2017 and 2016 and determine whether it is meeting its objective of paying trade creditors within 25 days (round calculations to two decimal places).

	2017	2016	2015
Cost of goods sold	$10,800,000	$9,350,000	$8,100,000
Accounts payable	890,000	654,500	565,000

QS 17-15 Solvency ratios LO4

The following information relates to three companies that operate similar businesses:

	Company A	Company B	Company C
Cash	$ 30,000	$ 65,000	$ 5,000
Accounts receivable, net	250,000	654,500	565,000
Inventory	760,000	590,000	190,000
Plant and equipment, net	640,000	1,850,000	985,000
Accounts payable	335,000	970,000	180,000
Notes payable secured by mortgages on plant and equipment	590,000	1,500,000	215,000
Common shares	700,000	500,000	450,000
Retained earnings	55,000	189,500	900,000

For each company, calculate the debt ratio, equity ratio, and pledged assets to secured liabilities. Identify which company has the *least favourable* performance in each ratio and why.

QS 17-16 **Times interest earned** LO4

The following information is available for Swing High Inc.:

Swing High Inc. Income Statement For Year Ended November 30, 2017		
Sales		$500
Cost of goods sold		190
Gross profit		$310
Operating expenses:		
Depreciation expense	$ 20	
Other expenses	200	
Total operating expenses		220
Profit from operations		$ 90
Interest expense		5
Income tax expense		10
Profit		$ 75

Required Calculate the times interest earned ratio for 2017 and compare it to the industry average in Exhibit 17.11. Explain why it compares favourably or unfavourably.

Use the following information to answer QS 17-17 to QS 17-22.

Flip to It Corp. Comparative Balance Sheet Information November 30 (millions of $)		
	2017	**2016**
Cash	$ 25	$ 5
Accounts receivable (net)	46	20
Inventory	80	95
Prepaid rent	30	15
Plant and equipment (net)	300	320
Accounts payable	40	22
Accrued liabilities	35	50
Income tax payable	7	2
Preferred shares[1]	50	50
Common shares[2]	100	100
Retained earnings[3]	249	231

Flip to It Corp. Income Statement For Year Ended November 30, 2017 (millions of $)		
Net sales		$500
Cost of goods sold		190
Gross profit		$310
Operating expenses:		
Depreciation expense	$ 20	
Other expenses	200	
Total operating expenses		220
Profit from operations		$ 90
Income tax expense		10
Profit		$ 80

[1] There were 1 million $5, non-cumulative, preferred shares issued and outstanding; no new shares were issued during 2016 or 2017.
[2] There were 25 million common shares issued and outstanding; no new shares were issued during 2016 or 2017.
[3] There are no dividends in arrears. Dividends totalling $62 million were declared and paid during 2017.

QS 17-17 **Profit margin** LO4

Calculate the profit margin for 2017 and evaluate the result against the industry average in Exhibit 17.11, explaining why it compares favourably or unfavourably (round to two decimal places).

QS 17-18 Gross profit ratio LO4

Calculate the gross profit ratio for 2017 and evaluate the result against the industry average in Exhibit 17.11, explaining why it compares favourably or unfavourably (round to two decimal places).

QS 17-19 Return on total assets LO4

Calculate the return on total assets for 2017 and evaluate the result against the industry average in Exhibit 17.11, explaining why it compares favourably or unfavourably (round to two decimal places).

QS 17-20 Return on common shareholders' equity LO4

Calculate the return on common shareholders' equity for 2017 and evaluate the result against the industry average in Exhibit 17.11, explaining why it compares favourably or unfavourably (round to two decimal places).

QS 17-21 Book value per common share LO4

Calculate the book value per common share for 2017 and evaluate the result against the industry average in Exhibit 17.11, explaining why it compares favourably or unfavourably (round to two decimal places).

QS 17-22 Earnings per share LO4

Calculate the earnings per share for 2017 and evaluate the result against the industry average in Exhibit 17.11, explaining why it compares favourably or unfavourably (round to two decimal places).

QS 17-23 Price–earnings ratio LO4

ABC Inc.'s common shares have a market value of $60 per share and its EPS is $3.50. XYZ Inc.'s common shares have a market value of $85 per share and its EPS is $4.10. You have done thorough research and are considering purchasing the shares of one of these companies.

Required
    a. Calculate the price–earnings ratio for each company (round to two decimal places).
    b. Which company's shares will you purchase based on your calculations in (a) above?

QS 17-24 Dividend yield LO4

Quick Video Inc. declared and paid an $8 per share cash dividend on its common shares during the current accounting period. The current market value of the Quick Video Inc. shares is $56 per share.

Required
    a. Calculate the dividend yield (express as a percentage rounded to two decimal places).
    b. Would the Quick Video Inc. shares be classified as growth or income shares?

Exercises

Exercise 17-1 Determining profit effects from common-size and trend percentages LO2,3

Common-size and trend percentages for a company's net sales, cost of goods sold, and expenses follow:

	Common-Size Percentages			Trend Percentages		
	2017	2016	2015	2017	2016	2015
Net sales	100.0%	100.0%	100.0%	106.5%	105.3%	100.0%
Cost of goods sold	64.5	63.0	60.2	114.1	110.2	100.0
Expenses	16.4	15.9	16.2	107.8	103.4	100.0

Required Determine whether the company's profit increased, decreased, or remained unchanged during this three-year period.

Exercise 17-2 **Current ratio—calculation and analysis** LO4

The following companies are competing in the same industry where the industry norm for the current ratio is 1.6.

	Current Assets	Current Liabilities	Current Ratio	Comparison to Industry Norm (F or U)
Company 1	$ 78,000	$31,000	_____	_____
Company 2	114,000	75,000	_____	_____
Company 3	60,000	99,000	_____	_____

Required

    a. Complete the schedule (round to two decimal places).

    b. Identify the company with the strongest liquidity position.

    c. Identify the company with the weakest liquidity position.

Analysis Component: You are more closely analyzing the financial condition of Company 2 to assess its ability to meet upcoming loan payments. You calculate its current ratio. You also find that a major account receivable in the amount of $69,000 is due from one client who has not made any payments in the past 12 months. Removing this receivable from current assets changes the current ratio. What do you conclude?

Exercise 17-3 **Quick ratio—calculation and analysis** LO4

Part of your job is to review customer requests for credit. You have three new credit applications on your desk and part of your analysis requires that the current ratios and quick ratios be compared.

    a. Complete the following schedule (round to two decimal places).

Account	1	2	3
Cash..	$2,520	$1,400	$ 1,540
Current non-strategic investments..................	$ 0	$ 0	$ 700
Current receivables.......................................	$2,800	$1,386	$ 280
Inventory..	$ 980	$1,400	$ 6,440
Prepaid expenses	$ 280	$ 840	$ 1,260
Land...	$4,200	$5,600	$23,800
Current liabilities	$3,080	$1,540	$ 5,110
Current ratio...	_____	_____	_____
Quick ratio	_____	_____	_____

    b. Based only on the information provided, which applications will you approve/not approve and why?

Exercise 17-4 **Accounts receivable turnover—calculation and analysis** LO4

	2017	2016	2015
Net sales	$1,440,000	$1,040,000	$960,000
Accounts receivable	352,000	86,400	65,600
Profit	392,000	408,000	417,600

You review the above information for your daycare business and it reveals decreasing profits despite increasing sales. You hire an analyst who highlights several points, including that "Accounts receivable turnover is too low. Tighter credit policies are recommended along with discontinuing service to those most delayed in payments." How do you interpret these recommendations? What actions do you take? Round calculations to two decimal places.

Exercise 17-5 **Days' sales uncollected—calculation and analysis** LO4

Western Windows constructs and installs windows for new homes. The sales staff are having a meeting and reviewing the following information to determine how to help reduce days' sales uncollected.

	2017	2016	2015
Accounts receivable	$ 534,000	$ 392,700	$ 339,000
Net sales	6,480,000	5,610,000	4,860,000

Required

a. Calculate the days' sales uncollected for 2015 to 2017 and identify whether the trend is favourable or unfavourable.

b. What can a salesperson do to improve days' sales uncollected?

Exercise 17-6 **Inventory turnover—calculation and analysis** LO4

		(millions of $)						
	Computer Inc.		Furniture Retailers		Fresh-cut Flowers Inc.		Custom Furniture Corp	
	2017	2016	2017	2016	2017	2016	2017	2016
Cost of goods sold	$1,350	$960	$2,940	$1,920	$2,160	$2,430	$2,190	$1,740
Inventory	150	120	105	60	15	9	45	120

a. Calculate the inventory turnover for 2017 for each company (round to two decimal places).

b. Can you compare these companies? Explain.

c. Review the turnover for Fresh-cut Flowers Inc. Does this result appear to be logical? Explain why or why not.

Exercise 17-7 **Days' sales in inventory—calculation and analysis** LO4

Refer to the information in Exercise 17-6 and calculate the days' sales in inventory for Furniture Retailers and Custom Furniture Corp for 2017 (round to two decimal places). Which company has the more favourable ratio? Explain why.

Exercise 17-8 **Liquidity and efficiency ratios—calculation and analysis** LO4

Airspace Technologies Inc.
Comparative Balance Sheet Information
November 30
(millions of $)

	2017	2016	2015
Cash	$ 61	$ 12	$ 24
Accounts receivable (net)	110	48	36
Inventory	192	228	188
Prepaid rent	72	36	24
Plant and equipment (net)	720	768	816
Accounts payable	96	53	43
Accrued liabilities	84	120	77
Income tax payable	17	5	12
Preferred shares	120	120	120
Common shares	240	240	240
Retained earnings	598	554	596

Airspace Technologies Inc.
Income Statement
For Year Ended November 30
(millions of $)

	2017	2016
Net sales	$1,200	$ 984
Cost of goods sold	456	384
Gross profit	$ 744	$ 600
Operating expenses:		
Depreciation expense	$ 48	$ 48
Other expenses	480	324
Total operating expenses	528	372
Profit from operations	$ 216	$ 228
Interest expense	17	7
Income tax expense	24	26
Profit	$ 175	$ 195

Required Refer to Exhibit 17.14 and calculate Airspace's liquidity and efficiency ratios for 2017 and 2016 (round answers to two decimal places).

Analysis Component: Identify whether the change in each ratio from 2016 to 2017 was favourable (F) or unfavourable (U) and why.

Exercise 17-9 **Solvency ratios—calculation and analysis** LO4

Focus Metals Inc. Comparative Balance Sheet Information November 30 (millions of $)		
	2017	2016
Cash	$ 14	$ 84
Accounts receivable (net)..................	378	224
Inventory	56	49
Plant and equipment (net).................	2,506	2,590
Accounts payable.............................	252	168
Long-term notes payable*	1,680	2,240
Common shares...............................	280	280
Retained earnings	742	259

*90% of the plant and equipment are secured by long-term notes payable.

Focus Metals Inc. Income Statement For Year Ended November 30 (millions of $)		
	2017	2016
Net sales..	$2,520	$1,722
Cost of goods sold..........................	882	672
Gross profit	$1,638	$1,050
Operating expenses:		
Depreciation expense...................	$ 84	$ 84
Other expenses	700	567
Total operating expenses..............	784	651
Profit from operations......................	$ 854	$ 399
Interest expense	100	134
Income tax expense	42	46
Profit...	$ 712	$ 219

Required Refer to Exhibit 17.14 and calculate Focus Metals' solvency ratios for 2016 and 2017 (round answers to two decimal places).

Analysis Component: Identify whether the change in each ratio from 2016 to 2017 was favourable (F) or unfavourable (U) and why.

Exercise 17-10 **Trend analysis, profitability ratios** LO2,4

Tia's Trampolines Inc. Comparative Balance Sheet Information November 30 (millions of $)			
	2017	2016	2015
Cash	$ 200	$ 588	$ 613
Accounts receivable (net)....	275	312	131
Plant and equipment (net)....	1,432	1,480	1,776
Accounts payable...............	55	131	184
Long-term notes payable	960	1,280	1,440
Preferred shares	160	160	160
Common shares.................	640	640	640
Retained earnings	92	169	96

The preferred shares are $0.50, non-cumulative

80 million preferred and 320 million common shares were issued and outstanding during each year.

Tia's Trampolines Inc. Income Statement For Years Ended November 30 (millions of $)			
	2017	2016	2015
Net sales.........................	$3,920	$6,240	$6,560
Cost of goods sold...........	2,744	4,368	4,592
Gross profit	$1,176	$1,872	$1,968
Operating expenses:			
Depreciation expense.....	$ 296	$ 296	$ 296
Other expenses	392	1,248	1,444
Total operating expenses	688	1,544	1,740
Profit from operations........	$ 488	$ 328	$ 228
Interest expense	58	77	87
Income tax expense	147	99	64
Profit..............................	$ 283	$ 152	$ 77

Required Refer to Exhibit 17.14 and calculate Tia's Trampoline Inc's profitability ratios for 2017 (round calculations to two decimal places). Also identify whether each of Tia's Trampoline Inc's profitability ratios compares favourably (F) or unfavourably (U) to the industry average by referring to Exhibit 17.11.

Analysis Component: Comment on the trend in sales, accounts receivable, cost of goods sold, and accounts payable for the three years 2017, 2016, and 2015.

Exercise 17-11 Ratio of pledged assets to secured liabilities LO4

CHECK FIGURE: Grant Inc. = 2.38

Use the following information to calculate the ratio of pledged assets to secured liabilities for both companies:

	Grant Inc.	Singh Inc.
Pledged assets	$379,000	$168,000
Total assets	385,000	343,000
Secured liabilities	159,000	160,000
Unsecured liabilities	186,000	273,000

Which company appears to have the riskier secured debt?

Exercise 17-12 Return on total assets LO4

CHECK FIGURE: 2017 = 11.0%

The following information is available from the financial statements of Landscape Enhancements Inc.:

	2017	2016	2015
Total assets, December 31	$304,000	$512,000	$1,200,000
Profit	45,000	58,000	93,000

Calculate Landscape Enhancements' return on total assets for 2016 and 2017. (Round answers to one decimal place.) Comment on whether the change in the company's efficiency in using its assets from 2016 to 2017 was favourable or unfavourable, including a comparison against the industry averages in Exhibit 17.11.

Exercise 17-13 Evaluating profitability LO4

CHECK FIGURES: 1. 2017 Total assets = $1,450,400 2a. 2017 = 12.2%

Spence Resources Inc.'s December 31 incomplete balance sheet information follows along with additional information:

	2017	2016	2015
Accounts payable	$360,920	$210,700	137,900
Accounts receivable, net	261,520	176,316	137,760
Cash	72,520	98,434	103,040
Common shares*	455,000	455,000	455,000
Long-term notes payable due 2020	273,000	287,000	231,000
Inventory	312,200	231,000	148,400
Plant assets, net	777,000	714,000	642,600
Prepaid expenses	27,160	26,520	11,200

	December 31, 2017	2016
Common shares market price	$30.00	$28.00
Annual cash dividends declared per share	0.60	0.30

*45,500 shares were issued and outstanding for all three years.

Required

1. Prepare a three-year comparative balance sheet for Spence Resources Inc.

2. To evaluate the company's profitability, calculate the ratios for each year shown in the following schedule and determine whether the change was favourable or unfavourable.

	2017	2016	Favourable or Unfavourable
a. Return on common shareholders' equity............			
b. Price–earnings...			
c. Dividend yield..			

Exercise 17-14 **Book value per common share** LO4

Western Grass Inc. Equity Section of Balance Sheet December 31, 2017	
Contributed capital:	
Preferred shares, $5 cumulative, 10,000 shares authorized, issued, and outstanding..	$ 120,000
Common shares, 100,000 shares authorized; 75,000 shares issued and outstanding..	450,000
Total contributed capital	$ 570,000
Retained earnings	534,000
Total equity..	$1,104,000

Required Using the information provided, calculate book value per common share assuming:

a. There are no dividends in arrears.

b. There are three years of dividends in arrears.

Exercise 17-15 **Book value per share** LO4

CHECK FIGURES: 3. Book value per common share = $92.00 4. Book value per common share = $90.75

Delta Tech Corporation's common shares are currently selling on a stock exchange at $85 per share, and a recent balance sheet shows the following information:

Delta Tech Corporation Equity Section of Balance Sheet April 30, 2017	
Contributed capital:	
Preferred shares, $2.50 cumulative, 1,000 shares authorized, issued and outstanding..	$ 80,000
Common shares, 4,000 shares authorized, issued, and outstanding.................	128,000
Total contributed capital	$208,000
Retained earnings	240,000
Total equity..	$448,000

Required

Preparation Component:

1. What is the market value of the corporation's common shares?

2. How much capital was contributed by the residual owners of the company?

3. If no dividends are in arrears, what are the book values per share of the preferred shares and the common shares?

4. If two years' preferred dividends are in arrears, what are the book values per share of the preferred shares and the common shares?

5. If two years' preferred dividends are in arrears and the board of directors declares dividends of $10,000, what total amount will be paid to preferred and common shareholders? What is the amount of dividends per share for the common shares?

Analysis Component: What are some factors that may contribute to the difference between the book value of common shares and their market value?

Problems

Problem 17-1A Calculation and analysis of trend percentages LO2

The condensed comparative statements of Uranium Mining Corporation follow:

Uranium Mining Corporation Income Statement ($000) For Years Ended December 31							
	2017	2016	2015	2014	2013	2012	2011
Net sales..	$957	$838	$762	$698	$652	$606	$504
Cost of goods sold.......................................	688	559	481	421	391	366	300
Gross profit from sales................................	$269	$279	$281	$277	$261	$240	$204
Operating expenses	204	160	147	108	94	92	78
Profit...	$ 65	$119	$134	$169	$167	$148	$126

Uranium Mining Corporation Balance Sheet ($000) December 31							
	2017	2016	2015	2014	2013	2012	2011
Assets							
Cash	$ 41	$ 53	$ 55	$ 56	$ 59	$ 58	$ 60
Accounts receivable, net.............................	288	302	274	210	185	175	122
Inventory...	1,043	758	662	559	502	426	312
Other current assets	28	25	14	26	23	23	12
Non-strategic investments	0	0	0	82	82	82	82
Plant and equipment, net............................	1,272	1,268	1,111	626	647	576	494
Total assets..	$2,672	$2,406	$2,116	$1,559	$1,498	$1,340	$1,082
Liabilities and Equity							
Current liabilities.......................................	$ 672	$ 563	$ 371	$ 308	$ 268	$ 254	$ 163
Non-current liabilities.................................	716	624	607	282	288	312	238
Common shares..	750	750	750	612	612	480	480
Retained earnings	534	469	388	357	330	294	201
Total liabilities and equity	$2,672	$2,406	$2,116	$1,559	$1,498	$1,340	$1,082

Required Calculate trend percentages for the items of the statements using 2011 as the base year.

Analysis Component: Analyze and comment on the situation shown in the statements.

Problem 17-2A **Calculating ratios and percentages** LO2,3,4   eXcel

The condensed statements of Independent Auto Inc. follow:

Independent Auto Inc. Income Statement ($000) For Years Ended December 31			
	2017	**2016**	**2015**
Net sales.....................	$207,200	$190,400	$165,200
Cost of goods sold.......	124,734	119,000	105,728
Gross profit from sales	$ 82,466	$ 71,400	$ 59,472
Selling expenses..........	$ 29,257	$ 26,275	$ 21,806
Administrative expenses	18,731	26,755	13,629
Total operating expenses	$ 47,988	$ 53,030	$ 35,435
Profit before taxes.......	$ 34,478	$ 18,370	$ 24,037
Income taxes	6,423	5,807	4,873
Profit.........................	$ 28,055	$ 12,563	$ 19,164

Independent Auto Inc. Balance Sheet ($000) December 31			
	2017	**2016**	**2015**
Assets			
Current assets..................	$33,936	$26,547	$35,454
Non-strategic investments...	0	350	2,604
Plant and equipment, net.............................	63,000	67,200	39,900
Total assets.....................	$96,936	$94,097	$77,958
Liabilities and Equity			
Current liabilities..............	$14,140	$13,972	$13,636
Common shares...............	56,700	56,700	42,000
Retained earnings............	26,096	23,425	22,322
Total liabilities and equity	$96,936	$94,097	$77,958

Required Rounding calculations to two decimal places:

1. Calculate each year's current ratio.

2. Express the income statement data in common-size percentages.

3. Express the balance sheet data in trend percentages with 2015 as the base year.

Analysis Component: Comment on any significant relationships revealed by the ratios and percentages.

Problem 17-3A **Analysis of working capital** LO4   eXcel

CHECK FIGURE: March 31 working capital = $360,000

Halifax Fisheries Inc. began the month of March with $750,000 of current assets, a current ratio of 2.5 to 1, and an quick ratio of 1.1 to 1. During the month, it completed the following transactions:

Mar.	6	Bought $85,000 of merchandise on account. (The company uses a perpetual inventory system.)
	11	Sold merchandise that cost $68,000 for $113,000.
	15	Collected a $29,000 account receivable.
	17	Paid a $31,000 account payable.
	19	Wrote off a $13,000 bad debt against Allowance for Doubtful Accounts.
	24	Declared a $1.25 per share cash dividend on the 40,000 outstanding common shares.
	28	Paid the dividend declared on March 24.
	29	Borrowed $85,000 by giving the bank a 30-day, 10% note.
	30	Borrowed $100,000 by signing a long-term secured note.
	31	Used the $185,000 proceeds of the notes to buy additional machinery.

Required Prepare a schedule showing Halifax Fisheries Inc.'s current ratio, quick ratio, and working capital after each of the transactions. Round calculations to two decimal places.

Problem 17-4A **Ratio analysis** LO2,4

North Exploration Inc. and Eagle Minerals Inc. are similar firms that operate within the same industry. The following information is available:

	North Exploration Inc.			Eagle Minerals Inc.		
	2017	2016	2015	2017	2016	2015
Current ratio..................	1.8	1.9	2.2	3.3	2.8	2.0
Quick ratio	1.1	1.2	1.3	2.9	2.6	1.7
Accounts receivable turnover......................	30.5	25.2	29.2	16.4	15.2	16.0
Inventory turnover..........	24.2	21.9	17.1	14.5	13.0	12.6
Working capital..............	$65,000	$53,000	$47,000	$126,000	$98,000	$73,000

Required The controller of your company has asked you to analyze the above two companies, so a decision can be made on whether you should invest in either. Prepare a paragraph on each of the below items that you can give to the controller in a memo.

    a. Compare the current ratios and quick ratios and discuss.

    b. Discuss the working capital for each and which company may have greater liquidity.

    c. Compare the receivable and inventory turnovers.

    d. How might obtaining industry standards affect the decision?

Problem 17-5A **Calculation of financial statement ratios** LO4

CHECK FIGURES: a. 2.81; b. 1.76; c. 19.7; d. 9.2; e. 34.9; f. 2.86; g. 6.6; h. 4.7; i. 2.07; j. 9.7; k. 14.5

The 2017 financial statements of Outdoor Waterworks Inc. follow:

Outdoor Waterworks Inc. Income Statement For Year Ended December 31, 2017	
Net sales...	$966,000
Cost of goods sold:	
Inventory, Dec. 31, 2016..............................	$ 75,360
Purchases	600,840
Goods available for sale	$676,200
Inventory, Dec. 31, 2017..............................	59,040
Cost of goods sold......................................	617,160
Gross profit from sales................................	$348,840
Operating expenses	273,360
Operating profit..	$ 75,480
Interest expense	11,400
Profit before taxes.......................................	$ 64,080
Income taxes	18,864
Profit...	$ 45,216

Outdoor Waterworks Inc. Balance Sheet December 31, 2017	
Assets	
Cash	$ 22,200
Current non-strategic investments	24,480
Accounts receivable, net...............................	52,080
Notes receivable	10,560
Inventory	59,040
Prepaid expenses...	5,760
Plant and equipment, net..............................	326,520
Total assets...	$500,640
Liabilities and Equity	
Accounts payable..	$ 48,840
Accrued wages payable	6,240
Income taxes payable	6,960
Long-term note payable, secured by mortgage on plant	114,000
Common shares, 160,000 shares.................	192,000
Retained earnings	132,600
Total liabilities and equity	$500,640

Assume all sales were on credit. Also assume the long-term note payable is due in 2020, with no current portion. On the December 31, 2016, balance sheet, the assets totalled $432,720, common shares were $192,000, and retained earnings were $107,640.

Required Calculate the following: (a) current ratio, (b) quick ratio, (c) days' sales uncollected, (d) inventory turnover, (e) days' sales in inventory, (f) ratio of pledged plant assets to secured liabilities, (g) times interest earned, (h) profit margin, (i) total asset turnover, (j) return on total assets, and (k) return on common shareholders' equity.

Analysis Component: Identify whether the ratios calculated above compare favourably or unfavourably to the industry averages in Exhibit 17.11.

Problem 17-6A Calculating book value LO4

CHECK FIGURES: Book value per common share
a. $37.00   c. $40.20

On December 31, 2017, University Security Inc. showed the following:

University Security Inc. Equity Section of Balance Sheet December 31, 2017	
Contributed capital:	
Preferred shares, $4, unlimited shares authorized, 14,000 shares issued and outstanding*	$ 308,000
Common shares, unlimited shares authorized, 35,000 shares issued and outstanding*	455,000
Total contributed capital	$ 763,000
Retained earnings	952,000
Total equity	$1,715,000

*All of the shares had been issued early in 2016.

Required

Part 1:

Calculate book value per common share and preferred share at December 31, 2017, assuming no dividends were declared for the years ended December 31, 2016 or 2017, and that the preferred shares are:

    a. Cumulative

    b. Non-cumulative

Part 2 (independent of Part 1):

Calculate book value per common share and preferred share at December 31, 2017, assuming total dividends of $91,000 were declared and paid in each of the years ended December 31, 2016 and 2017, and that the preferred shares are:

    c. Cumulative

    d. Non-cumulative

Problem 17-7A Calculation of financial statement ratios LO4

Alberta Playground Inc. produces, markets, distributes, and installs durable playground equipment. It is a new, growing playground distributor in Canada, and is hoping to expand to other provinces shortly. Its head office is in Edmonton, Alberta, and its 2017 and 2016 balance sheets and income statements follow.

Alberta Playground Inc. Balance Sheet ($000) Years Ended March 31		
	2017	**2016**
Assets		
Current assets		
Cash and cash equivalents	$ 77,491	$ 54,819
Receivables	460,807	367,069
Inventories........................	662,194	566,754
Prepaid expenses and other assets	50,940	29,494
Non-strategic investment.....	27,743	0
Other current assets..........	32,923	28,242
Total current assets...........	$1,312,098	$1,046,378
Portfolio investment	0	41,343
Property, Plant, & Equipment..................	1,027,150	1,038,756
Goodwill...........................	847,830	716,695
Trademarks and other intangibles....................	339,038	316,613
Other assets	138,193	93,666
Total assets	$3,664,309	$3,253,451
Liabilities		
Current liabilities		
Bank loans........................	$ 170,589	$ 61,572
Accounts payable and accrued liabilities	573,779	471,106
Income taxes payable........	198,638	149,377
Current portion of long term debt	28,199	8,639
Total current liabilities........	$ 971,205	$ 690,694
Non-Current Liabilities		
Long-term debt..................	378,480	380,790
Other liabilities.................	188,983	153,369
Total liabilities	$1,538,668	$1,224,853
Equity		
Common shares	$ 617,675	$ 584,749
Retained earnings................	1,507,966	1,443,849
Total equity	$2,125,641	$2,028,598
Total liabilities and equity	$3,664,309	$3,253,451

Alberta Playground Inc. Income Statement ($000) Years Ended March 31		
	2017	**2016**
Revenues	$6,025,470	$5,810,582
Cost of sales, selling and administrative expenses........	5,235,330	5,118,511
Depreciation and amortization expense	104,832	113,506
Operating profit........................	685,308	578,565
Interest on long-term debt.........	23,211	29,901
Other expenses.......................	14,263	5,161
Earnings before income taxes	647,834	543,503
Income taxes	196,715	160,789
Profit......................................	$ 451,119	$ 382,714

Assume the common shares represent 203,830 (thousand) shares issued and outstanding for the entire year ended March 31, 2017.

Required

1. Prepare a common-size balance sheet and income statement on a comparative basis for 2017 and 2016. Identify any significant changes from 2016 to 2017. Round calculations to two decimal places.

2. Calculate the 2017 ratios for Alberta Playground Inc. by completing the schedule below, including a comparison against the industry averages in Exhibit 17.11. Round calculations to two decimal places.

Ratio	Calculation	Favourable (F) or Unfavourable (U)
Current ratio...		
Total asset turnover		
Debt ratio...		
Equity ratio		
Times interest earned		
Profit margin		
Return on total assets		
Earnings per share..		

Analysis Component: Alberta's management monitors changes to the debt ratio closely to help maximize the company's return on total assets. Explain how a strategy for keeping a strong balance sheet by managing debt loads helps maintain the desired return on total assets.

Problem 17-8A Evaluating ratios L04

Web Structure Inc. calculated the ratios shown below for 2017 and 2016:

	2017	2016	Change F or U*	Comparison to Industry Average
Current ratio...	1.08:1	0.97:1		
Quick ratio	0.99:1	0.84:1		
Accounts receivable turnover	16	18		
Days' sales uncollected	35	31		
Inventory turnover...	6	7		
Days' sales in inventory...	49	37		
Total asset turnover	3.2	1.8		
Debt ratio..	67	47		
Times interest earned	2.2	6.3		
Profit margin	15	18		
Gross profit ratio	17	16		

*F = Favourable; U = Unfavourable

Required

1. Identify whether the change in the ratios from 2016 to 2017 is favourable (F) or unfavourable (U).

2. Assess whether the 2017 ratios are favourable or unfavourable in comparison to the industry averages shown in Exhibit 17.11.

Problem 17-9A Evaluating ratios L04

You have been given the opportunity to assist the board members of a charitable organization with their decision to invest excess funds into either Hemp Yoga Clothing Limited or Western Sport Clothing Inc., which are both clothing retailers. A number of factors have already been considered and the final decision will be based on an assessment of the ratios calculated below.

Ratio	Hemp Yoga Clothing Limited	Western Sport Clothing Inc.
Current ratio...	4.09	4.75
Inventory turnover...	5.14 times	2.57 times
Total asset turnover	1.66 times	2.09 times
Debt ratio..	20.36%	18.06%
Gross profit ratio	67.24%	54.74%

Required Prepare a paragraph comparing and evaluating each of the ratios above. For each ratio include which company is better, and what this means to both companies. You will give the comments to the board members of the charitable organization

Alternate Problems

Problem 17-1B **Calculation and analysis of trend percentages** LO2

The condensed comparative statements of Modern Health Inc. follow.

Required Calculate trend percentages for the items of the statements using 2011 as the base year.

Analysis Component: Analyze and comment on the situation shown in the statements.

Modern Health Inc. Income Statement ($000) For Years Ended December 31							
	2017	**2016**	**2015**	**2014**	**2013**	**2012**	**2011**
Net sales	$630	$658	$644	$686	$742	$728	$784
Cost of goods sold	266	276	272	291	307	297	300
Operating expenses	280	290	287	314	323	329	357
Profit before taxes	$ 84	$ 92	$ 85	$ 81	$112	$102	$127

Modern Health Inc. Balance Sheet ($000) December 31							
	2017	**2016**	**2015**	**2014**	**2013**	**2012**	**2011**
Assets							
Cash	$ 42	$ 46	$ 45	$ 50	$ 63	$ 59	$ 64
Accounts receivable, net	129	144	139	141	157	154	165
Inventory	200	209	206	219	223	237	227
Other current assets	28	30	31	34	32	36	39
Investments	112	84	56	122	122	122	126
Plant and equipment, net	507	515	521	402	409	416	423
Total assets	$1,018	$1,028	$ 998	$ 968	$1,006	$1,024	$1,044
Liabilities and Equity							
Current liabilities	$ 227	$ 237	$ 213	$ 170	$ 201	$ 240	$ 302
Non-current liabilities	182	203	224	245	266	287	308
Common shares	287	287	287	287	287	287	287
Retained earnings	322	301	274	266	252	210	147
Total liabilities and equity	$1,018	$1,028	$ 998	$ 968	$1,006	$1,024	$1,044

Problem 17-2B **Calculating ratios and percentages** LO2,3,4 e**X**cel

The condensed statements of Organic Grocery Corporation follow.

Organic Grocery Corporation Income Statement ($000) For Years Ended December 31			
	2017	**2016**	**2015**
Net sales.....................	$784,000	$659,200	$568,000
Cost of goods sold.......	436,000	346,400	270,400
Gross profit from sales	$348,000	$312,800	$297,600
Selling expenses.........	$104,800	$ 82,800	$ 87,200
Administrative expenses	78,400	83,600	76,000
Total expenses............	$183,200	$166,400	$163,200
Profit before taxes.......	$164,800	$146,400	$134,400
Income taxes	57,680	51,240	47,040
Profit..........................	$107,120	$ 95,160	$ 87,360

Organic Grocery Corporation Balance Sheet ($000) December 31			
	2017	**2016**	**2015**
Assets			
Current assets	$180,800	$100,000	$143,200
Investments...................	0	5,600	21,600
Plant and equipment, net...........................	408,000	424,000	313,600
Total assets...................	$588,800	$529,600	$478,400
Liabilities and Equity			
Current liabilities............	$ 88,000	$ 73,600	$ 61,600
Common shares.............	156,800	156,800	128,000
Retained earnings	344,000	299,200	288,800
Total liabilities and equity..................	$588,800	$529,600	$478,400

Required

1. Calculate each year's current ratio.

2. Express the income statement data in common-size percentages.

3. Express the balance sheet data in trend percentages with 2015 as the base year.

Analysis Component: Comment on any significant relationships revealed by the ratios and percentages.

Problem 17-3B **Analysis of working capital** LO4 e**X**cel

City Software Inc. began the month of March with $286,000 of current assets, a current ratio of 2.2 to 1, and an quick ratio of 0.9 to 1. During the month, it completed the following transactions:

Mar.	3	Sold for $55,000 merchandise that cost $36,000. (The company uses a perpetual inventory system.)
	5	Collected a $35,000 account receivable.
	10	Bought $56,000 of merchandise on account.
	12	Borrowed $60,000 by giving the bank a 60-day, 12% note.
	15	Borrowed $90,000 by signing a long-term secured note.
	22	Used the $150,000 proceeds of the notes to buy additional machinery.
	24	Declared a $1.75 per share cash dividend on the 40,000 shares of outstanding common shares.
	26	Wrote off a $14,000 bad debt against Allowance for Doubtful Accounts.
	28	Paid a $45,000 account payable.
	30	Paid the dividend declared on March 24.

Required Prepare a schedule showing the company's current ratio, quick ratio, and working capital after each of the transactions. Round to two decimal places.

Problem 17-4B **Ratio essay** LO2,4

Zhang Inc. and Black Inc. are similar firms that operate within the same industry. Black began operations in 2015 and Zhang in 2009. In 2017, both companies paid 7% interest to creditors. The following information is available:

	Zhang Inc.			Black Inc.		
	2017	2016	2015	2017	2016	2015
Total asset turnover	3.3	3.0	3.2	1.9	1.7	1.4
Return on total assets	9.2	9.8	9.0	6.1	5.8	5.5
Profit margin	2.6	2.7	2.5	3.0	3.2	3.1
Sales	$800,000	$740,000	$772,000	$400,000	$320,000	$200,000

Required The controller of your company has asked you to analyze the above two companies so a decision can be made on whether the company should invest in either company. Prepare a paragraph on each of the below items that you can give to the controller in a memo.

    a. Compare the profit margins of each company.

    b. Compare the trends of both companies, and comment on the effect the age of the company may have.

    c. Compare the asset turnover and discuss any conclusions that can be made about future maintenance expense.

    d. Comment on the relative success in employing financial leverage in 2017 for each company.

Problem 17-5B **Calculation of ratios and trends** LO2,4

CHECK FIGURES: 1a. 2017: 2.04 1c. 2017: 12.03 1e. 2017: 1.20 1g. 2017: 11.59 1i. 2017: 1.16

The 2017 four-year comparative financial statements of Digital Shelf Space Corp. follow:

Digital Shelf Space Corp. **Balance Sheet** **December 31**				
Assets	**2017**	**2016**	**2015**	**2014**
Cash..	$ 33,349	$ 27,718	$ 23,267	$ 20,938
Investments	56,000	72,000	56,000	40,000
Accounts receivable, net	120,207	50,086	31,304	17,200
Inventory..	10,018	6,637	4,830	3,784
Prepaid expenses	1,602	876	537	344
Plant and equipment, net	548,800	627,200	705,600	784,000
Total assets	$769,976	$784,517	$821,538	$866,266
Liabilities and Equity				
Accounts payable	$ 50,086	$ 33,182	$ 24,149	$ 18,920
Accrued wages payable...	16,028	8,765	5,366	3,440
Income taxes payable	36,662	19,370	12,823	8,706
Long-term note payable, secured by mortgage on plant assets..............	459,200	515,200	571,200	627,200
Common shares, 180,000 shares	176,000	176,000	176,000	176,000
Retained earnings...	32,000	32,000	32,000	32,000
Total liabilities and equity..	$769,976	$784,517	$821,538	$866,266

Digital Shelf Space Corp. Income Statement For Years Ended December 31				
	2017	**2016**	**2015**	**2014**
Net sales	$1,001,728	$626,080	$447,200	$344,000
Cost of goods sold	500,864	331,822	241,488	189,200
Gross profit...	$ 500,864	$294,258	$205,712	$154,800
Operating expenses..	320,553	175,302	107,328	68,800
Operating profit	$ 180,311	$118,956	$ 98,384	$ 86,000
Interest expense...	27,552	30,912	34,272	37,632
Profit before taxes	$ 152,759	$ 88,044	$ 64,112	$ 48,368
Income taxes..	36,662	19,370	12,822	8,706
Profit	$ 116,097	$ 68,674	$ 51,290	$ 39,662

Required

1. Calculate the following for 2017 and 2016 and identify whether the ratios compare favourably (F) or unfavourably (U) from 2016 to 2017: (a) quick ratio, (b) inventory turnover, (c) accounts payable turnover, (d) debt ratio, (e) ratio of pledged assets to secured liabilities, (f) times interest earned, (g) profit margin, (h) return on total assets, and (i) book value per common share.

2. Prepare a trend analysis for 2014 (the base year) through to 2017 using the income statement information.

Analysis Component: Compare and explain the trend in cost of goods sold, operating expenses, and profit to the trend in net sales. Explain why retained earnings are constant over the four years.

Problem 17-6B Calculating book value LO4

CHECK FIGURES: Book value per common share
a. $10.60   c. $11.00

On December 31, 2017, Warner Publishing Inc. showed the following:

Warner Publishing Inc. Equity Section of Balance Sheet December 31, 2017		
Contributed capital:		
Preferred shares, $0.75, unlimited shares authorized,		
62,500 shares issued and outstanding*	$500,000	
Common shares, unlimited shares authorized,		
156,250 shares issued and outstanding*	656,250	
Total contributed capital..		$1,156,250
Retained earnings...		1,093,750
Total equity		$2,250,000

*All of the shares had been issued early in 2016.

Required

Part 1:

Calculate book value per common share and preferred share at December 31, 2017, assuming no dividends were declared for the years ended December 31, 2016, or 2017, and that the preferred shares are:

    a. Cumulative

    b. Non-cumulative

Part 2 (independent of Part 1):

Assume no dividends were declared for the year ended December 31, 2016, and total dividends of $62,500 were declared and paid for the year ended December 31, 2017. Calculate book value per common share and preferred share at December 31, 2017, if preferred shares are:

    c. Cumulative

    d. Non-cumulative

Problem 17-7B Calculation of financial statement ratios LO4

Eco Play Ltd., with its head office in Vancouver, manufactures enviro-friendly, safe playground equipment for elementary schools. Its 2017 balance sheet and income statement follow.

Eco Play Ltd. Balance Sheet ($000) As at December 31		
	2017	**2016**
Assets		
Cash	$ 571	$ 2,928
Trade and other receivables	13,672	14,260
Inventories......................................	31,794	24,961
Prepaid expenses.............................	579	450
Other current assets	2,244	-0-
Property, plant, and equipment.........	46,195	39,719
Goodwill	1,084	-0-
Total assets.....................................	$96,139	$82,318
Liabilities and Equity		
Trade and other payables	$19,479	$18,061
Income taxes payable	-0-	377
Current loans..................................	11,104	2,512
Other current liabilities	1,297	639
Long-term loans	14,458	5,189
Other long-term liabilities.................	3,422	3,421
Share capital	17,724	17,724
Contributed surplus.........................	794	794
Retained earnings...........................	27,914	33,601
Accumulated other comprehensive loss	(53)	-0-
Total liabilities and equity	$96,139	$82,318

Eco Play Ltd. Income Statement ($000) For Years Ended December 31		
	2017	**2016**
Net sales....................................	$ 147,529	$ 138,185
Cost of sales	126,311	104,867
Gross Profit	21,218	33,318
Sales and marketing expenses ...	14,721	13,697
Distribution expenses................	7,352	7,882
General and admin expenses	6,410	5,315
Operating Profit (Loss)...............	7,265	6,424
Loss on disposal of property, plant, and equipment	57	-0-
Interest expense	714	142
Other revenues (expenses)	2,349	(1,779)
Profit (loss)................................	$ (5,687)	$ 4,503

Assume that the share capital is all common and that the weighted average number of shares outstanding in 2017 was 10,808,000.

Required

1. Prepare a common-size balance sheet and income statement on a comparative basis for 2016 and 2017. Identify any significant changes from 2016 to 2017. Round calculations to two decimal places.

2. Calculate the 2017 ratios for Eco Play by completing the schedule below, including a comparison against the industry averages in Exhibit 17.11. Round calculations to two decimal places.

Ratio	Calculation	Favourable (F) or Unfavourable (U)
Current ratio...		
Accounts receivable turnover		
Inventory turnover..		
Accounts payable turnover		
Debt ratio...		
Gross profit ratio		
Return on total assets		
Earnings per share...		

Analysis Component: As part of its cash flow management strategy, assume Eco Play requires a current ratio of 2:1. Calculate Eco Play's 2013 current ratio and explain the change from 2016 to 2017.

Problem 17-8B **Evaluating ratios** LO4

Silver Bullet Slide Company calculated the ratios shown below for 2017 and 2016:

	2017	2016	Change F or U*	Comparison to Industry Average
Current ratio...	1.14:1	1.23:1		
Quick ratio	1.00:1	0.99:1		
Accounts receivable turnover	11	9		
Days' sales uncollected	26	29		
Inventory turnover..	4.2	3.7		
Days' sales in inventory...	63	67		
Total asset turnover	1.8	2.0		
Debt ratio..	35	44		
Times interest earned	45	44		
Profit margin	11	9		
Gross profit ratio	14	15		

*F = Favourable; U = Unfavourable

Required

1. Identify whether the change in the ratios from 2016 to 2017 is favourable (F) or unfavourable (U).

2. Assess whether the 2017 ratios are favourable or unfavourable in comparison to the industry averages shown in Exhibit 17.11.

Problem 17-9B **Evaluating ratios** LO4

Sustainable Seafood Incorporated processes and markets frozen seafood products. Continental Pipelines Limited is in the oil and gas industry in Canada and abroad. Both companies are being considered as potential investment opportunities by the executive team of your company. In addition to research already performed, the following ratios need to be evaluated.

Ratio	Sustainable Seafood Incorporated Year Ended January 1, 2017	Continental Pipelines Limited Year Ended December 31
Profit margin	3.39%	17.87%
Total asset turnover	1.33 times	0.19 times
Accounts receivable turnover	10.62 times	7.13 times
Debt ratio..	54.42%	60.71%
Current ratio..	1.51:1	0.75:1

Required Prepare a paragraph comparing and evaluating each of the ratios above. For each ratio include which company is better and what this means. You will give the comments in a memo to the executive team of your company, who are primarily concerned about long-term profitability. Include a final paragraph discussing if it is reasonable to make the decision based on these ratios, and, if not, what other analysis or factors should be considered.

Analytical and Review Problems

A & R 17-1

Hope Bicycle Recycle Corporation Balance Sheet December 31, 2017	
Assets	
Cash...	$
Accounts receivable, net	
Inventory	
Plant and equipment, net	_____
Total assets	$ _____
Liabilities and Equity	
Current liabilities	$
12% bonds payable	
Common shares	
Retained earnings	
Total liabilities and equity.............................	$ _____

Selected Financial Information for Hope Bicycle Recycle Corporation From Fiscal 2017	
Net sales (all credit)......................................	$450,000
Liabilities to total assets	1 to 2
Income taxes...	$1,000
Profit	$36,000
Average collection period...............................	60.83 days
PPE asset turnover	3 times
Inventory turnover...	5 times
Expenses (including taxes of 40%).................	$114,000
Current ratio...	3 to 1
Total asset turnover	1.5 times
Retained earnings, Jan. 1, 2017....................	$10,000

Required Complete the balance sheet for Hope Bicycle Recycle Corporation. Round amounts to the nearest $100.

A & R 17-2

Wild Rafting Adventures Inc. began the month of May with $200,000 of current assets, a 2 to 1 current ratio, and a 1 to 1 quick (acid test) ratio. During the month, the following transactions were completed (assume a perpetual inventory system):

	Current Ratio			Quick Ratio		
	Increase	Decrease	No Change	Increase	Decrease	No Change
a. Bought $50,000 of merchandise on account.						
b. Credit sales: $70,000 of merchandise costing $40,000.........						
c. Collected an $8,500 account receivable.						
d. Paid a $30,000 account payable.....						
e. Wrote off a $2,000 bad debt against the allowance account.........						
f. Declared a $1 per share cash dividend on the 20,000 common shares outstanding........................						
g. Paid the dividend declared in (f).......						
h. Borrowed $25,000 by giving the bank a 60-day, 10% note.						
i. Borrowed $100,000 by placing a 10-year mortgage on the PPE assets....................................						
j. Used $50,000 of proceeds of the mortgage to buy additional machinery......................................						

Required

1. State the effect of each of the above transactions on the current ratio and the quick ratio. Give the effect in terms of increase, decrease, or no change. Use check marks to indicate your answers.

2. For the end of May, calculate the

   i. Current ratio   **ii.** Quick ratio   **iii.** Working capital

A & R 17-3

Both Dragon Corp. and Kent Inc. design, produce, market, and sell sports footwear. Key comparative figures (in thousands of dollars) from recent financial statements for these two organizations follow:

Key figures	Dragon	Kent
Cash and equivalents..	$ 445,421	$ 232,365
Accounts receivable	1,754,137	590,504
Inventory...	1,338,640	544,522
Retained earnings..	2,973,663	992,563
Cost of sales...	5,502,993	2,144,422
Income taxes...	499,400	84,083
Net sales	9,186,539	3,478,604
Total assets	5,361,207	1,786,184

Required

1. Calculate common-size percentages for the two companies for both years using the selected data provided.

2. Which company incurred a higher percentage of net sales as income tax expense?

3. Which company has retained a higher portion of total earnings in the company?

4. Which company has a higher gross margin on sales?

5. Which company is holding a higher percentage of total assets as inventory?

A & R 17-4 **Ratio analysis**

Rhondda McNabb always asks her advisor in-depth questions before acquiring a company's shares. Rhondda is currently considering investing in Simpson Scientific Corp. Simpson's annual report contains the following summary of ratios:

	2017	2016	2015
Net sales trend..	128.00%	117.00%	100.00%
Selling expenses to net sales.............................	9.8%	13.7%	15.3%
Quick ratio	0.8 to 1	1.1 to 1	1.2 to 1
Current ratio..	2.6 to 1	2.4 to 1	2.1 to 1
Inventory turnover...	7.5 times	8.7 times	9.9 times
Accounts receivable turnover	6.7 times	7.4 times	8.2 times
Return on equity..	9.75%	11.50%	12.25%
Profit margin	3.3%	3.5%	3.7%
Total asset turnover	2.9 times	3.0 times	3.1 times
Return on total assets	8.8%	9.4%	10.1%
Net sales to PPE assets......................................	3.8 to 1	3.5 to 1	3.3 to 1

Rhondda would like answers to the following questions about the trend of events over the three-year period covered in the annual report. Rhondda's questions are:

1. Is it becoming easier for Simpson to pay its current debts on time and to take advantage of cash discounts?

2. Is Simpson collecting its accounts receivable more rapidly?

3. Is Simpson's investment in accounts receivable decreasing?

4. Are dollar amounts invested in inventory increasing?

5. Is Simpson's investment in PPE assets increasing?

6. Is the shareholders' investment becoming more profitable?

7. Is Simpson using its assets efficiently?

8. Did the dollar amount of selling expenses decrease during the three-year period?

Ethics Challenge

EC 17-1

In your position as controller of Flashy Inc., a video production company, you are responsible for keeping the board of directors informed about the financial activities and status of the company. At the board meeting, you present the following report:

	2017	2016	2015
Net sales trend..	147.00	135.00	100.00
Selling expenses to net sales.............................	10.1%	14.0%	15.6%
Net sales to PPE assets.....................................	3.8 to 1	3.6 to 1	3.3 to 1
Current ratio...	2.9 to 1	2.7 to 1	2.4 to 1
Quick ratio	1.1 to 1	1.4 to 1	1.5 to 1
Inventory turnover...	7.8 times	9.0 times	10.2 times
Accounts receivable turnover	7.0 times	7.7 times	8.5 times
Total asset turnover	2.9 times	2.9 times	3.3 times
Return on total assets	9.1%	9.7%	10.4%
Return on equity..	9.75%	11.50%	12.25%
Profit margin	3.6%	3.8%	4.0%

After the meeting is over, you overhear the company's CEO holding a press conference with analysts in which she mentions the following ratios:

	2017	2016	2015
Net sales trend...	147.00	135.00	100.00
Selling expenses to net sales.............................	10.1%	14.0%	15.6%
Net sales to PPE assets.....................................	3.8 to 1	3.6 to 1	3.3 to 1
Current ratio...	2.9 to 1	2.7 to 1	2.4 to 1

Required

1. Why do you think the CEO decided to report 4 ratios instead of all of the 11 ratios that you prepared?

2. Comment on the possible consequences of the CEO's decision.

Focus on Financial Statements

FFS 17-1

Drinkwater Inc. reported the following information:

Drinkwater Inc. Adjusted Trial Balance March 31, (in thousands of Canadian dollars)			
	2017	**2016**	**2015**
Cash	$ 136,000	$ 98,000	$ 76,000
Accounts receivable	238,000	219,000	206,000
Allowance for doubtful accounts	2,300	2,100	2,000
Inventory	84,000	71,000	48,000
Prepaid insurance	50	30	25
Notes receivable, due in six months	600	400	150
Property, plant, and equipment assets	1,621,100	1,234,670	838,640
Accumulated depreciation	325,000	208,000	102,000
Accounts payable	219,000	174,000	145,000
Unearned sales	3,100	750	315
Notes payable, due in 2022	114,000	116,200	77,950
Preferred shares; $1 non-cumulative; 20,000 shares issued and outstanding	100,000	100,000	100,000
Common shares; 50,000 shares issued and outstanding	250,000	250,000	250,000
Retained earnings	772,050	491,550	294,300
Sales	943,000	798,000	503,000
Sales discounts	14,000	11,000	7,000
Cost of goods sold	424,000	335,000	196,000
Other operating expenses	141,000	103,000	50,000
Investment income	9,000	7,000	5,000
Interest expense	5,700	6,500	8,750
Income tax expense	73,000	69,000	49,000

Other information:

1. No shares were issued during the years ended March 31, 2017, and 2016.

2. No dividends were declared or paid during the years ended March 31, 2017, and 2016.

3. The market values per common share at March 31, 2017, and March 31, 2016, were $29 and $25 respectively.

4. Industry averages for 2017 were as provided in the chart on the following page.

Required

1. Using the information provided for Drinkwater Inc., prepare a comparative, single-step income statement and statement of changes in equity for the years ended March 31, 2017, and 2016, as well as a comparative classified balance sheet at March 31, 2017, and 2016.

2. Complete the chart below for Drinkwater Inc. (round all ratios to two decimal places):

	Calculate the Ratio for 2017:	Calculate the Ratio for 2016:	Favourable or Unfavourable Change From Previous Year	Favourable or Unfavourable Relative to Industry Average for 2017	
				Industry Average	Favourable or Unfavourable
a. Current ratio.....................................				1.96:1	
b. Quick ratio				1.42:1	
c. Accounts receivable turnover				4.35	
d. Days' sales uncollected				95.12	
e. Inventory turnover...........................				5.20	
f. Days' sales in inventory..................				75.08	
g. Total asset turnover				1.8	
h. Accounts payable turnover				8.45	
i. Debt ratio..				21%	
j. Equity ratio				79%	
k. Times interest earned				50.16	
l. Profit margin				30.14	
m. Gross profit ratio				52.16	
n. Return on total assets				17.20%	
o. Return on common shareholders' equity				31.00%	
p. Book value per common share.........				14.91	
q. Book value per preferred share........				$22.00	
r. Earnings per share........................				$4.32	
s. Price–earnings ratio				6.91	

FFS 17-2

Required

Refer to the financial statements for Danier Leather, Indigo, Telus, and WestJet in Appendix II. Calculate the following ratios for 2014 and 2013 for each company, indicating whether the change was favourable or unfavourable (round calculations to two decimal places).

1. Profit margin
2. Debt ratio
3. Current ratio
4. Can you compare these ratio results among these four companies? Explain why or why not.

Critical Thinking Mini Case

You are the new human resources manager and are reviewing the bonus policies as part of familiarizing yourself with the payroll system. The plant superintendent's bonus is calculated as the return on total assets ratio for the year times one month's salary. You have the information below and, recalling some basic accounting that you took while attending a post-secondary educational institution, you make a note to ask why double-declining balance depreciation is not being used, given the nature of the plant assets. Also, in speaking with one of the plant supervisors, you discover that the useful life of this type of machinery is typically 12 years and its residual value is $100,000.

	December 31			
	2017	2016	2015	2014
Net sales	$1,252,160	$ 782,600	$ 559,000	$ 430,000
Profit (loss) before tax...	194,844	101,469	63,146	38,714
Plant assets, net*	834,000	870,500	907,000	943,500
Total assets	1,109,969	1,066,872	1,051,754	1,046,226

*No plant assets have been purchased or sold since January 1, 2014; original cost $980,000; depreciation is calculated using straight-line; useful life 20 years; residual value $250,000.

Required

Using the elements of critical thinking described on the inside front cover, discuss the issues, define the problem, and identify the goal and assumptions and the facts. Before coming to a conclusion, you may want to prepare a schedule, calculating the adjusted profit and the adjusted total assets by adding back the straight line depreciation and then subtracting the double-declining-balance depreciation, and then calculate the adjusted return on assets.

Payroll Liabilities

The Payroll Liabilities Appendix can be accessed online through Connect.

Financial Statement Information

This appendix includes financial statement information from **Danier Leather Inc.**, **WestJet Airlines Ltd.**, **Indigo Books & Music Inc.**, and **Telus Corporation**. All of this information is taken from their annual reports. An **annual report** is a summary of the financial results of a company's operations for the year and its future plans. It is directed at external users of financial information, but also affects actions of internal users.

An annual report is also used by a company to showcase itself and its products. Many include attractive pictures, diagrams, and illustrations related to the company. But the financial section is its primary objective. This section communicates much information about a company, with most data drawn from the accounting information system.

This appendix includes the financial statements for:

- Danier Leather Inc.
- WestJet Airlines Ltd.
- Indigo Books & Music Inc.
- Telus Corporation

There are questions at the end of each chapter that refer to information in this appendix. We encourage readers to spend extra time with these questions as they are especially useful in reinforcing and showing the relevance and diversity of financial reporting.

More current financial information about these and other Canadian corporations can be found online at: www.sedar.com.

DANIER
ANNUAL REPORT 2014

CONSOLIDATED STATEMENTS OF EARNINGS (LOSS) & COMPREHENSIVE EARNINGS (LOSS)

(thousands of Canadian dollars, except per share amounts and number of shares)

	Years Ended	
	June 28, 2014	June 29, 2013
	52 weeks	*52 weeks*
Revenue	$141,930	$154,995
Cost of Sales (Note 13)	73,697	76,579
Gross profit	68,233	78,416
Selling, general and administrative expenses (Note 13)	79,086	76,620
Interest income	(118)	(236)
Interest expense	59	51
Earnings (loss) before income taxes	(10,794)	1,981
Provision for (recovery of) income taxes (Note 14)	(3,131)	570
Net earnings (loss) and comprehensive earnings	**($7,663)**	**$1,411**
Net earnings (loss) per share:		
Basic	**($2.00)**	**$0.34**
Diluted	**($2.00)**	**$0.33**
Weighted average number of shares outstanding:		
Basic	3,840,319	4,180,829
Diluted	3,948,336	4,323,619
Number of shares outstanding at period end	**3,854,168**	**3,832,168**

See accompanying notes to the consolidated financial statements

CONSOLIDATED BALANCE SHEETS

(thousands of Canadian dollars)

	June 28, 2014	June 29, 2013
Assets		
Current Assets		
Cash	$ 13,507	$ 24,541
Accounts receivable	638	1,197
Income taxes recoverable	3,461	358
Inventories (Note 5)	21,721	22,810
Prepaid expenses	643	803
	39,970	49,709
Non-current Assets		
Property and equipment (Note 6)	16,826	16,034
Computer software (Note 7)	1,459	1,143
Deferred income tax asset (Note 14)	2,374	2,163
	$ 60,629	$ 69,049
Liabilities		
Current Liabilities		
Payables and accruals (Note 9)	$ 9,185	$ 10,101
Deferred revenue	1,511	1,548
Sales return provision (Note 10)	94	99
	10,790	11,748
Non-current Liabilities		
Deferred lease inducements and rent liability	1,432	1,392
	12,222	13,140
Shareholders' Equity		
Share capital (Note 11)	11,772	11,533
Contributed surplus	1,040	954
Retained earnings	35,595	43,422
	48,407	55,909
	$ 60,629	$ 69,049

Contingencies, Guarantees and Commitments (Notes 16 and 17)

Approved by the Board of Directors
August 13, 2014

Jeffrey Wortsman

Jeffrey Wortsman, Director

Edwin F. Hawken

Edwin F. Hawken, Chairman

See accompanying notes to the consolidated financial statements

CONSOLIDATED STATEMENTS OF CASH FLOW (thousands of Canadian dollars)

	Years Ended	
	June 28, 2014	June 29, 2013
	52 weeks	*52 weeks*

Cash provided by (used in)
Operating Activities

Net earnings (loss)	($7,663)	$1,411
Adjustments for:		
Amortization of property and equipment	3,517	3,149
Amortization of computer software	791	412
Impairment loss on property and equipment	663	327
Amortization of deferred lease inducement	(75)	(100)
Straight line rent expense	115	121
Stock-based compensation	209	131
Interest income	(118)	(236)
Interest expense	59	51
Provision for (refund of) income taxes	(3,131)	570
Changes in working capital (Note 15)	883	1,348
Interest paid	(107)	(12)
Interest received	133	244
Income taxes (paid) recovered	(183)	(664)
Net cash generated from (used in) operating activities	**(4,907)**	**6,752**

Financing Activities

Subordinate voting shares issued	227	183
Subordinate voting shares repurchased (Note 11)	(275)	(11,399)
Net cash used in financing activities	**(48)**	**(11,216)**

Investing Activities

Acquisition of property and equipment	(4,972)	(4,498)
Acquisition of computer software	(1,107)	(829)
Net cash used in investing activities	**(6,079)**	**(5,327)**

Decrease in cash	**(11,034)**	**(9,791)**
Cash, beginning of period	24,541	34,332
Cash, end of period	**$13,507**	**$24,541**

See accompanying notes to the consolidated financial statements

CONSOLIDATED STATEMENTS OF CHANGES IN SHAREHOLDERS' EQUITY

(thousands of Canadian dollars)

	Share Capital	Contributed Surplus	Accumulated Other Comprehensive Income	Retained Earnings	Total
Balance - June 29, 2013	$11,533	$954	$ -	$43,422	$55,909
Net loss	-	-	-	(7,663)	(7,663)
Stock based compensation related to stock options	-	209	-	-	209
Exercise of stock options	350	(123)	-	-	227
Share repurchases (net of tax)	(111)	-	-	(164)	(275)
Balance - June 28, 2014	$11,772	$1,040	$ -	$35,595	$48,407

	Share Capital	Contributed Surplus	Accumulated Other Comprehensive Income	Retained Earnings	Total
Balance - June 30, 2012	$15,040	$925	$-	$49,526	$65,491
Net earnings	-	-	-	1,411	1,411
Stock based compensation related to stock options	-	131	-	-	131
Exercise of stock options	285	(102)	-	-	183
Share repurchases	(3,792)	-	-	(7,515)	(11,307)
Balance - June 29, 2013	$11,533	$954	$-	$43,422	$55,909

See accompanying notes to the consolidated financial statements

Executing on our strategies

WestJet Annual Report 2014

WESTJET

Consolidated Statement of Earnings
For the years ended December 31
(Stated in thousands of Canadian dollars, except per share amounts)

	Note	2014	2013
Revenue:			
Guest		3,599,157	3,337,569
Other		377,395	324,628
		3,976,552	3,662,197
Operating expenses:			
Aircraft fuel		1,090,330	1,039,448
Airport operations		507,743	460,566
Flight operations and navigational charges		458,146	408,951
Sales and distribution		376,676	356,988
Depreciation and amortization		226,740	200,840
Marketing, general and administration		224,783	222,567
Maintenance		193,685	169,197
Aircraft leasing expense		182,450	175,646
Inflight expense		171,741	176,907
Employee profit share		68,787	51,577
		3,501,081	3,262,687
Earnings from operations		475,471	399,510
Non-operating income (expense):			
Finance income		17,070	17,848
Finance cost		(51,838)	(43,447)
Gain (loss) on foreign exchange		(2,064)	1,136
Loss on disposal of property and equipment	7	(48,332)	(2,962)
		(85,164)	(27,425)
Earnings before income tax		390,307	372,085
Income tax expense (recovery):			
Current		114,521	154,964
Deferred		(8,171)	(51,601)
	11	106,350	103,363
Net earnings		283,957	268,722
Earnings per share:			
Basic		2.22	2.05
Diluted		2.20	2.03

The accompanying notes are an integral part of the consolidated financial statements.

Consolidated Statement of Financial Position
At December 31
(Stated in thousands of Canadian dollars)

	Note	2014	2013
Assets			
Current assets:			
Cash and cash equivalents	5	1,358,071	1,256,005
Restricted cash	6	58,149	58,106
Accounts receivable	18	54,950	42,164
Prepaid expenses, deposits and other	18	144,192	133,263
Inventory	18	36,658	36,722
Assets held for sale	7	78,306	–
		1,730,326	1,526,260
Non-current assets:			
Property and equipment	7	2,793,194	2,487,734
Intangible assets	8	60,623	58,691
Other assets	18	62,290	70,778
Total assets		4,646,433	4,143,463
Liabilities and shareholders' equity			
Current liabilities:			
Accounts payable and accrued liabilities	18	502,432	543,167
Advance ticket sales	18	575,781	551,022
Non-refundable guest credits	18	45,434	46,975
Current portion of maintenance provisions	9	54,811	76,105
Current portion of long-term debt	10	159,843	189,191
		1,338,301	1,406,460
Non-current liabilities:			
Maintenance provisions	9	191,768	142,411
Long-term debt	10	1,028,820	689,204
Other liabilities	18	13,150	8,834
Deferred income tax	11	296,892	306,714
Total liabilities		2,868,931	2,553,623
Shareholders' equity:			
Share capital	12	603,287	603,861
Equity reserves		75,094	69,079
Hedge reserves		(3,179)	105
Retained earnings		1,102,300	916,795
Total shareholders' equity		1,777,502	1,589,840
Commitments	16		
Total liabilities and shareholders' equity		4,646,433	4,143,463

The accompanying notes are an integral part of the consolidated financial statements.

On behalf of the Board:

Gregg Saretsky, Director   Hugh Bolton, Director

Consolidated Statement of Cash Flows
For the years ended December 31
(Stated in thousands of Canadian dollars)

	Note	2014	2013
Operating activities:			
Net earnings		283,957	268,722
Items not involving cash:			
Depreciation and amortization		226,740	200,840
Change in maintenance provisions		8,413	26,610
Change in other liabilities		(529)	1,782
Amortization of hedge settlements		1,400	1,400
Loss on disposal of property and equipment		48,332	2,962
Share-based payment expense	12	18,626	14,533
Deferred income tax recovery		(8,171)	(51,601)
Unrealized foreign exchange gain		(10,634)	(12,020)
Change in non-cash working capital		208,595	298,697
Change in restricted cash		(43)	(6,484)
Change in other assets		(6,833)	(1,374)
Cash interest received		17,243	19,079
Cash taxes paid		(204,489)	(147,868)
Purchase of shares pursuant to compensation plans		(10,989)	(7,131)
		571,618	608,147
Investing activities:			
Aircraft additions		(694,200)	(639,734)
Aircraft disposals		75,655	142
Other property and equipment and intangible additions		(46,586)	(75,580)
		(665,131)	(715,172)
Financing activities:			
Increase in long-term debt		613,885	318,075
Repayment of long-term debt		(303,573)	(178,647)
Shares repurchased	12	(39,431)	(112,362)
Dividends paid	13	(61,313)	(52,188)
Issuance of shares pursuant to compensation plans		96	106
Cash interest paid		(39,507)	(36,677)
Change in non-cash working capital		4,866	146
		175,023	(61,547)
Cash flow from operating, investing and financing activities		81,510	(168,572)
Effect of foreign exchange on cash and cash equivalents		20,556	16,378
Net change in cash and cash equivalents		102,066	(152,194)
Cash and cash equivalents, beginning of year		1,256,005	1,408,199
Cash and cash equivalents, end of year	5	1,358,071	1,256,005

The accompanying notes are an integral part of the consolidated financial statements.

Consolidated Statement of Changes in Equity
For the years ended December 31
(Stated in thousands of Canadian dollars)

	Note	2014	2013
Share capital:			
Balance, beginning of year		603,861	614,899
Issuance of shares pursuant to compensation plans		6,177	11,027
Shares repurchased		(6,751)	(22,065)
	12	603,287	603,861
Equity reserves:			
Balance, beginning of year		69,079	69,856
Share-based payment expense	12	18,626	14,533
Issuance of shares pursuant to compensation plans		(12,611)	(15,310)
		75,094	69,079
Hedge reserves:			
Balance, beginning of year		105	(5,746)
Other comprehensive income		(3,284)	5,851
		(3,179)	105
Retained earnings:			
Balance, beginning of year		916,795	793,296
Dividends declared	13	(61,313)	(52,188)
Shares repurchased	12	(32,680)	(90,297)
Purchase of shares pursuant to compensation plans		(4,459)	(2,738)
Net earnings		283,957	268,722
		1,102,300	916,795
Total shareholders' equity		**1,777,502**	**1,589,840**

The accompanying notes are an integral part of the consolidated financial statements.

Consolidated Statement of Comprehensive Income
For the years ended December 31
(Stated in thousands of Canadian dollars)

	2014	2013
Net earnings	283,957	268,722
Items to be reclassified to net earnings:		
Other comprehensive income, net of tax:		
Amortization of hedge settlements to aircraft leasing	1,400	1,400
Net unrealized loss on foreign exchange derivatives[(i)]	8,652	6,660
Reclassification of net realized gain on foreign exchange derivatives[(ii)]	(7,023)	(3,514)
Net unrealized gain (loss) on interest rate derivatives[(iii)]	(8,697)	522
Reclassification of net realized loss on interest rate derivatives[(iv)]	2,384	783
	(3,284)	5,851
Total comprehensive income	280,673	274,573

(i)   Net of income taxes of $(3,048) (2013 – $(2,347)).
(ii) Net of income taxes of $2,475 (2013 – $1,238).
(iii) Net of income taxes of $3,065 (2013 – $(183)).
(iv) Net of income taxes of $(841) (2013 – $(275)).

The accompanying notes are an integral part of the consolidated financial statements.

"We are what we repeatedly do. Excellence, then, is not an act, but a habit."

— Aristotle

!ndigo

Enrich your life™

Indigo   Chapters   Coles   indigo.ca

Consolidated Balance Sheets

(thousands of Canadian dollars)	As at March 29, 2014	As at March 30, 2013 restated (notes 4 and 22)	As at April 1, 2012 restated (notes 4 and 22)
ASSETS			
Current			
Cash and cash equivalents (note 6)	157,578	210,562	206,718
Accounts receivable	5,582	7,126	12,810
Inventories (note 7)	218,979	216,533	229,199
Prepaid expenses	5,184	4,153	3,692
Total current assets	387,323	438,374	452,419
Property, plant and equipment (note 8)	58,476	58,903	66,928
Intangible assets (note 9)	21,587	22,164	22,810
Equity investment (note 20)	598	968	961
Deferred tax assets (note 10)	44,604	48,731	48,633
Total assets	512,588	569,140	591,751
LIABILITIES AND EQUITY			
Current			
Accounts payable and accrued liabilities (note 19)	136,428	150,177	173,416
Unredeemed gift card liability (note 19)	46,827	47,169	42,711
Provisions (note 11)	928	2,168	232
Deferred revenue	12,860	13,733	11,234
Income taxes payable	–	11	65
Current portion of long-term debt (notes 12 and 18)	584	773	1,060
Total current liabilities	197,627	214,031	228,718
Long-term accrued liabilities (note 19)	2,896	4,004	5,800
Long-term provisions (note 11)	164	78	460
Long-term debt (notes 12 and 18)	227	705	1,141
Total liabilities	200,914	218,818	236,119
Equity			
Share capital (note 13)	203,812	203,805	203,373
Contributed surplus (note 14)	8,820	8,128	7,039
Retained earnings	99,042	138,389	145,220
Total equity	311,674	350,322	355,632
Total liabilities and equity	512,588	569,140	591,751

See accompanying notes

On behalf of the Board:

Heather Reisman
Director

Michael Kirby
Director

Consolidated Statements of Earnings (Loss) and Comprehensive Earnings (Loss)

(thousands of Canadian dollars, except per share data)	52-week period ended March 29, 2014	52-week period ended March 30, 2013 restated (notes 4 and 22)
Revenues	867,668	878,785
Cost of sales	(493,955)	(495,099)
Gross profit	373,713	383,686
Operating, selling and administrative expenses (notes 8, 9 and 15)	(403,693)	(383,319)
Operating profit (loss)	(29,980)	367
Interest on long-term debt and financing charges	(95)	(101)
Interest income on cash and cash equivalents	2,377	2,609
Share of earnings from equity investment (note 20)	789	1,315
Earnings (loss) before income taxes	(26,909)	4,190
Income tax recovery (expense) (note 10)		
Current	37	–
Deferred	(4,127)	98
Net earnings (loss) and comprehensive earnings (loss) for the period	(30,999)	4,288
Net earnings (loss) per common share (note 16)		
Basic	$(1.21)	$0.17
Diluted	$(1.21)	$0.17

See accompanying notes

Consolidated Statements of Changes in Equity

(thousands of Canadian dollars)	Share Capital	Contributed Surplus	Retained Earnings	Total Equity
Balance, March 31, 2012	203,373	7,039	145,220	355,632
Earnings for the 52-week period ended March 30, 2013	–	–	4,288	4,288
Exercise of options (notes 13 and 14)	417	(85)	–	332
Directors' deferred share units converted (note 13)	15	(15)	–	–
Stock-based compensation (note 14)	–	743	–	743
Directors' compensation (note 14)	–	446	–	446
Dividends paid (note 13)	–	–	(11,119)	(11,119)
Balance, March 30, 2013	203,805	8,128	138,389	350,322
Balance, March 30, 2013	203,805	8,128	138,389	350,322
Loss for the 52-week period ended March 29, 2014	–	–	(30,999)	(30,999)
Exercise of options (notes 13 and 14)	7	–	–	7
Directors' deferred share units converted (note 13)	–	–	–	–
Stock-based compensation (note 14)	–	1,242	–	1,242
Directors' compensation (note 14)	–	425	–	425
Dividends paid (note 13)	–	–	(8,348)	(8,348)
Repurchase of options (note 14)	–	(975)	–	(975)
Balance, March 29, 2014	203,812	8,820	99,042	311,674

See accompanying notes

Consolidated Statements of Cash Flows

(thousands of Canadian dollars)	52-week period ended March 29, 2014	52-week period ended March 30, 2013 restated (notes 4 and 22)
CASH FLOWS FROM OPERATING ACTIVITIES		
Net earnings (loss) for the period	(30,999)	4,288
Add (deduct) items not affecting cash		
Depreciation of property, plant and equipment (note 8)	16,358	17,638
Amortization of intangible assets (note 9)	11,123	10,245
Net impairment of capital assets (note 8)	2,604	250
Loss on disposal of capital assets	302	65
Stock-based compensation (note 14)	1,242	743
Directors' compensation (note 14)	425	446
Deferred tax assets (note 10)	4,127	(98)
Other	(206)	(482)
Net change in non-cash working capital balances (note 17)	(19,196)	1,089
Interest on long-term debt and financing charges	95	101
Interest income on cash and cash equivalents	(2,377)	(2,609)
Income taxes received	26	32
Share of earnings from equity investment (note 20)	(789)	(1,315)
Cash flows from (used in) operating activities	(17,265)	30,393
CASH FLOWS FROM INVESTING ACTIVITIES		
Purchase of property, plant and equipment (note 8)	(18,700)	(9,441)
Addition of intangible assets (note 9)	(10,546)	(9,621)
Distributions from equity investment (note 20)	1,159	1,308
Interest received	2,463	2,691
Cash flows used in investing activities	(25,624)	(15,063)
CASH FLOWS FROM FINANCING ACTIVITIES		
Notes payable (note 21)	–	190
Repayment of long-term debt	(814)	(1,200)
Interest paid	(110)	(160)
Proceeds from share issuances (note 13)	7	332
Dividends paid (note 13)	(8,348)	(11,119)
Repurchase of options (note 14)	(975)	–
Cash flows used in financing activities	(10,240)	(11,957)
Effect of foreign currency exchange rate changes on cash and cash equivalents	145	471
Net increase (decrease) in cash and cash equivalents during the period	(52,984)	3,844
Cash and cash equivalents, beginning of period	210,562	206,718
Cash and cash equivalents, end of period	157,578	210,562

See accompanying notes

2014 annual report

TELUS

the future is friendly®

Consolidated statements of income and other comprehensive income

Years ended December 31 (millions except per share amounts)	Note	2014	2013
Operating Revenues			
Service		$ 11,108	$ 10,601
Equipment		819	735
Revenues arising from contracts with customers		11,927	11,336
Other operating income	6	75	68
		12,002	11,404
Operating Expenses			
Goods and services purchased		5,299	4,962
Employee benefits expense	7	2,487	2,424
Depreciation	16	1,423	1,380
Amortization of intangible assets	17(a)	411	423
		9,620	9,189
Operating Income		2,382	2,215
Financing costs	8	456	447
Income Before Income Taxes		1,926	1,768
Income taxes	9	501	474
Net Income		1,425	1,294
Other Comprehensive Income	10		
Items that may subsequently be reclassified to income			
Change in unrealized fair value of derivatives designated as cash flow hedges		1	–
Foreign currency translation adjustment arising from translating financial statements of foreign operations		10	4
Change in unrealized fair value of available-for-sale financial assets		(4)	(13)
		7	(9)
Item never subsequently reclassified to income			
Employee defined benefit plan re-measurements		(445)	998
		(438)	989
Comprehensive Income		$ 987	$ 2,283
Net Income Per Equity Share	11		
Basic		$ 2.31	$ 2.02
Diluted		$ 2.31	$ 2.01
Total Weighted Average Equity Shares Outstanding			
Basic		616	640
Diluted		618	643

The accompanying notes are an integral part of these consolidated financial statements.

Consolidated statements of financial position

As at December 31 (millions)	Note	2014	2013
Assets			
Current assets			
Cash and temporary investments, net		$ 60	$ 336
Accounts receivable	25(a)	1,483	1,461
Income and other taxes receivable		97	32
Inventories	25(a)	320	326
Prepaid expenses		199	168
Current derivative assets	4(h)	27	6
		2,186	2,329
Non-current assets			
Property, plant and equipment, net	16	9,123	8,428
Intangible assets, net	17	7,797	6,531
Goodwill, net	17	3,757	3,737
Real estate joint ventures	18	21	11
Other long-term assets	25(a)	333	530
		21,031	19,237
		$ 23,217	$ 21,566
Liabilities and Owners' Equity			
Current liabilities			
Short-term borrowings	19	$ 100	$ 400
Accounts payable and accrued liabilities	25(a)	2,019	1,735
Income and other taxes payable		2	102
Dividends payable	12	244	222
Advance billings and customer deposits	25(a)	753	729
Provisions	20	126	110
Current maturities of long-term debt	21	255	–
Current derivative liabilities	4(h)	–	1
		3,499	3,299
Non-current liabilities			
Provisions	20	342	219
Long-term debt	21	9,055	7,493
Other long-term liabilities	25(a)	931	649
Deferred income taxes	9(b)	1,936	1,891
		12,264	10,252
Liabilities		15,763	13,551
Owners' equity			
Common equity	22	7,454	8,015
		$ 23,217	$ 21,566
Commitments and Contingent Liabilities	23		

The accompanying notes are an integral part of these consolidated financial statements.

Approved by the Directors:

W. A. MacKinnon

William A. MacKinnon
Director

D. Entwistle

Darren Entwistle
Director

Consolidated statements of changes in owners' equity

(millions except number of shares)	Note	Common Shares — Number of shares	Common Shares — Share capital	Non-Voting Shares[1] — Number of shares	Non-Voting Shares[1] — Share capital	Contributed surplus	Retained earnings	Accumulated other comprehensive income	Total
Balance as at January 1, 2013		349,821,092	$ 2,219	302,104,972	$3,360	$ 163	$ 1,904	$ 40	$ 7,686
Net income		–	–	–	–	–	1,294	–	1,294
Other comprehensive income	10	–	–	–	–	–	998	(9)	989
Dividends	12	–	–	–	–	–	(866)	–	(866)
Share option award expense	13(a)	–	–	–	–	6	–	–	6
Shares issued pursuant to cash exercise of share options	13(b)	–	–	200	–	–	–	–	–
Shares issued pursuant to use of share option award net-equity settlement feature	13(b)	2,534,586	18	152,160	2	(20)	–	–	–
Shareholder-approved and court-approved exchange of shares		302,257,332	3,362	(302,257,332)	(3,362)	–	–	–	–
Costs related to share transactions		–	(19)	–	–	–	–	–	(19)
Normal course issuer bid purchase of Common Shares	22(d)	(31,180,612)	(266)	–	–	–	(734)	–	(1,000)
Liability for automatic share purchase plan commitment pursuant to the 2014 normal course issuer bid for Common Shares		–	(18)	–	–	–	(57)	–	(75)
Balance as at December 31, 2013		623,432,398	$ 5,296	–	$ –	$ 149	$ 2,539	$ 31	$ 8,015
Balance as at January 1, 2014		623,432,398	5,296			149	2,539	31	8,015
Net income		–	–			–	1,425	–	1,425
Other comprehensive income	10	–	–			–	(445)	7	(438)
Dividends	12	–	–			–	(935)	–	(935)
Share option award expense	13(a)	–	–			3	–	–	3
Shares issued pursuant to use of share option award net-equity settlement feature	13(b)	1,447,207	11			(11)	–	–	–
Normal course issuer bid purchase of Common Shares	22(d)	(15,855,171)	(135)			–	(480)	–	(615)
Liability for automatic share purchase plan commitment pursuant to normal course issuer bids for Common Shares	22(d)								
Reversal of opening liability		–	18			–	57	–	75
Recognition of closing liability		–	(15)			–	(60)	–	(75)
Other		–	–			–	(1)	–	(1)
Balance as at December 31, 2014		609,024,434	$ 5,175			$ 141	$ 2,100	$ 36	$ 7,454

(1) At our annual and special meeting held May 9, 2013, our shareholders approved the elimination of the Non-Voting Shares from our authorized share structure and the elimination of all references to Non-Voting Shares from our Articles.

The accompanying notes are an integral part of these consolidated financial statements.

Consolidated statements of cash flows

Years ended December 31 (millions)	Note	2014	2013
Operating Activities			
Net income		$ 1,425	$ 1,294
Adjustments to reconcile net income to cash provided by operating activities:			
Depreciation and amortization		1,834	1,803
Deferred income taxes	9(b)	188	21
Share-based compensation expense	13(a)	74	24
Net employee defined benefit plans expense	14(b)-(c)	87	108
Employer contributions to employee defined benefit plans		(88)	(200)
Other		(49)	9
Net change in non-cash operating working capital	25(b)	(64)	187
Cash provided by operating activities		3,407	3,246
Investing Activities			
Cash payments for capital assets, excluding spectrum licences	25(b)	(2,373)	(2,035)
Cash payments for spectrum licences		(1,171)	(67)
Cash payments for acquisitions and related investments	25(b)	(49)	(261)
Real estate joint ventures advances and contributions	18(c)	(57)	(24)
Real estate joint venture receipts	18(c)	4	1
Proceeds on dispositions		7	12
Other		(29)	(15)
Cash used by investing activities		(3,668)	(2,389)
Financing Activities			
Dividends paid to holders of equity shares	25(b)	(913)	(852)
Purchase of Common Shares for cancellation	22(d), 25(b)	(612)	(1,000)
Issuance and repayment of short-term borrowings	19	(300)	(2)
Long-term debt issued	21, 25(b)	7,273	4,619
Redemptions and repayment of long-term debt	21, 25(b)	(5,450)	(3,375)
Other		(13)	(18)
Cash used by financing activities		(15)	(628)
Cash Position			
Increase (decrease) in cash and temporary investments, net		(276)	229
Cash and temporary investments, net, beginning of period		336	107
Cash and temporary investments, net, end of period		$ 60	$ 336
Supplemental Disclosure of Operating Cash Flows			
Interest paid	25(b)	$ (412)	$ (364)
Interest received		$ 2	$ 4
Income taxes paid, net	9	$ (464)	$ (438)

The accompanying notes are an integral part of these consolidated financial statements.

Chart of Accounts

Note: The blanks in the account names below allow students to specify account names.

Assets

CURRENT ASSETS

101 Cash
102 Petty cash
103 Investments
104 _____ investments
106 Accounts receivable
107 Allowance for doubtful accounts
108 GST receivable
109 Interest receivable
110 Rent receivable
111 Notes receivable
119 Merchandise inventory
120 _____ inventory
124 Office supplies
125 Store supplies
126 _____ supplies
128 Prepaid insurance
129 Prepaid _____
131 Prepaid rent

NON-CURRENT INVESTMENTS

141 Investment in _____ shares
142 Investment in _____ bonds
144 Investment in _____

PROPERTY, PLANT, AND EQUIPMENT (PPE)

151 Automobiles/Car/Vehicle
152 Accumulated depreciation, automobiles/Car/Vehicle
153 Trucks
154 Accumulated depreciation, trucks
159 Library
160 Accumulated depreciation, library
161 Furniture
162 Accumulated depreciation, furniture
163 Office equipment

164 Accumulated depreciation, office equipment
165 Store equipment
166 Accumulated depreciation, store equipment
167 _____ equipment
168 Accumulated depreciation, _____ equipment
169 Machinery
170 Accumulated depreciation, machinery
173 Building _____
174 Accumulated depreciation, building _____
175 Land
176 Leasehold improvements
179 Land improvements, _____
180 Accumulated depreciation, land improvements _____

INTANGIBLE ASSETS

191 Patents
192 Accumulated amortization, patents
193 Leasehold
194 Accumulated amortization, leasehold
195 Franchise
196 Accumulated amortization, franchise
197 Copyright
198 Accumulated amortization, copyright
199 Brand name

GOODWILL

200 Goodwill

Liabilities

CURRENT LIABILITIES

201 Accounts payable
202 Insurance payable

203 Interest payable
204 Legal fees payable
205 Short-term notes payable
206 Rent payable
207 Salaries payable
208 Wages payable
209 Estimated warranty liability
210 Income taxes payable
211 Common dividends payable
212 Preferred dividends payable
213 EI payable
214 CPP payable
215 Employees' medical insurance payable
216 PST payable
217 GST payable
218 _____ payable

UNEARNED REVENUES

230 Unearned consulting revenue
231 Unearned revenue
232 Unearned _____/ Unearned _____ revenue

LONG-TERM LIABILITIES

250 Long-term notes payable
251 Long-term lease liability
252 Bonds payable
253 Discount on bonds payable
254 Premium on bonds payable

Equity

301 _____, capital
302 _____, withdrawals

CORPORATE CONTRIBUTED CAPITAL

307 Common shares
310 Common share dividends distributable

313 Contributed capital from the retirement of common shares

315 Preferred shares

RETAINED EARNINGS

318 Retained earnings

319 Cash dividends

320 Share dividends

REVENUES

401 _____ revenue

403 _____ services revenue

405 Commission revenue

406 Rent revenue

407 Dividends income

408 Earnings from investment in _____

409 Interest income

413 Sales

414 Sales returns and allowances

415 Sales discounts

EXPENSES

COST OF SALES

500 Cost of goods sold

501 Purchases

502 Purchases returns and allowances

503 Purchases discounts

504 Transportation-in/freight-in

DEPRECIATION/

AMORTIZATION

600 Depreciation expense, automobiles/Car/Vehicle

602 Depreciation expense, _____

603 Amortization expense, copyrights

604 Amortization expense, _____

EMPLOYEE RELATED

EXPENSE

620 Office salaries expense

621 Sales salaries expense

622 Salaries expense

623 _____ wages expense

624 Employees' benefits expense

FINANCIAL EXPENSES

630 Cash over and short

633 Interest expense

634 Transaction fees

INSURANCE EXPENSES

636 Insurance expense, building

637 Insurance expense, _____

RENTAL EXPENSES

640 Rent expense

641 Rent expense, office space

642 Rent expense, _____

SUPPLIES EXPENSE

650 Office supplies expense

651 _____ supplies expense

OTHER EXPENSES

655 Advertising expense

656 Bad debts expense

659 Collection expense

661 Debit Card Expense

662 Credit card expense

663 Delivery expense/freight-out expense

667 Equipment expense

668 Food and drinks expense

671 Gas and oil expense

673 Janitorial expense

674 Legal fees expense

676 Mileage expense

682 Postage expense

683 Property taxes expense

684 Repairs expense, _____

688 Telephone /Cell phone expense

689 Travel and entertaining expense

690 Utilities expense

691 Warranty expense

695 Income taxes expense

696 _____ expense

OTHER INCOME AND

LOSSES

701 Gain on retirement of bonds

702 Gain on sale of machinery

703 Investment income

705 Gain on _____

805 Loss on retirement of bonds

806 Loss on sale of investments

807 Loss on sale of machinery

809 Loss on _____

CLEARING ACCOUNTS

901 Income summary

Index

SUMMARY OF FOCUS ON FINANCIAL STATEMENT ONLINE COMPANIES—VOLUME 2

EXTEND YOUR KNOWLEDGE (EYK) INDEX—VOLUME 2